MVS JCL and Utilities

MVS JCL and Utilities

Larry J. Brumbaugh
ILLINOIS STATE UNIVERSITY

Macmillan Publishing Company
NEW YORK
Maxwell Macmillan Canada
TORONTO
Maxwell Macmillan International
NEW YORK   OXFORD   SINGAPORE   SYDNEY

Acquisition Editor: Pamela S. Cooper
Project Editor: Mary C. Konstant
Production Management: Editing, Design, & Production, Inc.
Compositor: The Clarinda Company
Cover and Text Designer: Paul Adams Design Inc.

Macmillan Publishing Company
866 Third Avenue, New York, New York 10022

Macmillan Publishing Company is part
of the Maxwell Communication Group
of Companies.

Maxwell Macmillan Canada, Inc.
1200 Eglinton Avenue East
Suite 200
Don Mills, Ontario M3C 3N1

Library of Congress Cataloging-in-Publication Data

Brumbaugh, Larry J., 1943-
MVS JCL and utilities.

Includes index.
1. MVS (Computer system) 2. Job Control
Language (Computer program language) 3. Utilities
(Computer programs) I. Title.
QA76.6.B7773 1987 005.4′3 82-27936
ISBN 0-02-315970-7

Printed in the United States of America.

Print 3 4 5 6 7 Year 1 2 3 4 5

Contents

PREFACE ix

PART I MVS Job Control Language (JCL) 1

Chapter 1
The MVS Operating System: Its Role, History, and Major Components 3

Chapter 2
The Role of JCL in an MVS System 21

Chapter 3
JCL Syntax Fundamentals 29

Chapter 4
The JOB Statement and JES2 Statements 48

Chapter 5
The EXEC Statement and JES3 Statements 63

Chapter 6
Overview of DD Statements and Printed Data Sets 77

Chapter 7
DD Parameters for Disk and Tape Data Sets 99

Chapter 8
Procedures 150

PART II Major MVS Concepts 177

Chapter 9
Data Set Organizations and Access Methods 179
Chapter 10
Data Control Block 192
Chapter 11
(Non-VSAM) Record Formats 199
Chapter 12
Partitioned Data Sets (PDS) 212
Chapter 13
ISAM Data Sets 228
Chapter 14
Direct and Relative Data Sets 246
Chapter 15
Disk Data Sets 259
Chapter 16
Tape Data Sets 273
Chapter 17
Language Translators and (COBOL) PARM Options 292
Chapter 18
The Linkage Editor 307
Chapter 19
The Loader 337
Chapter 20
Flow of Control 352
Chapter 21
System Searches 363
Chapter 22
Dumps, Checkpoints, and Restarts 378
Chapter 23
The Sort/Merge Utility 385

PART III Utilities 401

Chapter 24
The IBM Utilities 403

Chapter 25
IEBGENER 410

Chapter 26
IEBPTPCH 424

Chapter 27
IEBUPDTE 436

Chapter 28
IEBCOPY 451

Chapter 29
IEBDG, IEBISAM, and IEBCOMPR 466

Chapter 30
IBM System Utilities 481

Chapter 31
IEHMOVE, IEHINITT, and IEHDASDR 496

Chapter 32
Using the IDCAMS Utility with Non-VSAM Data Sets 508

INDEX 523

Preface

What makes this textbook on JCL different from others? First, it covers much more than JCL, which, in fact, makes up only a third of the subject matter. The other two thirds discuss MVS programming concepts and utility programs. The book was written to be used as a textbook and the order of topics reflects this purpose. Second, it is the first and only textbook that covers JCL and related topics to such an extent that the book can truly be used as a reference tool. In fact, professional programmers will probably find the book more useful long range than textbooks they used in any of their other computer science or data processing courses. A wide variety of programming problems can be answered quicker using *MVS JCL and Utilities* than consulting the appropriate IBM manual.

More professionals program on MVS systems than on any other computer systems. The material in this book complements the knowledge of a programming language such as COBOL, PL/I, or assembler by developing the expertise required to work productively on large IBM computer systems. Knowledge of a specific programming language is not required. However, most features that require the use of JCL along with an application program are illustrated in COBOL since it is the most widely used language.

Most JCL textbooks go no further than an introduction to the subject and study of syntax. Many parameters are treated as independent entities, and important interrelationships among parameters and statements are often ignored. Such treatment shortchanges the reader in two ways. First, the degree of presentation is too low level to be of interest to the serious MVS student. Second, and equally important, JCL is not shown being used in a wide range of typical applications—which is the real reason for learning JCL. *MVS JCL and Utilities* overcomes these shortcomings. This book recognizes that unlike a high-level language, JCL should not be presented as a standalone subject.

Part I of *MVS JCL and Utilities* thoroughly describes MVS JCL syntax. Topics are covered in a natural ordering by statements and parameters. Practically every parameter and subparameter is used in a number of examples. Frequency of appearance is proportional to importance. Unlike other textbooks, information about a specific parameter is not divided and placed in two or more different parts of the book. Two complete job listings are included, which show the submitted JCL statements, JES messages, the printed JCL statements, and allocation messages. Part I is self-contained and could be used to teach a short course on JCL. Sections on JES2 and JES3 statements are included, since one of the two is required in conjunction with MVS. Chapter 1 contains a description of the major components of the MVS operating system with which an application programmer should be familiar.

Part II of *MVS JCL and Utilities* describes the relationship between JCL and the fundamental hardware and software components of an MVS system that are of interest to an application programmer. (Part I is a prerequisite for Part II.) Separate chapters cover disk (3350 and 3380) and tape processing. One chapter is devoted to each of the four important system services programs: compilers, the Linkage Editor, the Loader, and the Sort/Merge program. Rather than emphasizing how they work internally, the chapters explain the complete range of functions each program performs and show the necessary JCL and control statements required to use them. Each of the four non-VSAM data set organizations also is examined in a separate chapter. In particular, partitioned data set libraries are emphasized throughout the book. Two chapters thoroughly discuss the source and role of the dcb values associated with a data set. Several advanced JCL topics conclude Part II.

In Part III, the IEB/IEH utilities are presented. (Part III assumes a knowledge of Parts I and II.) Utilities are the single, best vehicle to use for developing a strong mastery of JCL. Students must actually write and execute JCL statements in order to learn JCL. Multi-step jobs using the utilities are the easiest way to do this. Most of the chapters in Part III have a large number of exercises. The exercises draw upon material from the first two parts of the book. Part III could also be used for a short course for a person with some JCL and MVS background.

One other major topic with which beginning application programmers on MVS systems should be thoroughly familiar is VSAM. The last chapter of *MVS JCL and Utilities* covers VSAM-related material.

Acknowledgments

Many colleagues, friends, and students helped in the development of this book—including several hundred students who have taken my ACS 372 course during the past seven years. Much of the content of the course is contained in this book.

I wish to gratefully acknowledge the following people who helped in the editing and reviewing of the manuscript, supplied technical assistance, or contributed moral support: Merle Bedell, Susan Brumbaugh, Larry Eggan, Kevin Fahling, Charles Kacmar, Robert Klasing, Priscilla Krampitz, Steve Krolak, William Puetz, Jeff Ricketts, Kevin Stolarick, Tim Stone, and Toni Wood. Throughout the development of the book, I received a great deal of support from the Illinois State University Computer Center. The center provided both computer resources and technical help. The examples in this book reflect the way MVS is actually implemented at one installation. Kup Tcheng and Robert Lee Moulic are responsible for a computer center that is excellently run and is a state-of-the-art facility for a school of its size. As is apparent from the examples throughout the book, our computer center uses JES2.

Special thanks go to the following people who played significant roles in the development of the book: Michael J. Powers, who initially convinced me to write this book; Douglas B. Auer, who provided a very detailed technical review of more than half of the original manuscript; David F. Kephart, who reviewed several chapters and has worked with me in developing and presenting a professional development seminar that covers a great deal of material from this book; and Diane C. Brumbaugh, who provided a tremendous amount of help and expertise in all aspects of the development of the book.

I would like to thank the following people for their helpful comments during the reviewing process: Dennis Adams, Texas Tech University; David L. Doss, University of Evansville; Ennio M. Gherardi, AIRCO Computer Learning Center; Evangeline Jacobs, Northern Arizona University; John Plotnicki, Colorado State University; Thomas Sheridan, DePaul University; and Elizabeth Sullivan, Cincinnati Technical College.

Even after several years of work and a great deal of help, there are, no doubt, some typographical and logical errors in the book. I will be grateful to be informed of any such errors. I also welcome your comments on any other aspects of this book.

LARRY J. BRUMBAUGH

PART I

MVS Job Control Language (JCL)

Chapter 1

The MVS Operating System: Its Role, History, and Major Components

Introduction

The material in this book is written primarily for two major audiences. The first group consists of college students who are preparing for future careers as programmers and expect to work with the Multiple Virtual Storage (MVS) operating system. For students this book can be used as a textbook, and the order of the chapters reflects this purpose. The second group consists of programmers who work on computer systems that use the MVS operating system. For programmers this book can be used as a reference. Both students and professional programmers can also use it for self study. To aim the book at such a specific audience might seem to severely restrict the number of potential readers. However, more people work with MVS than with any other computer operating system. In fact, more computer professionals work with the MVS operating system than with almost all other operating systems combined. This book can help members of both audiences work as productive application programmers on MVS systems.

This book is not meant to be used as a textbook for an MVS operating systems course. Rather, it clearly explains how an application programmer can quickly learn to use the MVS operating system effectively by mastering Job Control Language (JCL).

The book assumes that the reader can program in COBOL, PL/I, or Assembler, and contains very little high level language code. When it is necessary to examine a programming language feature, COBOL is emphasized. Although COBOL is the most restrictive of the three major languages, most application programming has been (and continues to be) done in COBOL. The manner in which relevant language features are implemented in PL/I and Assembler is discussed when they differ from COBOL.

A very detailed collection of exercises is included with aimost every chapter. Some of the exercises are straightforward and mechanical; others will challenge practically everyone who attempts them, even those with MVS experience.

MVS JCL and Utilities can be used as a detailed reference for most of the important topics related to executing batch programs on MVS systems. The book is designed to be used as a very thorough reference for important MVS topics. Obviously, it does not contain quite as much overall information as a collection of the various IBM manuals which discuss the same subject matter. However, two fundamental differences should be noted between this book and the group of IBM manuals. First, the manuals contain a great deal of redundant and irrelevant material. No irrelevant material is included in this book. A certain amount of redundancy is unavoidable, but repetition has been held to the bare minimum. Additionally, the presentation in this book is much clearer, better organized, and illustrated with more meaningful examples than those found in the manuals. This book contains the essential material that an MVS application programmer should know about JCL and utilities.

There are a great many IBM manuals, each of which contains some material that is discussed in at least one place in this book. Most MVS installations will have one or more copies of all of these manuals. The appropriate manual should be consulted for additional details on specific topics. These manuals are listed in Table 1–1. The numbers in parentheses identify the chapters in this book which contain material found in that manual.

TABLE 1–1
IBM Manuals

Title	*Manual Number*
OS/VS2 MVS Overview (1,22)	GC28-0984
MVS JCL Reference (2,3,4,5,6,7,8,20,21,22)	GC28-0692
IBM VS COBOL for OS/VS (9,10,11,13,14,17)	GC26-3857
IBM OS/VS COBOL Compiler and Library Programmer's Guide (9,10,11,13,14,17)	SC28-6483
OS/VS Sort/Merge Programmer's Guide (23) or *DFSORT Application Programming Guide* (23)	SC33-4035
MVS Data Management Services Guide (10,11,12,13,14)	GC26-3875
MVS Linkage Editor and Loader (18,19)	GC26-3813
MVS Linkage Editor and Loader Messages (18,19)	GC38-1007
MVS Supervisor Services and Macro Instructions (9,10,22)	GC27-6979
OS/VS Message Library: VS2 System Messages (every chapter)	GC38-1002
OS/VS Message Library: VS2 System Codes (every chapter)	GC38-1008
OS/VS Tape Labels (7,16)	GC26-3795
MVS Utilities (24,25,26,27,28,29,30,31)	GC26-3902
MVS Utilities Messages (24,25,26,27,28,29,30,31)	GC26-3920

IBM Operating Systems

Exactly what is the function of an operating system? An operating system is a program that controls the execution of all other programs running on the computer. Modern operating systems contain several major components. Four of the most important are the routines that manage jobs, tasks, input/output (I/O) operations, and error handling and recovery. All four of these components are absolutely essential in a computer system.

Job management and I/O management are the two components over which application programmers can exert the widest range of control. Most of the values coded with MVS JCL directly interact with either job or I/O management. A job is a programmers request to have MVS perform work. Job management monitors all jobs that are running on the computer from the time they are submitted for execution until they are purged from the system. Job management allocates and deallocates the various system resources that are needed by a job, and also monitors the printed output produced by jobs. I/O management is responsible for transferring data between the computer and secondary storage devices such as disk and tape drives. I/O management also allocates and deallocates disk storage (the details of I/O operations with terminal devices are not discussed in this book).

A job may consist of several components, called tasks. Most task management, along with error handling and recovery management, is not directly affected by the information coded in an application program's JCL. The major function of task management is to monitor the use of computer resources. This includes main memory and the central processing unit (CPU). Error handling and recovery management performs three basic functions: it handles abend processing and it also performs checkpoints and restarts. All three of these topics are discussed in Chapter 22.

Most large IBM mainframe computers currently use one of three major operating systems: Multiple Virtual Storage (MVS), Virtual Machine (VM), and Disk Operating System (DOS). DOS usually runs on the smaller IBM mainframes, and has the most limited capabilities. Both MVS and VM are available with large systems. VM is slightly older than MVS, but MVS is the more widely used of the two. A major advantage of the VM operating system is that it can be used to simulate several other operating systems, including MVS. This approach is used at some installations to allow MVS, DOS, and VM to run concurrently on the same computer. IBM shows every indication of maintaining MVS as its premier operating system into the 1990s.

MVS is one of the most sophisticated software systems ever developed; almost every conceivable bell and whistle have been built into it. This gives the user great power and tremendous flexibility. However, there is a price to pay for this power—a considerable amount of preliminary work must be done in order to program effectively with MVS. A major portion of this work consists of learning MVS JCL. JCL is a language which interfaces between an application program and the computer's operating system. The sheer complexity of the MVS environment can make even simple functions and requests difficult. Chapter 2 describes the potential problems involved in learning to program effectively with an MVS operating system.

Several of the major computer vendors, including National Advanced Systems (NAS) and Amdahl, sell IBM compatible mainframes called Plug Compatible Machines (PCM). These vendors have been able to successfully duplicate IBM hardware and sell it at a cheaper price. However, all Plug Compatible Machines use the actual (IBM) MVS operating system. This is possible because IBM software and hardware may be purchased independently. No other vendor is marketing a lookalike version of MVS. It would be extremely expensive to develop such an operating system. Historically, most companies that have tried to develop IBM compatible mainframe computer systems have failed, and have left the computer industry after suffering large financial losses.

Evolution of the Present MVS Operating System

As mentioned above, the operating system is the major software component that oversees all of the activities a computer performs. Early computers (designed in the 1940s and 1950s) did not need operating systems, since only one computer program or job ran at a time. All of the computer's resources were dedicated to this job. In a way, the executing job itself could be thought of as a temporary and very simplified operating system. The details of every I/O operation had to be handled by the application program. Only when the job was completely finished processing could another job be loaded into the computer. Hence, many of the important functions performed by a modern operating system were unnecessary in early computers.

The predecessors of the present MVS operating system were initially developed in 1964 when the IBM 360 computer was introduced. The development of this family of computers is still considered one of the most significant events in the history of data processing and computer science. It marked the beginning of the third generation of computers (previous computer systems had been classified as first and second generation).

One early operating system was called the Primary Control Program (PCP). It was a collection of common programs that were used by all data processing applications. The Basic Operating System (BOS) was an enhanced version of the PCP. BOS allowed the system to handle a wider range of application languages. The Tape Operating System (TOS), which permitted tape processing, followed next. With the development of disk devices, the Disk Operating System (DOS) was introduced. All of the early IBM 360 operating systems still permitted only one job at a time to reside in memory and execute. However, the delay between jobs was significantly reduced compared to older computer systems which did not have operating systems. Operating systems also greatly simplified the I/O processing for a program. System subroutines, called access methods, provided most of the necessary details. Until the late 1960s all instructions were executed in real memory, so the size of a program was limited by the amount of memory available.

IBM computer systems were substantially upgraded at that time by the introduction of two new operating systems, OS/MFT (Multiprogramming with a Fixed Number of Tasks) and OS/MVT (Multiprogramming with a Variable Number of Tasks). Both systems supported multiprogramming, which permits more than one program to reside in memory at the same time. The programs alternate using the central processor. For simplicity, multiprogramming is often imprecisely described as the capability to allow several programs to execute simultaneously. Multiprogramming requires the operating system to perform several additional functions. It is necessary to monitor the central processor to determine the order in which to execute programs and when to switch control back and forth between the various programs. Often, a program will execute until a specific condition occurs. At that point it is interrupted, and control is transferred to another program.

Multiprogramming produced a dramatic improvement in computer utilization, however with multiprogramming it became important to specify a job's processing requirements. An attempt was made to prohibit several programs that needed the same resources from executing concurrently. OS/MFT supported multiprogramming with a fixed number of tasks or programs. A maximum of sixteen programs could reside in memory at the same time. Memory was divided into regions, all of which were the same size. This practice resulted in wasting a large amount of main memory. OS/MVT allowed a variable number of tasks to execute concurrently; the amount of memory allocated to a program was based upon its actual needs. Hence, much of the wasted space found with OS/MFT did not occur with OS/MVT. The number of programs executing at a given time was limited by the total amount of storage required by the programs. The development of MFT and MVT marked the beginning of IBM's philosophy of vigorously supporting more than one major operating system for the same computer.

The next significant development in operating systems occurred in 1972, when IBM introduced their virtual storage (VS) operating systems. The development of virtual storage greatly expanded the potential size of application programs. Virtual storage allows programmers to address storage that does not physically exist in main memory. OS/MFT was replaced by OS/VS1, and OS/MVT by OS/VS2. Virtual storage systems had been available on Burroughs computers for some time prior to this, but IBM publicized and popularized the concept. A well known early release of OS/VS2 was called Single Virtual Storage (SVS). With SVS the total amount of virtual storage shared by all executing programs was 16 megabytes. MVS replaced SVS in 1974. MVS permits each individual program to concurrently access the complete amount of virtual storage available on the system. However, many installations permitted application programs to use a maximum of one or two megabytes of virtual storage. Since 1974 numerous upgrades and revisions have been made to MVS. Hence, the MVS operating system in use today represents over twenty years of refinement since the original IBM 360 operating systems.

Recently MVS/XA, the extended architecture version of MVS, has become available. This operating system allows real computer memories larger than 32 megabytes, which had been the absolute limit on an MVS system. However, only 16 megabytes could be accessed by a single program. MVS/XA provides a practically unlimited amount of virtual storage. Prior to MVS/XA, several computer systems had to be tied together if an installation needed more than 16 megabytes of virtual memory. This technique is called multiprocessing.

TABLE 1–2
IBM Operating Systems

Operating System	*Major Feature*
Primary Control Program (PCP)	Collection of commonly used programs
Basic Operating System (BOS)	Enhanced version of PCP
Tape Operating System (TOS)	Supported tape processing
Disk Operating System (DOS)	Supported disk processing
Multiprogramming with Fixed Number of Tasks (MFT)	First IBM multiprogramming operating system; all jobs ran in the same size region
Multiprogramming with Variable Number of Tasks (MVT)	Multiprogramming where the number of tasks and the region size can both vary
OS/VS1	MFT with virtual storage
OS/VS2	MVT with virtual storage
Single Virtual Storage (SVS)	Early version of OS/VS2
Virtual Machine (VM)	Can run MVS and other operating systems simultaneously
Multiple Virtual Storage (MVS)	Each user has up to 16 megabytes of virtual storage
Multiple Virtual Storage Extended Architecture (MVS/XA)	Programs larger than 16 megabytes are possible

The original Disk Operating System was also replaced by a virtual storage system called DOS/VS. Due to significant hardware and software design problems, DOS/VS was poorly received by the IBM users. A hardware extension to DOS systems (DOS/VSE) used microcode. IBM would like to replace all of their other existing operating systems with either MVS or VM, but thousands of small computer installations are still using various versions of DOS. A chronological listing of the major IBM operating systems is shown in Table 1–2.

Major MVS Concepts

It is unnecessary for an application programmer to understand most of the technical details concerning how MVS actually works. However, it is important to understand the basic role of some of the fundamental components of the MVS operating system and the related computer hardware. Major components include the (central) processor and the System Resource Manager; main memory, virtual storage, and paging; the Job Entry System; and the Job Scheduler. The processor is used to execute the actual instructions which comprise a program. Performing this work is the basic part of running a job. On a large MVS system hundreds of users may wish to run jobs at the same time. However, only a predetermined number of jobs can execute at one time. The system must make several major decisions to determine the order in which to execute jobs. First, the system must determine the order in which to select jobs to begin execution. Then, among the jobs executing concurrently, it must decide the order in which they get to use the processor. MVS and a program called the Job

Scheduler determine which jobs are selected for execution. The System Resource Manager (SRM), a major component of MVS, determines the order in which jobs use the processor.

The system must constantly monitor both the type of work and the maximum amount of work to perform on behalf of a user. Every request for work, whether explicit or implicit, contains information the system uses for this monitoring. Additionally, the system must determine if one job's request for resources conflicts with requests from other jobs in the system. These conflicts can involve hardware (can one job exclusively use a particular disk, tape, printer, or a number of such I/O devices?) or software (can one job have exclusive control to read or write records in a data set or to lock all other jobs out of an important library?).

What type of information must a job supply to MVS? The user must be identified, the account paying for the work must be known, and additional accounting information may need to be specified. Often it is necessary for security information to be provided.

Prioritizing System Utilization

The jobs submitted for execution on an MVS system are placed in different classes based on the types of resources that are needed. The classes are defined and used by the installation in such a way that there is usually a 'good' mixture of jobs running concurrently in the system. The following simplified example illustrates how classes may be defined and used.

Example 1: An installation assigns each job to one of five classes. The most important characteristics associated with each class are described in Table 1–3.

Note that classes A, B, and E are almost mutually disjoint. Class C jobs require operator intervention. Class D jobs are run infrequently, but should be executed as soon as possible. A separate queue is maintained for each of the five job classes. A queue is a "first in first out" structure. Hence, if all other factors are the same, the first job placed in the queue is executed first. When a job is submitted for execution, it is inserted into the appropriate queue based on its priority. A priority value specified by the programmer or the system is assigned to each job. The higher a job's

TABLE 1–3
Job Class Descriptions

Class	*Description*
A	Jobs which perform a large number of I/O operations. Such jobs are said to be I/O bound.
B	Jobs which have heavy processor requirements. These are called processor or CPU bound jobs. Number crunching programs are placed in this class.
C	Jobs in which substantial operator set-up is required. Most frequently one or more tape volumes must be mounted, or special printing done.
D	Very important production jobs.
E	Jobs which require very little execution time, and no operator set-up.

priority, the quicker it will be selected for execution. However, the higher the priority of the job, the smaller the maximum amount of storage and execution time allowed for the job. The Job Scheduler is responsible for placing the entry for a job into the appropriate queue. In particular, suppose each of the five queues contain jobs whose priorities are shown in the accompanying table. Note that, within a given class, the order in which jobs are selected for execution is determined first by their priority and second by the time they were submitted.

Class	*Jobs in the Queue (represented by their priority)*	*Number of Jobs*
A	6, 7, 7, 8	4
B	4	1
C	3	1
D	1, 2	2
E	10, 11, 12	3

Initiators are operating system programs that select jobs from the queues. An initiator prepares a job for execution and accompanies it through the execution process. When the job is finished the initiator performs a clean-up operation. The number of initiators available determines the maximum number of jobs that may execute concurrently in the system. In particular, suppose there are four initiators active in the system. The initiators are identified by numbers, and each has a list of job classes from which it may select jobs. Suppose the following classes are assigned to the four initiators:

Initiator	*Job Classes to Select From*	*Job Selected*
1	B, A, E	B-4
2	C, E	C-3
3	A, C, E	A-8
4	D, B, E	D-2

Here, the job selected is identified by its class and priority. The higher the priority of the job, the quicker it will be selected for execution from the queue for a specific class. However, an initiator examines jobs in the first class assigned to it before considering jobs in the remaining classes assigned to it. Hence, initiator 1 selected the class B job for execution, even though it had a lower priority than any of the class A or E jobs. Likewise, initiator 4 selects the class D job even though it has the second lowest priority of any job awaiting execution. Thus, the manner in which jobs are selected for execution is determined primarily by three values: each job's class, each job's priority, and the order in which the jobs were submitted for execution. As mentioned above, class values are assigned by an installation in such a way as to optimize computer throughput. In this example, it may not be wise to place class E last with every initiator, since such jobs consume very few resources. Likewise, if the only jobs submitted for execution were in class D, a serious and unnecessary bottleneck would develop.

The initiators, along with a job's class and priority, determine the jobs executing concurrently in the system. From among the jobs actually executing, the SRM decides the order in which to allow them to use the processor. Ordinarily, a job executes until it finishes or becomes suspended. A job can be suspended for several reasons. Three of the most common are paging (described later in this chapter), waiting for an I/O operation to complete, and having already executed for a specific amount of time. When a job is suspended the processor begins to work on another job. A second type of priority (called the dispatching priority) is used to determine the next job to use the processor. The dispatching priority can be explicitly coded in the JCL for the job, or a default value can be supplied by the Job Entry System. The dispatching priority value can change at different times during the job's execution.

JES3 Job Scheduling

The previous example used the JES2 job entry system. With JES3, some changes must be noted in the manner in which processing is performed. In particular, JES3 associates initiators with class groups.

JES3 works with initiators in determining the order in which jobs will be executed. Rather than classes, JES3 uses job class groups. A job class group is a collection of job classes. In addition, JES3 associates job class groups with specific processors and I/O devices. Nothing comparable is done with JES2. The job class groups are defined when the system is generated.

By using job class groups, JES3 can control more system resources than JES2. In particular, JES3 can control both the number of jobs in a specific class that can execute at the same time and the number of jobs that can run on one specific processor. JES3 also determines the I/O devices and storage that a job needs. Once JES3 has prepared a job to execute, it passes the job to an initiator. In many cases, since the resources that the job needs to execute have already been provided by JES3, the job can begin executing immediately. With JES2, the resources which a job needs are provided after the initiator selects it.

With JES3, the I/O devices are placed into one of three categories. A device can be managed exclusively by MVS or JES3, or be shared by MVS and JES3.

Virtual Storage

Virtual storage systems contain two types of memory, real and virtual. Real storage has always been available on computer systems. The development of virtual memory around 1970 has made it necessary to qualify the word *memory*. Real storage is the actual physical memory which is contained in the computer. It is a limited and very important resource. Virtual memory does not physically exist in the computer.

Rather, it is created and maintained on disk by the operating system. On an MVS system, the amount of virtual storage available is always 16 megabytes. In addition, every program has access to its own copy of virtual storage. Virtual storage can be used in the same manner as real storage. Thus every job can appear to have access to all of the main memory theoretically available on the system, and programs can be developed based on this assumption. Until recently the maximum amount of real storage permitted on an IBM system was 32 megabytes (a megabyte equals 1,048,576 bytes, which is 2 raised to the sixteenth power). However, many systems had considerably less than the maximum amount. MVS/XA permits more than 16 megabytes of virtual storage.

Every program executing on an MVS system is divided into sections called pages. The pages are stored on disk in virtual storage. Specific pages are copied from virtual storage to real storage as they are needed for execution. Only after this is done can the actual instructions on the page be executed. Virtual storage provides several major advantages over earlier operating systems. More programs can execute concurrently than can possibly fit into the available real storage. Additionally, only the active parts of an executing program need to be kept in real storage; the inactive pages can remain on disk until needed. This further increases the number of programs that can fit in real storage.

Some standard terminology is used when discussing virtual storage and paging. A *frame* is a block of real storage. A *page* is a block of virtual storage. A *slot* is a block of disk storage. Both real and virtual storage are always allocated in units of 4K blocks. Sixteen pages are grouped together to form a *segment* (64K bytes). The term *program address space* refers to the 16 megabytes of virtual storage available to an executing program. A *virtual address* is an address within the program address space. A *real storage address* is an address in main memory. The term *paging* is used to describe the movement of pages between real storage and virtual storage. The term *swapping* is used to describe the movement of a complete program or address space between virtual storage and auxiliary storage. *Page stealing* occurs when MVS takes a frame from one executing program and makes it available to another user. A *page fault* occurs when a page that is needed by an executing program is not currently in real storage.

Paging

In order to execute instructions, MVS must be able to rapidly convert virtual addresses to real addresses. This conversion is performed by an MVS feature called Dynamic Address Translation (DAT). MVS breaks the 16 megabytes of virtual storage into 256 segments of 64K bytes each. Each segment consists of 16 pages. A virtual address consists of the segment number, the page number within the segment, and a relative byte displacement within the page. To find the address of a particular instruction, MVS examines the segment table to find the segment address. This in turn provides a page table address. The page table contains the displacement for the instruction. The displacement is added to the frame address to yield the real storage address. As addresses are translated they are stored in a hardware buffer for later reference. In subsequent accesses MVS checks the buffer for an address before it uses the segment and page tables to determine the address. Therefore, the most active instruction addresses will be available quickly.

In order to perform a paging operation, MVS uses the DAT and other system components to determine where a page can be placed in real storage. Once a page is in real storage, it can be referenced by searching a table. A page fault requires that a paging operation be performed. Swapping and page stealing minimize the need for demand paging. Swapping causes an entire address space to be moved from virtual storage to auxiliary storage. To ensure that an adequate supply of real storage frames is available, the most inactive programs are moved. Page stealing moves the most inactive page from real storage to virtual storage, making the frame available for another program. A reference bit determines if a page is active; a change bit determines if the contents of the page have been modified. Modified pages are moved, but other pages are overlayed.

Example 2: Figure 1–1 illustrates the relationship between real, virtual, and auxiliary storage. Assume that a complete program occupies three pages in virtual storage. Currently page 3 is using the processor and, hence is in real storage (a frame). Copies of page 1 and page 2 are stored on disk in auxiliary slots. Page 1 is also in real storage since it was recently needed. The two versions of page 1 in real and virtual storage need not be identical.

Now suppose it is necessary to move page 2 to real storage. In addition, page 1 is moved from real to auxiliary storage by page stealing. Virtual and auxiliary storage can still be pictured as in Figure 1–1, although the contents of pages 1 and 3 have been modified. Page 1 and page 3 are no longer in real storage, but page 2 is.

Because of the manner in which paging is performed, there are some significant program design factors that should be considered. If a program is expected to execute rapidly, an effort should be made to minimize paging. The time required to move pages in and out of memory can considerably slow the program. This is especially true with on-line or interactive programs where a rapid response is desirable. Because of this, some of the fundamental principles of structured batch programming are often ignored when developing on-line programs. In particular, with on-line systems the use of straight in-line coding and duplicate code rather than subroutine calls will tend to keep active pages in memory. Performed paragraphs should be kept to a minimum

FIGURE 1–1

Real, Virtual, and Auxiliary Storage

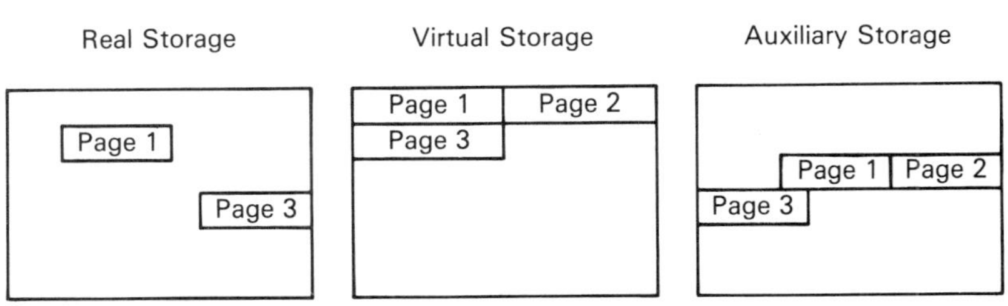

or not used. When programming in COBOL, the EXAMINE, INSPECT, TRANSLATE, and STRING verbs should be used sparingly, as they require dynamic subroutine calls or requests for storage that result in paging.

A significant advantage of virtual storage is that extremely large programs can be written to run on virtual systems, without worrying about overlay structures. Overlay structures are coding techniques used by programmers to segment large programs so that they can be run in a limited amount of real memory. More information on overlay programming is provided in Chapter 18. With the advent of virtual storage systems the use of overlay structures has practically disappeared.

MVS programmers are given a choice of using virtual storage or only real storage. Real storage has the advantage of much faster execution. The parts of a program executing in real storage are never paged out to disk. However, requesting real storage may cause execution to be slower for other users of the system, since less real storage will be available to support the paging process.

A user must select either real or virtual storage for each step in a job. Virtual storage is sufficient for almost all applications, so real storage must be specifically requested by the program (virtual storage is the default). Some installations may prohibit application programmers from requesting real storage. When using virtual storage, the parts of a program not currently needed may be paged out to disk. They will remain on disk until referenced again.

The Principal Areas in Main Memory

Figure 1–2 shows the three basic areas into which memory is divided. They are called the System Area, Common Area, and Private Area.

The System Area contains many of the essential parts of the MVS operating system, and is always placed in real storage. No part of it can ever be paged, and it cannot be swapped. It may optionally contain the fixed BLDL Table, which is described below.

The Common Area consists of the System Queue Area (SQA), Pageable Link Pack Area (PLPA), and Common Service Area (CSA). It may optionally contain the Pageable BLDL Table, which is described below. The SQA contains tables and queues used by the entire system, such as the page tables that describe the Common Area and the System Area. The PLPA contains heavily used system and user programs. These include the access methods (the routines responsible for performing I/O operations), supervisor call routines, and subroutines frequently used by high level language application programs. All programs in the PLPA are stored as load modules. This is a format that allows them to be immediately executed without further processing. Programs in the PLPA may be paged. However, they may not be modified during execution, and they must be re-entrant. That is, they can be used simultaneously by any number of executing jobs. The CSA contains data areas for both users and the system. It is also pageable. Several optional parts of the System and Common Areas are not discussed in this book.

One BLDL table can be included as part of the system. A BLDL table is a directory or table of contents for system disk libraries. If the library directory is

FIGURE 1–2

Divisions of Memory

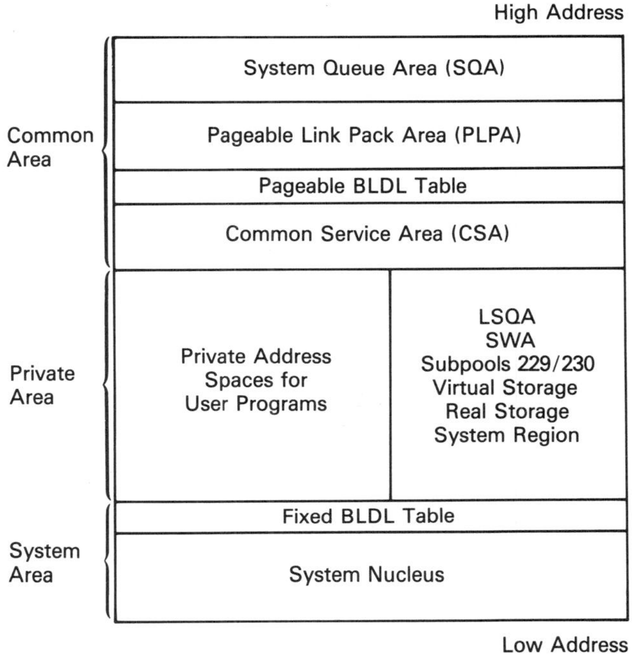

stored in memory there is no need to perform an I/O operation when referencing the information about a library member. This can save considerable time with a heavily used library. The two BLDL tables are mutually exclusive. A Fixed BLDL table is not pageable. It may be used with very important system libraries. A Pageable BLDL table is located in the Common Area and is pageable. Both types of BLDL tables are associated with libraries whose members for some reason cannot be stored in the Link Pack area. They may be very large or not re-entrant.

The Private Area is the part of memory that is available to application programs running on the system. It always contains the Local System Queue Area (LSQA), Scheduler Work Area (SWA), Subpools 229/230, and a System Region. The remainder of the Private Area is divided into two sections called the real region and the virtual region. The size of the real region is determined when the system is generated. A program that resides in the real region is never paged out. Parts of the real region that do not hold programs may be used for standard paging operations. Programs placed in the virtual region may be paged.

The LSQA contains tables and queues that are used by one of the executing programs. Hence, the LSQA contains control blocks and paging tables for one address space. The SWA contains the control blocks for a specific task. On pre-MVS systems this type of information was placed in one table, which was used by the entire system. This created contention problems for the executing programs. Subpools 229/230 contain additional control blocks. The System Region contains system programs that are performing work for a particular address space. The Private Area is pictured in more detail in Figure 1–3.

FIGURE 1–3
The Private Area

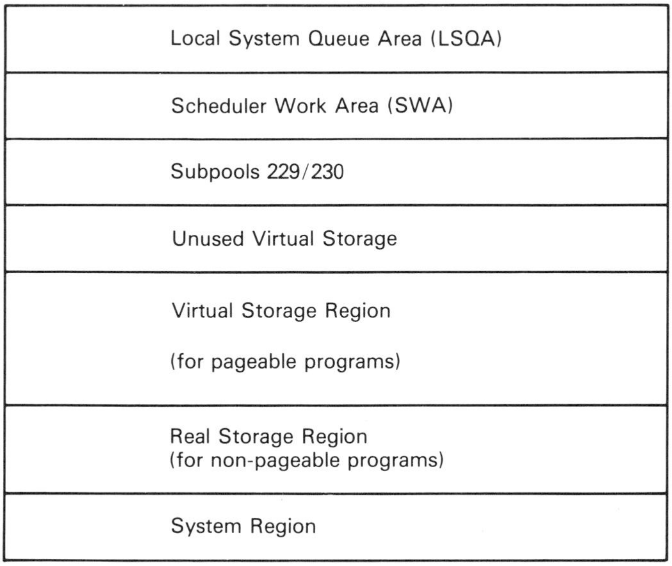

The System Resource Manager

It is the job of the System Resource Manager (SRM) to manage the MVS system resources. The SRM performs two basic functions. First, it allocates resources to the jobs currently executing in the system. These resources include main memory, CPU time, and I/O devices. Allocations must be made in accordance with an installation's performance specifications. These specifications concern response time and turnaround time for jobs in the system. Second, the SRM attempts to maximize the amount of system throughput. This maximizing centers mainly on the allocating of main memory, CPU time, and I/O resources. The fundamental decisions made by the SRM include the following: Which jobs should be paged in and paged out? When should pages be stolen, and which pages in particular? If an application program does not request a specific I/O device for a data set, which one should be allocated? When should the dispatching priority of an application program be changed (a process called *chapping*)?

The System Resource Manager itself consists of three basic components: SRM Control, the Workload Manager, and the Resource Manager. SRM Control determines which component of the SRM is needed to perform a specific function. It is also responsible for swapping address spaces. When making a swapping decision, SRM Control receives input from the other two components. The Workload Manager performs three basic functions: it monitors the use of system resources by the address spaces, makes swapping recommendations to SRM Control, and collects data on system utilization. The Resource Manager performs several major functions. Its chief function is to monitor system throughput and make recommendations to SRM control in order to optimize the throughput. It is also responsible for chapping, device allocation, and page stealing.

The Job Entry System

One major program or subsystem which must be available to work in conjunction with MVS is called the Job Entry System (JES). At present there are two versions available, JES2 and JES3. JES2 is a descendant of HASP (Houston Automatic Spooling Program), and JES3 developed from ASP (Asymmetric Multiprocessing System). There are many similarities between the two systems. The major functions of a Job Entry System are the following:

(a) Input job streams are read from card readers or internal readers and stored on disk in spool data sets. When the system is initialized, specific disk volumes are classified as spool volumes. Such volumes are used to hold input job streams. The contents of a job stream can be classified as JCL statements, in-stream data sets, or directions to the Job Entry System. The JCL and each in-stream data set become a separate spool data set.

(b) The syntax of the JCL in a job stream is checked for correctness. If no errors are detected, the JCL is converted to internal text.

(c) Jobs are selected for execution.

(d) All of the standard printed and punched output produced by the job is written to the spool volumes. The actual printing and punching is done at a later time. With this approach, the job does not have to wait on the much slower I/O devices during execution.

(e) The job is purged from the system.

Since the role of the Job Entry System is so important, it will be examined in more detail. The Job Entry System is not a part of the MVS operating system, but it runs as an executing batch job itself. When a job is submitted for execution on an MVS system, it first comes into contact with the Job Entry System. The Job Entry System is the actual link between the program's JCL and the MVS system. In order to perform the various processing components described above, JES interacts with several queues. The important queues used by MVS and the Job Entry System are shown in Figure 1–4. The six categories in the diagram are summarized below.

Jobs may be submitted for execution from a terminal through an internal reader or from cards through an actual card reader. These are the two major ways of submitting work. The statements which comprise the job stream are initially spooled to a disk volume.

Before any further processing takes place, the syntax of the JCL statements is checked by the Job Scheduler. If any syntax errors are found, no further processing occurs. Rather, a copy of the JCL statements and accompanying error messages is printed. This printing operation involves the spool disk volumes and is discussed below. If no syntax errors are found, the JCL statements are converted to a form of internal text understandable to both MVS and JES. The job may require that addi-

FIGURE 1–4
MVS Job Queues

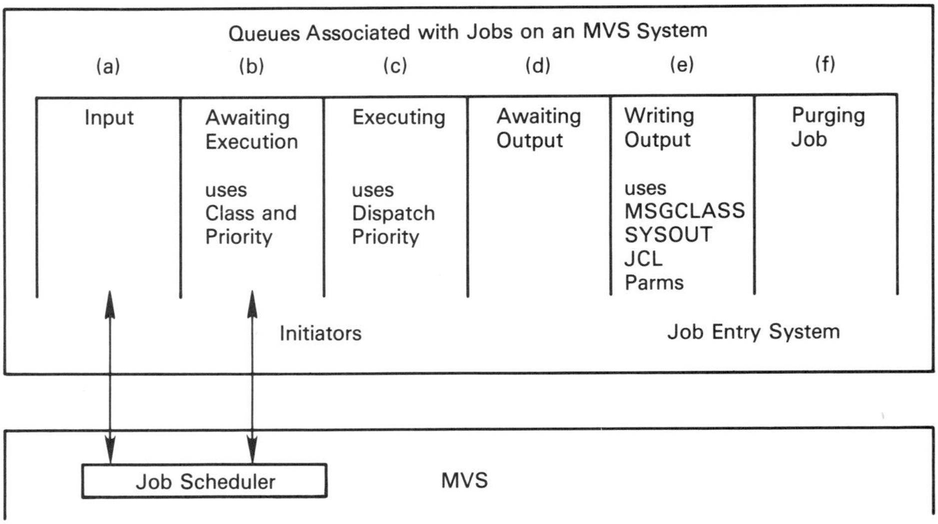

tional JCL be merged from the system JCL libraries. Some JCL statements in the job stream may generate additional JCL statements, which are also merged together. Even if there are no syntax errors, it is possible to request a printed copy of the statements in the job and then terminate processing. When scanning the job stream, every statement is classified as a JCL statement, a JES statement, or part of an in-stream data set. Each in-stream data set is given a unique temporary name and spooled to disk.

Each job is grouped with all other jobs in the same class awaiting execution. The jobs within a given class are ordered using their priority value. The higher the priority, the sooner the job will be selected for execution. The class and priority together determine how long a job must wait until it begins to execute. Additionally, all jobs executing in the system at the same time must have unique names.

When a job is scheduled for execution, it is an initiator that asks the Job Entry System for the next job. An initiator can be thought of as a subprogram associated with the Job Scheduler and JES.

Once a job begins executing, it must contend with the other jobs for system resources. The SRM determines how resources are allocated to the executing jobs. The most important resource is use of the processor. This is determined by the dispatching priority associated with the part of the job wishing to execute. The SRM also determines the disk packs on which to place data sets created by the job if the job does not specify a value. The initiator accompanies the job through execution. Most jobs produce printed (or occasionally punched) output. Such output is very rarely directed to a printer or punch. These devices are too slow when compared with the speed of the processor. Instead, the output is initially written to a spool data set, to be printed or punched at a later time. Standard printed and punched output is called a SYSOUT data set. This is the type of processing done in queue (e) in Figure 1–4.

When the job finishes execution, it must be purged from the system. All of the resources that the job used are released, including memory, data sets, and I/O devices. This is done primarily by the initiator assigned to the job. The spooled output data sets created by the job are printed whenever a printer becomes free.

Differences between JES2 and JES3

There are several important differences between JES2 and JES3. However, with a single processor system (one computer) there are few significant differences. Almost without exception, very large data processing centers use JES3.

Both JES2 and JES3 can perform *priority aging*. This process ensures that jobs that have been in the system waiting to run will be selected for execution before jobs that have just recently requested execution. JES2 increases the priority of a job awaiting execution based on the amount of time it has waited. JES3 increases the priority of a job based on the number of times it has not been selected for execution. JES3 provides *dependent job control*. This feature controls the order in which a specific group of jobs is to be executed relative to one another and to the other jobs in the system. A program can be bought to do this with JES2. JES3 also provides *deadline scheduling*. This process is used to specify that a job will begin executing prior to a specific time of day. JES2 allows all jobs of a specific type to be placed in one special class for faster processing (usually jobs which have very small execution times and use very few I/O devices).

Exercises

1. MVT, SVS, MVS, and MVS/XA have at one time all been the premier IBM operating system on their large computer systems. What are the fundamental differences among the four operating systems regarding the maximum amounts of real and virtual storage available to each user?

2. What are the major advantages of multiprogramming operating systems over the earlier operating systems? What are the major advantages provided by virtual storage operating systems? What are the major advantages of an extended architecture (XA) operating system?

3. Define the terms *multiprocessing, multiprogramming,* and *virtual storage*. For each term, with which operating system did it first become available?

4. Create a more thorough and realistic group of job classes than those defined in Example 1. Do this for two computer centers. Assume the first is at a university where half of the jobs are submitted by students in computer science classes and the rest are standard administrative production jobs. Assume the second computer center is part of a large bank.

5. Assume the same number of initiators and job classes associated with each initiator as in Example 1. Suppose that the collection of jobs awaiting execution includes the values

shown below. Which jobs will be selected? Notice that duplicate job names are present. Recall that all of the jobs executing at one time must have unique names.

Class	*Jobs in the Queue—Represented by Priority (and job name)*
A	5(IO1), 7(IO2), 8(IO3)
B	3(NUM)
C	3(P), 3(X), 5(Y)
D	2(X), 2(Y), 3(X), 3(X)
E	10(I), 10(I), 11(J), 11(J), 11(J)

Describe the potential problems inherent in the way that the classes and initiators are defined in Example 1.

6. List several factors that should be considered in determining the number of initiators that are active in the system. What problems can occur if the number of initiators is either too large or too small?

7. How can an MVS system limit the number of programs that wish to run in real storage and not be paged? Clearly some programs should have this capability, but the performance of the system may be negatively impacted if a large number of jobs wish to run in real storage.

8. Within the Private Area of memory, the Virtual Storage region and the Real Storage region are mutually exclusive areas. The size of the Real Storage region is fixed when the system is generated. What potential problems can occur if this Real Storage region is either too large or too small?

9. Where in main memory are each of the following parts of the system stored: heavily used re-entrant subroutines, the major parts of the MVS operating system itself, the system page tables, the scheduler work area, the access methods subroutines, and the virtual region used by an application program?

10. Describe the basic functions performed by a job entry system. How are these basic functions implemented with JES2 and JES3? Mention any significant differences in how they are handled by JES2 and JES3.

Chapter 2

The Role of JCL in an MVS System

Overview

JCL consists of ten distinct types of statements. Three of the ten must always be coded in order to perform meaningful work on an MVS System. These three statements are the JOB, EXEC (Execute), and DD (Data Definition) statements. All three statements have very specific roles that are described later in this chapter. Basic JCL syntax is covered in Chapter 3. The roles of the JOB, EXEC, and DD statements are discussed below.

The JOB statement identifies a request from a user to the computer's operating system (here, MVS) to perform work. It also identifies the user requesting the work. The JOB statement identifies a 'job stream' or job (these two terms are used interchangeably in this book). Almost always, the JOB statement marks the physical beginning of a request for service. A job is comprised of steps. Each step is a semi-independent entity. The JOB statement defines the fundamental unit of work in an MVS (batch) system. Loosely speaking, a job is analogous to a transaction in an on-line programming environment, such as CICS. A job step is similar to a CICS task.

The EXEC statement identifies a step within a job stream. The EXEC statement must be the first statement within the step. There need not be a specific relationship between two individual steps in a job stream. A single EXEC statement can consist of several sub-steps. When this occurs, the EXEC statement identifies an object called a procedure.

DD statements identify all of the data sets needed during a job. Over 50 percent of all JCL syntax involves the DD statement. Hence, it is the most complex of the JCL statements. Almost every DD statement must be coded after the EXEC statement that uses it. A few DD statements may be coded once and then are in effect throughout the entire job: these DD statements are placed after the JOB statement and before the first EXEC statement in the job stream.

Every job stream contains exactly one JOB statement, and must contain one or more EXEC statements. Each EXEC statement may be followed by as many as 1655 DD statements. Hence, within a job the order of the three major types of JCL statements is as follows:

```
JOB
  EXEC
    DD
    DD
  EXEC
    DD
```

The JCL statements coded in a job stream are used by the system to provide two general categories of information: global and local. Global JCL values identify the resources that are needed for the duration of the job. These resources include time, memory, security information, disk libraries, and operator instructions. Local JCL values identify the resources that are needed for one or more of the steps within a job. These resources include time, memory, data sets, disk storage, tape drives, printers, and operator assistance. Additionally, JCL places restrictions on the use of the resources in the job stream, and asks the following questions: Who can use the resources? What types of processing can they perform with them? When must resources be shared? How are the users' requests prioritized?

The JCL studied in this book was initially developed during the 1960s in conjunction with the creation of the IBM 360 computer, and the syntax of the present MVS JCL remains similar to that originally developed over twenty years ago. When JCL was initially introduced it was met with a very negative response from the application programmers of that era. They realized that the advent of JCL meant that more than just knowing a high-level programming language was required in order to run a program. JCL forced programmers to learn a new language, and also required them to become aware of the complete data processing environment in which they were working. When JCL was first introduced the accompanying version of the operating system contained numerous bugs. This made the transition to JCL even more difficult.

JCL is radically different from popular 'high-level' programming languages such as COBOL and PL/I. However, JCL is a computer language with its own syntax. The first step in mastering any language is to learn the syntax. The next six chapters cover the fundamentals of JCL syntax, which is similar to that of IBM assembler language. Like assembler language, JCL is not 'user friendly.' It has a very precise syntax. However, a person willing to spend as much time studying JCL as is ordinarily spent learning a high level language can quickly develop a great deal of JCL expertise. Learning JCL takes a concerted effort. A person cannot 'magically' master JCL through osmosis.

The Job Scheduler interprets and translates the JCL statements in a job stream, as described in Chapter 1. JCL diagnostic and error messages are written primarily by the Job Scheduler. These messages are preceded by the value IEFxxx, where xxx is a three digit numeric code. IEF is the identifier for the Job Scheduler messages.

Unlike high level programming languages, it is impossible to code complex logic in JCL within a job stream. In fact, most JCL consists of straight in-line coding with very little branching or conditionals. However, some moderate logic is possible in relation to the following topics: symbolic parameters, procedures, overriding operations, explicit and implicit backward references, forward references, concatenation, flow of control, the order in which the system searches for objects identified in the job stream, conflicting values from different statements in the job stream, checkpoints, and restarts.

A person without at least a minimal understanding of JCL simply cannot do much meaningful work on an MVS system. It is absolutely essential that MVS application programmers be able to write most of their own JCL, and be capable of reading and understanding the JCL written by other people. The major goal of this book is to develop and strengthen JCL skills. The fundamentals of JCL are discussed in Chapters 3 through 8. Other major JCL features are described in Chapters 20, 21, and 22, which also include discussion of other matters.

Problems with Learning JCL

Is JCL a difficult language to master? Perhaps it is! For most programmers it is apparently more difficult to learn JCL than to learn a new high level language. People give many reasons to explain why it is so hard to learn JCL. Most of the reasons are legitimate, but some are easier to overcome than others.

JCL does not contain several of the helpful convenience features found in many application programming languages. All of the major high-level languages have features designed to improve their user friendliness, including an English-like syntax with regard to grammar, punctuation, and abbreviations. High level languages also allow free formatting. They usually permit several distinct segments of code which produce the same results. Unfortunately, most of these features are either not available or have limited support with JCL.

JCL has a very precise syntax, which is very inflexible and unforgiving. If a single JCL syntax error occurs the entire job stream is scratched. A minor error, such as a misplaced comma or a misspelled keyword, causes the entire job to be cancelled before execution begins. Because JCL allows a large number of exceptional coding situations, JCL syntax is further complicated.

JCL also contains several exotic features which are rarely used. Programmers have difficulty developing familiarity with a feature used on a biannual basis.

There are several situations where potential JCL errors are allowed to go undetected. These include unnecessary duplication of information and coding JCL statements out of order. In such cases, no error or diagnostic messages are printed to warn the programmer.

When attempting to debug a JCL listing, a person can easily become confused by poorly worded diagnostic and error messages. Often a very confusing error message is used to 'explain' a common syntax error. A classic example is the message IEF210 UNIT FIELD SPECIFIES INCORRECT DEVICE NAME. This message is misleading, because frequently the UNIT parameter is not even coded on the statement that is flagged as being in error.

JCL permits a wide range of powerful and sophisticated operations. Unfortunately, this broad scope can often make it unnecessarily difficult to request simple functions.

The JCL 'mystique' frightens some people! JCL has developed a reputation as difficult to learn and troublesome to work with. Many people believe that it is necessary to go to a JCL 'guru' for help when JCL problems occur. Such gurus like to tell anyone who will listen that JCL is difficult to learn and troublesome to work with. Many JCL gurus are probably unfamiliar with a substantial portion of the material in this book.

JCL is a difficult subject to learn strictly through independent study. This is a culmination of all the reasons previously given. The best way to learn JCL is to take an organized course on the subject. It also helps to have an excellent JCL textbook available. Incidentally, numerous organizations offer Personal Development Seminars that teach JCL. Such seminars range in duration from one day to a week. There is a great demand in the data processing industry for JCL courses. Most such courses charge tuition of between $200 and $300 per day per student. Because of the cost, many data processing shops offer their own in-house JCL training to new programmers.

Advantages of Knowing JCL

It takes a considerable amount of work to learn JCL. Is this a worthwhile expenditure of time and energy? This book claims that the answer is a resounding 'yes' for any MVS application programmer, for the following reasons:

JCL permits a programmer to access all of the features available with an MVS computer system. By contrast, a programming language does not allow any type of processing that the language does not directly support.

Studying JCL leads to an understanding of how a sophisticated operating system such as MVS actually works. With this understanding comes the ability to use the operating system more advantageously.

There are numerous special features that are available in high level programming languages such as COBOL and PL/I that cannot be used unless the associated JCL concepts are understood. Several examples of COBOL related features are described in Chapters 9, 10, 11, 13, 14, and 17. Likewise, a programmer must know a moderate amount of JCL in order to combine programs written in two or more languages. This topic is discussed in Chapters 18 and 19.

Without a knowledge of JCL, a programmer on an MVS system must often depend on someone else when trying to determine why a program does not work correctly. Additionally, a person with a weak JCL background needs constant help in order to perform basic programming functions. Some interactive programming packages such as TSO/SPF make it very easy to perform specific JCL-related functions by masking the actual JCL from the programmer. However, a slight variation from a standard programming situation can cause problems for a person who does not understand JCL.

Ten years ago the author first began programming on IBM OS computer systems at a large university. The computer center employed a staff of JCL gurus who wrote and modified any JCL that an application programmer needed. For a person who did not know JCL this was a very convenient and effective arrangement from 8AM to 5PM, Monday through Friday, unless the gurus were busy. Unfortunately, JCL-related problems can also occur at night and on weekends.

JCL Statement Types

At this point, the specific types of information supplied on the JOB, EXEC, and DD statements are described in more detail. All information coded on the JOB statement is global. It affects the entire job stream. None of the JOB statement information can be qualified to apply it to specific steps. Information coded on an EXEC statement is local. For the most part, it affects only a single step. Almost all DD statements describe a data set only for the duration of the job step.

The JOB statement identifies a unit of work. It identifies the programmer doing the work, and the person paying for the work (these may be two different people). It also supplies necessary security information. The JOB statement specifies the resources that are needed for the duration of the entire job, and determines the course of action to take if an unexpected result occurs while any step in the job is executing.

The EXEC statement identifies either a program or procedure to be run (EXECuted) during a job step. It also either explicitly or implicitly identifies the specific program(s) to be executed. The EXEC statement identifies the resources that are needed for the duration of just that step. Some of the same type of information can be coded with both the JOB and EXEC statements. It is the scope to which the information applies that varies. The EXEC statement may also identify relationships between one job step and the prior steps in the job stream. It is possible to make information dynamically available to an executing program by coding the information on the EXEC statement. The JCL transmits the data to the program in the same manner in which a main program passes data to a subroutine.

The DD statement identifies (either directly or indirectly) a data set that is to be processed during a job step. It also specifies whether the data set already exists or if it is to be created during the present step. The DD statement determines the data set's status at the end of the step. It identifies the location of the data set and the type of I/O device used to process it. The DD statement also specifies the size of some data sets. For other data sets, it lists the processing characteristics of the records. The manner in which the processing is to be performed may also be included. Finally, the DD statement identifies related resources needed to process the records in the data set. All of the information described above must be supplied to the system for every data set used during the job step. All of the information can be explicitly coded on the DD statement, although some values can also be provided from non-JCL sources.

The more JCL experience a person has, the less JCL they need to write to accomplish a specific function. This surprising theme recurs throughout this book. There are two basic reasons for this. The JCL values most commonly required in specific situations are frequently the default values for those situations. Also, a person who understands JCL knows which values are redundant and which values are completely meaningless (and thus ignored except for syntax checks).

All ten JCL statements, including JOB, EXEC, and DD, consist of 80 byte records. Columns 73-80 are used for sequence numbers. Several JCL statements do not need most of this space, including the special purpose Null and Comment statements. The functions performed by these two statements are discussed below.

The Null Statement

The Null statement consists of two slashes (//) in the first two bytes of an 80 byte record. The remaining characters should all be blanks except possibly for sequence numbers. The Null statement should be the last statement in a job stream; if it is embedded in the middle of a job stream, the statements following it are not considered part of the job.

Several potential problems can occur when the Null statement is omitted. Suppose a job is read through a card reader, and a second job submitted immediately after it contains several JCL errors on its first statement (the JOB statement). The Job Scheduler may be unable to determine the end of the first job stream and the beginning of the second. When the Null statement is properly coded this problem can never occur.

Suppose a job is submitted for execution from a terminal through an internal reader. Extra or unused lines on the terminal screen following the end of the job may cause the Job Scheduler to print a warning or error message. Frequently this situation generates an unnecessary SYSIN DD statement in the JCL listing. Again, when the Null statement is properly coded this cannot occur.

The Comment Statement

The Comment statement also performs a limited function: documentation. Two slashes and an asterisk (//*) in the first three bytes of the 80 byte record identifies a JCL Comment statement. A Comment statement may be coded anywhere between the JOB statement and the end of the job stream. The remaining 77 bytes of the record are ignored by the Job Scheduler and can be used for documentation. JCL is usually documented in much the same manner and for the same purpose as high level language code. One standard format for documenting JCL is shown in the accompanying examples in this and the next chapter. Incidentally, under some circumstances the Job Scheduler also interprets a statement with // in columns 1 and 2 and spaces in columns 3–16 as a Comment statement. JCL documentation is discussed in more detail in the next chapter.

Example 1: The relative order of the JCL statements required to execute a job on an MVS system is outlined in Table 2–1. Only the statement type is identified; actual syntax is not shown. The skeleton of two simple yet typical job streams is shown. The listing on the left is a job stream consisting of one job step. The listing on the right is a multiple step job stream. An EXEC statement denotes the beginning of a step.

Notice that another type of statement is also included in Example 1. Any record in the job stream that contains /* in columns 1 and 2 and a keyword which begins in column 3 is not a true JCL statement. Rather, it is called a Job Entry System (JES) statement or Job Entry Control Language (JECL) statement. JES statements are syntactically and functionally similar to JCL. They are discussed in this book because they are one of the two non–JCL statements permitted in a job stream (the other is an in-stream data set). The syntax required for coding JES statements is examined in Chapters 4 and 5.

TABLE 2–1

Relative Order of JCL Statements

Job Stream 1	*Job Stream 2*	*Description of the Statement's Function*
`// JOB`	`// JOB`	On MVS systems, this statement denotes the beginning of a job stream.
`/*JOBPARM`	`/*SETUP`	/* identifies a JES statement.
`/*MESSAGE`	`/*ROUTE`	A second JES statement is coded.
`//******`	`//******`	Comment statements begin here,
`//* text`	`//* text`	and are continued here,
`//* text`	`//* text`	etc., forming a comment 'block.'
`//******`	`//******`	This is the final Comment statement.
`// EXEC`	`// EXEC`	EXEC requests the execution of a particular program or programs.
`// DD`	`// DD`	Each DD statement identifies a
`// DD`	`// DD`	data set to be used by the program
`// DD`	`// DD`	named on the previous EXEC statement.
`// DD`	`// EXEC`	This is a second program or group of programs to be executed in Job Stream 2.
`// DD`	`// DD`	A DD statement must be included for
`// DD`	`// DD`	every data set (file) used by the
`//`	`// DD`	program.
	`//`	The Null statement should always be the last statement in a job stream.

Exercises

1. Find the errors in the following job stream:

```
//*A COMMENT STATEMENT HERE
//XX   DD
//JOB1234     JOB
//XX   EXEC
//
//      EXEC    ABC
```

2. List some of the reasons why JCL syntax is less user friendly than that of a high level language such as COBOL or PL/I. In particular, why are features such as free-formatting, English-like syntax, and widespread use of abbreviations not available with JCL?

3. List the types of JCL statements discussed to this point in the book. Identify some of the major reasons why each statement type is used.

4. Discuss the order in which the various types of JCL statements may be coded. Specifically, which statements must precede or follow other statements? With which statements is the order of coding important?

5. Suppose JCL were not available on a computer system. How could the type of information that JCL provides be made available to the system? What would be the advantages and disadvantages of not having to code JCL?

6. Examine the part of the IBM Messages manual *OS/VS Message Library: VS2 System Messages* which contains the messages written by the Job Scheduler (these are the messages that begin with IEF). Note any patterns or relationships in the way the messages are numbered and the contents of the messages themselves.

7. Suppose that there were no JOB statement in MVS JCL. What effect would this have on the remaining JCL statements? List several advantages and disadvantages that would result from not having a JOB statement. Consider both a data processing shop and an academic environment.

8. Can a job stream contain no EXEC statements? If such a job were syntactically permissible, what functions could be performed by a job stream without EXEC statements? Can a job stream contain no DD statements? What meaningful functions could be performed by such a job stream?

Chapter 3

JCL Syntax Fundamentals

Overview

The ten types of JCL statements can be divided into two groups. Six statement types (JOB, EXEC, DD, OUTPUT, PROC, and PEND) employ a common syntax. The other four statements use different syntax types. A person just beginning to learn JCL will have no reason to code either the PROC or PEND statements, since they are used primarily with advanced JCL features. Their syntax shares many similarities with that of the JOB, EXEC, DD, and OUTPUT statements. The PROC and PEND statements are examined in detail in Chapter 8. The OUTPUT statement is used only with printed data sets and is discussed in Chapter 6.

The JOB, EXEC, DD, OUTPUT, PROC, and PEND statements are comprised of fields. All six statements contain a // in columns one and two. Following the //, as many as four fields can be coded on a single statement. From left to right these fields are coded in the following order:

```
//name field   operation field   operands field   comments field
```

The fundamental syntax rules associated with each of the four fields are examined below.

The Name Field

The JOB, EXEC, DD, OUTPUT, PROC, and PEND statements all may have name fields, which identify a specific JCL statement. The remaining four types of JCL statements do not contain name fields. Most system related messages use the name fields to reference a specific JCL statement. A programmer may use the name field in the same manner that statement labels or paragraph names are used in a high level language. Every JCL statement within the job can be uniquely identified if reasonable naming conventions are employed. One or two levels of qualification may be necessary to guarantee a unique name for each individual statement. This is further explained in Chapter 8.

With each of the six types of statements, the name must begin in column 3 immediately following the //. The name must consist of one to eight characters. The first character must be an alphabetic or national (#,@,$) character. Any additional characters must be alphabetic, numeric, or national. Several reserved names have a special role with the DD statement. There are several instances in which a name field is not required. These situations are described with the individual statement types later in Chapters 5 (EXEC), 6 and 7 (DD), 6 (OUTPUT), and 8 (PROC and PEND). The syntax rules for the name field are exactly the same with all six statement types.

Example 1: Each value on the left is a valid name for a JCL statement. The values on the right are invalid.

Valid	*Invalid*	*Reason Why Name Is Invalid*
ABCDEFGH	ABCDEFGHI	Over eight characters
@1A	1@A	Begins with a number
$$$	A$&	Ampersand not allowed
STEP1	STEP 1	Embedded blanks not allowed

In addition to identifying a statement, the name field serves different functions with each of these six types of JCL statements.

The name field on the JOB statement specifies the name of the entire job stream. Every job must have a name, and many installations have specific requirements for the job name. It is a good practice to code a job name that is different from those of other users of the system. Although MVS executes multiple user programs simultaneously, all of the jobs executing at a specific time must have unique names. When jobs with duplicate names are submitted for execution, all but one must be temporarily queued.

The name field on an EXEC statement supplies the name of the job step. Using a stepname is optional. However, a unique stepname should always be coded with each of the EXEC statements when there are more than two steps in a job. The default is a blank name field. This is a poor choice for a stepname, since blanks are not visible in a message statement printed by the system, and blank stepnames limit JCL programming capabilities (see Chapter 5). Although duplicate stepnames are permitted, this is risky, and no messages are provided warning of duplication. If an error message states that an abend occurred in step A and there are several steps named A, it is more difficult to detect where in the job stream the abend actually occurred. Specific installation coding standards for all of the name fields are very helpful. This is especially true for EXEC statements. More on this subject is included with the JCL coding guidelines later in this chapter.

The name field on a DD statement is called the DDname. A DDname must be coded, so the DD statement can be directly referenced from other parts of the job stream. This is also true of a stepname. However, not every DD statement must have a DDname, and there are two situations in which the DDname field should not be coded. The first is when a collection of sequential or partitioned data sets have been concatenated together for processing as a group. The second occurs when an ISAM data set is referenced using two or three DD statements. These topics are discussed further in Chapters 6 and 13 respectively. The most important function the DDname performs is to connect the actual physical data set and the corresponding logical file in an application program. A program does not contain the name of the data set or its location, so this information must be supplied on the DD statement.

The term *procedure* is used to identify a collection of EXEC and DD statements that are to be processed as a group. The PROC statement identifies a procedure. There are two types of procedures. With an *in-stream procedure* the procedure name field (procname) is required. The procname serves as an identifier for all of the statements comprising the in-stream procedure. With a *cataloged procedure* the procname is always optional, and procname is used primarily for documentation. With both types of procedures the procname permits referencing of statements within the procedure. The name used to identify the group of statements which comprise a cataloged procedure is usually supplied on a DD statement. Creating and referencing procedures are discussed in Chapters 8, 25, and 27.

A name field is never required with the PEND statement. A PEND statement may be coded only as the last statement in an in-stream procedure, where it is required. A PEND statement cannot be referenced by other JCL statements, and a pendname serves only as documentation. The PEND statement does not appear in the expanded JCL printed listing of the procedure. However, it does appear in the in-stream copy of the procedure. This can be seen in the complete JCL coding example in Chapter 8.

The name field is required with the OUTPUT statement. The names coded should be different for each OUTPUT statement throughout the entire job.

The Operation Field

The second field coded on a JCL statement identifies the operator or operation. The six JCL operators are JOB, EXEC, DD, OUTPUT, PROC, and PEND. Exactly one of these operators must be used to identify the statement type. The operator must be separated from the adjacent name and operand fields by one or more blanks. The operation field cannot be continued to another statement.

The Operand Field

The third field which may be coded on a JCL statement consists of one or more parameters separated by commas. There are three types of parameters: *positional, keyword,* and *symbolic*. The entire operand field must be separated from the adjacent operation and comment fields by one or more blanks. The operand field is required only with the EXEC and OUTPUT statements. However, it is usually coded with almost every JOB and DD statement. If the operand field is not coded with a DD statement, it implies that a process called *overriding within a concatenation* is to be performed.

There is no limit to the number of characters that may be coded in the operand field. The operand field can be continued to additional statements. Each continued statement should end with a comma, and the operand field itself must end with a complete parameter, not a comma. Except for symbolic parameters, each type of parameter can be coded only once on a single JCL statement. A symbolic parameter can theoretically be coded any number of times on the same statement. The PROC statement allows only symbolic parameters in the operand field. The JOB statement does not allow symbolic parameters in the operand field. The PEND statement does not have an operand field.

The Comment Field

The last of the four fields is used only for documentation purposes. It is not a required field with any of the six JCL statements. The comment field can be used as an alternative to the Comment statement, or coded in addition to the Comment statement. Like the operand field, comments can be continued to additional statements. However, it is not necessary to do this since Comment statements can be used instead.

The comment field must be separated from the preceding operand field by one or more blanks. Because of this, a blank accidentally coded in the middle of the operand field will cause all of the parameters following it to be treated as comments. This is a frequent cause of major JCL problems. The comment field cannot be coded on a JCL statement unless the operand field is also present (the PEND statement is the one exception to this rule since it has no operand field). Comments may be coded with all of the other types of JCL statement except the Null statement.

Summary of Fields

Table 3–1 classifies each of the four fields as required or optional for each of the ten types of JCL statements.

A field enclosed in parentheses is optional for that statement type. However, under most conditions the name and operand fields are coded. The six optional fields preceded by a plus sign (+) are always coded, except under specific and very restricted conditions. Additionally, the comments field is optional with the JOB, DD, and PROC statements, but it cannot be coded unless the operand field is also present. The PROC statement itself is optional with a cataloged procedure.

Example 2: Based on the syntax fundamentals discussed thus far and the information in Table 3–1, determine which of the following statements contain syntax errors. Specifically, why is a particular statement invalid? This is a drill in the syntax fundamentals discussed to this point.

```
//ABC     JOB    ALPHA
//ABC     EXEC   ALPHA   A COMMENT HERE
//ABC     EXEC   EXEC
//ABC     DD
//        DD
//        DD     DUMMY
//PROC           PROC    PROC=   PROC=
//##      EXEC   PGM=DD
//PEND    PEND   PEND
//JOB     EXEC   PROC    PEND    DD
//*XY     JOB    1234567890
//$       EXEC   PROC
//EXEC    EXEC
```

Surprisingly, only the last statement is invalid. Every EXEC statement must contain an operand field. All of the other statements coded here are syntactically correct, subject to a computer center's standards and the names of their procedures and jobs. Carefully reexamine any statements that appeared invalid. Suppose the last statement were corrected. Then, even more surprisingly, the thirteen statements form a syntactically correct job stream in the exact order in which they are coded. After learning more of the material in Part I of this book, it will be possible to confirm that this can be a valid job stream.

The information that is coded in the name and operation fields has a limited and very inflexible syntax. Any exceptions to the rules described for these two fields are flagged as syntax errors. However, these rules are very easy to learn. Once they are learned name and operator field errors should rarely occur. Most syntax errors involve the operand field. Most of this book examines the values that can be coded there.

JCL syntax is checked for correctness by the Job Scheduler. Both syntax errors and informatory messages are identified by an IEF message code. When analyzing JCL statements, the Job Scheduler makes several distinct passes through the job

TABLE 3–1
Summary of Fields

Type of JCL Statement	*Bytes 1 and 2*	*Beginning in Byte 3*	*The Final Two Fields*		
JOB	//	name	JOB	+(operand)	comments
EXEC	//	(name)	EXEC	operand	(comments)
DD	//	+(name)	DD	+(operand)	comments
OUTPUT	//	name	OUTPUT	operand	(comments)
PROC(in-stream)	//	name	PROC	+(operand)	comments
PROC(cataloged)	//	(name)	PROC	+(operand)	comments
PEND	//	(name)	PEND	(comments)	
Comment	//	*(comments)			
Null	//	nothing else allowed on statement			
Delimiter	/*	(comments)			
Command	/*	operation		+(operand)	comments

stream. It is possible to submit a job, discover JCL syntax errors, correct all of them, and make no other changes, yet have another group of entirely different syntax errors flagged when the job is resubmitted. After this second group of errors is corrected, a new group of syntax errors may be detected on the third attempt at running the job. If a single JCL syntax error occurs anywhere in the job stream, the entire job is scratched, and no steps are executed.

Types of Operand Parameters

As mentioned above, the three types of operand parameters are positional, keyword, and symbolic. A positional parameter must be coded in a specific location relative to the other parameters present on a JCL statement. MVS JCL contains exactly seven positional parameters, so it is easy to learn their identity and function. Additionally, six of the positional parameters use a very simple syntax format.

The great majority of the operand parameters are keyword. All keyword parameters use the format: keyword=value. The keyword parameters on a JCL statement may be coded in any order. However, they must follow any positional parameters that are coded on the same JCL statement. There are many keyword parameters; the DD statement alone has 32.

Symbolic parameters have the most complicated syntax of the three types, and are also the least frequently coded. With one exception, symbolic parameters must be coded either within a procedure or on the EXEC statement which invokes the procedure. Symbolic parameters are discussed in depth in Chapter 8.

All symbolic parameters coded within the body of a procedure begin with a single ampersand (&). Symbolic parameters on the EXEC statement which invoke the procedure and on the PROC statement itself use the keyword=value format, but the value does not begin with an ampersand. The positional parameters do not begin with an ampersand, and do not use the keyword=value format. In fact, there is no meaningful syntax property that is common to all seven positional parameters. The three types of parameters are described in more detail below.

All positional parameters must be coded before all the keyword parameters on a JCL statement. If two positional parameters are coded on the same statement, they must be written in a specific order. At present, two positional parameters can only be coded together on the same JOB statement. Two positional parameters may be coded on the JOB statement, one on the EXEC, and four on the DD. The JOB statement contains the Accounting Information and Programmer Name parameters. The EXEC statement contains one positional parameter, which is called the Program Name or PROC Name depending on its syntax. The DD statement contains the *, DATA, DUMMY, and DYNAM positional parameters. Only the Accounting Information parameter may consist of multiple values. The other six each supply a single value. The EXEC statement positional parameter is required; the other six are optional. A syntax error results if a positional parameter is not coded and a leading comma is coded to denote its omission.

All keyword parameters must follow any positional parameters that are present on the same statement. The actual ordering among the keyword parameters on a statement is syntactically irrelevant. The order in which keyword parameters should

TABLE 3–2

Parameters

Type of JCL Statement	*Number of Positional Parameters*	*Number of Keyword Parameters*	*Role of Symbolic Parameters*	*Common Ordering of Parameters*
JOB	2	14	not allowed	(P,)(P,)K,K,. . .
EXEC	1	10	permitted	P,K,K,K,. . .
DD	4	32	permitted	(P,)K,K,K,. . .
OUTPUT	0	29	not allowed	K,K,K,K,. . .
PROC	0	0	only symbolics	S,S,S,S,. . .
PEND	0	0	no parameters	

be coded is discussed with the JCL guidelines later in this chapter. There are two formats for keyword parameters: keyword = value and keyword = (value1,value2, . . .,valueN). Whenever both are permitted, the formats keyword = value1 and keyword = (value1) are identical.

A symbolic parameter is more flexible than either a positional or keyword parameter. In an analogy between JCL parameters and algebraic expressions, positional and keyword parameters are similar to constants while symbolic parameters function like variables. The same symbolic parameter can have different values assigned to it at different places in the job stream. In fact, the same symbolic parameter can be used as either a positional or keyword parameter at different times. In addition, symbolic parameters may follow or replace a positional parameter on the DD statement or the EXEC statement. They are the only type of parameter that can be coded on the PROC statement. Symbolic parameters are further discussed in Chapter 8.

The materials in this section is summarized in Table 3–2. Here P denotes a positional, K a keyword, and S a symbolic parameter. (P,) means that the positional parameter is optional. All keyword and symbolic parameters are optional. With the EXEC and DD statements, symbolic parameters may be interspersed with the other parameters and coded in any order on the statement.

Subparameters

Unlike positional parameters, many keyword parameters may be used to specify more than one value. These multiple values are called subparameters. When a keyword parameter contains subparameters, the format keyword = (value1,value2,. . ., valueN) must be used. Here, the parentheses are required. The individual subparameters may be either positional, keyword, or symbolic. The terms positional and keyword have the same basic meaning with subparameters as with parameters. Most subparameters are positional. Two DD statement subparameters may be coded as either positional or keyword. Keyword parameters can be classified as containing all positional, all keyword, or a mixture of both positional and keyword subparameters. Very few parameters allow a mixture of positional and keyword subparameters.

The Accounting Information parameter is the only positional parameter that contains subparameters. Hence, this topic is discussed in Chapter 4 with the JOB Statement. Symbolic parameters do not contain subparameters. However, symbolic parameters are the only type in which two or more adjacent parameters or subparameters can be coded without any separating commas.

When a keyword parameter contains all positional subparameters, the syntax used is: keyword=(subparm1,subparm2,. . .,subparmN). In this case, the omission of a positional subparameter that is not assigned a value must be denoted by coding a comma in its place. Thus, when the first positional subparameter has not been coded the syntax becomes: keyword=(,subparm2,. . .). A default value is frequently supplied when a positional subparameter is not coded. To a lesser degree this is also true with keyword subparameters. If several positional subparameters are not coded, their omission is denoted by coding commas in each of their places, unless one or more of them are consecutive and are the final positional subparameters coded. In this situation the trailing commas are unnecessary and should not be coded. A trailing comma may generate a JCL syntax error when it follows the last subparameter within a parameter or the last parameter on a JCL statement.

Example 3: Assume that all five positional subparameters of a keyword parameter are coded, with the following syntax: keyword=(A,B,C,D,E). When only the second, fourth, and fifth subparameters are coded, the syntax becomes keyword=(,B,,D,E). To code only the third and fourth subparameters, the syntax is keyword=(,,C,D). When only the second subparameter is coded, the syntax becomes keyword=(,B). A trailing comma after the last positional subparameter coded is unnecessary, so keyword=(,B,) should not be coded. However, all non-trailing commas must be coded.

As noted above, most subparameters are positional. When only the first positional subparameter is coded, it usually doesn't need to be enclosed in parentheses. To code just the first subparameter in the previous example, either keyword=A or keyword=(A) may be used. However, some parameters do not permit coding of only the first subparameter.

When a keyword parameter consists entirely of keyword subparameters, the syntax used is: keyword=(subparm1=value1,subparm2=value2,. . .,subparmN=valueN). Here, the subparm keywords can be coded in any order. Just as with positional subparameters, the keyword subparameters are separated by commas. Commas should not be coded when a specific keyword is not coded. If only one keyword subparameter is coded, it need not be enclosed in parentheses.

The DCB keyword parameter, which is coded on the DD statement, contains the most subparameters of any JCL parameter. All of the DCB subparameters are keyword. Several of the DCB subparameters "decompose" further into keyword sub-subparameter values. These sub-subparameter values are classified as keyword only because they are not positional. They can be coded in any order. However, they are not separated by commas or preceded by a keyword and an equal sign.

The COND keyword parameter may be coded on both the JOB and EXEC statements. It contains from one to eight subparameters which may be coded in any order, although they do not have a keyword subparameter syntax. The COND subparameters are composed of two or three positional sub-subparameters. Incidentally, there are no sub-sub-subparameters in JCL.

Example 4: Assume that a keyword parameter contains four keyword subparameters, all of which may be optionally coded. When all four are needed, the syntax may be coded as keyword=(X=value1,Y=value2,Z=value3,W=value4). The W=value4 subparameter consists of three sub-subparameter values: A, B, and C. Each sub-subparameter value may be coded independently of the other two. All of the following are syntactically correct.

```
keyword=(Z=value3,W=value4)     keyword=(W=AC,X=value1)
keyword=(Y=value2)              keyword=Y=value2
keyword=W=CB
```

Very few parameters permit a mixture of positional and keyword subparameters. LABEL and VOLUME are two keyword DD parameters whose final subparameter can be coded as either positional or keyword. With both parameters, the fifth subparameter is the final subparameter. Hence, for these two subparameters, keyword=(,,,,subparm5=value) and keyword=subparm5=value are equivalent. In fact, formats such as keyword=(,subparmI,subparmJ,subparm5=value) may also be coded, where I<J<5. Any of the first four positional subparameters may be coded in order followed immediately by the fifth subparameter. With both the LABEL and VOLUME parameters, subparm5 has the format: subparm5-keyword=value. Either of two distinct keywords can be coded with each parameter.

Continuing a JCL Statement

Frequently, a complete JCL statement is too large to fit on one 80 byte record. When this is the case additional records may be used to hold the rest of the statement. A JCL listing is easier to read if continued statements are coded in a sensible and consistent manner. The following rules describe the syntax required to code a JCL statement that occupies more than one 80 byte record:

1) Except for the last record in a continued statement, the operand field of every record which contains part of the statement should end with a complete parameter and its following comma or a complete subparameter and its following comma. Exceptions are noted in Rule 7 below.

2) Except for the first record in a continued statement, the first three characters in every record in the continuation must contain //b, where b represents a blank. The actual continuation text may be resumed anywhere in columns 4–16. Following a continued statement, if //x is coded in the first three bytes and x is any character other than a blank or an asterisk, a JCL syntax error results. If the continuation text begins after column 16, the entire 80 bytes is treated as a comment. The printed JCL listing of every statement that the system interprets as a Comment statement contains *** in the first three characters.

3) No JCL operands or commas can extend beyond column 71. Also, the complete operation field must be coded to the left of column 72 on the first statement of a continuation.

4) No embedded blanks are permitted between parameters in the operand field. All code which follows the first blank will be interpreted as a comment. This is a common source of JCL problems. Such problems are often difficult to detect, since they may not generate a syntax error message.

5) It is unnecessary to code a continuation character in column 72. Except when continuing the comment field, all coding in columns 72–80 is ignored. Columns 73–80 are frequently used to number the JCL statements in a job stream.

6) It is unnecessary to continue a comment field. When this is done, the following rules must be used: The statement being continued may end anywhere prior to column 72. Column 72 must contain a non-blank continuation character. The continued statement must contain // in columns 1 and 2. The continued comment may begin anywhere to the right of column 3.

7) Special continuation rules are used with the PARM parameter on the EXEC statement, and when assigning values to symbolic parameters on the EXEC statement. These topics are discussed in Chapters 5 and 8 respectively.

As mentioned above, *** precedes every Comment statement in the printed JCL listing. //* prints in front of any other type of coded JCL statement that contains only comments. Likewise, XX* identifies a non-Comment statement in a cataloged procedure which contains only comments. Finally, ++* denotes a similar statement in an in-stream procedure.

Example 5: The following statements illustrate several valid and invalid JCL continuations:

Valid JCL Continuations

```
//A    EXEC  PGM=ABCDEF,
//     REGION=256K,
//     COND=EVEN

//DD1 DD  DSN=X,DISP=(OLD,PASS)  THIS IS A          X
//                               CONTINUED COMMENT

//DD2 DD  DSN=X,DISP=SHR,DCB=(DSORG=DA,
//        LIMCT=3,OPTCD=E)
```

Invalid JCL Continuations	*Reason*
`//DD1 DD DSN=X,DISP=(OLD,PASS)` `// UNIT=3350,VOL=SER=WORK01`	no comma after DISP parameter
`//DD2 DD DSN=X,DISP=(OLD,PASS),` `// UNIT=3350,VOL=SER=WORK01`	continuation begins beyond column 16
`//DD3 DD DSN=X,DISP=(NEW,PASS),` `// DD UNIT=VIO,SPACE=(CYL,1)`	DD repeated on second statement

`//DD4 DD DSN=X,UNIT=3380,DCB=(OPTCD=I,`
`// LY,DSORG=IS),SPACE=(CYL,1),`
`// DISP=(,PASS)`
	continued in middle of subparameter

JCL Coding Standards

Many installations have developed JCL coding standards, which make it much easier to avoid and detect JCL problems. When everyone is using the same JCL format, it is also much easier to get help with JCL syntax problems. Finally, JCL coding standards produce more readable job listings. Some common JCL coding standards cannot be understood with only the small amount of JCL syntax described to this point, but many of the guidelines listed here should make sense. The complete set of guidelines should be reread after Chapters 4–8 are studied.

1. All DD operators should be aligned in the same columns. Likewise, the first parameter on each DD statement should begin in the same column. The same two rules hold for EXEC operators and the program or procedure name that follows the EXEC.

2. All continued statements should begin in the same column. This improves readability, and also makes it easier to detect syntax errors.

3. Keyword parameters should be coded in a specific relative order on JOB, EXEC, DD, and OUTPUT statements. Programmers may select their own orders. This makes it easier to avoid omitting a required parameter or coding the same parameter twice. Additionally, all statements of the same type look basically the same. For similar reasons keyword subparameters should be coded in a specific relative order.

4. Every step in a job should have a comment block that clearly and concisely describes the processing being performed in the step. Comments should not repeat information that can be readily determined from reading the JCL. For example, the statement

```
//*THIS  STEP USES THE PROGRAM OR PGM CALLED IKFCBL00
```

need not be included in a comment block, since the information the comment contains can be taken from the EXEC statement itself.

5. In order to highlight comments, enclose them in a block of asterisks. This appreciably improves the appearance of the JCL listing. Here is a suggested format:

```
//*******************************************************
//*
//*   CLEAR AND CONCISE COMMENTS SHOULD BE CODED HERE
//*
//*******************************************************
```

6. JCL comments should be included as part of a comment block as described in the previous guideline. In general, do not append a comment field to a non-Comment JCL statement. For example, the following is a valid JCL statement:

```
//A EXEC COBUCG  THIS IS A COBOL COMPILE AND GO PROCEDURE
```

However, all comment information should be placed in a comment block. Notice that the content of this comment also violates guideline 4 above.

7. Comments should be included with the job step they are describing. Place every comment block in front of or after the EXEC statements. Do not place them within an adjacent job step! This can require care when using cataloged or instream procedures, since comments placed after an overriding DD statement and immediately before the next EXEC statement will appear in the midst of the procedure following the overridden statement. This is undesirable since the comments apply to the upcoming job step.

8. Comments should be written in readable English, with all words spelled correctly. Spelling and grammar errors create an unfavorable impression when the listing is read.

9. Avoid using national characters (@,#,$) in the name fields of JCL statements. Many programmers are unaware that they are allowed, and others have trouble remembering which three symbols comprise the nationals.

10. Remove all GENERATED SYSIN DD statements from the JCL listing. Although these do not always lead to problems, they are frequently an indication of careless programming. This message results when a necessary DD * statement is omitted. This is a familiar occurrence with CICS and TSO users who allocate more lines than are really needed and submit their job before deleting the unused lines. Omitting a COB.SYSIN DD statement will also generate this message when a COBOL program is compiled with the COBUCG procedure.

11. With cataloged procedures, code a PROC statement which contains a procedure name.

12. All statements that begin with /* (JES2 statements such as /*ROUTE, /*JOBPARM, and /*MESSAGE) should be placed together after the JOB statement

and prior to the first EXEC statement. The /* PRIORITY statement must be coded in front of the JOB statement. There is no required order among the JES2 statements themselves, however. The same rule holds for JES3 statements. If JOBLIB, JOBCAT, or SYSCHK DD statements are present, they should also be coded consecutively following the JES statements.

13. Use /*MESSAGE statements with jobs that require tape mounts or special processing requests. Explain all pertinent information that the operators will need for the job on the /*MESSAGE statement.

14. Code the Null statement (//) as the last statement in a job stream.

15. Unless a new data set requires a specific disk volume, allow MVS to select the volume. This allows the system to better utilize resources, and requires less JCL to be coded.

16. Do not 'remove' JCL statements from a job stream by turning them into comments (by typing //* in the first three columns and allowing the statements to remain in the job stream). Rather, 'remove' statements by physically deleting them. This guideline applies only to the final copy of the program listing. During program development, this may be an acceptable practice.

17. Do not 'remove' a DD statement from a job stream by coding another DD statement with the same DDname in front of it in the same jobstep. Instead, physically remove it. Although JES2 will ignore the second of two distinct DD statements in the same jobstep that have the same DDname, leaving both generates a confusing JCL listing.

18. Following an EXEC statement, code the STEPLIB, STEPCAT, and message data set DD statements in the relative order shown here (provided that the statement type is present):

```
//STEP1       EXEC
//STEPLIB      DD   user load module library
//STEPCAT      DD   user catalog
//SYSPRINT     DD   message data set, other DDnames are
                    allowed, SYSPRINT is frequently used.
```

19. With job streams that consist of more than three jobsteps, use a straightforward pattern for naming the steps. The pattern should specify the relative location of each step within the job stream. For example, call the steps A, B, C, etc. Another common group of stepnames is STEP1, STEP2, STEP3, etc. This makes it quicker to locate a specific step in the listing. If a job stream consists of two or more steps, each step should have a unique name.

20. Do not code a COND parameter on the first EXEC statement in a job. COND is used to test the results of prior jobsteps, so it is meaningless in this case.

21. Within a job step, place all DD statements for in-stream data sets after all the other DD statements. It is possible to have more than one in-stream data set in a single job step.

22. Do not code unnecessary apostrophes to enclose a character string. In particular, apostrophes are rarely needed if the character string consists entirely of letters, numbers, and nationals.

23. Be consistent. If a function is to be performed two or more times within a job stream, do it the same way each time. Doing it differently implies that it is not the same function.

24. When reading records from a heavily used system data set, code DISP=SHR. When writing records to the same data set, code DISP=OLD.

Example 6: Carefully examine the job streams listed below. They illustrate how coding standards can improve the appearance and readability of a JCL listing. The

JCL with Standards

```
//USER123  JOB (Accounting Information),'F. Lastname',
//      CLASS=A,MSGCLASS=B,PRTY=6,MSGLEVEL=(1,1)
/*ROUTE PRINT TERM
/*JOBPARM COPIES=2
//**************************************************************
//* THE DEPARTMENT MASTER FILE IS MODIFIED IN STEP 1
//**************************************************************
//STEP1    EXEC PGM=UPDATE
//STEPLIB  DD   DSN=SYS1.XYZ,DISP=SHR
//SYSPRINT DD   SYSOUT=A
//MASTER   DD   DSN=OLD.MASTER,DISP=(OLD,PASS),
//              UNIT=3380, VOL=SER=WORK01
//WORKDS   DD   DSN=&&TEMP,DISP=(NEW,PASS),
//              UNIT=3380,SPACE=(CYL,(5,1))
//**************************************************************
//* A SORTED REPORT ON NEW TRANSACTIONS IS PRINTED IN STEP 2
//**************************************************************
//STEP2    EXEC PGM=REPORT
//SUMMARY  DD   SYSOUT=A,OUTLIM=5000,COPIES=10
//TEMP1    DD   UNIT=SYSDA,SPACE=(CYL,(10,5))
//TEMP2    DD   UNIT=SYSDA,SPACE=(CYL,(10,5))
//SYSIN    DD   *
  . . . in-stream data set
/*
//
```

first listing follows the standards outlined above; the second does not adhere to the standards. Although the second version is syntactically correct and performs exactly the same functions as the first, notice how much easier it is to read the first listing. Determine the specific coding guidelines that are broken in the second listing.

JCL with No Standards

```
//MYJOB    JOB  (Accounting Information),'ME',MSGLEVEL=(1,
//      1),PRTY=6,MSGCLASS=B,CLASS=A     TYPRUN=SCAN
// EXEC    PGM=UPDATE,COND=EVEN
//MASTER   DD DSN=OLD.MASTER,DISP=(OLD,PASS),VOL=SER=WORK01,
//         UNIT=3380
//WORKDS        DD         DISP=(NEW,PASS),
//         DSN=&TEMP,UNIT=3380,SPACE=(CYL,(5,10)),
//   VOL=SER=WORK02
//STEPLIB      DD      DSN=SYS1.XYZ,DISP=OLD
//SYSPRINT                  DD    SYSOUT=*
/*ROUTE PRINT TERM
//*STEP TWO HERE
//MFREPORT  EXEC  PGM=REPORT,COND=EVEN
//TEMP2    DD   SPACE=(CYL,(10,10)),UNIT=SYSDA
//TEMP1    DD   UNIT=VIO VIO DETERMINES THE SPACE VALUE
//TEMP2  DD   UNIT=VIO
/*JOBPARM N=2
//*UMMARY DD       COPIES=10,SYSOUT=A
//SUMMARY DD   OUTLIM=5000,COPIES=10,SYSOUT=A
  . . . in-stream data set
//*
```

Additional Syntax Rules

There are several additional general syntax rules. Parentheses must always be coded in pairs. No trailing parentheses can be omitted with any parameter. Parentheses are always required to enclose multiple subparameter values. With one keyword subparameter or a single leading positional subparameter, parentheses are optional.

Variable length character strings may be coded with several JCL parameters. Depending on the characters which comprise the string, the complete string may have to be enclosed in apostrophes. As a general rule of thumb, a character string must be enclosed in apostrophes unless it contains special characters. A special character is usually any symbol other than a letter, number, or national. Some slight variations in the definition of special characters occur with specific JCL parameters and subparameters. In some instances either parentheses or apostrophes may be used to enclose a character string.

Several specific combinations of adjacent characters are explicitly prohibited, including a period immediately after an opening parenthesis or immediately before a closing parenthesis.

Finally, a parameter, either positional or keyword, can only be coded once on a given JCL statement. Names of parameters and reserved word parameter values never exceed eight characters in length.

Chapter Summary

The material in this chapter should be thoroughly understood by a person wishing to master JCL. It is the basic information on which the next five chapters build. The final example illustrates this material using a moderately complex DD statement. It also illustrates that, as more JCL is learned, less must be coded to achieve a specific result.

Example 7: The DD statement coded below illustrates many of the syntax properties discussed in this chapter. The functions of the various DD parameters coded are unimportant, but the basic syntax should be examined carefully. The initial statement is coded when the data set is created, and it is syntactically correct. However, much of the information contained in the statement is completely unnecessary. In addition, some of the information could be supplied from non-JCL sources.

```
//ALPHA DD DSNAME=ALPHA.BETA,DISP=(NEW,KEEP,KEEP),
//          UNIT=TAPE,LABEL=(1,SL,,,RETPD=1),
//          DCB=(DSORG=PS,LRECL=100,BLKSIZE=16000,DEN=4,
//          RECFM=FBS,BUFNO=3),FREE=END,
//          VOLUME=(SER=TAPE01)
```

Several of the values coded are the defaults and need not be explicitly supplied. These default values include the first and third DISP positional subparameters, two keyword subparameters coded with DCB, and the first two positional subparameters coded with LABEL. END is the default value for the rarely coded FREE parameter. In addition, one of the RECFM sub-subparameter values is meaningless during data set creation. When all of these are omitted, the DD statement becomes:

```
//ALPHA DD DSN=ALPHA.BETA,DISP=(,KEEP),
//          LABEL=RETPD=1,UNIT=TAPE,
//          DCB=(LRECL=100,RECFM=FB,BLKSIZE=16000,BUFNO=3),
//          VOL=SER=TAPE01
```

Note that one leading comma is necessary to show that the first DISP subparameter was omitted. However, no commas should be coded to denote the omission of the last DISP subparameter or any DCB keyword parameters. The order of the UNIT and LABEL keyword parameters has been switched. The order of the DCB subparameters has also been changed. Abbreviations are used for both DSNAME and

VOLUME. Finally, the fifth LABEL subparameter is now coded as a keyword rather than a positional subparameter. Parentheses are not necessary with either the LABEL or VOL parameters.

Several of the remaining values may be selected by the system. For example, if DSNAME and VOLUME are not coded when creating a data set, the system generates a name for the data set and selects a volume on which to place it. In some situations the name and location of a data set are not important. Likewise, the system will pick a value for the BUFNO subparameter. By allowing the system to determine these three values, the amount of code in the DD statement is further reduced to:

```
//ALPHA DD DISP=(,KEEP),
//          LABEL=RETPD=1,UNIT=TAPE,
//          DCB=(LRECL=100,RECFM=FB,BLKSIZE=16000)
```

With a tape data set the second DISP subparameter values of KEEP and DELETE perform the same primary function, and DELETE is the default. In addition, all of the DCB values may also be supplied from the application program if it was written in COBOL, PL/I, or assembler. The LABEL value is essentially meaningless. Thus, the intent conveyed in the initial DD statement can also be achieved by coding only:

```
//ALPHA DD UNIT=TAPE
```

The original statement contained seven parameters and twelve subparameters; this final DD statement contains one parameter and no subparameters.

Exercises

1. For each of the following JCL statements, find the errors (if any). Some statements contain more than one error. Look only for syntax errors, since the actual meaning of most parameters has not yet been explained. Most of the statements are incorrect, but a few are valid.

```
a) //JOB    EXEC   PROC   DD     PEND
b) //A     DD    DSN=XYZ,SPACE=(TRK,
   //   (2,1),UNIT=3350,VOL=SER=DISK01
c) //EXECSTEP PGM=IEBGENER,PARM='1%&*@6>D",TIME=(,95)
d) //EXEC   EXEC   EXEC
e) //D   EXEC   PGM=X
   //
   //D   EXEC   PGM=Y
f) //ABC   DD DSNAME=DSNAME,DISP=(,KEEP),VOL=SER=DISK99,
   //UNIT=3380,SPACE=(CYL,5),DCB=(ALPHA1),
   //LABEL=RETPD=100
g) //SYSTMDUMP DD OUTLIM=100,COPIES=2,SYSOUT=*
h) //ABC DD DSN=ABCABCAB,DISP=(OLD,PASS),UNIT=SYSDA,
   //   SPACE=(TRK,20),UNIT=3350,DCB=(LRECL=80,RECFM=F),
   // VOL=(,RETAIN,SER=WORK99)
```

```
i) //DEF  DD DSN=DEFDEFDE,      A-BIZARRE-COMMENT-HERE      X
   // DISP=SHR  DISP=OLD
j) //GHI  DD               DSN=ABC.DEF.GHIJK, DISP=(OLD,PASS)
k) //JKL  DD DSN=X.X.X.X.X.XXX,UNIT=3380,VOL=SER=DISK98,
   //               SPACE=(CYL,1),DISP=(NEW,CATLG)
l) //BBBBBBBB DD DSN=X,DISP=(NEW,),SPACE=,UNIT=VIO
m)//JKL  DD DSN=XXXXXXXX,UNIT=3380 VOL=SER=DISK98,
   //          SPACE=(CYL,1),DISP=(,,CATLG)
n) //*$X   DD UNIT=VIO,DISP=(OLD,DESTROYED)
o) //DD-1     DD   DSN=OLDDATA.1SET,DISP=(OLD,,PASS,),
   //    DCB=(ALPHA1)
p) //DD3   DD   UNIT=,
   //          3350,TAPE=012345,DCB=BLKSIZE=1000
q) //DD4   DD   DSN=DUMMY,DISP=(OLD,PASS)
   //      DD   DUMMY,DISP=(NEW,PASS),UNIT=VIO
   //      DD   ,UNIT=VIO
r) //AAAAAAAA DD DSN=XYZ,SPACE=(CYL,(3,(2,(1))),
       DISP=NEW,VOL=SER=ABCDEF,UNIT=SYSDA
```

2. Describe a set of conditions under which the statements which follow a Null statement in the same job stream will be interpreted and processed as actual JCL statements, rather than merely ignored.

3. Describe the minimum number of fields that can possibly be coded on each of the following types of JCL statement: JOB, EXEC, DD, OUTPUT, PROC, and PEND. For each type of statement, illustrate the answer with an example.

4. Under what conditions are complete statements or parts of statements interpreted as comments? List at least four distinct situations where this occurs.

5. For each of the six major JCL statements, determine the location of the left–most character in which a comment field may begin. Consider an entire statement that is written on one 80 byte record, and also a statement that is continued to another record. With which statement types does the answer remain the same for both cases? State any assumptions used in determining your answers.

6. Determine if the parameter types specified are syntactically correct for each of the following statements. Explain why a given statement is invalid. Here P represents a positional parameter, K a keyword parameter, and S a symbolic parameter.

```
a) //A    EXEC P,K,S,K
b) //JOB  JOB  P,P,K,K,S
c) //ABC   DD  P,K,P,K,P
d) //ABC   DD  P,K,S,S,S
e) //ABC   DD  S,P,K,S
f) //ABC  EXEC K,K,K
g) //XYZ  PROC P,K,S
h) //JOB  JOB  ,P,K
i) //Q    PEND K,K
j) //EFG  EXEC S,S,K
k) //DD1   DD  ,K,K
```

7. For each of the following parameters, determine whether the syntax is correct. Here P represents a positional subparameter, K a keyword subparameter, and S a symbolic subparameter.

a) `parameter=(P,,P)`
b) `parameter=(K,P,S)`
c) `parameter=(S,S,P,P,K)`
d) `parameter=S`
e) `parameter=(P,K)`
f) `parameter=(SS)`
g) `parameter=(P,S,K)`

8. What do the following symbols specify when coded as the first three characters of a JCL statement? Some of the symbols are invalid. What do the same symbols mean when they appear in the printed listing of a job stream?

a) `//`
b) `//*`
c) `***`
d) `XX*`
e) `++*`
f) `**b←blank in column 3`
g) `/*b←blank in column 3`
h) `/*X←non blank`

9. Duplicate stepnames are permitted in a job stream. This is one of several instances in which it seems appropriate that a warning message be issued to inform the programmer of the duplication. What is the probable reason why no warning message is issued? Where else does duplication go undetected?

10. Which types of JCL statements may be coded in a job stream but do not appear in the printed JCL listing? Which types of JCL statements appear in the printed listing in a different format from that in which they are coded?

11. Which fields on JCL statements can be continued?

12. Develop some additional JCL coding standards to supplement the ones listed in this chapter. What are the reasons for each standard? This project should actually be on-going while working through the next five chapters.

Chapter 4

The JOB Statement and JES2 Statements

The JOB Statement

Overview

The general format of the JOB statement is as follows:

```
//jobname  JOB  Accounting Information,Programmer Name,
//  keyword parameters   optional comment field
```

The JOB statement is required for every job stream, and is usually the first statement in the job stream. Only certain JES statements may precede it in the job stream. The jobnames must be unique for jobs concurrently executing in the system. The two positional parameters, Accounting Information and Programmer Name, are optional; an installation may require either, neither, or both. Most commonly both are required. Accounting Information is placed first in the operand field when both are coded. If one or both is not required, a comma must not be coded to denote the omitted parameter. All keyword parameters are also optional. The JOB statement contains seventeen keyword parameters. Fourteen of these parameters are discussed in this chapter; the COND, RD, and RESTART keyword parameters are discussed in other chapters. If the operand field is present, comments may also be coded on the JOB statement.

JOB statement parameters are examined below. The positional parameters are covered first, followed by the keyword parameters. Symbolic parameters are not permitted on the JOB statement.

Accounting Information

Accounting Information is the first positional parameter. The syntax of the Accounting Information parameter is completely determined by the installation. Accounting Information can be enclosed in parentheses or quotes. Some examples of Accounting Information parameters are shown below:

Accounting Information Parameter Syntax	*Meaning of the Accounting Information Subparameters*
(xxxx,yyy)	xxxx = programmer identification
(xxxx,yyy,zzzzzzzzz)	yyy = department identification
(xxxx,yyy,zzzzzzzzz,pp)	zzzzzzzzz = Social Security number
	pp = project number
(xxxx,yyy,cccccccc)	cccccccc = security code/password
(A,B,C,D,E,F,G,H,I)	specific JES2 positional subparameters

Each of the nine fields has a standard interpretation with JES2. The letters have the following meanings: A = Account Number, B = Room Number, C = Time in Minutes, D = Line Count in Thousands of Lines, E = Number of Cards Punched, F = Special Forms, G = Number of Copies of the Complete Output Listing, H = Print the JES Job Log, and I = Number of Lines per Page.

Programmer Name

The Programmer Name field is optional, but is required at most installations. If Accounting Information is also coded, Programmer Name is the second positional parameter. The Programmer Name field may contain up to 20 characters. If the value coded contains special characters, the field must be enclosed in apostrophes. Standard MVS conventions for using apostrophes apply here. Hence, to code O'BRIAN as the Programmer Name, 'O''BRIAN' must actually be written. With Programmer Name, special characters include all symbols except alphabetics, numerics, nationals, hyphens, and leading and embedded periods. As shown in Table 4–1, the definition of special characters is different from the standard IBM definition.

TABLE 4–1
Special Characters

Terminology	*Character Set*	*Number*
Alphabetics	A through Z	26
Numerics	0 through 9	10
Nationals	@, #, and $	3
Alphanumerics or Alphamerics	A through Z, and 0 through 9	36
Special Characters	All characters except Alphanumerics and Nationals	

It is unnecessary to code apostrophes when they are not needed. However, many programmers always code apostrophes with the Programmer Name value.

The Programmer Name value prints on the front and back separator pages of the program listing, making it easier to identify. This alone is a good reason to require that Programmer Name be coded. A common format for Programmer Name is 'F. LASTNAME'.

The remaining JOB statement parameters are keyword. On the JOB statement, the COND parameter determines if and when the entire job will be terminated. COND is a very complex parameter, and is discussed as a separate topic in Chapter 20. The RD and RESTART parameters are used with restarts and checkpoints. These are among the most complex of the JOB statement parameters, and are discussed in Chapter 22.

ADDRSPC

The ADDRSPC parameter is used if all of the steps within the job should be executed in real storage or all should be executed in virtual storage. Either VIRT or REAL must be specified. When ADDRSPC=VIRT is coded, the steps in the job can be paged. With ADDRSPC=REAL, they cannot be paged. If ADDRSPC is also coded on an EXEC statement, the value coded on the JOB statement overrides it. The default is VIRT.

Requesting real storage places a much heavier demand on system resources. Hence, ADDRSPC=REAL is rarely coded in a standard application program. However, there are two common situations in which REAL is needed: in a banking environment when sorting checks, and when an executing channel program must be modified.

CLASS

The CLASS parameter assigns each job to a specific job class. There are 36 possible job classes, which are identified by either letters (A-Z) or numbers (0-9). Each installation individually defines the various classes and the types of jobs they hold. Classes should be defined in a manner that will ensure a good mixture of jobs running concurrently in the system at all times. The correct use of the CLASS parameter and the assignment of class values is meant to avoid situations where most of the jobs running are predominantly the same type (i.e., all number crunching programs or all jobs which perform a large amount of I/O). Recall that each job initiator selects jobs only from certain classes. The CLASS parameter supplies this value to the initiators. Hence, the delay until a job is selected for execution is controlled by this parameter and the status of other jobs currently executing and submitted for execution. The role of the CLASS parameter is examined in more detail in Chapter 1.

Example 1: At one installation, the CLASS values and their meanings are defined as follows:

Class	*Definitions*
A	All jobs, other than IMS batch, which use less than 5 CPU minutes and require no operator set-up
B	IMS batch jobs, which use less then 5 CPU minutes and require no operator set-up
M	Night jobs that require no operator set-up
N	Jobs that require operator set-up, special print forms, or tape mounts
V	Night Production
W	Day Production
X	CICS
Z	All other jobs except for class 1
1	Jobs that require less than 1 minute of CPU time

GROUP

The GROUP parameter is used with RACF, the Resource Access Control Facility program, which is an IBM security programming product. The GROUP parameter allows a programmer to access resources protected by RACF. Most commonly the resources are data sets. If GROUP is coded on the JOB statement, the USER and PASSWORD parameters must also be coded. If GROUP is not coded and USER is, the default RACF group for the user is selected.

MSGCLASS

The MSGCLASS parameter identifies the output class used for printing system messages, JCL statements, and allocation messages. The 36 permissible MSGCLASS values are letters (A-Z) and numbers (0-9). Each individual installation assigns the various MSGCLASS values and determines their meanings. Similar to CLASS, the MSGCLASS values are defined to ensure that the desired type of output is being produced.

To route output data sets that are created during the job to the same destination as the MSGCLASS value, code either SYSOUT=*, SYSOUT=$, or SYSOUT=the-MSGCLASS-value on the DD statement. The asterisk (*) and dollar sign ($) are used to reference the value coded on the JOB statement. In this situation a DD statement value is supplied from the MSGCLASS parameter on the JOB statement.

MSGLEVEL

The MSGLEVEL parameter determines the specific amount of output (JCL and allocation messages) that is to be written to the MSGCLASS output device. The JES log and some system messages are unaffected by the MSGLEVEL parameter. MSGLEVEL is composed of two positional subparameters. Standard positional subparameter conventions must be followed when coding MSGLEVEL. The exact syntax is MSGLEVEL=(X,Y), where X specifies the amount of JCL which is to be printed and Y determines if the allocation messages are written.

The following values may be coded for X:

Value	*Meaning*
0	Only the JOB statement is printed.
1	Every JCL statement in the job stream is printed. Cataloged and in-stream procedure statements are also included.
2	Only the JCL statements actually coded are printed. No statements copied from cataloged or in-stream procedures are printed.

The following values may be coded for Y:

Value	*Meaning*
0	Unless the job abends, no messages are written.
1	Under all circumstances all of the allocation messages are written.

With JES2 the default MSGLEVEL value is determined by the CLASS parameter. With JES3 the default value is determined by the reader supplying the job. The two most common default values are MSGLEVEL=(0,0) and MSGLEVEL=(1,1), which produce the least and most printed output respectively. During program development and testing MSGLEVEL=(1,1) should almost always be used.

NOTIFY

The NOTIFY parameter sends a message to a TSO user when a background job has finished executing. TSO (Time Sharing Option) is a major IBM program product which is used at almost every MVS installation. If the user identified on the NOTIFY parameter is not logged on when the job finishes, the message is saved and displayed when the user logs on again. The person notified need not be the person who submitted the job. The actual syntax is NOTIFY=TSO-user-identification.

PASSWORD

Like GROUP and USER, the PASSWORD parameter is used with RACF. PASSWORD is composed of two positional subparameters. Standard positional subparameter conventions must be followed when coding the PASSWORD parameter. When PASSWORD is coded, the USER parameter must also be coded on the JOB statement. The PASSWORD parameter performs two functions: the first subparameter identifies the user's current password, and the second subparameter is used to select a new password. If a password expires a new password must be coded. This is common at many installations. Coding PASSWORD=(ALPHA,BETA) specifies that ALPHA is the present RACF password and BETA is to become the new password.

PERFORM

The PERFORM parameter assigns a job to a performance group. Performance groups are entirely installation defined. PERFORM specifies the processing rate for a job within the performance group, based on the existing system workload. If PERFORM is also coded on an EXEC statement, the value coded on the JOB statement overrides it. If PERFORM is not coded on either statement, the Job Entry System selects a default value. The value coded with PERFORM can be unimportant when the system workload is relatively light. During heavy system utilization, however, the PERFORM value is crucial to determining system performance. Whether the PERFORM value is meaningful depends on the other jobs running concurrently on the system, since PERFORM attempts to dynamically prioritize the jobs that are executing. This should be contrasted with the CLASS and PRTY parameters which statically prioritize the jobs submitted for execution. A value from 1 to 255 must be coded with PERFORM. Thus, to assign a job to performance group 3, code PERFORM=3.

PRTY

The PRTY parameter determines the priority in which a job is selected for execution. The value coded with PRTY is meaningful only within the CLASS in which the job is placed. The system initiators select jobs with the highest priorities within a specific CLASS first. With JES2 values from 0 to 15 may be coded, where 15 is the highest value. With JES3 values range from 0 to 13. Specific system resources, such as CPU time and amount of memory, can be assigned maximum values based on the PRTY value. For example, PRTY=8 may provide a maximum of 1 minute of CPU time and a region of 500K. If PRTY is not coded, a default value is assigned by the installation. The role of the PRTY parameter is examined in more detail in Chapter 1.

REGION

The REGION parameter establishes the amount of memory available for the duration of the job. This parameter is coded as REGION=valueK. To request 400K bytes of memory code REGION=400K, not REGION=400. The REGION value coded on the JOB statement overrides any REGION parameter coded on an EXEC statement. An even number should be specified for the REGION value. A default REGION value is set by the installation (usually determined by the PRTY parameter). There is also a maximum REGION value set by the installation. A common default value for REGION is 512K. A common maximum REGION value is 1500K. The actual type of memory provided is determined by the ADDRSPC parameter.

TIME

The TIME parameter specifies the amount of CPU time allowed for the entire job. If the TIME parameter is also coded on an EXEC statement, both parameters are in effect for the duration of that step. Note that this is different from most other parameters, that are coded on both the JOB statement and an EXEC statement. Timing can also be controlled in a third location, on a /*JOBPARM JES statement. The TIME parameter consists of two positional subparameters. Standard positional subparameter syntax conventions must be followed when coding the TIME parameter. Code TIME=(minutes,seconds), where minutes ranges from 0 to 1440, and seconds ranges from 0 to 59. To specify that the job not be timed, code TIME=1440. Some imprecision is possible with the TIME parameter values used on both the JOB and EXEC statements. TIME must be coded in order to request an execution time less than the maximum permitted within a given CLASS and PRTY.

Example 2: Two steps in a job may each execute for one minute of CPU time. However, the logic of the job is such that both steps together should run in less than 90 seconds of total CPU time. This can be accomplished by coding:

```
//JOB1      JOB    ...,TIME=(1,30)
//STEP1     EXEC   PGM=X,TIME=1
    ...
//STEP2     EXEC   PGM=Y,TIME=(1)
```

TYPRUN

The TYPRUN parameter is used to request special JES processing. Four possible values may be coded: HOLD, JCLHOLD, SCAN, and COPY. When TYPRUN=HOLD is coded the job is held for execution until it is released by the operator. TYPRUN=HOLD is convenient when the successful execution of the job is dependent on some event which may not have occurred. If a job contains JCL syntax errors, it will not be held.

JCLHOLD is the least frequently used of the four values. When TYPRUN=JCLHOLD is coded the job is not processed by the JCL converter until it is released by the operator. An example of a situation where JCLHOLD might be used is shown in Chapter 27, Example 1.

When TYPRUN=SCAN is coded the JCL is checked for syntax errors, but the job is not executed. With JES2 this checking includes invalid keywords and characters and parentheses errors, but does not include all possible syntax errors. JES3 also checks for excessive parentheses and parameter value errors.

TYPRUN=COPY converts the entire job stream, JCL and in-stream data, into a (printed) SYSOUT data set. The job is not executed, and no other processing is performed. The MSGCLASS parameter determines the SYSOUT class used.

USER

The USER parameter is the third RACF parameter allowed on the JOB statement. It permits a user to access RACF protected resources. When USER is coded, PASSWORD must also be specified. USER is required if either GROUP or PASSWORD is coded.

Summary of Job Statement Parameters

Example 3: Code the JOB statement needed to run a class X job which has a priority of 11. The job needs at most 45 seconds of CPU time, and requires a maximum of 256K bytes of virtual storage. There are four steps in the job. When the job finishes executing, inform TSO user T123X. Suppress all JCL and allocation messages. The job must be released by the operator.

```
//FMLXXXX JOB (1125,515),'L BRUMBAUGH',CLASS=X,PRTY=11,
//    TIME=(,45),ADDRSPC=VIRT,REGION=256K,NOTIFY=T123X,
//    MSGLEVEL=(0,0),MSGCLASS=A,TYPRUN=HOLD
```

Example 4: Run the same job as in the previous example, but let CLASS and PRTY determine default values for TIME and REGION. Eliminate the operator releasing the job, and do not inform the TSO user. Print the maximum amount of JCL and allocation messages. Printed output should go to message class C. The job should execute in real storage.

```
//FMLXXXX JOB (1125,515),'L BRUMBAUGH',CLASS=X,PRTY=11,
//    ADDRSPC=REAL,MSGLEVEL=(1,1),MSGCLASS=C
```

Exercises

1. For each of the following JCL statements, find the errors (if any). Some statements contain more than one error. Look mainly for syntax errors.

```
a) //A    JOB   MSGCLASS=8,MSGLEVEL=(1,2),REGION=1000,
   //     ADRSPC=REAL,CLASS=*,TYPRUN=JCLSCAN
b) //B    JOB   1,X,TIME=4096
c) //C    JOB   (1,2,3),LARRY,ADDRSPC=REAL,MSGCLASS=A,
   //     REGION=4000K,CLASS=A
```

2. Why are the CLASS and PRTY parameters coded only on the JOB statement and not on the EXEC statement? Why is PERFORM coded with both statement types? Note that all three parameters supply the same general category of information.

3. Write the parameters to allocate 300K bytes of real memory to every step in a job. What effect might this have on the other jobs executing on the system? Write the parameters to allocate 300K bytes of virtual memory to every step in a job.

4. Suppose two jobs with the same jobname are submitted for execution. The jobs have different PRTY and CLASS values coded on their JOB statements. In what order do the jobs get executed? Can both jobs be executing in the system at the same time?

5. What occurs when TIME=1440 is coded on a JOB statement? What is the significance of the numeric value 1440?

6. Two job streams are read through a card reader one after the other. The first job does not end with a Null Statement. Describe several different conditions under which the second job will be interpreted as a continuation of the first.

JES2 Statements

Overview

Seven JES2 control statements are discussed in this section. JES2 statements are not actual JCL statements. Rather they are used to request that the Job Entry System perform specific functions while processing a job. JES2 control statements are also called JECL (Job Entry Control Language) statements. JES2 statements are coded within a job stream and are interspersed with the JCL. One JES2 statement, the PRIORITY statement, must be placed in front of the JOB statement. The other six must follow the JOB statement. Traditionally all other JES2 statements are coded together immediately after the JOB statement and before the first EXEC or DD statement. Like the JOBLIB and JOBCAT DD statements, a JES statement is in effect for the entire job. However, JES statements may be coded anywhere within the job stream. There is no required order among the six other JES statement types.

As with JCL, specific syntax rules must be observed when coding JES2 control statements. There are several significant differences between JES2 and JCL syntax, including the following: The first two characters of each statement must contain a /*. There is no name field on any of the JES2 statements. Rather, the operator begins in byte three and also serves as the statement identifier. The complete JES2 statement format contains two fields and is coded as follows:

```
/*operator          operands
```

Since the operator field is required, this format distinguishes a JES2 statement from the JCL Delimiter statement. After the operator one or more blanks must precede the first operand. With older releases of JES2 the spacing between operator and operand fields varied with the different JES statements. A good practice is to code exactly one blank between the operator and operand fields.

The format of the operand field varies from statement to statement. Two JES2 statements, JOBPARM and OUTPUT, consist of a large number of keyword parameters. One statement, ROUTE, consists of two positional parameters. The SETUP statement requires a list of volume names. The other three statements require one specific value each.

Continuation is permitted only with the OUTPUT statement. However, multiple control statements of the same type may be coded. If two statements of the same type are coded, and both contain the same parameter, the parameter on the second statement has priority. If two parameters of the same type are coded on a single statement, the second parameter is used and the first ignored. JES2 statements are ignored if placed in a procedure. A detailed examination of the seven JES2 control statements follows.

JOBPARM

Twelve keyword parameters may be coded with JOBPARM. All of them supply values that are in effect throughout the entire job. Much of the information they supply cannot be specified in other places in the job stream. The parameters may be coded in any order. Most parameters use a standard keyword syntax of keyword= value. Ten of the most commonly coded parameters are described below.

`CARDS=xxxxxxx` This identifies the maximum number of punched cards produced by the job. Up to 10 million cards may be punched. CARDS may be abbreviated as C.

`COPIES=xxx` When this is coded xxx copies of the complete output listing are printed. COPIES may be abbreviated as N. Here xxx can be any value from 1 to 255 inclusive.

`LINECT=xxx` This identifies the number of lines to print on each page of output. Values from 0 to 255 may be coded. LINECT may be abbreviated as K. LINECT=0 may cause printing over the page separators.

`LINES=xxxx` This identifies the maximum number of printed lines produced by the job. The value coded specifies thousands of lines. Up to 10 million lines may be printed. LINES may be abbreviated as L.

`NOLOG` If NOLOG is coded the JES2 job log will not be printed at the beginning of the listing. NOLOG may be abbreviated as J.

`PROCLIB=DDname` This identifies the procedure library which is to be searched to locate the cataloged procedures coded in the job stream. DDname references a DD statement in the JES2 cataloged procedure. The default procedure library is SYS1.PROCLIB. PROCLIB may be abbreviated as P.

ROOM=xxxx — This prints the programmer's room number on the page separators between jobs. This helps with the identification and distribution of listings. A maximum of four characters may be coded. ROOM may be abbreviated as R.

TIME=xxx — This specifies the execution time in minutes of real time. The TIME parameters coded on the JOB and EXEC statements identify actual CPU execution time. Values range from 0 to 279,620. TIME may be abbreviated as T.

RESTART=Y or RESTART=N — This performs the same basic function as the RESTART parameter on the JOB and EXEC statements. If for some reason the job cannot be restarted from a checkpoint or job step; RESTART=Y will restart the job from the beginning after it is queued to be executed again. RESTART=N is the default. RESTART may be abbreviated as E.

Any values coded with JOBPARM override comparable values (JES2 format) on the JOB statement. This format is described earlier in this chapter in relation to the Accounting Information parameter.

Example 5: A programmer in room 666 wishes to print 25 copies of the complete job listing, with 50 lines per output page. However, the JES2 log, the JCL, except for the JOB statement, and allocation messages are not to print on these copies. Additionally, cataloged procedures are to be located in the library SYS1.PROC123. The procedure library is associated with the DDname P123 in the JES2 cataloged procedure. A maximum of 75,000 lines should be printed by the job. Finally, the job should not execute for more than 5 minutes of CPU time or one hour of real time. The following code performs all of the desired functions. In addition, multiple JOBPARM statements are used, and the same keyword parameter is used more than once in one statement. The TIME parameter on the last statement overrides the TIME=999 value on the previous JOBPARM statement.

```
//LARRY JOB   ...,MSGLEVEL=(0,0),TIME=5
//*MSGLEVEL=(0,0) SUPPRESSES THE JCL AND ALLOCATION MESSAGES
/*JOBPARM ROOM=666,NOLOG,N=15,N=25
//*25 IS USED, 15 IS IGNORED ON THE PREVIOUS STATEMENT
/*JOBPARM PROCLIB=P123,TIME=999,LINECT=50,LINES=75
/*JOBPARM TIME=60
```

MESSAGE

This statement is used to send messages to the operator. If it is coded after the JOB statement, the job's number is included with the message. Otherwise a message is identified with the input device which submitted the job.

```
/*MESSAGE  DO NOT START THIS JOB UNLESS THE BACKUP
/*MESSAGE  RAN SUCCESSFULLY LAST NIGHT
```

The MESSAGE statement is often used when special processing is required, to handle job failure situations, or to request that the operator notify the programmer when a job finishes.

OUTPUT

The OUTPUT statement is used to specify options for SYSOUT data sets. There are approximately twenty keyword parameters that can be coded. Some of the OUTPUT keywords can also be specified on SYSOUT DD statements. Most of the OUTPUT keywords can also be coded on the OUTPUT JCL statement. IBM recommends using the OUTPUT JCL statement rather than the JES2 OUTPUT statement. The values specified on the JES2 OUTPUT statement will override the comparable values coded on certain SYSOUT statements. The syntax of the OUTPUT statement is:

```
/*OUTPUT   code   keyword parameters
```

The code value identifies the specific SYSOUT data sets in the job stream that are affected by the OUTPUT statement. The third positional subparameter on the SYSOUT statement may also contain a code. The OUTPUT statement will affect all SYSOUT statements with matching codes. An asterisk (*) in the code field is used to continue the previous OUTPUT statement. The original statement and the continuation do not need to be adjacent.

Almost every OUTPUT keyword parameter value may also be supplied on a DD statement. For the seven parameters described below, all except CKPTPGS may also be coded as DD parameters. A more thorough description of the functions these parameters perform is given with the description of the corresponding DD parameters in Chapter 6.

The OUTPUT keyword parameter values include:

BURST=Y or N — Tells the system to burst the output from a 3800 printer into separate sheets rather than continuously folding the paper. BURST is the comparable DD parameter.

CKPTPGS=xxx — Identifies the number of pages to print before the next checkpoint (checkpoints are discussed in Chapter 22).

COPIES=xxx — Identifies the number of copies of the SYSOUT data set to print. The maximum value is 255.

COPYG=xxx — Identifies the number of copies of a single page to group together when using a 3800 print. The COPIES DD parameter performs the same function as COPIES and COPYG.

DEST=xxx Identifies the destination of the SYSOUT data set. DEST is the comparable DD parameter.

FCB=xxxx Identifies the forms control block.

UCS=xxxx Identifies the universal character set. FCB and UCS are the comparable DD parameters.

Example 6: For all SYSOUT data sets with a code of P01, print five copies of the output. These should be printed in groups of one, two, and two copies. The output goes to a 3800 printer, and the output is to be burst. For all SYSOUT data sets with a code of XYZ, three copies of the output are to be printed. Additionally, four copies of the complete job listing are to be printed. Finally, five copies of the output identified by the DDname ALPHA are to be printed. The COPIES DD parameter is discussed in Chapter 6.

```
//*   THE JOBPARM STATEMENT PROVIDES THE FOUR COMPLETE JOB LISTINGS
/*JOBPARM   COPIES=4
/*OUTPUT P01 COPIES=5,COPYG=(1,2,2)
/*OUTPUT *   BURST=Y
/*OUTPUT XYZ COPIES=3
. . .
//PRINT   DD   SYSOUT=(D,,P01)  USES FIRST TWO OUTPUT STATEMENTS
//ALPHA   DD   SYSOUT=A,COPIES=5
//BETA    DD   SYSOUT=(C,,XYZ),COPIES=2 THIS COPIES VALUE IS OVERRIDDEN
```

PRIORITY

This statement assigns a priority to a job. PRIORITY contains one parameter. An integer between 0 and 15 should be coded. All other values cause a JECL error. This is the same type of error as results from coding, for example, Accounting Information incorrectly. Priority can also be coded on the JOB statement. If it is coded in both places, the JES2 value has priority over the PRTY parameter. This is one JES2 statement which must be coded before the JOB statement; otherwise it is ignored. The value coded with PRIORITY has meaning only with the queue associated with the job's class. If neither PRIORITY nor PRTY are coded, a job's priority is assigned based upon the Accounting Information.

ROUTE

ROUTE specifies the location to which output should be routed. ROUTE is ignored with SYSOUT data sets for which the DEST DD parameter is coded. Two positional parameters separated by spaces must be coded with ROUTE. The first contains the value PRINT, PUNCH, or XEQ, depending on the type of output being routed. The second parameter specifies the location where the output should be routed. ROUTE is an installation-dependent statement. With PRINT or PUNCH, the second parameter most commonly identifies a local or remote terminal. When XEQ is coded, the job is routed to a specific node for execution.

```
/*ROUTE PRINT RMT345
/*ROUTE PUNCH LOCAL
```

SETUP

The SETUP statement identifies volumes needed for execution. All volumes listed in the operand field should be separated by commas. To identify three work volumes, code the following:

```
/*SETUP  WORK01,WORK02,WORK03
```

This tells the operator that the three volumes must be mounted before the job is executed. The operator releases the job after the volumes are mounted. This should be contrasted with using the VOLUME parameter on the DD statement to identify volumes. Additional SETUP statements may be coded.

XEQ

This statement specifies that the job is to be routed to a given node in the system for execution. The same results can be gotten with the JES2 ROUTE statement. To route a job to the Chicago computer center for execution, the following may be coded:

```
/*XEQ  CHICAGO
```

Exercises

1. With JES2 statements the same keyword parameter may be coded more than once on a single statement. What results when this is done? With MVS JCL statements, what occurs if the same keyword parameter is coded more than once on a single statement? What occurs if a positional parameter is coded more than once on the same JCL statement? Determine the reason for this syntax inconsistency between JCL and JES2 statements.

2. A specific JES2 statement may be coded two or more times in a single job stream. What results when this is done? With MVS JCL statements, what occurs when two statements of the same type are included in a single job stream? Consider the ten types of JCL statements. What happens when two statements with the same name are coded in a single job step? Consider several possible cases.

3. Many of the OUTPUT keyword parameters have matching DD parameters that perform the same function. Under what conditions is it preferable to code one of these OUTPUT keyword parameters rather than the comparable DD parameter?

4. For the three SYSOUT data sets identified below, determine how many copies of each are printed. Note that N=2 is coded on the JOBPARM statement.

```
/*JOBPARM   N=2
/*OUTPUT A COPIES=4,COPYG=(1,2,1)
//ALPHA   DD   SYSOUT=(A,,B),COPIES=5
//BETA    DD   SYSOUT=(B,,A)
//GAMMA   DD   SYSOUT=(A,,A),COPIES=7
```

5. Why do JES2 statements not contain name fields?

Chapter 5

The EXEC Statement and JES3 Statements

The EXEC Statement

Overview

The general format of the EXEC statement is as follows:

```
//stepname EXEC PGM=xxx,keyword parameters     comments            or
//stepname EXEC [PROC=]xxx,keyword parameters  comments
```

The EXEC statement identifies the beginning of a job step. Each EXEC statement contains exactly one positional parameter, which identifies the program to execute or the procedure to invoke. This parameter does not have a default value. Ten keyword parameters may be coded on the EXEC statement. All of the keyword parameters are optional. Comments may follow the operand field.

Although the stepname is optional, it is strongly recommended. Many of the reasons for coding names on JCL statements apply here. Several additional points should be noted. It is helpful to have specific conventions for stepnames. All stepnames within a job should be different. Although uniqueness is not required, duplicate stepnames can cause confusion. Several important JCL features can be used only with EXEC statements which have a stepname. These features include using referbacks later in the job stream to reference information on statements inside the step; performing step or checkpoint restarts; using the COND parameters to test the results of the present step in subsequent steps; overriding and adding DD statements in a procedure; and overriding, adding, and nullifying keyword parameters on an EXEC statement which invokes a procedure.

The EXEC statement parameters are described below. As with the JOB statement, the COND and RD parameters are discussed separately in Chapters 20 and 22 respectively. The RESTART parameter is not coded on the EXEC statement. Coding of symbolic parameters on an EXEC statement is discussed in Chapter 8. The relationship of the ten EXEC statement keyword parameters within a procedure for adding, overriding, and nullifying is discussed below.

PGM or PROC

There is one positional parameter, and it is required. The PGM or PROC parameter identifies the program(s) to be executed. Either a program or procedure must be specified. PGM=program name directly identifies the program to execute; PROC=procedure name indirectly identifies the program(s) to execute. The word PROC is optional. Hence, coding EXEC PROC=X and coding EXEC X are equivalent. The values coded with this parameter can be specified in three distinct ways:

1. Direct identification of the one program to execute:

```
EXEC PGM=program name (or an equivalent alias name)
```

2. Referback identification of the one program to execute:

```
EXEC PGM=*.stepname.DDname                                or
EXEC PGM=*.stepname.procstepname.DDname
```

3. Direct identification of the procedure (this implies indirect identification of one or more programs to execute):

```
EXEC PROC=procedure name                                  or
EXEC procedure name
```

A detailed discussion of the three formats available for coding PGM is presented in Chapters 18 and 19, in conjunction with the Linkage Editor and the Loader, respectively. PROC can identify either a cataloged or in-stream procedure. Procedures are examined in Chapter 8.

For an IBM supplied program the value coded with PGM is used for one other purpose on MVS systems. Clearly, coding

```
EXEC  PGM=ABCDEFGH
```

identifies the name of the program to execute (in this case ABCDEFGH). In addition, all informatory, warning, and error messages produced by the program are identified by a code which begins with ABC, the first three letters in the program name. Knowing this fact makes it easier to determine where and when specific messages were written. It is also possible to identify the actual software which wrote the message.

Keyword Parameters

The ten remaining EXEC statement parameters are all keyword. Six of the ten can be coded on the JOB statement also. With the ADDRSPC, PERFORM, RD, and REGION parameters, the value coded on the JOB statement overrides the corresponding EXEC value. For the COND and TIME parameters, both the JOB and EXEC values are in effect during the step.

When the COND parameter is coded on an EXEC statement it determines whether the job step will actually be executed or skipped. The COND parameter is discussed in detail in Chapter 20.

The restart definition (RD) parameter may be coded on both the JOB and EXEC statements. The RD value coded on the JOB statement overrides that on the EXEC. The RD parameter performs two functions: It determines how automatic step restart facilities are to be used with the CHKPT macro, and determines whether automatic restart is permitted or suppressed. The RD parameter is discussed in detail in Chapter 22.

ACCOUNT

The ACCOUNT parameter is used to specify additional accounting information. Like the Accounting Information parameter on the JOB statement, this operand may contain subparameters. The ACCOUNT fields and values are installation-defined. The values supplied apply to only one jobstep. The ACCOUNT parameter is used very rarely.

ADDRSPC

The ADDRSPC parameter performs the same function on both the EXEC and the JOB statements. When coded on both statements, the JOB value has precedence. ADDRSPC is used to request either virtual or real storage. Either ADDRSPC=VIRT or ADDRSPC=REAL must be coded. VIRT is the default. ADDRSPC=REAL is more frequently coded on an EXEC statement than on the JOB statement, but should rarely be coded on either statement.

DPRTY

The DPRTY parameter assigns a dispatching priority to an address space. The DPRTY value is used by the System Resource Manager (SRM), not the Job Scheduler. Each individual step can have its own dispatching priority. Step priority is not related to the PRTY value coded on the JOB statement. The syntax is DPRTY=(value1,value2). With JES2 and JES3 both value1 and value2 range between 0 and 15 inclusive. Both subparameters are positional, and standard syntax for positional subparameters must be used. The formula dispatching-priority= (value1*n) + value2 determines the actual dispatching priority value. Here n is assigned its value by the installation (usually 16). The greater the dispatching priority, the faster the step will execute. The DPRTY parameter is rarely coded.

DYNAMNBR

The DYNAMNBR parameter is coded to reserve space for dynamically allocated resources. DYNAMNBR can be specified rather than coding individual DYNAM parameters on the DD statements. DYNAMNBR is coded primarily by TSO users.

PARM

The PARM parameter is used to pass data from a JCL statement to an executing program. The information that is passed frequently changes each time the program is executed. With an application program if the PARM information is a constant value it is simpler to include it in the WORKING-STORAGE section of the program. PARM should identify 100 or less bytes of data. If this condition cannot be met, the data can be read in from a disk, tape, or card data set. The PARM parameter is a convenient feature that saves a production program from repeated recompilation or unnecessary I/O operations. If any special characters are included in the PARM value, the entire value must be enclosed in parentheses or apostrophes.

Example 1: Both of the following PARM operands pass the same data to an executing program, which in this case is the COBOL compiler:

```
PARM='STATE,SXREF,FLOW=50'
PARM=(STATE,SXREF,'FLOW=50')
```

The three individual values that are passed are separated by commas. The PARM value delimiters are not passed to the program. When apostrophes are coded, any character string may be included between them. However, when parentheses are used, any character string that contains special characters must also be first included in apostrophes. Here special characters are all characters except alphabetics, numerics, and nationals. Individual character strings are separated by commas.

While both PARM = STATE and PARM = 'STATE' are syntactically correct, the second example uses unnecessary apostrophes. In order to pass a single apostrophe or ampersand to an executing program, it is necessary to code two of them within a PARM value. Hence, to specify &O'BRIAN as a PARM value, code PARM = '&&O''BRIAN'. This approach is standard on MVS systems when using apostrophes. The two ampersands are needed to distinguish the actual data value from a symbolic parameter. A single ampersand denotes the beginning of a symbolic parameter which may also be included within the PARM field as part of the data value. For example, in PARM = A&XYZ.Q&W the &XYZ and &W are not part of the actual character string passed to the application program. Rather, values must be assigned to both symbolic parameters somewhere else in the job stream.

Since a maximum of 100 characters can be passed to a program from the PARM operand, it is possible to continue the PARM value at one or more locations within the character string. Character strings enclosed in apostrophes cannot be continued, and must be completely coded on a single statement. With continuation, it is important to enclose the value in parentheses and not apostrophes. A continuing comma must be coded, and it is considered part of the PARM value.

Example 2: Suppose that an EXEC statement is coded as:

```
//A   EXEC   PGM=COBOLPGM,PARM='''ALPHA12345'''
```

The twelve byte character string is passed to the LINKAGE SECTION of a COBOL program. The first two fields in the LINKAGE SECTION must be defined with the attributes shown below. The PARM value itself is placed in the PARM-DATA field. PARM-LENGTH, the first field in the LINKAGE SECTION, contains the number of bytes received from the EXEC statement (here 12).

COBOL Code	*Field Contents*
`LINKAGE SECTION.`	
`01  PARM-LENGTH    PIC S9(4) COMP.`	(the value 000C or +12)
`01  PARM-DATA      PIC X(100).`	(the value 'ALPHA12345' ...)
`. . .`	
`PROCEDURE DIVISION USING PARM-DATA.`	

To use continuation with the PARM parameter, the EXEC statement could also be coded as:

```
//A    EXEC    PGM=COBOLPGM,PARM=('AL',
//    'PHA12345')
```

Here, the comma must be detected and removed by the COBOL program.

PERFORM

Values coded with the PERFORM parameter have installation-defined meanings. PERFORM can also be coded on the JOB statement; in which case it overrides the value specified on the EXEC statement. Values from 1 to 255 may be coded on both the JOB and EXEC statement. The role of the PERFORM parameter is described in more detail in Chapter 4.

REGION

The REGION parameter determines the amount of memory available for a job step. It is coded as REGION=valueK. If REGION is also coded on the JOB statement, the EXEC value is overridden. An even number should be coded for the REGION value (odd values will be rounded up). A default REGION value may be set by the installation for each PRTY value. Otherwise, one default value is in effect for every one.

TIME

The TIME parameter specifies the maximum amount of CPU time allowed for the job step. When TIME is also coded on the JOB statement, both values are in effect. TIME is coded with two positional subparameters: TIME=(minutes,seconds), where minutes is any value less than or equal to 1440 and seconds is any value from 0 through 59. When TIME=1440 is coded the step will not be timed. If the total time remaining for the entire job is less than the value coded on an EXEC statement, the EXEC value is replaced by the amount of time remaining. Some imprecision may occur with the TIME parameters both on the JOB statement and on the EXEC statement, because of the way the system calculates time.

Keyword Parameters with Procedures

All of the EXEC statement keyword parameters may be coded on a statement which invokes a procedure. Recall that a procedure may contain multiple steps. When this is the case care must be taken to identify the step or steps to which the keyword parameter applies. In particular, does the value coded apply to every step in the procedure? Nine parameters have the same meaning when they are coded without specifying or qualifying the steps to which they apply (PARM is the exception). In Table 5–1 it is assumed that the keyword and a value are coded without indicating to which step the value applies. In addition, the syntax keyword= can be used to nullify the keyword values in the procedure.

With a procedure both keyword and symbolic parameters may be coded together on an EXEC statement. Symbolic parameters can also be qualified by stepname. All parameters associated with a single step should be coded together in the order in which the steps occur in the procedure. Any unqualified parameters should be placed in front of the qualified parameters. This is further discussed in Chapter 8.

Example 3: One step of a multistep job is to be executed. A program called UPDATE requires 400K bytes of virtual storage and takes 2 minutes and 30 seconds of CPU time. The character string 12/23/88*05 must be passed to the program during execution. Five DD statements are to be dynamically allocated. The step belongs in

TABLE 5–1
Keyword Parameters

Parameter	*Effect on the Steps in the Procedure*
ACCOUNT	overrides every ACCOUNT value in the procedure
ADDRSPC	overrides every ADDRSPC value in the procedure
COND	overrides every COND value in the procedure
DPRTY	overrides every DPRTY value in the procedure
DYNAMNBR	overrides every DYNAMNBR value in the procedure
PARM	overrides PARM value in first step, nullifies every other PARM value
PERFORM	overrides every PERFORM value in the procedure
RD	overrides every RD value in the procedure
REGION	overrides every REGION value in the procedure
TIME	overrides every TIME value in the procedure

performance group 1 and should have a high dispatching priority. Code the EXEC statement to do this as follows:

```
//A    EXEC   PGM=UPDATE,REGION=400K,ADDRSPC=VIRT,
//     TIME=(2,30),PARM='12/23/88*05',DYNAMNBR=5,
//     PERFORM=1,DPRTY=(15,15)
```

Exercises

1. For each of the following JCL statements, find the errors (if any). Some statements contain more than one error. Look mainly for syntax errors (there are also some logic errors).

```
a) //EXECSTEP PGM=IEBGENER,PARM='1%&*@6',TIME=(,95)
b) //EXECSTEP EXEC PROGRAM=IEBGENER,TIME=(5,0)
c) //SYSPRINT  DD PGM=IKFCBL00,PARM='STATE,PMAP'
d) //B   EXEC    PROC=PROCEDURE,TIME=(5,59),CLASS=C,
   //            PRIORITY=13,REGION=512K
e) //EXEC    PGM=IEFBR14
f) //    EXEC   PROC=TWOSTEP,COND.ONE=EVEN,TIME.TWO=(0,5),
   //        REGION.ONE=1000K,PARM=ALPHA
g) //X   EXEC   REGION=400K,COND=,PROC=PGM
h) //Y   EXEC   PGM=PROC,COND=,REGION=400K
```

2. A job called GAMMA is to be run. The accounting information for the job consists of three positional subparameters with values A, BC, and DEF respectively. The job consists of two steps, ALPHA and BETA. These steps execute programs ALPHA1 and BETA2 respectively. Write the complete JCL stream for this job (exclusive of DD statements). Comment only the second jobstep. Do not allow any step within the job to use over 200K of virtual memory or any real memory. The first step should execute for no more than 15 seconds and the second step for no more than 75 seconds. Running the job requires operator intervention. Print the maximum number of JCL and allocation messages.

3. Make the following modifications to job GAMMA: It is a class Z job and has as high a priority as possible. Neither step should execute for over 30 seconds. Suppress as many of the JCL and allocation messages as possible. Also suppress the JES2 log. The job should be released by the operator, and 100 copies of the complete job should be printed. The second step requires that the value *05*04*43* be passed to it while it is executing. Additionally, the second step should be run in real memory.

4. The job GAMMA has been submitted for execution. What factors determine when GAMMA will actually be run? Specifically, which JCL parameters play a role in this process? What are the exact roles of each parameter?

5. While running job GAMMA, what 'security' features can be included in the JCL?

6. Which parameters may be coded on both the JOB and EXEC statements? When such parameters are coded on both statements, which parameter values are in effect?

7. Which of the following PARM values contain syntax errors? For each PARM value which is invalid, what specifically is incorrect?

   a) `PARM=&&&PARM`
   b) `PARM=('STATE')`
   c) `PARM='PARM'`
   d) `PARM=PARM`
   e) `PARM=('A,B,C',ABC,'...')`
   f) `PARM='A,B,C,ABC,...'`
   g) `PARM='A-B-C'`
   h) `PARM=`

JES3 Control Statements

Overview

JES3 control statements can be coded in the job stream along with JCL statements. Like JES2, JES3 uses the same basic syntax as JCL. Also, like JES2, there are a few additional rules that must be followed. With two exceptions (Commands and the PAUSE statement), JES3 statements should be coded after the JOB statement. If any of the other JES3 statements are coded before it or between two statements in a continued JOB statement, they are ignored. Like JES2 statements, if JES3 statements are coded within a cataloged procedure, they are ignored. However, JES3 statements are valid within in-stream procedures, JES2 statements are ignored in in-stream procedures. JES3 statements processed by JES2 are treated as comments. A JES2 statement processed by JES3 may generate a syntax error. A JES3 statement contains //* in its first three columns. The operator field begins in column 4.

The syntax of a JES3 control statement is as follows:

```
//*operator  keyword-operands
```

Note that JES3 statements do not contain either a name field or a comment field. Unlike most JES2 statements, JES3 statements can be continued. This is done by ending a line by coding a keyword operand and its following comma. The continued statement contains //* followed by the resumption of the operands in column 4. This is illustrated in Example 5. Like JES2, some types of JES3 statements may be coded more than once, but a keyword parameter should be coded only once on a given statement; for example, multiple FORMAT statements are coded in Example 4.

JES3 contains more control statements with more options than JES2 has. Only the three most important JES3 statements are discussed in detail in this book. The other JES3 statements are described in the MVS JCL manual.

The FORMAT statement is used to perform several functions. Only its role in determining the special processing properties and the destination for printed data sets is examined in this book. FORMAT is similar to the JES2 OUTPUT statement. The JES3 MAIN control statement specifies processing information which holds for the complete job stream. It contains more parameters, but it performs the same basic role as the JES2 JOBPARM statement. The JES3 NET statement describes the relationships which hold between multiple jobs that are to be executed. There is no comparable JES2 statement. With JES3, it is sometimes advantageous to decompose a single job stream into multiple disjoint jobs. The primary reason for this is the way JES3 manages I/O devices.

The FORMAT Statement

The first FORMAT operand parameter is positional. All remaining operands are keyword, and almost all are optional. The first parameter must be one of the four values AC, NJP, PR, or PU. They are coded respectively with TSO users, network processing, printed data sets, and punched data sets. Only printed data sets are considered here. The exact syntax of the FORMAT statement for printed data sets is as follows:

```
//*FORMAT  PR,DDNAME=DDname or reserved word,optional,
//*keyword parameters
```

Some of the same PR operands are also used with AC, NJP, and PU. The three reserved words JESJCL, SYSMSG, and JESMSG may be coded in addition to DDNAME. JESJCL is a listing of the JCL and JES3 statements in the job stream. SYSMSG identifies system messages. Finally, JESMSG contains the JES3 job log including operator messages. If a DDname is coded, the FORMAT statement applies to the specifically identified DD statement. DDname may contain up to three levels of qualification with procedures. Full qualification is required.

There are sixteen optional keyword parameters that may also be coded. Several of these describe options that are also available with JCL DD parameters, when processing printed data sets. These JES3 FORMAT keyword parameters are CHARS, COPIES, FCB, FLASH, MODIFY, and STACKER (the BURST DD parameter is equivalent). These processing options are all described in Chapter 6 in detail.

Example 4: The JCL listing and system messages are to be printed by one device and the JES3 job log by another. In addition, 10 copies of the JCL are to be printed. Finally, 50 copies of the data set with DDname MASTER are to be printed on a 3800 laser printer.

```
//*FORMAT PR,DDNAME=JESJCL,COPIES=10
//*FORMAT PR,DDNAME=SYSMSG
//*FORMAT PR,DDNAME=JESMSG
//*FORMAT PR,DDNAME=MASTER,COPIES=50
```

The MAIN Statement

The MAIN control statement can be used to specify some of the processing requirements for the entire job. There are approximately 25 keyword parameters that may be coded with MAIN, all of which are optional. Roughly half of them have default values. Like the JOBPARM statement, MAIN controls the number of lines printed, number of cards punched, operator intervention, and cataloged procedure libraries. It also contains several parameters for which there is no JES2 equivalent, such as selection of a processor, allocation of devices, the I/O and CPU resource utilization, and scheduling the job. The most important parameters are briefly described here.

SYSTEM identifies the specific processor or any processor within a class on which the job is to be run. With MVS, five values may be coded. SYSTEM=/(main-name1,main-name2,. . .) can be used to exclude all of the identified processors from consideration. ANY means that any processor may be used and is the default value. JLOCAL and JGLOBAL identify local or global processors respectively. The SYSTEM parameter is clearly only meaningful in a multiple processor environment. JES2 does not contain a comparable parameter.

TYPE can be used to select the operating system to use in the same way that SYSTEM is used to select the processor on which to run a job. Several values that reference pre-MVS operating systems may specifically be coded. TYPE=VS2 identifies MVS. TYPE=AU means any operating system may be used, and is the default. JES2 does not contain a comparable parameter.

LINES and CARDS may be coded to estimate respectively the number of lines printed or cards punched during the entire job. Both keyword parameters contain two subparameters. Both parameters have the format keyword=(xxx,action). With LINES, xxx is the number of lines printed in thousands. With CARDS, xxx is the number of cards punched in hundreds. With both LINES and CARDS, three action values may be coded. If WARNING is coded and the value is exceeded, a warning message is issued, and the job continues. With the other two values, CANCEL and DUMP, if the value coded is exceeded, the job is cancelled. With DUMP, following the cancellation, an abend dump results. It may be either a SYSUDUMP or a SYSABEND dump. All three actions may be identified by an abbreviation which consists of the first letter in the name of the action. Hence, W, C, and D are all valid action values.

The HOLD parameter must specify either YES or NO. HOLD=YES is equivalent to coding TYPRUN=HOLD on the JOB statement. With both parameters, if the job has no JCL errors, it will be held until released by the operator. HOLD=NO implies that operator intervention is not required when a job is submitted for execution. HOLD=NO is the default.

CLASS is used to identify the job's class. This is the same information and values that can be coded on the JOB statement. The value coded with JES3 overrides the value on the JOB statement.

PROC identifies a private procedure library that is to be used to locate cataloged procedures invoked during the job. PROC=ST specifies the standard procedure library and is the default. PROC=xx means that the last two characters of a DDname which identifies the new procedure library are xx in the JES3 cataloged procedure. With PROC=xx, SYS1.PROCLIB, the default procedure library is not searched. If xx is an invalid value, the job is scratched. The xx values are installation defined. PROC is equivalent to the JES2 PROCLIB parameter.

UPDATE identifies a procedure library that is to be updated while the job is executing. When UPDATE is coded, none of the members in the libraries used in the job can also be used by other jobs until this job finishes. All jobs requiring those libraries are suspended until that time. UPDATE may specify either ST or xx. Both have the same meanings as with the PROC parameter. JES2 does not contain an operand comparable to UPDATE. The TYPRUN=JCLHOLD JOB parameter can be used for the same basic purpose with JES2. This is illustrated in Example 1 in Chapter 27.

The JOURNAL parameter must specify either YES or NO. YES implies a job journal for the job. NO implies no job journal. Job journals are used with restarts.

IORATE is used to specify the proportion of I/O processing to CPU processing. It is used to produce a good mixture of jobs executing concurrently on the system. When IORATE is coded, it overrides the installation defaults for job selection. Three values may be coded to estimate the ratio of I/O to CPU processing, LO, MED, and HIGH.

DEADLINE is used for deadline scheduling. A specific time may be coded in one of three possible formats:

xM	schedule job within x minutes where $x \leq 1440$
xH	schedule job within x hours where $x \leq 24$
hhmm	is the actual time in 24 hour clock time by which the job should be scheduled

A date can also be coded in mmddyy format with DEADLINE. Several other values may also be coded for jobs that are run on a periodic basis such as daily, weekly, monthly, or annually.

SETUP is used to allocate devices to a job. With JES3, these devices are allocated before execution begins. Specific devices can be allocated or not by coding SETUP=(DDname1,DDname2,. . .) or SETUP=/(DDname1,DDname2,. . .) respectively. In addition, four other values may be coded, JOB, HWS, THWS, and DHWS. The MVS JCL manual contains a lengthy explanation of these important terms. It should be noted that each device on an MVS system with JES3 falls into one of three categories. It is either managed by MVS, by JES3, or jointly by MVS and JES3.

Example 5: For the accompanying job stream, a maximum of 150,000 lines are to be printed and 3000 cards punched. The job is class E and is to be held until released by the operator. The job is an MVS job to be run on processor X1. Cataloged procedures are to be retrieved from the procedure library identified in the JES3 procedure with the DDname ABCDEF. The job must be run within the next four hours. The CLASS parameter on the JOB statement is overridden and the TYPRUN parameter is unnecessary.

```
//JOB1    JOB   ...,CLASS=A,TYPRUN=HOLD
//*MAIN   LINES=(150,WARNING),CARDS=(30,W),CLASS=E,HOLD=YES,
//*SYSTEM=X1,TYPE=VS2,PROC=EF,DEADLINE=4H
```

The NET Statement

A *net* is a collection of jobs that are interrelated and must be executed in a specific sequence. In order to use the NET statement, it is first necessary to determine the order in which jobs in the net must be executed. Specifically, which jobs must be executed prior to a given job and which jobs should be executed immediately after a given job. There are three parameters on the NET statement which specify this information. NETID identifies the net name and should contain the same value for every job in the net. RELEASE identifies the jobnames of subsequent jobs which can be run only after the present job completes execution. NHOLD identifies the total number of jobs that must be executed prior to this job. As a very simple example, suppose three jobs called A, B, and C are to be executed in that order. The following table shows the NET parameter values associated with each job.

Jobname	*Net Name*	*Number of Predecessor Jobs*	*Names of Successor Jobs*
A	NETID=X1	NHOLD=0	RELEASE=(B)
B	NETID=X1	NHOLD=1	RELEASE=(C)
C	NETID=X1	NHOLD=1	

Only job A is not dependent on a previous job to finish execution. For job B, one previous job in the net must have been executed. This must be job A which, in fact, releases job B. When A releases B, the NHOLD value for B is decremented by 1. When B finishes execution, it releases job C.

Example 6: Consider the accompanying job net. Note that jobs B and E require that multiple jobs must be executed immediately prior to both of them. The information in the net can be summarized as follows:

Jobname	*Net Name*	*Number of Predecessor Jobs*	*Names of Successor Jobs*
A	X2	0	B
B	X2	2	C,E
C	X2	1	E
D	X2	0	B,E
E	X2	3	—

The five JES3 statements needed to implement the above net are as follows:

Jobname	*NET Control Statement*
A	`//*NET NETID=X2,RELEASE=(B)`
B	`//*NET NETID=X2,NHOLD=2,RELEASE=(C,E)`
C	`//*NET NETID=X2,NHOLD=1,RELEASE=(E)`
D	`//*NET NETID=X2,NHOLD=0,RELEASE=(B,E)`
E	`//*NET NETID=X2,NHOLD=3`

Exercises

1. Find the syntax errors in the following JES3 statements:

```
//*
//*MAIN
//X3       JOB Statement
//*MAIN
//*NET       NETID=X3
//*FORMAT   PR DDNAME=SYSMSG
```

2. Why do JES2 and JES3 statements not contain name fields? What advantages/disadvantages does this cause?

3. Compare the keyword parameters available with JES2 JOBPARM and JES3 MAIN statements. Comment on the omissions from one to the other: e.g., UPDATE with JES3 but not JES2. Make the same comparison between OUTPUT with JES2 and FORMAT with JES3.

4. Printing of JESJCL, SYSMSG, and JESMSG output can be controlled by the FORMAT statement. What determines, if any, where these three data sets are printed with JES2?

5. Write the necessary JES3 NET statements to implement the following net of jobs. How could such processing be done with JES2 or if the NET statement were not used with JES3? Letters of the alphabet denote job names and arrows imply predecessor jobs. That is A and B must both be run prior to D.

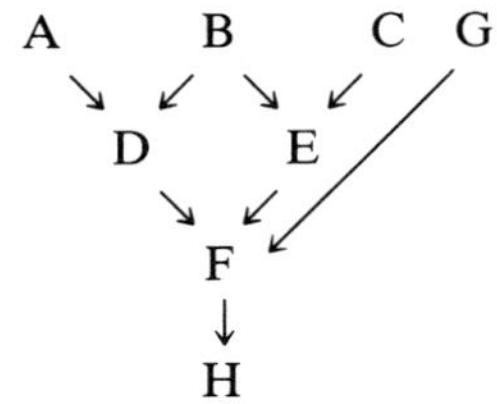

6. Write the JES3 control statements to perform the same functions as specified with JES2 in Example 6 in Chapter 4. Note that some JES2 functions cannot be duplicated with JES3.

Chapter 6

Overview of DD Statements and Printed Data Sets

A DD statement must be coded for every data set a program processes. These DD statements can be either coded in the JCL or supplied as a part of a cataloged or in-stream procedure. The role of the DD statement within procedures is discussed in Chapter 8. In this chapter and the next the emphasis is on the parameters which may be coded on a DD statement, rather than the location of the DD statement.

The DD statement is used to perform numerous important functions. For every data set a program uses the DD statement can be used to do some or all of the following functions:

1) Describe the characteristics of the records in the data set and the manner in which they are to be processed. These characteristics include logical record length, physical record length, record format, data set organization, and key information. Buffering information and special processing options can also be coded on the DD statement. The operating system must have all of this information in order to successfully process the records in the data set.

2) Specify whether an existing data set will be used or a new data set is to be created in this job step. In either case the DD statement also determines what should be done with the data set at the end of the jobstep.

3) Describe the particular type of device where an existing data set resides or a new data set is to be written. This is usually some type of disk drive, tape drive, or unit record device. The term *unit record* refers to printers, card readers, and card punches. If there are many devices of the same type, a specific one can be identified. With most tape and disk devices the particular volume to mount on the device can also be specified.

4) For an existing data set, determine the order in which the operating system will search to locate the data set; for a new data set, determine the locations where information about it should be stored in the system; for an old data set, tell whether any of the existing system information describing it should be modified during the step.

5) Give a new data set a name or allow the system to create a default name for it; for an existing data set, use its name to simplify identifying it.

6) Associate various types of security with the data set.

7) For a new disk data set, estimate its size; for a printed data set, limit its size.

With the material in this chapter and Chapter 7 it should be possible to tell which specific DD parameters and subparameters supply the information for each of the above categories. In fact, this is the last exercise at the end of Chapter 7. All of the information described above can be explicitly coded on a DD statement. However, much of it is optional in the sense that, if a specific parameter is not coded, the system will supply a default value. In fact, it is possible to create a disk data set and code just one parameter on the DD statement. Typically an existing disk or tape data set is retrieved by coding just two parameters. One parameter is usually sufficient to reference unit record data sets (printer, card reader, and card punch).

In each of the four major programming languages specific statements within the source code imply the existence of a corresponding DD statement in the accompanying JCL for that job step. The relationship between logical files and actual data sets for COBOL, PL/I, Assembler, and FORTRAN is shown in Table 6–1.

TABLE 6–1
Logical Files and Data Sets

Programming Language	*Source Code Statement*	*Associated DD Statement*

COBOL	SELECT file-name
	ASSIGN TO xy-3-DDname
	--- 	
	ALTERNATE KEY IS aix-key
	--- 	
		//DDname DD
		
		//DDname1 DD
		(DSN=pathname)

PL/I	DECLARE DDname FILE or TITLE option	//DDname DD
Assembler	DCB -- macro keywords --, DDNAME=DDname,---	//DDname DD
FORTRAN	FORTRAN Unit Number nn	//FTnnF001 DD

All of the occurrences of DDname can also be coded as //stepname.DDname DD. When the DD statement is part of a procedure, any of the occurrences of DDname on a JCL statement can be coded as //stepname.procstepname.DDname DD.

Additionally, programs may use data sets not identified in the programming language in the manner shown above. For example, with a COBOL program the following DDnames are often coded during execution:

SYSOUT, SYSDBOUT, SYSCOUNT, SYSUDUMP, and SORTMSG.

All of these DDnames identify data sets that produce some type of printed output. The roles of SYSOUT, SYSDBOUT, and SYSCOUNT are discussed in Chapter 17; SYSUDUMP is described in Chapter 22 and SORTMSG is explained in Chapter 23. When these data sets are used it is unnecessary (and actually meaningless) to specify a SELECT statement for them. Similarly, in PL/I it is unnecessary to explicitly declare SYSIN and SYSPRINT as files.

With PL/I and COBOL a 'system' sort requires several extra DD statements. Usually these work data sets are specified in the JCL by coding:

```
//SORTWKii   DD UNIT=SYSDA,SPACE=(CYL,n)
```

where ii = 01, 02, 03,. . . and n is the requested number of cylinders. This is discussed further in Chapter 23.

It is possible that two distinct files within a program can both reference the same DD statement. For example, in a COBOL program FILE1 and FILE2 can be two files each of which is defined by its own unique FD. However, the SELECT statements for these files may be coded as:

```
SELECT FILE1                      and    SELECT FILE2
     ASSIGN TO DA-q-XYZ                       ASSIGN TO DA-q-XYZ
     ACCESS IS SEQUENTIAL                     ACCESS IS RANDOM
     ---.                                     ---.
```

Both of these files will be associated with the same data set. It will be coded on a DD statement with DDname XYZ:

```
//XYZ  DD DSN=non-sequential-data-set,...
```

This type of coding is very common when processing a non-VSAM data set, where it is necessary to access the data set both sequentially and randomly in the same program. Here q identifies the particular data set organization, indexed, relative, or direct. Accessing a data set in two distinct ways can be accomplished in a much easier fashion with a VSAM data set by coding ACCESS IS DYNAMIC in a single SELECT statement.

Summarizing, it is possible for a DD statement to be referenced by more than one SELECT statement. At the other extreme, one SYSOUT DD statement may serve multiple purposes in a COBOL program. A single such DD statement can be used with all DISPLAY, EXHIBIT, and READY TRACE statements. Most often there is a one-to-one pairing between SELECT statements and DD statements. If there are n SELECT statements in a COBOL program and m accompanying DD statements, it is possible to have m less than n, or n less than m, but most commonly m equals n. An experienced MVS application programmer should probably be able to tell the exact function performed by every DD statement coded in their JCL.

Unnecessary and Duplicate DD Statements

What happens when a DD statement identifies a data set that is never processed by the application program? Such a JCL statement is syntax checked and all requested resources are allocated to it, but those resources are never used. This may keep other jobs from using the same resources, and the entire job will be scratched if the DD statement contains syntax errors. Thus, nothing good ever results from coding unnecessary DD statements.

What happens when two DD statements with the same DDname are coded within the same job step? With JES2 only the first DD statement is actually used for I/O operations, and the second is ignored. However, resources are allocated to it. No messages are printed concerning the presence of this second statement. The second statement functions somewhat like a comment. In fact, some programmers intentionally turn statements into comments (usually temporarily) by inserting a DD statement into the job step with the same DDname as the statement to be 'commented out.' This is a questionable programming practice. With JES3 multiple DD statements with the same DDname in the same job step generate a JCL error message, and cause the job to be cancelled.

What happens when two DD statements within the same job step but with different DDnames identify the same data set? This is permissible and can be associated with meaningful processing. This topic is examined further in Chapters 18 and 21.

Reserved DDnames

Nine DDnames have special reserved meanings. They should only be coded for the specific purpose for which they are intended. These nine can be grouped into four categories, depending on the type of object they identify:

System Catalogs	*Program Libraries*	*Abend Dumps*	*Checkpoints*
JOBCAT	JOBLIB	SYSABEND	SYSCHK
STEPCAT	STEPLIB	SYSMDUMP	SYSCHEOV
		SYSUDUMP	

A very brief discussion of these nine statements is included below.

Both JOBCAT and STEPCAT identify system catalogs. Such catalogs contain important information about data sets in the system. This information can greatly simplify the amount of JCL a programmer must code when accessing a cataloged data set. One JOBCAT statement may be coded in the job stream. It must follow the JOB statement and precede the first EXEC statement. The STEPCAT statement may be coded with each EXEC statement in the job stream. Traditionally STEPCAT is the first DD statement following the EXEC statement, although syntactically it can be placed anywhere among the DD statements for the step. These two DD statements and catalogs in general are discussed in detail in Chapter 21.

Both JOBLIB and STEPLIB identify program libraries. These libraries are used to locate a specific PGM value identified on an EXEC statement. One JOBLIB statement may be coded in the job stream. It must follow the JOB statement and precede the first EXEC statement. If JOBCAT is also coded the JOBLIB statement must precede it. The STEPLIB statement may be coded with each EXEC statement in the job stream. Traditionally STEPLIB is the first DD statement following the EXEC statement. If both STEPLIB and STEPCAT are coded the STEPLIB statement is ordinarily placed first. Syntactically the STEPLIB statement may be placed anywhere among the DD statements within the step. These two DD statements and accessing program libraries are discussed in detail in Chapter 21.

When a job step abends the system prints an error message telling the type of abend that occurred. If additional information is desired the programmer can request an abend dump. On MVS systems no dump prints by default. Rather, a DD statement with a DDname of SYSABEND, SYSMDUMP, or SYSUDUMP must be coded within the step where the abend occurred. Each of these three provides a different format for the dump. Most commonly the dump is sent to a printer. Dumps are discussed further in Chapter 22.

SYSCHK and SYSCHEOV have meaning only when checkpoints are employed within a program. These two DDnames and checkpoints in general are further discussed in Chapter 22.

Example 1: The following job stream illustrates the placement of eight of the special DDnames described above. For illustration purposes all of them are used with a two step job.

```
//...        JOB
//JOBLIB      DD ...
//JOBCAT      DD ...
//SYSCHK      DD ...
//A         EXEC PGM=FIRST
//STEPLIB     DD library which contains program FIRST
//STEPCAT     DD ...
//other DD statements
//SYSABEND    DD SYSOUT=A
//B         EXEC PGM=SECOND
//STEPCAT     DD ...
//other DD statements
//SYSCHEOV    DD ...
//SYSUDUMP    DD SYSOUT=A
```

DD Statement Syntax

There are four positional parameters that may be coded on a DD statement. They are:

```
*    DATA   DUMMY    DYNAM
```

At most one positional parameter can be coded on a specific DD statement. None of the four positional parameters contain subparameters. A positional parameter must precede any keyword parameters that are coded on the statement. Very few keyword parameters are permitted on the same DD statement with any of the four positional parameters. If no positional parameter is coded the DD statement may begin with any keyword parameter. Never code a leading comma to denote the omission of a positional parameter on any JCL statement; this causes a JCL syntax error.

Each of the four positional parameters has a limited role and is used in a very specific situation. DATA and * denote the presence of an in-stream card image data set. DUMMY is used to suppress I/O operations from being performed. DYNAM is coded by a TSO user in conjunction with the dynamic allocation of resources.

Except for two very specific situations a DD statement must always contain a DDname field and at least one operand. One exception occurs when data sets are concatenated, in which case DDname is not coded and the operand field need not be coded. Concatenation is a process which allows two or more data sets to be joined together as input to a program. Initially the program reads records from the data set on the first DD statement until end of file is reached. At that point records from the second data set are automatically supplied to the program. This continues for each data set contained in the concatenation. After the last record is read from the Nth data set, the first record is read from the N+1th data set. Concatenation is denoted by omitting the DDname on every DD statement which follows the first one. For example, to concatenate three data sets together code:

```
//ALPHA DD DSN=X,DISP=SHR
//      DD DSN=Y,DISP=SHR,UNIT=3380,VOL=SER=DISK11
//      DD DSN=Z,DISP=SHR
```

Here the cataloged data sets X and Z, and the kept data set Y are processed as one file by the application program. With COBOL one SELECT and one OPEN statement are used to process all of the data sets in the concatenation. Concatenation is restricted to data sets used for input.

Up to 256 sequential data sets may be concatenated. The data sets being concatenated must have 'similar' dcb values. This is discussed in Chapter 7. Up to 16 partitioned data sets may also be concatenated. Concatenation has a somewhat different meaning with partitioned data sets. In this case any member in any of the concatenated libraries can be retrieved. Here also the libraries must have 'similar' dcb values. 'Similar' has a more flexible meaning with partitioned data set libraries than with sequential data sets. ISAM data sets cannot be concatenated, nor can direct data sets.

The other situation in which it is valid to not code a DDname occurs with ISAM data sets that are identified by more than one DD statement. The components of the ISAM data set are then grouped together. More details on this are given in several examples in Chapter 13.

It is permissible to code a DD statement which does not contain an operand field only when concatenated data sets in a procedure are overridden. This complex subject is examined in detail in Chapter 8. This is the only place in MVS JCL where it is syntactically correct to code a DD statement with no operands.

It is syntactically correct to code a keyword parameter or subparameter and assign no value to it. For example, the following statement assigns no value to the keyword parameter OUTLIM and none to the DCB subparameter BLKSIZE.

```
//NULLIFY   DD SYSOUT=A,OUTLIM=,
//             DCB=(LRECL=80,BLKSIZE=,RECFM=F)
```

This type of syntax can be coded on any DD or EXEC statement. However, it is meaningful only with procedures, where it nullifies an existing value. This is further discussed in Chapter 8.

Some DD statement parameters are mutually exclusive and cannot be coded on the same statement. If they happen to be coded together, the following error message prints:

IEF652 MUTUALLY EXCLUSIVE KEY WORDS-KEY WORD IN THE xxx FIELD IS MUTUALLY EXCLUSIVE WITH KEY WORD ON THE yyy STATEMENT.

This message most frequently occurs when statements within a procedure are overridden or symbolic parameters are assigned values on the EXEC statement which invokes a procedure. All of this is discussed in Chapter 8. IEF652 is also printed if the same parameter is coded twice on a JCL statement.

The maximum number of DD statements that may be coded in a single jobstep is 1635. The results are unpredictable if this figure is exceeded.

Backward and Forward References

With three of the DD parameters it is possible to reference information that has been coded on a prior DD statement in the same (or an earlier) jobstep. This technique is called a 'backward' reference (or referback). It is identified by using one of the following three formats, each of which begins with an asterisk:

(1) `keyword=*.DDname`
(2) `keyword=*.stepname.DDname`
(3) `keyword=*.stepname.procstepname.DDname`

Here keyword must be replaced by one of the three keyword parameters, DSNAME (abbreviated DSN), DCB, or VOLUME=REF (abbreviated VOL=REF). Format

(1) is used when referencing a prior DD statement within the same jobstep. Format (2) references a DD statement in an earlier jobstep. The third form of the backward reference can only be used with procedures, and is discussed in Chapter 8.

Referbacks are strictly a convenience feature. Only after a fair mastery of JCL has already been developed should a user begin coding referbacks. A referback is handled somewhat differently, with each of the three parameters, and each has different advantages associated with using a referback. All three backward references are thoroughly examined when the specific keyword parameters are discussed in Chapter 7.

Example 2: Consider the following segment of code used to create three temporary disk data sets. Here each referback used is format (1), since all occur within the same step.

```
//A      EXEC PGM=IEFBR14
//DD1    DD  DSN=TEMP1,DISP=(NEW,PASS),UNIT=3350,
//       VOL=SER=DISK01,SPACE=(CYL,1),
//       DCB=(LRECL=80,RECFM=FB,BLKSIZE=6160)
//DD2    DD DSN=*.DD1,DISP=(NEW,PASS),UNIT=3380,
//       VOL=SER=WORK02,SPACE=(TRK,2),DCB=*.DD1
//DD3    DD DSN=TEMP2,DISP=(NEW,PASS),UNIT=3350,
//       VOLUME=REF=*.DD1,SPACE=(CYL,10),
//       DCB=(*.DD1,LRECL=240)
```

The DSN and DCB parameters on the second DD statement are assigned the same values as the corresponding DD parameters on the statement with DDname DD1. The VOLUME and DCB parameters on the last DD statement are assigned the same values as the VOLUME and DCB parameters coded on the first DD statement. The DCB parameter on the last statement is then subsequently modified.

It is also possible to code a 'forward reference.' This technique is used to identify information that is to be supplied from a DD statement coded later in the step. Forward references are specified by coding the DDNAME keyword parameter. This parameter informs the system that an upcoming DD statement may be necessary to supplement the information contained on the present DD statement. The identification between the two statements is made by matching the DDname field on the second statement with the DDNAME value on the present statement. The DDNAME parameter is ordinarily used only to concatenated in-stream data sets to other data sets in a procedure. DDNAME is discussed in Chapter 7.

Classification of DD Keyword Parameters

There are 32 keyword parameters that may be coded on MVS JCL DD statements. These parameters will be classified into one of three categories depending on type and frequency of use. Each keyword parameter's subparameters are classified as positional or keyword. The lists below note default values for all of the positional and several of the keyword subparameters.

THE EIGHT MOST FREQUENTLY USED DD KEYWORD PARAMETERS

Seven of the eight parameters listed here form the major topic in Chapter 7. SYSOUT is used with printed data sets, and is discussed later in this chapter.

DCB All subparameters are keyword. There are a great many subparameters. Several, such as DSORG and BUFNO, have default values, but most do not. Many values coded with this parameter can also be supplied from non-JCL sources. More syntax errors occur with DCB than with any other JCL parameter.

DISP There are three positional subparameters. All have default values. Some values can be assigned from non-JCL sources.

DSNAME There are no subparameters. However, many different syntax formats are allowed for various types of qualification. Values cannot be specified anywhere else.

LABEL There are five positional subparameters. The first two and the fifth have default values. The fifth can also be referenced as a keyword subparameter.

SPACE There are five positional subparameters. The last three have vacuous default values.

SYSOUT There are three positional subparameters. Only the first has a default value.

UNIT There are three positional subparameters. The second and third have vacuous default values.

VOLUME There are five positional subparameters. The third and fourth have vacuous default values. The fifth can also be referenced as a keyword subparameter.

THIRTEEN OCCASIONALLY USED DD STATEMENT PARAMETERS FOR TAPE AND DISK DATA SETS

ACCODE There are no subparameters.

AMP All subparameters are keyword. Several, such as BUFND and BUFNI, have default values. Most values coded with this parameter can be supplied from other sources. For VSAM data sets this is the equivalent of the DCB parameter.

CHKPT	There are no subparameters.
CNTL	There are no subparameters. An earlier statement name is coded.
DDNAME	There are no subparameters. An earlier statement name is coded.
DEST	There is one keyword subparameter. The value LOCAL may be coded. All other values are installation dependent.
DSID	There are two positional subparameters.
FREE	There are no subparameters. Two possible values may be coded: END and CLOSE.
MSVGP	There are two positional subparameters.
PROTECT	There are no subparameters. Two possible values may be coded: YES and NO.
QNAME	There are no subparameters.
SUBSYS	There can be one or more positional subparameters.
TERM	There are no subparameters.

ELEVEN OCCASIONALLY USED DD STATEMENT PARAMETERS FOR PRINTED AND IN-STREAM DATA SETS

BURST	There is one keyword parameter. Two possible values may be coded: Y and N.
CHARS	There can be one or more keyword subparameters.
COPIES	There can be one or two positional subparameters.
DLM	This keyword parameter has no default value. It can be assigned an arbitrary two character value.
FCB	There are two positional subparameters.
FLASH	There are two positional subparameters.
HOLD	There are no subparameters. Two possible values may be coded.
MODIFY	There are two positional subparameters.

OUTLIM There are no subparameters.

OUTPUT From 1 to 128 keyword subparameters may be coded. They identify OUTPUT JCL statements coded in the job stream.

UCS There are three positional subparameters.

The Positional Parameters and SYSOUT

There are four positional DD parameters. Three of them, *, DATA, and DUMMY, are frequently used. The fourth positional parameter, DYNAM, is rarely used. In fact, a non-TSO user rarely has reason to code it. DYNAM is used with TSO to dynamically allocate resources for subsequent use. The SYSOUT parameter is not positional. However, it is traditionally grouped with the positional parameters, and is routinely coded first on DD statements.

DUMMY

As with any positional parameter, DUMMY must precede all keyword parameters on the DD statement. The only keyword parameter commonly coded with DUMMY is DCB. The DCB subparameter BLKSIZE is coded to allocate storage for the data set's buffers. If BLKSIZE is not coded and blocking information is not provided in some other way, an S001-4 abend completion code may result when the first I/O statement is executed. Coding DUMMY is equivalent to specifying DSN=NULLFILE on a DD statement. If DUMMY is coded any DSN value on the DD statement is ignored. The same applies to almost all other DD statement parameters coded with DUMMY. Hence, when

```
//DD1   DD DUMMY,DSN=X,DISP=(NEW,PASS),UNIT=VIO
```

is coded the three keyword subparameters are ignored.

When DUMMY is coded on a DD statement no actual I/O operations take place with the data set. End of file occurs on the first attempt to read a record from the data set. Nothing is written on any write operation to the data set. DUMMY must be used carefully within a concatenation; if it is included in the concatenation it results in end of file, and all of the following DD statements in the concatenation are ignored.

DUMMY has several principal uses. It can be used to test whether a program's logic can correctly handle an empty input file. Before actual data are available a program can still be compiled and executed. DUMMY can also be used to suppress irrelevant printed output. Some message data sets fall into this category. DUMMY can be coded on an overriding DD statement with a procedure to suppress an abend dump.

In-stream Data Sets (*) and the Delimiter Statement (/*)

The * positional parameter identifies card image data sets in the input stream. Every statement in a job stream falls into one of three categories: a JCL statement, a JES or JECL statement, or a member of an in-stream data set. An in-stream data set is usually preceded by a DD statement containing either * or DATA. Hence * is used as follows:

```
//DDname    DD   *
   . . .
```

In-stream data goes here. It consists of any collection of statements that does not include JCL or JES statements.

```
   . . .
/*
```

The /* JCL statement is used in conjunction with the DD * statement. It is usually called the Delimiter statement. Like the Null and Comment statements, it is a limited function JCL statement. The /* statement signals the end of an in-stream data set. The /* statement is not actually required when using the * parameter, but it is good defensive programming practice to include it. Any statements that do not contain either // or /* in columns 1 and 2 can be placed between the DD * and the Delimiter statements.

In many programming situations both the DD * and /* statements may be omitted and processing will still be correctly performed. Suppose there are statements in the job stream that are all non-JCL and non-JES and are not preceded by either a DD * or DD DATA statement. The system generates a DD statement to reference them. In the JCL listing this statement appears as:

```
//SYSIN  DD *  GENERATED STATEMENT
```

Allowing the system to generate this statement reduces the amount of JCL coded. However, this same message may occur because of logic errors contained in the JCL code. The presence of a GENERATED SYSIN statement should be interpreted as a warning that there are potential JCL problems. When the /* statement is omitted the next JCL or JES statement in the job stream signifies the end of the in-stream data set. Even when coded, the /* statement never appears in the printed JCL listing.

In-stream Data Sets (DATA) and the DLM Parameter

Quite frequently on MVS systems JCL statements are included as part of an in-stream data set. When this happens code:

```
//DDname  DD DATA
   . . .
```

in-stream data (possibly containing JCL statements)

```
   . . .
/*
```

Statements which contain // in columns 1 and 2 will be read in the same manner as non-JCL statements. The system will interpret every statement it reads as a member of the in-stream data set until a statement with /* in columns 1 and 2 is encountered. Failure to code a /* statement following the in-stream data set can cause actual JCL to be ignored. A SYSIN DD DATA statement will never be generated by the system.

If an in-stream data set contains statements that have a /* in columns 1 and 2, a further refinement is necessary. This is the one situation in MVS JCL where the DLM keyword parameter is needed, as follows:

```
//DDname   DD DATA,DLM=xy
  . . .
in-stream data (possibly containing /* in columns 1 and 2 and any type of JCL statement)
  . . .
xy
```

Either * or DATA must precede DLM on the DD statement or a syntax error results. Here xy delimits the in-stream data set. The characters x and y can be any two EBCDIC characters. When used with the DLM parameter they replace /* as the delimiter for the in-stream data set. Because of their special syntax properties, ' (apostrophe) and & (ampersand) should be avoided as delimiters on MVS systems. With both, two characters must be coded for each one needed. If either or both x and y are special characters, then xy should be enclosed in apostrophes. This is consistent with the JCL rule that any character string which contains one or more special characters must be enclosed in apostrophes. Here a special character is any character that is not alphabetic, numeric, or national.

DLM is a simple DD parameter, and performs only this single function. It may be coded only with DATA or *. Using DLM any statement consisting of two characters and the remainder spaces can be used as a JCL statement.

Example 3: To place three JCL statements and a JES statement within an in-stream data set, code the following:

```
//INPUT   DD   DATA,DLM=@@
/*JOBPARM COPIES=2
   THIS STATEMENT IS NEITHER JCL NOR JES
/*
//DD1     DD   DSN=XYZ,DISP=OLD
//
@@
```

DLM performs a slightly different role with * and DATA. When coded with * the end of the in-stream data set can be specified by the DLM value or the first JCL statement in the job stream following the DD statement containing DLM. With DATA the in-stream data set may be ended only when a statement that contains the DLM value is encountered; even a Null statement placed in the in-stream data set will not end it.

Whether * or DATA is coded on a DD statement, the following comments apply:

1) A single job step can contain more than one card image in-stream data set. This is true even when the job is submitted through an actual card reader.

2) All in-stream data sets are initially spooled to disk by the Job Scheduler prior to processing. Hence, when a card image is read the data actually resides on disk.

3) The delimiter for an in-stream data set, whether /* or a two character string delimiter, never appears in the printed JCL listing.

4) If one or more consecutive statements in a job are not JCL or JES and not preceded by a DD * or DD DATA statement, a SYSIN DD * statement will be generated and placed in the JCL listing. Every occurrence of this message in the printed JCL listing should be carefully examined.

Example 4: Consider an in-stream data set composed of PL/I source code and PL/I comment statements:

```
//A    EXEC   PLIXCG
//PLI.SYSIN   DD *
    A:PROC OPTIONS(MAIN);
       ...
   /* THIS IS A COMMENT   */
       ...
    END A;
/*
//GO.PRINTER   DD ...
//B    EXEC   PLIXCG
    B:PROC OPTIONS(MAIN);
       ...
   /* THIS IS A COMMENT  */
       ...
     END B;
//GO.PRINTER   DD ...
```

The statements between the PLI.SYSIN statement and the /* statement comprise an in-stream data set. This data set is the input to the PL/I compiler. If the PLI.SYSIN statement is omitted the system responds by generating a SYSIN statement for the in-stream data. Likewise, if the /* statement is omitted the system uses the GO.PRINTER statement to determine that an in-stream data set has ended. Hence, both steps A and B give the same results.

Some programming languages and utilities, such as PL/I and IDCAMS respectively, permit comment statements which begin with /*. The /* must be coded between columns 2 and 71. Such a statement is coded correctly in Example 4. If the single comment shown here had begun in column 1 the in-stream data would be interpreted as two distinct data sets. The second would be preceded by a GENERATED SYSIN statement, and would be ignored since it had the same DDname as the first one. The actual JCL listing is shown below.

```
//B      EXEC    PLIXCG
//SYSIN DD   *    GENERATED STATEMENT
      B:PROC OPTIONS(MAIN);
         ...
/*       THIS IS A JCL DELIMITER NOW
//SYSIN DD   *    GENERATED STATEMENT
         MORE PL/I SOURCE CODE
         ...
        END B;
//GO.PRINTER  DD ...
```

The SYSOUT Parameter

The SYSOUT parameter is used to direct output to a printer or card punch. The meaning of the values that are coded with SYSOUT are very installation-dependent. Although there are three positional subparameters that may be coded, ordinarily only the first is used. When this is the case it appears as SYSOUT=x. Here x may take on any of 38 possible values, A-Z, 0-9, *, or $. If a letter or number is coded, the output is directed to the same destination as for MSGCLASS=x on the JOB statement. To get the job listing and any printed data sets sent to the same output device make the SYSOUT and MSGCLASS values the same.

A type of backward reference can also be coded with SYSOUT. If SYSOUT=* or SYSOUT=$ is coded this data set is automatically sent to the same output class as that specified with the MSGCLASS parameter on the JOB statement. The complete syntax of the SYSOUT parameter is:

```
SYSOUT=(class name,program name,form name or)
                                code name
```

All three subparameters are positional and optional. However, at least one of the three should be coded, except when overriding a statement in a procedure. The parentheses are not required with SYSOUT when just the first subparameter is coded. If the first subparameter is omitted but either the second or third is coded, the class name will default to the MSGCLASS value on the JOB statement.

Program name may be coded when the data set is to be written by an installation developed program rather than by JES2 or JES3. The installation written program is not executed under the control of JES2 or JES3, but rather is controlled by an external writer. Two program names, INTRDR and STDWTR, have reserved meanings with JES2 and JES3. When INTRDR is coded, the SYSOUT data set is processed as a job stream. Using INTRDR, which stands for Internal Reader, the SYSOUT data set from one job is submitted as a second job.

Form name identifies a special form that is to hold the SYSOUT data set. Code name is used only with JES2. The code name value is used to identify the JES2 OUTPUT statement that will supply additional information concerning the creation of the SYSOUT data set. Code name is illustrated in several examples in Chapter 4. For both form name and code name, one to four characters (alphabetic, numeric, and national) may be coded.

Additional Keyword Parameters for Printed Data Sets

All of the remaining keyword parameters are used only with printed data sets. Several of these parameters may be used only with an IBM 3800 or comparable laser printer. This includes BURST, CHARS, FLASH, and MODIFY. Additionally, the COPIES and FCB parameters have expanded roles with the 3800 printer.

BURST

BURST may only be coded when using a 3800 printer. The 3800 printer has two different stackers to hold printed output. BURST determines the stacker to which the output sheets will be directed. With BURST=Y, the output is burst and trimmed into individual sheets. This is typically used with letters or forms. With BURST=N the printed output is continuously folded. Only Y and N may be coded. Most frequently BURST=N is the default. The same results can be achieved from coding the OUTPUT statement.

Example 5: To use the 3800 printer to create a printed data set of form letters to be used in a mass mailing, the following can be coded:

```
//PRINTED  DD  SYSOUT=A,BURST=Y
```

CHARS

When printing a data set on the 3800 printer the CHARS parameter is used to select the names of one or more character tables. The character tables are used to identify specific types of printed output (they can be thought of as fonts). A table name consists of from one to four characters, all of which must be letters or numbers. If only one table is coded parentheses are not necessary. Character tables can also be coded with the CHARS parameter on the JES2 OUTPUT statement and the OUTPUT JCL statement. Some character tables are provided with the system; others can be created using a utility called IEBIMAGE. If CHARS=DUMP is coded a high-density dump of 204 characters per line is printed.

Example 6: A data set requires two special character tables. Additionally, a high-density dump is to be printed if an abend occurs during the step. The two SYSOUT data sets are coded as follows:

```
//DD1       DD SYSOUT=A,CHARS=(SPCL,GS01)
//SYSUDUMP  DD UNIT=3800,CHARS=DUMP,FCB=STD3
```

Here, a special character set and a Gothic character set are used to print the first data set. When FCB=STD3 is coded the high-density dump is printed with eight lines per inch along with the 204 characters per line.

COPIES

The COPIES parameter is used to print multiple copies of a SYSOUT data set. If SYSOUT is not coded on the same DD statement the COPIES value is ignored and one copy of the data set is produced. Hence, it should not be coded with disk or tape data sets. In the simplest case a value from 1 to 255 is coded. COPIES=5 creates five printed copies of the output data set. Recall that when COPIES=5 is coded on the JES2 JOBPARM statement five copies of the entire job output are produced. If both are coded, 25 copies of the data set are printed. As with BURST and CHARS, the information supplied by COPIES may also be coded on the COPIES parameter on the JES2 OUTPUT statement.

The complete syntax of the COPIES parameter is:

```
COPIES=(xxx,(group1 value,group2 value,...,group8 value))
```

Here the second subparameter determines the number of copies of each page that are to be printed together.

Example 7: Five copies of a data set are to be printed. Three consecutive copies of each page of output are to be grouped together, followed by two separate copies of the entire data set. This can be accomplished by coding:

```
COPIES=(5,(3,1,1))
```

Group values may be coded only for a 3800 printer. When group values are coded two sets of parentheses are required. Each group value may range from 1 to 255, but the sum of the group values coded cannot exceed 255 and a group value of 0 is not allowed. Standard sub-subparameter syntax must be used. If group values are specified but SYSOUT is not coded on the DD statement the first group value determines the total number of copies printed. When group values are coded the first subparameter value is ignored.

Example 8: The following DD statements illustrate three common formats of the COPIES parameter. DD1 prints 100 copies of the data set. Any type of printer may be used. Six copies of the data set are produced on a 3800 printer with DD2. The output contains 3, 1, and 2 consecutive copies of each individual page. On a non-3800 printer four copies of the output are produced. With DD3 SYSOUT is not coded, so three copies of the data set are printed.

```
//DD1 DD SYSOUT=C,COPIES=100
//DD2 DD SYSOUT=A,COPIES=(4,(3,1,2))
//DD3 DD UNIT=3800,COPIES=(4,(3,1,2))
```

FCB

When printing a SYSOUT data set the FCB parameter identifies the forms control buffer to be used. The complete syntax of the FCB parameter is:

```
FCB=(image-code,ALIGN  or)
                VERIFY
```

The image-code identifies the image module to be loaded into the forms control buffer. The image-code value consists of one to four characters which must all be alphabetic, numeric, or national. The image-code is used to control vertical spacing on the printer. Prior to the introduction of the forms control buffer spacing was performed by a paper carriage control tape. Some COBOL syntax still specifies this with printed data sets. The same results can be achieved by coding the OUTPUT JCL statement or the FCB parameter on the OUTPUT JES2 statement.

When ALIGN is coded the operator must examine the alignment of the paper in the printer before allowing the data set to print. VERIFY specifies that the operator should determine whether the image on the printer is the correct one. If necessary the operator can also align the paper at this time. One particular image-code (FCB = STD3) produces a dump which occupies eight lines per inch. STD3 is often coded along with the CHARS = DUMP parameter. Both ALIGN and VERIFY are ignored for SYSOUT data sets. FCB is used primarily with 3800 printers.

Example 9: Two data sets are printed. DD1 uses the FCB image-code of ABC. Additionally, if an abend dump is produced it is printed at 8 lines per inch and 204 characters per line.

```
//DD1       DD SYSOUT=C,FCB=ABC
//SYSABEND DD SYSOUT=A,FCB=STD3,CHARS=DUMP
```

FLASH

The FLASH parameter is used only with the 3800 printer. Its role is to specify a forms overlay which should be used for printing the data set. The complete syntax is as follows:

```
FLASH=(overlay name,xxx)
```

The syntax rules for overlay name are exactly the same as those for image-code with the FCB parameter. The value coded for xxx specifies the number of copies of output for which the forms overlay is to be used, and must not exceed 255. Additionally, it cannot exceed the values codes on the COPIES parameter.

Example 10: To produce five copies of a SYSOUT data set and use forms overlay Z with the first three, code the following:

```
//PRINTER DD SYSOUT=A,FLASH=(Z,3),COPIES=5
```

HOLD

The HOLD parameter may only be coded with a SYSOUT data set. It holds a data set from printing until it is released by an operator or a TSO user. Two values may be coded, YES and NO. HOLD=NO is the default, and any value other than YES is treated as the default value. However, incorrect values will generate an informatory message. This parameter is in some ways similar to TYPRUN=HOLD on the JOB statement.

MODIFY

The MODIFY parameter is used only with the 3800 printer. It is often used in conjunction with the CHARS parameter to identify a copy modification module.

OUTLIM

The OUTLIM parameter is used to control the number of records printed in a SYSOUT data set. It is ignored if coded on a DD statement that does not contain SYSOUT. An unsigned number from 1 to 16,777,215 should be specified with OUTLIM. For example, OUTLIM=5000 means that a maximum of 5000 lines of output will be printed for this data set. The basic function of the OUTLIM parameter is to avoid infinite print loops. It can also be used to print only the first part of a very large data set. If OUTLIM is not coded a system default value (usually quite large) is used. If the OUTLIM value is exceeded, an S722 abend occurs.

OUTPUT

The OUTPUT DD parameter is used to connect the DD statement on which it is coded with one or more OUTPUT JCL statements. The OUTPUT parameter should be used with SYSOUT data sets. Only the three standard referback formats may be coded with the OUTPUT parameter. Hence, one of the following must be coded:

```
OUTPUT=*.DDname
OUTPUT=*.stepname.DDname
OUTPUT=*.stepname.procstepname.DDname
```

Any combination of these three formats can be included with one OUTPUT parameter. For example, to associate a single SYSOUT parameter with three OUTPUT JCL statements the following could be coded:

```
OUTPUT=(*.DD1,*.STEPB.DD2,*.A.PROCX.DD3)
```

Here three separate data sets will be printed, each with the characteristics coded on the referback OUTPUT JCL statements.

The value coded with DDname should identify an OUTPUT statement coded in the same step or an OUTPUT statement coded after the JOB but before the first EXEC statement. The OUTPUT parameter provides an explicit connection between a DD statement and an OUTPUT statement. Implicit connections can also be made. If OUTPUT is coded with a non-SYSOUT DD statement, it has no effect. Note that parentheses are unnecessary if only one value is coded. Since the subparameters are not positional, leading and unnecessary embedded commas should not be coded.

UCS

The UCS parameter identifies the universal character set (UCS) image that the JES is to use to print the accompanying SYSOUT data set. The complete syntax of the UCS parameter is:

```
UCS=(character-set-code,FOLD,VERIFY)
```

The subparameters are positional and only the first is required. The character-set-code must identify a universal character set. Values coded depend on the particular printer being used. All values should consist of one to four characters which are alphabetic, numeric, or national. FOLD is available only with JES2 and can be used to print upper and lower case data entirely in upper case. VERIFY specifies that the opperator should determine whether the character set image which is displayed on the printer is the correct one.

The OUTPUT JCL Statement

OUTPUT is a relatively new statement type which was added to MVS JCL several years ago. It is used to provide additional processing options with SYSOUT data sets. It should not be used with non-SYSOUT data sets. The link between a specific SYSOUT data set and the OUTPUT statement is the OUTPUT DD parameter coded on the DD statement with SYSOUT. The OUTPUT parameter uses a referback syntax to identify one or more OUTPUT DD statements.

Example 11: The SYSOUT data set coded with DDname PRINTR is to be created in two formats. One set of processing options are provided for VERSN1, while VERSN2 supplies a second set of values.

```
//VERSN1 OUTPUT BURST=Y,DEFAULT=N,COPIES=3
//VERSN2 OUTPUT LINECT=55,FORMS=STD
   ...
//PRINTR DD SYSOUT=A,OUTPUT=(*.VERSN1,*.VERSN2)
```

The above code is equivalent to having the PRINTR DD statement coded twice and having both data sets actually print. In reality, if both have the same name in the same job step the second one will be ignored. However, the effect will be as shown here:

```
//PRINTR DD SYSOUT=A,BURST=Y,DEFAULT=N,COPIES=3
//PRINTR DD SYSOUT=A,LINECT=55,FORMS=STD
```

Thus, with printed data sets values may be supplied from three sources: the DD statement which contains SYSOUT, the OUTPUT JCL statement, and JES control statements such as OUTPUT and FORMAT.

Values coded on the SYSOUT statement override comparable values on the OUTPUT statement. This is a complete override if subparameters are coded. Likewise, JES values are also overridden.

Approximately 30 keyword parameters may be coded with the OUTPUT DD statement. Many of the important parameters supply information that can be coded on a DD statement or JES statement. The BURST, CHARS, COPIES, FCB, FLASH, MODIFY, and UCS parameters may be coded on a DD statement or with the OUTPUT statement. The basic function is the same in both places. Only two additional OUTPUT parameters are discussed here: CLASS and DEFAULT.

The CLASS parameter determines the output class for a SYSOUT data set. The same values may be coded as with the MSGCLASS parameter on the JOB statement. In order to use the CLASS parameter, the SYSOUT value cannot be coded on the DD statement. Recall that the DD statement value overrides the comparable OUTPUT parameter. Hence, to identify the output class the following two statements could be coded:

```
//ALPHA OUTPUT CLASS=D
//DD1    DD      SYSOUT=(,),OUTPUT=*.ALPHA
```

The DEFAULT parameter determines whether the OUTPUT data set can be used in implicit references. Two values can be coded: YES or NO. When YES is coded, the accompanying OUTPUT statement can be implicitly referenced by SYSOUT DD statements. With DEFAULT=NO, only an explicit reference can use the OUTPUT statement. Y and N can also be coded. NO is the default value for DEFAULT.

Exercises

1. For each of the following JCL statements find and explain the errors (if any). Some statements contain more than one error. Look mainly for syntax errors.

a) `//EXEC DD     DUMMY-JOB`

b) `//EXEC DD     DUMMY JOB`

c) `//EXEC DD     PROC  JOB`

d)
```
//ABC DD DSNAME=XZXZXZ,DISP=(,KEEP),VOL=SER=DISK99,
//UNIT=3380,SPACE=(CYL,5),DCB=(ALPHA1),LABEL=RETPD=100
```

e)
```
//ABC DD DSN=ABCABCAB,DISP=(OLD,PASS),UNIT=SYSDA,
//   SPACE=(TRK,20),UNIT=3350,DCB=(LRECL=80,RECFM=F),
//   VOL=(,PRIVATE,SER=WORK99)
```

f)
```
//X   DD UNIT=VIO,DISP=(OLD,DESTROYED)
```
g)
```
//AAAAAAAA DD DSN=XYZ,SPACE=(CYL,(3,(2,(1))),
    UNIT=SYSDA,DISP=NEW,VOL=SER=ABCDEF
```
h)
```
//DD1#1 DD  DSN=OLDDATA.1SET,DISP=(OLD,,PASS,),
//  DCB=(ALPHA1)
```
i)
```
//DD2  DD   DSN=A.B.C.D.,DISP=(,,PASS),UNIT=,
//      VOL=REF=.*.STEPA.DD1
```
j)
```
//DD3  DD   UNIT=
//       3350,TAPE=012345,DCB=BLKSIZE=1000
```
k)
```
//DD4  DD   DSN=DUMMY,DISP=(OLD,PASS)
//      DD   DUMMY,DISP=(NEW,PASS),UNIT=VIO
//      DD   ,UNIT=VIO
```
l)
```
//JOB123    JOB  ...
//JOBCAT     DD  ...
//SYSCHEOV   DD  ...
//DD1      EXEC  PGM=X
//JOBLIB     DD  ...
/*OUTPUT         ...
//DD2        DD  ...
//STEPLIB    DD  ...
```
m)
```
//ALPHA   EXEC IDCAMS
//SYSIN     DD *
/*  AN IDCAMS COMMENT*/
    PRINT IDS(XYZ)
/*  ALSO A COMMENT
    LISTCAT ENT(PQR)
/*
//ABC  JOBB (X,Y),'NEW JOB'
```
n)
```
//C  EXEC   PGM=X
... ABC ...
... DEF ...
//GO   DD   SYSOUT=5,OUTLIM=1000
```
o)
```
//D    DD   DSN=*.X,DISP=(OLD,PASS),SPACE=*.Y.1,
//          VOL=REF=(*.Y),DCB=(WHATEVER,LRECL=80)
```
p)
```
//SYSIN  DD   DATA,DLM='  '
ABC
'

/*
00
''
//C      EXEC  PGM=Y
//
```
q)
```
//CONCATEN DD  DSN=pds-library,DISP=SHR
//         DD  DSN=seq-data set,DISP=SHR
//         DD  DSN=isam-data set,DISP=SHR
//         DD  DSN=NULLFILE,DISP=SHR
//         DD  DSN=2nd-pds-library,DISP=SHR
//         DD
```

Chapter 7

DD Parameters for Disk and Tape Data Sets

Over half of this chapter is devoted to describing the seven major DD parameters used with Disk and Tape Data Sets: DSNAME, UNIT, VOLUME, DISP, SPACE, LABEL, and DCB. The material for each of the seven parameters contains an overview describing the role of the parameter, a detailed examination of the syntax, and numerous coding examples. Following this the remaining DD parameters are examined. Finally, the output from an actual job is thoroughly examined.

The DSNAME Parameter

Overview

Some system facilities must be available to allow existing data sets to be easily and quickly located. When new data sets are created these facilities must be rapidly accessed and updated. Disk data sets have their names stored in a Volume Table of Contents (VTOC) located on the disk volume where the data set resides. Likewise, all tape data sets with standard labels (SL, SUL, AL, AUL) have their names written in their header and trailer labels. Data set names may also be stored in system catalogs and the system 'pass mechanism.' MVS uses these four types of facilities (VTOCs, tape labels, catalogs, and the 'pass mechanism') to efficiently manage data sets.

The DSNAME parameter is the connection between the data sets used by a program and the four facilities where the system stores data set names. DSNAME performs two major functions: When a disk or tape data set is created DSNAME may be used to assign it a specific name; when an existing data set must be retrieved DSNAME is coded to identify it. Every data set on an MVS system is assigned a name when it is created. The data set name may be specified with DSNAME. If DSNAME is not coded when a data set is created the system generates a name for it. A data set can be classified as temporary if it is created and deleted in the same job and no entries are placed in any system catalog during the job. System-generated names should be avoided with permanent data sets. With temporary data sets they are often acceptable.

DSNAME may be abbreviated as DSN (the abbreviation is used throughout this book). Only one operand may be coded with DSN: the name of the data set itself, DSN=dsname. In two cases on MVS systems a part of a data set may also be identified with the DSN parameter. In both cases the syntax becomes DSN=dsname(part of data set). Additionally, several data sets may share the same name. In some cases they can be distinguished by using a notation similar to subscripts, DSN=dsname(subscript). The names of data sets in a catalog must be unique. The names of data sets in the VTOC of a specific disk volume must also be unique.

Temporary Data Set Names

The syntax rules for coding data set names fall into two categories. Syntactically, every data set is classified as either temporary or permanent. The syntactical definition of temporary is more restrictive than the broad description of temporary given above. A (syntactically) temporary data set name begins with two ampersands, which identify a data set as temporary. The remainder of the characters define the actual name, consisting of one to eight characters, all of which must be either alphabetic, numeric, national (@, $, #), a hyphen, or +0 the (12-0) punch with punched cards. The first character following the two ampersands must be alphabetic or national.

Example 1: All of the entries on the left are valid temporary data set names. All entries on the right are invalid.

Valid	*Invalid*	*Reason for Invalid DSNAME*
DSN=&&X	DSN=&&&	& not allowed for actual name
DSN=&&X@#1	DSN=&&1A2B3C	1 not alphabetic or national
DSN=&&TEMP123	DSN=&&ABCDEFGHI	9 characters in data set name
DSN=&&$ABC	DSN=&&	no name coded
DSN=&&A-B-C	DSN=&&A.B.C.D	periods not allowed with name

Variations of the last invalid DSN parameter are often inadvertently coded because many people are unaware of the syntax differences between temporary and permanent data set names. DSN=A.B.C.D is a valid name for a permanent data set.

One significant variation is permitted in the rules for constructing a temporary data set name: the name may also begin with a single ampersand. When this change is made the five valid examples above remain correct. In MVS JCL a single ampersand denotes the beginning of a symbolic parameter. However, if the symbolic parameter is coded inside a procedure as DSN=symbolic parameter and not assigned a value, it is then interpreted as a temporary data set name. Incidentally, this is the only situation in which a symbolic parameter not assigned a value will not generate a syntax error. When one ampersand is used to begin a temporary data set name the remaining characters must also satisfy the syntax rules for a symbolic parameter. The major distinction between a temporary data set name and a symbolic parameter name is that the latter contains one to seven characters following the ampersand. Symbolic parameters are discussed in Chapter 8.

Example 2: Several additional examples of valid and invalid DSN values which begin with a single ampersand are shown below.

Valid	*Invalid*	*Reason for Invalid DSNAME*
DSN=&AEIOU	DSN=&ABCDEFGH	8 characters in name
DSN=&$	DSN=&	no name coded
DSN=&A1@	DSN=&-A-1-@	hyphen not alphabetic or national

Permanent Data Set Names

In this context permanent means that the name of the data set does not begin with one or two ampersands. With permanent data sets the DSN parameter allows a more flexible syntax. A data set does not actually become permanent until the DISP parameter is used to give it a permanent status. In particular, it must be categorized as kept or cataloged.

If the leading ampersands are removed from a temporary data set name a valid permanent data set name is created. Such names are called permanent unqualified data set names. Additionally, two or more permanent unqualified data set names may be concatenated together and separated by periods to produce longer data set names. The characters between the periods must obey the rules for temporary data set names without ampersands, and are called *levels of qualification*. Hence, DSN=A.B.C.D and DSN=X.X1$@.A-B are valid names. The maximum length of a qualified data set name is 44 bytes including periods. This permits five character strings eight bytes in length to be coded together. A maximum of 22 levels of qualification are possible if each qualifier is a one byte character string.

Example 3: All of the names on the left are valid, and all those on the right are invalid.

Valid	*Invalid*	*Reason for Invalid DSNAME*
DSN=A1.B2.A-B	DSN=A-B-C-D-E	9 character qualifier
DSN=A.B.C.D.E.F.G	DSN=A..B+C	..is invalid
DSN=ALPHA.BETA12.XX	DSN=O"BRIAN	quote
DSN=A&B	DSN=A&B	& invalid unless symbolic
DSN=A-	DSN=A.B.	cannot end with period

Additional DSNAME Properties

The character string that starts with the first letter of the data set name and continues up to the first period is called the *first level of qualification* for a data set name. The group of valid data set names in Example 3 contained the first level qualifiers A1, A, and ALPHA. Some installations permit only certain character strings to be used as first levels of qualification. A security package such as RACF can be used to require programmers to work within a specific collection of first level qualifiers. Additionally, the first level of qualification may be used to determine the appropriate catalog when cataloging a data set or referencing a data set through its catalog entry. This is discussed further in Chapter 21. The remaining levels of qualification are ordinarily left to the user's discretion. However, several important utility programs perform *generic processing,* in which all of the data sets in a given group with one or more of the same levels of qualification may be processed together. Several variations of generic processing are allowed. Thus, DSN=ABC.* can identify all data sets with first level qualifier ABC and any further qualifier values. DSN=A.*.C can identify all data sets whose first and third qualifier are A and C respectively. Here all data sets whose qualifiers are the same can be processed as a group without giving the complete data set name for any of them. Hence, programmers and installations may wish to develop their own standards for additional levels of qualification. Generic values cannot be coded on JCL statements. They must be supplied by utility control statements.

Characters other than alphabetics, numerics, nationals, hyphens, +0, and periods for qualification may be coded with DSNAME. When this is done the entire DSNAME value must be enclosed in apostrophes. From one to eight characters separated by periods may be coded in each level of qualification.

It was mentioned earlier that system-generated names should be avoided with permanent data sets. The generated name consists of five levels of qualification with eight bytes in some levels, and begins with SYS. It includes the time and date when the data set was created, along with the jobname and assorted other information.

Incidentally, the system uses each programmer-supplied temporary data set name to generate a qualified name with basically the same format as a system-generated name. However, the programmer-supplied name is sufficient for future references in the job stream. Coding a system-generated name when later referencing a permanent data set can easily create errors. However, a system-generated name is always adequate for a temporary data set used in only one job step; there is no reason to code a DSN value in this situation. Due to the manner in which the system generates names it is impossible for two temporary data sets to have the same name even if they are created at the same time.

Referbacks may also be coded with DSN. There are two specific reasons for using referbacks with DSN. Suppose a data set name occurs repeatedly throughout a job stream. If the DSN value needs to be changed it must be changed in each location. However, only one change must be made in the JCL if referbacks are coded for every DSN value after the first reference to the data set. Additionally, a data set name with several levels of qualification can be quite lengthy to code, and using a referback results in less typing. A referback can identify a DD statement that does not contain a DSN parameter.

Referencing Parts of a Data Set

Three special formats are permitted with DSN. They are used with partitioned data sets (pds), Generation Data Groups, and ISAM data sets. Each involves following the name of the data set with a value enclosed in parentheses. In each case the value in parentheses identifies a particular part of a larger entity.

Partitioned data set libraries are composed of members, each of which is a data set itself. The pds is a convenient way to group multiple data sets together. Suppose XYZ is a pds with members A, B, and C. The following formats are permitted to reference one or more member:

Syntax	*Explanation*
`//DD1 DD DSN=XYZ`	This references the entire pds.
`//DD2 DD DSN=XYZ(A)`	This references just member A.
`//DD3 DD DSN=XYZ(C)`	This references both members C and A.
`// DD DSN=XYZ(A)`	Note that concatenation is used here.
`//DD4 DD DSN=XYZ(C,A)`	This is a JCL syntax error. Only one member name can be coded on a DD statement.

A pds can also be temporary. Hence, in the above examples both &&XYZ and &&XYZ(A) can be coded. Partitioned data sets are discussed in detail in Chapter 12. Member names must be one to eight characters in length and consist entirely of alphabetics, numerics, and nationals.

Generation Data Groups have two sets of naming conventions. Like partitioned data sets, they are a topic in their own right. ISAM data sets are also a separate topic, and are covered in Chapter 13.

The UNIT Parameter

Overview

The UNIT parameter specifies the type of I/O device to assign to a data set. A wide range of device types may be identified. For example, UNIT could specify a certain type of tape drive (800 BPI, 6250 BPI, cartridge, etc.) or a specific type of disk drive (3350,3380,etc.). On MVS systems a UNIT value may be explicitly coded using any of three different formats. First, UNIT can be assigned the value of a device's system address, a three digit hexadecimal value which uniquely identifies a specific I/O device. The actual format is UNIT=XYZ. The system address describes the path by which the device is physically connected to the computer. Second, UNIT can identify a device type by using its IBM product name. Hence UNIT=3380 requests that a 3380 disk be used and UNIT=3480 identifies a cartridge tape drive. Some device types are qualified by hyphenation, such as 3330-1 or 3420-6. Even when a hyphen is used it is unnecessary to enclose the UNIT value in apostrophes. Third, UNIT can be assigned a group or generic name. Group names and the devices they identify are defined when the system is generated, and are chosen by the installation. The value of the UNIT parameter can also be implicitly determined in a variety of ways.

The complete syntax of the UNIT parameter showing the three positional subparameters is:

```
       device address                        or unit count or
UNIT=(device type                            or P              ,DEFER)
       installation defined (group) name  ,
```

Group Names and Device Types

These two forms of the UNIT parameter do not ordinarily identify a specific device. For example, coding the device type format UNIT=3420-6 means that any nine track model 3420-6 tape drive may be used. Likewise, group name UNIT=SYSSQ implies that any disk or tape drive may be used. Hence, device type and group name forms are designed to allow the system considerable flexibility in selecting a device to associate with a volume. If the VOL parameter identifies a volume which is permanently mounted on a device, such flexibility is not available. Coding a specific VOL value for a permanently mounted volume determines the UNIT selected whether device type or group name is used.

The following list includes some of the most frequently used group names, along with their typical meanings at many installations.

Group Name	*Usual Meaning*
UNIT=SYSDA	any disk drive within a particular group; SYSDA is often used with temporary or work data sets; it is unnecessary to code a VOL parameter with UNIT=SYSDA
UNIT=DASD	same meaning as UNIT=SYSDA
UNIT=DISK	same meaning as UNIT=SYSDA; SYSDA, DASD, and DISK can all be used to identify different groups of disk devices
UNIT=SYSSQ	any device which can hold a sequential data set, including a mixture of disk and tape drives
UNIT=TAPE	any tape drive
UNIT=WORK	a disk drive used to hold work data sets
UNIT=VIO	VIO data sets are not true disk data sets, and are described at the end of this section.

Notice that coding UNIT=group name does not ordinarily identify a specific volume. Rather, it classifies the I/O device associated with the volume.

System Device Addresses

One situation in which the UNIT value identifies a specific device is when a system address is coded. Since system addresses are unique there is no ambiguity about the device or volume requested for a permanently mounted volume, such as a 3350 or 3380 disk. In this case the UNIT value determines the VOL value. If an installation has only one device in a particular device type or group and it contains a permanently mounted volume, coding UNIT=device type or UNIT=group name also determines the volume. Most installations recommend that the system address format not be coded with UNIT. The system address is by far the most restrictive of the three UNIT parameter formats. A non-shared device, such as a tape drive or printer, can only be allocated to a job if no other job is requesting it. The average user rarely knows the system addresses of the I/O devices. However, these addresses are included with the JCL allocation messages. This can be seen in the complete job listing at the end of this chapter in the IEF237 messages.

All I/O devices are connected to a control unit, which is connected to the computer by a channel. This approach is standard on MVS systems. The meaning of the three hexadecimal digits is shown in Figure 7–1, where UNIT=36B:

FIGURE 7–1
System Device Addresses

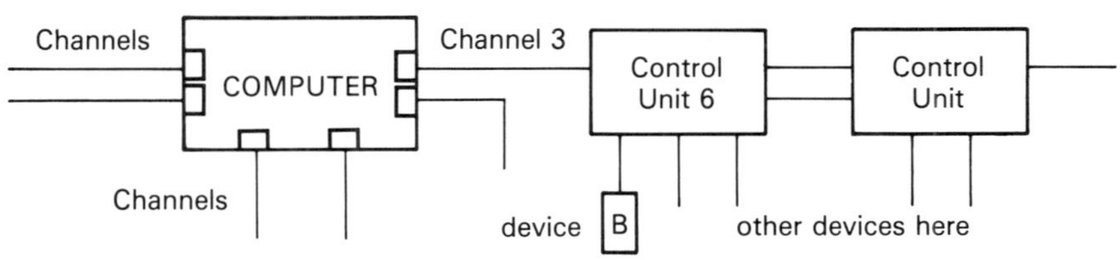

Here I/O device B is attached to control unit 6, which is connected to the computer by channel 3. This is the standard method by which all I/O devices are connected to the computer. Control units can be thought of as limited function computers which manage a group of I/O devices. Hence, a device's unit address (UNIT=XYZ) describes the path between the device and the CPU. Although X, Y, and Z are each one byte fields, the complete three digit number can be decomposed in many ways to identify the channel, control unit, and device numbers. One popular approach allows for 16 channels, 8 control units per channel, and 32 devices per control unit. In this case, X, Y, and Z occupy 4, 3, and 5 bits respectively.

Conditions for Coding the UNIT Parameter

UNIT must be coded whenever a disk or tape data set is created. There are no exceptions to this statement. UNIT does not have a default value for disk and tape data sets. In fact, UNIT is required whenever a disk data set is created, even though in one case the SPACE parameter is not required (when UNIT=VIO is coded a default SPACE value is supplied). If this value is too small a SPACE parameter can be coded.

For existing data sets there are several important situations when it is unnecessary to code the UNIT parameter. First, UNIT is never required with DUMMY data sets, and it is ignored if coded. UNIT is also unnecessary with in-stream and SYSOUT data sets, although it can be coded with either to identify a specific I/O device type.

There are also three important situations with disk and tape data sets where it is unnecessary to code UNIT. First, it is unnecessary to code UNIT with an existing cataloged data set. For such data sets unit and volume information is stored in a system catalog along with the name of the data set. Hence, it is sufficient to instruct the system to use the catalog to retrieve these two values. This is done by omitting both the UNIT and VOL parameters from the DD statement which references the data set. It is important that the VOL parameter not be coded on the DD statement, since the system will not use the catalog to retrieve UNIT information if VOL is coded. This is the first of several situations where UNIT and VOL are paired together. Frequently either both or neither parameter is coded.

Second, it is unnecessary to code UNIT when retrieving an existing data set which has been passed, if it can be referenced through the pass table or pass mechanism. As with cataloged data sets, unit and volume information is stored in the pass table along with the data set name. Thus, when requesting that the system get UNIT and VOL values from this table it is unnecessary to code them on the DD statement. In fact it is the omission of these two parameters on the DD statement that instructs the system to go to the pass table. As with cataloged data sets, the VOL parameter must not be coded or the system will not go to the pass table to retrieve UNIT information. More details on referencing both cataloged and passed data sets are provided in Chapter 21. In summary, it is unnecessary to code UNIT and VOL when retrieving a data set that is cataloged or has been previously passed, unless the data set is to be extended to an addition volume. Then, even with cataloged and passed data sets, UNIT and VOL should be coded. Considerably more information on this subject and other exceptional conditions is found in Chapter 21.

The third major situation in which UNIT is not required is with VOL=REF=referback or VOL=REF=dsname. With VOL=REF=referback the UNIT value is taken from the referenced DD statement. With VOL=REF=dsname the UNIT value is supplied from the passed or cataloged data set coded with VOL. VOL=REF is the third situation where UNIT and VOL are paired together. If a multi-volume data set is identified with the VOL=REF format it may be necessary to code a UNIT parameter. However, the value specified must be a subset of the referenced unit type. In all other cases any UNIT value coded with VOL=REF is ignored.

As noted above, the UNIT parameter frequently interacts strongly with the VOL parameter. If VOL is coded on a DD statement UNIT should usually be coded, and vice versa. There are two major exceptions to this pairing. The first occurs when VOL=REF is coded to reference an existing data set, as described above. The second is when a non-specific volume request is made when creating or extending a data set. In this situation UNIT is coded but a VOL parameter is not present. Either UNIT=device type or UNIT=generic name should be coded when making a non-specific volume request.

Second and Third Positional Subparameters

The second and third UNIT subparameters are used with multi-volume data sets. It is possible to request more than one unit on a DD statement by coding the second positional subparameter. The device address format of UNIT is rarely used when this is done.

Example 4: To reference a data set that occupies three volumes, any of the following may be coded:

```
//DD1 DD UNIT=(3380,3),VOL=SER=(DISK01,DISK02,DISK03),...
//DD2 DD UNIT=TAPE,VOL=SER=(TAPE01,TAPE02,TAPE03),...
//DD3 DD UNIT=(3380,3),no VOL parameter,....
```

With DD1 each volume is assigned to a different device. With DD2 all three volumes share the same device. With DD3 three 3380 disk volumes are selected by the system since the VOL parameter is not specified. A maximum of 59 units can be specified on one DD statement.

The value P, which requests parallel mounting, can also be coded for the second positional subparameter. This means that all volumes must be mounted at the same time. P is most commonly coded with an existing multi-volume data set. Sufficient devices must be available to hold the volumes which comprise the data set. When parallel mounting is used the job does not have to wait for an operator to mount an additional volume, allowing a job to execute faster.

Example 5: Both forms of the second positional subparameter are used to request three tape drives.

```
//DD1   DD UNIT=(TAPE,P),VOL=SER=(ABC001,ABC002,ABC003),...
//DD2   DD UNIT=(TAPE,3),VOL=SER=(ABC001,ABC002,ABC003),...
```

With DD1 the three tape volumes must all be mounted on separate tape drives before the job step begins execution. The same type of tape drive will be selected for all three volumes. With DD2 the volumes will be mounted on separate tape drives only as they are needed.

The third UNIT positional subparameter is used to request deferred mounting, in which the volume holding the data set does not need to be mounted until the data set is opened. This has two disadvantages: the device is allocated before the data set is needed and the job must wait while an operator mounts the requested volume or volumes when the data set is opened. Hence,

```
//DD3 DD UNIT=(TAPE,3,DEFER),VOL=SER=(ABC001,ABC002,ABC003),...
```

will allocate three tape drives to the data set and the volumes will be mounted when it is opened.

The UNIT=AFF Format

A second syntax format available with UNIT is the AFF format, which functions like a referback. It is:

```
UNIT=AFF=DDname
```

The UNIT value is copied from the DD statement identified by DDname. Coding UNIT=AFF minimizes the number of devices needed during a jobstep. The volumes identified on the two DD statements are said to have UNIT affinity. Notice that UNIT=AFF is syntactically more restrictive than a true referback, since the DDname must be contained within the same jobstep. The restriction is reasonable since the purpose of this format is to assign different volumes to the same I/O devices during a single job step. The DDname statement must be coded before the UNIT=AFF statement which references it.

Example 6: A job step requires that ten tape volumes be processed. However, only three tape drives are available and it is unreasonable to request all of them for this one program. The volumes can all be processed using just one tape drive by coding:

```
//DD1   DD   UNIT=581,VOL=SER=TAPE01,...
//DD2   DD   UNIT=AFF=DD1,VOL=SER=TAPE02,...
//DD3   DD   UNIT=AFF=DD1,VOL=SER=TAPE03,...
//DD4   DD   UNIT=AFF=DD1,VOL=SER=TAPE04,...
  ...
```

One limitation associated with this code is that only one of the volumes may be processed at any one time. Hence, considerable operator intervention is required.

VIO Data Sets

VIO data sets may be used as an alternative to standard disk data sets. VIO data sets are available on all MVS systems, and have the advantage of allowing I/O to be performed much faster than when conventional disk data sets are used. With VIO the I/O operations are performed using the operating system's paging routines, rather than through true disk I/O operations. Hence, VIO operations function at the speed of main memory rather than at the speed of the disk device, which is much slower. If SPACE is not coded on the DD statement with UNIT=VIO a default SPACE parameter of (1000,(10,50)) is automatically provided. If additional space is necessary the SPACE parameter should be coded.

Example 7: Two VIO data sets are to be used as work data sets. Each requires ten cylinders. These can be created by coding:

```
//DD1   DD   UNIT=VIO,SPACE=(CYL,10)
//DD2   DD   UNIT=VIO,SPACE=(CYL,10)
```

There are several limitations associated with using VIO data sets. They cannot be used with permanent data sets, which prohibits their use with VSAM data sets. They are also not allowed with ISAM data sets. Specific volumes should not be identified on a DD statement which contains UNIT=VIO. When the system is generated certain volumes are selected for use with VIO data sets. UNIT=VIO should not be used with very large work data sets or major system problems may result.

The VOLUME Parameter

Overview

This parameter is used to determine the volume or volumes that are to contain the data set being processed. Either disk or tape volumes may be coded with VOLUME. Most frequently all of the volumes that contain a data set are the same type. Under some circumstances different types of volumes may be used to hold parts of the same data set. For an existing data set VOLUME identifies the volume(s) which contains the data set. For a new data set VOLUME specifies where to write the data set. The

VOLUME parameter may be abbreviated as VOL. VOL contains five positional subparameters; the first four have very limited and specific roles, and the fifth supports a wide range of coding options. The last subparameter can also be referenced as a keyword subparameter, as with the fifth LABEL subparameter. When it is used as a positional subparameter as many as four of the preceding subparameters or commas may be coded. Along with DSN and DCB, the fifth subparameter permits standard JCL referbacks. It also shares a second similarity with the DCB parameter; a nonstandard referback format may be coded with VOL.

The complete syntax of the VOL parameter showing the five positional subparameters is:

```
VOLUME=(PRIVATE,RETAIN,volume sequence,maximum number,x)
                       number          of volumes
```

The fifth subparameter can assume any of these six formats: SER=(volser) or SER=volser specifies a single volume data set. SER=(volser1,volser2,. . ., volserN) identifies a multi-volume data set. REF=dsname references a cataloged or passed data set. The three standard referback formats (REF=*.DDname, REF=*.stepname.DDname, and REF=*.stepname.procstepname.DDname) are also allowed.

A volser name may be up to six characters in length. When all of the characters are alphabetic, numeric, national, or hyphens the name need not be enclosed in apostrophes. In every other case apostrophes should be used with the volser value.

VOL=SER and VOL=REF Subparameters

When most data sets are referenced only the fifth VOLUME subparameter needs to be used. In this situation it is simplest to code it as a keyword subparameter. For example, when referencing a data set which resides on volume ABCDEF any of the following six formats may be coded:

Positional Syntax	*Keyword Syntax*
VOL=(,,,,SER=ABCDEF)	VOL=(SER=ABCDEF)
VOL=(other subparameters,SER=ABCDEF)	VOL=SER=ABCDEF
VOL=(,SER=ABCDEF)	VOL=SER=(ABCDEF)

Multiple volumes must be separated by commas. When referencing a data set which occupies disk volume WORK01, WORK02, and WORK03 either of the following can be coded:

Keyword	VOL=SER=(WORK01,WORK02,WORK03)
Positional	VOL=(,,,,SER=(WORK01,WORK02,WORK03))

VOL=REF has two formats that are syntactically the same as referback formats coded with DCB. VOL=REF=dsname can be used to retrieve volume information from an existing cataloged or passed data set. With the DCB parameter only cataloged data sets may be referenced. VOL=REF also allows all of the three standard referback formats. With a referback both VOLUME and UNIT information are copied from the referenced DD statement, so it is unnecessary to code a UNIT parameter on the same statement with VOL=REF=*. If UNIT is coded it is ignored, except under very restrictive conditions. When a VOLUME referback is used with tape data sets the first two LABEL subparameters are also copied from the referenced data set. If these subparameters are also coded on the same DD statement with VOL=REF=* the coded values are ignored.

The VOL=REF=dsname format also copies both VOLUME and UNIT parameters from the referenced data set. Here again UNIT need not be coded. The dsname identified with VOL=REF must be found by the system without benefit of UNIT and VOL information. The standard way this can be done is by searching a pass table or catalog (in that order) for the dsname value. As always any technique that minimizes the amount of JCL coded is worthwhile. Hence, VOL=REF should be used when appropriate.

Example 8: Three examples of using the VOL=REF syntax are shown here. On statement DD1 volume and unit information is taken from the cataloged data set SYS1.PROCLIB. On statement DD2 these values are taken from the ALPHA DD statement coded earlier in the jobstep. On statement DD3 unit, volume, and label information is taken from the BETA DD statement. The LABEL=(2,NL) value is ignored.

```
//ALPHA   DD  DSN=OLD.Y,DISP=SHR,VOL=SER=(ABCDEF,GHIJKL),UNIT=DISK
//BETA    DD  DSN=OLD.Z,DISP=(OLD,DELETE),VOL=SER=TAPE01,
//            UNIT=TAPE,LABEL=(2,SL)
//DD1     DD  DSN=X,DISP=SHR,VOL=REF=SYS1.PROCLIB
//DD2     DD  DSN=Y,DISP=SHR,VOL=REF=*.ALPHA
//DD3     DD  DSN=Z,DISP=SHR,LABEL=(2,NL),VOL=REF=*.BETA
```

The First Four VOL Subparameters

When PRIVATE is coded no data sets may be written to the volume unless the DD statement specifically requests the volume. When the jobstep is finished the volume will be dismounted unless RETAIN or DISP=PASS is coded. All tape volumes are PRIVATE.

RETAIN keeps the volume from being dismounted at the end of the jobstep. When processing a tape volume that is used in multiple job steps RETAIN is coded to minimize operator intervention.

The third and fourth VOL subparameters are meaningful only with multi-volume data sets. The third subparameter identifies the specific volume where processing is to begin; the default value is 1. Ordinarily the third subparameter value will correspond to a volume listed in the fifth subparameter. If the third subparameter value is greater than the maximum number of volumes value, an additional non-specific volume request is made for additional volumes. Volume sequence number is coded in two common situations: when extending a multi-volume data set and when the processing of a multi-volume data set does not begin with the first volume that contains the data set.

The fourth subparameter identifies the total number of volumes in the data set. It is compared to the actual list of volumes in the fifth subparameter and the second UNIT subparameter. The largest of these three numbers determines the maximum number of volumes associated with the data set. In addition, these three values determine the relationship between volumes and unit devices.

Example 9: Two multi-volume data sets are to be processed. Data set XYZ occupies three tape volumes: TAPE01, TAPE02, and TAPE03. Only records in the second and third volumes are to be read. Data set YYY is to be created on three tape volumes which are to be selected by the system. Data set YYY also is used in the following job step. This can be accomplished by coding:

```
//DD1     DD   DSN=XYZ,DISP=SHR,UNIT=TAPE,
//             VOL=(,,2,3,SER=(TAPE01,TAPE02,TAPE03))
//DD2     DD   DSN=YYY,DISP=(NEW,PASS),UNIT=TAPE,
//             VOL=(,RETAIN,,3)
```

Conditions for Coding the VOL Parameter

A detailed description of when VOLUME should and should not be coded is included in the section with the UNIT parameter earlier in this chapter. The relationship between UNIT and VOL is also further discussed there. The conditions for which VOL must be coded are summarized below.

When creating a tape or disk data set VOL must be coded unless a non-specific volume request is desired. The System Resource Manager determines the volumes to use in this case. The SRM selects volumes to optimize the use of system resources.

When accessing an existing tape or disk data set VOL must be coded unless one of three conditions is satisfied: if the data set is passed, cataloged, or a DUMMY data set, VOL need not be coded. If the data set is to be extended onto additional volumes it is still necessary to specify VOL with passed and cataloged data sets if specific volumes are desired.

The DISP Parameter

Overview

The DISP parameter identifies the status of a data set prior to the beginning of the jobstep and after the jobstep completes. Two distinct DISP values may be specified for the end of the jobstep, one for normal termination and one for when an abend occurs. Thus three positional subparameters may be coded with DISP. Chapter 21 examines several of the topics discussed in this section in more detail.

The complete syntax of the DISP parameter showing the three positional subparameters is:

```
       beginning status after  status
DISP=( status   ,  normal     ,following)
                termination   an abend
```

The three subparameters may assume four or five possible values. The values that may be coded with each subparameter are:

```
       NEW KEEP     KEEP
       OLD DELETE   DELETE
DISP=(SHR,CATLG   ,CATLG    )
       MOD UNCATLG UNCATLG
           PASS
```

The possible default values for each subparameter are underlined. Notice that there are two default values for the second subparameter, and under certain circumstances each of the four values used with the third subparameter can be the default. For the second and third subparameters the default value chosen depends on the preceding values. When NEW is the first subparameter DELETE is the default for the second and third if neither is coded. When the second and third subparameters are not coded but OLD or SHR is, KEEP is the default for the second and third subparameters. The defaults can be summarized by saying that an existing data set is kept by default and a new data set is deleted. MOD can be interpreted as either NEW or OLD. If the second subparameter is coded its value becomes the default value for the third subparameter except for PASS.

Example 10: The following examples illustrate the default values used with the DISP parameter.

DISP Value Coded	*Default Values Supplied*
DISP=NEW	DISP=(NEW,DELETE,DELETE)
no DISP parameter coded	DISP=(NEW,DELETE,DELETE)
DISP=(,PASS)	DISP=(NEW,PASS,DELETE)
DISP=(,KEEP)	DISP=(NEW,KEEP,KEEP)
DISP=(OLD,,CATLG)	DISP=(OLD,KEEP,CATLG)
DISP=(MOD,,DELETE)	DISP=(MOD,KEEP or,DELETE) DELETE
DISP=MOD	DISP=(MOD,KEEP or,KEEP or) DELETE DELETE
DISP=(,,CATLG)	DISP=(NEW,DELETE,CATLG)

The meanings of the specific values are explained below.

The First DISP Subparameter Values

DISP=NEW is the default value for the first positional subparameter. When a data set is created the disposition must be NEW or MOD. The accompanying DSN value for a new data set must not duplicate any existing data set name on the specific disk volume where it is placed or in a catalog, if it is cataloged. UNIT information must be supplied with a NEW data set. If a data set is to be created, closed, and then opened again for additional processing in the same step, one DD statement should be coded with DISP=(NEW,. . .). No additional reference to the data set specifying DISP=OLD on a second DD statement should be made. In fact, attempting this may abend the job. Rather, the value coded for the first subparameter reflects the data set's status before the step is executed.

DISP=OLD and DISP=SHR both identify existing data sets. Often only the DSN parameter is coded with DISP=OLD or DISP=SHR. Other times UNIT and VOL parameters are also coded to help locate an existing data set. If the accompanying DD parameters are not sufficient to locate the data set the message IEF212 DATA SET NOT FOUND is printed and the job ends.

When DISP=OLD is coded other jobs cannot simultaneously access the data set. They receive the message IEF099 JOB WAITING FOR DATA SETS. When this occurs the operator may cancel a job that is waiting to use a data set. DISP=OLD is usually coded when adding records to a data set; this prohibits other jobs from reading two different versions of the records in the data set. It is a poor programming practice to code DISP=OLD when merely reading records in a heavily used data set. Such coding could cause a system bottleneck. When adding or modifying a member in a library DISP=OLD keeps other users from accessing any members in the library. This can also cause a serious system bottleneck. When DISP=OLD is coded adding a new member whose name matches an existing pds member name results in the automatic replacement of the existing member. The same replacement occurs with DISP=SHR. However, DISP=SHR is very rarely coded when writing members to a pds library.

SHR allows multiple jobs to access the same data set simultaneously. This is the only significant difference between OLD and SHR. When reading the records in a data set SHR should be coded. Any number of jobs can simultaneously access a shared data set.

MOD can be interpreted as either NEW or OLD. Initially the system assumes that the data set exists and attempts to locate it using the information on the DD statement. If the data set is found the appropriate processing is performed. If the data set is sequential DISP=MOD allows additional records to be appended to the end of the data set. If the data set is a pds additional new members can then be added. When DISP=MOD is coded and an attempt is made to add a member whose name is already in the pds directory the jobstep abends. If a data set is not found then MOD is treated as being the same as NEW and a data set is created. If VOL is coded with DISP=MOD, the data set is assumed to be on the specified volume. If it is not, no attempt is made to create a new data set. Rather, the job ends with a DATA SET NOT FOUND message.

The Second and Third DISP Subparameter Values

The second and third DISP subparameters have the same basic meaning whether the step terminates normally or abends. If a step abends a data set cannot be passed to a subsequent step. Hence, PASS is not permitted as a third subparameter value. KEEP and DELETE are related to CATLG and UNCATLG respectively. KEEP can be thought of as a subset of CATLG (both create or maintain a permanent data set). Likewise UNCATLG is in some ways a subset of DELETE with some data sets. Either KEEP or DELETE are the defaults for the second and third subparameters depending on the value of the first subparameter.

Coding PASS makes the data set available to upcoming steps in the job by placing an entry for the data set in the pass mechanism or pass table. Subsequent references to the data set can be directed to the pass table which contains the UNIT and VOLUME values for a data set, rather than to the volume that contains the data set. Hence, these two parameters need not be coded when retrieving a passed data set. In fact, the pass table is automatically searched for the location of the data set when UNIT and VOL are not coded.

The pass table can be thought of as a directory of passed data sets. The directory is dynamic in that all of the passed data sets are associated with the job currently executing in the system. When a job ends any entries in the pass table associated with it are removed. Thus the disposition of a passed data set that is not subsequently referenced is either DELETE or KEEP. Every time a data set is passed an additional entry is placed in the table. Hence, one data set can have several entries in the pass table. A data set can be retrieved from the pass table only as many times as it has been passed. Retrievals take place in the same order that entries were put in the table. Once a data set is passed it can be retrieved in any subsequent step. It need not be retrieved in every intervening step.

When a tape data set is passed the two LABEL subparameters, file sequence number and label type, are also stored in the pass table. Hence UNIT, VOL, and LABEL can all be omitted when retrieving a passed tape data set. A data set should only be retrieved as many times as it has been passed. However, no matter how many times a temporary data set is passed it can be retrieved from the pass table only one time in a single jobstep. Since retrieving passed data sets requires coding less JCL, data sets should be passed whenever possible.

CATLG shares several similarities with PASS. CATLG places an entry in a system catalog. The entry is used to simplify the amount of JCL needed for future references to the data set. For both tape and disk data sets the catalog entry includes UNIT and VOLUME information. For tape data sets the file sequence number is also included. When retrieving a cataloged disk data set only the DSN and DISP parameters need to be coded to locate it. LABEL=(,format type) must also be coded for a tape data set that does not contain Standard Labels or is to be processed without the Standard Labels.

Unlike a passed data set, the entry for a cataloged data set is permanent and remains in a catalog until an uncatalog operation is performed. After a data set is uncataloged it can still be retrieved. Either UNIT and VOL (and LABEL for some tape data sets) must be coded, or an entry in the pass table may be used. A data set can be retrieved through the catalog any number of times in the same jobstep. Since referencing cataloged data sets requires coding fewer DD parameters, data sets should be cataloged whenever possible. Hence, cataloged data sets are preferred over kept data sets. All data set names in a specific catalog must be unique, but there can be multiple catalogs in a system. The same data set can be both cataloged and passed, in which case it is retrieved using the entry in the pass table.

UNCATLG performs only one function: it removes the data set's entry from a system catalog. UNCATLG does not delete the data set from the disk or tape volume. Rather, it turns a cataloged data set into a kept data set. UNCATLG is only meaningful with a permanent cataloged data set. If the data set cannot be uncataloged the message

```
IEF287 dsname NOT UNCTLGD X
```

is printed. This could mean that the data set is not cataloged or that there is insufficient information to locate the data set's entry in a catalog. In the IEF message X is a numeric value that gives the specific reason for the failure of the uncatalog operation. It is impossible to uncatalog a data set if UNIT and VOLUME values are coded on the same DD statement, since they do not permit catalog access. A data set can also be uncataloged without using JCL by using the IEHPROGM or IDCAMS utility programs.

Coding KEEP creates a permanent data set which exists after the jobstep ends. However, KEEP does not place an entry in a catalog or pass table. In order to retrieve a kept data set UNIT, VOL, and (perhaps) LABEL parameters must be coded. Since kept data sets require additional code for subsequent references, both cataloged and passed data sets are preferable. After a kept data set is initially referenced in the job stream it can be passed, and then future references within the job can use the pass table.

KEEP is commonly coded when it is necessary to create a data set with the same name as an existing cataloged data set. Since data set names in a catalog must be unique, the new permanent data set must be kept. There is no other good reason to create a permanent data set and not catalog it. The same data set name can occur on every disk and tape volume, however. When a data set is created coding DISP=(NEW,CATLG) implies a KEEP operation followed by cataloging the data set. An existing kept data set can also be cataloged by coding DISP=(OLD,CATLG). The operation will not be performed unless either the data set is referenced through the pass table or UNIT, VOLUME, and (perhaps) LABEL are coded on the DD statement.

DELETE is used to remove a data set (scratch it) from a volume. With a disk data set the entry in the Volume Table of Contents (VTOC) is removed and the space the data set formerly occupied is returned to the available space on the volume. Subsequent references to the data set result in the message:

```
IEF212 dsname DATA SET NOT FOUND
```

A tape data set is not physically deleted until it is overwritten. Subsequent references will retrieve a 'deleted' tape data set.

When DELETE is coded additional processing may occur with a cataloged data set. For DISP=(OLD,DELETE), if the data set is referenced through the catalog or pass table, the data set is first uncataloged and then deleted. Either of these situations implies that UNIT and VOLUME are not coded on the DD statement. When a cataloged data set is deleted the following messages result:

```
IEF285   dsname UNCATALOGED
IEF285   dsname DELETED
```

With a cataloged data set, when UNIT and VOLUME are coded on a DD statement which also contains DISP=(OLD,DELETE) the catalog is not accessed, but the data set is scratched from the volume. However, an entry remains in the catalog pointing to the volume which formerly contained the data set. Suppose that a later attempt is made to create and catalog a data set with the same name as the old data set. System messages may imply that it is created successfully but cannot be cataloged. However, if the new data set is placed on the same volume as the former data set the existing catalog entry can be used to reference it. System 213 abends frequently occur in this situation when there is a catalog entry but no corresponding VTOC entry.

DELETE performs one additional function with tape data sets: it leaves the tape positioned at the end of the data set just processed. Both KEEP and PASS rewind the tape to a previous location on the volume (the beginning of the volume and the beginning of the data set respectively).

DISP should not be coded with SYSOUT and in-stream data sets. It is a conflicting DD parameter with them. DISP processing is ignored with a DUMMY data set.

The SPACE Parameter

Overview

The SPACE parameter is used to request a specific amount of disk storage. SPACE should be coded only with disk data sets. If it is coded with UNIT=SYSSQ and a tape device is allocated, it is ignored. With the SPACE parameter the system ordinarily selects the portion of the disk to assign to the data set, although the programmer may pick a specific area. The SPACE parameter is almost always coded when creating a disk data set, and may also be coded with an existing disk data set. Syntactically SPACE can be coded on the DD statement with any existing disk data sets. However, nothing meaningful is ordinarily accomplished when this is done, and the resulting JCL will probably confuse anyone trying to read the listing. A JCL syntax error or abend can result from coding an unneeded SPACE parameter.

All requests for disk space are categorized as either primary or secondary allocations. When a data set is created exactly one primary allocation is made. The entire amount of primary space requested must be available on a single disk volume. If the volume identified on the VOL parameter on the DD statement does not contain sufficient space the job is cancelled. To avoid this it is advisable to let the system select a volume which contains sufficient storage. If the VOL parameter is not coded when a data set is created the system will check every volume of the type identified on the UNIT parameter until it finds one with sufficient unused space. This technique of having the system select a volume is called making a non-specific volume request. This technique may always be used unless a particular disk volume is required. The SRM attempts to select the least used volume in the requested UNIT type to satisfy the request.

Once the entire primary space allocation becomes filled secondary allocations may be made. A maximum of fifteen secondary allocations can be made on the volume which contains the primary allocation, and the maximum value of fifteen is allowed only if a contiguous amount of the requested size is available on the disk volume whenever disk storage is needed. A contiguous amount of disk storage is called an *extent*. Two to five non-contiguous extents are combined if no single extent is large enough to satisfy the secondary allocation. Hence fifteen areas (or extents) on the volume are used for secondary allocations. The primary space allocation may also be satisfied by up to five non-contiguous extents. If user labels are present they occupy one complete extent. Both situations reduce the number of secondary allocations. Space allocations and extents are discussed further in Chapter 15.

Additional secondary allocations may also be requested on other disk volumes. When this is necessary the VOL or UNIT parameter must request two or more volumes. The primary and initial secondary allocations are all made on the first volume. Once all possible secondary allocations have been made on the first volume, or if there is insufficient space remaining on the volume, additional allocations are made on the second volume. Once all allocations are made on the second volume, or if there is insufficient space remaining on the volume, allocations are made on the third volume, and so on. The additional volumes need not be requested or identified when the data set is created. Rather, they can be requested when they are needed. The size of the secondary allocations can change at any time by coding a new SPACE parameter with a different secondary allocation value.

The complete syntax of the SPACE parameter showing the five positional subparameters is:

```
       CYL or                                         ALX   or
SPACE=(TRK or,(primary,secondary,index   or ),RLSE,MXIG or,ROUND)
       block  request request   directory         CONTIG
```

Cylinders, Tracks, and Blocks

Disk space can be allocated in three distinct units. The first positional subparameter specifies either cylinders (CYL), tracks (TRK), or blocks (an unsigned positive integer which gives the length of a physical record). Since there is no default value one of the three must be coded. Cylinders and tracks are device-dependent. A track on a 3380 can hold considerably more data than a track on a 3350. Likewise, the number of tracks which comprise a cylinder is different on various disk types. Blocks are device-independent. The system converts block allocations into tracks. Every block allocation is 'rounded up' into a whole number of tracks and cylinders. A data set is never allocated part of a track.

Example 11: The three versions of the SPACE parameter shown on the left all allocate 30 tracks of disk storage on an IBM 3350 disk. The numeric values coded with the second and third parameters reflect properties of a 3350 disk (one cylinder consists of 30 tracks and 19,069 bytes of user data may be stored on one track). When 30 tracks are allocated, they need not all be on the same cylinder. The parameters on the right illustrate a secondary allocation of 30 tracks.

```
SPACE=(CYL,1)              SPACE=(CYL,(1,1))
SPACE=(TRK,30)             SPACE=(TRK,(30,30))
SPACE=(19069,30)           SPACE=(19069,(30,30))
```

CYL allocates space in cylinders. Some applications such as ISAM may require that CYL be used, and CYL is the most convenient unit to select with large data sets. CYL is usually selected when it is uncertain how much space is required to hold the records in a data set. Unfortunately, TRK is more appropriate for many data sets. Chapter 15 describes the methods used to store data sets on disk. Once this is understood it is possible to make an accurate estimate of the disk storage requirements for any data set. Even if the formulas and overhead for calculating storage on a particular disk volume are not known tables are usually available to help determine the amount of space needed.

TRK allocates space in tracks. For small data sets TRK comes closest to fitting the actual space requirements. When block size is coded space is rounded up to the number of tracks needed to hold the blocks which are also allocated in tracks.

In many situations coding a block size is the most convenient way to request disk space. When this is done the system calculates the number of tracks or cylinders that are needed to hold the data set. To determine a reasonable primary or secondary value it is only necessary to know the approximate number of logical records in the data set and the blocking factor: no properties of the disk need be known. However, it is important to understand the factors that are used to select a good blocking factor and hence utilize the disk effectively. This is thoroughly examined in Chapter 15. The block size is independent of the device, which is convenient when moving a data set to a different type of disk. Additionally, block size is usually coded when writing parts of the same data set on different types of disk volumes. For a data set that contains variable length blocks the value specified for block size should be the average block length. With RECFM=F or RECFM=FB the value coded for block size should be the same value coded with the DCB BLKSIZE subparameter. For any data set which has keys set block size=BLKSIZE+KEYLEN where KEYLEN is the length of the disk KEY field.

There are only two situations where the third allocation sub-subparameter of the SPACE parameter is coded. With an ISAM data set it specifies the size of the index component exclusive of the track indexes found on each cylinder. Space for an ISAM data set must always be requested in cylinders. When the third sub-subparameter is coded with TRK the amount requested must be equivalent to a whole number of cylinders. ISAM data sets are discussed in Chapter 13. With a partitioned data set the third sub-subparameter specifies the number of 256 byte directory blocks created. Space for these blocks is taken out of the primary allocation. Chapter 12 contains more information on this subject. Whenever the third sub-subparameter is coded it implies a default DSORG value of PO. Hence, when creating an ISAM index it is often necessary to code DCB=(DSORG=IS,. . .).

The Final Three SPACE Subparameters

The RLSE subparameter is used to return allocated space that is not needed to the disk volume. When RLSE is coded all unused space is released and becomes available for other data sets to use. However, when a job abends unused space is not released. Furthermore, space is only released if the data set was open for output and the last I/O performed was a WRITE operation. If space is requested by coding TRK or block size it is released in terms of unused tracks. RLSE should not be coded with a sequential data set that may be extended at a later time by coding DISP=MOD. Likewise, RLSE should not be coded with a pds that will have either additional members added to it or existing members replaced.

The CONTIG, MXIG, and ALX subparameters are meaningful only with the primary allocation. CONTIG, the most commonly coded of the three, specifies that the entire primary allocation must be contained within a single extent. When MXIG is coded the largest contiguous amount of unused space on the disk volume becomes the primary allocation if it is at least as large as the value actually requested. ALX allocates five disjoint areas on the disk volume. Each area must be greater than or equal to the primary allocation value.

The ROUND subparameter is meaningful only when block size is coded. The amount of space requested is rounded up to the next whole cylinder. This is only in effect during the primary allocation.

The ABSTR Format of the Space Parameter

A second format of the SPACE parameter allows the allocation of specific tracks on the disk if those tracks are available. It is considerably more restrictive than the format described above. The second format is:

```
SPACE=(ABSTR,(primary,address of first track,index or))
              allocation                      directory
```

ABSTR stands for absolute track address, the actual location where the data set will be stored. To use this format the disk CCHH address must be converted to a relative track address. CC and HH identify a specific cylinder and a track on the cylinder. The primary allocation value specifies the total number of tracks allocated to the data set. Note that there is no secondary allocation. The roles of the index and directory are the same with both formats of the SPACE parameter.

Example 12: Create a data set that occupies seven tracks beginning with track five on cylinder two of an IBM 3350 disk where a cylinder contains 30 tracks. The data set is partitioned and three directory blocks are needed.

```
//DD1   SPACE=(ABSTR,(7,65,3)),...
```

The LABEL Parameter

Overview

Of the seven major DD parameters used with disk and tape data sets, only LABEL deals with several very different types of information. LABEL consists of five positional subparameters. The final subparameter shares several syntax properties with the fifth VOL subparameter. Both can also be coded as a keyword subparameter. Two distinct keywords are available with each subparameter, SER and REF with VOL and EXPDT and RETPD with LABEL. Additionally, if one or more of the consecutive subparameters that immediately precede the fifth subparameter is not coded it is unnecessary to code their commas.

The complete syntax of the LABEL parameter is as follows:

```
LABEL=(file     ,label,PASSWORD or,IN or,RETPD=xxx or)
       sequence  type  NOPWREAD    OUT   EXPDT=yyddd
       number
```

File Sequence Number and Label Type

The first LABEL subparameter is used only with tape data sets, and is coded to identify a specific data set on a tape volume. Tape data sets are numbered consecutively starting with one. One is the default value for the file sequence number. If zero is coded this is interpreted as one. The file sequence number is discussed in Chapter 16.

The second LABEL subparameter serves two functions: it determines whether a data set has labels, and if labels are present it identifies the type. Eight possible label type values may be coded, but only two may be used with disk data sets. Hence most of the discussion of this subparameter is also postponed until Chapter 16.

The two label types that may be coded with disk data sets are SL and SUL. SL identifies Standard Labels, IBM disk data set labels which are automatically written in the Volume Table of Contents (VTOC) of the disk volume for every disk data set when it is created. The contents of the labels are described in Chapter 15. SL is the default value for label type with both disk and tape, and need not be coded. SUL identifies Standard User Labels: combinations of the standard system labels provided by SL and user labels. The contents of user labels are written by the application program. SUL cannot be used with ISAM or partitioned data sets. When LABEL=(,SUL) is coded the first track of the disk data set is reserved for user labels. The user labels track is part of the primary space allocation and no other data may be written on the track. From one to eight unblocked 80 byte records are written on the track and followed by an End of File marker. The first four bytes of each record contain the characters UHLx where x is a value from one to eight. The remaining 76 bytes may contain any values.

User labels may be written by a utility program such as IEBGENER, IEBDG, or IEBUPDTE. They can also be created by a COBOL application program. In a COBOL program the DECLARATIVES SECTION must be used for processing user labels. This holds for both writing and reading them. In the FD for the data set the clause

```
LABEL RECORDS ARE recordname1, recordname2, ... ,recordname8
```

must be coded. Here each of the recordnamei variables should identify an 80 byte field in the WORKING-STORAGE SECTION. Some additional automatic user label processing can be performed with COBOL. See the IBM VS COBOL for OS/VS manual for more details on processing standard user labels in a COBOL program.

Protecting Data Sets

The three remaining LABEL subparameters are all concerned with various aspects of data set access or security. The third subparameter is used with password protected data sets. When this subparameter is coded a field in the data set label is initialized to one of the two values. When PASSWORD is coded an operator must enter the password for the data set in order to do any processing with it. If NOPWREAD is coded it is not necessary to enter the data set's password when reading the data set. However, the password must be supplied for an output operation or to delete the data set. Either IEHPROGM or TSO can be used to assign a password to a data set. If the correct password is not supplied the job abends. The password subparameter is no longer widely used; it has been replaced by security packages such as RACF.

The fourth LABEL subparameter is used to control the type of I/O operations that may be performed. When IN is coded the data set may be read only; any other operation is not allowed. When OUT is coded only output operations may be performed with the data set. This subparameter is used only with BSAM and BDAM data sets. IN and OUT are used to qualify I/O verbs in programs that can perform both types of processing. This subparameter is commonly used with FORTRAN programs.

The fifth LABEL subparameter assigns an expiration date or retention period to the data set. It is used to protect the data set from accidental or careless deletion until a specified date is reached. The date can be coded as a specific day in a specific year or as a specific number of days after the present date. For example, assume the present date is January 2, 1988. To specify January 12 as the date after which the data set may be deleted, code any of the following:

Keyword	*Positional*
`LABEL=(EXPDT=88012)`	`LABEL=(,,,,EXPDT=88012)`
`LABEL=(RETPD=11)`	`LABEL=(,,,,RETPD=11)`

The expiration date with EXPDT must be coded as the last two digits of the year followed by a day value of from 001 to 366. With RETPD any value up to 999 days may be coded. The parentheses are unnecessary with both of the keyword examples. With the positional examples one, two, or three commas may be omitted.

Either IEHPROGM or IDCAMS must be used to delete a data set before its expiration date has been reached. With each utility the PURGE operand must be coded on a standard delete request. It is impossible to circumvent the expiration date by coding only JCL. If the deleted data set was cataloged the catalog entry still remains and must be removed. This can also be done with either IEHPROGM or IDCAMS or strictly through JCL.

There are several situations where EXPDT and RETPD should not be coded. Neither should be used with a temporary data set whose name begins with one or two ampersands. Additionally, if the data set is created and deleted in the same step EXPDT and RETPD will not have any effect.

Example 13: A data set is to be created with standard user labels. It is to be protected from accidental deletion for the next six months. During creation only output operations are allowed. Afterwards a password must be supplied for all operations except reading the data set. Notice that it cannot be determined if this is a disk or tape data set from the information in the LABEL parameter.

```
LABEL=(,SUL,NOPWREAD,OUT,RETPD=183)
```

The DCB Parameter

Overview

The DCB parameter describes the characteristics of the records in a data set. It also specifies the conditions under which the records are to be processed. The DCB parameter contains a large number of subparameters. The four most frequently coded are LRECL, BLKSIZE, RECFM, and DSORG; less commonly coded subparameters include BUFNO, BUFTEK, CYLOFL, DEN, EROPT, KEYLEN, LIMCT, NTM, OPTCD, and RKP. In this chapter the complete syntax of the DCB parameter and the general functions associated with the DCB subparameters are discussed. Many of the subparameters are further discussed as parts of individual topics at other places in the book. In those chapters, the emphasis is on both syntax and using the subparameters in an application. A complete index to the locations in the book which contain more information on the individual DCB subparameters is included in Chapter 9, along with a thorough discussion on the role of many of the DCB subparameters. Several infrequently coded DCB subparameters are not discussed in this book.

Probably more errors occur when coding the DCB parameter than with any other single JCL parameter. The large number of subparameters available with the DCB parameter is partially responsible for this. Additionally, more special formats and unusual processing options are available with the DCB than with any other parameter. Historically this has always been true. At one time the DCB parameter could be continued to another statement after any subparameter and its following comma, although continuation following a subparameter was invalid with almost every other JCL parameter. There are still several instances in JCL where the DCB parameter obeys slightly different rules than the other DD parameters. It is especially important to be aware of these differences when coding the DCB parameter within procedures. It is also very important to realize that much of the information commonly coded with the DCB parameter is often unnecessary, and may duplicate, override, or invalidate correct information. This aspect of DCB coding is examined in Chapter 10, where the construction of the data control block (dcb) and Job File Control Block (JFCB) are discussed in detail.

All DCB subparameters are keyword. Hence, the standard DCB format is:

```
DCB=(subparameter1=value1,subparameter2=value2,...,
     subparameterN=valueN)
```

The keyword subparameters can be coded in any order. When only one subparameter is coded the parentheses are unnecessary. The syntax subparameterI=, may also be used to nullify a subparameter value. Ordinarily it is only used with procedures. A discussion of the individual DCB subparameters follows. With few exceptions the value coded with one DCB subparameter interacts with the values coded with other subparameters.

LRECL (Logical Record Length)

The LRECL subparameter value specifies the size of the records that the application program is actually processing. The concept of a logical record is discussed in detail in Chapter 9. The LRECL value cannot be too large or too small for the type of I/O device associated with the data set. For example, with tape data sets the LRECL value can range from 18 to 32,760 bytes. With a 3350 disk the values coded can range from 1 to 19,069, which is the number of usable bytes on one track. When the track overflow feature is used a single logical record may be written on more than one track. In general the maximum LRECL value permitted is 32K bytes. If a larger logical record value is desired it is necessary to code LRECL=X and use spanned records. With variable length records the first four bytes of each logical record are used to hold the length of the record. Variable length records are discussed further in Chapter 11. The LRECL value can also be specified within the application program or taken from the data set label of an existing data set.

BLKSIZE (Block Size): Physical Record Length

The BLKSIZE subparameter value specifies the size of a physical record. A physical record or block consists of the data that is actually written to or read from an I/O device in one operation. The concept of a physical record is discussed in detail in Chapter 9. The same lower and upper limits apply to BLKSIZE as to LRECL. With variable length records the first four bytes of each physical record are used to hold the length of the block. Variable length records are further discussed in Chapter 11. BLKSIZE values can also be specified within the application program or taken from the data set label of an existing data set. The size of a physical record helps determine the amount of storage required for buffers (discussed in Chapter 9). The LRECL, BLKSIZE, and RECFM subparameters are strongly interrelated. The most important relationships among the three are described below and in Chapter 11.

RECFM (Record Format)

The values coded with the RECFM subparameter perform several functions. RECFM specifies whether logical and physical records are fixed in length or may vary in size. It also describes the relationship between physical and logical records. If carriage control characters are present RECFM identifies the type used. It also specifies whether the records contain EBCDIC or ASCII code and identifies any special features present with them. Multiple values may be coded with one RECFM subparameter.

RECFM classifies every data set into one of five categories. Two factors determine the classification: the relationship between logical and physical record size, and whether all logical records are the same size. Between them they determine the record format for a data set. The five possible logical record values are:

F Fixed length records

V Variable length records

U Undefined or unspecified records (also variable length)

VS (Variable) Spanned records

D (Variable) ASCII records

The first four formats are EBCDIC. Five additional letters may be coded with RECFM. Each of them interacts with one or more of the above five values.

B The logical records in the data set are blocked. B should not be coded with U, but it is allowed with the other four values defined above.

T The track overflow feature is to be used with disk data sets. Specifically, records larger than one track can be written, and parts of the same record can be written on different tracks. S should also be coded.

S There are two possible meanings, depending on whether F or V is coded along with S: Standard and Spanned.

FSxy Fixed Standard (Blocked). Every block is the same size except (perhaps) for the last one in the data set. Here x and y denote any values compatible with F, S, and each other, such as RECFM=FSBA.

VSxy Variable Spanned (Blocked). A complete logical record need not be contained within one physical record. Here x and y have the same meaning as above, such as RECFM=VSB.

When a data set is printed the first byte of each logical record may be used for carriage control. One of two values may be coded to identify the type of carriage control used:

A The first byte of each record is used as an ANSI carriage control character.

M The first byte of each record is used as a machine carriage control character.

Chapter 11 contains a very detailed discussion of RECFM, LRECL, and BLKSIZE. The interrelationships among RECFM, LRECL, and BLKSIZE are also thoroughly examined. RECFM values can also be specified within the application program or taken from the data set labels of an existing data set.

Example 14: Some of the most commonly coded RECFM values are listed below.

RECFM=F All logical records are the same size. Each physical record contains exactly one logical record. The accompanying LRECL and BLKSIZE values should be the same, so usually only BLKSIZE is coded in the JCL.

RECFM=FB All logical records are the same size. As many complete logical records as will fit are placed in a block, so RECFM=FB should be accompanied by a BLKSIZE value which is an integral multiple of the LRECL. The same results occur when RECFM=BF is coded. The RECFM sub-subparameter values may be coded in any order.

RECFM=FBA or RECFM=FBM — With one addition both of these values yield exactly the same results as coding FB. Here the first byte of each logical record is used for carriage control. Likewise, RECFM=FA or RECFM=FM identify fixed unblocked records whose first byte is used for carriage control.

RECFM=FBS — With one addition this is also the same as coding RECFM=FB. There should be no embedded short blocks in the data set; it is the programmer's responsibility to ensure this is actually true. Short blocks are discussed in Chapter 11.

RECFM=V or RECFM=VB — Both logical and physical records are variable length. The first four bytes of each logical record contain its length. The LRECL value must specify the length of the largest possible record in the data set +4. With RECFM=V the BLKSIZE=LRECL+4. For RECFM=VB the BLKSIZE must be greater than or equal to LRECL+4. The notion of a true blocking factor is used only with fixed length records; it does not make sense with variable length records. Hence BLKSIZE need not be set equal to 4 plus a multiple of the LRECL.

RECFM=VBS — With two exceptions this is equivalent to RECFM=VB. Here segments from one logical record can be written in different blocks. In addition the LRECL value can be larger than BLKSIZE.

RECFM=VS — This implies everything included with the description of VBS above. Additionally, although parts of a logical record can be stored in several physical records, one physical record cannot contain more than one logical record or one logical record segment. Thus parts of two distinct logical records cannot be placed in the same block. Spanned records are discussed in Chapter 11.

RECFM=U — Undefined records are variable length. However, they do not contain a field which holds their length. With undefined records each block contains exactly one logical record, so it is sufficient to code just BLKSIZE and omit LRECL.

DSORG (Data Set Organization)

The value coded with the DSORG subparameter specifies one of the four non-VSAM data set organizations. The DSORG value can also be specified within the application program or taken from the data set labels of an existing data set. Data set organization is determined when the data set is created, and cannot be changed subsequently. Surprisingly, in one instance data set organization is determined by the SPACE parameter rather than the DSORG subparameter. Each of the four data set organizations allow two formats, x and xU. Coding U specifies that the data set contains unmovable data. This means that the data set must reside at a specific location on a disk volume. Important data sets that are heavily used may have U specified. The ABSTR format of the SPACE parameter is often coded when creating an unmovable data set. The four DSORG values that can be coded are PS, IS, DA, and PO.

PS Physical Sequential. This is the default value and need not be coded. Chapter 9 examines sequential data set processing.

IS Indexed Sequential. This identifies an ISAM data set. DSORG=IS should be coded whenever an ISAM data set is created and occasionally when an existing data set is retrieved. Other DCB subparameters commonly coded when creating an ISAM data set (DSORG=IS) include CYLOFL, KEYLEN, NTM, OPTCD, and RKP. Chapter 13 describes ISAM data sets.

DA Direct Access. This includes both direct and relative data sets in COBOL and the three Regional data sets in PL/I. DA should be coded whenever a direct access data set is created and occasionally when it is retrieved. DCB subparameters commonly coded with direct data sets (DSORG=DA) include KEYLEN, LIMCT, and OPTCD. Chapter 14 discusses direct data sets.

PO Partitioned Organization. DSORG=PO identifies a partitioned data set or library. Throughout this book the abbreviation pds is used for partitioned data set. DSORG=PO is coded only for documentation. The third allocation amount sub-subparameter of the SPACE parameter specifies that a directory or table of contents is to be created for a pds. The directory must be constructed when a partitioned data set is created. In fact, it is meaningless to code DSORG=PO during data set creation without an accompanying request for directory space. It is rarely necessary to code DSORG=PO when retrieving an existing pds. Chapter 12 discusses partitioned data sets.

Example 15: Code the DCB values that describe a physical sequential card image data set whose records are blocked using a blocking factor of 10. Here the DSORG value is coded only for documentation.

```
DCB=(LRECL=80,BLKSIZE=800,RECFM=FB,DSORG=PS)
```

Example 16: Create a partitioned data set that will contain variable length logical records which may contain as many as 100 bytes of actual data. No block should exceed 500 bytes in length including all overhead. Additionally, five directory blocks should be created.

```
DCB=(LRECL=104,BLKSIZE=500,RECFM=VB,DSORG=PO),
SPACE=(CYL,(1,1,5))
```

Here the DSORG value is coded only for documentation. It is the presence of the sub-subparameter 5 in the SPACE parameter that makes the data set a pds. Note that with variable length records four bytes must be added to the maximum length of the data in a logical record.

Additional DCB Subparameters

The remaining DCB subparameters are used less frequently than the four already discussed. Ten additional subparameters are described here in alphabetical order. Most of the ten are discussed further later in the book. Some, such as BUFNO, BUFTEK, KEYLEN, OPTCD, and RKP may be supplied from non-JCL sources.

BUFNO This subparameter specifies the number of buffers to assign to the data set. Depending on the data set organization the default value ranges from two to five. BUFNO is especially important when processing a sequential data set or a member of a pds library. Buffering is discussed in Chapter 9.

BUFTEK This subparameter specifies the buffering technique to use. With each data set organization there are several to choose from. For example, with sequential data sets the choices include simple, exchange, and locate.

CYLOFL With an ISAM data set CYLOFL specifies the amount of disk space to use for the cylinder overflow area. OPTCD=Y must also be coded in the same DCB parameter. CYLOFL is discussed in Chapter 13.

DEN This subparameter specifies tape density. It identifies the amount of data which can be placed on a fixed amount of tape. DEN is discussed in detail in Chapter 16.

EROPT This subparameter specifies the type of processing to perform when an I/O error occurs while reading or writing a block of data. Three values may be coded:

`EROPT=ACC` - ACCept the bad block of data.
`EROPT=SKP` - SKiP the bad block of data.
`EROPT=ABE` - ABEnd the jobstep.

ABE is the default. SKP is sometimes coded when processing a very large data set with a few bad records where it is not necessary to process every record in the data set.

KEYLEN This subparameter gives the length in bytes of the key field associated with ISAM and some types of direct access data sets. KEYLEN should not be coded with the other data set organizations. In addition, it should not be specified with a COBOL Relative data set or a PL/I Regional I data set. With ISAM data sets the RKP subparameter is usually coded with KEYLEN. KEYLEN is discussed in Chapters 13 and 14.

LIMCT — This subparameter is used only with a direct access data set. It specifies that the extended search feature is to be used when adding new records and locating existing records. OPTCD=E must also be coded in the same DCB parameter. LIMCT is described in more detail in Chapter 14.

NTM — This subparameter is used only with an ISAM data set. It specifies that a high level index structure is to be created. OPTCD=M must also be coded in the same DCB parameter. NTM is discussed in Chapter 13.

OPTCD — This subparameter identifies one or more special processing options. Each option is represented by a letter of the alphabet. For example, with an ISAM data set OPTCD=ILMY may be coded. The letters I, L, M, and Y identify four special processing options. With OPTCD the letters can be permuted in any order without changing the meaning. It is unnecessary to enclose the string of letters in quotes. Although most of the values shown below do not illustrate this, the same letter can have a different meaning with two distinct data set organizations. The most commonly coded values used with each data set organization are listed here along with the chapter references in this book where more information on some of them can be found.

PS (Chapter 9) - B,Q,T,W
PO (Chapter 12) - B,Q,T,W
IS (Chapter 13) - I,L,M,R,U,W,Y
DA (Chapter 14) - A,R,E,W

RKP — This subparameter identifies the relative key position. This is the displacement from the beginning of the logical record to the first byte of the key field. Hence RKP=7 if a key field begins in byte 8. RKP should only be coded with ISAM data sets. Although some types of direct access data sets have keys, the keys do not have to be written on the disk within the logical record. Whenever RKP is coded KEYLEN should also be coded. RKP is discussed in Chapter 13.

Example 17: The records in a very large physical sequential data set are to be read. The logical records are 100 bytes in length and blocked using a blocking factor of 40. Five buffers should be allocated to the data set. If any bad blocks are encountered they should be ignored. The DCB parameter necessary for this is coded as follows:

```
DCB=(LRECL=100,BLKSIZE=4000,RECFM=FB,DSORG=PS,
     BUFNO=5,EROPT=SKP)
```

Example 18: Create an ISAM data set which contains 100 byte logical records. The first four bytes in each record are the key. A blocking factor of 5 is used. A cylinder overflow area and a high level index should be created for the data set. The DSN, DISP, and DCB parameters may be coded as follows:

```
//DD1    DD   DSN=ISAM.DATA.SET,DISP=(NEW,PASS),
//            DCB=(LRECL=100,RECFM=FB,BLKSIZE=500,DSORG=IS,
//            OPTCD=MY,CYLOFL=10,NTM=3,KEYLEN=4,RKP=0),...
```

Example 19: Create a COBOL Direct data set. This is called Regional III in PL/I. Use the same logical records described in the previous example. One additional byte is included at the beginning of each record. It is to be used as a delete byte. Here the records are to be unblocked. The extended search option should be used.

```
//DD1    DD   DSN=DIRECT.DATA.SET,DISP=(NEW,PASS),
//            DCB=(LRECL=101,RECFM=F,BLKSIZE=101,DSORG=DA,
//            OPTCD=E,KEYLEN=4,LIMCT=3),...
```

Special DCB Formats

When coding the DCB parameter two special formats are available. The first is the standard JCL referback. All of the three referback formats allowed with DSN and VOL are also valid with the DCB. The second format references the DCB values stored in the data set labels of an existing cataloged data set. Unlike the VOL parameter, passed data sets cannot be used with this format.

Example 20: The following segment of code illustrates the use of a standard referback to copy DCB values from one DD statement to another within the same job step:

```
//DD1    DD   DSN=X,DCB=(LRECL=80,BLKSIZE=4000,RECFM=FB),...
  ...
//DD2    DD   DSN=Y,DCB=*.DD1,...
```

Here the three DCB subparameter values from DD statement DD1 are also in effect with statement DD2. Since the DCB parameter frequently contains several subparameters, using a referback minimizes the amount of coding. As always, coding less JCL reduces the chance for syntax errors.

Often some of the subparameter values coded with the DCB parameter are desired on the referback but others should be modified. In this example suppose data set Y requires an LRECL value of 80 and a RECFM of FB, but the BLKSIZE value should be 6160. This can be accomplished by coding DD2 as:

```
//DD2   DD   DSN=Y,DCB=(*.DD1,BLKSIZE=6160),...
```

Here all of the DCB values are copied from DD1. However, the keyword subparameter values following *.DD1 override the corresponding values on the statement with DDname DD1. In this example only the BLKSIZE value is overridden. When overriding with a referback the parentheses are required. DCB is the only parameter which permits a referback to be both modified and extended. Continuing the example, it is possible to code:

```
//DD2   DD   DSN=Y,DCB=(*.DD1,BLKSIZE=6160,LRECL=,DSORG=IS),...
```

Here the three subparameters coded after the referback on DD2 respectively modify, nullify, and add to the values coded with DD1. Notice that this is a legitimate use of the syntax keyword-subparameter=. Whenever subparameters are coded the entire DCB value must be enclosed in parentheses.

Example 21: Suppose it is desired to code the same DCB values on a DD statement as those stored in the data set labels of an existing cataloged data set. For example, suppose SYS1.TEST is a cataloged data set. Then coding:

```
//DD3   DD   DSN=Y,DISP=(NEW,PASS),DCB=(SYS1.TEST),...
```

supplies the same DCB values as those found in the data set labels of SYS1.TEST. The parentheses are not required. No UNIT and VOLUME information is available to provide the system with the location of the data set supplying the values, so SYS1.TEST is referenced through its catalog entry. This DCB format supports the same type of modifications as the standard referback. Thus DD3 can be coded as:

```
//DD3   DD   DSN=Y,DCB=(SYS1.TEST,BLKSIZE=6160,LRECL=,DSORG=IS),...
```

When using the DCB=(dsname) syntax, the message

```
IEF212   DDname DATA SET NOT FOUND
```

can reference either the data set coded in the DCB parameter or the data set identified with DSN. Both possibilities must be considered. Note that DCB=(dsname) cannot be used to reference a data set from the pass table.

Infrequently Used DD Statement Keyword Parameters for Disk and Tape Data Sets

Ten additional keyword parameters are described below. Each parameter performs one specific function. These parameters are included in this chapter rather than the previous one because they are not used with either the SYSOUT parameter or in-stream data sets. Other limited function keyword parameters are coded with either SYSOUT or in-stream data sets, as described in the previous chapter. The CHKEOV parameter is discussed in Chapter 22. The AMP parameter is used only with VSAM data sets.

ACCODE

The ACCODE parameter is used to protect certain tape data sets. It can be coded only with ISO/ANSI/FIPS Version 3 tape data sets. ACCODE cannot be used with SL tape data sets. The ACCODE parameter is coded as follows:

```
ACCODE=Access-code value
```

The value used must be a letter of the alphabet. One to seven additional characters may optionally be coded. If the application program cannot supply the correct access-code value the data set cannot be used and the job abends. ACCODE is meant to be used in conjunction with RACF or a volume access code. If PASSWORD or NOPWREAD is coded on the LABEL parameter of the same DD statement then ACCODE is ignored.

Example 22: To process a data set with an access-code of X the following should be coded:

```
//ANSITAPE DD DSN=TAPEFILE,DISP=OLD,ACCODE=X,
//            UNIT=TAPE,VOL=SER=ABCDEF,LABEL=(,AL)
```

If LABEL=(,AL,NOPWREAD) is coded on the above statement the ACCODE value is ignored.

CNTL

The CNTL parameter is one of the newest JCL parameters. CNTL identifies a group of control statements which are contained within a CNTL/ENDCNTL group coded earlier in the job stream. This parameter uses a syntax almost identical to the three standard formats of a backward reference. The control statements are executed within the present step. The only difference in syntax between CNTL and a true referback is that a label rather than a DDname is coded with all three CNTL formats. Hence, the three ways to code CNTL are as follows:

```
//LABL  DD CNTL=*.LBL123              *LBL123 is a label
//STEP  DD CNTL=*.STEPA.LBL123        *STEPA is a stepname
//PROC  DD CNTL=*.STEPA.PROC1.LBL123*PROC1 is a procstepname
```

Example 23: Here the simplest form of the CNTL parameter is used with a 3800 printer subsystem:

```
//STEP1    EXEC  PGM=PRINT
//ALPHA    CNTL  *
//PRGCNTL  PRINTDEV BUFNO=10,PIMSG=YES,DATACK=BLOCK
//BETA     ENDCNTL
//PRINT1   DD   UNIT=3800-3,CNTL=*.ALPHA
```

The 3800-3 subsystem uses the BUFNO, PIMSG, and DATACK options of the PRINTDEV control statement to print the data set on a 3800 model 3 printer.

DDNAME

There are numerous places in JCL where various types of backward references may be coded. However, the DDNAME parameter is the only example of a forward reference in JCL. The DDNAME parameter postpones defining a data set until later in the job stream. It is coded almost exclusively within procedures. By using DDNAME the data set need not be defined until the procedure is invoked. Only the AMP parameter and the DCB subparameters BLKSIZE, BUFNO, and DIAGNS may be coded on the same statement as DDNAME. To illustrate the use of the DDNAME parameter, consider the following job step:

The Actual JCL Coded	*The JCL Interpretation*

`//A      EXEC PGM=ABC`
`//DD1     DD  DDNAME=DD3`
`//DD2     DD  an unrelated`
`              data set`
`//DD3     DD  DSN=X,DISP=SHR`
	`//A      EXEC PGM=ABC`
	`//DD1     DD  DSN=X,DISP=SHR`
	`//DD2     DD  an unrelated`
	`              data set`

Most commonly DDNAME is coded within a procedure to identify a statement where it would be convenient to code an in-stream data set. However, JCL syntax prohibits in-stream data sets within a procedure, so DDNAME is used. Several cataloged procedures which use the Linkage Editor employ DDNAME for this reason to reference control statements. This is illustrated in Chapter 18. If a DDNAME parameter is coded and no subsequent DD statement in the step contains a matching DDname, the informatory message

```
nnn IEF686   DDNAME REFERRED TO ON DDNAME KEYWORD
             IN PRIOR STEP WAS NOT RESOLVED
```

is printed. Here nnn is the number of the EXEC statement after the step which contained the DDNAME parameter. Hence an unresolved DDNAME value is equivalent to coding DUMMY on the DD statement. Additionally, the referenced DD statement must follow the statement containing the DDNAME parameter or the same message is printed. Note that DDNAME can only reference a data set in the same jobstep. A maximum of five DDNAMEs can be coded in the same step. Each must specify a different value.

Complications can occur when DDNAME is used in the same step with backward references. Recall that true backward references may be coded with the DSN, DCB, and VOL parameters. UNIT=AFF is also a type of backward reference. Each of these four parameters may be used to refer back to a DD statement where the DDNAME parameter is coded. Here the backward reference identifies the DDname on the statement, not the value coded with DDNAME. Additionally, the statement identified on the DDNAME parameter cannot contain a backward reference to any statement which follows the statement containing the DDNAME parameter, and any statement which contains UNIT=AFF=DDname-value must follow the statement whose DDname is value.

Example 24: The code shown here illustrates the points discussed in the previous paragraph. The referbacks coded on statements DD2 and DD3 are resolved using the values coded on the statement with DDname ALPHA. Notice that no backward references can be coded with statement ALPHA because DD1 is the first DD statement in the step. Finally, statement DD4 must follow ALPHA.

```
//A      EXEC PGM=ABC
//DD1     DD  DDNAME=ALPHA,DCB=(BLKSIZE=4000)
//DD2     DD  DSN=*.DD1,DISP=SHR,VOL=REF=*.DD1
//DD3     DD  DSN=BETA,DISP=OLD,DCB=(*.DD1,LRECL=40)
//ALPHA   DD  DSN=A.B.C,DISP=SHR,UNIT=3350,VOL=SER=DISK98,
//            DCB=(LRECL=80,RECFM=FB,BLKSIZE=6160)
//DD4     DD  DSN=&&TEMP,DISP=NEW,UNIT=AFF=DD1
```

DSID

The DSID parameter is used with the 3540 diskette unit to identify a specific diskette. The diskette identified may be used for an input or output operation. If a diskette data set is read for input either * or DATA must be coded along with DSID. For an output diskette data set both SYSOUT and DSID must be coded. For more information on using this parameter, see the manual *IBM 3540 Programmer's Reference*. The syntax for the DSID parameter is

```
DSID=Id        or
DSID=(Id,V)
```

Here the value coded for Id obeys exactly the same syntax rules as a JCL name field. V is used with SYSIN data sets that have been verified.

Example 25: To read from one diskette data set and write to another, the following may be coded:

```
//A      EXEC PGM=ABC
//DD1     DD  *,DSID=(ALPHA,V),VOL=SER=ABCDEF
//DD2     DD  SYSOUT=A,DSID=BETA
```

FREE

The FREE parameter is used to determine the length of time that the system resources identified on the DD statement are allocated to the jobstep. Its function is to allow more efficient utilization of system resources among the jobs currently executing in the system. More precisely, FREE controls dynamic deallocation. Two values may be coded with FREE: FREE=END deallocates the data set at the end of the jobstep; FREE=CLOSE deallocates the data set when the application program closes it. By using FREE=CLOSE to release the data set when it is no longer needed several types of system resources are better utilized. FREE=END is the default value.

There are several situations where the FREE parameter has no effect. If the same DD statement contains DISP=(. . .,PASS) and FREE=END the data set remains allocated until it is processed in a following jobstep or the job ends. The same result occurs when FREE=CLOSE is coded with a passed data set. In some programming applications a data set must be repeatedly opened and closed. In this situation the program can override FREE=CLOSE and cause it to be ignored. Most commonly this approach is used in an assembler language program. FREE=CLOSE does not deallocate the data set if an abend occurs or the data set is contained within a concatenation. Likewise, FREE=CLOSE should not be coded on a DD statement which is identified on a referback.

There are several types of resources that can be released by the FREE parameter. If DISP=OLD had been coded on the same DD statement the exclusive control of the data set is ended. When FREE=CLOSE is coded with a tape data set the tape volume becomes available to other jobs. With FREE=CLOSE the UNIT device also becomes available to other jobs.

Example 26: A multi-step job processes three data sets. During the first step records in a heavily used system library are modified, a tape volume that other jobs may also require is read, and a temporary disk data set is created and passed to a subsequent step. Coding FREE=CLOSE probably serves a worthwhile function with the first two DD statements. The FREE parameter on the final DD statement in step A is ignored. In step B the SYSOUT data set is scheduled for printing as soon as it is closed. The temporary data set &&X is deallocated after the step ends.

```
//A    EXEC PGM=CHANGLIB
//DD1  DD   DSN=PDSLIB,DISP=OLD,FREE=CLOSE
//DD2  DD   DSN=TAPEXY,DISP=OLD,UNIT=TAPE,VOL=SER=TAPE02,
//          LABEL=(2,SL),FREE=CLOSE
//DD3  DD   DSN=&&X,DISP=(NEW,PASS),UNIT=SYSDA,FREE=END
//B    EXEC PGM=REPORT
//DD1  DD   SYSOUT=A,FREE=CLOSE
//DD2  DD   DSN=&&X,DISP=(OLD,DELETE)
```

MSVGP

The MSVGP parameter is used only with Mass Storage Systems (MSS). When a non-specific volume request is made it creates a data set on one of a group of mass storage volumes. There are three possible values that may be coded with MSVGP:

```
MSVGP=Id                or
MSVGP=(Id,DDname)       or
MSVGP=SYSGROUP
```

Id identifies the group of mass storage volumes. The syntax rules for Id names are the same as those for a JCL name field. When DDname is used it identifies a DD statement coded earlier in the same jobstep. With this syntax the present volumes selected must be different from the volumes that hold the earlier data set. SYSGROUP allocates a default group of mass storage volumes.

Example 27: Three data sets are created on MSS. It is assumed that a default SPACE allocation is made for each data set. Additionally, specific volumes should not be requested on the same statement with MSVGP.

```
//DD1   DD   DSN=X,DISP=(NEW,CATLG),VOL=(,,,2),MSVGP=ABC
//DD2   DD   DSN=Y,DISP=(NEW,CATLG),MSVGP=(ABC,DD1)
//DD3   DD   DSN=Z,DISP=(NEW,CATLG),MSVGP=SYSGROUP
```

PROTECT

The PROTECT parameter can be used only when the system is protected by RACF. Code PROTECT=YES when creating a non-temporary disk data set that will exist after the present step. Likewise, PROTECT=YES may be coded to afford RACF protection to an existing tape data set. A tape data set must be the first on a labeled volume and the data set must be opened for an output operation. The RACF protection then applies to the entire tape volume. PROTECT=Y may also be coded. With an existing tape data set where PROTECT is coded standard labels and DISP=OLD must be specified.

QNAME

The QNAME parameter is coded only with jobs which use TCAM (Tele-Communications Access Method) for data communications. It is questionable how much longer IBM will continue to support TCAM. For the most part it is being phased out and replaced by VTAM (Virtual Telecommunications Access Method). The value coded with QNAME references a specific TCAM macro instruction in the program. The macro in turn identifies a message queue. The message queue may be created or an existing queue can be accessed. There are two formats for the TCAM parameter:

```
QNAME=macro name                  or
QNAME=macro name.TCAM jobname
```

In both cases macro name must match the name field in the TPROCESS macro command. TCAM jobname is the actual name of a job that may process the messages in the queue. The five DCB subparameters LRECL, BLKSIZE, RECFM, OPTCD, and BUFL are the only other values which may be coded on the same DD statement.

Example 28: The following jobstep illustrates the two formats of the QNAME parameter:

```
//A      EXEC   TCAMPGM
//DD1    DD     QNAME=ALPHA
//DD2    DD     QNAME=BETA.PROG1
```

Here ALPHA identifies a TCAM queue to which messages are routed. The messages routed to the BETA queue will be processed by program PROG1.

SUBSYS

The SUBSYS parameter is coded whenever a data set is to be processed by a subsystem. Additionally, one or more parameter values may also be passed to the subsystem. The syntax of the SUBSYS parameter is as follows:

```
SUBSYS=(subsystem,parmvalue1,parmvalue2,...,parmvaluen)
```

Subsystem names must be composed of from one to four alphabetic, numeric, or national characters. Any characters may be coded as parm values. However, if special characters are coded the entire parm value must be enclosed in apostrophes. Up to 254 parm values may be passed. Many common JCL parameters either cannot be coded with SUBSYS or are ignored if they are coded.

Example 29: Three examples of the SUBSYS parameter are shown. The last two illustrate passing parm values to a subsystem. The third DD statement illustrates that the first positional parm value is not present:

```
//A      EXEC   PGM=SUBSYSTM
//DD1    DD     DSN=ALPHA,DISP=OLD,SUBSYS=PRNT
//DD2    DD     DSN=BETA,DISP=OLD,SUBSYS=(X1,A,'TEST=X1')
//DD3    DD     DSN=GAMMA,DISP=OLD,SUBSYS=(LAST,,
//              '01/01/87',LAST,'X=Y*Z')
```

TERM

The TERM parameter is coded only by a TSO user. TERM specifies that the data set is either input or output to the TSO user's terminal. Only the SYSOUT and DCB parameters may be meaningfully coded with TERM. All other parameters are either invalid, ignored, or cause the TERM parameter itself to be ignored.

TERM may be interpreted in two ways, depending on whether it is part of a foreground or background job. With a foreground job TERM=TS identifies a data set going to or from the TSO user's terminal. If a SYSOUT parameter is also coded it denotes an input data set. With a background (batch job) the TERM=TS parameter is treated the same as if SYSOUT=* were coded provided no other parameters are coded on the DD statement. If other parameters are coded on the DD statement then TERM=TS is ignored.

Example 30: Two basic situations exist when coding TERM=TS: either it is the only parameter coded or other parameters are coded on the same statement. For each case a different result occurs depending on whether a foreground or background job is executing.

```
//DD1   TERM=TS
//DD2   TERM=TS,SYSOUT=A
//DD3   TERM=TS,DSN=X,DISP=OLD,...
```

With a foreground job these are interpreted as an input data set, an output data set, and an ignored line.

Complete JCL Job Listing: Example 1 A four-step job is used to illustrate some of the basic JCL syntax discussed in Chapters 3 through 7. The job stream also illustrates the appearance of output produced by JES2. The first step sequentially updates a master file using an in-stream transaction file or data set. In addition, an exception report and a log of all records processed are printed. The five data sets are easily identified by their accompanying DDnames. The second step uses a utility program to create a back-up copy of the new master file created in the previous step. In the third step the original master file is deleted, and the new disk master file is cataloged. In the last step the trailer labels for the tape data set are printed to determine the number of records in the data set. The actual JCL is shown first. This is followed in Figure 7–2 by the three parts of the printed job listing produced when the job is executed. In order, these are the JES2 log, the JCL listing, and the allocation messages.

```
//LARRY JOB (1125,515,YRRAL),LARRY,PRTY=8,CLASS=A
/*ROUTE PRINT TERM
//A         EXEC  PGM=UPDATE
//*************************************************************
//* THE IN-STREAM DATA SET CONTAINS TRANSACTION RECORDS
//* WHICH ARE USED TO UPDATE AN EXISTING MASTER FILE.  A
//* NEW MASTER FILE IS CREATED.  TWO PRINTED REPORTS ARE
//* ALSO PRODUCED.
//*************************************************************
//STEPLIB    DD DSN=ACSSTU.MYLIB,DISP=SHR
//SYSPRINT   DD SYSOUT=*
//EXCPTINS   DD SYSOUT=A
//OLDMASTR   DD DSN=ACSSTU.MASTER,DISP=SHR
//NEWMASTR   DD DSN=ACSSTU.MASTER,DISP=(NEW,PASS),UNIT=3380,
//              SPACE=(CYL,(10,2)),
//              DCB=(BLKSIZE=1000)
//TRANS      DD *
   ... in-stream data set
/*
```

```
//B         EXEC  PGM=IEBGENER,COND=(4,LT,A)
//*********************************************************
//* A BACKUP OF THE NEW MASTER FILE IDENTIFIED ON THE
//* SYSUT1 DD STATEMENT IS MADE.  THE BACKUP IS THE DATA
//* SET WITH DDNAME SYSUT2.  SYSPRINT IDENTIFIES THE
//* MESSAGE DATA SET AND THE SYSIN DATA SET IS DUMMIED
//* OUT SINCE IT IS NOT NEEDED.  STEP B IS NOT RUN
//* UNLESS STEP A EXECUTED 'SUCCESSFULLY'.
//*********************************************************
//SYSPRINT  DD SYSOUT=$
//SYSUT1    DD DSN=*.A.OLDMASTR,DISP=(OLD,PASS)
//SYSUT2    DD DSN=TAPE.BACKUP.NEW.MASTER,DISP=(NEW,KEEP),
//             UNIT=TAPE,VOL=(,RETAIN,SER=LJB500),LABEL=(1,SL),
//             DCB=(ACSSTU.MASTER)
//SYSIN     DD DUMMY,DSN=ACSSTU.CONTROLS,DISP=SHR
//C        EXEC PGM=IEFBR14,COND=(0,NE)
//*********************************************************
//* IF THE NEW MASTER FILE IN STEP A AND THE BACKUP IN
//* STEP B WERE BOTH CREATED SUCCESSFULLY, THE ORIGINAL
//* OLD MASTER IS DELETED, AND THE DISK VERSION OF THE
//* NEW MASTER IS CATALOGED.
//*********************************************************
//DD1       DD DSN=*.A.OLDMASTR,DISP=(OLD,DELETE)
//DD2       DD DSN=ACSSTU.MASTER,DISP=(OLD,CATLG),
//             VOL=REF=*.A.NEWMASTR
/*
//D         EXEC PGM=IDCAMS,REGION=500K
//*********************************************************
//* THE RECORDS IN THE TAPE DATA SET ARE PRINTED.
//*********************************************************
//SYSPRINT  DD SYSOUT=A
//DD1       DD DISP=OLD,UNIT=TAPE,LABEL=(3,BLP),VOL=SER=LJB500,
//             DCB=(LRECL=80,RECFM=F,BLKSIZE=80)
//SYSIN     DD *
    PRINT   INFILE(DD1)
/*
//
```

When this job is submitted the output shown in Figure 7–2 is produced by MVS.

The following comments describe the statements that appear in Figure 7–2. Each comment is prefaced by the statement number to which it applies.

1 Accounting information is installation dependent. For security reasons, the actual values do not print in the JCL listing. The JES2 ROUTE statement is not numbered. In addition, /*ROUTE appears in the printed listing as ***ROUTE. Here, the job output is routed to an IBM 6670 laser printer.

2 In step A, program UPDATE is executed. Comment statements are not numbered in the JCL listing. In addition, //* appears in the printed listing as ***.

3 The UPDATE program is not in the system program library (SYS1.LINKLIB). Hence, a STEPLIB (here) or JOBLIB DD statement is coded to identify the library that holds UPDATE. The three remaining programs in the job are all in SYS1.LINKLIB, so no other STEPLIB statements are coded.

4 The SYSPRINT output is sent to message class A since it is the default MSGCLASS value.

5 The EXCPTINS output is also sent to message class A. The SYSPRINT output prints before the EXCPTINS output since it is coded first in the jobstep, and both are message class A.

6 OLDMASTR identifies the data set ACSSTU.MASTER which is located through its catalog entry. This occurs since this is the first step in the job and it cannot be retrieved from the pass mechanism and UNIT and VOL are not coded. At the end of this step, the data set is kept. Hence, it cannot be retrieved as a passed data set in subsequent steps. Note that this data set is on volume WORK02 (IEF237 message on p. 143).

7 A new data set also called ACSSTU.MASTER is created on a different volume (WORK01) than the data set in the previous statement. ACSSTU is a first level qualifier that selects a specific catalog SYS1.ACSCTLG1. Only one entry for ACCSTU.MASTER can appear in this catalog. Hence, this data set cannot be cataloged. At the end of the step, ACSSTU.MASTER is passed. A non-specific volume request was made and the SRM selected a SYSDA volume with sufficient space.

8 In-stream records do not appear in the printed JCL listing. These transaction records are initially written to a spool volume. DATA could also be used in place of * if transaction records required it. Notice that the /* statement does not appear in the JCL listing.

9 In step B, the IBM utility IEBGENER is executed. IEBGENER is described in Chapter 25. It is contained in the SYS1.LINKLIB program library. IEBGENER can be used to create a back-up copy of an existing sequential data set. The COND parameter is coded on the EXEC statement. It is used to skip step B if the new master file was not successfully created in the first step. The COND parameter is dicussed in Chapter 20. The Complete JCL Job Listing: Example 2 in Chapter 8 contains an allocation message which results when a step is skipped because of the COND parameter. For the remainder of this job listing, the role of the COND parameter can be ignored since every step ran successfully.

10 Messages generated by IEBGENER are sent to message class A ($=*=A).

11 The ACSSTU.MASTER data set is identified via the DSN referback. Since UNIT and VOL are not coded, the pass mechanism successfully located the data

FIGURE 7–2

JCL Job Output, Example 1

```
                     J E S 2   J O B   L O G

-------- JOB  512  IEF097I LARRY    - USER ACS1125  ASSIGNED
15.57.32 JOB  512  $HASP373 LARRY    STARTED - INIT  2 - CLASS A - SYS 8000
15.57.32 JOB  512  IEF403I LARRY - STARTED - TIME=15.57.32
15.57.36 JOB  512 *IEF233A M 842,LJB500,,LARRY,B,TAPE.BACKUP.NEW.MASTER
15.58.19 JOB  512  IEC705I TAPE ON 842,LJB500,SL,6250 BPI,LARRY,B,TAPE.BACKUP.NEW.MASTER
15.58.22 JOB  512  IEC502E K 842,LJB500,NL,LARRY,D,SYS86327.T155732.RA000.LARRY.R0000001
15.58.22 JOB  512  IEF471E FOLLOWING VOLUMES NO LONGER NEEDED BY LARRY
                           LJB500.
15.58.22 JOB  512  IEF404I LARRY - ENDED - TIME=15.58.22
15.58.22 JOB  512  $HASP395 LARRY    ENDED
```

```
 1      //LARRY JOB (XXXXXXXXXXXXXX),LARRY,PRTY=8,CLASS=A                          JOB  512
        ***ROUTE PRINT 16670                                                              002
 2      //A         EXEC  PGM=UPDATE                                                     0030
        *****************************************************************                0040
        *** THE IN-STREAM DATA SET CONTAINS TRANSACTION RECORDS                          0050
        *** WHICH ARE USED TO UPDATE AN EXISTING MASTER FILE.  A                         0060
        *** NEW MASTER FILE IS CREATED.  TWO PRINTED REPORTS ARE                         0070
        *** ALSO PRODUCED.                                                               0070
        *****************************************************************                0080
 3      //STEPLIB    DD DSN=ACSSTU.MYLIB,DISP=SHR                                         0090
 4      //SYSPRINT   DD SYSOUT=*                                                          0100
 5      //EXCPTINS   DD SYSOUT=A                                                          0110
 6      //OLDMASTR   DD DSN=ACSSTU.MASTER,DISP=SHR                                        0150
 7      //NEWMASTR   DD DSN=ACSSTU.MASTER,DISP=(NEW,PASS),UNIT=3380,                      0120
        //              SPACE=(CYL,(10,2)),                                              0130
        //              DCB=(BLKSIZE=1000)                                               0140
 8      //TRANS      DD *                                                                 0160
 9      //B         EXEC PGM=IEBGENER,COND=(4,LT,A)                                      0200
        ***************************************************************                  0210
        *** A BACKUP OF THE NEW MASTER FILE IDENTIFIED ON THE                            0220
        *** SYSUT1 DD STATEMENT IS MADE.  THE BACKUP IS THE DATA                         0230
        *** SET WITH DDNAME SYSUT2.  SYSPRINT IDENTIFIES THE                             0240
        *** MESSAGE DATA SET AND THE SYSIN DATA SET IS DUMMIED                           0250
        *** OUT SINCE IT IS NOT NEEDED.  STEP B IS NOT RUN                               0260
        *** UNLESS STEP A EXECUTED 'SUCCESSFULLY'.                                       0260
        ***************************************************************                  0270
10      //SYSPRINT   DD SYSOUT=$                                                          0280
11      //SYSUT1     DD DSN=*.A.OLDMASTR,DISP=(OLD,KEEP)                                  0290
12      //SYSUT2     DD DSN=TAPE.BACKUP.NEW.MASTER,DISP=(NEW,KEEP),                       0310
        //              UNIT=TAPE,VOL=(,RETAIN,SER=LJB500),LABEL=(1,SL),                 0320
        //              DCB=(ACSSTU.MASTER)                                              0330
13      //SYSIN      DD DUMMY,DSN=ACSSTU.CONTROLS,DISP=SHR                                0340
14      //C        EXEC PGM=IEFBR14,COND=(0,NE)                                          0360
        ***************************************************************                  0370
        *** IF THE NEW MASTER FILE IN STEP A AND THE BACKUP IN                           0380
        *** STEP B WERE BOTH CREATED SUCCESSFULLY, THE ORIGINAL                          0390
        *** OLD MASTER IS DELETED, AND THE DISK VERSION OF THE                           0400
        *** NEW MASTER IS CATALOGED.                                                     0400
        ***************************************************************                  0430
15      //DD1        DD DSN=*.A.OLDMASTR,DISP=(OLD,DELETE)                                0440
16      //DD2        DD DSN=ACSSTU.MASTER,DISP=(OLD,CATLG),                               0450
        //              VOL=REF=*.A.NEWMASTR                                             0460
17      //D         EXEC PGM=IDCAMS,REGION=500K                                          0480
        ***************************************************************                  0490
        ***                                                                              0500
        ***************************************************************                  0510
18      //SYSPRINT   DD SYSOUT=A                                                          0520
19      //DD1        DD DISP=OLD,UNIT=TAPE,LABEL=(3,BLP),VOL=SER=LJB500,                  0530
        //              DCB=(LRECL=80,RECFM=F,BLKSIZE=80)                                0540
20      //SYSIN      DD *                                                                 0550
        //                                                                               0580
```

```
IEF236I ALLOC. FOR LARRY A
IEF237I 26C  ALLOCATED TO STEPLIB
IEF237I 265  ALLOCATED TO SYS00185
IEF237I JES2 ALLOCATED TO SYSPRINT
IEF237I JES2 ALLOCATED TO EXCPTINS
IEF237I 14D  ALLOCATED TO OLDMASTR
IEF237I 14C  ALLOCATED TO NEWMASTR
IEF237I JES2 ALLOCATED TO TRANS
IEF142I LARRY A - STEP WAS EXECUTED - COND CODE 0000
IEF285I   ACSSTU.MYLIB                                   KEPT
IEF285I   VOL SER NOS= WORK03.
IEF285I   SYS1.ACSCTLG1                                  KEPT
IEF285I   VOL SER NOS= ISU013.
IEF285I   JES2.JOB00512.S0000103                         SYSOUT
IEF285I   JES2.JOB00512.S0000104                         SYSOUT
IEF285I   ACSSTU.MASTER                                  KEPT
IEF285I   VOL SER NOS= WORK02.
IEF285I   ACSSTU.MASTER                                  PASSED
IEF285I   VOL SER NOS= WORK01.
IEF285I   JES2.JOB00512.SI000101                         SYSIN
IEF373I STEP /A       / START 86327.1557
IEF374I STEP /A       / STOP  86327.1557 CPU    0MIN 00.07SEC SRB    0MIN 00.00SEC VIRT    32K SYS   252K
IEF236I ALLOC. FOR LARRY B
IEF237I JES2 ALLOCATED TO SYSPRINT
IEF237I 14C  ALLOCATED TO SYSUT1
IEF237I 842  ALLOCATED TO SYSUT2
IEF237I 265  ALLOCATED TO SYS00187
IEF237I DMY  ALLOCATED TO SYSIN
IEF142I LARRY B - STEP WAS EXECUTED - COND CODE 0000
IEF285I   JES2.JOB00512.S0000105                         SYSOUT
IEF285I   ACSSTU.MASTER                                  KEPT
IEF285I   VOL SER NOS= WORK01.
IEF285I   TAPE.BACKUP.NEW.MASTER                         KEPT
IEF285I   VOL SER NOS= LJB500.
IEF285I   SYS1.ACSCTLG1                                  KEPT
IEF285I   VOL SER NOS= ISU013.
IEF373I STEP /B       / START 86327.1557
IEF374I STEP /B       / STOP  86327.1558 CPU    0MIN 00.08SEC SRB    0MIN 00.01SEC VIRT    40K SYS   268K
IEF236I ALLOC. FOR LARRY C
IEF237I 14D  ALLOCATED TO DD1
IEF237I 265  ALLOCATED TO SYS00189
IEF237I 14C  ALLOCATED TO DD2
IEF142I LARRY C - STEP WAS EXECUTED - COND CODE 0000
IEF285I   ACSSTU.MASTER                                  UNCATALOGED
IEF285I   VOL SER NOS= WORK02.
IEF285I   ACSSTU.MASTER                                  DELETED
IEF285I   VOL SER NOS= WORK02.
IEF285I   SYS1.ACSCTLG1                                  KEPT
IEF285I   VOL SER NOS= ISU013.
IEF285I   ACSSTU.MASTER                                  CATALOGED
IEF285I   VOL SER NOS= WORK01.
IEF373I STEP /C       / START 86327.1558
IEF374I STEP /C       / STOP  86327.1558 CPU    0MIN 00.01SEC SRB    0MIN 00.00SEC VIRT     4K SYS   228K
IEF236I ALLOC. FOR LARRY D
IEF237I JES2 ALLOCATED TO SYSPRINT
IEF237I 842  ALLOCATED TO DD1
IEF237I JES2 ALLOCATED TO SYSIN
IEF142I LARRY D - STEP WAS EXECUTED - COND CODE 0000
IEF285I   JES2.JOB00512.S0000106                         SYSOUT
IEF285I   SYS86327.T155732.RA000.LARRY.R0000001          KEPT
IEF285I   VOL SER NOS= LJB500.
IEF285I   JES2.JOB00512.SI000102                         SYSIN
IEF373I STEP /D       / START 86327.1558
IEF374I STEP /D       / STOP  86327.1558 CPU    0MIN 00.10SEC SRB    0MIN 00.01SEC VIRT   196K SYS   252K
IEF375I  JOB /LARRY   / START 86327.1557
IEF376I  JOB /LARRY   / STOP  86327.1558 CPU    0MIN 00.26SEC SRB    0MIN 00.02SEC
RCS176I  1125 015150000


IDCAMS  SYSTEM SERVICES


LISTING OF DATA SET -SYS86327.T155732.RA000.LARRY.R0000001

RECORD SEQUENCE NUMBER - 1
000000  C5D6C6F1 C2C1C3D2 E4D74BD5 C5E64BD4   C1E2E3C5 D9D3D1C2 F5F0F0F0 F0F0F1F0   *EOF1BACKUP.NEW.MASTERLJB50000010*
000020  F0F0F140 40404040 4040F8F6 F3F2F740   F0F0F0F0 F0F0F0F0 F0F0F0F1 C9C2D440   *001        86327 000000000001IBM *
000040  D6E261E5 E240F3F7 F0404040 40404040                                         *OS/VS 370                        *


RECORD SEQUENCE NUMBER - 2
000000  C5D6C6F2 C6F0F1F0 F0F0F0F0 F1F0F0F4   F0D3C1D9 D9E84040 4061C240 40404040   *EOF2F010000010040LARRY    /B      *
000020  40404040 4040C240 4040F6F0 F0F0F040   40404040 40404040 40404040 40404040   *      B    60000                  *
000040  40404040 40404040 40404040 40404040                                         *                                  *

IDC0005I NUMBER OF RECORDS PROCESSED WAS 2

IDC0001I FUNCTION COMPLETED, HIGHEST CONDITION CODE WAS 0
```

set. It is unnecessary to use a catalog. The entry in the pass mechanism is then removed. Note that the NEWMASTR data set is processed even though DSN references the OLDMASTR data set. If the OLDMASTR data set is passed, the results will be different. If, however, in addition, the order of the OLDMASTR and NEWMASTR DD statements are switched, the NEWMASTR data set will be referenced on this statement even if both are passed.

12 The backup copy of the new master file is created as the first data set on a Standard Label tape. The DCB values for the new data set are taken from the labels of the cataloged data set ACSSTU.MASTER on volume WORK02.

13 Since DUMMY is coded, the other two parameters are ignored. There need not be an ACSSTU.CONTROLS data set anywhere in the system. This programming situation can be better handled using symbolic parameters as described in the Chapter 8.

14 In step C, program IEFBR14 is executed. IEFBR14 is described in Chapter 21. The dispositions of two copies of the master file are changed. No logical records are processed during this step. Rather, the status of the data sets themselves are changed. The COND parameter will cause this step to be skipped unless the first two steps executed successfully.

15 The referback identifies ACSSTU.MASTER. The appropriate version of the data set is located through its catalog entry. The allocation messages show that the data set is first uncataloged and then deleted from volume WORK02.

16 The new version of the master file created in the first step is now cataloged. It could not be cataloged in the user catalog associated with the first level qualifier ACSSTU until the existing data set name with the same entry was removed or deleted. UNIT and VOL must be coded to locate the data set. This would have been unnecessary if the data set had been passed in an earlier step.

17 In step D, the IBM utility IDCAMS is executed. This step is always executed unless a previous step abended. If the tape data set was not created, the job abends. IDCAMS requires a substantial amount of memory.

18 Both messages generated by the IDCAMS program and the printed copy of each output record are written to messages class A.

19 The (trailer) labels for the backup copy of the master file on tape value LJB500 are printed. Here, just a portion of the tape data set is referenced. The trailer labels contain the number of records in the data set. Both trailer labels are further described in Chapter 16 and are pictured on p. 143.

20 SYSIN identifies one or more control statements. Here, the PRINT statement requests a listing of the INFILE DD1 data set. Note the JES messages.

Exercises

1. Which of the following DSN parameters are invalid? For each invalid parameter, explain why it is invalid.

```
DSN=&#$
DSN=$&-1
DSN=$&.1
DSN=A-----B.--C
DSN=*.A.STEP1.A.B
DSN=(ALPHA.BETA)
DSN=*.ABC
DSN=A.B..C.D
DSN='A+B*C'
DSN=&
DSN=DSN
DSN=A-.B-
DSN=A(X,Y)
DSN=ISAM(DATA)
(DSN=ABC.DE)
DSN=A.BC.DEF.GHIJ.KLMNO.PQRSTU.VWXYZ1
```

2. List several specific conditions for which a DSN parameter need not be coded on a DD statement which identifies a disk or tape data set. Consider data sets which are used in just one step and data sets used in multiple steps. Further classify the data sets as either new or existing. An additional situation with tape data sets related to this exercise is described in Chapter 16.

3. The computer system described here is referenced in several of the following questions. The system contains twelve 3350 disk volumes, and six 3420 tape drives. There are three system catalogs. The disk volumes have names of the form DISKxx, where xx ranges from 01 to 12.

How many data sets named ALPHA can exist in the system at a given time? At a specific time how many of these are disk data sets, tape data sets, cataloged data sets, or passed data sets?

4. The six tape drives can be referenced in a variety of ways with the UNIT parameter:

`UNIT=SYSSQ`	all tape and disk drives
`UNIT=TAPE`	all six tape drives
`UNIT=3420`	two of the six tape drives-581 and 582
`UNIT=581,582,..., and 586`	the tape drive unit addresses

Code the appropriate UNIT and VOL parameters to correctly and efficiently perform the following types of processing. For the first five questions, assume the tape volumes have serial values of TAPE01, TAPE02, and TAPE03.

a) A three way tape merge is to be performed. This begins by using the three tape volumes as input and a fourth volume for output. Then the single volume is used for input and the three original tape volumes for output. This process is repeated until all of the records are sorted.

b) A report is to be produced which sequentially lists the records in the data set on the three tape volumes TAPE01, TAPE02, and TAPE03 in that order.

c) The same report as in the previous step is to be produced. However, now the records are to be listed in the reverse order. Assume the application program can specify reading the tapes backwards. Should the JCL be changed to reverse the order in which the volumes are processed.

d) Some additional records are to be added to the end of the third volume of the data set, which is the last volume. The first two volumes remain unchanged.

e) On some occasions the report described in step b is not to be produced. Program logic will dictate when this is the case. The tape drives should not be tied up under these conditions.

f) For each of the five processes described above, two work data sets must be available for the duration of the steps. How should the DD statements for these two data sets be coded?

g) Suppose the same data set used in the above steps occupies ten tape volumes rather than three. Which of the steps a through e can still be performed? In each case show the necessary UNIT and VOL parameters.

h) What is the maximum number of tape volumes that can be processed during a single jobstep? What is the maximum number of tape volumes that can be processed simultaneously on this system? Specifically, what do the digits in UNIT=581 represent?

5. Suppose UNIT=688 is a 3350 disk drive. What happens if //A DD UNIT=688,VOL=SER=TAPE01,. . . is coded? Note that there are several problems here. Suppose UNIT=188 is coded for a 3350 disk along with VOL=SER=DISK99, whose unit address is actually 161. What happens? Suppose UNIT=581 is coded on a DD statement along with VOL=SER=TAPE03, which is presently on UNIT=583. What happens?

6. A data set named A.B.C has been created. Parts of it reside on three 3350 disk volumes, DISK01, DISK02, and DISK03. Except when otherwise noted (f and g), assume that the records in the data set are to be read only. Code all necessary parameters to reference the data set in each case described below. Do not code unnecessary DD parameters. Consider the following seven situations:

a) The data set is cataloged.

b) The data set has been passed in an earlier step.

c) The data set is cataloged and also has been passed.

d) A.B.C is a kept data set.

e) A.B.C is a kept data set but the cataloged data set A.B.C resides on the same three disk volumes.

f) The data set is cataloged and is to be extended by adding records to the end of the data set on volume DISK03.

g) The data set is cataloged and is to be extended by adding records to volume DISK04.

7. For each of the following SPACE parameters determine the largest amount of space which can be allocated on a single 3350 disk volume. Assume a maximum number of secondary allocations. Give all answers in tracks. For a 3380 disk volume compute the largest amount of space for those values which change. Note that several of the SPACE parameters are invalid.

```
SPACE=(TRK,(5,2))
SPACE=(CYL,(1,1))
SPACE=(TRK,(,2))
SPACE=(TRK,50)
SPACE=(1,(1,1))
SPACE=(1,1,1)
SPACE=(20000,(2,1))
SPACE=(TRK,0)
SPACE=(TRK,(0,1))
SPACE=(TRK,(1,1),RLSE)
SPACE=(CYL,200,,ALX)
SPACE=(CYL,(100,50),RLSE,CONTIG,ROUND)
```

8. Suppose a disk data set is contained entirely on one volume. What is the maximum number of extents that the data set may have? What is the maximum number of space allocations that will exhaust all of the secondary allocations even if unused space remains on the volume? Illustrate both answers with SPACE=(TRK,(10,5)). Does either answer change if SPACE=(TRK,(3,2)) is coded? What do the two answers become if the data set is allowed to occupy five disk volumes rather than just one?

9. When processing tape data sets what JCL features are available to keep a volume mounted on the tape drive between steps? What additional features are available to minimize operator intervention when processing a multi-volume tape data set?

10. Suppose that a 3350 disk volume contains seven unused extents. The actual values are shown below. For simplicity all values are given in cylinders. Assume space is always allocated from lowest to highest cylinder address.

Extent	*Cylinders*
1	1-3
2	5-7
3	10-50
4	60-90
5	92-92
6	100-100
7	150-170

For each SPACE parameter coded below determine which of the above cylinders are allocated to the data set. Assume all of the seven extents are available when processing each parameter.

```
SPACE=(CYL,4)
SPACE=(CYL,(20),,CONTIG)
SPACE=(CYL,(10),,ALX)
SPACE=(CYL,(10),,MXIG)
SPACE=(TRK,100)
SPACE=(CYL,4,RLSE,CONTIG) and two tracks are used
SPACE=(ABSTR,0120,60)
SPACE=(CYL,75)
```

11. Can part of a data set be stored on disk and the rest stored on tape? Justify your answer.

12. Three collections of records are to be processed. Their significant properties are shown below:

Record Group	*Logical Record Length in Bytes*	*Record Format*
(1)	80	Fixed
(2)	100 (including 4 bytes of overhead)	Variable
(3)	2000 (no overhead)	Undefined

Code the appropriate DCB parameter values to describe a data set with the following properties:

a) Using group (1), a physical sequential data set, triple buffering, and a blocking factor of 10.
b) Using group (2), an unblocked physical sequential data set, one buffer, and spanned records.
c) Using group (3), an unblocked direct data set, single buffering, and a nine byte key field.
d) Using group (1), an ISAM data set, single buffering, and a blocking factor of 3. There is a 12 byte key field in bytes 60 through 71.
e) Using group (2), a member of a pds, variable blocked records with a maximum block-size of 500, and five buffers.
f) Using group (1), an ISAM data set, unblocked records, an additional delete byte preceding the data, a cylinder overflow area, a master index, reorganization statistics, and the same 12 byte key as in d) above.

13. Which DCB subparameters are stored in each of the following locations?

a) Pass Table
b) System Catalogs
c) Data Set Labels (See Chapters 15 and 16)

What UNIT, VOL, and LABEL information is stored in each of the above locations? Determine why VOL=REF=dsname allows dsname to be either a cataloged or passed data set while DCB=dsname allows only cataloged data sets. Why is DCB=(dsname, additional values) permitted, while VOL=REF=(dsname, additional values) is not allowed?

14. Find the JCL syntax and logic errors in each of the following DCB parameters:

```
DCB=(LRECL=1000,RECFM=FB,BLKSIZE=2500)
DCB=(BLKSIZE=,BUFNO=0,RECFM=U,OPTCD=PQRS)
DCB=(DSORG=DA,RECFM=F,KEYLEN=12,RKP=5,RECFM=F,LRECL=80)
DCB=(DSORG=IS,OPTCD='ILYRWM',RECFM=VB,LRECL=100,
     KEYLEN=12,RKP=90,BLKSIZE=500)
DCB=(DSORG=PO,RECFM=U,BLKSIZE=100,BUFNO=3,LRECL=96)
```

15. Describe specific situations where the SPACE parameter should be coded with existing data sets.

16. Can the unit coded on the primary SPACE request (CYL, TRK, or blocksize) be changed for the secondary? Can the secondary value be changed?

17. Can different UNITs (i.e., 3350,3380, etc.) be mixed on the same DD statement? What limitations are in effect when this is done? Can this be done with referbacks?

18. Which DD parameters permit a true referback? Which allow a 'pseudo' referback? Other than with the DD statement, where else in JCL may a referback be coded?

19. The beginning of Chapter 6 describes the type of information provided by the DD statement. For each of the basic seven functions identify the specific parameters and subparameters that provide this type of information.

Chapter 8

Procedures

Overview

Procedures are not a required part of JCL; a programmer can work on an MVS system for years and never use a procedure. Rather, procedures are a convenience feature that can be used to minimize and optimize the coding of JCL. Because JCL is difficult to code, syntax errors occur more frequently when writing JCL than when using a high level language. Chapter 2 contains a lengthy discussion of the problems involved with coding JCL. For these reasons many programmers are content to write JCL that merely works, rather than trying to write the best JCL to run a job. Since heavily used procedures are commonly written by JCL experts, they usually contain the best and most flexible JCL for a particular situation. Procedures also contribute to JCL standardization. If everyone is using the same basic JCL to perform a function, it is easier to find and correct JCL errors when they do occur.

A procedure is a collection of JCL statements that is inserted into a job stream when the name of the procedure is coded on an EXEC statement. Either of the following formats may be used:

```
//A    EXEC PROC=procedure name                  or
//A    EXEC procedure name
```

Example 1: A procedure can be written to compile a program and link edit the object module into a load module library. In this procedure two EXEC statements and numerous DD statements are coded. If the source program is written in COBOL the procedure might consist of the statements shown below. The individual parameters coded on the EXEC and DD statements which comprise the body of the procedure should be familiar by now. The reasons for coding the specific EXEC and DD statements are explained in Chapters 17 and 18. The role of the individual DD statements is not important here.

```
//COB       EXEC PGM=IKFCBL00,PARM='STATE,XREF',REGION=256K
//SYSPRINT DD   SYSOUT=A
//SYSUT1    DD   UNIT=SYSDA,SPACE=(460,(400,100))
//SYSUT2    DD   UNIT=SYSDA,SPACE=(460,(400,100))
//SYSUT3    DD   UNIT=SYSDA,SPACE=(460,(400,100))
//SYSUT4    DD   UNIT=SYSDA,SPACE=(460,(400,100))
//SYSUDUMP DD   SYSOUT=A
//SYSLIB    DD   DSN=SYS1.COPYLIB,DISP=SHR
//SYSLIN    DD   DSN=&LOADSET,DISP=(MOD,PASS),
//              SPACE=(CYL,(1,1)),UNIT=SYSDA
//SYSPUNCH DD   DUMMY
//LKED      EXEC PGM=IEWL,PARM='LIST,LET,XREF'
//SYSPRINT DD   SYSOUT=A
//SYSLIB    DD   DSN=SYS1.COBLIB,DISP=SHR
//SYSUT1    DD   UNIT=SYSDA,SPACE=(CYL,1)
//SYSLIN    DD   DSN=*.COB.SYSLIN,DISP=(OLD,DELETE)
//SYSLMOD   DD   DUMMY
```

Notice that a substantial amount of non-trivial JCL is included in the two steps. The above code does not show how a name is assigned to the procedure. When a COBOL program must be compiled and link-edited, the JCL necessary to use the above code is:

```
//A     EXEC       procedure-name
//COB.SYSIN        DD  *
  COBOL source program code
/*
//LKED.SYSLMOD  DD   DSN=LOADMOD.PDS(ALPHA),
//      DISP=(NEW,CATLG),UNIT=3350,VOL=SER=DISK99,
//      SPACE=(CYL,(1,,1))
```

When using the procedure in this way a total of one EXEC and two DD statements must be coded. However, 17 JCL statements are needed if a procedure is not available. Because important procedures such as this one are generally written by someone who knows the best JCL for a given situation, the procedure should be flexible, efficient, and free of syntax errors. Anyone using the procedure need only code the statements necessary to customize it for their particular application. In the example above the location of the COBOL source program (DDname COB. SYSIN) and the library where the output program is stored (DDname LKED.SYSLMOD) must be identified at runtime. Additionally, the output load module is given the name ALPHA. A programmer does not have to understand all the JCL statements that comprise the procedure in order to use it successfully.

Types of Procedures

What is coded for the procedure name on the EXEC statement that invokes the procedure? The answer depends on the type of procedure being used. There are two kinds, cataloged and in-stream. The two types share many similarities.

Cataloged Procedures

Cataloged procedures are permanent members of a system procedure library. The name of the procedure is its member name in the library. At most installations the main procedure library is called SYS1.PROCLIB. Each member of the library consists of fixed length 80 byte records. To use a procedure stored in SYS1.PROCLIB code:

```
//A   EXEC member name
```

The procedure described in Example 1 is usually a member of SYS1.PROCLIB. Often it is given the member name COBUCL. The reasons for choosing this name are explained later in this chapter. Hence, to use this procedure it is sufficient to code:

```
//A EXEC COBUCL
```

Other procedure libraries can also be created and used. The library to be used for a given job stream must be identified on the /*JOBPARM statement with JES2 and the //*MAIN statement with JES3 if it is not SYS1.PROCLIB. Procedure libraries should not be modified while their members are being used. For more information on placing members in a card image library and on updating the members, see Chapter 27. Multiple job streams may simultaneously access the same procedure, with each user receiving a separate copy.

In-Stream Procedures—The PROC and PEND Statements

In-stream procedures are temporary. They are available only within the job stream where they are coded. In-stream procedures must begin with a PROC statement. The final statement in an in-stream procedure must be a PEND statement. The fundamental syntax of the PROC and PEND statements is discussed in Chapter 3. The role of both statements is discussed below. The four fields in the PROC statement appear as:

```
//procname   PROC   symbolic-parameters   comments
```

The value coded for procname identifies an in-stream procedure in the same way the member name identifies a cataloged procedure. Symbolic parameters are optional on the PROC statement. Comments cannot be coded if there are no symbolic parameters on the statement. With cataloged procedures the PROC statement is optional. In order to assign values to symbolic parameters PROC must be coded, however.

The PEND statement is coded as follows:

```
//pendname   PEND   comments
```

Both the pendname and comments fields are optional. Neither are commonly coded. The PEND statement cannot be used with cataloged procedures.

Up to 1-5 in-stream procedures may be coded within a job. They are traditionally coded after the JOB statement and before the first EXEC statement. However, they may also be coded at later locations in the jobstream. An in-stream procedure must be coded prior to an EXEC statement that invokes it. The same in-stream or cataloged procedure may be invoked more than once during a job.

Example 2: To illustrate the placement of in-stream procedures, consider a job stream containing two of them, each of which is subsequently invoked. The first procedure is invoked a second time in the third step.

```
1       //    JOB statement
        //PROC1     PROC
              .
              . body of procedure PROC1
              .
        //ENDPROC1 PEND    END OF PROC1 IN-STREAM PROC
        //PROC2     PROC        X=,ABC=
              .
              . body of procedure PROC2
              .
        //ENDPROC2 PEND    END OF PROC2 IN-STREAM PROC
2       //A    EXEC PROC1
3       ++PROC1     PROC
4       ++
              .
              . body of procedure PROC1
              .
n       ++ last statement associated with PROC1
n+1     //B    EXEC PROC2 X=CYL,ABC=3380
n+2     ++PROC2     PROC        X=,ABC=
n+3     ++
              .
              . body of procedure PROC2
              .
n+m     ++ last statement associated with PROC2
n+m+1 //C    EXEC PROC1
n+m+2 ++PROC1     PROC
```

Notice that, when the procedure is invoked, the in-stream procedure statements are inserted with // replaced by + +. If PROC1 had been a cataloged procedure the //

would have been replaced by XX. If there are both cataloged and in-stream procedures named PROC1, the in-stream procedure is always inserted in the job stream. Note that the statements in the in-stream procedure are not numbered until they are invoked. JCL syntax checking for the in-stream procedure statements is also deferred until they are invoked. The PEND statement is never printed in the numbered JCL listing. Its only function is to identify the end of an in-stream procedure.

There are certain JCL statements that cannot be coded in a procedure. They include the following:

Statement Type	*Explanation*
JOB	A JOB statement must precede all other JCL statements in a job stream.
Null	Everything following the Null Statement is ignored, including the PEND statement and the rest of the job stream.
JOBLIB	If a JOBLIB statement is coded it must come immediately after the JOB statement. This is impossible for a JOBLIB statement in a procedure. However, STEPLIB DD statements are permitted in procedures.
JES	If either JES2 or JES3 statements are placed inside a procedure they are ignored.
DD * and DATA	In-stream data sets are prohibited in the body of a procedure.
/*	This goes together with not permitting in-stream data sets in a procedure.
EXEC procname	Procedures cannot be nested.

Since in-stream data sets are not allowed within procedures, the DDNAME parameter is often used to allow in-stream data to be included within a concatenation when the procedure is invoked. This is the most common situation for coding DDNAME.

Dynamic Modification of Procedures

If a procedure must have the same format every time it is invoked its usefulness will be severely restricted. For this reason four methods are available to modify or customize a procedure when it is invoked. All four are temporary in that the procedure itself remains unchanged. They are the following:

1) Additional DD statements may be added to the procedure.

2) Existing DD statements within the procedure may be modified (i.e., have their values overridden).

3) Keyword parameters coded on EXEC statements within the procedure may be modified or nullified. New parameters may be added to the EXEC statements.

4) Symbolic parameters may be coded on the EXEC and DD statements within the procedure.

When the procedure in Example 1 was invoked the COB.SYSIN statement was added to the first step and the LKED.SYSLMOD statement in the second step was overridden. The four dynamic modification techniques will now be illustrated using the same simple procedure with all examples.

Adding and Overriding DD Statements

Example 3: Suppose that, in order to minimize the amount of coding involved, a one–step procedure is used to list data sets to the printer. The procedure will use the utility program IEBGENER. (For a detailed discussion of IEBGENER, see Chapter 25.) The procedure consists of the following five statements:

```
//GENER    PROC
//GENER    EXEC PGM=IEBGENER
//SYSPRINT DD   SYSOUT=A
//SYSUT2   DD   SYSOUT=A
//SYSIN    DD   DUMMY
```

IEBGENER requires four DD statements. However, the SYSUT1 DD statement (which identifies the data set to be printed) is not coded within the procedure. The parameters coded with SYSUT1 will change each time the procedure is used. Hence, whenever procedure GENER is invoked one additional DD statement must be supplied. On the other hand, the remaining three DD statements will contain the same parameters every time the procedure is used. To print the records in the data set OLD.CATLOGED.DATASET the following two JCL statements are coded:

```
//A        EXEC GENER
//SYSUT1   DD   DSN=OLD.CATLOGED.DATASET,DISP=SHR
```

Assume that GENER is a cataloged procedure. The statements in GENER are merged with the two coded statements. The printed JCL listing will appear as follows:

```
//A        EXEC GENER
XXGENER    PROC
XXGENER    EXEC PGM=IEBGENER
XXSYSPRINT DD   SYSOUT=A
XXSYSUT2   DD   SYSOUT=A
XXSYSIN    DD   DUMMY
//SYSUT1   DD   DSN=OLD.CATLOGED.DATASET,DISP=SHR
```

All added DD statements are listed after the statements in the procedure. The XX symbols show that the statements are part of a cataloged procedure. If GENER were an in-stream procedure the XX symbols would be replaced by + + in the printed listing and a PEND statement would be the final statement in the procedure itself.

Example 4: Suppose the SYSIN statement also had been included when the procedure was created. Then two DD statements must be supplied every time the procedure is invoked.

```
//A       EXEC GENER
//SYSUT1  DD   DSN=OLD.CATLOGED.DATASET,DISP=SHR
//SYSIN   DD   *
  in-stream data set
/*
```

Added DD statements can be coded in any order. Note that this particular SYSIN statement could not have been coded within the procedure because it contains the * parameter.

To modify or override one of the DD statements within the procedure merely code a DD statement with the same DDname as the statement in the procedure.

Example 5: The SYSUT2 statement identifies where the copy of the SYSUT1 data set is to be written. To direct the output from GENER to the card punch rather than the printer, and also specify a limit of 1000 cards, code:

```
//A        EXEC GENER
//SYSUT2    DD   SYSOUT=B,OUTLIM=1000
//SYSUT1    DD   DSN=OLD.CATLOGED.DATASET,DISP=SHR
```

The operand field of the SYSUT2 DD statement is now completely changed. In the expansion of the procedure the new SYSUT2 statement above will precede the original SYSUT2 statement coded in the procedure:

```
//SYSUT2   DD   SYSOUT=B,OUTLIM=1000
X/SYSUT2   DD   SYSOUT=A
```

The X/ means that the SYSUT2 statement occurs in the procedure but has been overridden by a new DD statement with the same DDname. Any DD statement in a procedure can be overridden. However, two rules must be followed: First, all overriding DD statements must precede all added DD statements. Second, the overriding statements must be coded in exactly the same order (by DDname) as they appear within the procedure. If either of these rules is not followed the resultant procedure will not contain the intended statements, and no warning messages will be generated in the JCL listing.

When DD statements are coded with an EXEC statement that invokes a procedure, the DD statements included with the EXEC and the DD statements within the procedure are merged. The merge is performed as follows. The DDname on the first coded DD statement is compared with the DDnames in the procedure, beginning with the first one. If a match is found the coded DD statement overrides the statement in the procedure. If no match is found the coded statement is considered an added statement. The DDname on the second coded DD statement is then checked against the remaining DDnames in the procedure beginning with the DD statement following the one where the previous match occurred. This process is repeated for each coded DD statement. When a DD statement's DDname does not match any contained in the procedure, that statement and all remaining coded statements are interpreted as added DD statements. Hence, this is a one-pass merge.

Suppose that in the previous example SYSUT1 and SYSUT2 had been coded in reverse order. Since SYSUT1 does not occur as a DDname in the procedure, it is treated as an added statement as intended. After SYSUT1 is added to the procedure the SYSUT2 statement which follows is also considered an added statement, contrary to the programmer's intentions. Now there are two DD statements in this jobstep with the name SYSUT2. With JES2 the first is used and the second ignored. Output will go to the printer, not the card punch. An easy way to see if a statement has been successfully overridden is to look for X/ or +/ in the JCL listing. In this situation, the statements

```
XXSYSUT2  DD  SYSOUT=A
//SYSUT2  DD  SYSOUT=B,OUTLIM=1000
```

and

will both occur in the listing. With JES3 the same thing happens.

Multi-Step Procedures

When a procedure contains more than one step the rules for adding and overriding DD statements hold for each step. For example, to correctly use the procedure in Example 1 that compiles and link-edits a COBOL program, all DD statements included with the invoking EXEC statement must be coded in the following order:

-- all overriding DD statements for the compile step, in the order in which they occur in the procedure

-- all additional DD statements for the compile step in any order

-- all overriding DD statements for the link-edit step, in the order in which they occur in the procedure

-- all additional DD statements for the link-edit step in any order

With multi-step procedures DD statements must identify the specific step with which they are associated, either explicitly or implicitly. To do this the DDname may be qualified with the name of the appropriate step (the stepname on one of the EXEC statements in the procedure). With most IBM cataloged procedures COB is the procedure step name for a COBOL compile, LKED for a link-edit, and GO for a load and go or go step. Hence, when doing a COBOL compile and link-edit all statements with

```
//COB.DDname  DD  .........
```

should precede all statements with

```
//LKED.DDname   DD .....
```

When step names are coded out of the order in which they occur within the procedure the JCL error message IEF611 OVERRIDDEN STEP NOT FOUND IN PROCEDURE terminates the job. If a qualifying procedure stepname is not coded in a multistep procedure a default value is used. Specifically, the most recently coded qualifying stepname is applied to every following DD statement until a new procedure stepname is coded to qualify a DDname. If no procedure stepname is coded on the first DD statement(s) they are associated by default with the first step within the procedure.

Example 6: Consider the following four DD statements that are coded with the compile and link-edit procedure in Example 1. The first three groups of statements give the same results. The SYSLIB statement in the COB step and the SYSLMOD statement in the LKED step are overridden. The SYSIN statement is added to the COB step and the SYSUDUMP statement is added to the LKED step. With Format 1 every DDname is qualified. Format 3 uses the minimum amount of qualification to achieve the correct results. A JCL error results with Format 4 since the qualifiers are not in order.

Format 1	*Format 2*	*Format 3*	*Format 4*
//COB.SYSLIB	//COB.SYSLIB	//SYSLIB	//SYSLIB
//COB.SYSIN	//SYSIN	//SYSIN	//LKED.SYSLMOD
//LKED.SYSLMOD	//LKED.SYSLMOD	//LKED.SYSLMOD	//SYSUDUMP
//LKED.SYSUDUMP	//SYSUDUMP	//SYSUDUMP	//COB.SYSIN

Overriding Individual Parameters

To this point we have simplistically implied that in the overriding operation one statement completely replaces another. However, when an overriding DD statement is coded the statement in the procedure is overridden on an individual DD parameter basis. Parameters coded on the overriding statement can either be added to the parameters in the procedure, replace the same parameter value in the procedure, or nullify the parameter.

Hence, when the SYSUT2 statement with SYSOUT=B,OUTLIM=1000 was coded for the GENER procedure in Example 5, the value B replaced A on the SYSOUT parameter and the OUTLIM parameter was added. An existing parameter in a procedure can be nullified by coding parameter=. Note that no value follows the equal sign. Although this is syntactically correct in other contexts, it is meaningless to code parameter= except when nullifying a parameter or subparameter in a procedure.

Example 7: The accompanying DD statement is used to illustrate the range of possibilities that can occur when overriding a DD statement.

```
//PROCDD DD DSN=X,DISP=(NEW,KEEP),UNIT=3350,
//          VOL=SER=DISK95,SPACE=(CYL,2)
```

The statement is overridden by the following DD statement:

```
//PROCDD DD DSN=X,SPACE=(TRK,(0,5)),DISP=OLD,
//             UNIT=,VOL=SER=,LABEL=(RETPD=14)
```

The parameters on the overriding statement do not need to be coded in the same order as on the statement in the procedure. Here the UNIT and VOL parameters are nullified. Hence the data set will be accessed through a catalog or the pass table, rather than through the VTOC of volume DISK95. Both the SPACE and DISP parameters have been modified, the DISP partially and the SPACE parameter completely. Incidentally, there is no reason for coding DSN=X on the overriding statement, since the same value is present on the original DD statement. If DSN=ABC had been coded, ABC would override X. Since the LABEL parameter did not occur on the DD statement in the procedure, it is added to the parameters on the original DD statement.

It is unnecessary to nullify an existing DD parameter if a mutually exclusive parameter is coded on the overriding statement. For example, if UNIT is coded on the statement in the procedure and SYSOUT is coded on the overriding statement, the UNIT parameter is automatically nullified. The same result occurs when DSN is coded on the overridden statement. However, in this case a warning message is issued. The *OS/VS2 MVS JCL* manual contains a table which shows which pairs of parameters are mutually exclusive.

Overriding Subparameters

One exception to the general rules for overriding DD statements occurs with the DCB parameter. Here adding, modifying, and nullifying are done on an individual subparameter basis. For example, if

```
DCB=(LRECL=80,RECFM=FB,BLKSIZE=8000)
```

is coded on a DD statement in a procedure, then coding

```
DCB=(LRECL=160)
```

on an overriding statement will modify the original LRECL value but leave the RECFM and BLKSIZE values unchanged. To nullify an entire DCB parameter each subparameter must be nullified. In this example it is necessary to code:

```
DCB=(LRECL=,BLKSIZE=,RECFM=)
```

If the DCB value in the procedure is either a referback or the name of a cataloged data set, values may still be added, nullified, or modified. Coding

```
DCB=(OLD.CATLOGED.DATASET,LRECL=75,BLKSIZE=,BUFNO=5)
```

is interpreted as taking all DCB values from the data set label of DSN= OLD.CATLOGED.DATASET, except for LRECL, which gets a different value, and BLKSIZE, which is nullified. BUFNO does not occur in the data set labels and is an added subparameter. Similarly,

```
DCB=(*.STEPA.DD1 ,LRECL=75,BLKSIZE=)
```

modifies the LRECL and nullifies the BLKSIZE found in the DCB parameter identified on the referback statement. The last two DCB parameters are also allowed even when procedures are not used.

Developing Procedures

Before adding a member to a procedure library it is essential to test it as an in-stream procedure, since errors are more easily corrected in that format. When testing a procedure, invoke it at least once without any overriding statements. If this is not done potential problems such as conflicting DD parameters may go undetected.

Modifying EXEC Parameters

The third way in which a procedure can be dynamically modified applies only to the EXEC statement. Any EXEC statement keyword parameters within the procedure can be modified or nullified by coding the same parameter on the invoking EXEC statement. New parameters can be added to the procedure. Suppose a TIME parameter is desired with the GENER procedure in the earlier examples. When the procedure is invoked, code:

```
//A    EXEC   GENER,TIME=(,30)
```

This will have the same effect as if the EXEC statement within the procedure had been coded as:

```
//GENER   EXEC   PGM=IEBGENER,TIME=(,30)
```

Hence, any EXEC keyword parameter can be specified when the procedure is invoked. If the same parameter was coded on the EXEC statement in the procedure, this value overrides it. If the parameter was not coded in the procedure it is added. If parameter= is coded the value coded on the EXEC statement in the procedure is nullified. The only EXEC statement parameter that cannot be overridden, added, or nullified is PGM.

When there are multiple steps in a procedure the rules become more complicated. The compile and link-edit procedure is used to illustrate this. All parameters that apply to the EXEC statement for the compile step must be specified first. They may be coded in any order and may add, nullify, or modify keyword parameters. Each parameter should be coded as follows:

`parameter.COB=value` or `parameter.COB=`

Here COB is the step name on the first EXEC statement in the procedure. For example, if the STATE and FLOW PARM options and a REGION value are needed but were not coded on the EXEC statement in the procedure, the following EXEC statement could be used:

```
//A   EXEC   COBUCL,PARM.COB='STATE,FLOW',REGION.COB=400K
```

After all parameters for the compile step are coded those for the link-edit step should be listed. Failure to keep the parameters together and in order by job step will result in the same syntax error as coding the DD statements out of order by procedure step: IEF611 OVERRIDDEN STEP NOT FOUND IN PROCEDURE.

Example 8: Suppose the following EXEC statement is used to invoke the procedure described in Example 1:

```
//A   EXEC COBUCL,PARM.COB='PMAP,STATE,FLOW',TIME.COB=2,
//         REGION.COB=,COND.LKED=(8,LE,COB)
```

Here the PARM value on the EXEC statement for the COB step is overridden, the REGION value in the first step is nullified, the TIME value is added, and a COND parameter is added to the LKED step.

If the procedure step name is not used to qualify a parameter then (in most cases) the parameter applies to every step within the procedure. If REGION=400K is coded on an EXEC statement which invokes a multi-step procedure, 400K overrides any REGION value coded on an EXEC statement within the procedure, and 400K is added to the EXEC statement if a REGION parameter is not coded. Coding REGION= nullifies the REGION parameter on each EXEC in the procedure where it is coded and has no effect on the steps where REGION is not coded.

There is one exception to the rule for omitting the procedure step name on an EXEC parameter: If PARM is coded without qualification its value applies to the first EXEC statement in the procedure, and any PARM values coded on subsequent statements in the procedure are nullified.

Symbolic Parameters

The final way in which a procedure can be modified involves symbolic parameters. Unlike the previous three methods, symbolic parameters can be used with both EXEC and DD statements. A symbolic parameter can be used to make any parameter, subparameter, or character string within the procedure into a variable. As a variable it must then be assigned a value each time the procedure is invoked. If a value is not explicitly coded for a symbolic parameter a default value must be supplied by the procedure on the PROC statement.

Symbolic parameters may be used within macros when programming in PL/I and assembler language. Symbolic parameters have more flexibility when used with the two programming languages than with JCL. However, in both settings their basic role is the same: they identify a variable that must be assigned a value before any further processing can be performed.

Symbolic parameters can be easily identified in a procedure because they always begin with a single ampersand. The ampersand is then followed by one to seven alphanumeric or national characters. The first character must be alphabetic or national. Although it is easy to determine where the name of a symbolic parameter begins, Examples 10 and 11 reveal that determining where it ends can be more complicated.

Example 9: Symbolic parameters can be used to make the procedure GENER more flexible. Notice that the three symbolic parameters &PROG, &OUT, and &DATASET are coded within the procedure. In addition, two of the three are also listed as operands on the PROC statement, but without the leading ampersands.

```
//GENER    PROC OUT=,PROG=
//GENER    EXEC PGM=IEB&PROG
//SYSPRINT DD   SYSOUT=A
//SYSUT2   DD   SYSOUT=&OUT
//SYSIN    DD   DUMMY
//SYSUT1   DD   DSN=&DATASET,DISP=SHR
```

Since a symbolic parameter can be assigned any value, it need not represent a complete parameter or subparameter value. For example, on the EXEC statement the value assigned to &PROG will be concatenated to the character string IEB. The result of the concatenation must be syntactically correct and identify an existing program. Recall that overriding cannot be used to change a PGM value in a procedure. As shown here, a symbolic parameter makes all or part of it a variable.

In the above code two of the three symbolic parameters have been nullified on the PROC statement. In this case the symbolic parameters &PROG and &OUT must be assigned values when the procedure is invoked. There are two ways to assign values. First, default values can be assigned on the PROC statement. In this situation the PROC statement can be written as:

```
//GENER  PROC  OUT=A,PROG=GENER
```

These two values will replace the symbolic parameters when the procedure is executed. If GENER is an in-stream procedure the statements within the procedure will be interpreted as:

```
++GENER    EXEC PGM=IEBGENER
++SYSPRINT DD   SYSOUT=A
++SYSUT2   DD   SYSOUT=A
++SYSIN    DD   DUMMY
++SYSUT1   DD   DSN=&DATASET,DISP=SHR
```

Two substitutions messages will print following the JCL listing. They will show the parameters coded with the EXEC and SYSPRINT statements following the assignment of values to the symbolic parameters. Symbolic parameters can also be assigned values on the EXEC statement that invokes the procedure. When GENER is invoked, coding

```
//A   EXEC   GENER,OUT=A,PROG=GENER
```

will give the same values to the symbolic parameters as assigning them on the PROC statement. Note that a comma is used to separate the procedure name and the first symbolic parameter value. On the PROC statement a blank precedes the first symbolic parameter.

Every symbolic parameter must either be assigned a value or nullified. Both operations can be performed on the PROC statement or the EXEC statement. If different values are assigned to the same symbolic parameter on the PROC and the EXEC statements, the EXEC value has precedence. Ordinarily the most common value that the symbolic parameter will assume should be coded on the PROC statement. This minimizes having to code the symbolic parameter on the EXEC statement. A second coding philosophy assigns default symbolic parameter values, each of which generates a syntax error. This calls the role of the parameter to the programmer's attention in a very dramatic way.

The same symbolic parameter can be coded more than once on both the PROC and EXEC statements. On either statement the first appearance determines the value assigned on the statement. Since all operands on the PROC statement are keyword they can be coded in any order. The same is true for symbolic parameters on the EXEC statement, except that they must come after the procedure name. In a multistep procedure the symbolic parameters should be qualified in the same way as the other keyword parameters coded on the EXEC statement. Likewise, they should be coded in order by stepname.

The fact that symbolic parameters can be coded on the EXEC statement puts an additional restriction on naming conventions: they should not be given the same name as any value that can appear as a keyword parameter on the EXEC statement. Hence COND, TIME, REGION, PARM, etc. cannot be used as symbolic parameter names. However, the value assigned to any of these parameters may be a symbolic parameter. &REGION is invalid but REGION=&REGVALU is acceptable.

If the value assigned to a symbolic parameter contains special characters the value must be enclosed in apostrophes. Special characters include all symbols except alphabetic, numeric, and national characters. If the output from GENER is to be assigned to SYSOUT=* and the data set used as input is ALPHA.BETA.GAMMA, then the EXEC statement invoking it is coded:

```
//A   EXEC  GENER,PROG=GENER,OUT='*',
//          DATASET='ALPHA.BETA.GAMMA'
```

The apostrophes are not inserted into the generated code.

Several other syntax rules must be observed when using symbolic parameters. The assigned value cannot be continued to the next statement. The length of the assigned value added to the length of all operands and delimiters in a single JCL statement cannot exceed 120 characters. If an ampersand is required on a JCL statement && should be coded. Otherwise a single ampersand will be interpreted as the beginning of a symbolic parameter. If DSN=&symbolic parameter is not assigned a value it is treated as a temporary data set name. For this reason &DATASET need not be assigned a value in Example 9. In every other context a symbolic parameter must be assigned a value or nullified. If this is not done the following error message results:

```
mmm IEF657I THE SYMBOL xxxxx WAS NOT USED IN THE
            PROCEDURE INVOKED BY STATEMENT nnn.
```

The statement numbered mmm is the first statement following the invoked procedure.

Whenever two ampersands (&&) or apostrophes ('') are coded on the same statement as a symbolic parameter, the symbolic parameter must precede the double ampersands or apostrophes in order for the correct substitution to occur.

Symbolic Parameter Syntax

Some of the potential problems associated with symbolic parameters are illustrated below; along with their solutions.

Example 10: Suppose the following SPACE parameter is coded on a DD statement in a procedure:

```
SPACE=(&AMOUNT,1)
```

If AMOUNT=TRK is specified on the PROC or EXEC statement the syntactically correct expression SPACE=(TRK,1) results. Now suppose that

```
SPACE=(&AMOUNT1)
```

appears in the procedure and AMOUNT='TRK,' is coded on the PROC or EXEC statement. A JCL syntax error results because the character "1" is taken to be part of the symbolic parameter name. Actually there are two errors in this code. AMOUNT=TRK is coded on the EXEC statement to assign a value to the symbolic parameter AMOUNT. However, there is no symbolic parameter within the procedure with this name. In addition, the symbolic parameter AMOUNT1 is coded within the procedure but is not assigned a value or nullified. Hence the two messages

```
IEF657I THE SYMBOL xxxxx WAS NOT USED IN THE
        PROCEDURE INVOKED BY STATEMENT nnn.

IEF670I NO VALUE ASSIGNED TO THE SYMBOLIC PARAMETER
        ON PROC STATEMENT VIA THE EXEC STATEMENT.
```

are printed. In this situation the problem is caused by the manner in which the end of the name of the symbolic parameter is determined. Characters such as commas or parentheses can be used to clearly delimit symbolic parameter names.

When a symbolic parameter immediately precedes a character string and is not followed by a comma it is often impossible to determine where the name of the symbolic parameter ends. This occurs when the character(s) immediately following the symbolic parameter are all alphabetic, numeric, and national. In such cases the symbolic parameter should be followed with a period which serves as a delimiter. Following the substitution the period will not be present in the invoked code. For example, using

```
SPACE=(&AMOUNT.1)
```

and assigning AMOUNT='TRK,' provides the correct result.

Example 11: Suppose a symbolic parameter is the second level of qualification in a data set name:

```
DSN=ALPHA.&NAME.GAMMA
```

If NAME=BETA is coded on a PROC or EXEC statement the result generates a syntax error:

```
DSN=ALPHA.BETAGAMMA
```

This occurs because the period following NAME is treated as a delimiter rather than a qualifier. To correct this situation code

```
DSN=ALPHA.&NAME..GAMMA
```

The first period is the delimiter and the second is the name qualifier.

Symbolic Parameter Positional and Keyword Syntax Problems

The most common syntax problems related to symbolic parameters concern leading and trailing commas. It is essential that after symbolic parameters have been assigned values or nullified the resulting JCL be syntactically correct. Different situations arise depending on whether the symbolic parameter is used to represent a positional parameter, a keyword parameter, or a subparameter of either type.

Symbolic parameters used as positional parameters should be followed by a period rather than a comma. If a comma is coded and the positional parameter is nullified a leading comma will cause a syntax error.

Example 12: If the following statement is coded:

```
//PROCDD   DD   &FIRST.DSN=&DSN,DISP=...
```

and FIRST= is coded on the PROC or EXEC statement the result will be

```
//PROCDD   DD              DSN=&DSN,DISP=...
```

Note that if &FIRST had been followed by a comma rather than a period a syntax error would have resulted. On the other hand, if FIRST='DUMMY,' is coded the substitution is

```
//PROCDD   DD    DUMMY,DSN=&DSN,DISP=...
```

With this substitution all of the parameters which follow DUMMY are ignored. If FIRST=DUMMY is coded the statement contains

```
//PROCDD   DD    DUMMYDSN=&DSN,DISP=...
```

This is also a syntax error.

Keyword parameters are of the form keyword=value. With symbolic parameters keyword=&value may be coded. Since a comma follows &value no problems occur when the complete keyword value is made the symbolic parameter.

Positional subparameters can cause problems when one or more trailing subparameters are nullified.

Example 13: Suppose the following three positional subparameters are coded with the DISP parameter:

```
DISP=(&FIRST,&SECOND,&THIRD)
```

If FIRST=value1, SECOND=value2, or both are coded the statement is syntactically correct as long as the THIRD parameter is not nullified. However, when THIRD= is coded the result is

```
DISP=(value1,value2,) or DISP=(value1,,)
```
or
```
DISP=(,value2,)
```

Because of the trailing comma a syntax error results in all three cases. To deal with this potential problem the following could be coded:

```
DISP=(&FIRST,&SECOND&THIRD)
```

Then whenever &THIRD is to be assigned a value, THIRD=',value' should be used. To handle situations where both SECOND and THIRD may be nullified code

```
DISP=(&FIRST&SECOND&THIRD)
```

Keyword subparameters, like keyword parameters, should not cause any syntax problems since subparameter=&value is syntactically correct.

Any portion of the operand field of a DD or EXEC statement operand can be coded in a symbolic parameter. If &ALL is the only operand on a DD statement code

```
//PROCDD   DD   &ALL
```

The assignment ALL='DSN=&&TEMP,UNIT=VIO,SPACE=(CYL,(5,1))' could be used to completely define a temporary work data set. Symbolic parameters cannot be coded as part of either the stepname, DDname, or operator fields, however.

Symbolic Parameters and Overriding DD Statements

What happens when values are assigned to symbolic parameters in a procedure and the DD statements that contain these values are overridden? To answer this question it is necessary to know which gets performed first, assigning a symbolic parameter value or overriding a value. Symbolic parameters are assigned values prior to any overriding. Thus, it is possible that a value assigned on an EXEC or PROC statement will not be the eventual value of the parameter. Symbolic parameters should not be coded on overriding statements because there is no way that a value can be later assigned to them. Only DSN=&symbolic parameter should be coded on an overriding statement.

The system makes several distinct passes through the JCL in a job stream in order to check syntax. Consider a job step that contains referbacks, symbolic parameters, and overriding statements. If all of these features are coded incorrectly the Job Scheduler rejects the job because of the JCL errors. However, it flags only the symbolic parameter errors and the errors in the overriding statements. If these are corrected and the job is resubmitted, it is rejected because of the referback errors. When these are corrected the job may finally be run.

When designing a procedure some thought should be given as to how easily it can be modified. Consider whether a symbolic parameter or an overriding statement is the more appropriate method for modifying a procedure. Overriding is usually the more complicated of the two; it is necessary to know the names and order of the steps within the procedure and the names and order of the DD statements within the step which is to be modified. While symbolic parameters merely require coding the desired value on the invoking EXEC statement, more preplanning is necessary to create the procedure. In order to use a symbolic parameter it is necessary to know its name, the step in which it occurs, and its role in the procedure.

In order to illustrate many of the points discussed with regard to symbolic parameters, a common programming situation is discussed below.

Example 14: Assume that there are several standard label tape datasets, all on the same volume, which must be copied to disk. Rather than using overriding statements for each data set, symbolic parameters are coded in the procedure. This allows the procedure to be invoked and changes the tape and disk names for each data set without coding any overriding JCL statements:

```
//GENER      PROC TNAME=,TAPELBL=,DSNNAME=,UNIT=,AMT=
//A          EXEC PGM=IEBGENER
//SYSPRINT    DD  SYSOUT=A
//SYSIN       DD  DUMMY
//SYSUT1      DD  DSN=&TNAME,UNIT=TAPE,DISP=(OLD,PASS),
//              VOLUME=(,RETAIN,SER=098765),LABEL=(&TAPELBL,SL)
//SYSUT2      DD  DSN=ABCDEF.&DSNNAME,DISP=(NEW,CATLG),
//              UNIT=3350,VOL=SER=DISK02,SPACE=(&UNIT&AMT)
//           PEND
```

Since all symbolic parameters must be assigned a value either in the procedure or when the procedure is invoked, the following can be coded to copy the first tape data set to disk:

```
//STEP1       EXEC    GENER,TNAME='FIRST.TAPE',TAPELBL=1,
//     UNIT=TRK,AMT=',12',DSNNAME=ALPHA
```

TAPELBL may also be omitted since 1 is the default value for the first LABEL subparameter. If this procedure is to be used on a regular basis several of the symbolic parameters will assume the same values quite frequently. These parameters should be assigned their most common values on the PROC statement, as follows:

```
//GENER       PROC    TAPELBL=1,UNIT=TRK,AMT=',10',
// DSNNAME=,TNAME=
```

To invoke the procedure and use these default values code only

```
//STEP1       EXEC    GENER,TNAME='FIRST.TAPE',DSNNAME=ALPHA
```

It is unnecessary to list every symbolic parameter on the PROC statement. However, it is a good programming habit since by looking at this statement it is clear which ones have been given default values and which ones must be assigned values on the EXEC statement.

Concatenating Data Sets Within Procedures

It is permissible to concatenate sequential data sets or libraries within a procedure. Standard concatenation rules apply. Symbolic parameters can be coded on any of the DD statements in the concatenation. Overriding one or more statements within the concatenation is also allowed. However, this situation can lead to a JCL syntax oddity.

Example 15: Four data sets are concatenated together and it is necessary to override just the second and third data sets. Suppose the procedure contains

```
//SYSLIB  DD  DSN=ALPHA,DISP=SHR
//        DD  DSN=BETA,DISP=SHR
//        DD  DSN=GAMMA,DISP=SHR
//        DD  DSN=DELTA,DISP=SHR
```

The overriding statement should be coded as

```
//SYSLIB  DD
//        DD  DSN=REPLACE1
//        DD  DSN=REPLACE2
//        DD
```

The statements in the concatenation that are not to be overridden have no operands coded. This is the only situation where a DD statement can be coded with no operands. In this example the first and fourth DD statements will have none of their parameters modified or nullified and no new parameters will be added. The DSN parameter will be modified on the second and third DD statements. There is no reason to recode DISP=SHR on these two overriding statements since it is already in effect.

Important Procedures

Every system procedure library contains a group of procedures that are used with the language translators, Linkage Editor and Loader. These procedures are especially convenient for people who do not have a thorough understanding of JCL or of these important system programs. The procedures are discussed and illustrated in depth in Chapters 17, 18, and 19. Six procedures are available to make six fundamental functions easier to use. In this chapter, the six procedures and their programming languages are listed. The xxx value identifies the language, such as COB for COBOL and PLI for PL/I. The y value identifies a particular version of the language. LKED and GO do not adhere to these rules since they are language independent.

Procedure Name	*Chapter Reference*	*Basic Function*	*COBOL Procedure*
xxxyC	17	Compile a program	COBUC
xxxyCL	8,18	Compile and link–edit a program	COBUCL
xxxyCG	17,19	Compile, load, and execute a program	COBUCG
xxxyCLG	18	Compile, link–edit, and execute a program	COBUCLG
L (or LKED)	8,18	Link–edit a program	LKED
G (or GO)	19	Load and execute a program	GO

Complete JCL Job Listing: Example 2 The following three-step job is used to illustrate in-stream and cataloged procedures and symbolic parameters. This example includes the actual listing generated by running the job stream shown here. Between the JOB and the first EXEC statement an in-stream procedure name COPY is defined. Its first step can be used as a general purpose utility program to create a back-up copy of an existing data set. The default back-up copy generated by the procedure is a printed listing of the original data set. An input data set must be specified. There is no default. Three symbolic parameters are used to identify the existing input data set (&X), the back-up copy (&SYSOUT), and the location of the input data set &UNITVOL respectively. The second step in the procedure can be used to create new data sets or catalog, uncatalog, or delete existing data sets. In other words, the second step is used to disposition process data sets. This process and the IEFBR14 program are described in more detail in Chapter 21.

In the first step in the job, the sequential disk data set ACSSTU.MASTER is copied to the existing pds library ACSSTU.X, where it is stored as member ALPHA. In addition, in step two of the procedure an existing cataloged data set is uncataloged. In the second jobstep the in-stream procedure is invoked again. A printed copy of the input data set is produced and the second procedure step is skipped. The JCL comment is incorrect. In the final jobstep, a member of the load module library ACSSTU.MYLIB is processed by the program IEWL, and then placed back in the library.

```
//LARRY  JOB (1125,515,YRRAL),LARRY,PRTY=8,MSGCLASS=A,CLASS=B
/*ROUTE PRINT TERM
//COPY          PROC X=,SYSOUT='SYSOUT=A',
                UNITVOL='UNIT=SYSDA,VOL=SER=WORK01'
//*********************************************************************
//* THIS IN-STREAM PROCEDURE CONSISTS OF TWO STEPS.  STEP
//* COPYPGM CREATES A PRINTED LISTING OF THE SEQUENTIAL DATA
//* SET IDENTIFIED IN THE 'INPUT' DD STATEMENT.  THE SECOND
//* STEP CAN BE USED TO PERFORM ADDITIONAL DISPOSITION
//* PROCESSING.
//*********************************************************************
//COPYPGM       EXEC PGM=BACKUP
//STEPLIB        DD  DSN=ACSSTU.MYLIB,DISP=SHR
//MESSAGES       DD  SYSOUT=*
//INPUT          DD  DSN=&X,DISP=SHR&UNITVOL
//OUTPUT         DD  &SYSOUT
//CONTROLS       DD  DDNAME=DUMMY1
//CLEANUP       EXEC PGM=IEFBR14
//ENDCOPY       PEND END OF THE COPY IN-STREAM PROCEDURE
//A             EXEC COPY,X='ACSSTU.MASTER',REGION.COPYPGM=500K,
//              SYSOUT='DSN=ACSSTU.X(ALPHA),DISP=SHR',UNITVOL=
//*********************************************************************
//* THE RECORDS IN THE DATA SET ACSSTU.MASTER ARE COPIED
//* TO PDS MEMBER ALPHA.  THE PDS ITSELF ALREADY EXISTS.
//*********************************************************************
```

```
//OUTPUT        DD   DISP=OLD
//MESSAGES      DD   DUMMY
//DUMMY1        DD   DUMMY
//CLEANUP.DD1  DD DSN=ACSSTU.OLD.DATASET,DISP=(OLD,UNCATLG)
//B            EXEC COPY,COND.CLEANUP=(ONLY,(0,LE))
//             X='ACSSTU.MASTER'
//***********************************************************
//* FIRST STEP IS SKIPPED AND A NEW DATA SET IS CREATED.
//***********************************************************
//CLEANUP.DD1  DD   DSN=ACSSTU.NEW.DATASET,DISP=(NEW,CATLG),
//             UNIT=SYSDA,SPACE=(CYL,1)
//***********************************************************
//* A CATALOGED PROCEDURE IS USED TO PROCESS A LOAD MODULE.
//***********************************************************
//C            EXEC LKED,COND=EVEN
//SYSLMOD       DD   DSN=ACSSTU.MYLIB,DISP=OLD
//SYSIN         DD   *
   . . .in-stream data set
//
```

Just as the printed output of the *Complete JCL Job Listing: Example 1* was given in Figure 7–2 at the end of Chapter 7, the three major printed listings generated by this job are shown in Figure 8–1. Since this job performs no tape processing, the JES2 Job Log is much simpler. Notice that the allocation messages begin with the substitution messages that are used to assign values to the symbolic parameters in the in-stream procedure. Under no conditions should these be considered error or warning messages.

Exercises

1. Write an in-stream procedure to use IEBGENER or IDCAMS to copy a disk data set. The copy must also be a disk data set on either the same volume or a different volume as the original. Include only the EXEC statement and message and control DD statement data sets. Do not use symbolic parameters. Now use the procedure to copy the records in the cataloged disk data set ALPHA.BETA to volume DISK99 where they will be called BETA.ALPHA. Now use the procedure to copy the tape data set TAPE.ALPHA.BETA to volume DISK99. The tape data set is the only data set on the SL tape volume 012345.

2. Modify the one step procedure developed in the previous exercise. Include SYSUT1 and SYSUT2 DD statements for the input and output data sets respectively. On each statement code those DD parameters that will be in effect almost every time the procedure is invoked. Use the procedure to create the same two disk and tape data sets as in the last exercise. Determine the amount of coding that is now necessary when using the revised version of the procedure.

3. Continue to modify the procedure used in the two previous exercises. Code symbolic parameters for all remaining DD statement parameters that may be necessary. Where appropriate initialize the symbolic parameter to the most common default value. Again,

FIGURE 8–1

JCL Job Output, Example 2

```
                          J E S 2   J O B   L O G

 -------- JOB  122  IEF097I LAR      - USER ACS1125  ASSIGNED
 10.33.43 JOB  122  IEF677I WARNING MESSAGE(S) FOR JOB LAR      ISSUED
 10.33.43 JOB  122  $HASP373 LAR        STARTED - INIT  1 - CLASS B - SYS 8000
 10.33.43 JOB  122  IEF403I LAR - STARTED - TIME=10.33.43
 10.33.47 JOB  122  IEF404I LAR - ENDED - TIME=10.33.47
 10.33.47 JOB  122  $HASP395 LAR        ENDED


 1   //LAR     JOB (XXXXXXXXXXXXXX),LARRY,PRTY=8,MSGCLASS=A,CLASS=B          JOB  122
     ***ROUTE PRINT 16670                                                         002
     //COPY          PROC X=,SYSOUT='SYSOUT=A',                                  0030
     //              UNITVOL=',UNIT=SYSDA,VOL=SER=WORK01'                        0031
     //*******************************************************                  0032
     //* THIS IN-STREAM PROCEDURE CONSISTS OF TWO STEPS.  STEP                   0033
     //* COPYPGM CREATES A PRINTED LISTING OF THE SEQUENTIAL DATA                0034
     //* SET IDENTIFIED ON THE 'INPUT' DD STATEMENT.  THE SECOND                 0035
     //* STEP CAN BE USED TO PERFORM ADDITIONAL DISPOSITION                      0036
     //* PROCESSING.                                                             0037
     //*******************************************************                  0038
     //COPYPGM       EXEC PGM=BACKUP                                             0040
     //STEPLIB        DD  DSN=ACSSTU.MYLIB,DISP=SHR                              0050
     //MESSAGES       DD  SYSOUT=*                                               0060
     //INPUT          DD  DSN=&X,DISP=SHR&UNITVOL                                0070
     //OUTPUT         DD  &SYSOUT                                                0080
     //CONTROLS       DD  DDNAME=DUMMY1                                          0090
     //CLEANUP       EXEC PGM=IEFBR14                                            0100
     //ENDCOPY       PEND END OF THE COPY IN-STREAM PROCEDURE                    0110
 2   //A             EXEC COPY,X='ACSSTU.MASTER',REGION.COPYPGM=500K,            0120
     //              SYSOUT='DSN=ACSSTU.X(ALPHA),DISP=SHR',UNITVOL=              0130
     ************************************************************                0140
     *** THE RECORDS IN THE DATA SET ACSSTU.MASTER ARE COPIED TO PDS             0150
     *** MEMBER ALPHA.  THE PDS ITSELF ALREADY EXISTS.                           0151
     ************************************************************                0160
 3   ++COPY          PROC X=,SYSOUT='SYSOUT=A',                                  0030
     ++              UNITVOL=',UNIT=SYSDA,VOL=SER=WORK01'                        0031
     *******************************************************                     0032
     *** THIS IN-STREAM PROCEDURE CONSISTS OF TWO STEPS.  STEP                   0033
     *** COPYPGM CREATES A PRINTED LISTING OF THE SEQUENTIAL DATA                0034
     *** SET IDENTIFIED ON THE 'INPUT' DD STATEMENT.  THE SECOND                 0035
     *** STEP CAN BE USED TO PERFORM ADDITIONAL DISPOSITION                      0036
     *** PROCESSING.                                                             0037
     *******************************************************                     0038
 4   ++COPYPGM       EXEC PGM=BACKUP                                             0040
 5   ++STEPLIB        DD  DSN=ACSSTU.MYLIB,DISP=SHR                              0050
 6   ++MESSAGES       DD  SYSOUT=*                                               0060
 7   ++INPUT          DD  DSN=&X,DISP=SHR&UNITVOL                                0070
 8   //OUTPUT         DD  DISP=OLD                                               0170
     +/OUTPUT         DD  &SYSOUT                                                0080
 9   ++CONTROLS       DD  DDNAME=DUMMY1                                          0090
10   //MESSAGES       DD  DUMMY                                                  0180
11   //DUMMY1         DD  DUMMY                                                  0190
12   ++CLEANUP       EXEC PGM=IEFBR14                                            0100
13   //CLEANUP.DD1 DD DSN=ACSSTU.OLD.DATASET,DISP=(OLD,UNCATLG)                  0200
14   //B             EXEC COPY,COND.CLEANUP=(ONLY,(0,LE)),                       0210
     //              X='ACSSTU.MASTER'                                           0211
     ************************************************************                0220
     *** FIRST STEP IS SKIPPED AND A NEW DATA SET IS CREATED.                    0230
     ************************************************************                0240
15   ++COPY          PROC X=,SYSOUT='SYSOUT=A',                                  0030
     ++              UNITVOL=',UNIT=SYSDA,VOL=SER=WORK01'                        0031
     *******************************************************                     0032
     *** THIS IN-STREAM PROCEDURE CONSISTS OF TWO STEPS.  STEP                   0033
     *** COPYPGM CREATES A PRINTED LISTING OF THE SEQUENTIAL DATA                0034
     *** SET IDENTIFIED ON THE 'INPUT' DD STATEMENT.  THE SECOND                 0035
     *** STEP CAN BE USED TO PERFORM ADDITIONAL DISPOSITION                      0036
     *** PROCESSING.                                                             0037
     *******************************************************                     0038
16   ++COPYPGM       EXEC PGM=BACKUP                                             0040
17   ++STEPLIB        DD  DSN=ACSSTU.MYLIB,DISP=SHR                              0050
18   ++MESSAGES       DD  SYSOUT=*                                               0060
19   ++INPUT          DD  DSN=&X,DISP=SHR&UNITVOL                                0070
20   ++OUTPUT         DD  &SYSOUT                                                0080
21   ++CONTROLS       DD  DDNAME=DUMMY1                                          0090
22   ++CLEANUP       EXEC PGM=IEFBR14                                            0100
23   //CLEANUP.DD1 DD  DSN=ACSSTU.NEW.DATASET,DISP=(NEW,CATLG),                  0250
     //              UNIT=SYSDA,SPACE=(CYL,1)                                    0260
     ************************************************************                0270
     *** A CATALOGED PROCEDURE IS USED TO PROCESS A LOAD MODULE.                 0280
     ************************************************************                0290
24   //C             EXEC LKED,COND=EVEN                                         0300
25   XXLKED      EXEC PGM=IEWL,PARM='XREF,LIST,LET,NCAL',REGION=196K         00000010
26   XXSYSPRINT DD  SYSOUT=$,DCB=(RECFM=FB,LRECL=121,BLKSIZE=1210)           00000020
27   XXSYSLIN   DD  DDNAME=SYSIN                                             00000030
28   //SYSLMOD        DD  DSN=ACSSTU.MYLIB,DISP=OLD                              0310
     X/SYSLMOD  DD  DSN=&&GOSET(GO),SPACE=(1024,(50,20,1)),                  00000040
     XX         UNIT=VIO,DISP=(MOD,PASS)                                     00000050
29   XXSYSUT1   DD  UNIT=VIO,SPACE=(1024,(200,20))                           00000060
30   //SYSIN          DD  *                                                      0320
     //                                                                          0360
```

```
 STMT NO. MESSAGE
 -
    7      IEF653I SUBSTITUTION JCL - DSN=ACSSTU.MASTER,DISP=SHR
    8      IEF653I SUBSTITUTION JCL - DSN=ACSSTU.X(ALPHA),DISP=SHR
   19      IEF653I SUBSTITUTION JCL - DSN=ACSSTU.MASTER,DISP=SHR,UNIT=SYSDA,VOL=SER=WORK01
   20      IEF653I SUBSTITUTION JCL - SYSOUT=A
   22      IEF686I DDNAME REFERRED TO ON DDNAME KEYWORD IN PRIOR STEP WAS NOT RESOLVED
IEF236I ALLOC. FOR LAR COPYPGM A
IEF237I 26C  ALLOCATED TO STEPLIB
IEF237I 265  ALLOCATED TO SYS04017
IEF237I JES2 ALLOCATED TO MESSAGES
IEF237I 14D  ALLOCATED TO INPUT
IEF237I 14D  ALLOCATED TO OUTPUT
IEF237I DMY  ALLOCATED TO CONTROLS
IEF237I DMY  ALLOCATED TO MESSAGES
IEF142I LAR COPYPGM A - STEP WAS EXECUTED - COND CODE 0000
IEF285I   ACSSTU.MYLIB                                  KEPT
IEF285I   VOL SER NOS= WORK03.
IEF285I   SYS1.ACSCTLG1                                 KEPT
IEF285I   VOL SER NOS= ISU013.
IEF285I   JES2.JOB00122.S0000102                        SYSOUT
IEF285I   ACSSTU.MASTER                                 KEPT
IEF285I   VOL SER NOS= WORK02.
IEF285I   ACSSTU.X                                      KEPT
IEF285I   VOL SER NOS= WORK02.
IEF373I STEP /COPYPGM / START 86326.1033
IEF374I STEP /COPYPGM / STOP  86326.1033 CPU    0MIN 00.07SEC SRB    0MIN 00.00SEC VIRT    28K SYS   288K
IEF236I ALLOC. FOR LAR CLEANUP A
IEF237I 26C  ALLOCATED TO DD1
IEF237I 265  ALLOCATED TO SYS04019
IEF142I LAR CLEANUP A - STEP WAS EXECUTED - COND CODE 0000
IEF285I   ACSSTU.OLD.DATASET                            UNCATALOGED
IEF285I   VOL SER NOS= WORK03.
IEF285I   SYS1.ACSCTLG1                                 KEPT
IEF285I   VOL SER NOS= ISU013.
IEF373I STEP /CLEANUP / START 86326.1033
IEF374I STEP /CLEANUP / STOP  86326.1033 CPU    0MIN 00.02SEC SRB    0MIN 00.00SEC VIRT     4K SYS   276K
IEF236I ALLOC. FOR LAR COPYPGM B
IEF237I 26C  ALLOCATED TO STEPLIB
IEF237I 265  ALLOCATED TO SYS04021
IEF237I JES2 ALLOCATED TO MESSAGES
IEF237I 14C  ALLOCATED TO INPUT
IEF237I JES2 ALLOCATED TO OUTPUT
IEF237I DMY  ALLOCATED TO CONTROLS
IEF142I LAR COPYPGM B - STEP WAS EXECUTED - COND CODE 0000
IEF285I   ACSSTU.MYLIB                                  KEPT
IEF285I   VOL SER NOS= WORK03.
IEF285I   SYS1.ACSCTLG1                                 KEPT
IEF285I   VOL SER NOS= ISU013.
IEF285I   JES2.JOB00122.S0000103                        SYSOUT
IEF285I   ACSSTU.MASTER                                 KEPT
IEF285I   VOL SER NOS= WORK01.
IEF285I   JES2.JOB00122.S0000104                        SYSOUT
IEF373I STEP /COPYPGM / START 86326.1033
IEF374I STEP /COPYPGM / STOP  86326.1033 CPU    0MIN 00.06SEC SRB    0MIN 00.00SEC VIRT    24K SYS   288K
IEF202I LAR CLEANUP B - STEP WAS NOT RUN BECAUSE OF COND=ONLY
IEF272I LAR CLEANUP B - STEP WAS NOT EXECUTED.
IEF373I STEP /CLEANUP / START 86326.1033
IEF374I STEP /CLEANUP / STOP  86326.1033 CPU    0MIN 00.00SEC SRB    0MIN 00.00SEC VIRT     0K SYS     0K
IEF236I ALLOC. FOR LAR LKED C
IEF237I JES2 ALLOCATED TO SYSPRINT
IEF237I JES2 ALLOCATED TO SYSLIN
IEF237I 26C  ALLOCATED TO SYSLMOD
IEF237I 265  ALLOCATED TO SYS04023
IEF237I VIO  ALLOCATED TO SYSUT1
IEF142I LAR LKED C - STEP WAS EXECUTED - COND CODE 0000
IEF285I   JES2.JOB00122.S0000105                        SYSOUT
IEF285I   JES2.JOB00122.SI000101                        SYSIN
IEF285I   ACSSTU.MYLIB                                  KEPT
IEF285I   VOL SER NOS= WORK03.
IEF285I   SYS1.ACSCTLG1                                 KEPT
IEF285I   VOL SER NOS= ISU013.
IEF285I   SYS86326.T103343.RA000.LAR.R0000001           DELETED
IEF373I STEP /LKED    / START 86326.1033
IEF374I STEP /LKED    / STOP  86326.1033 CPU    0MIN 00.11SEC SRB    0MIN 00.01SEC VIRT   196K SYS   308K
IEF375I  JOB /LAR     / START 86326.1033
IEF376I  JOB /LAR     / STOP  86326.1033 CPU    0MIN 00.26SEC SRB    0MIN 00.01SEC
RCS176I  1125 015150000
```

use the procedure to create the same two data sets as in the last two exercises. Note that when using the procedure the amount of coding is further reduced.

4. The procedure used in the three previous exercises is to be replaced by a two step procedure. In the first step the program IEFBR14 will be used to create the disk or tape data set. In the second step the existing data set's records are to be copied to the data set created in step one. Invoke the procedure to create the same two data sets as in the last exercise.

5. Consider the following procedure where data set X is passed in each step:

```
//ABC PROC
//A   EXEC PGM=A
//DD1 DD   DSN=X,DISP=(OLD,PASS)
//DD2 DD   DSN=X,DISP=(MOD,PASS)
//B   EXEC PGM=B
//DD3 DD   DSN=X,DISP=SHR
```

Invoke the procedure twice. Note that during the second invocation the data set retrieved in Step B is a copy of X passed in Step A of the first invocation. Explain this result.

6. Determine which of the symbolic parameters in the following procedure are invalid:

```
//TEST     PROC PGM=,DATA=,OP=DD,PROG=GENER,PRT=PRINT,*='*'
//A        EXEC &PGM=IEB&PROG
//SYS&PRT &OP   SYSOUT=&DATA
//SYSIN    DD   &*
//PEND
```

Comment on any other problems with the procedure. Is this a cataloged or an in-stream procedure? What must be done to convert it to the other type of procedure?

7. As in the previous exercise, determine all of the errors associated with the accompanying in-stream procedure and the statement that invokes it. There are at least ten major errors. The procedure is a bad solution to Exercise 4.

```
//        PROC
//A       EXEC PGM=IEFBR14
//DD1       DD DSN=ALPHA,DISP=(NEW,PASS),
//             UNIT=SYSDA,VOL=SER=WORK01,SPACE=(CYL,(1,1)),
//             DCB=(LRECL=80,BLKSIZE=6160,RECFM=FBS)
//B       EXEC PGM=IEBGENER
//SYSPRINT DD SYSOUT=A
//SYSUT1    DD DSN=&DSN,DISP=(&FIRST&SECOND
//             UNIT=&UNIT,VOL=SER=&VOLSER
//SYSUT2    DD DSN=&DSN,DISP=(&THIRD,&FOURTH),
//             UNIT=&UNT,DCB=(&LRECL,&BLKSIZE,&RECFM)
//SYSIN     DD DUMMY
//        PEND
//FIRST   EXEC   ,DSN=,FIRST=OLD,SECOND=,PASS),
//              VOLSER='(WORK01,WORK02)',DSN=ALPHA,THIRD=,
//              UNT=DISK,LRECL=,BLKSIZE='BLKSIZE=1000,',
//              FORMAT=FBS
```

8. Which of the following symbolic parameters are valid? They are classified by the statement type on which they are coded.

Coded on DD statement	*Coded on EXEC statement*
a) `&DSN`	g) `&DSN`
b) `&SYSOUT$`	h) `&ALPHA123`
c) `DISP=&PARENS&F&S&PARENS`	i) `&GO.TEMP`
d) `&DISP=DISP`	j) `&A&B.&C`
e) `DDNAME=&ALPHA`	k) `&.A.B.C`
f) `DSN=&A...&B`	l) `&COND`

9. Read the material on using macro statements in assembler language or in PL/I. What additional options are available with macros that cannot be done with symbolic parameters and procedures? Compare the role of the symbolic parameters with macros and procedures. True macros are not available with COBOL. Why do PL/I and assembler support a wider range of macro processing than JCL?

10. Under what conditions would user procedure libraries be a good idea? Many installations prohibit programmers from creating their own procedure libraries. Why is this the case?

11. Can both a cataloged and an in-stream procedure have the same name? In this case which one is invoked? Would there ever be a legitimate reason for coding an in-stream procedure with the same name as a cataloged procedure?

12. List all of the differences between cataloged and in-stream procedures. Consider syntax and role. Under what conditions should each be used?

13. Can two or more steps within a procedure have the same name? Why or why not? Can a symbolic parameter be coded more than once in a procedure? Why or why not? Can a symbolic parameter be coded on an EXEC statement and a DD statement in the same step? Can a procedure contain a referback to a statement outside of the procedure?

14. Why is the nesting of procedures not allowed (i.e., an EXEC procedure statement cannot be coded inside a procedure)? Why is a STEPLIB statement permitted inside of a procedure while a JOBLIB statement is not allowed?

15. Describe the differences between the syntax rules for one level of a qualified data set name and the allowable syntax for a symbolic parameter exclusive of the ampersand.

PART II

Major MVS Concepts

Chapter 9

Data Set Organization and Access Methods

Overview

This chapter contains an introduction and overview of three of the major topics presented in Part II. Chapters 10 and 11 are concerned with dcb values, how they are determined, and what they mean. Chapters 12, 13, and 14 discuss the three non-sequential non-VSAM data set organizations. Chapters 15 and 16 describe disk and tape data sets. Some of the material in this chapter should be reread after studying Chapters 15 and 16. The material in this chapter is not a prerequisite to the remaining chapters in Part II, but several of the major topics discussed in Chapters 10 through 16 are first introduced here. Sequential data sets are used for illustration purposes with several important topics, including blocking, buffering, and the access methods. These same topics are then re-examined with regard to non-sequential data sets.

This chapter begins the study of the data set organizations available on an MVS system. There are seven distinct types of data sets. The four types of non-VSAM data sets are examined in this chapter and Chapters 12, 13, and 14.

There are four non-VSAM data set organizations: sequential, indexed, direct, and partitioned. Most large computer systems have their own version of these four types; they are not restricted to MVS or IBM systems. In this chapter an overview of the four data set organizations is presented. A fundamental goal in this and the following chapters is to answer questions like the following: What are the prominent characteristics of these four data set organizations? How are they similar? How do they differ? What criteria should be used to determine which of these four (if any) is appropriate for a particular application? The best place to begin the study of the non-VSAM data sets is by examining their physical organization.

Sequential Data Sets

Sequential data sets are the simplest to understand and use. A sequential data set can be used with any type of I/O device: tape, disk, or unit record (printer, card reader, or card punch). All processing of a sequential data set involves consecutive record processing. The Nth record must be processed before processing the N + 1st record. When it is necessary to process every (or almost every) record in a data set, sequential data set organization is an excellent choice. Usually one field within the records is used to order them for a particular application. A second application may need to sort the records before processing them. To retrieve one specific record from a sequential data set can be very time consuming, especially if the record is not near the beginning of the data set.

A very limited range of I/O operations is permitted with sequential data sets. Consecutive records can be read and written starting at the beginning of the data set. A record can be read and rewritten as long as its length is not changed. Records can also be added onto the end of an existing sequential data set. Unlike the other three data set organizations, there is no additional physical overhead associated with the records in a sequential disk data set.

ISAM Data Sets

A non-VSAM indexed data set is called an ISAM data set. ISAM stands for Indexed Sequential Access Method. An ISAM data set must be stored on disk. Backup copies can also be stored on tape. However, a back up ISAM data set is stored on tape with sequential organization.

The records in a non-VSAM data set must be processed in one of two different ways: sequentially (consecutively) or randomly. With random processing an individual record can be accessed without starting at the beginning of the data set. Random processing is restricted to disk data sets. The system must have some way of quickly determining the record's location in the data set.

Records in an ISAM data set can also be processed sequentially. However, the processing is not as efficient as sequentially processing a data set whose organization is sequential. The reason for this is that an ISAM data set has two overhead components that are not present with a sequential data set. Each record in the data set contains a key; and there are one or more indexes that associate key values with the location of the record that contains that specific key value. Although this index/key combination slows down sequential processing, it permits random retrieval of an individual record in the data set. Random processing cannot be done with sequential data sets.

An extremely wide range of I/O operations can be performed with ISAM data sets. These include all of the operations permitted with sequential data sets. It is also possible to randomly read, write, and rewrite records, and logical deletion is allowed. Finally, random positioning to a specific record preliminary to sequential processing (using the START verb) is allowed. The index must be used with every I/O operation performed, even sequential processing. An ISAM data set uses more disk storage than a comparable sequential data set, due to the presence of the two overhead components, indexes and keys.

Direct Data Sets

Direct data sets are sometimes called BDAM data sets. Direct is in some ways a poor name choice. The direct data set organization decomposes into sub-categories; none of the other three data set organizations allow this. In PL/I these are called REGIONAL I, REGIONAL II, and REGIONAL III. A COBOL application program can process two types of direct data sets, relative and direct. Note that the word direct is being used in two contexts, as a data set organization and as an example of a particular type of direct data set organization. Direct data sets are the most complicated of the four data set organizations. They require the most work on the part of the application programmer who creates and uses them. Most collections of records are not good candidates for being stored as direct data sets. All direct data sets are stored on disk. Every other data set organization has at least one specific utility that can be used to create backup copies on tape. The utility IEBGENER can backup a direct data set, although this is not usually considered one of its major functions.

Other than creating a backup copy it is rare to process a direct data set sequentially. Direct data sets are used when the fastest possible random record retrieval is desired. Hence it is usually irrelevant to compare the sequential processing efficiency of a direct data set with either sequential or ISAM data sets. For random processing direct is faster than the other data set organizations. The major reason for this superiority is that direct data sets do not have indexes. Some direct data sets (relative and REGIONAL I) do not have keys; others (direct and REGIONAL III) do. A wide range of I/O operations is possible with a direct data set, including the standard sequential operations and a variety of random read, write, and rewrite operations. Logical deletion and random (START) positioning are also allowed.

Because it is extremely difficult to process most collections of records as direct data sets, indexed data sets are much more common. Each record of a direct data set must have some field that can be used to determine where the record should be placed on disk. Interaction between the application program code and the system programs (access methods) supplied by MVS can then be used to find this same disk location when it is necessary to retrieve the record.

Partitioned Data Sets (PDS)

A partitioned data set is a collection of sequential data sets. It is possible to process only one member or every member of a pds. When processing the entire partitioned data set (all the members) certain restrictions are in effect. In particular all the members should have compatible dcb values. A partitioned data set allows grouping of data sets.

A directory or table of contents is used to manage the members in a partitioned data set. This directory precedes the member area. Directory processing is very different from sequential processing. Most directory processing is handled automatically and does not require work on the part of an application program. Within the directory record keys are employed. A partitioned data set must be stored on disk, but can be backed up to tape. As with an indexed data set, when this is done the partitioned data set is stored as a sequential data set.

Summary of Data Set Organizations

The above information is summarized in Table 9–1.

It is clear that the type of processing required strongly influences the data set organization selected for a collection of records. If all processing is to be sequential then there is no reason to consider ISAM or direct data set organizations. If random processing is necessary either indexed or direct organization must be used. If the speed of the random processing is the most important criteria then direct organization is preferable. Note that direct can only be used if the records that comprise the data set will permit it. Most collections of records easily can be made into an ISAM data set; any collection of records can be turned into a sequential data set.

Access Methods

Once a data set organization has been selected two or more access methods are available from MVS to help process the records in the data set. An access method is a system program that performs the actual I/O requested by an application program. When an I/O operation is to be executed a call is made to the access method, and appropriate parameters are passed to it. After the I/O is performed the access method returns control to the application program which called it. As mentioned above, there are two or more access methods associated with each of the four data set organizations. The nature of the I/O request determines which access method performs the function. An application program cannot ordinarily request a specific access method directly. Rather, a particular access method is chosen based on the other parameters involved in the operation being performed. Table 9–2 identifies the access methods that are available with the four data set organizations.

The letters 'AM' stand for access method, 'Q' stands for queued, and 'B' stands for basic. Note that there are two access methods available with sequential data sets, QSAM and BSAM. Both QSAM and BSAM are also available to process the members of a partitioned data set. Recall that the members are themselves sequential data sets. The BPAM access method is also available with a partitioned data set. It is used only for processing the directory. With direct data sets two basic access methods are supplied. With both sequential and indexed organization there is one queued and one basic access method. Finally, notice that the BSAM access method is available with both sequential and direct data sets. This implies that some type of similarity must exist between these two data set organizations.

TABLE 9–1

Data Set Organizations

Data Set Organization	*Common Names*	*I/O Devices Allowed*	*Backup Utility*	*Sequential Processing*	*Random Processing*	*Disk Overhead*
Sequential	QSAM BSAM	unitrecord tape disk	yes IEBGENER	excellent fastest	not possible	none
Indexed	ISAM	disk	yes IEBISAM	slower than sequential	good	index keys
Direct	direct relative REGIONAL BDAM	disk	possibly IEBGENER	very rarely done except for backup	excellent	possibly keys
Partitioned	library or pds	disk	yes IEBCOPY	excellent for the members in the pds	not possible for the members	directory keys

There are three major distinctions between the queued and basic access methods: the amount of work the access method is responsible for performing, the complexity of the processing, and how control is returned to the application program. The queued access methods handle blocking and buffering automatically, with no work or worry on the programmers' part. When a basic access method is used the application program is responsible for all blocking and buffering. Blocking and buffering

TABLE 9–2

Access Methods

Data Set Organization	*Access Methods*	
Sequential	QSAM (Queued Sequential)	BSAM (Basic Sequential)
Indexed	QISAM (Queued Index Sequential)	BISAM (Basic Index Sequential)
Direct	BSAM (Basic Sequential)	BDAM (Basic Direct)
Partitioned	QSAM and BSAM (for the members)	BPAM (Basic Partitioned for the directory)

are examined in more detail below. Both topics can be quite complex, so in most situations a programmer is only too happy to assign the blocking and buffering responsibilities to the access method. The queued access methods support a more limited range of I/O operations than do the comparable basic access methods. The queued access methods are used with sequential processing, while basic access methods are used for both sequential and random processing. The third major difference between the queued and basic access methods concerns their methods of returning control to the application program: queued do not return control until the operation is complete. Hence the application program is suspended during the I/O operation. Basic access methods return control when the operation is scheduled. The application must then determine when the operation is finished. In an assembler program this involves issuing a CHECK macro instruction after every READ or WRITE operation. The CHECK statement suspends execution until the operation is complete.

It is possible to perform I/O operations without calling an access method. This is usually only done in an assembler language program. It requires a great deal of additional work on the programmer's part.

Blocking and Buffering

At this point it is necessary to define the terms physical record (block), logical record, and buffer.

A physical record is a contiguous area of data stored on an I/O device. It is physically disjoint from the adjacent physical records that precede and follow it. When an application program requests an I/O operation to be performed, it is a physical record that is read or written. A physical record is often referred to as a block.

A logical record consists of the data that an application program 'appears' to be reading or writing as the result of one specific I/O statement. An I/O device is completely unaware of the concept of a logical record. The application program and access method combine to determine where one logical record ends and another begins. Most frequently a logical record is a subset of a physical record. It may be a proper subset of a physical record, or may occupy the entire physical record. With one type of record format a single logical record may occupy several physical records. The word 'record,' when unqualified, can imply either physical or logical record. Often the meaning can be determined from the context in which it is used. The major point to be noted is that application programs process logical records and I/O devices process physical records.

A buffer is an area in memory that is contained within the application program's region or address space. A buffer is used in two situations: it holds data preliminary to writing it to an I/O device, and holds the data after it is read from an I/O device. Hence data passes through a buffer on its way to and from the I/O device. Ordinarily two or more buffers are provided for each data set processed by a program.

The queued access methods can distinguish between physical and logical records. With the basic access methods all I/O statements in an application program process physical records. This places strong restrictions on the data set organizations and processing that are permitted. The language translator used to write a program can also influence the choice of an access method. For example, the COBOL compiler selects QSAM with almost all sequential data sets.

The definitions for physical record, logical record, and buffer will be clarified by considering how I/O is performed in a COBOL application program using QSAM.

Example 1: Assume that a disk data set consists of several physical records of 300 bytes each. Each physical record contains three logical records. Logical records are 100 bytes in length. Suppose there are 10 logical records and 4 physical records in the data set. The last physical record or block contains only 100 bytes. The other blocks are 'full' and contain 300 bytes each. The corresponding file description and 01 level in the COBOL program is written as

```
FD   DISK-FILE
     BLOCK CONTAINS 3 RECORDS
     RECORD CONTAINS 100 CHARACTERS
     LABEL RECORDS ARE STANDARD.
01   DISK-REC          PIC X(100).
```

Two 300 byte buffers are provided to hold the data as it is read in from disk. After the first READ statement is executed both buffers have been filled with the contents of the first two physical records from disk. The status of the buffers is pictured in Figure 9–1, where Li represents logical record i:

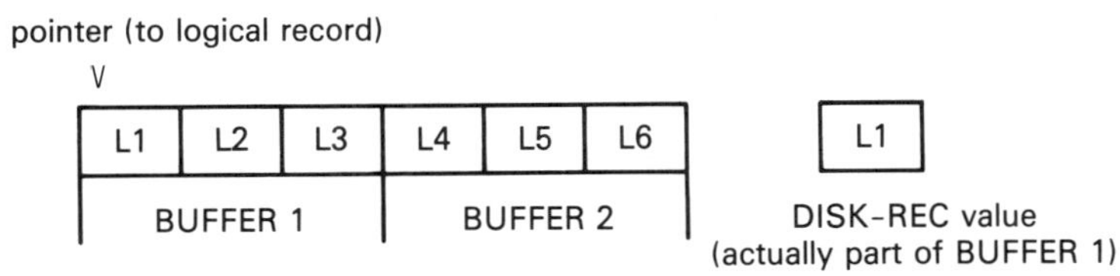

FIGURE 9–1
Buffers After First Logical READ

In addition to reading the first two physical records from disk (a total of 2 I/O operations), a pointer is set to the logical record currently being processed (here L1, the first logical record in the data set). The contents of L1 may be referenced through the COBOL variable DISK-REC, the 01 level in the FD. Thus it is possible to identify the 01 level associated with an FD as part of the buffer area.

When the second READ statement is executed no actual I/O is performed. Rather, the logical record pointer advances to L2, the second logical record. The contents of L2 are now available through DISK-REC. Unless the contents of L1 had been moved to a storage area within the region prior to the second READ, the data in L1 can no longer be referenced. The contents of the buffers at this point are pictured in Figure 9–2.

When the third READ statement executes the logical record pointer advances to L3. The contents of L3 are now accessible through DISK-REC. Note that no actual I/O is performed when the second and third READ statements execute.

FIGURE 9–2
Buffers After Second READ

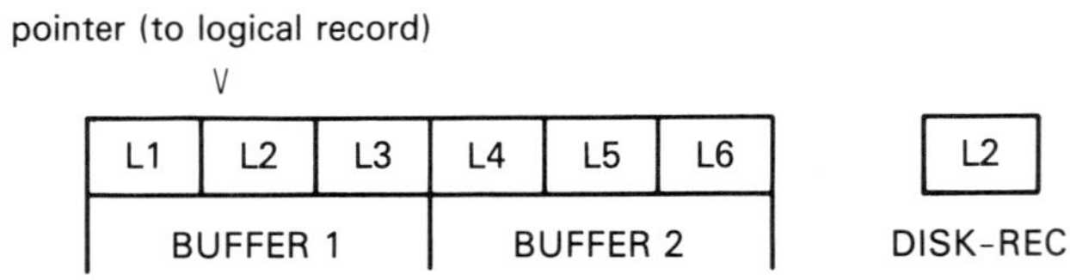

The fourth READ statement advances the logical record pointer to L4, the first logical record in the second physical record. The contents of L4 are now available through DISK-REC. Concurrent with this an additional I/O operation is performed: the third physical record is read into BUFFER 1. The contents of the buffers at this point are pictured in Figure 9–3.

After three more logical records are processed a fourth physical READ is performed: L10 is read into buffer 2. The final four READS are all logical, since all of the disk data has been read. The eleventh READ statement detects that End of File (EOF) has been reached; there are no records left to process. A READ following End of File will ordinarily cause the program to abend. Once End Of File is reached no more processing is possible, and the data set should be closed.

In addition to double buffering, several other variations are possible. A data set can be processed with a single buffer or more than two buffers. With a single buffer only one physical record is available in the application program's region. This means that the program requires less memory. However, when only one buffer is available I/O operations cannot be overlapped with other processing. Suppose a single buffer is used with the data set in Example 1. When the fourth READ statement is executed the application program must wait for the I/O to be performed before processing can continue. When two buffers are used the disk I/O can be performed preliminary to the actual READ request. This is often called anticipatory buffering. When large data sets with small blocking factors are processed double buffering can save considerable time. This is the reason that the default number of buffers for a sequential data set is usually two or more.

If double buffering is good, is triple buffering better? Here three buffers are initially filled. Following this a physical record is read whenever all the logical records in a buffer have been processed. Clearly, the I/O operations can overlap other processing in the program. A disadvantage of triple buffering is that the application program requires more memory. Are there any advantages? This depends on whether the time it takes to read a physical record into the buffer is greater than the time needed for the overlapped processing with double buffering. If it is then the program must still wait for I/O to be performed, and triple buffering will decrease processing time. If it is not then double buffering is just as good as triple buffering. The same

FIGURE 9–3
Buffers After Fourth READ

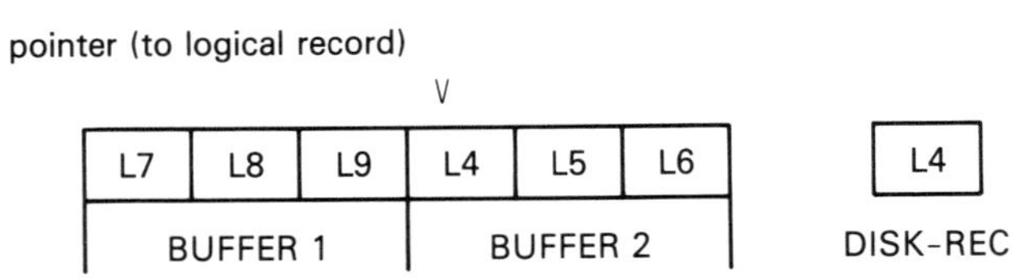

considerations apply when deciding to use four or more buffers. The number of buffers can be specified either through JCL or within the application program. It is not stored as part of the data set labels or in the pass table for an existing data set.

EXCP stands for execute channel program. A channel program must be executed whenever an I/O operation is performed. The channel program is executed concurrent with the CPU processing application programs. When the channel program finishes executing it may interrupt the CPU to inform it that it is done. With MVS/XA, the I/O subsystem does not interrupt MVS. A counter keeps track of the number of real I/O operations performed. In a printout EXCPS = xxxxx means that xxxxx I/O operations were performed by the program. Many computer installations have a specific charge for each EXCP performed. Hence, the more real I/O operations performed, the greater the cost of running the program. This is a very significant benefit derived from blocking the records in a data set. In fact, performing fewer I/O operations is one of the two most important reasons for blocking. To save money and computer resources a program should minimize the number of I/O operations performed. One way to do this is to block the records. The other major reason for blocking records is to conserve storage on the I/O device. This is examined in detail in Chapters 15 and 16.

The above discussion on blocking and buffering applies to a queued access method. With both QSAM and QISAM the physical records are automatically deblocked on input by the access method. The access method then supplies the specific logical record to the application program. On output logical records are 'written' until a buffer is filled. Then the contents of the buffer are written to disk.

Example 2: Suppose that the FD defined in Example 1 is used to write records to a tape or disk data set. Hence, three 100 byte logical records comprise one physical record. When the data set is opened the two buffers have undefined values. The logical record pointer references the first 100 bytes of BUFFER 1. Values are moved to the fields in DISK-REC or to an area in WORKING-STORAGE. A WRITE DISK-REC or WRITE DISK-REC FROM WORKING-STORAGE-FIELD statement is executed. The pointer then advances to the beginning of the second logical record. The contents of the buffers following the first WRITE statement are pictured in Figure 9–4.

This is why a DISPLAY statement should always precede a WRITE statement when both reference the contents of an output buffer area. After the second and third logical records are written the first physical write takes place. At this point both buffers again contain undefined values.

With the basic access methods there is no logical record concept. Hence all blocking and deblocking must be performed by the application program. This is an

FIGURE 9–4

Buffers After First Logical WRITE

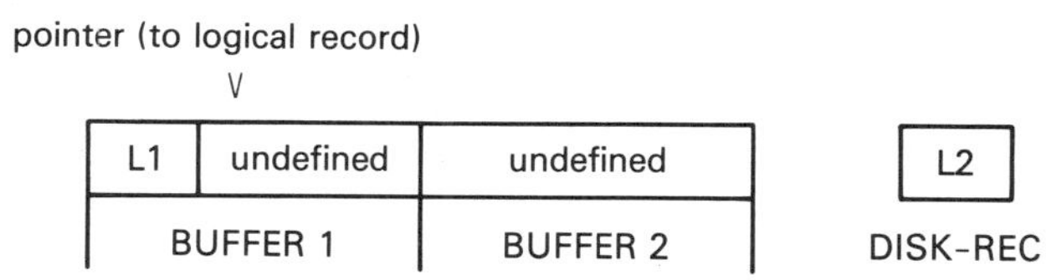

additional burden for the application programmer to handle. It is often said that the basic access methods do not support blocked records, but this is not completely true. Blocking is permitted: however, the access method does not provide help. The program itself must do the work. This includes monitoring the number of logical records contained in a physical record, determining the boundaries of the logical records, acquiring and releasing storage for buffers, and processing short blocks.

When should a data set not be blocked? If the access method makes the application program responsible for the blocking, records are usually unblocked. Hence partitioned data set directories and direct data sets are not blocked. Even with direct data sets blocking could be performed. The access methods used with the data set organization do not perform the blocking automatically.

Records are blocked in order to process as many of them as quickly and cheaply as possible. With random processing one specific record must be read or written. If the record is part of a block the entire block must be processed, because only physical records may be read or written. Thus, for an indexed data set where most processing is random, records are often not blocked at all. If they are blocked a small blocking factor is used. Large blocking factors are appropriate if the transactions that determine the records to be randomly retrieved are batched and sorted into ascending order before processing.

When most processing of an indexed data set is sequential the data set should be blocked like a sequential data set. Since sequential data sets do not support random processing, they should routinely be blocked. The best blocking factor for a sequential data set is one that makes optimal use of the I/O device and performs the desired function of the processing program. With disk data sets the rule of thumb is to block as large as possible without wasting large portions of the disk surface, exceeding one track in size, or using exorbitantly large amounts of storage for buffers. With tape data sets the rule of thumb is to block as large as possible without using exorbitantly large amounts of buffer storage.

Remember that when a data set is blocked, buffers the size of the physical records must be supplied from the region allocated to the application program. Buffers occupy real storage during an I/O operation. If several data sets which have large block sizes are all opened by the same program, additional storage may need to be requested by the program. On modern virtual storage systems like MVS this should not be used as a reason for failing to adequately block sequential data sets. However, it is also important not to go overboard on blocking. Many large buffers can monopolize I/O paths and channel time.

Chapters 15 and 16 discuss ideal block sizes. The minimum and maximum sizes of physical records are also covered there. Chapters 12, 13, and 14 discuss blocking with regard to the data set organizations they describe.

I/O Concepts and JCL

It will be made clear in Chapter 10, that it is usually unnecessary to specify the values for blocking, buffering, physical and logical records, and access methods through JCL. Other ways exist to supply these values to the system. Except for the access method and type of processing (sequential or random), all the topics discussed in this chapter can be specified as part of the DCB parameter on a DD statement associated with a data set. The access method cannot be explicitly requested on a JCL statement. Rather, as explained earlier, it is a combination of the other factors in the processing that determine the choice of access method. Likewise, only the application program can specify sequential or random processing.

The size of a physical record is specified by the BLKSIZE subparameter. The size of a logical record is given by the LRECL subparameter. Data set organization is specified with the DSORG subparameter. The number of buffers available for processing the data set is coded on the BUFNO subparameter. Special processing options are listed on the OPTCD subparameter. The format of the logical records and their relationship to physical records is specified on the RECFM subparameter. A detailed discussion of the RECFM subparameter appears in Chapter 11. A summary of these important DCB subparameters, their meanings, and where they are further discussed in this text appears below. Recall that a detailed description of each subparameter with an emphasis on JCL syntax is presented in Chapter 7.

DCB Subparameter	*General Description*	*Additional Material in Text*
BLKSIZE	physical record size	RECFM,Disk,Tape,DCB
LRECL	logical record size	RECFM,Disk,Tape,DCB
RECFM	record format	RECFM,DCB,IEBGENER
DSORG	data set organization	RECFM,DCB,Disk
BUFNO	number of buffers	DCB
BUFTEK	type of buffering	
KEYLEN/RKP	record keys (length and location)	DCB,ISAM,DIRECT
OPTCD	special processing options	DCB,ISAM,DIRECT,Disk Tape

Table 9–3 shows the relationship between the DCB subparameters on a DD statement and the corresponding COBOL syntax.

TABLE 9–3
DCB Subparameters and COBOL Syntax

DCB Subparameter on DD Statement	*COBOL Program FD or SELECT Statement*
RECFM	RECORDING MODE clause or a default selected by compiler
BLKSIZE	BLOCK CONTAINS clause - if no clause, then file is unblocked; BLOCK CONTAINS 0, defers to value in the JCL or labels
LRECL	01 structure in the FD not the RECORD CONTAINS clause
KEYLEN	KEY clause in SELECT statement and PIC clause with data item
RKP	KEY clause in SELECT statement and offset in the 01 structure
BUFNO	RESERVE x AREAS clause
OPTCD	some values can be specified in the I-O-CONTROL SECTION
DSORG	ASSIGN clause in SELECT statement

TABLE 9–4
Storage of DCB Values

DCB Subparameter on DD Statement	*Data Set Label Disk and Tape*
BLKSIZE	YES
LRECL	YES
RECFM	YES
DSORG	YES(Disk) Tape = PS
KEYLEN	YES(Disk) Tape = not applicable
RKP	YES(Disk) Tape = not applicable
BUFNO	NO
OPTCD	SOME

Table 9–4 shows which DCB values are stored in the data set labels for disk and tape data sets.

Exercises

1. Suppose that a disk data set is to be written with logical records of length 100 bytes and blocked with a blocking factor of 2. An application program has 3 buffers provided in which to build the physical records prior to writing them to disk. Describe the exact steps needed to write the eleven records in the data set to disk using QSAM. Show the contents of the buffers and the current logical record at every step in the processing. If BSAM is to be used, how will the processing change?

2. The records in the data set created in the previous exercise are to be read. Describe the exact steps needed to read the eleven records. Show the contents of the buffers and the current logical record at every step in the processing. Assume that BUFNO = 2 has been coded on the DD statement for the data set.

3. The 01-level of an FD in a COBOL program must be examined. Which of the following combinations of statements will give a correct value for the DISPLAY? For the other DISPLAY statement, what values will be displayed?

```
DISPLAY DISK-REC.        or        WRITE   DISK-REC.
WRITE   DISK-REC.                  DISPLAY DISK-REC.
```

4. It is claimed that random updating can be performed more efficiently if the transaction records are presorted into ascending order prior to processing. List several specific advantages of this approach. List several specific disadvantages. Which of the four data set organizations supports more efficient random processing if the transaction records are presorted?

5. For each of the non-VSAM data set organizations, list the access methods that may be used to process the records in it. Describe their basic processing properties.

6. Select the best data set organization for each of the following applications. Describe the underlying file structure and defend your choice of a particular data set organization.

a) A payroll program for a very large company which is run every other week.
b) Updating the amount of money in a bank checking account.
c) Determining the owner of a car based on the license plate number.
d) Using an automatic teller to determine the balance in a checking account.
e) Determining a person's correct name based on knowing just the first several letters.
f) Using Social Security number to retrieve tax information for a specific year at the main IRS computer center.
g) Making a grade change in a student records file.
h) Producing a monthly summary statement showing all transactions in a checking account.

Chapter 10

Data Control Block

Overview

In order to process a non-VSAM data set, a data control block (dcb) must be constructed for it. The dcb contains information about the records in the data set that the system requires in order to perform I/O operations with the data set. There are a great many fields in a dcb. The important entries are logical record length (LRECL), physical record length (BLKSIZE), record format (RECFM), data set organization (DSORG), key length and location (KEYLEN and RKP), buffer information (BUFNO and BUFTEK), special processing options (OPTCD), the types of I/O operations permitted (MACFM), end of file processing (EODAD or AT END in COBOL), the number of outstanding I/O requests (NCP), and the name of the accompanying DD statement (DDNAME). All of the dcb fields should be assigned values before attempting to use the data set in an I/O operation. Hence the dcb for a data set should be constructed when the data set is initially opened.

How do values get placed in the dcb? There are three major sources that supply these values: the DCB macro instruction in the application program itself, the DCB parameter on the associated DD statement in the JCL, and for an existing disk data set or Standard Label tape data set the data set labels. Some dcb fields may be assigned a value from any one of these three sources or from all of them. Logical record length and physical record length are two such entries. At the other extreme, some dcb entries can be assigned a value from exactly one of the three sources. For example, the types of I/O macros allowable for processing the data set can be specified only in the DCB macro in the application program. Different macros may be selected if the data set is processed a second time. DCB macro is an assembler language term. In a COBOL program the DCB macro for a data set is constructed from a combination of the entries found in the SELECT, FD, and OPEN statements. Note the terminology used here. The DCB macro is one of three sources used to construct the data control block (dcb). During data set creation the dcb entries are assigned values from just two sources since data set labels are not present to supply values. In fact, it is at this time that the labels are created from the entries in the dcb.

An abend usually occurs when processing a data set whose dcb contains incorrect or uninitialized entries. For example, an S001-4 abend occurs when a COBOL program attempts to read a blocked data set and the FD for the file contains either no BLOCK CONTAINS clause or a clause with too small a value. The data set can be opened successfully; but on the first READ the abend results when an attempt is made to retrieve a physical record whose size is greater than the buffer size for the data set. With COBOL this problem can be avoided by coding BLOCK CONTAINS 0 RECORDS in the FD for the file. This phrase means that the COBOL application program will not supply the physical record length. Rather, the BLKSIZE value is gotten from the JCL or the data set labels. When a COBOL program creates a data set and BLOCK CONTAINS 0 RECORDS is coded, the BLKSIZE parameter must be coded in the JCL.

Construction of the dcb

Every field in the dcb must be assigned a unique value. However, it is possible that a distinct value can be provided from each of the major sources. When this happens the value in the DCB macro has precedence over the other two. The value coded on the DD statement has a higher priority than the value found in the data set label. There are also situations where a dcb can be completed or have values modified after the data set is opened. These latter two possibilities are usually restricted to assembler language programs.

The construction and use of a dcb is a seven step process. Although these seven steps are language–independent the discussion here emphasizes a COBOL program that is to be compiled and then executed. The basic ideas remain the same for all of the major programming languages.

Example 1: Consider the following job stream which contains the cataloged procedure to perform a COBOL Compile and Go:

```
//A     EXEC COBUCG
//COB.SYSIN DD *
   . . .
   COBOL source code is placed here. It includes a SELECT
   and FD for each data set the program processes. For
   example,
   . . .
     SELECT DISK-FILE
     ASSIGN TO UT-S-XYFILE.
   . . .
     FD DISK-FILE
   . . .
/*
//GO.XYFILE DD DSN=ABC.DEF,DISP=(NEW,PASS),UNIT=3350,
//     SPACE=(CYL,(1,1)),DCB=(BLKSIZE=800,RECFM=FB,LRECL=80)
```

The Job Scheduler reads the above JCL, and a Job File Control Block (JFCB) is created for each DD statement coded. The JFCB contains all the information that can be explicitly or implicitly determined about the data set using just the information coded on the DD statement. The information placed in the JFCB is not accessed until the data set is opened.

The COBOL compiler analyzes the source code and constructs a DCB macro for every FD in the program. The DCB macro code is included as part of the object module. Either the loader (above) or the linkage editor is then used to create a load module which is eventually placed into memory. It is only during program execution that the information from the DCB macro and the corresponding JFCB are combined. With COBOL they are tied together by the ASSIGN clause of the SELECT statement. Here XYFILE implies that a DD Statement with DDname XYFILE or GO.XYFILE should be associated with the FD DISK-FILE. The DSN parameter on the DD statement is then used to connect the JFCB and the data set itself. This process is pictured in Figure 10–1.

Notice that the COBOL program does not know the name of the data set or even what type of device contains it (disk, tape, or unit record). The seven steps involved in the construction and use of a dcb are pictured in Figure 10–2.

A detailed description of the processing which takes place in each of the seven steps follows:

Step 1 The dcb is constructed when the application program opens the data set. All values coded in the DCB macro are assigned to corresponding fields in the dcb. With COBOL these values are supplied by the SELECT, FD, OPEN, and the I/O–related statements associated with the file. In assembler they come directly from the DCB Statement. In PL/I they are supplied by the DECLARE, OPEN, and I/O-related statements.

Step 2 When the JCL for the job step is initially scanned by the Job Scheduler a Job File Control Block (JFCB) is created to hold all information about the data set that can be gathered from the DD Statement. This is done for every DD Statement in the job stream, even DUMMY data sets.

Step 3 When the data set is opened the fields in the JFCB that have not been assigned a value may get a value from the data set label. This can only occur when labels for the data set already exist. If the data set is opened for input this takes place with both disk data sets and Standard Label tape data sets.

FIGURE 10–1
The Three Sources of Data Control Block Values

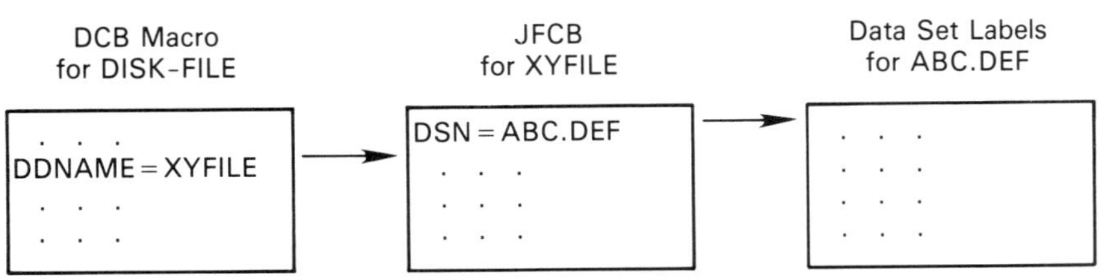

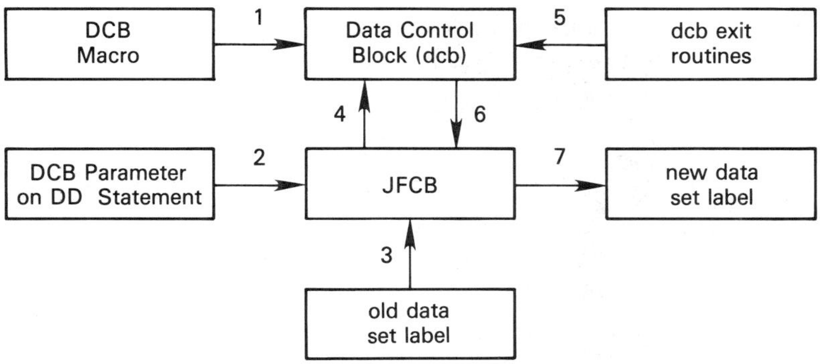

FIGURE 10–2
Construction and Use of a Data Control Block

Notice that if a value had been assigned on the DD statement the corresponding value in the data set label will not be used. This ignored value is usually the 'correct' value. At this point some fields in the JFCB may still be uninitialized. For more information on the fields that are contained within the data set labels see Chapters 15 and 16.

Step 4 Every field in the dcb that has not been assigned a value will now get one from the corresponding field in the JFCB if that field in the JFCB has been assigned a value. All fields in the dcb that contain values prior to Step 4 remain unchanged during the step. In most cases Step 4 completes the construction of the dcb.

Step 5 After a data set is opened any missing dcb values can be provided and existing values can be modified. This is not ordinarily done in a COBOL program.

Step 6 When processing is completed the data set is closed. If the data set had been used for an output operation (either creation or extension) all dcb fields except for DSORG are unconditionally copied into the corresponding JFCB fields. The DSORG field in the JFCB gets a value from the dcb only if it is undefined. If the data set is used for input, values are copied from the dcb to the JFCB only when the corresponding JFCB field has not been assigned a value.

Step 7 After the data set is closed the dcb is restored to the state it had before the data set was opened. Also, if the data set had been used for an output operation the modified JFCB (as constructed in Step 6) is used to write the labels for the data set. This can lead to potential problems with partitioned data sets. Specifically, it allows members with different dcb properties to be stored in the same pds. Because of Step 7 it is also possible to extend a sequential data set and assign different dcb properties to the extension than those which the existing data set had. Both of these dcb irregularities are further examined in the exercises.

When processing is finished the data set should be closed. If the application program does not close it the system will automatically close all non-VSAM data sets except for ISAM when the step is completed.

Example 2: To further illustrate the fundamental steps involved in building the dcb, carefully examine Figure 10–3. Step numbers are the same as above. Consider the five objects in Figure 10–3 (the DCB macro, the DCB parameter on the DD statement, the data set label, the JFCB, and the dcb) as tables. Each table entry can hold a specific dcb value. For simplicity it is assumed here that the dcb consists of exactly seven fields all the same size. To clarify the discussion assume that these fields can be referenced using the values 1 through 7. If a slot in a table is blank the corresponding field has not been assigned a value. The four values supplied by the DCB macro (relative positions 1, 3, 4, and 7) become entries in the dcb. The three remaining dcb fields must be assigned values from the other two sources. Note that the four values coded on the DD statement are all present in the JFCB. The two remaining JFCB fields are assigned values from the data set labels. Most of the values in the data set label are ignored. The middle position in the JFCB is undefined. Finally, in Step 4 three of the values from the JFCB are copied to the dcb.

FIGURE 10–3
Building the Data Control Block

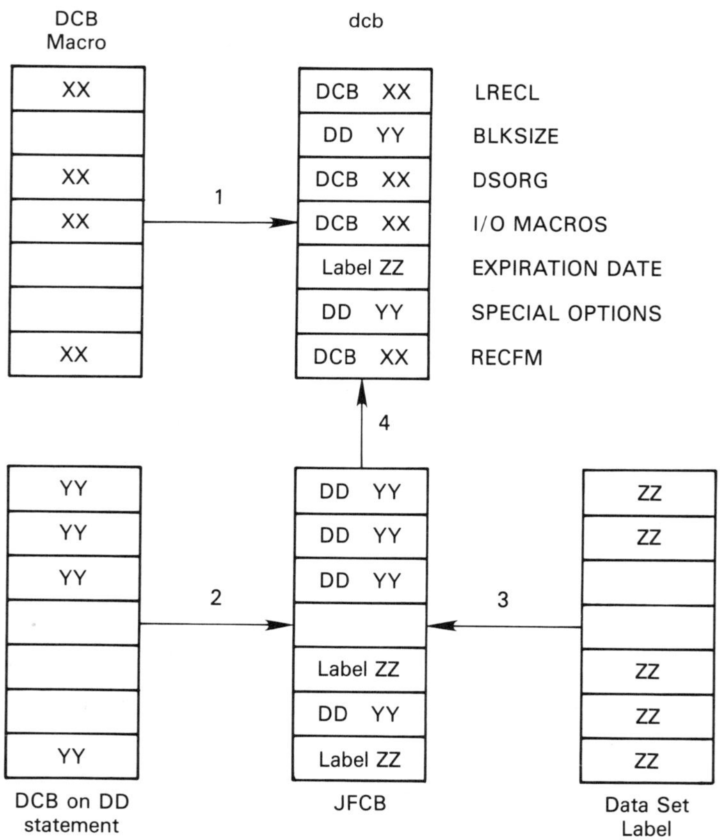

Programming Techniques Related to the Data Control Block

MVS programmers should understand how the dcb is constructed. This is another area in which a person who understands it codes considerably less JCL. Three major points should be noted:

1. It is unnecessary to supply a specific dcb value from two or three different sources; one will suffice. In particular, if a data set has labels let the system use the values in those labels. Coding the same values on the DD statement is redundant and error prone. When differences exist between the two the incorrect values are used. This applies to all the standard DD parameters, including BLKSIZE, RECFM, and LRECL. Of course the application program values can still override the JFCB values.

2. Values coded in the DCB macro will always appear in the dcb, so it is unnecessary to repeat them on the DD statement. In a COBOL program, for example, all the common DD parameters will be assigned values by the DCB macro. A possible exception to this is BLKSIZE. Coding BLOCK CONTAINS 0 RECORDS means that the blocking factor is not being supplied by the DCB macro and must come from one of the other two sources. Coding any other BLOCK CONTAINS value or omitting the clause altogether means that the block size has been assigned a value. Consequently a BLKSIZE subparameter coded on the DD statement will be ignored. When constructing the dcb JCL values coded for RECFM, LRECL, DSORG, KEYLEN, and RKP are ignored with a COBOL program since the COBOL compiler always supplies these values. Some important OPTCD values must be supplied through JCL or data set labels since they cannot be specified in a COBOL program.

3. The amount of coding in the DCB parameter on the DD statement should be minimized. A great deal of the coding in the DCB serves no purpose except as an invitation to trouble.

Exercises

1. For each of the major dcb fields (LRECL, BLKSIZE, RECFM, DSORG, KEYLEN, RKP, BUFNO, BUFTEK, OPTCD, MACFM, EODAD, and DDNAME) describe the specific COBOL syntax used to assign it a value in the DCB Macro.

2. Under what conditions can a value coded with a COBOL application program (for example LRECL, BLKSIZE, RECFM, DSORG, KEYLEN, RKP, BUFNO, BUFTEK, OPTCD, MACFM, EODAD, and DDNAME) not be placed in the resulting dcb for a data set?

3. When creating an ISAM data set with a COBOL program, is it necessary to code KEYLEN and RKP in the DCB parameter on the accompanying DD statement? What values should

be coded in the DCB parameter when creating an ISAM data set with a COBOL program? When processing an existing ISAM data set, what values should be coded in the DCB parameter on the DD statement? Explain the reason for each value selected.

4. When creating a DIRECT data set with a COBOL program, is it necessary to code KEY-LEN and RKP in the DCB parameter on the accompanying DD statement? What values should be coded in the DCB parameter when creating a DIRECT data set with a COBOL program? When processing an existing DIRECT data set, what values should be coded in the DCB parameter on the DD statement? Explain the reason for each value selected.

5. This exercise requires some additional material from Chapter 11. Each of the following four DCB subparameter values may possibly be placed in the dcb when coded on the DD statement with a COBOL application program: RECFM, BLKSIZE, DSORG, and OPTCD. Give specific circumstances when each parameter must be coded in order to get the correct results. For each such circumstance create a simple example, omit the parameter, and examine the resulting output.

6. Create a disk data set consisting of twenty 80 byte records. Block them using a blocking factor of 5 and close the data set. Open the data set and add 30 additional records to it. These should be 125 byte records, blocked with a blocking factor of 10. In a separate step print out all the records in this data set in one pass. Use either a COBOL program or a utility. Create the same data set on Standard Label tape. Examine the header and trailer labels. They contain different dcb values! This is explained in Chapter 16.

7. Create a pds and add three members to it. Each should be added in a separate job step. Select a different LRECL, BLKSIZE, and RECFM value for each of the three members. In a single jobstep print out the records in the three members.

Chapter 11

(Non-VSAM) Record Formats

Overview

Five record formats are available on MVS systems. They are available with every major programming language. In this book all five record formats are considered as completely distinct. In actuality some are subsets of others. The D or ASCII record format is used so rarely that only its existence is mentioned here. For more information about record formats in general, consult the IBM manual *MVS DATA MANAGEMENT SERVICES GUIDE*.

A non-VSAM data set contains records classified in one of the five categories listed below:

F format or fixed length records

V format or variable length records

U format or undefined or unspecified records

S format or (variable) spanned records

D format or ASCII records (the other four formats are EBCDIC records)

Two of the five record formats, V and S, can also be used when processing VSAM data sets, since VSAM treats fixed-length records the same as variable-length records. The equivalent of F, V, and S formats are available with VSAM.

Data sets that contain fixed length records are the easiest to visualize and use in programming. Every logical record in the data set must contain the same number of bytes. It is unnecessary to include additional overhead bytes to hold the actual length of a record. The length of every logical record can be determined from the data control block. Any logical record in a physical record can be located by determining its displacement from the beginning of the block. For example, in a physical record (block) which contains fixed length card images, logical record 6 begins at byte displacement 400. Here 400 = (6-1) * 80.

Unfortunately, not all data sets lend themselves to representation with fixed length records. Suppose a data set exists where each record includes the courses and grades that a student has taken while in college. A freshman record will be considerably smaller than that of a graduating senior. It would be tremendously wasteful to 'pad' all records out to the size of the maximum possible record associated with any student. In situations such as this the record format should be specified as variable, undefined, or spanned. These three formats allow physical and logical records of different lengths in the same data set. However, all three record formats can cause complications not present with fixed length records.

If logical records are not fixed length some method must be used to determine where each record begins. With variable and spanned a header field is added to each logical record. This field identifies the beginning of a record. Undefined records are unblocked, and every physical record contains one logical record.

Advantages and Disadvantages of V, U, and S Record Formats

Format V records may be used when the length of the logical records in a data set can vary. It is possible to 'pad' such records with a fill character to make them the same length for processing as format F. Often this is impractical because of the wide range in lengths among the records. Since the number of bytes in the records within the data set is variable, some additional information is included with each logical record. This overhead includes the length in bytes of the logical record. Since physical records are composed of logical records, blocks can also vary in size. Thus every physical record also needs some accompanying overhead information that will enable the appropriate number of bytes to be transmitted to or from an I/O device. Determining if a variable length record format should be used for a data set is often a difficult question. Will the savings gained from using the exact size to store each record outweigh the disadvantages? The disadvantages include the overhead associated with every physical and logical record, the strong possibility of programming logic more complicated than with fixed length records, and limitations on the ways a data set can be organized.

Format U records are a second type of variable length record format. The records in such a data set can again take on a range of values. Here no overhead information precedes the records. Rather, each physical record contains exactly one logical record, and the physical record length equals the logical record length. When format U records are written to disk the logical (or physical) record length is placed in the COUNT field. The typical application program uses variable records more often than undefined records, since undefined records are not blocked by the system. However, there are several common situations where undefined records are encountered. The Linkage Editor writes format U records when creating a load module. If variable length records were somehow created without overhead fields, they could not be processed as format V records, but could be processed as format U records. To examine the overhead fields associated with a variable record it can be processed as an undefined record. To determine the contents of an NL tape data set the physical records it contains can be printed by specifying DCB values of RECFM=U and BLKSIZE=maximum-value with a utility such as IDCAMS. Transmitted data that can be of varying length can be represented as format U records.

Format S records are a third type of variable length record format. Here a logical record need not be contained within a single physical record. Logical records can also exceed physical records in size. There are several advantages to using spanned records. Device dependency is reduced. If data are stored on a 3330 disk all blocks must be less than 13,030 bytes in length. If this data set is moved to a 3350 disk longer blocks can be written. With spanned records there is no reason to worry about the maximum block size. Rather, specify the block size that is appropriate for the data set. Pick a value that optimizes the use of disk space and buffer space. When using spanned records it is possible to specify that records be split between two or more tracks. Code OPTCD=T to do this. For some data sets adroit usage of spanned records can utilize an I/O device even more efficiently than V format does. Like variable records, spanned records may be blocked. Since S format records are a subset of V format records, they include all the disadvantages associated with V format records. There are also additional disadvantages associated with spanned records. They require a more elaborate (and larger) buffer area for dealing with the multiple physical records which may comprise one logical record. An additional piece of overhead required with every part of a logical record is an indicator identifying it as the beginning, middle, or end segment of the logical record or as an unsegmented record. Spanned records are not permitted in partitioned data sets, although they are allowed with sequential data sets.

Either variable, undefined, or spanned must be specified for the record format if the logical records in a data set do not have the same length. If logical records can exceed physical records in size the data set must be S format. No matter which of the four record formats is coded when the data set is created, it can later be processed as a format U data set. If this is done and the records had originally been blocked the application must somehow deblock them.

Specifying a Record Format

When creating a data set there are several ways to specify a record format. It can be coded as a subparameter of the DCB keyword parameter on a DD statement (e.g., DCB=(RECFM=x, . . .) where x is F, V, U, VS, or D). Other letters can be concatenated to these, such as RECFM=BF or RECFM=VBA. Here B specifies that the records are blocked and A specifies that the first byte of each record can be used as a carriage control character. More information on the syntax of the RECFM subparameter can be found in the discussion of the DCB parameter in Chapter 7.

Record format can also be specified in an application program, either explicitly or implicitly. With COBOL, the clause RECORDING MODE IS x may be coded in the FD for a file. Here x is either F, V, U, or S. When uncertain as to how the COBOL compiler will select a default record format value, code the RECORDING MODE clause. If the record format is specified within an application program then in almost every case the value coded in the DCB parameter on the associated DD statement for the data set will be ignored. Exceptions are very rare.

The COBOL compiler considers three factors when selecting a default record format.

(1) Are all logical records in the file the same size? This occurs when either of the following hold:

(a) There is one record description (01 level) for the file and it contains no OCCURS DEPENDING ON clause.
(b) There is more than one record description for the file but all of them contain the same number of bytes and no OCCURS DEPENDING ON clauses.

(2) How are logical records and physical records related? When a BLOCK CONTAINS 0 CHARACTERS or BLOCK CONTAINS 0 RECORDS clause is coded this relationship cannot be determined by the COBOL compiler.

(a) If a BLOCK CONTAINS clause specifies BLOCK CONTAINS a TO b CHARACTERS and b is less than the length of the largest 01 record, then the file will be interpreted as S format. This can occur even when all of the logical records are the same size.
(b) If b is greater than or equal to the maximum length of the 01 records S format will never be selected by default.
(c) If a BLOCK CONTAINS clause is not coded format S will never be selected by default.

(3) How is the data set organized? Whether the file is sequential, indexed, direct, or relative has a bearing on the default record format selected. With COBOL all ISAM and relative files must contain fixed length records. Direct files and sequential files can contain any of the four record formats.

The COBOL compiler selects a default record format as follows: A file is F format if all records are the same size and b as defined above is greater than or equal to the length of the 01 record(s). The file is U format if the length of a logical record does not exceed that of a physical record, the file has direct organization, and the records in the file can have different lengths. The last can occur if the FD for the file contains two or more level 01 record descriptions of different length, if a record description for the file contains an OCCURS DEPENDING ON clause, or if a RECORD CONTAINS clause specifies a range of record lengths. The manner in which a file is classified as V format is exactly the same as for U format except that physical sequential file replaces direct file in the SELECT statement. Format S is the default only when a BLOCK CONTAINS clause specifies fewer characters than a logical record may contain.

No matter which record format is coded when a data set is created, any compatible record format can be used to subsequently process the data set. Hence a data set created with RECFM=V could be successfully processed with RECFM=U if the records were unblocked. If the original records were blocked and RECFM=U was then coded they would have to be unblocked in the application program.

Fixed Length Records

Fixed length records can be blocked or unblocked. Format F records can be used with all of the four non-VSAM data set organizations. Coding RECFM=FS or FBS does not denote fixed length spanned records. Rather, with F the S specifies Standard. This means that all physical records (except perhaps for the last one in the data set) are 'full.' There are no 'short' blocks in the middle of the data set. A standard data set can be processed more efficiently than a non-standard data set using QSAM. Be careful specifying DISP=MOD when adding records to an FBS record format data set. When using QSAM to extend a sequential data set a 'short' block at the end of the data set is never filled when records are subsequently added to the data set. Standard can only be coded with true physical sequential data sets, not pds members.

Example 1: A data set is created with 100 byte logical records and a blocking factor of 3. Five records are written to the data set. It is then closed and later reopened. Four additional records are then added to the end of the data set. The records and blocks in the data set are shown in Figure 11–1, where Li denotes logical record i.

Variable Length Records

Format V records can be used with all non-VSAM data sets except Relative. Variable records with ISAM are not allowed with COBOL. Unlike records in a format F data set, variable length records are preceded by fields which contain control information. One field is associated with every logical record and one field with every physical record. All control fields are four bytes in length. The first two bytes hold the length of the record (logical or physical); the last two bytes are reserved for future system usage and contain binary zeros. Consider a format V data set with unblocked records. A typical record is shown in Figure 11–2.

FIGURE 11–1
Example 1 Embedded and Nonembedded Short Blocks

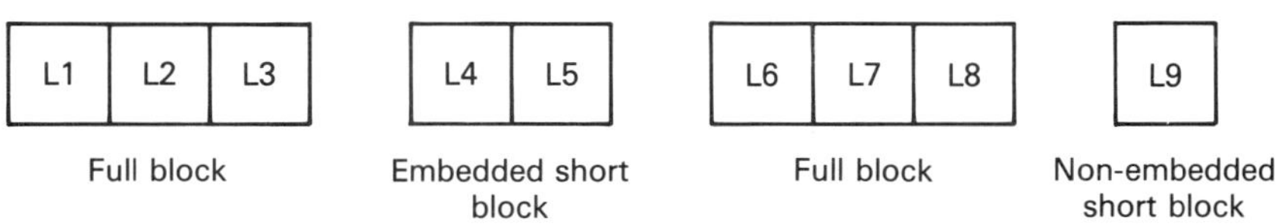

FIGURE 11–2
An Unblocked Variable Length Record

4 bytes (BDW)		4 bytes (RDW)		
LL	RR	ll	rr	actual data

LL and RR contain control data for the physical record;
ll and rr contain control data for the logical record.

LL, RR, ll, and rr are all two bytes in length. If the data portion of the record is 100 bytes in length the ll field will contain the value 104 (100 + 4) and the LL field the value 108 (100 + 4 + 4). LL and RR together are referred to as the Block Descriptor Word (BDW) or Block Descriptor Field (BDF). Likewise, ll and rr together are called the Record Descriptor Word (RDW) or Record Descriptor Field (RDF). If there are two records of length 100 and 28 bytes respectively blocked together in a variable format data set their ll fields will contain the values 104 and 32 respectively. The LL field for the block will contain 140. To determine the actual length of a physical record in a V format data set the following formulas are used:

For Unblocked Records: LL Length = 4 + 4 + data length
For Blocked Records: ll Length = 4 + (4 + length of record 1) +
(4 + length of record 2) + . . .

Variable length record descriptions in a COBOL application program should not define space for RDW fields and need not do so for the BDW. This is handled automatically by the system. The BDW and RDW fields are present in the buffers for the data set and the buffers are allocated in such a manner that there will be room for them. They are not directly accessible to the application programmer during variable record processing. When variable length records are moved from buffers to working storage the control information is stripped from the records. Going the other direction control fields are added to the records. Special care must be taken when processing variable length record fields outside the buffers.

There are two ways in which variable format files can be processed in a COBOL program: with either an OCCURS DEPENDING ON clause or multiple 01 records of different lengths. The two methods can also be combined in the same FD.

Example 2: An OCCURS DEPENDING ON clause is used to process a file containing variable length records. The OCCURS DEPENDING ON clause can be coded anywhere within the record description. It needs not be coded last as shown here. Multiple OCCURS DEPENDING ON clauses can be coded within the same 01 level.

```
FD  VAR-FILE
    RECORDING MODE IS V
    BLOCK CONTAINS 43 TO 85 CHARACTERS
    RECORD CONTAINS 35 TO 77 CHARACTERS
    LABEL RECORDS ARE STANDARD
    DATA RECORD IS VAR-REC.
```

```
01   VAR-REC.
     05  A                   PIC X(33).
     05  B                   PIC 99.
     05  C                   OCCURS 0 TO 6 TIMES
                             DEPENDING ON B  PIC 9(7).
```

The RECORD CONTAINS clause specifies the smallest and largest logical records that can be associated with this file. The BLOCK CONTAINS clause specifies these values plus an additional 8 bytes for the BDW and RDW. Note that the file is unblocked. The RECORDS CONTAINS clause is used for documentation only. The data control block for this file will have the LRECL value 81. This is the size of the largest possible logical record plus four bytes for the RDW. The compiler computes this by actually adding up the maximum number of bytes in the 01-level of the FD and adding four. Unlike the RECORD CONTAINS clause, the BLOCK CONTAINS clause always specifies the actual BLKSIZE value for the file, in this case 85 bytes. The BLOCK CONTAINS clause is never treated as documentation. When a BLOCK CONTAINS clause is coded any BLKSIZE subparameter value coded on the DD statement for the data set and the BLKSIZE value in the data set label is ignored. The value 43 is treated as documentation. Any value between 0 and 84 may be coded in place of 43 and will be acceptable to the compiler.

Now suppose the same logical records are to be written and blocked using a blocking factor of three. There are several ways this can be accomplished. One way is to code a new BLOCK CONTAINS clause specifying BLOCK CONTAINS 121 TO 247 CHARACTERS. Here the 121 is coded strictly for documentation and the BLKSIZE parameter in the data control block is assigned the value 247. Note that 247=4+(3*(4+77)). A second approach is to code either

```
BLOCK CONTAINS 0 CHARACTERS or
BLOCK CONTAINS 0 RECORDS
```

in the FD, and specify DCB=(BLKSIZE=247, . . .) in the associated DD statement. This gives exactly the same result. Finally, coding

```
BLOCK CONTAINS 3 RECORDS
```

also gives the BLKSIZE a value of 247. Surprisingly, no matter which of the three approaches is used, more than three logical records can be placed in a single physical record!

Example 3: Suppose the same data set as in Example 2 is being created with one exception. Assume that BLOCK CONTAINS 3 RECORDS is coded and the first 6 records to be written have lengths of 35, 42, 35, 35, 49, and 63 bytes respectively. Then four logical records can be placed in the first physical record. This occurs because the total length of the four records is

$$4 + (4 + 35) + (4 + 42) + (4 + 35) + (4 + 35) = 167$$

and 167 is less than 247. Clearly there is sufficient space in the block for the fourth record, so it gets placed in the block. Is there room in the block for the fifth record, which is 49 bytes in length? Since 167 + 4 + 49 = 220 (which is less than 247), there is room for the record. However, after a COBOL program writes a record to a variable format file a test is made to determine if another record of maximum length can be added to the block. In this case after writing the fourth record the test is

167 + (4 + 77) = 248

which is greater than 247. Since the maximum record size associated with the file could not fit in the block, the block is truncated and written to the I/O device without considering the length of the next logical record. Logical record 5 becomes the first record in the next physical block. As an exercise try to determine the circumstances under which the second block contains four logical records. Note that it can never contain more than four. In this example BLKSIZE=(3 * LRECL) + 4. In reality there does not need to be such a relationship. BLKSIZE must only be at least 4 bytes larger than LRECL. The term blocking factor is meaningful only with fixed length records.

Example 4: Here multiple 01 levels of different lengths are used to construct a variable format data set with the same data used in the previous examples.

```
ENVIRONMENT DIVISION.

I-O-CONTROL SECTION.
APPLY WRITE-ONLY ON VAR-FILE-2.

FILE-CONTROL SECTION.

FD   VAR-FILE-2
     RECORDING MODE IS V
     BLOCK CONTAINS 3 RECORDS
     RECORD CONTAINS 35 TO 77 CHARACTERS
     LABEL RECORDS ARE STANDARD
     DATA RECORDS ARE VARREC0, VARREC1, VARREC2,
     VARREC3, VARREC4, VARREC5, VARREC6.
01   VARREC0                   PIC X(35).
01   VARREC1                   PIC X(42).
01   VARREC2                   PIC X(49).
01   VARREC3                   PIC X(56).
01   VARREC4                   PIC X(63).
01   VARREC5                   PIC X(70).
01   VARREC6                   PIC X(77).
```

The FD will be used to illustrate that a higher level of I/O efficiency can be achieved when writing a variable length file. It is possible to request a test on when to truncate a buffer other than the "maximum record next" test used in Example 3. If an APPLY WRITE-ONLY ON VAR-FILE-2 statement is present in the I-O-CONTROL SECTION of the program then a record is added to a block if there is room for it. Using the same records as in Example 3 the first five records get placed in one block. In general APPLY WRITE-ONLY results in a more efficient utilization of I/O devices and fewer I/O operations. When the APPLY WRITE-ONLY clause is used all WRITE statements must include the FROM clause. Hence a record must be written with one of the 01 levels listed here.

Undefined Records

Example 5: A file with an undefined record format has a very simple FD structure. The same logical records that were written in Example 2 are to be read using an undefined format. Note that this is not the format with which they were created. Recall that the records are unblocked. If the RECORDING MODE clause is not coded, the COBOL compiler will select either variable or undefined for the record format depending on the value in the ASSIGN clause.

```
FD   UDEF-FILE
     RECORDING MODE IS U
     LABEL RECORDS ARE STANDARD
     RECORD CONTAINS 43 TO 85 CHARACTERS
     DATA RECORD IS UDEF-REC.
01   UDEF-REC.
     05  HEADER-INFO         PIC 9(16) COMP.
     05  A                   PIC X(33).
     05  B                   PIC 99.
     05  C                   OCCURS 0 TO 6 TIMES
                             DEPENDING ON B PIC 9(7).
```

If a BLOCK CONTAINS clause is coded, the COBOL compiler issues a warning message since blocking is not permitted with U format records. In addition, if the original records are to be processed by this FD care must be taken because the BDW and RDW fields are now interpreted as data and read into the HEADER-INFO field.

Spanned Records

Example 6: In order to understand the structure of a data set that contains spanned records, consider the following FD from a COBOL program:

```
FD   SPAN-FILE
     RECORD CONTAINS 10 TO 50 CHARACTERS
     BLOCK CONTAINS 25 CHARACTERS
     LABEL RECORDS ARE STANDARD
     DATA RECORDS ARE SPAN-REC1, SPAN-REC2.
01   SPAN-REC1             PIC X(50).
01   SPAN-REC2             PIC X(10).
```

Several points should be noted about the FD structure. Although no RECORDING MODE clause is present, the BLOCK CONTAINS clause implies spanned records. Because the file is spanned it must be either sequential or direct. Neither an ISAM nor a relative data set can contain spanned records. The SELECT clause specifies the data set organization.

FIGURE 11–3

Segments in Each Block With Spanned Records

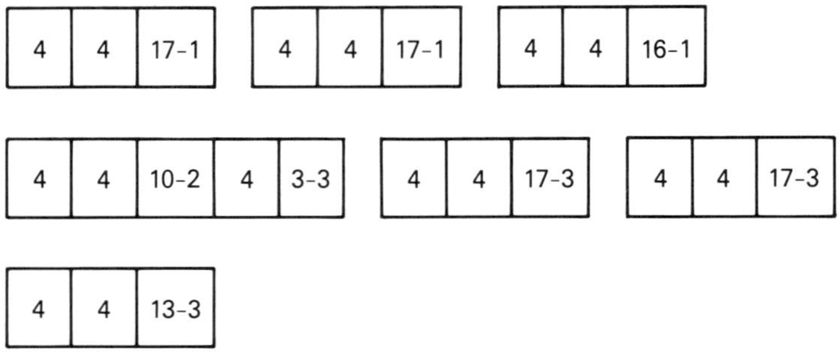

Suppose that three records to be written to this data set are 50, 10, and 50 bytes in length respectively. There are 110 bytes of actual data. This data is segmented and placed into physical blocks of length 25 bytes or less. In each block at least eight bytes are used for overhead. Figure 11–3 shows the number of bytes in each segment within the seven blocks of 25 bytes or less (X-Y means X bytes from logical record Y).

The first three physical records are required to hold the first logical record. Thus 25 + 25 + 24 = 74 bytes are required to hold the 50 bytes of data. Block three contains only 24 bytes. Physical record 4 contains all of logical record 2 and can contain seven additional bytes. These bytes are used to hold the Segment Descriptor Word (SDW) for logical record 3 and the first three bytes of data from that record. With a spanned data set a SDW replaces an RDW. The remaining 47 bytes of logical record 3 are contained in physical records 5 (17 bytes), 6 (17 bytes), and 7 (13 bytes). If there had been a fourth logical record no part of it or its SDW would have gone in physical record 8.

The SDW for the first three physical records specify that they contain a beginning, middle, and end segment respectively. This information is written in the two bytes that contained binary zeroes in the RDW. The first two bytes of the SDW also contain the length of the segment. Physical record 4 contains 12 bytes of overhead since it contains two SDW. The SDW for logical record 4 specifies that it is not segmented. Because logical record size is independent of physical record size with spanned records, it is perhaps surprising that a subtle change in the above example can dramatically change the physical layout of the records.

Example 7: The three logical records in Example 6 are to be written to disk. The JCL associated with the data set that will hold them contains the following code: DCB=(LRECL=50,BLKSIZE=25,RECFM=VS). Unlike Example 6, the spanned records in this data set are unblocked. This means that each physical record must contain either one logical record or one logical record segment. Segments from two distinct records cannot be placed in the same block.

For the records above the first three physical records remain unchanged. The fourth block is 18 bytes in length (8 bytes overhead and 10 bytes for logical record 2). The fifth block now contains the first 17 bytes of logical record 3. With this change the 3 logical records still occupy seven physical records. The fourth logical record still begins in physical record 8.

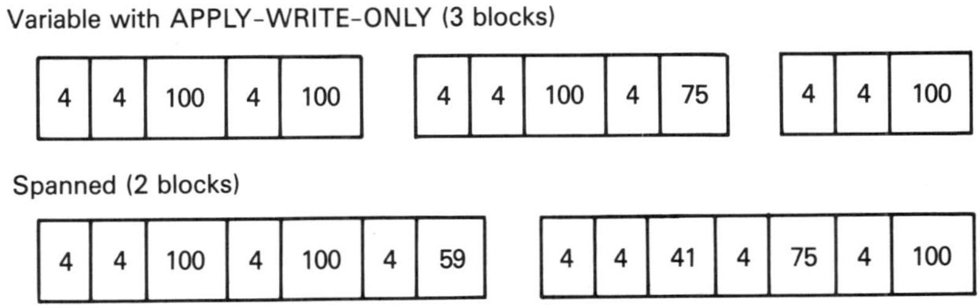

FIGURE 11–4
Comparing Variable and Spanned Records

There are situations in which using a spanned format rather than a variable format will save space on the I/O device. This saving can be realized even if the variable file is written with an APPLY WRITE-ONLY clause. Conversely, with other data sets a variable format is preferred to a spanned format.

Example 8: Consider a data set with a blocksize of 275 bytes and a logical record length from 50 to 100 characters (Figure 11–4). The five logical records in the data set contain 100, 100, 100, 75, and 100 bytes of data respectively. If the file is created as variable records with the APPLY WRITE-ONLY clause, the first two records are placed in block 1, the next two are placed in block 2, and the last in block 3. If the file is spanned the first two records are written in block 1 along with 59 bytes of record 3. The remainder of record 3 and the last 2 logical records are placed in block 2.

What is the best record format to use when creating a data set with variable length records? There is no clear answer. Rather, the contents of the records themselves along with the applications that will process them determine the best record format for a specific data set.

Relationship Between Record Formats and Data Set Organization

Table 11–1 shows the data set organizations that are permitted with a given record format. An X means the record format-data set organization pair is valid.

TABLE 11–1
Data Set Organizations and Record Formats

Data Set Organizations	*Record Formats*			
	Fixed	*Variable*	*Undefined*	*Spanned*
Sequential	X	X	X	X
ISAM	X	X		
Direct	X	X	X	X
Relative	X			
Partitioned (Member)	X	X	X	

With any particular language not all of these may be possible. For example, COBOL permits only fixed length records with an ISAM data set.

Exercises

1. Describe how to create a data set which contains fixed blocked records where there is more than one 'short' block. Once created such a data set should not have RECFM=FS or RECFM=FBS coded on its accompanying DD statement.

2. Describe numeric conditions under which it is possible to determine if a data set comprised of fixed blocked records contains embedded blocks that are not completely filled. Assume that the number of logical records, the number of physical records, and the blocking factor are known.

3. Why should DISP=MOD not be coded when processing an existing sequential data set with RECFM=FBS? Can problems occur when coding DISP=MOD with RECFM=FS?

4. Under what conditions should RECFM=FBS not be used with a data set that is stored on tape? Can RECFM=FS be used safely with a tape data set?

5. Why should the COBOL compiler be influenced by data set organization in implicitly selecting a record format?

6. Using a blocksize of 100 and a logical record size between 25 and 50, determine a group of logical records where the number of blocks needed to hold the records will differ depending on whether variable, variable with APPLY WRITE-ONLY, or spanned is specified.

7. Extend the example in the last exercise by selecting a collection of logical records that will give four different block counts for the three formats described in that exercise, and also spanned unblocked records.

8. In Example 2 in this chapter what is the maximum number of logical records that can ever comprise one physical record? What does the answer become if BLOCK CONTAINS 2 RECORDS is coded in the FD?

9. Suppose that the following SELECT, FD and DD statements are included in a COBOL program.

```
SELECT DCB-FILE               FD  DCB-FILE
    ASSIGN TO UT-S-DCBETC         BLOCK CONTAINS 0 RECORDS
                                  RECORD CONTAINS 80 CHARACTERS
                                  RECORDING MODE IS V
                                  LABEL RECORDS ARE STANDARD.
                              01  DCB-REC          PIC X(80).

//DCBETC    DD   DCB=(LRECL=150,BLKSIZE=1500,RECFM=FB),
//               DSN=DCB.DATASET,...
```

DCB.DATASET is an existing data set that contains the values LRECL=84, BLKSIZE=844, RECFM=VB, and DSORG=PS in its labels. What values (LRECL, BLKSIZE, and RECFM) will be placed in the dcb for this data set when it is first opened? What values will be placed in the dcb if BLOCK CONTAINS 0 RECORDS is coded? What will occur when the first record is read from the dataset? What values will go in the dcb if there is no BLOCK CONTAINS clause and no RECORDING MODE clause in the FD? Starting with the original COBOL code and JCL shown above, what will be placed in the dcb if the data set is new and is being created in this jobstep? What will be written in the data set labels in this case?

10. A data set contains variable length records. Each logical record contains three fields which have the following formats:

```
A-FIELD         PIC X(10).
B-FIELD         PIC X.
C-FIELD         OCCURS 0 TO 9 TIMES
                DEPENDING ON B-FIELD PIC X(50).
```

The records are unblocked. Can such records be processed as format U records? If so, how? Specify DCB values. Can such records be processed as format S records? If so, how? Specify DCB values. Can such records be processed as format F records? If so, how? Specify DCB values. Do the answers to these three questions change if the original records are blocked?

11. Based on the size of the BDW and RDW fields, what is the maximum possible size of a variable length logical record? A variable length physical record? What are the minimum sizes of variable length logical and physical records? Do any of these answers change for undefined or spanned records?

12. List some specific criteria for determining the 'best' record format to use when creating a data set with variable length records. Some of the criteria should be numeric.

13. Can a spanned unblocked data set ever be created by a COBOL program? If so, under what conditions can it be done? If not, why not?

14. Do either PL/I or assembler provide two different techniques for creating variable length record formats as the COBOL compiler does?

15. What is the difference between RECFM=F and RECFM=FS? What is the difference between RECFM=V and RECFM=VS?

16. Use the utility IEBGENER to create a variable format data set. Determine which algorithm IEBGENER uses when writing format V records, ''maximum record next'' or APPLY WRITE-ONLY. Carefully choose the BLKSIZE and LRECL values for the records.

Chapter 12

Partitioned Data Sets (PDS)

Overview

A partitioned data set (pds) is substantially different from the other three non-VSAM data set organizations. It is the only one of the four that is indispensable on an MVS System. It is also the only one that does not have an equivalent VSAM data set organization.

A pds is a *single* disk data set that is organized in a partitioned manner. It consists of a *collection* of data sets all of which are physical sequential. A pds is often called a library. With a pds, it is possible to process all the sequential data sets together as one entity. Some utilities (IEBCOPY, IEHMOVE, and IEBPTPCH) can automatically process every member in a pds when they recognize a data set as partitioned. This process is not the same as concatenation. It is also possible to process just one data set within the pds as a separate object. The data sets within the pds are called *members*. Since all PGM values coded on EXEC statements must be members of a pds, it is the one non-VSAM data set organization that must be present to perform meaningful work on an MVS system.

A pds consists of two adjacent components, a directory and a member area. As will be explained in Chapter 15, disk data sets are formatted in two distinct ways. The directory and member areas each have different formats. The directory serves as an index or table of contents for the sequential data sets stored in the member area. The directory tells where they are stored within the member area. It may also contain other useful information about the individual members. The member area holds the actual sequential data sets. The member area usually comprises a large percentage of the disk space the pds occupies. In terms of locating a data set and disposition processing it, the system considers a pds a single data set. Finding a pds in a system catalog or VTOC is handled no differently than locating other types of data sets. It is only after the PDS is actually found that an individual member can then be accessed. A pds can be temporary or permanent and cataloged, kept, or passed. A large pds may contain several thousand members.

A pds must be stored on disk in order to use it as a pds. A pds can be copied to tape for use as a backup or for transportability. When this is done the pds is stored as a sequential data set and individual members cannot be referenced from tape. The IEBCOPY utility is used for creating backup copies on tape. More on this topic is covered with the IEBCOPY utility, which is the primary utility for maintaining a pds.

There are three places in JCL syntax where a data set can be identified as partitioned. DSORG=PO may be coded as a DCB subparameter. However, this is coded strictly for documentation. DSN=data set name(member name) identifies a pds and one member within it. JCL syntax does not allow multiple member names to be coded with the DSN parameter. However, neither the DSORG nor DSN code is meaningful unless a request for directory space is included as part of the SPACE parameter when the pds is created.

Creating a PDS

The beginning part of the pds always holds the directory. The size of the directory is determined at the same time that space is requested for the entire pds on a DD statement in the JCL. Code SPACE=(a,(b,c,d),...) where a can be CYL, TRK, or blocksize, b is the number of primary allocation units, c is the number of secondary allocations, and d is the number of 256-byte blocks that will be used to hold the directory of the pds. Note that the (d) sub-subparameter is independent of the unit in which space for the member area is requested. CYL, TRK, or blocksize may be used for the member area. It is the presence of the (d) sub-subparameter that actually creates a partitioned data set organization.

Example 1: When attempting to create a pds and place a member ALPHA in it, the following JCL is coded. Despite the DSN and DCB syntax a sequential data set is created.

```
//DD1    DD   DSN=PDSLIB(ALPHA),DISP=(NEW,PASS),
//            UNIT=SYSDA,SPACE=(CYL,(1,1)),
//            DCB=(LRECL=80,RECFM=F,DSORG=PO)
```

If SPACE is changed to (CYL,(1,,1)) a pds is created.

Example 2: SPACE=(CYL,(3,0,5)) requests three cylinders for the member area and five 256-byte blocks for the directory. The five blocks are taken out of the three primary cylinders. Hence, the actual member area actually contains less than three cylinders. These cylinders occupy 3*n tracks where n is the number of tracks per cylinder for a disk device. Thus (3*n)-1 full tracks are reserved for the member area and part of one track for the directory. The five directory blocks are written on the first track. If there is still room on the track for data blocks from the first members after writing the five blocks, then member blocks will share the track with the directory. On pre-MVS systems a track was not split between the directory and the member area. Hence any unformatted space on a directory track was wasted.

To avoid splitting a track between the directory and the member area request sufficient directory blocks to fill an entire track or tracks. For example, since exactly 36 blocks fit on one track of a 3350 disk, select a multiple of 36 directory blocks. When the exact format of the directory is discussed below it will become clear that exactly 36 blocks fill the track.

In the next four examples no secondary allocations are requested. There are two reasons for this. First, it is irrelevant to the discussion of directory size since the primary space allocation contains the directory blocks. Also, secondary allocations always cause a data set to be processed less efficiently. This is especially true with a very complex structure like a pds.

Example 3: SPACE=(TRK,(4,,36)), allocates four tracks to the pds. Three tracks are for the member area and one is for the directory. This assumes a 3350 disk, as does the next example.

Example 4: SPACE=(TRK,(1,,36)) is coded. The 36 directory blocks completely fill the single primary track. Since there is no space left for the member area, the jobstep will not be executed. The same result occurs even if a secondary allocation is coded.

Example 5: SPACE=(CYL,(2,1)) is coded. Since no directory blocks have been allocated, this data set is not a pds. Without a request for directory blocks this data set will be sequentially organized.

Example 6: SPACE=(TRK,(1,,1)) is coded. This is the 'world's smallest' pds measured in either of two different ways that the size of a pds can be specified. The same results occur when SPACE=(1,(1,,1)) is coded.

Recall that the primary space allocation for a disk data set is made just once. The space for the directory comes out of the primary amount. Hence, after it is created the directory can never be increased in size. It is important to keep this in mind when creating a pds. Directory size can limit the future growth of a pds.

The pds shown in Figure 12–1 was created with SPACE=(TRK,(4,x,y)) specified where x is the secondary allocation and y is the number of directory blocks allocated on the first track. On an intuitive level a pds can be thought of as pictured here. EOF represents an End of File marker. Note that every member (along with the directory) is followed by an End of File marker.

The DD statement used to create this pds and add the first member (E) to it in the same job step can be coded as follows:

```
//DD1    DD   DSN=NEWPDS(E),DISP=(NEW,CATLG),
//            UNIT=SYSDA,SPACE=(TRK,(4,0,1)),
//            DCB=(LRECL=80,BLKSIZE=6160,RECFM=FB,DSORG=PO)
```

FIGURE 12–1

A PDS with Four Members

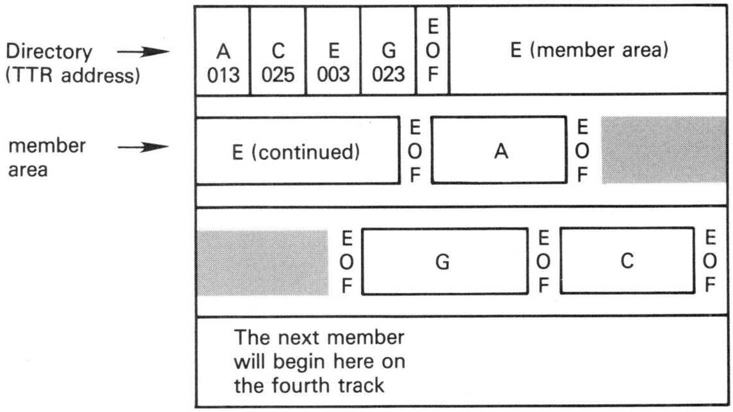

DSORG=PO is coded only for documentation. To create the pds but not place any members in it the DSN parameter should be changed to

```
DSN=NEWPDS
```

No other changes are necessary.

Several important points should be noted. The directory contains the names of the pds members and their addresses in the member area. The member names in the directory are in alphabetical order, but the members themselves are not in alphabetical order. The members are not all the same size, or even contiguous. Note the unused space (the shaded area) in the midst of the member area.

The PDS Directory

The directory always occupies the beginning of the area allocated to the pds. The directory is an index for the contents of the member area. It stores the member names and aliases in ascending EBCDIC collating sequence order. An alias is an additional name for a pds member. A member can have one 'true' name but numerous aliases. The directory is dynamic; it immediately reflects any changes in the member area. For example, when a member is deleted its entry is removed from the directory. When a member is added to the pds an entry is inserted into the directory in the appropriate location. Numerous other programmer requests can also cause changes in the directory. These include adding or deleting an alias, updating a member, renaming a member, and recording user data in the directory. The system automatically maintains the directory. It determines which functions to perform based on JCL and utility code. Following the usable portion of the directory the system may store garbage in a directory block and all subsequent blocks.

The directory can also be maintained by an application programmer. This involves using the FIND, BLDL, and STOW macros to search and update it. Part of a typical directory is pictured in Figure 12–2.

FIGURE 12–2
A Complete PDS Directory Block Plus Overhead

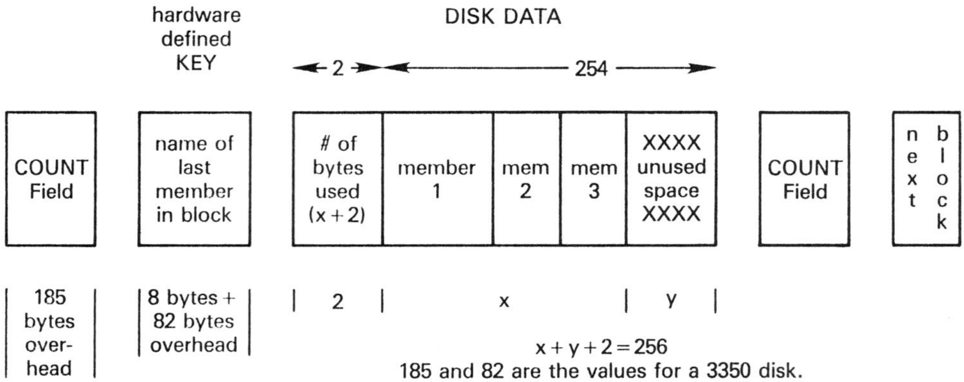

If the directory were a data set it would have dcb values BLKSIZE = 256 and RECFM = U. With undefined records it is unnecessary to specify an LRECL value. Do not code these dcb values when creating a pds or accessing pds members. Although the directory is a part of the pds its dcb values never change. The dcb values coded with a pds should reflect the properties of the members. In fact, with some utilities when DCB = (BLKSIZE = 256,RECFM = U) is coded the directory rather than the member area is automatically processed.

The member names are stored in ascending EBCDIC collating sequence. The last entry in the last used directory block is X'FFF...FFF' (B'111...111' or HIGH-VALUES in COBOL). This name denotes the end of the directory entries. All following values are meaningless.

The directory entry associated with a specific member contains either three or four fields. These fields are shown in Figure 12–3.

The name field identifies a member name or an alias. It consists of one to eight alphanumeric characters left-justified and padded on the right with blanks when less than eight characters are specified. If more than eight characters are coded in a DD statement it is a JCL syntax error. When the member name is referenced on a utility control statement or in an assembler program the same rules apply.

The TTR field is three bytes in length. It is a pointer to the first physical record (or block) of the member. TT identifies the track number relative to the beginning of the data set. The first track is 0. R identifies the block number relative to the beginning of the track. The first block on a track is 1. The TTR value for a new entry is created by adding 1 to the TTR of the last block of the last member (which is always the EOF mark). Thus, an EOF mark also constitutes a block. If track TT is full the next block begins at record 1 of track TT + 1 and the directory pointer will then be set to this value. The system locates the block by searching in multi-track mode using TT(R − 1) as a search argument.

FIGURE 12–3
Directory Fields for a Member

(always present)			(optional)
NAME	TTR	C	(user data area) TTRN TTRN TTRN other data
8 bytes	3	1	0 to 62

The C field contains three types of information. Since only one byte is used for the C field individual bits are used to represent these three items. The bits are numbered from 0 to 7 while going from left to right.

Bits			*Information in the field*
0	1 bit	2 values	0 if a real or true name. 1 if the name is an alias.
1–2	2 bits	4 values	The number of user data TTRNs. The values 00, 01, 10, and 11 represent 0 to 3 TTRNs respectively. More than three TTRNs are possible using a NOTE list record. TTRNs are described in detail below.
3–7	5 bits	32 values	Values can range from 0 to 31. This is the number of halfwords in the optional user data area. This includes the space used by TTRN pointers in user data field.

One role of the user data field is to provide data as input to the routines which manipulate the directory (STOW macro). If pointers to locations within the member (TTRN) are provided they are four bytes long and are placed first in the user data field.

The utility IEBUPDTE provides the keyword parameter SSI to allow four bytes of user data to be written in the directory entry when adding a member to a pds. These four bytes are commonly used for identification. The Linkage Editor routinely writes over 20 bytes of user data whenever it adds a member to a load module library. With an assembler language program the full 62 bytes of user data may be written.

Example 7: To clarify the role of the C field, two common C values are examined. C=X'80' implies that the name is an alias and that no user data follows. C=X'5E' specifies the member is a true name. Additionally, there are 60 bytes of user data and two TTRN values. This is apparent from converting X'5E' to binary and getting 0 10 11110.

The user data field is pictured in Figure 12–4.

FIGURE 12–4

The User Data Field

The user data area may be pictured as follows:

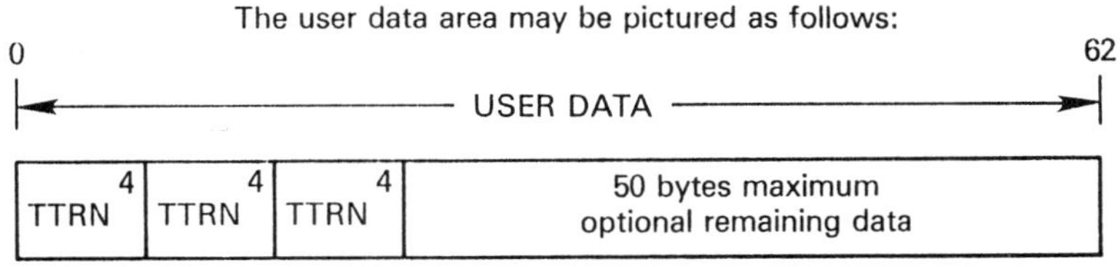

TT = relative track address of the NOTE list or area being referenced.
R = relative block number on that track.
N = binary value — the number of additional pointers contained in a NOTE list pointed to by the TTR. If the pointer is not a NOTE list, N = 0. Hence, for a simple pointer, N = 0.

FIGURE 12–5

A PDS Member Without a NOTE List

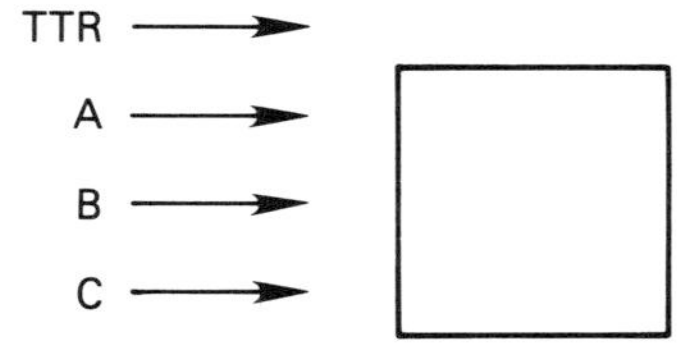

Without a NOTE list, a maximum of 3 internal points within a PDS member, say A, B, and C, can be accessed directly.

A NOTE list consists of additional pointers to blocks within one member of a pds. A member can be divided into subgroups; a pointer to the beginning of each subgroup is stored in the NOTE list. For example, if one member is a load module with many CSECTS, each CSECT becomes a subgroup pointed to by an entry in the note list. This pointer to the beginning of the subgroup is created by using the NOTE macro instruction after writing the first record of the subgroup. Remember that the pointer to the first record of the member is automatically stored by the system in the directory entry in the three bytes immediately following the member name. Figure 12–5 shows a pds member without a NOTE list.

Example 8: Suppose either IEBUPDTE or IEBGENER is used to create a pds and place two members in it. The SPACE parameter specified is SPACE=(CYL,(1,,2)). The members are called ALPHA and BETA. ZETA is an alias for ALPHA. ALPHA contains five logical records and BETA contains eight. The data set label for the pds specifies LRECL=4000, BLKSIZE=8000, and RECFM=FB. Hence two physical records fit on one track of a 3350 disk. After this jobstep has executed the first directory block contains the following values:

```
  NAME     TTRCNAME     TTRCNAME     TTRCNAME          TTRC
32ALPHAbbb0040BETAbbbb0130ZETAbbbb0048(HIGH-VALUES)0000. . .
```

The four digits following the member names are the TTR and C fields. Note that both ALPHA and ZETA contain the same TTR value. However, the C field shows that ALPHA is a true name and ZETA is an alias. The R value is 4 since the EOF marker for the directory is record 3. The X‘32’ at the beginning of the block implies that 50 bytes of directory information are present in this block. This includes 12 bytes for the null member. Member BETA begins on the second track in the third block. None of the directory entries contain user data.

The pds is now modified by rewriting ALPHA, adding two additional logical records to the back of the member, adding a new member GAMMA, and deleting BETA. After these changes have taken place the first directory block now contains the following:

```
  NAME     TTRCNAME     TTRCNAME     TTRCNAME          TTRC
32ALPHAbbb0330GAMMAbbb0530ZETAbbbb0048(HIGH-VALUES)0000...
```

TABLE 12–1
Standard Transactions and Their Effect on the Directory

Transaction	*Effect on Directory*	*JCL or UTILITY*
Add	Insert new entry in EBCDIC sequence.	DSN=PDS(name),DISP=MOD
Delete	Remove directory entry. Compress that block.	Use IEHPROGM or IDCAMS since IEFBR14 won't work.
Update (regular)	Entry in same location has new TTR value.	DSN=PDS(name), DISP=OLD or Linkage Editor NAME name(R).
Update (inplace)	Entry in same location has same TTR value.	IEBUPDTE with UPDATE=INPLACE specified.
Change directory information	Depends on the function.	Probably a utility or assembler program.

Notice that the values following ALPHA have been modified, while those following ZETA are unchanged. Hence the alias points to the original version of ALPHA.

Processing a pds member is identical to processing a sequential data set. Either QSAM or BSAM can be used. With QSAM the directory can not be altered, but it can be processed. The STOW, BLDL, and FIND macros are available for locating a member in the directory or processing the directory.

Table 12–1 shows the effect on the directory when standard transactions involving a PDS member are performed.

The Member Area

The member area differs from the directory in several significant ways. It is not maintained in collating sequence. Rather, the data sets in the member area are stored in the order in which they were added to the pds. The old members are at the beginning immediately following the directory and the new are at the end. There are holes or 'dead spaces' in the member area corresponding to where members were deleted or updated. For either of these two situations the space in that member's area is no longer available to the pds. To reclaim this space it is necessary to reorganize or 'compress' the pds. The space allocated to an individual member is fixed and cannot be increased. Hence, unless an update of a member yields a member exactly the same length as the original, the new version must be added at the end of the pds. The old member becomes dead space. This is why a pds can become 'full' even though the members in the pds which are currently 'active' occupy only a small percentage of the member area.

A summary of the effects of the standard transactions on the member area now follows.

Transaction	*Effect on Member Area*
Add	The member is added at the end of the existing member area. The new member always starts a new block. Each member is followed by its own End of File marker.
Delete	There is no longer a TTR in the directory for the member area. However, the deleted member still occupies space and this space is now inaccessible. An alias will still point to the original member area.
Update (regular)	The old copy of this member is now treated exactly the same as a deleted member. There is no TTR pointing to it. The new copy is treated like an added member and is placed at the end of the member area.
Update (inplace)	The new copy occupies exactly the same area as the old member. The only output operation permitted is rewriting a record.

Advantages of Using a PDS to Group Data Sets Together

1. A pds allows for easier management of the individual members by making them part of a group. By placing related data sets together in one entity documentation becomes simpler.

2. With some types of pds processing only one OPEN statement will make every member available to a program. I/O operations are minimized.

3. With some applications the entire pds can be processed. That is, every member is processed as part of a group, not individually. No member names need to be specified.

4. Addresses in the TTR are relative addresses, not absolute. Hence, the entire pds can be moved without changing entries in the directory. It is convenient to consider a pds as one contiguous set of tracks regardless of how space is actually allocated.

5. Although a member of a pds can be found by searching the directory blocks, there are more efficient ways to locate an individual member. In fact, once the pds is opened it is possible to retrieve any individual member without searching the entire data set directory. This involves using the BLDL macro, which is described below.

6. It is easy to create a backup of an entire pds. Several utilities perform this function. The backup can be a true pds or a sequential data set which contains the pds.

7. Additional information can be stored with an individual member in the user data area. This user information gets placed in the directory either by a utility or assembler program.

8. It is simpler to use symbolic parameters to reference a pds member than a sequential data set; since a member name cannot be qualified.

Disadvantages of Using a PDS

1. When the directory becomes full additional members can not be added; nor can updates be done except inplace. In this situation members can still be added in two ways: by deleting an existing member from the directory or by creating a new pds with a larger directory, and using the utility IEBCOPY to copy members from the old pds to the new pds. Remember, once the directory of a pds is created its size can never be changed.

2. The member area can become filled. This can happen in a variety of ways. When it does, no more adding or updating (except inplace) can be done to the pds. There are three ways to deal with this: run the utility IEBCOPY to compress the pds to regain any dead space, create a new pds with a larger member area and copy the old pds into it, or when adding the next member ask for secondary space allocations if they have not already been used.

3. The data set needs reorganization. It often happens that a pds is not full but just wasteful of disk space. In this case, IEBCOPY should be run to reclaim this wasted space.

4. When used with a pds secondary extents can lead to processing inefficiency problems.

5. Inconsistent DCB subparameters can cause problems when processing a pds. The DCB parameter on a DD statement for the pds should be specified when creating the pds. All subsequent references to the pds (especially when adding members) should be consistent with these subparameters. For an existing pds, it is usually unnecessary to specify DCB subparameters following the IEFBR14 program or other program that created the pds. It is the programmer's responsibility to be certain that all members added to the pds have the same DCB attributes.

6. Spanned records are not permitted with a pds. The other three non-VSAM record formats are allowed.

7. A pds must be entirely contained on one volume.

8. A pds cannot contain user labels.

9. A maximum of 16 pds's can be concatenated. On the other hand, up to 256 sequential data sets may be concatenated.

Automatic Replacement

The first DISP subparameter on the DD statement (NEW,MOD,OLD, or SHR) determines which directory action parameter will be chosen by the system for the STOW macro instruction when adding a member.

If DISP=OLD is specified on the DD statement a STOW instruction with the R option will be issued. This means that the member name will be inserted into the directory. If that name already occurs in the directory an automatic replacement will take place. If the name does not occur in the directory the member will be added.

If DISP=NEW or MOD is specified the STOW will contain the A option. If the member name is not in the directory, it will be added. If the member name is already in the directory it will not be added (or replaced). In this case, the jobstep will abnormally terminate with an S013 abend.

To force a member into an existing pds code DISP=OLD. Use DISP=MOD to add members to an existing pds; a member currently in the pds with the same name will not be inadvertently destroyed.

The Three Fundamental Macros for PDS Manipulation

The three macros to be discussed in the next several sections are fundamental to most pds manipulation. Unless programming is done in assembler the three will probably never be used directly. However, by requesting certain functions when using utilities and by selecting specific JCL parameters and subparameters, these macros are indirectly invoked. It is very difficult to understand how pds's actually work without some knowledge of these macros. All three macros are members of SYS1.MACLIB, the system macro library.

Macro	*Function*
BLDL	Creates a list of pds directory entries within the program's region in memory.
FIND	Locates a member of the pds for subsequent processing. This can be done by supplying either a member name(s) or a TTR value(s).
STOW	Is used to add, delete, replace, or change a member entry in the directory.

To use any of these macros, either DSORG=PO or POU must be specified in the DCB macro instruction. Also, all preceding I/O operations should be checked for successful completion prior to issuing any of these.

BLDL

The BLDL macro involves the BuiLDing of a List or table. This list is shown in Figure 12–6.

These names must be in collating sequence regardless of whether the members are from the same or different libraries.

The programmer supplies the following:

a) FF—the number of member names in the following list. Never specify over 64K names in the list.

b) LL—the number of bytes for each entry in the table, giving the length of every entry. This must be an even number between 14 and 76 bytes.

c) member names—eight bytes, left justified, padded with blanks, etc. These member names must be in ascending EBCDIC collating sequence even if the members are from different libraries. These member names can, of course, be aliases.

The a,b, and c values must be supplied prior to issuing the BLDL macro. BLDL then supplies:

TTR	the member's starting location.
K	0 if there is only one pds; otherwise the actual number if it is included within a concatenation. K is not required if there is no user data.
Z	denotes the source of the directory entry: 0 = private library; 1 = link library; 2 = job or step library. Z is not required if there is no user data.
C	the same C field as was discussed with the directory above. It gives the number of user data halfwords.
USER DATA	includes as much as will fit in an entry.

FIGURE 12–6
Using The BLDL Macro

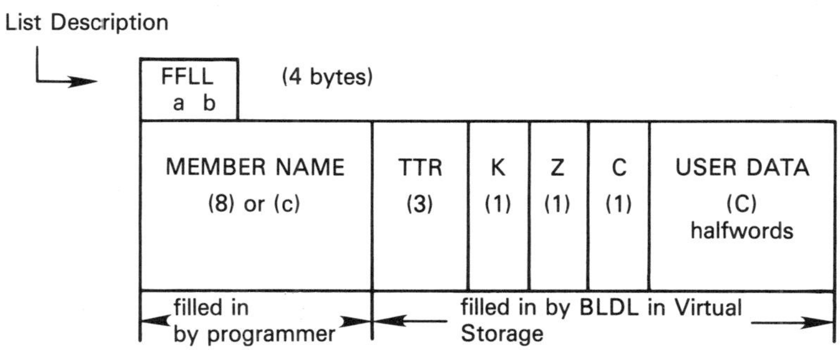

Once a BLDL has been issued the list it supplies can be used over and over again. In fact, retrieval time for a pds member can be optimized by directing subsequent FIND macros to the BuiLD List rather than the directory when trying to locate the member to be processed.

The format of a BLDL instruction is:

```
BLDL      dcb address,list address
```

Here dcb address is the address of the data control block for an open pds, and list address gives the location of a list similar to the one pictured above. BLDL then fills in the five fields on the right. Specific examples of where BLDL may be used are included with the discussions of FIND and STOW.

FIND

This macro is used to locate the starting address of a specific member, i.e., the TTR of the member. The system responds by placing the disk address in the data control block in a field called the DCBRELAD field. Following this a subsequent I/O operation may begin processing at that point.

When using the FIND macro, there are two ways to request the system to locate the correct address:

(1) Specify the address of an area containing the name of the member. The system responds by searching the data set's directory for the relative track address (TTR).

(2) Specify the address of the TTR field of the entry in a BuiLD List created using the BLDL macro. In this case, no directory search is required since the relative track address is in the BuiLD List entry. A variant of this approach is used to locate members in SYS1.LINKLIB.

The system will also search a concatenated series of directories when either a DCB is supplied that is opened for a concatenated pds or a DCB is not supplied, in which case either JOBLIB or STEPLIB (themselves concatenated) followed by SYS1.LINKLIB are searched.

Suppose only one member of a pds is to be processed. It can then be processed as a sequential data set. In this case specify DSORG=PS. Either QSAM or BSAM can be used. Identify the member by coding DSN=PDSname(member). The system automatically does a type (1) FIND to locate the data set. No BLDL (or STOW) is necessary. When the data set is opened the system places the member's starting address in the data control block so that a subsequent GET or READ macro instruction will begin processing at that point. FIND, BLDL, and STOW cannot be used directly when processing one member as a sequential data set.

Since the DCBRELAD address in the dcb is updated when the FIND macro is issued, the FIND macro should not be issued after WRITE and STOW processing without first closing the data set and reopening it for input processing.

The format for the FIND macro instruction is:

```
FIND     dcb address,name address,D                    or
         dcb address,relative address list,C
```

where name address is an eight byte field containing the data set's name. D means that the member name has been provided. The access method will respond by searching the directory of the pds specified in the data control block for the member name.

Relative address is the address of an area that contains the TTR for that member. The relative address is usually a list entry completed by using a BLDL macro. C means a relative address has been given. There is no reason to search the directory. The address is used directly by the access method.

STOW

When adding several members to a pds a STOW macro instruction must be issued after writing each member. This places an entry for the member in the directory. When using STOW specify DSORG=PO or POU in the DCB macro instruction.

STOW performs several other functions in addition to adding members to the directory. It can be used to delete, replace, or change a member name in the directory. It can also store or modify user information within the directory entry. A member in the pds can be referenced by more than one name using the concept of an alias. An alias can be stored in the directory in exactly the same manner as a member name. It is important to be consistent in altering all aliases associated with a given member. For example, if a member is replaced (updated) then any related alias entries should be deleted or changed so that they point to the new (updated) member. In most situations this is not handled automatically. It is the programmer's responsibility to keep track of aliases.

When adding only one member to a pds and specifying the member name as DSN=PDSname(member) on a DD statement it is unnecessary to use BPAM and STOW. In this case it is possible to use BPAM and STOW, or BSAM, or QSAM. If either sequential access method is used, or if BPAM is used and a CLOSE macro is issued without issuing a STOW macro, the system will issue a STOW using the member name that was specified on the DD statement.

What happens when the system issues a STOW? When this occurs the directory entry is the minimum length, 12 bytes. This automatic STOW macro will not be issued if either the CLOSE macro is a TYPE=T or the task is being abnormally terminated when the dcb is closed.

The format for the STOW macro instruction is

```
STOW     dcb address,list address,directory action
```

Here list address is the address where the information the STOW macro needs to process the directory has been placed. The actual format of this field varies depending on what action is requested.

The directory actions are:

A add an entry to the directory

C change the name of a member or alias from its present value in the directory

D delete an entry in the directory (member name or alias)

R replace an existing directory entry with a new directory entry (if R is specified but the old entry is not found, the new name is added to the directory)

Exercises

1. Suppose an MVS system did not support partitioned data sets. What restrictions would this place on executing programs?

2. How many 256 byte directory blocks will fit on one track of an IBM 3380 disk?

3. Create a pds on a 3350 disk drive. Specify SPACE=(CYL,(1,,36)). Use either ADRDSSU or IEHDASDR to examine the portion of the disk that contains the directory. Verify that 36 directory blocks fit on the first track of the pds. Note also that it takes more than one track to hold the complete directory. Does a comparable situation occur when writing a track of directory blocks on a 3380 disk drive? Clarify the comments that accompany Example 4 in light of this exercise.

4. How much space is present in the member area when SPACE=(TRK,(1,,35)) is coded with an IBM 3350 disk? If x directory blocks occupy one track of an IBM 3380 disk, what is the comparable value when SPACE=(TRK,(1,,x-1)) is coded?

5. Are some member names actually moved from one directory block to the next to facilitate insertion? To answer this question, construct an appropriate example and see what happens. Use IEHLIST or IEBPTPCH to print the contents of the directory. Use SYS1.PROCLIB or SYS1.MACLIB if possible. Construct an example that will contain garbage following the HIGH-VALUES entry in the directory.

6. A pds is created and one member added to it using the JCL shown here:

```
//DD1 DD DSN=ALPHA(BETA),DISP=(NEW,CATLG),
//        SPACE=(CYL,(1,,2)),
//        DCB=(LRECL=2000,BLKSIZE=8000,RECFM=FB),
//        UNIT=3350,VOL=SER=CLIC18
```

Six logical records are written to the member in this jobstep. A control statement specifies an alias of BABABA for this member. Sketch the complete contents of the pds directory at this point. Also sketch the member area. Label relevant parts of your picture.

The following members are created/accessed/deleted, etc. in the next (separate) jobstep. The members are referenced in the order shown here.

```
//DD1  DD  DSN=ALPHA(GAMMA),DISP=MOD,---  8 records written
//DD2  DD  DSN=ALPHA(BETA),DISP=OLD,---  1 record written
```

Sketch the complete contents of the pds directory at this point. Also sketch the member area. Label relevant parts of your picture. Would reversing the order of the two DD statements change your answer?

The following members are created/accessed/deleted in the next (separate) jobstep. The members are referenced in the order shown here.

```
//DD1  DD  DSN=ALPHA(MU),DISP=OLD,---  16 records written
//DD2  DD  DSN=ALPHA(ZETA),DISP=OLD,---  2 records written
//DD3  DD  DSN=ALPHA(BETA),DISP=MOD,---  8 records written
```

ZETA has aliases of Z1 and Z2. All members and aliases created here contain 62 bytes of user data.

Sketch the complete contents of the pds directory at this point. Also sketch the member area. Label relevant parts of your picture. Would permuting the order of the DD statements change your results?

The following members are created/accessed/deleted, etc. in the next (separate) jobstep. The members are referenced in the order shown here.

```
//DD1  DD  DSN=ALPHA(MU),DISP=OLD,---  UPDATE=INPLACE
//DD2  DD  DSN=ALPHA(ZETA),DISP=OLD,---  delete this member
```

Sketch the complete contents of the pds directory at this point. Also sketch the member area. Label relevant parts of your picture. Would switching the order of these two DD statements change your results?

7. What is the maximum number of member entries that can be placed in one directory block? What is the minimum number of entries that can completely fill a directory block?

8. Example 6 describes the smallest possible pds, measured in two ways. What is the third way to measure the size of a pds? What constitutes the smallest value for this measurement on a 3350 disk?

9. There is an error in one of the TTR values in Example 8. It occurs in the final listing of the contents of the first directory block. Find the error and correct it.

10. The following DD statement has been coded in an attempt to create a a very large pds and add two members to it. Find all of the errors in the code:

```
//DDPDS    DD DSN=PDS(MEM1,MEM2),DISP=(NEW,PASS),
//    UNIT=SYSDA,VOL=SER=(DISK01,DISK02),
//    SPACE=(CYL,(10,36)),LABEL=(,SUL,,,EXPDT=90366),
//    DCB=(LRECL=100,BLKSIZE=50,RECFM=VBS,DSORG=PDS)
```

11. How can the partitioned data set organization be redesigned in order to more efficiently use the disk space allocated to it? Discuss any necessary changes to the directory and member areas that will result in decreasing the need to periodically compress a pds.

Chapter 13

ISAM Data Sets

Overview

ISAM is the abbreviation for Indexed Sequential Access Method. Throughout the 1970s ISAM was the most widely used and the best known example of an indexed data set. IBM is in the process of gradually withdrawing programming support from ISAM. Beginning in 1985 ISAM could no longer be used with new releases of CICS, the popular IBM teleprocessing monitor product. It seems certain that most future indexed data sets will be VSAM KSDS's. However, because there are so many existing ISAM data sets it will remain an important topic for the next several years.

There are two major reasons why it is important to have some knowledge of ISAM data sets. First, despite the growing popularity of VSAM, there are still a substantial number of ISAM data sets in use. Some installations have shown a great reluctance to convert all their ISAM data sets to VSAM. Second, ISAM serves as a good introduction to VSAM data set organizations. ISAM and the VSAM KSDS represent the two most popular techniques for creating and processing indexed data sets.

From an academic viewpoint it is easier to begin the study of indexed data sets with ISAM. ISAM data sets are in many ways simpler to understand and easier to work with.

An indexed data set is a collection of records that are logically ordered based on the value in a key field within each record. This key field or key must be the same length and in the same position within each record. It can be from 1 to 255 bytes in length. The key cannot be part of a variable length field that may not be present in some records. By using the key fields ISAM can locate an individual record much faster than if a sequential search is used. Such a process is called random (or direct) record retrieval.

There are two standard types of indexed data sets. With one an overflow area disjoint from the original area is used to hold records which cannot fit in the original area. The overflow area approach is typified by ISAM. The second type of indexed data sets reserves room for future additional records in the original area. If this area becomes full a dynamic reorganization of the original area takes place. This is the approach used with a VSAM KSDS.

An indexed data set is a compromise between sequential and direct data sets. The records in a sequential data set are meant to be processed sequentially. Ordinarily it is impossible to process them randomly (except for a VSAM ESDS). Records in a direct data set can be processed randomly. However, sequential processing of a direct data set is frequently meaningless as far as an application is concerned. Note that the words sequential and direct (or random) are being used here in two different contexts. First, they may identify a data set organization; second, they may identify a method of accessing the records in a data set.

The records in an indexed data set can be meaningfully processed both sequentially and randomly. An indexed data set cannot be sequentially processed as efficiently as a data set with sequential organization. The reasons for this will become clear when the structure of the indexed data set is described. Likewise, random processing with an indexed data set is not as fast as with a data set with direct organization. Direct data sets do not have indexes. The indexes increase the processing time, as does the sequential track search that concludes randomly locating a specific record. When a large amount of both sequential and random processing is required, an indexed data set is usually the best data set organization to choose. These comments apply to both ISAM and VSAM KSDS indexed data sets. The remainder of this chapter discusses only ISAM data sets.

ISAM Data Set Components

An ISAM data set consists of data and index components. Depending on the size and complexity of the ISAM data set both the data and index may contain several disjoint subcomponents. There can be up to five levels of indexes and three distinct data areas. An ISAM data set may be written on more than one direct access volume. In fact, the data, part of the index, and the data overflow areas all can be placed on distinct volumes.

The index serves as a partial table of contents for locating the records in the data area. The index is written in a special index area. An index consists of key values along with the location of the records which contain that key value. Not all records have their keys listed in the index. Hence the index is non-dense.

Data records are written in either a prime data area or one of two overflow areas. When the data set is initially created all records are written in the prime data area.

ISAM data sets must be stored on disk. ISAM data sets are well suited for use with 3330 and 3350 disks, but are processed less efficiently with 3380 disks. An ISAM data set occupies an integral number of cylinders. Space can only be requested by asking for cylinders or ABSTR addresses that correspond to a whole number of

FIGURE 13–1

ISAM Data Set

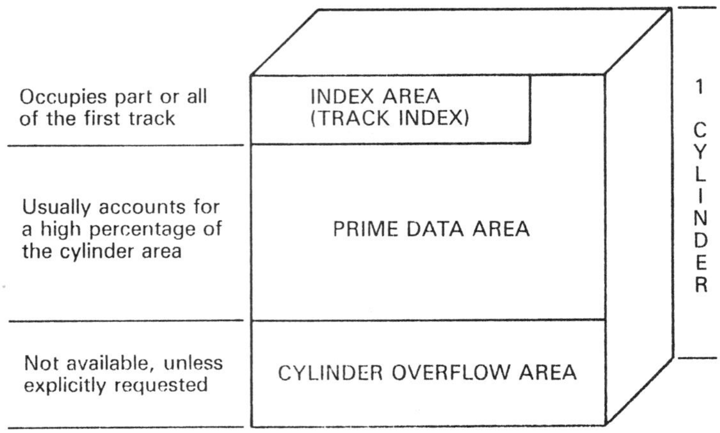

cylinders. The smallest ISAM data set occupies one cylinder. Such a data set has the organization shown in Figure 13–1.

The index area consists of a pair of records for each track in the prime data area. These two index records determine the range of key values for records associated with the track. In this book they are called index record 1 and index record 2. Both index records consist of an address and a key value.

Index record 1 identifies a track in the prime data area. It also contains the highest key value associated with the records stored on that track.

A shortage of space on a prime data track causes records to be bumped into the overflow area. Under some circumstances records are added directly to the overflow area. Index record 2 contains the highest key value from among all the records that have been bumped from the prime data track identified in index record 1 to the overflow area or added directly to the overflow area associated with the prime data track. It also contains the address of the record with the lowest key value that has been bumped from that track or added directly. When an ISAM data set is created both index record 1 and index record 2 contain the same value for highest key. This occurs because no records are written to the overflow area during the creation process. The lowest key value address in index record 2 is initialized to binary zeros.

Tracks in the overflow area do not have specific index records associated with them. Rather, the overflow area can only be accessed through the index records for the tracks in the prime data area.

The index area always begins on the first track of the cylinder. If the index area does not fill the entire track the rest of the track contains the beginning of the prime data area. Theoretically the index area could occupy more than one track. However, this is impossible with 3330, 3350, and 3380 disks. Index record 1 and index record 2 have the same format. Both index records are present even when there is no overflow area on the cylinder. Both records are stored in COUNT-KEY-DATA format as shown in Figure 13–2. This format is further described in Chapter 15. For now it is sufficient to know that COUNT, KEY, and DATA are three disjoint adjacent disk fields. The COUNT field contains the same basic types of information for every data set organization.

FIGURE 13–2
The COUNT-KEY-DATA Format for Index Records

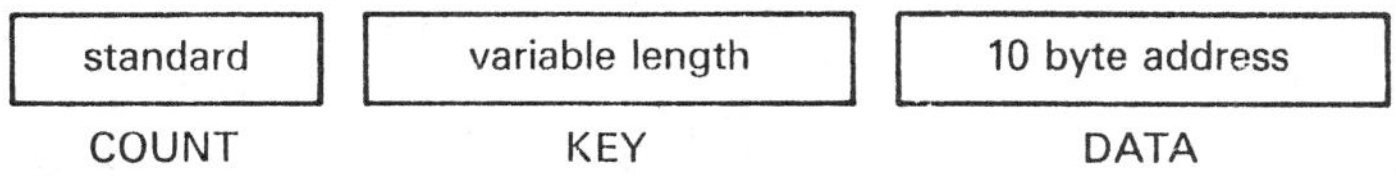

For index record 1 the KEY field contains the highest key value on the track. The size of the KEY field is determined when the data set is created. The DATA field contains the address of the prime track. It is a ten byte field. Index record 2 contains the corresponding values for the records placed in the overflow area that are associated with the prime track. These are both the highest key value bumped from the track and the address of the record with the lowest key value placed in the overflow area associated with the prime track. Note that index record 1 contains the address of a track, while index record 2 identifies a specific overflow record. The function of the index records is to locate as quickly as possible the track that contains a record with a given key value. Indexes are used in the same manner for both adding and retrieving records randomly. Once the desired track is determined it must then be searched sequentially for the required record.

Sequential Data Set Creation

When an ISAM data set is initially created the records placed in it must be sequentially written in the prime data area. This process is similar to the creation of a sequential data set. During creation the records must be written in ascending order based on the values in their key fields. Input records with duplicate keys or key values out of order are not written to the data set. In a COBOL program such records activate an INVALID KEY condition. This causes the records to be skipped, and processing continues with the next valid record. Tracks are filled until the data set is created or the prime area on the cylinder becomes filled. During the creation of an ISAM data set records are never added to the overflow area. Records that do not fit on the first cylinder are written to the prime data area on a second cylinder, and so on. After the prime data area on a cylinder has been filled the associated index entries are written on the first track. After the data set is initially created all of the records in the prime data area are in both logical and physical order.

Records can also be sequentially added to an existing ISAM data set. They are written in the prime data area immediately following the existing records. DISP=MOD should be coded on the corresponding DD statement for the data set. With a COBOL program the data set should be opened for EXTEND. As with data set creation, when a data set is sequentially extended the records must be written in ascending key order.

When sequentially adding records to a data set every track is completely filled, with the exception of the last track which contains records. Dummy records can be written anywhere within the prime data area to reserve space for future use. An ISAM dummy record is created by placing hexadecimal 'FF' (binary '11111111' or COBOL HIGH-VALUES) in the first byte of the logical record. Additionally, OPTCD=L must be coded in the DCB parameter when the data set is created.

Dummy records may serve as place holders. Dummy records can be replaced subsequently by active records. This involves rewriting the dummy records. Often the first part of a track will contain active records and the rest of the track dummy records. Following the last track used to hold data in the prime area one entire track is used as an end-of-file marker for the data set. The index structure is responsible for the extravagant size of the end-of-file marker. With this approach the fields in the index records remain consistent throughout the data set.

After a track has been filled sequentially the two index records for the track are written. Following sequential creation both index records contain the same key values. However, the address of the track and the address of the (non-existent) overflow area are different. Two of the four index values associated with the records on a track never change, no matter what processing takes place. These are the prime track address in index record 1 and the key value in record 2. As will be seen, the last record sequentially placed on the track is always the first record bumped into the overflow area. No record with a higher key will be placed on that track or in its associated overflow area.

Following the sequential creation of an ISAM data set the overflow area is empty. The address of the first available location where an overflow record may be written is stored in the track capacity record (RO) of the index track. Whenever a new record is added to the overflow area or an old active record is bumped to the overflow area the RO value determines where it is written. Following either of these operations the value in RO is updated. More information on RO can be found in Chapter 15.

Each cylinder in the prime data area uses the same number of tracks for cylinder overflow. This number must be specified in the JCL when the data set is created. It cannot be subsequently changed. ISAM may use some of the overflow area to hold high level indexes if specific space is not requested for this purpose. A cylinder overflow area is not required. Although rare, this may be desirable for a data set where only sequential processing and random retrieval take place. Note that specific tracks in the overflow area are not paired off with individual tracks in the prime area to hold overflow only from those tracks. Rather, space in the overflow area is available on a first come, first serve basis for any active record bumped from the prime data area or initially placed in the overflow area during a direct add. Overflow space is allocated in a left to right, top to bottom fashion. One linked list structure is created in the overflow area for each prime data track which has had an active record bumped from it. This is further illustrated in the next example.

Example 1: The accompanying illustration shows the appearance of an ISAM data set following its sequential creation on a 3350 disk. The data set has DCB values of LRECL=1750, RECFM=FB, and BLKSIZE=3500. The key field is 255 bytes in length and is contained within the 1750 bytes of data. If non-embedded keys are used the appearance of the data set will be changed (non-embedded keys are discussed in the exercises). Twenty-five records are written to the data set. These records have key values of 100, 150, 200, 250, 300, 350 . . . 1300, each preceded by sufficient leading zeroes. Twenty-five of the thirty tracks are reserved for cylinder overflow. The sizes of the records, keys, and overflow area have been chosen to construct an example that serves two important purposes. With just a few records it

FIGURE 13–3
ISAM Data Set Following Sequential Creation

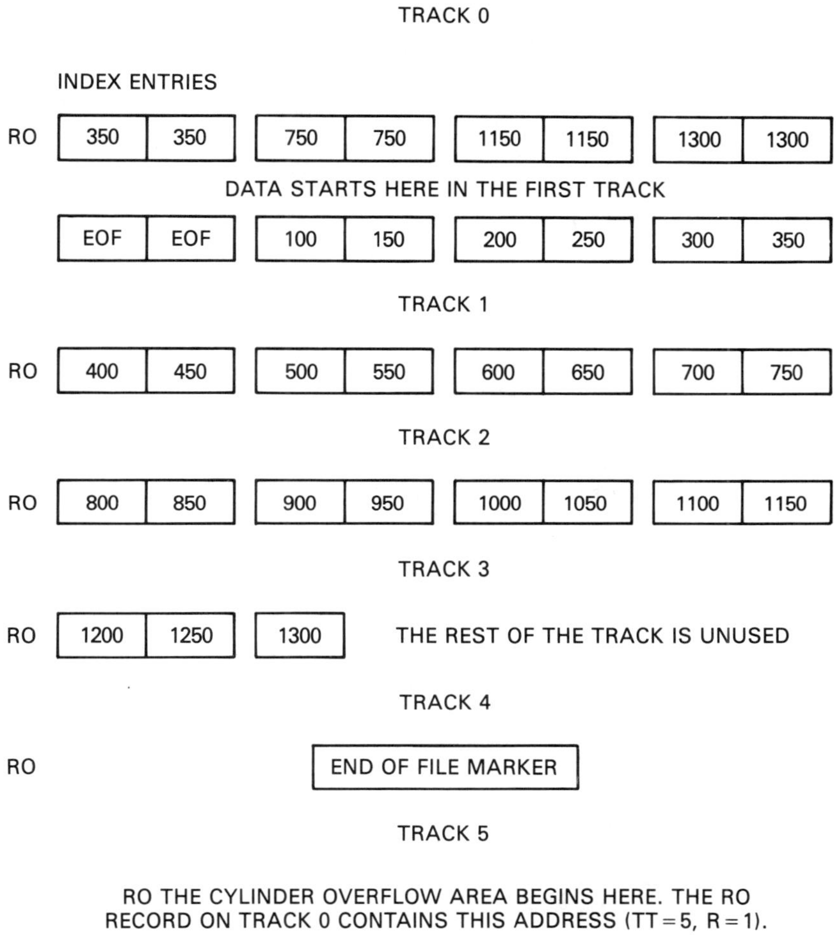

can be easily used to illustrate many significant features of ISAM processing. Additionally, with these sizes the example given here is technically correct in every detail. The data set is pictured in Figure 13–3. Only key values are shown in the index records. Likewise the data records are identified by their key value.

Sequentially Processing an Existing Data Set

After an ISAM data set is created it can be processed either sequentially or randomly. Sequential processing is conceptually similar to processing a physical sequential data set.

When reading an ISAM data set sequentially the QISAM access method retrieves records in logical order. To do this it is necessary for ISAM to use the key values in the index area. Otherwise overflow records will be retrieved following the prime data records and hence appear out of sequence. Records can be rewritten during sequential processing. A record must be read before it can be rewritten. Sequential processing can begin with any record in the data set. In COBOL the START verb is used to accomplish this. The beginning location is found using the key value and the indexes. The first READ statement retrieves the record located by the START. It is important to remember that every type of processing, including sequential, uses the index.

Random Processing

With random processing ISAM uses a three step technique to locate a record. In Step 1 and Step 3 the key of the desired record is used as a search argument. In Step 1 the KEY field values in the track index are examined sequentially in order to determine the first KEY value that is greater than or equal to the search value. The KEY value determined can be either the highest key value on a track or the highest key value in the overflow area associated with a specific track. In Step 2 the corresponding DATA field of the index record is examined to determine the starting address of the area to be searched. The search moves from the index to either the prime data area or the overflow area. Finally, in Step 3 the track or linked list overflow area associated with the track is searched sequentially. If records are blocked the key of the last record in the block is placed in the disk KEY field which precedes the block. Hence only one physical record is actually read. Random processing with an ISAM data set is summarized in Table 13–1.

TABLE 13–1
Random Processing with an ISAM Data Set

Step	*Action*
1	The index for the cylinder is sequentially searched. KEY field values in both types of index records are examined.
2	The search moves to either a track in the prime data area or a linked list in the overflow area associated with a track.
3	To find the desired record a sequential search is made of the data records on the track or in the linked list.

This approach works because the key values in the index and the records on an individual track are in ascending order. Records in the overflow area are placed in disjoint linked lists. There can be one linked list for each track in the prime data area. Within each linked list the records are chained together in logical ascending order by pointers.

Example 2: The ISAM data set created in the previous example is now used to illustrate the direct retrieval process. It is necessary to locate the record with a key value of 500. Since 500 is greater than or equal to 350 the record is not on the first track or in the (non-existent) overflow area associated with the first track. Since 500 is less than or equal to 750 the required record (if it exists) is on the second track.

Now the disk KEY fields on Track 2 are examined. With a blocked ISAM data set, the highest record key in the block is written in a disk KEY field preceding the block. The highest key value is always in the last record in the block. Since 500 is greater than or equal to 450, the first KEY value, the record is not in the first block. Because 500 is less than or equal to 550, if the desired record is in the data set it must be in the second block. The physical record is read into a buffer and the embedded keys of each logical record are sequentially examined. The desired record is found as the first record in the block.

For a given key value it is possible that no record with that key exists in the data set. In COBOL this also causes an INVALID KEY condition. This is not an error, but rather a method for obtaining information about the data set. If the search value exceeds the highest value in the track index no such record is contained on that cylinder.

Adding Records Randomly

In addition to retrieval two other types of random processing are possible. New records can be directly added to the data set. In order for the records in the data set to remain in ascending logical order some existing records may have to be moved. Finally, existing records may be rewritten.

Example 3: Several records are added to the data set created in Example 1. To add a record with key = 625 the records following it on Track 1 must be moved down the track. The last record on the track (with key=750) will be bumped into the overflow area. The location where a record will be added is found using the same three step process as used in random retrieval. If the record is to be added to a prime track other records must be moved and the track index records for that track will then need to be updated. Either one or two of the index values will change. The two index records for track 1 now contain the values shown in Figure 13–4.

If a record is added directly to the overflow area then at most one of the index values will change. Suppose a record with key=725 is to be added. Since 700 is less than or equal to 725 and 725 is less than or equal to 750, the record becomes part of the overflow area associated with track 1. The capacity record on the index track determines where the overflow record will be placed. Physically the new record follows the record with a key of 750 on track 5. Logically the new record precedes it, and consequently the track index entry identifies it as the first record in the overflow area associated with track 1. A ten byte pointer field is appended to each record written in the overflow area. For the record with key=725 the pointer contains the address of the record with key=750. After a record is added to the overflow area

FIGURE 13–4
Index Records After Random Add Operation

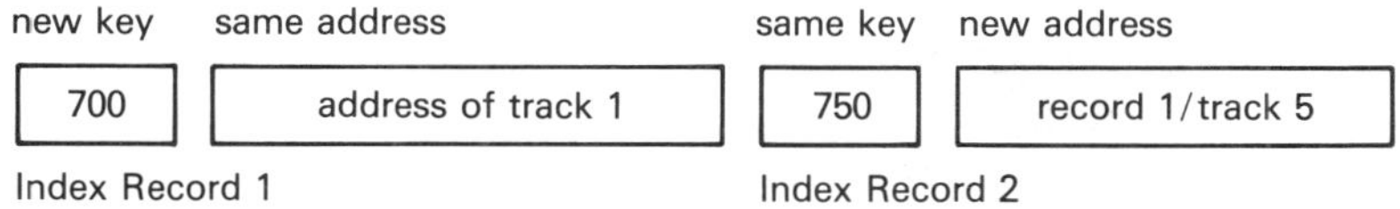

the track capacity record is updated. Even if blocking is specified for the data set all records in the overflow area are unblocked. At this point the index records for track 1 contain the values shown in Figure 13–5.

FIGURE 13–5
Current Status of Index Records

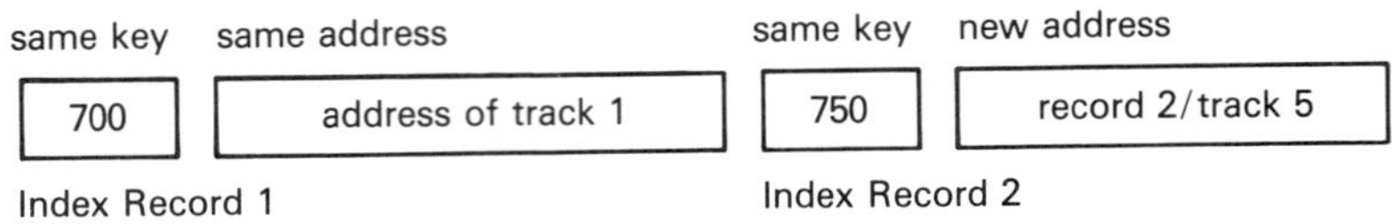

The first two COUNT-KEY-DATA triples on track 5 are pictured in Figure 13–6.

FIGURE 13–6
The First Two COUNT-KEY-DATA Triples on Track 5

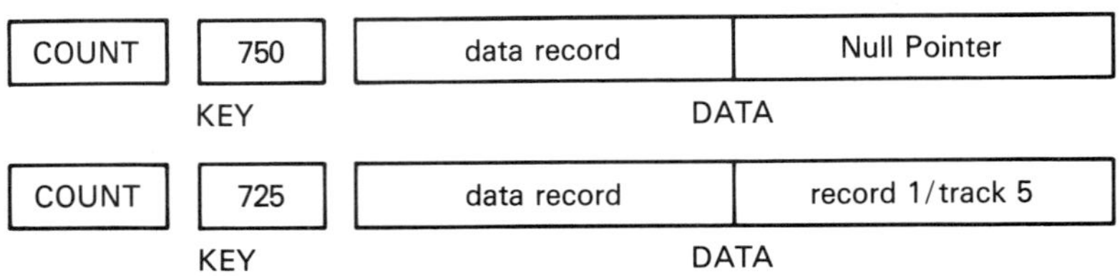

At this point RO on the index track contains the address of record 3 on track 5.

Suppose that a record with key = 730 is to be added to the data set. The index records determine that it belongs with the overflow records from track 1. However, it is necessary to follow the linked list pointers and retrieve each record individually until the correct location of the record is determined. In this case the entire linked list must be examined. Neither of the index records are changed. At this point, the records on track 5 contain the values shown in Figure 13–7.

FIGURE 13–7
Current Status of Records on Track 5

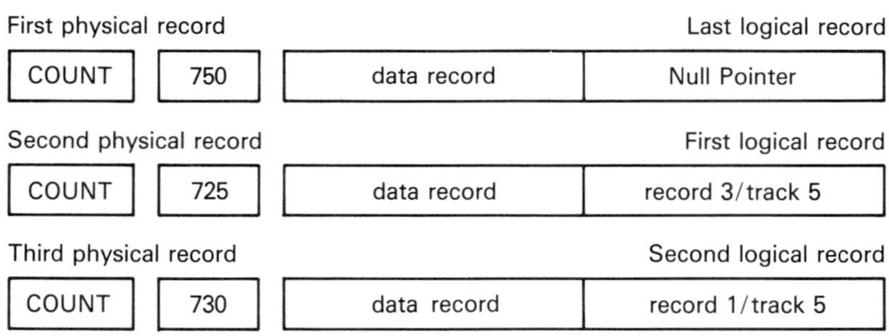

If the next record added to the data set has key = 825 then the record on track 2 with key = 1150 will be bumped into the overflow area. It will become record 4 on track 5. It will have a null pointer to reference the next overflow record in its linked list. Index record 2 for track 2 will contain the values 1150 and record 4 on track 5. Finally, suppose a record with key = 600 is to be added. In the process of determining where to write the record an existing record with the same key value will be found. This will raise the INVALID KEY condition.

Since the index track is required for all ISAM data set processing it is usually read into main memory preliminary to processing. It is modified in memory and written back to disk when processing is completed or when the buffer containing it is needed for something else.

Random Rewriting and Deletion

Rewriting an existing record is the other type of random processing. As with sequential processing, a record must be read before it can be rewritten. With fixed length records none of the index entries are changed during a rewrite operation. Complications can occur with variable length records whenever the length of a record is changed. This is not a problem with COBOL application programs since COBOL cannot process ISAM data sets that contain variable length records.

Deletion is a special case of rewriting. Records are logically deleted by moving X'FF' to the first byte of an ISAM record prior to rewriting it. A logically deleted record is ignored during subsequent sequential processing. However, random processing retrieves logically deleted records. In this case the application program and not ISAM must determine if the record is marked as deleted. Logical deletion is an ISAM option that must be requested when the data set is created. The programmer should code OPTCD=L in the DCB parameter on the accompanying DD statement if this option is desired.

An application program cannot physically delete an ISAM logical record. The simplest way to physically delete records is to first mark them as logically deleted and then sequentially create a new copy of the entire ISAM data set. During the copy operation the logically deleted records are skipped. Hence the new data set will not contain the logically deleted records. Additionally, all of the active records in the overflow area will be placed in the prime data area in the new data set. This reorganization should be done periodically to any ISAM data set from which records are being logically deleted or with an overflow area containing many records. The utility IEBISAM (described in Chapter 29) can be used to reorganize an ISAM data set.

A record can be physically deleted during random processing. When a logically deleted record is bumped from a prime data track it will not be added to the overflow area. Suppose the record with key=1150 in Example 1 is logically deleted. Following this a record with key=1125 is added to the data set. The new record becomes the last record on track 3 and the record with key=1150 is bumped off the track. However, it is not added to the overflow area. Note that if the two operations are reversed the record is logically deleted while in the overflow area.

If there are variable length records in an ISAM data set rewriting one record on a track and changing its length could cause all logically deleted records following it on the track to be physically deleted. With ISAM data sets that contain fixed length records this cannot occur. When ISAM data sets contain blocked records inserting a record can cause the rest of the records on the track to be reblocked. It is possible that a record in the overflow area that is logically deleted will never be read during either sequential or direct processing. In Exercise 3 an example is constructed to study this situation.

ISAM Data Sets Larger Than One Cylinder

For each cylinder that holds some of the prime data records the prime data area always contains the same number of tracks. It occupies the same location on every cylinder in the data set (two exceptions are noted later).

When an ISAM data set occupies more than one cylinder the index structure becomes more complex. First, a cylinder index is created automatically. It contains one entry for each cylinder in the data set. The entry identifies the highest key value found on that cylinder. During processing the cylinder index is initially searched. Following this the appropriate track index is examined. Hence two levels of index must be searched for each random I/O operation. With a very large data set the cylinder index itself can become big. When this occurs a master index can be created. If a master index is desired it must be requested in the DCB parameter when the data set is created. As with several other special processing options, two subparameters must be supplied. For a master index code DCB=(OPTCD=M, NTM=x, . . .). Here x determines the relationship between the master index and cylinder index entries. For each x tracks in the cylinder index an entry will be placed in the master index. This minimizes the need for long sequential searches through the cylinder index. IBM recommends a master index whenever a cylinder index exceeds four tracks. Entries in the master index have the same format as entries in the cylinder index. The highest key value found in the x tracks is stored in the master index.

With very large data sets higher levels of master index will automatically be created by ISAM. There can be up to three levels of master index. Only extremely large data sets require the second or third level of master index.

Overflow records can be placed in either of two locations. With the cylinder overflow areas discussed above records remain on the cylinder where they logically belong. To request a cylinder overflow area code DCB=(OPTCD=Y,CYLOFL =x, . . .). This specifies that x tracks on each cylinder are reserved for overflow records. If this optional overflow area is desired it must be requested when the data set is created. The data set in Example 1 had DCB=(OPTCD=Y,CYLOFL=25, . . .) coded when it was created.

A second general overflow area can also be created for an ISAM data set. It is called the independent overflow area. It must be identified by its own DD statement when the data set is created. Like the prime area, space must be requested in cylinders. These cylinders need not be adjacent to the prime area or even on the same volume. Linked list addresses must specify volume, cylinder, track, and records with independent overflow records. If cylinder overflow is not requested the overflow records from all the prime cylinders are written in the independent overflow area. If both cylinder and independent overflow areas are requested the cylinder overflow area handles all overflow for a cylinder until it becomes full. At that point additional overflow from the cylinder goes to the independent area.

Both overflow areas are optional. Neither, both, or exactly one of the two can be coded. Each has a significant processing advantage. When processing a data set the use of a cylinder overflow area minimizes access arm movement. Access arm movement is required to process the independent overflow area whenever it is on the same disk as the prime data area. However, it is usually on a different volume. Cylinder overflow wastes space if the amount of overflow is not relatively constant throughout the prime cylinders. It is often a good idea to allow for both types of overflow. Of course, if records are not randomly added to the data set an overflow area is unnecessary.

As random processing takes place the overflow areas eventually contain longer and longer record chains. Processing the data set then becomes inefficient. This is true for both random and sequential processing. To help determine the status of the overflow area three special fields in the format-2 data set control block (dscb) in the VTOC are used by ISAM to hold processing statistics. These values can be accessed by an application program. Based on their content a decision can be made as to whether or not the data set should be reorganized. These fields contain the following information:

— The number of cylinder overflow areas that are completely full.

— The number of unused tracks in the independent overflow area.

— The number of total references to overflow records other than the first reference.

These values can be examined at leisure or they can be used to dynamically decide whether to immediately reorganize the data set. The latter can be done as follows: With a COBOL program the contents of these fields can be used to select a value to move to the RETURN-CODE register. For a specific value a reorganization of the data set should be performed. The value moved to RETURN-CODE can be tested on the COND parameter in subsequent steps within the job stream. In COBOL the three reorganization fields should be coded as follows:

```
I-O-CONTROL SECTION.
    APPLY CORE-INDEX ON isam-file-name.
    APPLY REORG-CRITERIA TO reorg-data ON isam-file-name.

WORKING-STORAGE SECTION.
01  reorg-data.
    05  cylinder-overflow       PIC S9(4) COMP.
    05  ind-overflow-tracks     PIC S9(4) COMP.
    05  overflow-activity       PIC S9(8) COMP.
```

The possible values that may be coded with the OPTCD subparameter for an ISAM data set are summarized in Table 13–2. In order to use L and R the application program must contain the necessary code. The other four values are not directly affected by application code.

The relevant JCL needed to create and access ISAM data sets is examined below. The first example shows the JCL needed to create a very simple ISAM data set. It occupies only one cylinder, allows logical deletion of records, and has a cylinder overflow area.

TABLE 13–2
OPTCD Values For an ISAM Data Set

OPTCD Value	*Additional Subparameter*	*Meaning*
I		An independent overflow area is created.
L		The first byte of each logical record is used as a delete byte. The first byte should not be part of the key field.
M	NTM	A master index is created.
R		Reorganization statistics are maintained by ISAM.
W		A write operation is verified.
Y	CYLOFL	A cylinder overflow area is created on each cylinder.

Example 4: It is necessary to create an ISAM data set on a 3350 disk. The data set will contain approximately 500 one hundred byte records. The first five bytes of each record contain the numeric key value. Once created very few records will be added to or deleted from the data set. Most processing will consist of direct retrieval. Such a data set can be created with either a (COBOL) application program or the IEBDG utility described in Chapter 29.

```
//DD1   DD   DSN=ISAM.DATASET,DISP=(NEW,CATLG),
//           UNIT=3350,VOL=SER=DISK99,SPACE=(CYL,1),
//           DCB=(DSORG=IS,LRECL=101,BLKSIZE=303,RECFM=FB,
//           RKP=1,KEYLEN=5,CYLOFL=21,OPTCD=LY)
```

Since 99 logical records will fit on one track, eight tracks contain sufficient space for the prime data area. The last track holding data is followed by an End of File mark on the next track. Hence the 21 remaining tracks on the cylinder can be designated as the cylinder overflow area. Notice that a delete byte has been appended to the front of each logical record. If a COBOL application program is used to create the data set the DCB coding can be simplified to

```
DCB=(DSORG=IS,CYLOFL=21,OPTCD=LY)
```

The LRECL, BLKSIZE, RECFM, RKP, and KEYLEN values can all be determined from the FD and SELECT statements.

Suppose the same 500 records are used to create an unblocked ISAM data set. Additionally, after each active record is written it should be followed by two dummy records. If the active record has key value x the dummy records should have key values of x + 1 and x + 2. This will not cause any INVALID KEY conditions during data set creation. Suppose also that the data set will grow appreciably larger. With these conditions the data set will now occupy two cylinders unless the overflow area is reduced. The SPACE and DCB parameters need to be recoded as follows:

```
SPACE=(CYL,(1,1)),DCB=(DSORG=IS,LRECL=101,RECFM=F,
BLKSIZE=101,RKP=1,KEYLEN=5,CYLOFL=5,OPTCD=ILYM)
```

Note that the OPTCD subparameter specifies an independent overflow area and a master index. For this small data set probably neither are needed. Additionally, the independent overflow area needs additional disk space.

Example 5: It is possible to create an ISAM data set using either two or three distinct DD statements. Each DD statement references one or more of the data set's three major components: index, prime data area, and overflow area. Note the similarity between the DSN values coded here and those used to reference individual partitioned data set (pds) members.

```
//DD2    DD   DSN=ISAM.DATA.SET(INDEX),DISP=(NEW,KEEP),
//            UNIT=3350,VOL=SER=DISK01,SPACE=(CYL,1),
//            DCB=(DSORG=IS,BLKSIZE=101,RECFM=F,RKP=1,KEYLEN=5,
//                 OPTCD=ILM,NTM=4)
//       DD   DSN=ISAM.DATA.SET(PRIME),DISP=(NEW,KEEP),
//            UNIT=3350,VOL=SER=DISK02,SPACE=(CYL(10,5)),
//            DCB=DSORG=IS
//       DD   DSN=ISAM.DATA.SET(OVFLOW),DISP=(NEW,KEEP),
//            UNIT=3350,VOL=SER=DISK03,SPACE=(CYL,5),
//            DCB=DSORG=IS
```

Several significant JCL features are present in the DD statements. Notice that the second and third DD statements do not contain a DDname. The syntax is identical to concatenation with sequential and partitioned data sets. With ISAM it is used to show that the three DD statements are to be processed together. The syntax DSN = x(y) implies either a pds member or one of the three components of an ISAM data set. INDEX, PRIME, and OVFLOW are reserved words in this process. The three DD statements should be coded in the order shown here. An ISAM data set can also be created and processed using two DD statements. The complete DCB parameter needs only to be specified with the first statement. It is sufficient to code just DCB = DSORG = IS with the other two. KEEP is specified as the disposition for the data set on all three DD statements. CATLG cannot be specified when multiple DD statements are used to create an ISAM data set. In a subsequent step the IEHPROGM or IDCAMS utility can be used to catalog the data set.

ISAM JCL syntax shares another similarity with pds JCL syntax. Each allows a third sub-subparameter with the SPACE parameter. With ISAM it specifies index size.

When SPACE = (CYL,(x,y,z)) is coded it means that z cylinders are allocated for the index of an ISAM data set. These cylinders are in addition to the x cylinders in the primary allocation. This form of the SPACE parameter is never necessary with ISAM data sets that occupy one cylinder and contain only a track index. In fact, even with data sets that occupy several cylinders it is not needed. If space for the index is not specifically requested then one or more cylinders are taken from the primary allocation and used for this purpose. Hence, coding SPACE = (CYL,(2,,1)) and SPACE = (CYL,3) both result in two cylinders being allocated to the prime data area and one to the index area.

Example 6: An ISAM data set is to be created with a primary allocation of 100 cylinders. In addition, five cylinders should be used to hold the cylinder and master indexes. All this can be accomplished by coding

```
SPACE=(CYL,(100,,5))
```

Example 7: Create a data set that contains variable length records. Assume the dcb and key values for the data set are identical to those in Example 1 except that maximum length (actual data) of a record is 100 bytes. Several DCB subparameters must be modified. The key field cannot be located in the first five bytes of a record. The DCB parameter must now be written as

```
//           DCB=(DSORG=IS,LRECL=105,BLKSIZE=319,RECFM=VB,
//               RKP=5,KEYLEN=5,CYLOFL=21,OPTCD=LY)
```

Example 8: To retrieve the ISAM data set created in Example 4 code only the following:

```
//DD5    DD   DSN=ISAM.DATASET,DISP=(OLD,PASS),
//            DCB=(DSORG=IS)
```

The above code is sufficient if the ISAM data set is cataloged or passed. If this is not the case then UNIT and VOL must also be coded. It is unnecessary to recode any of the other DCB parameters that were coded during data set creation. Those values are available in the format-1 and format-2 data set control blocks on the VTOC of the volumes that contain the data set. DCB=DSORG=IS should always be coded unless the data set was passed.

Many important ISAM data sets are very large. Often they occupy multiple disk volumes. With data sets of this size a Master Index should be created. The indexes and independent overflow areas should be placed on separate volumes from the prime data area.

Example 9: Create an ISAM data set that will occupy 100 cylinders on each of three disk volumes. An index of five cylinders and an independent overflow area of 25 cylinders should also be allocated.

```
//DD7    DD   DSN=ISAM.DATA.SET(INDEX),DISP=(NEW,KEEP),
//            UNIT=3350,VOL=SER=DISK01,SPACE=(CYL,5),
//            DCB=(DSORG=IS,BLKSIZE=101,OPTCD=ILMRY,NTM=4,
//            CYLOFL=5)
//       DD   DSN=ISAM.DATA.SET(PRIME),DISP=(NEW,KEEP),
//            UNIT=3350,VOL=SER=(DISK97,DISK98,DISK99),
//            SPACE=(CYL,100),DCB=*.DD7
//       DD   DSN=ISAM.DATA.SET(OVFLOW),DISP=(NEW,KEEP),
//            UNIT=3350,VOL=SER=DISK02,SPACE=(CYL,25),
//            DCB=*.DD7
```

Here a referback is used with the second and third DD statements. This is an alternative to coding DCB=DSORG=IS. Unlike sequential data sets, 100 cylinders are allocated on all three of the volumes identified as the prime data area.

Problems With ISAM Data Sets

ISAM data sets have some inherent processing inefficiencies. These occur primarily because of the index structure and the overflow area. At first glance there may not seem to be many problems with the index. However, this is only because such problems are overshadowed by problems with the overflow area. Records in either overflow area wreak havoc with either random or sequential processing. The fact that all overflow records are unblocked worsens the problem. Data sets with large overflow areas must be reorganized on a regular basis.

Many features associated with processing an ISAM data set are very inflexible. This includes requesting space in cylinders for the data and index components, storing the entire key in the index record, sequentially searching the track index, separate index record blocks for each data track, assigning exactly one index record per track, and not allowing physical deletions. From an application programming perspective it involves a substantial effort to process an ISAM data set on a secondary key and to distinguish between logical and physical deletion. A data set cannot be concurrently processed sequentially and randomly. The culmination of the above problems was the primary reason for developing the VSAM KSDS to replace ISAM.

Exercises

1. Each of the following DD statements is an attempt to create an ISAM data set. Find the problems with the three statements.

```
//DD1    DD   DSN=&&X,DISP=(,PASS),SPACE=(CYL,(1,,1)),
//            UNIT=VIO

//DD2    DD   DSN=ISAM(ALPHA),UNIT=SYSDA,
//            SPACE=(CYL,(5,1)),VOL=SER=WORK01,
//            DCB=(DSORG=IS,RKP=0,KEYLEN=9,OPTCD=ILMR,
//            BLKSIZE=100)

//DD3    DD   DSN=ISAM(INDEX),DISP=(NEW,CATLG),
//            UNIT=3350,VOL=SER=WORK01,SPACE=(CYL,5),
//            DCB=(RKP=90,KEYLEN=10,CYLOFL=10,
//            LRECL=100,RECFM=FB,BLKSIZE=4000,OPTCD=IRW)
//       DD   DSN=ISAM(OVRFLOW),DISP=(NEW,PASS),
//            VOL=REF=*.DD3,SPACE=(CYL,10),
//            DCB=(*.DD3,RECFM=F,BLKSIZE=100)
//       DD   DSN=ISAM(PRIME),DISP=(NEW,KEEP),
//            UNIT=3380,VOL=SER=(DISK01,DISK02),
//            DCB=DSORG=IS,OPTCD=I
```

2. Give a specific example that illustrates why the index is necessary in order to sequentially process an ISAM data set.

3. Logically delete a record in the overflow area. Determine if any changes take place in the pointers in the overflow area. Suppose the record deleted is the physically last record written in the overflow area. Does the answer change in this case?

4. Describe how to construct the smallest possible ISAM data set that requires a master index with 3350 disks. Specify actual dcb values and the size and type of the overflow areas used.

5. When creating an ISAM data set on a 3350 disk, which of the following are not valid SPACE parameter values? For each invalid parameter specify why it is invalid.

```
SPACE=(ABSTR,address,900)
SPACE=(CYL,(10,5))
SPACE=(CYL,(10,5,1))
SPACE=(TRK,(300,30))
SPACE=(19069,(1,2,3))
```

6. How much space in bytes will the index for a one cylinder ISAM data set occupy on a 3350 disk? Give the largest and smallest possible values. Include disk overhead. Note that the answer depends on the amount of cylinder overflow specified and the size of the key field.

7. With PL/I and Assembler it is possible to create an ISAM data set where the key field need not be part of the logical record. Such keys are called non-embedded keys. They cannot be used with a COBOL program. With non-embedded keys the key field is written in front of the logical record when it is placed on disk. What limitations on processing occur when using non-embedded keys? What advantages may be gotten from using non-embedded keys?

8. Describe the details required to dynamically reorganize a data set based on the three values in the reorganization statistics fields. Include both the relevant COBOL code and the following step in the job stream which may perform the reorganization.

9. Suppose a record is to be added to a track in the exact location where there is a logically deleted record. Will it replace the deleted record? Are there any additional conditions that must be met before the new record will replace the logically deleted record? Do the answers change if the new record and the logically deleted record contain the same key value?

10. Suppose it is desired to create an ISAM data set randomly rather than sequentially. How can this be done? Under what conditions might this be desirable?

11. Describe in detail the processing needed to perform the following I/O operations with the ISAM data set shown in Example 1. Discuss all three steps performed during random processing. Suppose the operations are performed in the order shown here and following the addition of the records with keys of 725, 730, and 750.

- Read the record with key = 1200
- Add the record with key = 0925
- Add the record with key = 0675
- Read the record with key = 1330

12. Under what conditions can a rewrite operation cause a value in the track indexes to change? Consider this first for fixed length records and then for variable length records.

13. List all of the possible operations mentioned in this chapter that can cause an INVALID KEY condition to be raised. Do any other operations also seem to be reasonable candidates?

Chapter 14

Direct and Relative Data Sets

Overview

The direct data set organization allows several different physical structures. Relative and true direct are the most popular and are the only two permitted with COBOL. The others are available with PL/I and Assembler.

Direct Data Sets

Direct data sets are available with all three of the major programming languages: COBOL, PL/I, and Assembler. They are even available with Fortran! In COBOL they are called Direct data sets, while in PL/I they are called REGIONAL III data sets. Direct data sets require a more complex disk structure than relative data sets. Some of the processing options that are available with direct data sets cannot be used with relative ones. There is no VSAM equivalent of a direct data set.

All direct data sets must be written on a direct access device. Like ISAM data sets, direct data sets are stored on disk in COUNT-KEY-DATA format. Unlike ISAM, a record's key need not be physically present within the disk DATA field. Hence the value contained in the disk KEY field need not also be included in the disk DATA field, although it often is. Whether it is or not is left to the discretion of the programmer. It is the responsibility of the application program to supply two values when referencing a record in a direct data set. The first value is a relative track number. With direct data sets each track is a slot. Records are associated with a specific slot. Hence a slot may contain several records. A relative data set slot holds exactly one record. The second value supplied is the disk KEY field value, which is written on the track preceding the record. When writing a record to a direct data set the record is written on the specified relative track in the first available location on the track that does not contain a record. Hence if 04 and ABC denote the relative track and key respectively a record is written on disk as shown in Figure 14–1. The character string ABC need not be repeated in the DATA field.

Programming Considerations

The above description of direct addressing implies two potential problems. When adding a record, what happens if the requested track is completely full? What if the desired track has available space but already contains a record with a disk KEY field that contains the same value as the record to be written? Within certain limitations both of these situations must somehow be handled by the application program.

When a track becomes full a request can be made to add a new record to the next available track that contains sufficient space to hold the record. The system can be instructed to do this automatically. If the track is full and this is not done the request to write the record will be rejected. Other approaches can be developed by the programmer.

It is possible that several records on one track may contain the same value in their disk KEY fields. When trying to randomly access any of these records only the first record can ever be retrieved. The others will be ignored. The ones that are ignored will include the most recently written. One of these is probably the desired record. Once a record is written it cannot be physically deleted to allow its space to be reused. Hence it is the application program's responsibility to, if possible, avoid writing multiple records with the same KEY value on a single track.

All four non–VSAM record formats are allowed with a direct data set. Fixed length records are handled in one way, while variable, undefined, and spanned records are processed using a second technique. A spanned record may occupy several blocks. BSAM and BDAM are used to process direct data sets, and blocking and deblocking of logical records are not performed by the basic access methods. When the data set is created secondary allocations may be coded with the SPACE parameter. However, once the data set is initially closed its size cannot subsequently be increased.

With the variable record formats the track capacity record R0 is used to monitor the available unused space on the track. This is one of only two situations where an application program interacts with the capacity record. ISAM uses the R0 record in the track index to point to the overflow area. Initially the track capacity record specifies an empty track. As processing occurs two values are stored in R0. They are

FIGURE 14–1
A Record in a Direct Data Set

written as CCHHR and LL. Here CCHHR is the address of the last record written on the track and LL is the number of unused bytes remaining on the track. In the majority of applications direct data sets contain fixed length records. This chapter emphasizes this situation. Hence, assume unblocked fixed length records unless otherwise stated.

When all records are fixed length the same number of records is written on each track. Each physical record contains one logical record. When the data set is first opened, every track in the primary allocation is preformatted with dummy records. A dummy record is identified by binary ones (HIGH-VALUES) in the first byte of the disk KEY field of that record. This method of creating and identifying dummy records is handled entirely by the BSAM and BDAM access methods. Application programs should not try to retrieve dummy records by moving HIGH-VALUES to the first byte in the KEY field in an attempt to match a KEY value on disk. Likewise, an application program may do both logical and physical deletions. The first byte in the disk DATA field is commonly reserved for logical deletions.

Data Set Creation

Both a relative and direct data set can be created in two different ways. With relative data sets both techniques are sequential; with direct, creation can be either sequential or random. Random is the most commonly used. It is roughly equivalent to sequentially creating a relative data set using the NOMINAL KEY. Secondary extents are never used if the data set is created randomly. Hence with random creation the entire data set will be placed on one volume. With sequential creation the secondary allocations may be used. Sequential creation is similar to the sequential creation of a relative data set without using the NOMINAL KEY.

As mentioned above, two values must be supplied to identify where a record is to be written: the relative track number and the disk KEY field. In COBOL terminology these fields can be described as follows:

Field	*COBOL Attributes*
Relative Track Number	1 Fullword (PIC S9(8) COMP)
Disk KEY field	1 to 255 bytes of data (PIC X to PIC X(255))

These same two values must be supplied to retrieve an existing record. Both fields should be contained within the same group item and in the order specified above. It is the combination of these two values in the application program that determine the disk location. The first byte in the disk KEY field should be reserved for use as a delete byte by the access method. In a COBOL program the group item which contains the relative track field and the disk KEY field is called the ACTUAL KEY. The ACTUAL KEY must be defined in the WORKING-STORAGE SECTION (most commonly), the LINKAGE SECTION, or the FILE SECTION. When the key field is defined in the FILE SECTION it cannot be part of the particular FD for which it is the ACTUAL KEY.

How are values assigned to the two elementary items that comprise the key field? Ordinarily the disk KEY field is the most straightforward of the two with which to work. A specific field present within each record is used for this purpose. If at all possible the KEY field values should be unique. If there is no unique record field present a concatenation of several fields can be used. For example, when Social Security number is present it is a good candidate for the key field. The concatenation of a complete name (first, middle, and last) and address might also suffice. The smaller the number of bytes used as a KEY field, the less space used on the disk. However, this is not ordinarily a significant factor in selecting a key field. Likewise, the KEY field is often unnecessarily duplicated within the DATA field. When nonunique KEY values occur processing becomes more complicated.

Usually there is no straightforward pairing between a specific data field (or fields) within a record and the track or slot the record occupies on disk. This situation occurs because it is difficult to find a field that contains the value 0 to n equally distributed. Rather, some specific field in the records is selected. Its contents are then mathematically manipulated using an algorithm of some type to determine a unique relative track. Such manipulation is often referred to as a *hashing algorithm*. The algorithm must satisfy two properties. If there are N tracks in the data set the value the algorithm yields should be between 0 and N-1. It should also attempt to evenly distribute the records throughout all N tracks. Additionally, a record should be placed in the slot initially selected by the algorithm. It is uncommon for a data field within the records to directly satisfy these three conditions without some type of manipulation. If such a field does exist it should be used to determine the relative track slot.

Example 1: Suppose that a direct data set is defined on five tracks of an IBM 3350 disk. Each record contains 4000 bytes of data. Hence exactly four records fit on a track. A nine byte field in each record contains a Social Security number. There are five records in the data set. The keys for the records are shown in Table 14–1. The relative track selected to hold the record is determined by a simple quotient and remainder algorithm. The remainder that results from dividing the last two digits of the Social Security number by 5 is used. For example, since 08 divided by 5 gives 3 as a remainder, the record with key 101010108 is written on track 3. Table 14–2 shows the order in which the records are placed on the tracks during the random creation.

TABLE 14–1

Record Keys

Record	*Key Value*	*Relative Track Number*
1	000111225	0
2	123456789	4
3	987654321	1
4	000000011	1
5	000012330	0

TABLE 14–2
Direct Data Set following the Random Creation

Track of Data Set	Records
0	1,5
1	3,4
2	—
3	—
4	2

It is important to note that this simple algorithm is not practical if there are more than a few records in the data set, although it probably will satisfy the even distribution property. Most courses in Data Structures include examining and evaluating hashing algorithms. The records in the data set can be used to determine an acceptable algorithm.

Updating a Direct Data Set

Example 2: Suppose the above direct data set is to be updated. It is necessary to add five additional records, modify two existing records, and perform both types of deletion. The complete list of transactions is shown in Table 14–3.

The first two records are added to track 0. Following these additions track 0 is full. It contains four active records. Transaction three reads the first record on track 1 into a buffer area, modifies the appropriate fields within it, and rewrites it. The rewritten record remains the first record on the track.

Transaction four writes a third record on track 1. No check is made to see if there is an existing record on this track with the same KEY field as this record, which happens to be the case here. At this point the second and third records on track 1 contain the same KEY field.

TABLE 14–3
Transactions in Updating the Direct Data Set

Transaction Number	Social Security Number (DISK) KEY	Relative Track Number	Type of Transaction
1	112233430	0	Add
2	112233435	0	Add
3	987654321	1	Update
4	000000011	1	Add
5	001100110	0	Add (track 1)
6	000000011	1	Update
7	123456789	4	Delete (logical)
8	000000000	0	Add (track 2)
9	000111225	0	Delete (physical)

Transaction five attempts to add a record to track 0. Since track 0 is full the system if so instructed will write this record on the first subsequent track that contains sufficient space to hold the record. If this approach is not used when a track is full then the application program must have its own specific routine to determine where to place the record or the record will not get added.

Transaction six requires updating the record on track 1 with KEY 000000011. When the READ is executed the first of the two records with this KEY is moved to the program's buffer area. Thus the older copy of the record is updated, not the most recent copy. This may not be the intent of the application!

The logical deletion requested in transaction seven consists of reading the designated record, modifying the first byte in the record itself, and then rewriting the record. Transaction eight attempts to add a record to track 0. Since this track is full an attempt is made to add this record to track 1. Since track 1 is also full the record is eventually written as the first record on track 2.

Transaction nine performs a physical deletion of the first record on track 0. This consists of changing the first byte in the KEY field to binary ones. The access method does this. If the last two transactions had been specified in reverse order the record with key 000000000 would have been added to the correct track and the delete would also have taken place. This is an important point; even though the processing is random, the order in which the transactions are processed can affect the correctness and efficiency of the update. Points such as this should be noted whenever transactions are batched.

JCL for Direct Data Sets

In order to request the use of the next available track that contains sufficient space to hold the record, the OPTCD subparameter must be coded on the accompanying DD statement for the data set. Code DCB=(LIMCT=x,OPTCD=E,DSORG=DA, . . .). The value of x determines the number of additional tracks that may be searched in order to find sufficient space. OPTCD=E requests the extended search feature. Additional space to add or retrieve a record is examined. Hence the OPTCD value must also be coded during retrieval. In order to locate records that were placed on tracks other than where they should have been written, the same two parameters must be coded when retrieving records. If duplicate KEY values occur the records involved may end up written on different tracks. This can make it very difficult to retrieve the desired record. It is not required to code the same value with LIMCT during retrieval as was coded during creation, or even to code this DCB subparameter at all. When different values are coded it is possible that (pick one from each pair) an existing/non-existing record may/may not be found. LIMCT supports 'wrap around.' When the value coded exceeds the remaining number of tracks the tracks at the beginning of the data set will be searched if necessary. The default for LIMCT is that every track in the data set is searched and that wrap around is used.

Example 3: A DD statement to create a direct data set with the DCB values used in Example 1 may be coded as shown below. The SPACE parameter value implies that there are more than five records in the data set.

```
//DIRECT DD DSN=DIRECT.DATASET,DISP=(NEW,PASS),
//          UNIT=DISK,VOL=SER=DISK01,SPACE=(TRK,(50,10)),
//          DCB=(LRECL=4001,BLKSIZE=4001,RECFM=F,DSORG=DA,
//          KEYLEN=10,LIMCT=2,OPTCD=E)
```

Direct data sets can only be created on a direct access device. They may be permanent or temporary. Secondary allocations are used during sequential creation if they are needed. Once created the data set cannot be extended. It is necessary to specify the length of the KEY field in the DCB parameter or in the application program. Since the key field value need not be embedded within the logical record, the RKP subparameter should not be coded with a direct data set. Incidentally, LIMCT=2 means that the designated track and (if necessary) one additional track will be examined when processing a record. Thus, in the previous example transaction eight will not add a record if LIMCT equals 1 or 2. Notice that the values 4001 and 10 (not 9) are coded to allow the two types of deletion.

Example 4: To access the existing direct data set created in the previous example code the following JCL:

```
//DIRECT DD DSN=DIRECT.DATASET,DISP=(OLD,PASS),
//          DCB=(DSORG=DA,OPTCD=E,LIMCT=2)
```

The only JCL that is coded here specifically for a direct data set is the DCB parameter. OPTCD and LIMCT are coded as a pair. Suppose that one or both of these had not been coded. If an attempt is made to find the record with key 001100110 every track in the data set will be searched if necessary. If it is in this data set the record will be found. DSORG must be coded since the default for this parameter is a physical sequential data set. This code assumes that the data set has been cataloged or passed. Hence UNIT and VOLUME need not be coded.

Relative Data Sets

Relative data sets are available in COBOL. With PL/I the same type of data set is called a REGIONAL I data set. Naturally, they also can be processed with an assembler program. The basic idea behind relative data set organization is to access a record based on its relative location within a disk data set. This is done by requesting an initial primary allocation of disk storage. This storage is then formatted into physical records all the same size. For example, suppose ten tracks are allocated and 800 byte records are to be processed. On an IBM 3350 exactly nineteen such records fit on a track. Hence the allocated storage is thought of as 190 slots on the disk. These slots are numbered from 0 to 189. To determine the location of slot 72 the system can calculate that it is the fifteenth record in the fourth track in the data set. Likewise, to find the location of an arbitrary slot N divide N by 19. This results in a quotient of x and a remainder of y. The slot is the yth record on track x-1. In any disk data set relative tracks are numbered beginning with 0 and relative records are numbered from 1 on a given track. With a relative data set the slot numbers are independent of specific tracks or cylinders as far as the program is concerned.

Clearly a relative data set requires that all physical records must be the same size. With this assumption the same number of records fit on every track. Blocking can be permitted. However, it is the responsibility of the application program to perform all of the blocking and deblocking.

Programming Considerations

Because no secondary allocations are allowed after the data set is created the value coded on the SPACE parameter should be carefully selected. Once the data set is initially created no further expansion is possible. To use a relative data set a programmer must be willing to accept three fundamental limitations: all records are fixed length, no blocking is performed by the access method, and no secondary allocations may be used. Secondary allocations may be coded on the SPACE parameter. However, no secondary allocations are actually made. All processing requests should be within the primary allocation.

With a relative data set no key field needs to be present within the data records. Recall that an ISAM data set requires a key within each logical record. The key field value is used for retrieving and adding records randomly. With a direct data set a record also need not have a key within the logical record itself. Likewise, a relative data set is written on a disk in COUNT DATA format, instead of the COUNT KEY DATA format which is used with both ISAM and direct data sets. However, a key field is necessary for processing a relative data set.

When processing a relative data set a key field must be specified in the application program. However, it is not contained within the record itself. In a COBOL program the key field must be in the WORKING-STORAGE SECTION or LINKAGE SECTION. On a WRITE statement the value in the key field identifies the slot where the record is written. On a READ statement the value in the key field determines the slot whose contents are read into the program's buffer area. Sometimes a particular field within the record will also contain the same value as the key field. In such a situation that particular field was probably selected because it contained unique values that all fell within the set of possible slot numbers. This is the ideal situation in which to use a relative data set. For example, if a field within each record in the data set contains a unique three digit number then a relative data set with 1000 slots can be used to hold the records. There may be considerably less than 1000 records in the data set. The number of slots must be greater than or equal to the largest possible value found in this field.

Because relative data sets have no disk overhead they can randomly access records considerably faster than either ISAM or direct data sets. ISAM processing must use the index first and then conclude with a sequential search of a track. A direct data set identifies a specific track that must be sequentially searched for the desired record. Because a relative data set is the fastest way to randomly process records, it should be used when speed is the highest priority in processing. In actuality there are few relative data sets. The primary reason for this is that most data sets do not contain a field that can be used to identify the slot number where the record is to be stored. Such a field must either directly or indirectly provide a non-negative integer value. The records in the data set should occupy a 'reasonable' number of the available slots. Reasonable can be defined as anywhere between 10% and 70%. Ideally the field which determines the slot should identify unique values. When duplicates occur some approach must be found to handle the duplicate records. The more duplication, the more problems.

The most common approach with duplicate key values is to write the record in the first available empty slot following the one that should contain the record. A delete byte is usually used to determine whether a slot is empty. The first byte in a record is used for this purpose. The delete byte is logical, not physical. It is the complete responsibility of the application programmer. The common convention is that if the delete byte contains binary ones (HIGH-VALUES) the slot is empty. Hence moving HIGH-VALUES to the delete byte logically deletes a record. A slot which contains an active record should have binary zeroes in the delete byte. Before writing a record to a relative data set move LOW-VALUES to the delete byte. During program development it is a good idea to use printable characters for the two states of the delete byte.

Creating a Relative Data Set

When a relative data set is created any slots that do not have records written to them are marked as deleted by the BSAM access method. The actual values coded in the delete byte are left to the discretion of the application programmer. The usual approach is to mimic the way ISAM works. However, with relative data sets deleted records are retrieved both sequentially and randomly. All processing decisions are handled by the application program. The following example illustrates the construction of a relative data set.

Example 5: A relative data set is to be created. Each record is 4000 bytes in length, and four tracks of space are allocated on an IBM 3350 disk. Hence there are 16 slots in the data set. Slots 0, 1, 2, and 3 are on track 0. Slots 4, 5, 6, and 7 are on track 1, etc. Each record that is to be written to this data set contains a two byte field. The values in this field are not necessarily unique, and they range from 00 to 99. In order to assign a record to a specific slot the value in this field is divided by 16 and the remainder is used to identify the slots. For example, if this field contains the values 17, 19, 37, 07, 57, 59, 13, and 63 respectively, then slots 1, 3, 5, 7, 9, 11, 13, and 15 have records written to them. During data set creation the WRITE verb is used to add a record to a slot.

This assumes that the data field within the record is used to determine the corresponding slot number value before each WRITE statement. Following this the value of the slot number must be moved to the NOMINAL KEY in working storage. In a COBOL program the NOMINAL KEY must be defined as PIC S9(8) COMP. When this is done the record is written in this slot if it is empty. If the NOMINAL KEY is not used in this process then the record is written to the next available slot. Ordinarily this is the slot following the one just written to. If the file had just been opened the record is placed in slot 0. Hence creation of a relative data set can be done one of two ways: specifying the slot number in the NOMINAL KEY field or allowing the BSAM access method to place the records in consecutive slots. With the second approach some method must be found to keep track of the record in a given slot. One approach is for the application program to maintain a table identifying the records in a given slot.

Using the value in the key field to determine the slot leads to two methods employed by BSAM. First, records are assumed to be in ascending order. When they are not, the record that is out of order is written in the next available slot.

Example 6: If records with slot numbers of 1, 3, 2, 5, 4, 10, 7, and 11 were to be written to a relative file they would be placed in slots 1, 3, 4, 5, 6, 10, 11, and 12 respectively. Second, all slots that are not assigned an active record have their first byte initialized to HIGH-VALUES. In Example 5 this will be every even numbered slot. The data portion of these records will have the same contents as the record currently in the buffer for the data set. In Example 6 this implies that slots 7, 8, and 9 will be identical to slot 10 except for the delete byte.

When records are written without using the key field order is not important. In Example 5 the eight records to be written would occupy slots 0 through 7. Retrieving these records in subsequent applications may well be difficult since nothing within the record correlates to the slot that the record occupies. For this reason records are usually written using the key field.

No matter which technique is employed, once the file is closed for the first time it cannot be subsequently extended. Hence, even if only part of the last track has been accessed, it is still preformatted with dummy records. The entire relative data set must be placed on one volume since it consists only of the primary allocation.

When creating a relative data set access must be specified as sequential and the file must be opened for output. In fact, for sequential processing only the WRITE verb may be used. To read the records in a relative data set the programmer uses random processing and the file is opened for input. With random processing the file can also be opened for I/O. When this is done both the READ and REWRITE verbs may be used.

Updating a Relative Data Set

Suppose we wish to update the records in a relative data set. The transactions to be performed include add, delete, and update operations. Only one verb is necessary for all three types of operations: the REWRITE verb. No matter which action is specified it is necessary to READ the record using the key field to determine the slot number.

The following logic can then be used:

Transaction Type	*Contents of Delete Byte*	*Logic*
Add	HIGH-VALUES	Move the new record's fields to the 01 level; issue a REWRITE for the new record.
Add	LOW-VALUES	Invalid transaction; there is an active record in this slot.
Delete	HIGH-VALUES	Invalid transaction; there is no logical record in this slot.
Delete	LOW-VALUES	Move HIGH-VALUES to the delete byte; issue a REWRITE to logically delete the record.
Update	HIGH-VALUES	Invalid transaction; there is no logical record in this slot.
Update	LOW-VALUES	Modify the fields in the 01 level getting new values; issue a REWRITE to change the record on disk.

When doing any of these operations the record in question must first be read to determine the status of the delete byte. The logic for all three types of transactions is controlled by the value found in that field. Care should be taken to REWRITE the same record that was just READ. If the value in the program that determines slot number is changed between the READ and the REWRITE this will not be the case.

JCL for Relative Data Sets

The JCL used when creating a relative data set could typically be coded somewhat like the following:

```
//RELATIVE    DD   DSN=XYZ,DISP=(NEW,CATLG),UNIT=DISK,
//          VOL=SER=DISK99,SPACE=(CYL,10),
//          DCB=(LRECL=100,BLKSIZE=100,RECFM=F,DSORG=DA)
```

If DSORG=DA is not coded problems can result.

To reference an existing relative data set that has been cataloged or passed code

```
//RELATIVE    DD   DSN=XYZ,DISP=(OLD,PASS),DCB=DSORG=DA
```

Nothing else need be coded.

Duplicate Slot Numbers

Consider the problem of duplicate slot numbers occurring. When this happens two common techniques are available. First, the record is written in the next available free slot following the desired slot. Ideally this is within the next several slots. To make this work for the largest slot numbers wrap-around must be used where the records at the beginning of the data set (slot 0, etc.) logically follow the last slot in the data set. This implies that there is a field within each record that has a unique value and is coded in its entirety within each disk record. Without this individual records cannot be positively identified when it is necessary to retrieve them.

A second approach involves chaining records with duplicate key values in a designated overflow area. With this approach space must be preformatted with dummy records when the file is initially created. Because no tracks can be used following the one which contains the last active record, a programmer must code a routine to preformat as many additional tracks as are desired. The first slot can be used to identify the first available empty slot in the overflow area. Call this the control slot. Now when an attempt is made to add a record to a slot that contains an active record the following occurs: the control slot is checked to determine the next available free slot in the overflow area; the new record is written to this slot; the value in the control slot is incremented by one. An additional pointer field must now be included with every record in the data set. It will be used to identify additional records that were assigned to the same slot number. As records are logically deleted from the overflow area they can be reused. This implies that all records in the overflow area that do not contain active records are also linked together in a list. In this situation the control slot will always identify the slot at the beginning of this list. This will require more complicated programming.

Clearly both of the above approaches involve moderately complex programming. Neither is needed when duplicate keys do not exist. However, duplication is the norm, not the exception. As an intermediate approach, try to determine a scheme for assigning slot numbers that will leave about 50% of all slots empty. As the number of empty slots drops below this value processing efficiency drops off dramatically.

Exercises

1. Create a direct data set that consists of 101 byte records. Bytes two through ten should be used as the key. Use the last digit of the key to select the relative track. Hence, code SPACE=(TRK,10). Use the preceding two digits as the disk KEY field. Following this use either ADRDSSU or IEHDASDR to dump out the contents of the disk tracks that hold the data set. Examine the contents of the COUNT, KEY, and DATA fields, including the delete bytes.

2. Update the direct data set created in the previous exercise. Use a variety of transaction types. Following the update use either ADRDSSU or IEHDASDR to again dump out the contents of the disk tracks that hold the data set. Again examine the contents of the COUNT, KEY, and DATA fields, including the delete bytes.

3. Create a direct data set that consists of variable length records. First create the data set sequentially, then recreate it randomly. Use either ADRDSSU or IEHDASDR to examine the contents of the data set, especially the contents of the RO records.

4. Rather than using LIMCT, develop your own algorithm to handle the situation where a record should be written to a track that is already full. Hint: reserve a specific area within

the data set that is to be used only for overflow records. This is similar to the approach described with relative slots.

5. Suppose a hashing algorithm favors certain relative tracks. That is, it produces those track numbers more frequently than other numbers. What programming adjustments will this force in maintaining a direct data set?

6. In Example 1 why do exactly four records fit on one track of a 3350 disk? Suppose that 1000 records of this size were to be made into a direct data set using Social Security number as the key. How much disk space will be required? What hashing algorithm could be used? Following the creation of the data set, what percentage of records will be active?

7. In Example 2 problems occur when processing the fourth and sixth records. How can the processing be performed in order to avoid the problems with these two transactions? Two records with the same key field should not be placed on track 1. Additionally, suppose that there are two records on a track with the same key. How can the second record be updated?

8. Write a program to maintain a relative data set using the next available empty slot to hold a record when the desired slot is full.

9. Write a program to maintain a relative data set using an independent overflow area. Consider two approaches. First, the overflow area is adjacent to the prime data area within the same data set. Second, assume the overflow area is another relative data set.

10. Why would secondary allocations ordinarily be useless with a relative data set even if they were permitted? Describe a situation where secondary allocations would be convenient.

11. Use a relative data set to create and update a linked list structure.

12. What percentage of slots must contain active records for a relative data set to need reorganization (if it is 90% full the search for an empty slot is very time consuming)? How does this affect the two approaches for duplicates going to the same slot?

Chapter 15

Disk Data Sets

Overview

Data is stored on the IBM 3350 and 3380 disk drives (and also on the older 3330 model) in one of two formats: COUNT DATA and COUNT KEY DATA. The choice between the two is determined automatically by the data set organization of the records being stored on disk. If the records can be written and read using physical keys then the COUNT KEY DATA format is selected. The KEY values can be provided by the programmer as with indexed or direct data sets. They can also be supplied by the access method as with the directory of a pds or the index of an ISAM data set. Data sets with ''sequential–like'' organization are stored with COUNT DATA format. This includes physical sequential data sets, partitioned data set members, and relative data sets. Recall that physical keys are not created or used when processing a relative data set. Rather, with relative data sets the physical location of the record relative to the beginning of the data set is used to access the record. All VSAM data sets are stored in COUNT DATA format.

Throughout this chapter a track is pictured as a rectangle. An identification is always assumed between the left and right hand sides of the rectangle. Think of the accompanying figures as resulting from cutting the concentric circle that is the track and then flattening the resulting figure. Furthermore, assume that the cut was made at the 'beginning' of the track. One particular location on each track called the index point denotes the start of the track. The index point is followed by three disjoint fields, the Home Address (HA), the COUNT field for Record 0, and Record 0 itself. An application program is not allowed to directly process these fields. Since these fields cannot be used to store actual user data, their size is not included when later determining how many bytes of a given data set can fit on one track of a particular disk drive.

Disk Format

The beginning portion of each disk track is pictured in Figure 15–1.

The gaps on the track of the disk exist in order for specific hardware functions to take place as the gap moves past the read/write mechanism. The size of the gap varies depending upon where on the track it occurs. An application programmer need never be concerned with these gaps other than being aware that they exist and knowing their size when they occur within the user data area of the track.

The Home Address is a nine byte field which contains information about the entire track. The nine bytes contain the following five fields:

Field	*Length*	*Description*
physical address	2 bytes	this is the actual hardware address of the track
flag	1 byte	used to identify several categories such as: Is the track functional or defective? Is this a primary or an alternate track?
cylinder number	2 bytes	denoted as CC
head number	2 bytes	denoted as HH
cyclic check	2 bytes	this field is used for error detection

The four bytes in the cylinder and head number fields also identify the track. They can be thought of as a logical address. These bytes may not contain the same value as in the physical address field.

The Home Address field is followed by a special record called Record 0 or R0. It is used in several specific application programming situations. Two uses are discussed in the chapters on ISAM and direct data sets. A high level language application program can not explicitly read or write R0. Since both R0 and HA are always present but cannot be explicitly accessed they will not be shown in any of the subsequent pictures of tracks. Likewise, they have no role in calculating available space on the track. R0 itself is preceded by a COUNT field. The format of the COUNT field is described below.

A track formatted as COUNT DATA is pictured in Figure 15–2.

FIGURE 15–1

The Beginning of Each Disk Track

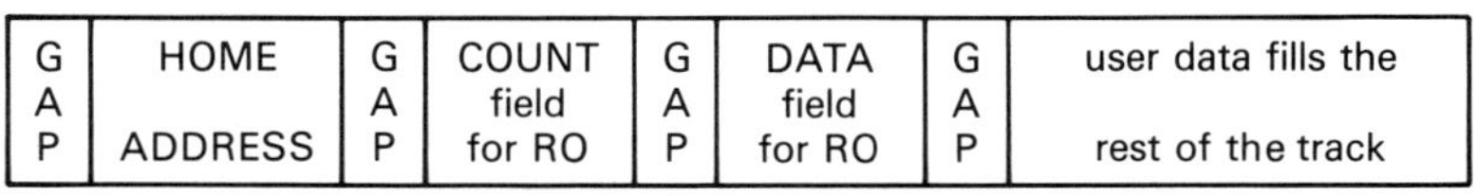

FIGURE 15–2
A Track Formatted as COUNT DATA

HA RO etc.	COUNT field for R1	G A P	PHYSICAL RECORD 1	G A P	COUNT field for R2	G A P	PHYSICAL RECORD 2	G A P	

Following the HA and R0 fields the remainder of the track alternates between a COUNT field and a user data field. The COUNT field contains thirteen bytes of data and consists of eight values. These fields are:

Value		*Length*	*Description*
physical address		2 bytes	same as in HA field
flag		1 byte	same as in HA field
cylinder number	(CC)	2 bytes	same as in HA field
head number	(HH)	2 bytes	same as in HA field
record number	(R)	1 byte	not included in HA field
key length	(K)	1 byte	not included in HA field
data length	(DD)	2 bytes	not included in HA field
cyclic check		2 bytes	same as in HA field

The CCHHR value identifies one specific physical record on the disk. Record values (R) range from one up to the highest number on the track. This value must be less than 256. With a 3350 disk the highest possible value is 103. With the COUNT DATA format the key length field contains binary zeroes since there is no disk KEY field. The data length field contains the number of bytes in the upcoming physical data record.

Bytes 4 through 11 are often collectively identified by the letters CCHHRKDD. The COUNT field and its associated gap together occupy 185 bytes on a 3350 disk.

A track formatted as COUNT KEY DATA is pictured in Figure 15–3.

When this format is used a physically disjoint KEY field is inserted between each COUNT and DATA pair. The KEY field is then followed by a gap to separate it from the DATA component. When records are stored in COUNT KEY DATA format the one byte key length field in the COUNT field contains the number of bytes in the KEY field.

Example 1: Suppose that several 500 byte physical records are written to a 3350 disk. Each record contains a nine byte key field. Assume that the records are

FIGURE 15–3
A Track Formatted as COUNT KEY DATA

HA RO etc.	COUNT field for R1	G A P	K E Y	G A P	PHYSICAL RECORD 1	G A P	COUNT field for R2	G A P	K E Y	G A P	PHYSICAL RECORD 2	

part of either an ISAM or direct data set. For the first record on track 3 of cylinder 20 in this data set the CCHHRKDD value in the COUNT field is:

```
00  14  00  03  01  09  01  F4
C   C   H   H   R   K   D   D
```

Suppose the same data are written to the same location on disk, but the record is part of a sequential data set and does not have a KEY field. The eight bytes will then contain the value:

```
00  14  00  03  01  00  01  F4
C   C   H   H   R   K   D   D
```

Since one byte is used to number the physical records on a track a maximum of 255 physical records can be written on a track. After the size of the COUNT, KEY, and DATA fields is discussed it will be apparent that 255 distinct records can never actually be placed on the same track. Note that a maximum of 255 bytes may be used for a key field. This is standard with keys throughout MVS systems. A two byte data field allows for a theoretical maximum record length of 64K. Ordinarily the number of bytes that will fit on one track serves as the upper bound for record size. There are no values in the COUNT field specifically related to either logical record length or record format. The disk drive interprets all records as physical. Likewise, the notion of record format is irrelevant to the disk. It considers all (physical) records as variable length unless told otherwise. In a sense the KDD portion of the COUNT field functions similar to a Block Descriptor Record with variable length records.

Even when records have been written to disk with RECFM=FB coded it is still possible for different block sizes to occur. This results when a data set is written to disk and the number of logical records is not an integral multiple of the blocking factor. For example, if a data set contains seven records and a blocking factor of three is used, the physical records will contain three, three, and one logical record respectively. Furthermore, whenever a data set is closed and then opened with EXTEND (DISP=MOD) specified an additional short block can be written. If five additional logical records are added to the seven logical records, blocks four and five contain three and two records. If a data set contains all blocks of the same size it can be processed more efficiently than a data set whose blocks vary in size. The next highest level of processing efficiency occurs when only one block is of a different size than all the others and it is the last block in the data set. These two types of data sets are called standard data sets. When such a data set exists, inform the system by coding RECFM=FBS in the accompanying DCB parameter. Processing can then be performed more efficiently. Standard cannot be specified within a COBOL application program.

Physical records are ordinarily written entirely on a single track. It is possible to write a record that is split between two or more tracks, by coding OPTCD=T in the DCB parameter on the accompanying DD statement. This requests the track overflow feature. This option often leads to processing inefficiencies. With OPTCD=T only spanned records are permitted. For more information on this topic see Chapter 11.

Disks and JCL

An MVS user initially interacts with a disk drive through JCL. To request a specific amount of disk storage the SPACE parameter is coded on a DD statement. There are three ways to request space: in cylinders, in tracks, and in physical records. The amount of space is actually allocated in tracks or cylinders. The system never allocates just part of a track. Physical records are device–independent. Hence 20 records on a 3350 remain 20 records on a 3380. However, there is a considerable difference in size between a 3350 and a 3380 disk. Thus, the amount of space allocated in tracks or cylinders varies appreciably from one type of disk drive to another.

No matter which of the three SPACE parameter formats is used one primary space allocation is made. A maximum of 15 secondary allocations may also be made on a specific disk volume. The number of secondary allocations can actually range from a high of 15 allocations to a low of 3, depending on whether the allocations are contiguous. With multi-volume data sets these secondary allocation values are in effect for every volume that holds part of the data set. Hence, if

```
SPACE=(CYL,(5,2)),VOL=SER=(DISK01,DISK02)
```

is coded five cylinders on volume DISK01 are initially allocated to the data set. When a specific volume is requested the primary space must be available for allocation on that volume or the job is cancelled. With a non-specific volume request the system searches for a volume of the type specified on the UNIT parameter with sufficient space for the primary allocation. With the secondary allocation request of two cylinders a maximum of 15 allocations will be made. Hence up to 35 cylinders on volume DISK01 may be allocated to this data set. If the entire amount of either the primary or secondary allocation is not available in contiguous storage on the volume up to five non-contiguous areas will be allocated to satisfy the secondary storage request. Since CYL is specified above, up to two non-contiguous cylinders may be allocated. If this is done on every secondary allocation the maximum amount of space allocated to the data set will be 20 cylinders.

When using a multi-volume data set up to 15 secondary allocations can also be made on volume DISK02. Just as with DISK01, this can result in from 16 to 30 cylinders being allocated on that volume.

The primary allocation is made only once. This occurs when the data set is created. A SPACE parameter that specifies a primary allocation may also be coded with any existing disk data set. It is checked for syntax by the Job Scheduler. However, no additional primary SPACE is actually allocated. Hence there is reason to code a primary space allocation with an existing data set.

A secondary allocation may be meaningfully coded with an existing data set. If no secondary allocation was initially coded the coded value becomes the secondary allocation. If a previous secondary allocation was coded the new value replaces it. The new value can specify more or less space in different units, for example, switching from tracks to cylinders. Additional volumes can also be requested when extending a multi-volume data set. There is no limit to the number of volumes to which a data set can be extended. Since the primary and secondary allocation amounts are positional sub-subparameters, a secondary allocation can be coded as SPACE=(TRK,(,2)).

A third sub-subparameter can be coded when requesting disk storage. It is used only when creating a pds or with an ISAM data set. For more information on this third sub-subparameter, see Chapters 12 and 13.

The values coded with any of the three amount sub-subparameters must be unsigned integers. If 0 is coded as the primary space value and no secondary value is coded, an entry is made in the directory (VTOC) of the volume but no space is actually allocated. Subsequently space can be requested through secondary allocations. A value of 0 can also be coded in order to code a subparameter that follows the amount subparameter. This is necessary since SPACE=(,,additional parameters) generates a JCL syntax error.

Volume Table of Contents (VTOC)

To understand more about the SPACE parameter and the way it works it is necessary to examine the Volume Table of Contents (VTOC). Every disk drive has a VTOC. The VTOC contains the names and locations of the data sets on the volume. The location is given as a CCHH address. It is the information in this directory that interacts with the SPACE parameter. The VTOC also manages the unused space on the volume. When a data set is to be either initially written or extended on the volume, this component of the VTOC determines where space is actually allocated. The VTOC must also keep track of its own used and unused space.

The entries in the VTOC are placed into one of seven categories. These classifications are called format-X data set control blocks where X is a value between 0 and 6. For example, every data set contained on the disk volume is represented by a format–1 data set control block in the VTOC. This is usually abbreviated as a format–1 dscb. Each dscb is 140 bytes in length. A format–1 dscb contains the name of the data set, its location on the volume (primary and up to two secondary allocations), and its pertinent dcb values (LRECL, RECFM, BLKSIZE, etc.). Additional secondary allocation information is stored in a second dscb which is chained to the original one. The format–1 dscb is the most common entry in the VTOC. When a data set is to be created on a disk volume the format–1 dscb's are sequentially searched until one that is unused is found. Hence the first format–1 dscb's are the most heavily used.

Since an ISAM data set contains more volume and dcb information than a sequential data set, it is represented by a format–1 and a format–2 dscb. This is one reason why DCB=(DSORG=IS, . . .) is coded when processing an ISAM data set. If the JCL implies a sequential data set and a format–2 dscb is found on the volume an abend results.

The exact role of the seven dscb types is shown in Table 15–1.

Numeric Calculations

The next several examples illustrate the amount of data that can be placed on a disk track. The two most important notions are those of blocking factors and data set organizations.

TABLE 15–1
The Seven DSCB Types

Types of DSCB	*Functions of DSCB*
0	A format–0 dscb is an unused dscb.
1	A format–1 dscb is associated with each data set written to the disk drive. If there are more than three contiguous areas in the data set a format–3 dscb is used. It is chained to the format–1 dscb.
2	These contain supplemental information for ISAM data sets only. The format–1 dscb for the ISAM data set points to a format–2 dscb.
3	These contain up to 13 extends for a data set in addition to the three extents stored in the format–1 dscb.
4	There is only one format–4 dscb. It describes the contents of the rest of the VTOC. In particular it monitors the unused dscb's in the VTOC. It also contains a pointer to the last entry in the format–1 dscb linked list.
5	A format–5 dscb keeps track of unused space on the disk drive. One format–5 dscb can monitor up to 26 extents. There are three fields associated with each extent: the beginning address of the extent and the number of cylinders and tracks which comprise it.
6	Format–6 dscb's are not used on MVS systems.

Example 2: Suppose that unblocked card images are written to an IBM 3350 disk. How many records will fit on a track? What percentage of the track actually contains data (and not overhead for the COUNT field)? Since the track alternates between 185 bytes of overhead and 80 bytes of data there are

$$\frac{19254}{265\ (=185+80)} = 72 \text{ physical (and logical) records per track}$$

The actual quotient is 72.65. However, part of a physical record cannot be placed on a track unless OPTCD=T is coded. Track overflow is not used in any of the examples in this chapter.

Additionally, only

$$\frac{80}{185+80} = \frac{80}{265} = 30.2\%$$

of the usable disk surface holds data. If there are 1000 records in the data set 1000 actual I/O operations will be necessary to write them to disk since they are unblocked. On a 3350 these records will occupy 14 tracks.

Example 3: Suppose that the same 1000 card images from the previous example are to be written to disk and blocked using a blocking factor of 20. Here a total of 200 logical records will fit on one track. This occurs because there are:

$$\frac{19254}{1785\ (=\ 1600+185)} = 10 \text{ physical records per track.}$$

Since $\frac{1600}{1785} = 90\%$,

most of the track is being used to hold data. Fifty actual write operations are necessary to create the data set. The data set now occupies five tracks.

Example 4: The 1000 card images are written to a 3350 disk and as many logical records as will fit on a track will comprise a block. To determine the largest possible blocking factor subtract 185 from 19254. This gives 19069. When 19069 is divided by 80 the quotient is 238.36. Hence, the blocking factor is 238. With this blocking factor

$$\frac{19040}{19040 + 185} = \frac{19040}{19225} = 99\%$$

of the track is holding data. Note that 19040 = 238*80. Actually the value 19254 should replace 19225 in the above fraction since the remaining 29 bytes cannot be used for storing additional data. The complete data set can be written to disk with just five write operations. This is one advantage associated with increasing the blocking factor from 20 to 238. Notice that for both blocking factors the data set occupies five tracks! There are two reasons why surprising results such as this often occur when working with disk data sets. First, the disk has a very low percentage of overhead associated with a large block. Second, since only complete blocks are written to a track the remaining portion of the track remains unused and wasted. In both Example 2 and Example 3 the unused space on the end of the track was ignored. When these unusable bytes are included, the percentage of data on a track decreases.

Unlike tape data sets, a disk data set does not necessarily use the track in a more efficient manner as the blocking factor increases. This is because of the unused space on the end of the track. If the size of a physical record plus the 185 bytes of overhead is greater than 19254/2 (= 9627), then the remainder of the track is unused. Hence, blocking card images with a blocking factor of 120 result in 9785 (= (80*120) + 185) bytes per block. There are 9469 wasted bytes on the track (almost half the track). It is a good idea to check a potential blocking factor to determine the portion of a track that will be unused. This can be a much more important consideration than the 185 bytes of overhead associated with each block. Remember that a large blocking factor is not necessarily better than a smaller blocking factor. In fact, large values can sometimes be disastrous.

Even if a large blocking factor results in very little wasted space on a track, it may be only slightly more efficient in percent of actual data on the track when compared to a considerably smaller blocking factor. If the buffer size is an important consideration the smaller blocking factor may be the appropriate choice.

Example 5: Determine an ideal blocking factor for card images on a 3350 disk. To conserve storage for buffers try to select a physical record size between 4K and 6K, approximately. Larger blocks require substantial buffer space. Smaller blocks result in too many unnecessary I/O operations, and also utilize a smaller percentage of the track for data. For values near 4K either four or five blocks will fit on a track. For values near 6K exactly three blocks will fit on a track. The best blocking factor (N) that will place three records on one track can be determined by noting that when

(80*N) + 185 is divided into 19254 the quotient must be 3 and the remainder should be as small as possible. Hence

$$3*(80*N + 185) + \text{remainder} = 19254$$
$$240 * N + 555 + \text{remainder} = 19254$$
$$\text{and } 240 * N + \text{remainder} = 18699$$

Dividing both sides by 240 gives

$$N = 77 \text{ and remainder} = 219$$

Thus, 231 (= 77*3) logical records fit on a track. Hence, as in Examples 2 and 3 above, the entire data set occupies five tracks. A total of 13 actual I/O operations are necessary to create the data set and subsequently access it. This compares to the values 50 and 5 in the previous examples. The trade-off between the blocking factor of 77 and the blocking factor of 238 is that the former uses approximately three times as many I/O operations to process the data set as the other. Since the actual blocksize is 6160 bytes this record is slightly larger than 6K (6144 bytes).

All of the previous discussion and examples concerned sequential disk data sets. Since a pds member falls into this category all of the above calculations also apply to a member. Likewise, a relative data set is stored in the same COUNT DATA format. It is impossible to distinguish between a sequential and relative data set by examining the dump of the disk tracks that hold the data set. All other non-VSAM data set organizations are represented in the more complex COUNT KEY DATA format. This applies to ISAM and direct data sets and also to the directory of a pds. For all three of these data sets KEY fields are written between the COUNT and DATA fields. These KEY fields are physically disjoint from both COUNT and DATA fields. Like the COUNT field, there is a space overhead associated with the KEY field. With a 3350 disk the KEY field overhead is 82 bytes. Unlike the COUNT field, a variable amount of information can be written in the KEY field. Keys range from 1 to 255 bytes in length. The following two examples illustrate the effect of this KEY field in processing.

Example 6: Unblocked ISAM card images are written to disk. A 9 byte Social Security number within each record is used as the key. How many such records will fit on one track? Here the 80 bytes of data has 276 bytes of overhead associated with it. Hence

$$\frac{19254}{356\ (= 80+185+82+9)} = 54$$

records will fit on one track. This value compares with 72 physical sequential unblocked card images on one track. Notice that only

$$\frac{80}{356} = 23\%$$

of the track holds actual data.

Example 7: Determine the number of partitioned data set directory blocks that can be placed on one track. Since every directory block is 256 bytes and each block has an 8 byte key, there are

$$\frac{19254}{531\ (=\ 256+8+185+82)} = 36$$

directory blocks per track.

This example is discussed in more detail in Chapter 12.

Since both direct data sets and pds directories must be unblocked only an ISAM data set can have a KEY field associated with it and at the same time contain blocked records. Each logical record within the block contains its own key. The key from the last logical record in the block is written in the disk KEY field. Hence with card images blocked with a factor of 20 and a 9 byte key the 1600 bytes of data will have 276 bytes of overhead. If each logical record also contains a leading delete byte then there will be

$$\frac{1620}{1620+276} = \frac{1620}{1896} = 85\%$$

of actual data on the disk. Because a great deal of the processing associated with an ISAM data set is random, it is unusual to select large blocking factors with ISAM. Hence the percentage of the track that contains data is appreciably lower with ISAM data sets than with sequential data sets.

ISAM data sets can be created and processed with non-embedded keys. This means that the key is not part of the logical record in the application program. In fact, the key is concatenated to the front of the logical record when written to the data field on disk. If non-embedded keys are used each record now occupies 90 bytes (1+9+80). Hence a physical record is 1800 bytes and

$$\frac{1800}{2076} = 87\%$$

of the disk holds data, exclusive of unused space at the end of the track. Unfortunately, only nine physical records can now fit on the track versus ten with the embedded keys. Since the above fraction ignores wasted space on the end of the track, the appearance of a higher percentage of utilization is misleading.

Why Block a Disk Data Set?

There are two fundamental reasons why a disk data set should be blocked. First, a blocked data set uses the disk drive more efficiently. This means that with blocking the amount of disk overhead is reduced. By picking a good blocking factor a very high percentage of the track will actually hold data (versus COUNT and KEY fields or wasted space on the end of the track). Second, with blocking the number of actual

I/O operations needed to process the data set is reduced. Most installations charge a specific amount for each I/O operation performed. This is usually identified as the total number of execute channel programs (EXCPs). Hence the larger the blocking factor, the cheaper the cost of performing the I/O. Note that some data set organizations do not permit blocking.

The 3380 Disk Drive

The current top of the line disk drive used on MVS systems is the model 3380. As with the 3350, a data set is stored on the 3380 in either COUNT DATA or COUNT KEY DATA format. In terms of calculating space requirements the 3380 differs significantly from the older 3350. With a 3380 all space is allocated in increments of 32 bytes. If a particular physical record length or KEY value is not an integral multiple of 32 the value is rounded up to the nearest multiple. All space is measured in these 32 byte increments. Overhead is also measured in the same way. For a data set without keys (COUNT DATA) the overhead is 15 blocks. For a data set with keys (COUNT KEY DATA) the overhead is 22 blocks plus the key itself. Each track can hold 47,968 bytes of data. This is equivalent to 1499 blocks of 32 bytes each. The standard technique for determining the number of physical records that can fit on one track is to use the formula

$$\frac{1499}{\text{OVERHEAD}+\text{DATA}(+\text{KEY})}$$

Here if there is no key OVERHEAD = 15. For a data set with keys OVERHEAD = 22.

To determine the number of 32 byte increments required to hold the DATA and KEY fields the following formulas should be used:

$$\text{DATA} = \frac{\text{blocksize} + 12}{32} \qquad \text{KEY} = \frac{\text{key length} + 12}{32}$$

It is important to remember to add 12 to both blocksize and keylength and round the quotients up to the next highest integer whenever they are not integers. With COUNT DATA, KEY = 0.

Example 8: For a data set that contains unblocked 80 byte physical records this formula gives

$$\frac{1499}{15+3+0} = \frac{1499}{18} = 83$$

records per track. This is a somewhat shocking result since 72 records of the same size fit on one track of a 3350, which contains less than half as many bytes per track. Notice that the 80 bytes of data required that three of the 32 byte blocks be used since 92(= 80 + 12)/32 = 2.9 which is rounded up to 3.

TABLE 15–2
The 3350 and 3380 Overheads

	COUNT Overhead	*KEY Overhead*	*Total Overhead (in bytes)*
3350	185 bytes	82 bytes	267
3380	15 blocks = 480 bytes	7 blocks = 224 bytes	704

Now suppose these card images are blocked using a blocking factor of 20. Since a physical record is 1600 bytes the formula becomes

$$\frac{1499}{15+51+0} = 22$$

physical records per track. Hence 440 logical records are written. This compares to 200 logical records on a 3350.

Why does the 3380 disk seem to perform under expectation with the unblocked records and then function more or less as expected with a blocking factor of 20? In the second case a track on the 3380 holds 2.2 times as many records as a track on the 3350. The primary reason for such results is the high overhead associated with each physical record on the 3380. Table 15–2 contrasts the overheads on the two devices. In addition both the blocks and keys themselves are subject to rounding up.

Example 9: Determine the number of partitioned data set directory blocks that can be written on one track of a 3380. Since the data and KEY fields occupy 256 and 8 bytes respectively the formula becomes

$$\frac{1499}{15+7+\left(\frac{8+12}{32}\right)+\left(\frac{256+12}{32}\right)} = \frac{1499}{22+1+9} = \frac{1499}{32} = 46.8 \text{ or } 46$$

directory blocks per track.

Disk Timing Considerations

Three factors affect the speed at which disk processing is performed. These are the rotation of the disk itself, the movement of the read/write heads to the desired cylinder, and the actual rate of data transfer between the disk and the buffer in memory. These are usually referred to as rotational delay, access arm movement, and rate of data transfer respectively. Whenever possible an effort should be made to minimize the amount of time needed for each of these operations. Writing relatively large records and utilizing most of a track both contribute to greater efficiency in all three areas.

Rotational delay can be reduced by supplying the records in the actual order in which they are processed. With VSAM multiple copies of a single record can be placed throughout the track. With JCL there is no specific technique that will reduce rotational delay.

Access arm movement can be reduced by placing the data set on adjacent (or contiguous) cylinders. This can be done (with some limitations) through JCL. The fourth SPACE subparameter is used for this purpose. Three values may be coded, CONTIG, MXIG, and ALX. Each of them is meaningful only with the primary allocation. Each allocates space in terms of cylinders. CONTIG specifies that the cylinders must be adjacent. Recall that in general a primary allocation can be made in terms of five non-contiguous areas. With CONTIG the job is cancelled if the available space for the primary allocation is not contiguous. Clearly contiguous cylinders minimize access arm movement. MXIG allocates the single largest area of contiguous storage on the same volume as the primary allocation for the data set. This area must be at least as large as the amount of space requested. ALX allocates five contiguous areas on the disk, all of which must be at least as big as the amount of space requested. As with CONTIG, both MXIG and ALX minimize access arm movement.

If too much disk storage has been requested the unused space may be returned to the volume. This is done with the RLSE subparameter. Unused tracks and cylinders are returned to the volume and the format–5 dscb is modified. RLSE should not be coded with sequential data sets that will be extended or with partitioned data sets that will either have additional members written to them or have members modified.

Exercises

1. Suppose the same unblocked card images that were written to disk in Example 2 are also written to tape. Which data set (disk or tape) uses the I/O device most efficiently, i.e., which device contains a higher percentage of actual data?

2. If the unused space at the end of the track is included in the calculations in Examples 2, 3, and 6 what actual percentage of the track holds data?

3. Verify that the largest R value that can occur in a CCHHR address is 103 for a 3350 disk. Determine the comparable value for a 3380 disk. Explain why the two values are almost the same.

4. Describe the relationship between the NOMINAL KEY used in a COBOL application program to reference a record in a relative data set and the exact location on the disk where the record is stored. How is the PIC S9(8) COMP value from the COBOL program converted to a CCHHR value? Specify the algorithm used by BSAM and BDAM.

5. What are some significant reasons for not blocking a disk data set with the largest possible blocking factor? Illustrate each reason with an example.

6. Suppose a multi-volume disk data set is identified on a DD statement as NEW. Which entries in the VTOC of the disk volumes must be accessed and modified in order to create the data set?

7. Given an IBM 3350 disk that has a data set written on it, determine how many logical records will fit on one track. The data set organization and blocking factors will determine your answers. Only an integer number of records can fit on a track. Do not give fractional answers. All records in the data set consist of 80 bytes of data—of which 10 bytes within each record can be used as a key if necessary.

DSORG		*Blocking Factor (BF)* Unblocked	BF=3	BF=10	Largest BF Possible
PS			++		
*IS	key embedded		++		
	key non embedded		++		
*DA	direct				
	relative		++		
PO	member area				
	directory		XXXXXX	XXXXX	BF=1 (unblocked)

add a delete byte for IS and DA data sets.

Complete the following pictures to show what the first 2 physical records will look like in each of the four cases denoted by "++" above. Show all relevant COUNT, KEY, and DATA fields.

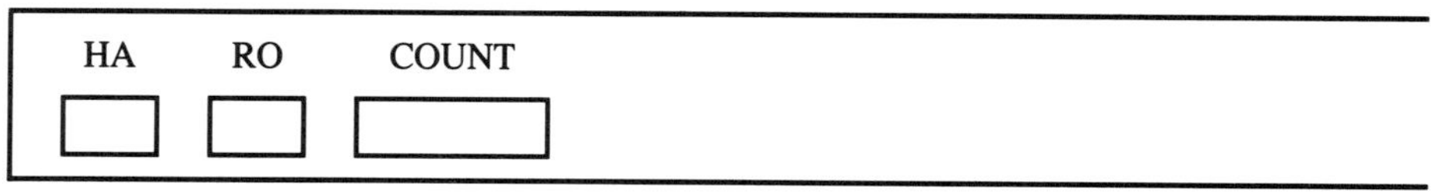

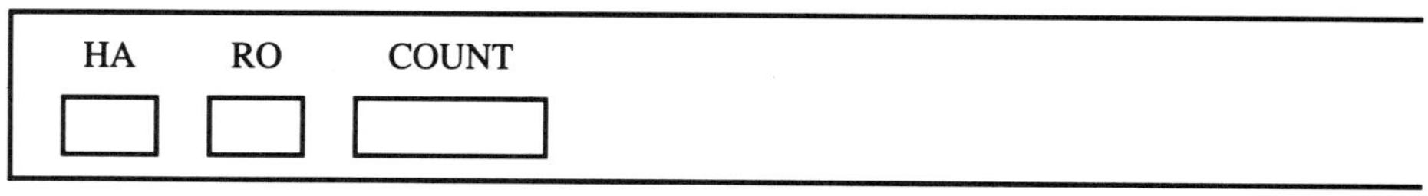

Now repeat the above calculations and pictures for an IBM 3380.

8. For the unblocked data sets in the previous question determine the actual percentage of the track which contains data. This should be done for both the 3350 and the 3380.

Chapter 16

Tape Data Sets

Overview

Magnetic tape is heavily used with MVS systems for both storing and processing data sets. The use of tape as a secondary storage medium began prior to the development of disk drives. In fact, an ancestor of the MVS operation system was called the Tape Operating System (TOS). It was some time after TOS was introduced that IBM developed the Disk Operating System (DOS). With the growing popularity of direct access storage devices the importance of tape data sets has diminished. Today tape volumes are used primarily for two purposes, backup and transportability. In some instances production jobs may process tape data sets. This situation most commonly occurs with very large data sets that span several tape volumes or with data sets that are infrequently processed.

Tape volumes are inexpensive and take up a small amount of storage space. They are also quite reliable. These points make them ideal candidates for backing-up the contents of disk volumes on a periodic basis. Practically every computer installation copies the contents of their disk volumes to tape on some type of periodic basis. Depending on the contents of the disk this may be done daily, every other day, or on a weekly basis. This backup serves as insurance against the accidental modification, destruction, or deletion of the disk data sets or an entire disk volume. Because a tape volume and tape drive are in many ways much simpler than a disk drive, fewer things can go wrong with them.

Tape volumes are used to physically transport data sets from one system to another. The factors that make tape a good choice for backing-up disks are also important for transportability. These include the low cost, physical size, and reliability of tape volumes.

There are disadvantages associated with using tape data sets. The most significant disadvantage is that tape volumes are stored off-line. When a particular tape volume is requested an operator must physically locate it and then mount it. Large installations may have tens of thousands of tape volumes. This human intervention creates time delays and other problems that do not occur when processing disk data sets. Tape requests are time consuming in two ways. In addition to searching the computer room or the tape library, the operator must postpone other functions when tape processing is performed. IBM and vendors who make plug compatible I/O devices are attempting to minimize these problems with tape.

A second disadvantage of tape processing is that it is slower than disk processing. When equivalent I/O operations are done with both disk and tape the disk I/O is performed quicker.

There is another significant reason why specific operations take longer to perform with tape. Tape data sets must have sequential organization. All tape volumes have to be processed sequentially. Because of this the only data sets that can be copied to tape and retain the same format they had on disk are sequential data sets and pds members. Recall that pds members are sequential even though the organization of the data set itself is partitioned. It is possible to copy any of the other data set organizations (both non-VSAM and VSAM) to tape. IBM supplies utilities that perform this important function for each of these data set organizations. It is important to realize that the tape copy of the data set does not retain the original data set organization. Rather, the data sets are transformed by the utility into sequential data sets. However, the original non-sequential data set can always be easily recreated from the tape data set. Usually this recreation involves using the same utility that initially created the tape data set. Copying a non-VSAM data set to tape is called *unloading* the data set. With VSAM this is referred to as *exporting* the data set. The process of recreating the data set from the unloaded copy is called *loading* or *importing* the data set. The specific details on copying data sets to and from tape are found in the chapters listed below.

Data Set Organization	*Utility*	*Chapter*	*Terminology*
Sequential and Direct	IEBGENER and IDCAMS	25	Copy
ISAM	IEBISAM	29	Unload/Load
Partitioned	IEBCOPY and IEHMOVE	27 31	Unload/Load

Representing Data on Tape

Data are stored on tape by magnetizing certain spots on the tape. At present there are two types of tape available on MVS systems: 7 track and 9 track. The 7 track tape is rarely used, and will not be discussed in this book. For more information on

7 track tape consult the IBM manuals *OS/VS2 MVS JCL* and *IBM Tape Labels*. The 9 in 9 track means that 9 bits are necessary to represent one byte of information. Eight of these bits consist of a standard EBCDIC representation of the byte or character. The extra bit is called a parity bit. Most 9 track tape is approximately 2400 feet in length and one-half inch in width. Smaller lengths also exist. The 9 track tape can be thought of as composed of 9 bands which run the length of the tape, partitioning the one-half inch of tape surface. To illustrate this some of the common EBCDIC values are pictured as they could be stored on tape if they were visible.

track 1	(8)	1	1	1	1	1	1	1	1	1	1	1	1	1	0	0	1
track 2	(4)	1	1	1	1	1	1	1	1	1	1	1	1	1	1	1	1
track 3	(2)	0	0	0	0	0	0	0	0	0	0	1	1	1	0	0	1
track 4	(1)	0	0	0	0	0	0	0	0	0	1	1	1	1	0	1	1
track 5	(8)	0	0	0	0	0	0	0	1	1	0	0	0	0	0	1	1
track 6	(4)	0	0	0	1	1	1	1	0	0	0	0	0	0	0	1	1
track 7	(2)	0	1	1	0	0	1	1	0	0	0	0	1	1	0	0	0
track 8	(1)	1	0	1	0	1	0	1	0	1	1	1	0	1	0	0	0
track 9	(parity)	1	1	0	1	0	0	1	1	0	0	1	1	0	1	0	0
Character		A	B	C	D	E	F	G	H	I	J	1	2	3	b̸	*	longitudinal
EBCDIC value		C1	C2	C3	C4	C5	C6	C7	C8	C9	D1	F1	F2	F3	40	5C	FC parity

Notice that all of the characters are represented in EBCDIC using the top eight bits. To see this evaluate the top four bits as one hexadecimal character and the next four as a second hexadecimal character. Hence A, which has an EBCDIC representation of C1, is stored as 1100 0001. The ninth track contains the parity bit. Each character (or eight bits) has one parity bit associated with it. The parity bit allows certain types of relatively simple I/O errors to be detected. When a byte is written the parity bit is assigned a value that will cause all the one bits in that representation to sum to an even number. With the EBCDIC representation of A there are three one bits. Hence the parity bit for A is set to one. This gives four one bits altogether in the representation. Likewise, with C there are four one bits in the EBCDIC representation and the parity bit is set to zero. Whenever the tape is subsequently read the tape drive checks to determine if the parity is correct. If it is incorrect some type of machine or I/O error has occurred and the data are invalid. For example, if the bit pattern 101010101 is detected the data are in error. Clearly not all errors can be detected by using a parity bit. Even if a simple parity error is detected, it cannot ordinarily be corrected.

A second level of error detection is provided by a parity check associated with each of the nine tracks. This is called a longitudinal parity check. It consists of one additional byte that is included following each block of data. The bit values are determined as described above. Hence, since track 1 contains 13 one bits, its longitudinal parity bit is set to one. For track 8 the longitudinal bit is set to zero since there are eight one bits in the block on that track.

The amount of data that can be stored on a fixed length of tape is selected by the programmer. This amount is given in Bytes of data Per Inch of tape (BPI) and is called the tape density. Some people interpret BPI as bits per inch. With this interpretation it is the number of bits that can be placed on one track in one inch of tape. MVS supports three tape densities: 800, 1600, and 6250 BPI. When two or more densities are available a good rule of thumb is to select the highest value. There is never a good reason for recording at a density other than the highest available. Most tape drives will record at two densities. There are two standard combinations, 800 and 1600 BPI drives and 1600 and 6250 BPI drives.

The DEN subparameter of the DCB parameter is used to select the tape density. Three coded values may be specified with DEN. The meanings of the three values are the following:

DEN=2	800 BPI
DEN=3	1600 BPI
DEN=4	6250 BPI

Most installations have the highest BPI value specified as the default for the DEN parameter. Hence DEN usually need not be coded at all. Note that DEN values are related to the tape drive used. DEN=4 cannot be used with a drive that records only at 800 or 1600 BPI.

Types of Tape Data Sets

Through JCL a format is selected for a tape data set when it is created. There are four commonly used formats, IBM standard label (SL), no label (NL), by-pass label processing (BLP), and standard user label (SUL). The LABEL parameter is coded on the DD statement that references the tape data set. The LABEL parameter contains five subparameters. The first two, which are positional, are the only ones relevant to the material in this chapter. The syntax of the two subparameters is as follows:

```
LABEL=(file sequence number,format)
```

Here the file sequence number is an unsigned positive integer that can range from 1 to N. If 0 is coded it is interpreted as 1. The value N implies that there are N distinct data sets on the tape volume. Format is ordinarily one of the four values SL, NL, BLP, or SUL. A specific tape data set is referenced using a combination of the LABEL, VOLUME, and UNIT parameters. When referencing the data set a different value from the one coded when it was initially created can be specified with LABEL. However, it must be a compatible value. If the label parameter is not coded or if the second subparameter is not specified, standard label is the default. Hence

LABEL=(2,SL) and LABEL=(2)

both reference the second data set on a tape volume. This data set must have standard labels or problems will occur when processing the data set. Likewise,

LABEL=(1,SL), LABEL=(,SL), LABEL=1, and no LABEL parameter

TABLE 16–1
Values on the LABEL Parameter

Label Type	*LABEL subparameter value (second subparameter)*
System supplied Labels	SL
By-pass the existing Labels during processing	BLP
System and User Labels combined	SUL
No Labels	NL and BLP
Non-Standard Labels	NSL
Leading Tape Mark	LTM
ANSI Standard Labels	ASL
ANSI and User Labels combined	AUL

all refer to a standard label data set which is the first data set on the volume. This occurs because 1 is the default value for file sequence number.

As discussed in Chapter 7, LABEL can be coded with both tape and disk data sets. LABEL's second positional subparameter determines the format or type of label associated with the data set. Data set labels for tape and disk can be categorized as system supplied only, user supplied only, a combination of both system and user labels or no labels at all. With tape data sets any of these four possibilities may occur. The various values that can be coded on the LABEL parameter and their relationship to these four categories are pictured in Table 16–1. Those entries below the line are very rarely used.

SL Tape Data Sets

SL tape data sets are the most commonly used. They are also the easiest to work with and to understand. Every SL tape data set actually consists of three disjoint components: header labels, the data set itself, and trailer labels. This is pictured in Figure 16–1.

Here TM denotes a tape mark that is used to separate the three components of the data set. A tape mark is written by the tape drive and is three inches wide. Existing tape marks can be detected by the drive and are used to locate specific data sets on the volume. When an SL data set is the first data set on a tape volume two changes must be made to the picture in Figure 16–1: the previous data set and its following tape mark are not present and, the header labels will be larger. Except for the header labels for the first data set on a volume, every set of headers and trailers for an SL tape data set consists of two unblocked 80 byte records. The header labels

FIGURE 16–1
An SL Tape Data Set

previous data set	TM	Header Labels	TM	Actual Data Set	TM	Trailer Labels	TM	next data set

for the first data set on the volume consist of three unblocked 80 byte records. The first of these records is the volume header. It is unrelated to the first data set except for the fact that it is written within that data set's header labels. The complete contents of the header and trailer records are described in Table 16–2. More details on the various fields within the labels can be found in the manual *IBM Tape Labels*.

NL Tape Data Sets

NL is the second most common type of tape data set. A NL data set consists of only the data set itself. No headers or trailers are present on the tape. If the same tape data sets represented as SL above had been written as NL they would appear as shown in Figure 16–2.

When an NL data set is the first data set on the volume the previous data set and its following tape mark will not be present. The volume header label which identifies an SL volume is not permitted with NL data sets. Because they do not have labels NL data sets are more difficult to process than SL data sets. This disadvantage far outweighs the small amount of tape overhead saved when NL processing is used.

NL and SL data sets cannot be mixed on the same tape volume. When a DD statement specifies an SL data set the volume header (VOL1–the first of the three 80 byte records in the header labels for the first data set on the volume) is checked to see if the correct volume has been mounted. The VOLUME value coded on the DD statement must occur in bytes 5 through 10 of the header record. If the two values are different an incorrect volume was mounted. However, operator intervention can still cause the correct volume to be mounted. If it is not the volume requested it cannot be processed.

BLP with Tape Data Sets

BLP is similar to NL processing. When creating tape data sets both NL and BLP create a data set without labels. When retrieving existing data sets BLP provides considerably more flexibility. BLP is compatible with both SL and NL.

As an illustration of how BLP processing works with existing data sets, suppose that two SL data sets are written to a tape volume. When processing either data set as SL the contents of the volume are pictured as shown in Figure 16–3.

FIGURE 16–2
Tape Data Sets Written as NL

previous data set	TM	actual data set	TM	next data set

FIGURE 16–3
Data Sets Processed as SL

HD1R	TM	DATA SET 1	TM	TR1L	TM	HD2R	TM	DATA SET 2	TM	TR2L	TM

TABLE 16–2

Header and Trailer Records

HDR1/EOF1/EOV1 Record Formats

Byte Position	*No. Bytes*	*Contents of the 80 byte records*
1	4	Characters 'HDR1' or 'EOF1' or 'EOV1'.
5	17	Data set name. Rightmost 17 characters, left justified, padded on right with blanks.
22	6	Volume serial number. Right justified, padded on left with blanks. For a multivolume file the serial number of first volume.
28	4	Volume sequence number (0001-9999). Sequence number of a multivolume file; 0001 for single volume file.
32	4	File sequence number (0001-9999). Number of the file on tape.
36	4	Generation number (0001-9999) for generation data group.
40	2	Version number (00-99) for generation data group.
42	6	Creation date 'ƀyyddd'.
48	6	Expiration date 'ƀyyddd'.
54	1	Data set security. 0-no protection, 1-PASSWORD protection, 2-NOPWREAD protection.
55	6	Block count of blocks in file. Zero in HDR1.
61	20	Special codes.

HDR2/EOF2/EOV2 Record Formats

Byte Position	*No. Bytes*	*Contents of the 80 byte records*
1	4	Characters 'HDR2' or 'EOF2' or 'EOV2'.
5	1	Record format. F-fixed length, V-variable length, U-undefined length.
6	5	BLKSIZE.
11	5	LRECL.
16	1	DEN (2-800BPI, 3-1600 BPI, 4-6250 BPI).
17	1	Data set position. 1-volume switch has occurred; otherwise 0.
18	17	'job-name/job-step' that created the data set.
35	2	TRTCH (7-track tape only).
37	1	Control characters. A-ASCII, M-machine, ƀ-no control characters.
38	1	Reserved.
39	1	Block attribute. B-blocked, S-spanned, R-blocked and standard or spanned, ƀ-unblocked records.
40	8	Reserved.
48	1	Contains 'C' if file contains checkpoint data set.
49	32	Reserved.

VOL1 Record Format

Byte Position	*No. Bytes*	*Contents of the 80 byte records*
1	4	Characters 'VOL1'.
5	6	Volume serial number. Left justified, padded on right with blanks.
11	70	Unused characters.

FIGURE 16–4
Data Sets Processed as BLP

was	HDR1		DS1		TRL1		HDR2		DS2		TRL2	
now	DATA SET 1	TM	DATA SET 2	TM	DATA SET 3	TM	DATA SET 4	TM	DATA SET 5	TM	DATA SET 6	TM

If the data sets on the same volume are processed as BLP the information on the volume is interpreted as shown in Figure 16–4.

Here every tape mark is interpreted as a separator between two data sets. With BLP processing the concept of header and trailer labels does not exist. In fact, existing labels are interpreted as data sets in their own right. For example, the header labels for the second SL data set can be processed as data by referencing them as LABEL=(4,BLP). To reference the first actual data set on this volume code either LABEL=(1,SL) or LABEL=(2,BLP). With the second format all necessary information about the data set must be supplied within the application program or through JCL since there are no data set labels available.

There is a simple formula to relate how the same data set can be referenced as either SL or BLP. If the data set is the Nth on an SL volume then code either LABEL=(N,SL) or LABEL=(3*N-1,BLP). Going the other direction, with BLP processing code LABEL=(N,BLP) and LABEL=((N+1)/3,SL) where data set M=(N+1)/3 is a standard label data set and M-1 and M+1 are its headers and trailers respectively.

Now consider the appearance of a tape volume which has exactly two NL data sets written to it, as shown in Figure 16–5. Notice that no headers or trailers are present. The two data sets can be referenced by coding LABEL=(x,NL) or LABEL=(x,BLP) where x=1 and 2.

Blocking Tape Data Sets

Since every data set stored on tape is sequentially organized blocking is a very important consideration. Blocking strategies are much simpler with tape data sets than with disk data sets. The only reason for not blocking a tape data set as large as possible may be a limitation on the amount of memory available for buffers. None of the other reasons discussed in Chapter 9 for minimizing buffer size or prohibiting blocking altogether have any meaning with tape. Hence large blocking factors should be the rule rather than the exception. Several examples are presented to illustrate the advantages gained from blocking tape data sets.

FIGURE 16–5
A Tape Volume with Two NL Data Sets

DATA SET 1	TM	DATA SET 2	TM	TM

Example 1: Unblocked card images are written to an 800 BPI tape. What portion of the tape holds data and what portion consists of inner block gaps (IBGs)? The gaps separate physical records and are necessary in order to start and stop the tape. Since a physical record occupies 1/10 inch of tape and an IBG 6/10 inch, the data set comprises 14.3% of the tape surface. The IBGs occupy the remaining 85.7%. If there are 1000 records in the data set it will take 1000 actual physical reads (EXCPS) to retrieve them. This example illustrates how wasteful and expensive it is to store unblocked data on tape. Naturally large logical records, even if unblocked, will result in a more effective utilization of the tape.

Example 2: The same card image data set is written to tape using a blocking factor of 20. Now what percentage of the tape holds data? Since a physical record occupies 2 inches ((80 bytes * 20)/800 bytes/inch) the ratio of data to total tape becomes

$$\frac{2}{2+.6} = \frac{2}{2.6} = 77\%$$

To retrieve the 1000 records now takes 50 physical reads.

Example 3: The same 1000 card images are now blocked as large as possible. Since the largest physical record that can be written on tape is approximately 32K bytes this results in a blocking factor of 409 for card images. A 32,720 byte block occupies 40.9 inches of tape. Thus the data set itself occupies

$$\frac{40.9}{40.9+.6} = \frac{40.9}{41.5} = 98.5\%$$

of the tape surface, the highest possible utilization for card images. All of the records in the data set can be retrieved with just three read operations since 1000 = 409 + 409 + 182. With double buffering 65,440 bytes of main memory must be used to hold the records.

Example 4: Suppose 100 byte records are being written to a 6250 BPI tape. With 6250 BPI tape an IBG is .3 inches. Pick a blocking factor that comes closest to utilizing 50% of the tape for data. Here it is necessary to create a block that occupies X inches of tape where

$$\frac{X}{X+.3} = .5$$

Solving this equation for X gives .3 inches. Since .3 inches of the tape can hold 1875 bytes of data, a blocking factor of 19 comes closest to the required 50%. This example is merely used to develop familiarity with tape calculations. There is no good reason to try to utilize exactly 50% of a tape. Rather, an attempt should be made to utilize as much as possible.

Tape I/O Operations

This section describes the processing that takes place on the tape volume and in the application program's region when standard I/O operations are performed. There are four general situations to examine: a data set can be read or written, and the data set in question either does or does not have labels. Either QSAM or BSAM may be used in all four processing situations described here.

CASE I. READING A DATA SET THAT DOES NOT CONTAIN (STANDARD) LABELS

There are several reasons to code a DSN parameter on the DD statement that references such a data set. Suppose that it is to be passed to a subsequent job step or cataloged. In this case future retrievals using DSN will require less JCL coding. If the data set is passed or cataloged then the DSN value can be used to locate the data set. When referencing both passed and cataloged data sets it is unnecessary to code UNIT and VOLUME parameters. When the data set is opened the read/write mechanism of the tape drive is positioned to the beginning of the data set. All dcb information for the data set must be supplied by the application program or coded on the accompanying DD statement. The data set itself does not have a permanent name. When the data set is closed its contents are left completely unchanged. Buffers are filled in an identical manner as with disk data sets.

CASE II. WRITING A DATA SET THAT DOES NOT CONTAIN (STANDARD) LABELS

This takes place in basically the same manner as in Case I. If a DSN parameter is coded on the DD statement for the data set it supplies a name for the duration of the job only, unless the data set is cataloged. No label information is available to help in processing and none is created.

CASE III. READING A STANDARD LABEL DATA SET

Here the DSN parameter must be coded on the accompanying DD statement. When the data set is opened the JCL DSN value is compared to the name coded in bytes 5 through 21 in the first header record. In order for processing to continue these names must agree. When they are not identical an S813 abend occurs. (Actually, since only the 17 rightmost bytes of the name are stored in the labels, some discrepancies are allowed without abending the job.) Once the data set name is verified the values in the data set labels are used to complete any entries in the JFCB that have not been assigned values on the DD statement. See Chapter 11 for more on this topic. Actual processing of the records in the data set is identical to processing for a data set without labels. When the data set is closed the trailer labels remain unchanged.

CASE IV. WRITING A STANDARD LABEL DATA SET

When an SL data set is created on tape the DSN value coded on the DD statement is written in the first header record. Most of the values that are placed in the two header records are supplied from two sources. Many are provided from the accompanying JCL for the program doing the writing. These include jobname, stepname, and the date. See Table 16–2 for the complete set of values. The dcb values written in the labels are provided both from the application program and the accompanying DD statement. If DSN is not coded a temporary name will be generated and placed in the label. Since it makes subsequent SL processing more difficult this is not a good programming practice.

A count of physical records is maintained as the blocks are written. This count is placed in the first trailer record. When this data set is later processed as an input data set and the end of the data set is reached, the count field is checked to make sure all blocks have been read. After a data set has been created all fields in the trailer records are identical to the comparable field in headers except for the block count. It is initialized to binary zeroes in the header record.

Records can also be appended to the back of an existing data set by coding DISP=MOD. In a COBOL program code OPEN EXTEND file-name. After the data set is extended the trailer records must be rewritten. The block count is incremented to reflect the new physical record total. After records are added to an existing data set it is possible that the dcb values in the trailer records will disagree with the comparable values in the headers. This results from the manner in which a dcb is constructed and modified. It is the direct consequence of an application program or DD statement specifying dcb values that conflict with the actual values of the data set. This situation should be avoided when possible.

When a tape data set contains embedded short blocks do not code RECFM=FBS. If this is done and an embedded short block is encountered the application program will abend with an S522. Processing an embedded short block on disk causes the same abend during standard processing.

SUL and LTM Tape Data Sets

When user labels and system labels are both present processing becomes more complex. When programming in COBOL user labels are created and retrieved by using the DECLARATIVES SECTION of the PROCEDURE DIVISION. The accompanying DD statement for the data set must contain both LABEL=(n,SUL) and DCB=(OPTCD=Q, . . .). Up to eight header and eight trailer records may be written by a user application program. The first four bytes of each user label must contain 'UHLx' or 'UTLx', depending on whether it is a header or trailer being written. If other values are specified they are overwritten. Any values can be coded in the remaining 76 bytes. The x represents the integers 1 through 8. The user labels immediately follow the system supplied labels. The tape mark is written after the user labels. Like the system labels, the user labels are unblocked.

FIGURE 16–6
The Beginning of an SUL Data Set

VOL HDR	IBG	HDR 1 80 byte	IBG	HDR 2 80 byte	IBG	USER HDR1 80 byte	IBG	USER HDR2 80 byte	IBG	USER HDR3 80 byte	TM	DATA SET BEGINS

Example 5: Suppose the first data set on an SL volume contains three user header labels. The contents of the tape up to the first tape mark are pictured in Figure 16–6. The application program must reserve additional buffer space when processing user header and trailer records.

Data sets created on a DOS system often contain a tape mark which precedes the first data set on the volume. To successfully use such a tape on an MVS system Leading Tape Mark (LTM) processing should be used. This will cause the system to skip over the leading tape mark and then treat all the data sets on the volume as NL format. Attempting to read an LTM tape using any other format (such as (1,SL), (1,NL), or (1,BLP)) will produce incorrect results.

Tape Processing Guidelines

The guidelines listed here are some of the fundamental rules that should be followed in order to successfully process tape data sets. Extreme care should be taken not to violate any of these rules. Breaking a rule will usually either destroy one or more data sets or cause an abend!

1. The LABEL=N+1 data set on a tape volume cannot be created until after the LABEL=N data set has been created. This holds for N=1,2,3,. . . . Hence it is impossible to reserve space for a tape data set that is to be created following the creation of the present one.

2. If the Nth data set on a tape volume is written, rewritten, or extended, all data sets that follow it on the volume are destroyed (i.e., the N+1, N+2, N+3, . . . data sets). This is a consequence of the tape drive writing two tape marks following any output operation to a data set on a tape volume. For an SL data set the tape marks are written after the trailer labels. If an attempt is made to retrieve these lost data sets an SA13 abend occurs. This abend code implies attempting to access a tape data set whose file sequence number exceeds the highest file sequence number on the tape volume. To protect against the accidental destruction of tape data sets in this way, many installations allow only one data set per tape volume. When this policy is used rules 1 and 2 become meaningless.

3. Two data sets on the same tape volume cannot be opened or processed at the same time. Opening a tape data set results in reading the labels (when present) and then positioning the read/write mechanism to the beginning of the first block of data. Obviously, it is impossible to position one read/write head to two distinct locations simultaneously. When an attempt is made to concurrently open two or more data sets on the same volume an S513 abend results.

4. SL and NL data sets cannot be stored on the same tape volume. Any attempt at combining them causes an abend to occur.

5. There are several other common sense rules that should be kept in mind when processing tape data sets. These include the following: Never read an FBS data set backwards. Never open a data set BACKWARDS EXTEND. Never write physical records smaller than 18 bytes. Unless all relevant dcb values are specified in the application program it is important to remember to code a DCB parameter when processing NL and BLP data sets. Use care when coding VOL REF with tape data sets; unusual situations can result.

JCL for Tape Data Sets

The important DD parameters that are coded with tape data sets are now examined. For more general information about DD parameters see Chapters 6 and 7.

DSN

With two exceptions any valid sequential disk data set name may also be used with tape. The DSN parameter must not imply an ISAM data set or a pds member. A temporary DSN value may be coded but the data set will not be deleted at the end of the job. With standard label processing the rightmost 17 bytes coded with DSN are checked against the value in the first label record of an existing data set. These values must agree in order to allow processing to begin. Generation Data Sets may be stored on tape.

DISP

Every possible DISP value is permitted. SHR is rarely coded since it is extremely unlikely that there will be two simultaneous requests for the same tape data set. The values PASS, KEEP, and DELETE all result in a kept data set. PASS also places an entry in the pass mechanism. Since all three values result in a permanent (but uncataloged) data set, which should be coded in a specific situation? When the step ends each of the three subparameter values positions the tape to a different location. KEEP rewinds the tape volume back to the load point, which immediately precedes the first data set on the volume. PASS rewinds the tape volume to the beginning of the data set that was just processed. DELETE leaves the tape where it was after processing of the data set is finished. With DELETE there is no rewinding. The appropriate value to select from among these three depends on which data set (if any) is to be processed next on the volume. When a data set is passed the first two subparameters of the LABEL parameter are also placed in the pass table. Hence, when the data set is referenced through the pass table these values need not be coded.

DCB

When using SL processing most common DCB subparameters are available from the data set labels. These subparameters include LRECL, RECFM, BLKSIZE, and DEN. DSORG need never be coded with a tape data set. Any additional DCB subparameters that are desired must be coded either in the application program itself or on the accompanying DD statement.

SPACE

This parameter is never coded with a tape data set. It is considered a conflicting DD parameter whenever either LABEL=(N) or UNIT=(tape) is coded on the same DD statement.

UNIT

As with disk data sets, one of three categories can be coded here. A specific tape drive can be requested by coding its three hexadecimal digit address, e.g., UNIT=582. An installation may define generic names to reference groups of like units. UNIT=TAPE may be coded to mean that any 9 track drive can be used for processing. UNIT=LODENS may be used to identify an 800/1600 BPI tape drive. UNIT=SYSSQ is often used to denote any available sequential device, tape or disk. It is also possible to identify a UNIT by model number. For example, 3400–5 and 3420–6 are specific tape drives. The 3480 is the new cartridge tape drive.

The second format of the UNIT parameter is frequently used with tape processing. UNIT=AFF=ddname is commonly coded whenever the number of tape volumes to be mounted during a step exceeds the number of tape drives available. UNIT=AFF allows more than one volume to be mounted on a single drive during a step. Coding UNIT=AFF is contingent on only one volume at a time being requested by the application.

VOLUME

This has several commonly coded subparameters that are more important with tape than disk. PRIVATE, the first positional subparameter, applies to every tape volume and need not be explicitly coded. The second subparameter, RETAIN, may be specified to keep a tape volume mounted between steps in a multi-step job. This subparameter is used to minimize operator intervention. Volume count and volume number must be coded with applications that use a multi-volume tape data set. SER and REF have three different types of syntax. They may identify a specific volume or volumes, reference an existing volume by name, or reference an existing volume by identifying its DDname. When VOL=REF is coded UNIT need not be coded.

LABEL

This has already been described in detail earlier in the chapter. The last three LABEL subparameters have no special significance when coded with tape or disk.

To illustrate tape processing consider the following four step job. In Step A two tape data sets are created, one SL and one NL. In Step B both data sets are referenced. In Step C both are referenced a second time and then disposition processed. The last example describes a method for printing header and trailer labels for an SL data set.

Example 6: The two tape data sets are created. An entry for data set XYZ is made in the pass mechanism. This entry includes UNIT, VOL, and LABEL information. Hence in subsequent references to XYZ it is only necessary to code DSN and DISP. DCB is rarely coded with an existing SL data set. At most installations DEN=4 is the default. The &&XYZ data set becomes a permanent data set, the ampersands notwithstanding. There is no such thing as a temporary tape data set. Additionally, there is no purpose whatsoever to coding DSN with an NL data set that is not cataloged or passed.

```
//STEPA EXEC ---
//DD1     DD  DSN=XYZ,DISP=(NEW,PASS),UNIT=TAPE,
//            VOL=SER=123456,LABEL=(1,SL),
//            DCB=(LRECL=100,BLKSIZE=20000,RECFM=FB,DEN=4)
//DD2     DD  DSN=&&XYZ,DISP=(,DELETE),UNIT=TAPE,
//            VOL=SER=999999,LABEL=(,NL),DCB=BLKSIZE=4000
```

Example 7: Here the two tape data sets created in the previous example are referenced as input. Data set XYZ is located through its entry in the pass table. No other DD parameters need be coded. Since &&XYZ is an NL kept data set, the DCB, VOL, and LABEL parameters must be coded. The data set will also be located successfully if the DSN parameter is not coded. UNIT is supplied from the VOL referback.

```
//STEPB EXEC ---
//DD1    DD  DSN=XYZ,DISP=(OLD,CATLG)
//DD2    DD  DSN=&&XYZ,DISP=(OLD,PASS),
//           VOL=REF*.STEPA.DD2,LABEL=(,NL),
//           DCB=(*.STEPA.DD2)
```

Example 8: Data set XYZ is deleted. However, it will actually remain on volume 123456 until it is overwritten. The temporary data set is now referenced through its entry in the pass table created in STEPB.

```
//STEPC EXEC ---
//DD1    DD  DSN=XYZ,DISP=(OLD,DELETE)
//DD2    DD  DSN=*.STEPB.DD2,DISP=(OLD,PASS),
//           DCB=(*.STEPA.DD2),VOL=REF=(*.STEPA.DD2)
```

Example 9: The header and trailer labels for data set XYZ are to be printed. This is possible because the data set remains on the volume even though DELETE was specified in the previous step. To access the labels as data sets BLP processing is used. The two input data sets are concatenated. The DCB parameter must be coded.

```
//STEPD    EXEC  PGM=IEBGENER
//SYSPRINT DD    SYSOUT=A
//SYSUT1   DD    UNIT=TAPE,VOL=SER=123456,LABEL=(1,BLP),
//         DCB=(LRECL=80,BLKSIZE=80,RECFM=F),
//         DISP=(OLD,DELETE)
//         DD    UNIT=TAPE,VOL=SER=123456,LABEL=(3,BLP),
//         DCB=(LRECL=80,BLKSIZE=80,RECFM=F),
//         DISP=(OLD,DELETE)
//SYSUT2   DD    SYSOUT=A
//SYSIN    DD    DUMMY
```

Processing Multi-Volume Tape Data Sets

Multi-volume data sets present additional programming complications. They also illustrate some additional JCL syntax. Only the UNIT and VOL parameters need to be changed. Several specific examples are contained in Chapter 7. In particular, see Examples 4, 5, and 9.

Cartridge Tape Drives

Recently IBM introduced a new generation of tapes and tape drives. These are generally referred to as cartridge tapes because they are similar to audio tape cassettes. IBM calls this the 3480 Magnetic Tape Subsystem. The new tape systems are faster, more reliable, and less sensitive to the environment. They consist of 18 tracks and support a density of 38000 BPI. The tapes are enclosed in a cartridge that is 4″ by 5″ by 1″. They are inserted into the tape drive and thus the tape does not come into contact with the operator's hands or the computer room environment. The 3480 cartridge is approximately 25% the size of a standard tape reel and can hold 20% more data.

The tape drive itself contains a microprocessor. The microprocessor performs some of the tape handling functions previously done by operators. The microprocessor contains a 512K byte buffer. The buffer can be used to hold records before an application requests them or to write to tape after the application is finished. Because of the buffer and other features the data set transfer rate is three megabytes per second.

The same JCL is used with the cartridge tapes and drives as with the older equipment. Plug compatible cartridge tape drives have now been developed. Eventually the cartridge tape drive will become the industry standard.

The IBM 3480 cartridge tape drive was introduced in the early 1980s. It is a radically new type of drive that signals the beginning of a new era of tape technology.

Exercises

1. What types of errors can be detected and corrected using the two sets of parity bits? Categorize your answer in terms of the number of bits in error.

2. Determine the maximum number of 100 byte records that can be placed on a 6250 BPI tape where the records are blocked as large as possible. Assume this is the only SL data set on the volume. Account for both the header and trailer data sets and the four tape marks on the volume. Assume a 2400 foot tape volume. What does the answer become when using NL tape?

3. Using the same tape and records as in the previous question, what are the comparable answers when 1600 BPI tape is used? What are the comparable answers if 800 BPI tape is used to hold this data set?

4. Create an SUL tape data set that contains several user header and trailer records. Either a COBOL program or the IEBGENER utility can be used. Dump out the headers and trailers to confirm their existence. Can anything comparable be done on disk? If so, demonstrate how. Discuss meaningful uses for SUL data sets.

5. Take an SL tape volume and turn it into an NL tape. Then take an NL tape and turn it into an SL tape. Determine what happens when an SL tape is processed as NL and vice-versa. Are there any circumstances where labeled and unlabeled data sets can be on the same tape volume? How can this be done? Is order important? What is the equivalent of an NL data set on disk?

6. A tape volume has arrived without any information concerning its contents. It is probably NL, but this is not yet confirmed. Determine what is actually in the first data set on the volume. Discuss and implement strategy(s) to print out the contents of this data set. Try to do this in only a few runs.

7. Write a general purpose utility that can be used to list the two trailer records associated with X sequential standard label data sets where X is a value from 1 to 20 inclusive and all are on the same tape volume. Do a minimum of editing. Your program may abend to signal completion!

8. Copy a direct data set, an ISAM data set, and a pds to tape. Dump out the printed version of the resulting sequential data sets. Comment on the dcb values found in the headers. Can NL versions of these three data sets be created? If so, how?

9. Modify the information in the header or trailer label of a tape data set. Do not destroy the data set while doing this. In particular change the block count and DSNAME fields.

Comment on subsequent processing oddities if any. Is it possible that this can also be done with disk data set labels?

10. A tape volume contains data set names that do not conform to standard MVS syntax conventions. The names of the SL data sets are of the form ASCSSTU-LJB-XYZ . . ., etc. Print out the data sets themselves. Use SL processing if possible. If not, find something that works. How could these strange data set names get into the headers?

11. Create a true multi-volume data set. Print out all header and trailer labels associated with this data set. This can be a very expensive project; do it as economically as possible. Check the tape and JCL manuals carefully before starting. Contrast this with multi-volume disk data set processing. Do an example of this also.

12. Examine problems that can occur when processing a tape data set that specifies RECFM=FSB. Can comparable problems occur on disk? Why or why not? Determine ways that standard data sets will abend tape jobs where nonstandard data sets will not.

13. Create a RECFM=D data set and place it on tape. This is ASCII format. Try to process it. If possible practice the creation on disk first. You will probably have to use a COBOL program to create the data set. Code OPTCD=Q.

14. Do any of the LABEL formats (SL, NL, BLP, SUL, LTM, etc.) have any meaning on disk? Which other subparameters of the LABEL parameter can be used with disk data sets? Discuss syntax problems when these subparameters are incorrectly or inappropriately used.

15. Without benefit of BLP processing create a data set whose headers and trailers contain different dcb values (if this is possible). How can this be done? What happens during subsequent processing of the data set? Under what conditions will an abend result?

16. Use tape data sets with the COBOL compiler and/or linkage editor as their work data sets. Dump out their contents afterwards. Try UNIT=SYSSQ and specify tape volume(s). Try to make some sense out of the output.

17. Write a short paper on future concepts in tape processing on large IBM computer systems. As discussed in this chapter major new product announcements have been made recently in this area. More are expected soon.

18. Create a GDG where you place several members on tape and several others on disk if possible. Evaluate problems associated with tape Generation Data Sets that would not be present with disk GDSs.

19. Create seven tape data sets in the same job step. Each should be on a different volume. Try to do something meaningful with each. Can all seven be opened at the same time? Assume that only two tape drives are available.

20. Are there any advantages to using tape data sets with the SORT/MERGE utility? Can you specify a 'tape sort'? How does it differ from a 'disk sort'?

21. What role does tape play when working with VSAM data sets?

22. Three data sets were written to the same reel of magnetic tape. All three data sets were created with the same value in the second subparameter of the LABEL parameter. These values were SL, NL, BLP, and SUL respectively. Determine the data sets (or labels, etc.) that are identified when the value at the left is specified for each of the four LABEL subparameters listed at the top in Figure 16–7.

FIGURE 16–7
Exercise 22

created as → processed as ↓	3 SL data sets	3 NL data sets	3 BLP data sets	3 SUL data sets
LABEL = (2,NL)				
LABEL = (4,BLP)				
LABEL = (2,SL)				
LABEL = (3,SUL)				

Chapter 17

Language Translators and (COBOL) PARM Options

Language Translators

Overview

Language translators consist of compilers and assemblers. The primary distinction between these two is that compilers are used with the high level languages (COBOL, PL/I, FORTRAN, etc.) and assemblers are restricted to assembly languages. There is very little actual difference between the way IBM compilers and assemblers are manipulated through JCL statements. Both employ essentially the same types of data sets for input, output, and work files. The basic function of a language translator is to construct an object module out of a source program (the code written by an application programmer). An object module is often imprecisely referred to as machine language, binary code, or hexadecimal code. In this chapter the COBOL compiler will be examined in detail. The PL/I Optimizing compiler and F-level assembler will be discussed only by pointing out how they differ from the COBOL compiler.

None of the material in this chapter discusses the actual procedure by which a compiler turns a source program into an object module (for information on this interesting subject see any book on compiler design). Rather, the material in this chapter explains how JCL is used to request specific processing functions from a compiler.

The COBOL U compiler uses up to seven types of data sets when turning a COBOL source module into an object module. Ten actual data sets are involved. Each data set is categorized as being used for input, output, or a work area. A thorough description of the functions of each data set follows. The DDname identifies the basic role the data set performs. For example, a DDname of SYSIN references the source program. Following the descriptions of the data sets several coding examples are examined. Several rarely used optional data sets are not described.

Required Data Sets (Identified by DDname)

SYSIN

SYSIN identifies the primary input. It is used to identify the data set that contains the COBOL source code. The SYSIN data set must always be present to do a compile; it cannot be dummied out. Most frequently SYSIN identifies an in-stream data set consisting of 80 byte card images. A sequential disk or tape data set or a member of a pds can also be specified with SYSIN. When disk or tape data sets that have a large blocking factor are used, additional storage may be required for buffers. The records in the SYSIN data set should have DCB values that include LRECL=80 and RECFM=F or FB. SYSIN can also identify a collection of concatenated data sets.

SYSLIB

SYSLIB identifies the secondary input. With COBOL this input is called a COPY library. This is a pds whose members contain segments of COBOL source code. A member is inserted into the primary input wherever a corresponding COPY statement is located. Like SYSIN, if the COPY library contains large physical records it may be necessary to request additional storage for the buffers.

Example 1: Suppose ALPHA and BETA are members of a COPY library. ALPHA contains three MOVE statements and BETA consists of a PERFORM and STOP RUN statement. References to COPY members cause the statements they contain to be inserted into the COBOL source code that was read from the SYSIN data set. The primary input is coded as follows:

```
PERFORM PARA-A.
COPY ALPHA.
MOVE X TO Y.
COPY BETA.
```

Members ALPHA and BETA are retrieved from the COPY library and inserted into the COBOL source code as follows:

```
      PERFORM PARA-A.
      COPY ALPHA.
C     MOVE A1 TO B1.
C     MOVE A2 TO B2.
C     MOVE A3 TO B3.
      MOVE X TO Y.
      COPY BETA.
C     PERFORM LOOP.
C     STOP RUN.
```

Note that all the inserted statements are preceded by a C in the printed listing of the COBOL program. This substitution operation is performed prior to the actual compilation of the source code. Hence, if a major problem occurs while processing a COPY member, compilation is abandoned. In fact, a common case of a return code of 16 occurring during a compile is insufficient buffer space for COPY members.

Through concatenation SYSLIB can be used to reference multiple COPY libraries. When this is done the library with the largest blocksize should be listed first in the concatenation. If all the libraries have the same blocksize list the most frequently referenced first. When two or more DD statements are present the libraries they identify are searched in the order they are coded to find the member whose name was specified on a COPY statement in the COBOL source code. If the same member name occurs in more than one library the first member found is inserted into the source code. For information on building a COPY library see Chapters 25 and 27.

A DD statement with a DDname other than SYSLIB may also be used to identify a COPY library. The COPY library is the only data set used with the COBOL compiler whose DDname may be selected by the programmer. When this approach is used the COPY statement in the COBOL program must specify the member name and also identify the DDname. The DD statement in turn contains the data set name of the library. Suppose a member BETA occurs in two libraries, LIB1 and LIB2. ALPHA is in LIB1. Then to include the BETA from LIB2 the COPY statements can be coded as:

```
   COPY ALPHA.
   COPY BETA IN SECOND.
```

The accompanying JCL should contain the following two DD statements:

```
//SYSLIB DD  DSN=LIB1,DISP=SHR
//SECOND DD  DSN=LIB2,DISP=SHR
```

With this approach multiple members with the same name can be referenced in a program. The order of the DD statements can be reversed.

The COPY statement is a very convenient feature of the COBOL language. It should be used whenever appropriate. It reduces COBOL syntax errors and leads to a great deal of consistency in coding. It is especially helpful when many programmers are writing a large computer system. Alias names many be assigned to COPY library members. For more information on the COPY statement consult the IBM manual *OS/VS COBOL*.

SYSLIN

SYSLIN identifies the primary output produced by the compiler, which is the object module. Like the source program, the object module consists of 80 byte records. It contains four types of statements. They are called the External Symbol Dictionary (ESD), the Relocation Dictionary (RLD), the actual computer instructions or text (TXT), and a delimiting statement (END) which marks the end of the module. An object module is pictured in Figure 17–1.

FIGURE 17–1

Four Parts of the Object Module

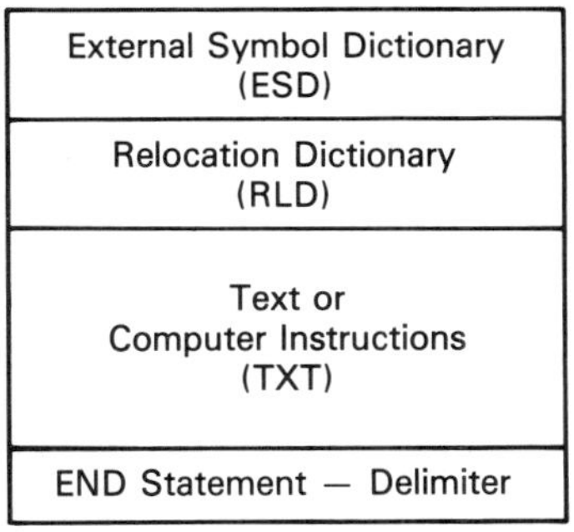

The ESD, RLD, and TXT statements need not be constructed together in groups as shown here. An object module has sequential organization and may be stored either as a sequential data set or as a member of a pds. The structure and role of the object module are further examined in the next two chapters. The contents and roles of the ESD and RLD statements are described in Chapter 18.

If several COBOL source programs are each compiled in separate steps in the same jobstream the resulting object modules can be concatenated together into a single sequential data set. Cataloged procedures perform this by specifying a DISP parameter of (MOD,PASS) on the SYSLIN DD statements in the procedure. The first time the data set is referenced MOD is interpreted as NEW. All subsequent references to this data set result in MOD being interpreted as OLD. Hence the object modules are concatenated together. The END statements separate the modules. Coding MOD can lead to more potential problems than any of the other three DISP subparameter values. An alternate approach is to compile all of the programs in the same step. This is done by coding CBL in columns one to three on a statement preceding each COBOL program to be compiled. This technique is illustrated in Example 6. With this approach all of the source programs are placed in the same SYSIN data set. The compiler will create separate object modules out of each source program. Hence all of the object modules will be placed in the same SYSLIN data set just as with DISP=MOD and the cataloged procedure. Again, the END statements separate the modules.

There is no one-to-one pairing between the statements in a source module and the object module constructed from it. As much object code as will fit is placed in each statement. Hence the equivalent of several lines of high level language code may be stored in one object module record. When trying to analyze the structure of an object module it is simplest to use an assembler program. The assembler source statements are not further decomposed during the translation. Individual statements can be easily located in the object module. To examine the complete structure of an object module it can be printed in hexadecimal using either the IEBPTPCH or IDCAMS utilities.

If an object module is not to be created the SYSLIN data set can be dummied out. This may occur when the only service required from the compiler is a syntax check of the COBOL source code. In this case the cost of the step is noticably reduced. If an object module is not to be created code the NOLOAD option on the PARM parameter. NOLOAD means that an object module is not to be built. There is no NOOBJECT option.

SYSPRINT

SYSPRINT identifies the message data set, which is also an important output data set. The message data set is ordinarily sent to the printer. It contains a numbered listing of the statements in the SYSIN data set. It also shows where members from COPY libraries have been inserted. In addition, all diagnostic and error messages that are produced during the compilation are listed in the SYSPRINT data set. These messages are labeled IKFxxxx. This occurs because the name of the program which compiles COBOL source programs is IKFCBL00. A listing of all the PARM options in effect during the compilation is also printed.

A large variety of optional information can also be included as part of the SYSPRINT data set. These features include such items as an assembler–like translated listing of the COBOL code, a table of every variable name used in the COBOL program along with the statement numbers where the name occurs (a cross reference listing), a similar listing where the variable names have been sorted into alphabetical order (a sorted cross reference listing), execution time debugging options, and many others. The *COBOL Programmer's Guide* describes all of the available PARM options. The second part of this chapter describes many of the commonly coded PARM options. The actual content of the SYSPRINT data set is determined by the options selected either explicitly or implicitly on the PARM parameter on the EXEC statement. If SYSPRINT DD DUMMY is coded the message data set is not written.

SYSUT1, SYSUT2, SYSUT3, and SYSUT4

SYSUT1, SYSUT2, SYSUT3, and SYSUT4 identify work data sets that are used by the compiler during the process of translating the COBOL source code into an object module. All four should be coded and all four should contain the same DD parameter values. Since these are temporary data sets only the UNIT and SPACE parameters are required. VIO is often coded for the UNIT value. The IBM–supplied (recommended) values for the SPACE parameter are ordinarily used. This is shown in Example 3. If desired, data set name may be explicitly coded in order to force these data sets onto different volumes. Several optional work data sets may also be coded. They have DDnames of SYSUT5 and SYSUT6 and are described in the *COBOL Programmer's Guide*.

Optional Data Sets

SYSPUNCH is also an output data set which is used to produce a punched copy of the card images in the object module. Since only one copy of the object module is ordinarily needed the SYSLIN data set is usually sufficient. Hence SYSPUNCH is frequently dummied out. If SYSPUNCH is not to be used code the NODECK option on the PARM parameter. The SYSPUNCH data set exists primarily for historic reasons. In the 1960s it was a common practice to punch the object module onto cards and use the cards in subsequent processing.

SYSUDUMP is also an output data set. Its role is the same with all programs, although it functions differently with the compiler. It is used to identify the data set that will hold an abend dump if one occurs during the compilation. This should not be confused with the dump that results when an application program abends during execution. Rather, it means that for some reason the COBOL compiler itself abended while translating the source code. Examining the dump should give some indication as to the source code that was responsible for the abend. Typically some incorrect COBOL syntax could not be properly handled by the compiler and the abend resulted. Whenever the compiler abends all relevant information including the dump should be called to the attention of the systems programming department. Chapter 22 contains additional information on dumps.

JCL and the COBOL Compiler

All seven types of data sets described above may be explicitly coded when using the COBOL compiler. However, when a cataloged procedure is used to invoke the compiler most of these data sets are defined within the procedure. Frequently only the SYSIN DD statement needs to be coded with a procedure.

Example 2: A one step cataloged procedure is available with each programming language to compile a source program written in that language. The name of the procedure is usually of the form xxxyC where xxx identifies the language and y denotes a particular version of the compiler or assembler. Hence, to compile a COBOL program it is sufficient to code

```
//A            EXEC COBUC
//COB.SYSIN DD    *           or //SYSIN   DD *
      COBOL source program
/*
```

COBU identifies the U-level COBOL compiler. With one exception the statements within the COBUC procedure are the same statements in the first step of the procedure used in the next example. With COBUC the SYSLIN data set is usually dummied out. If an object module is to be produced SYSLIN must be overridden. DDnames do not need to be qualified with a one step procedure.

Example 3: To compile a COBOL program and then execute it (usually called a COBOL Compile and Go) the following procedure may be used:

```
//A      EXEC  COBUCG,PARM.COB='STATE,PMAP,other options',
//       other COB (compile) parameters,GO step parameters
//COB.SYSIN   DD  *
    COBOL source code is placed here.
/*
//GO.DDname1 DD  Data sets used during the GO step by
//GO.DDname2 DD  the Loader or by the COBOL application
//...            program are placed here.
```

The other DD statements needed by the compiler are included in the COBUCG cataloged procedure. The XX in columns 1 and 2 mean that those statements were inserted into the jobstream from the cataloged procedure. At most installations the complete JCL listing should look something like the following:

```
//A        EXEC COBUCG,PARM.COB='STATE,PMAP,other options',...
XXCOB      EXEC PGM=IKFCBL00,REGION=128K,PARM=CLIST
XXSYSPRINT  DD  SYSOUT=A
XXSYSUT1    DD  UNIT=VIO,SPACE=(460,(700,100))
XXSYSUT2    DD  UNIT=VIO,SPACE=(460,(700,100))
XXSYSUT3    DD  UNIT=VIO,SPACE=(460,(700,100))
XXSYSUT4    DD  UNIT=VIO,SPACE=(460,(700,100))
XXSYSLIN    DD  DSN=&LOADSET,DISP=(MOD,PASS),
XX              UNIT=SYSDA,SPACE=(80,(500,100))
XXSYSLIB    DD  DSN=SYS1.COBCOPY.LIBRARY,DISP=SHR
XX          DD  DSN=SYS1.COBCOPY2.LIBRARY,DISP=SHR
XXSYSUDUMP  DD  SYSOUT=A
XXSYSPUNCH  DD  DUMMY
//COB.SYSIN DD  *
     The COBOL source code is placed here, but this is not
     evident from the JCL listing. Likewise, the /* which
     denotes the end of the in-stream data set does not
     appear in the printed listing.
XXGO       EXEC PGM=LOADER,COND=(5,LT,COB),REGION=128K
XXSTEPLIB
XX...               DD statements which are coded in the
XX...               procedure for the GO step appear here.
//GO.DDname1 DD     Added statements are coded last.
```

Example 4: Another common programming situation occurs when most of the DD statements within the cataloged procedure are acceptable as coded but some require modification. Those DD statements with parameters that need to be modified can be overridden. For example, suppose a different COPY library is needed with the COBUCG procedure. Additionally, the SYSUDUMP data set is to be dummied out. To make both of these modifications invoke the COBUCG cataloged procedure with the three DD statements shown here:

```
//A    EXEC   COBUCG,PARM.COB='STATE,PMAP,other options',...
//COB.SYSLIB     DD
//               DD  DSN=NEW.COPY.LIBRARY
//COB.SYSUDUMP DD    DUMMY
//COB.SYSIN      DD  *
    . . . the rest of the code from the previous example
          remains unchanged
```

Recall that all DD statements that override existing statements in the cataloged procedure are coded prior to the SYSIN statement, which is an added statement. Only the second COPY library is overridden by this code. Note that SYSLIB and SYSUDUMP are coded in the same order in which they occur within the procedure.

A person using the COBOL compiler is not required to use cataloged procedures. All the required DD statements can be coded directly in the jobstream. This is rarely done since the cataloged procedures almost always contain a considerable amount of usable code. As always, the less JCL coded, the less can go wrong. If overriding is not being done the procedure should almost always be used. However, when uncertain about how an overriding DD statement should be coded it may be safer to code all the statements. Subtle errors can easily occur when using procedures and overriding.

Figure 17–2 shows the seven types of data sets that are used during a COBOL compile.

FIGURE 17–2
Data Sets Used During a COBOL Compile

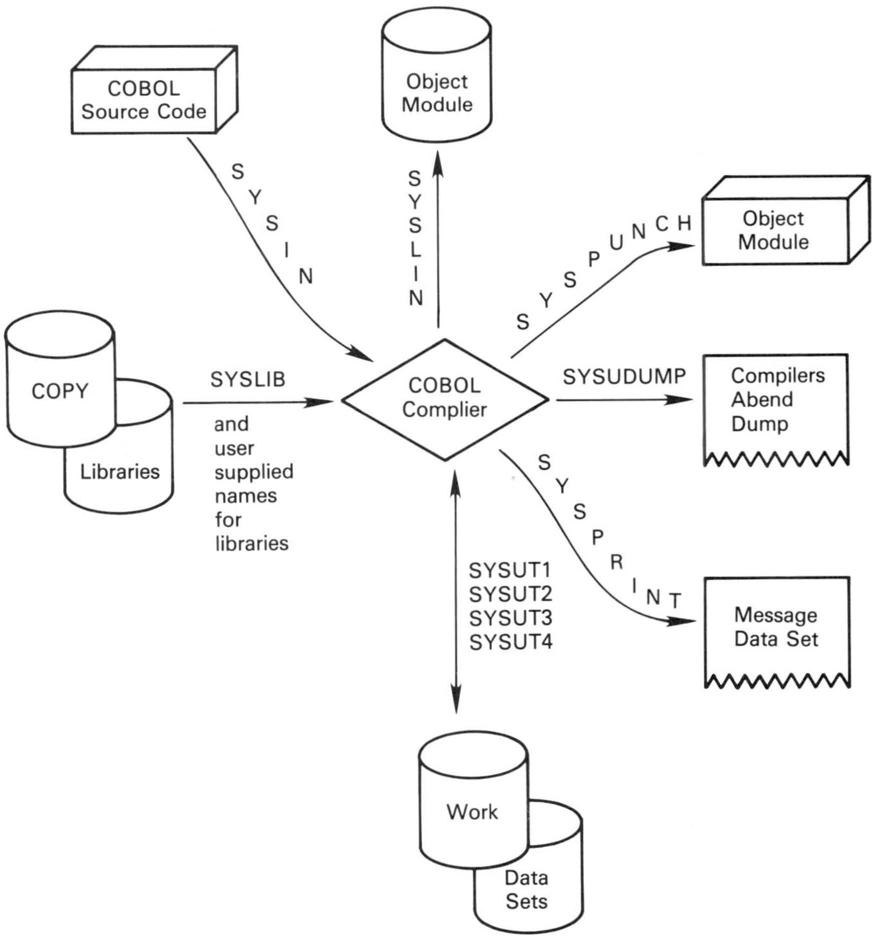

PL/I and Assembler Data Sets and DDnames

Both PL/I and assembler use almost the same DDnames and types of data sets as COBOL. With the PL/I compiler all of the above data sets retain the same DDnames and roles as with COBOL except for the work data sets. PL/I uses only one work data set, and it has a DDname of SYSUT1. Some other minor changes related to the differences between the two languages also occur. For example, %INCLUDE is used to insert additional source code with PL/I rather than the COPY statement. Hence SYSLIB may be more accurately said to denote an INCLUDE library. Like COBOL, the PL/I compiler permits using DDnames other than SYSLIB when referencing INCLUDE libraries. PL/I also permits variable length source code in the SYSIN data set.

The F-level assembler data sets also vary very little from the DD statements used with COBOL. With assembler the object module is identified by the DDname SYSGO rather than SYSLIN. The SYSLIB statement can be used to identify both COPY libraries and MACRO libraries. The newest IBM assembler uses SYSLIN rather than SYSGO as the DDname for the object module. Additionally, both assemblers require only three work data sets, SYSUT1, SYSUT2, and SYSUT3.

Example 5: Assembler source code is stored in member ALPHA of the cataloged pds SOURCE.CODE. It is to be assembled and the resulting object module is to be written in the same library and called BETA. Because of their similar DCB properties source and object modules can be safely stored in the same library if care is taken. This can be accomplished as follows:

```
//A          EXEC PGM=IFOX00
//SYSIN       DD  DSN=SOURCE.CODE(ALPHA),DISP=SHR
//SYSGO       DD  DSN=SOURCE.CODE(BETA),DISP=OLD
//SYSPRINT    DD  SYSOUT=A
//SYSLIB      DD  DSN=SYS1.MACLIB,DISP=SHR
//            DD  DSN=SYS1.COPYLIB,DISP=SHR
//SYSUT1      DD  UNIT=VIO,SPACE=(CYL,(5,1))
//SYSUT2      DD  UNIT=VIO,SPACE=(CYL,(5,1))
//SYSUT3      DD  UNIT=VIO,SPACE=(CYL,(5,1))
//SYSPUNCH    DD  DUMMY
```

COBOL PARM Options

Overview

A wide range of options is available when using the COBOL Compiler. The desired options are specified with the PARM parameter on the EXEC statement. There are approximately 50 PARM options. The most important ones are described below. The complete list of PARM options can be found in the *COBOL Programmer's Guide*.

PL/I and assembler have their own comparable PARM options, and they include many of the COBOL PARM values.

There are two ways to supply PARM values to the compiler, implicitly and explicitly. Implicit PARM values are the set of default values which are provided with the compiler. They can be modified by an installation's systems programming staff. Explicit PARM values are coded on an EXEC statement. With the COBOL compiler most of the PARM values are implicitly supplied; the programmer need only supply PARM values for special cases. Several of the PARM values are opposites and mutually exclusive (e.g., DECK or NODECK, SEQ or NOSEQ, PMAP or CLIST). If two mutually exclusive values are specified, usually the last one coded is in effect. A PARM value coded on the EXEC statement will override its counterpart default value. If a cataloged procedure invokes the compiler all of the PARM values on the EXEC statement within the procedure are overridden by the PARM values on the EXEC proc name statement.

```
//A      EXEC  COBUCG,PARM.COB=overriding PARM values
XXCOB    EXEC  PGM=IKFCBL00,PARM=explicitly coded values
        PARM values are overridden by PARM.COB values
         Default (implicit) PARM values are specified as
         part of the COBOL compiler program (IKFCBL00).
         They can only be overridden on an individual
         basis.
```

Important COBOL PARM Options

The COBOL compiler PARM values that an MVS COBOL programmer should be familiar with are described below. Some of the values require that an additional DD statement be coded during execution. Other values considerably increase the compilation time.

SIZE

This specifies the number of bytes of main storage available for compilation. The default is 128K bytes.

CLIST

This specifies that a condensed listing is to be produced. A condensed listing consists of each verb in the PROCEDURE DIVISION along with its hexadecimal offset from the beginning of the program. The default is NOCLIST. CLIST and PMAP are mutually exclusive. When both NOCLIST and NOPMAP are coded the message data set still contains verb references, global tables, the literal pools, register assignments, and information about the WORKING-STORAGE SECTION.

PMAP

This specifies that in addition to global tables, literal pools, register assignments, and information about the WORKING-STORAGE SECTION, the assembler language equivalent of the COBOL source program is also listed in the SYSPRINT data set. PMAP is usually coded whenever it is necessary to read a dump that results from a COBOL application program abending. The default is NOPMAP. If it is necessary to read a dump either PMAP or CLIST should be coded. Both supply the address of the instruction that caused the abend.

FLOW

This specifies that a formatted trace of the flow of program execution is to be printed. This is done only when an abend occurs. The SYSDBOUT DD statement must be included at execution time, not during the compilation. It contains the printed listing of the paragraphs in the order they were executed. The FLOW option is an alternative to the use of the READY TRACE statement in the COBOL program itself. Both the FLOW and STATE options usually require a STEPLIB DD statement that identifies the COBOL automatic call library, SYS1.COBLIB. The role of this library is discussed in the next two chapters. A trace of just the last nn paragraphs executed may be requested by coding FLOW=nn. The default is NOFLOW.

STATE

This specifies a powerful debugging option that is used only when an abend occurs. The number of the source statement that was executing at the time of the abend, the type of abend, and additional diagnostic messages are printed. When the STATE option is used the SYSDBOUT DD statement must be present at execution time, not during the compilation. Like FLOW, some additional overhead information is required in the object module to support the STATE feature. For this reason STATE and FLOW are not routinely used in a production environment. A STEPLIB DD statement which identifies SYS1.COBLIB is also usually required with STATE. The default is NOSTATE.

COUNT

This specifies that a detailed summary is to be printed of both the absolute number and the percentage of times each statement in a COBOL program is executed. Each verb is identified by procedure name and by statement number. Also included is the number of times it was used. Percentages are calculated for each verb with respect to the total number of executed statements. When COUNT is used both the

SYSDBOUT and SYSCOUNT DD statements must be present at execution time. Both should identify SYSOUT data sets. COUNT requires a substantial amount of overhead. It should not be used unless the information it produces is actually needed. It can be used to optimize the segments of code that are executed most frequently. NOCOUNT is the default.

XREF

This specifies that a cross reference listing of data names and procedure names is to be produced. Accompanying each name is a list of all statement numbers where the name is used. The default is NOXREF.

SXREF

This also produces a cross reference listing. However, the data names and procedure names are first sorted. XREF and SXREF are mutually exclusive. SXREF requires more overhead than XREF, but SXREF is the more convenient of the two. Both are useful for debugging COBOL syntax errors and modifying existing programs. The default is NOSXREF.

DECK

This specifies that the object module is to be written to the SYSPUNCH data set. The default is NODECK. If NODECK is coded the SYSPUNCH data set is not used.

LOAD

This specifies that the compilation should produce an object module. When LOAD is coded the SYSLIN DD statement must be included with the compiler JCL. If NOLOAD is coded the compilation will not produce an object module. NOLOAD merely checks the syntax of the COBOL source code. NOLOAD is often specified in the COBUC catalogued procedure. The default is LOAD.

SEQ

This specifies that the compiler should check the sequence numbers coded in the first six columns of each source statement. If any sequence numbers are out of order a single warning message is printed specifying the number of sequence errors. SEQ is the default. When NOSEQ is coded the compiler does not check the order of the values in the sequence number field of the source code.

APOST

This specifies that the apostrophe (') will be used to enclose literals. Although the IBM default is QUOTE ("), most installations have replaced QUOTE with APOST to provide compatibility with IBM software packages.

LISTER

This is the group name for a large number of options that deal with the content and appearance of the message data set. LISTER provides facilities to print or punch the source statements in a readable format with indenting, spacing, and cross referencing of information. The LISTER option requires heavy overhead and appreciably increases the cost of a compilation. It should be used sparingly, and only after all syntax errors have been removed from the source code. The default is NOLST.

LIB

This specifies that the automatic copy libraries will be searched to locate COPY members coded in the source program. If there are no COPY statements NOLIB should be coded. NOLIB will result in a faster compilation since the initial scan of the source code can be omitted. The default is LIB.

BATCH

This specifies that two or more COBOL programs are to be compiled in a single jobstep. Each program is preceded by a CBL statement. The *PROCESS statement is used for the same purpose in PL/I. Additional compiler PARM options may be listed on the CBL statement. They apply only to the program they precede. Otherwise the options coded on the EXEC statement apply to all of the programs. The default is NOBATCH.

Example 6: The following code illustrates how the PARM options are coded and also shows the necessary accompanying DD statements that they require:

```
//A    EXEC  COBUCG,
//     PARM.COB='STATE,FLOW,SXREF,BATCH,COUNT,PMAP'
XXCOB EXEC  PGM=IKFCBL00,PARM='CLIST,DECK'
XX...
//COB.SYSIN DD *
CBL
  main COBOL program here
CBL  XREF,CLIST
  first external subroutine placed here
  ...
```

```
/*
//GO.SYSDBOUT DD SYSOUT=A
//GO.SYSCOUNT DD SYSOUT=A
//  other DD statements needed during execution
```

Because STATE and FLOW are coded the SYSDBOUT statement is necessary. SYSCOUNT must be used with COUNT. BATCH implies multiple programs in the SYSIN data set. Each program is preceded by a statement with CBL in the first three bytes. The output from SXREF and PMAP is written to the SYSPRINT data set during the compile step. Output from COUNT, STATE, and FLOW is printed during the program execution step. The latter two print only if an abend occurs. The CLIST and DECK options in the procedure are overridden. The XREF and CLIST options are only in effect during the compilation of the second program.

Exercises

1. A COBOL source module is contained in the sequential data set COBOL.SOURCE. The following jobstep has been written to create an object module out of this code. Find and correct all of the logic and syntax errors in the following code:

```
//DISASTER EXEC PGM=IKFCBL00,PARM='PMAP,CLIST,XREF,STATE,OBJ'
//SYSPRINT   DD  SYSOUT=A
//SYSDBOUT   DD  SYSOUT=A
//SYSUT1     DD  UNIT=VIO,SPACE=(CYL,(1,1))
//SYSUT2     DD  DSN=*.SYSUT1,UNIT=VIO,SPACE=(CYL,(1,1))
//SYSUT3     DD  DSN=*.SYSUT1,UNIT=VIO,SPACE=(CYL,(1,1))
//SYSUT4     DD  DSN=*.SYSUT1,UNIT=VIO,SPACE=(CYL,(1,1))
//SYSLIB     DD  DSN=SYS1.PROCLIB,DISP=SHR
//SYSUDUMP   DD  DUMMY
//SYSIN      DD  DSN=COBOL.SOURCE,DISP=SHR
//SYSLIN     DD  DSN=SYS1.LINKLIB(ALPHA),DISP=OLD
//SYSPRINT   DD  SYSOUT=*
```

2. List the DDnames that may be coded in a jobstep that uses the COBOL compiler. For each DDname list the following information for the accompanying data set: required or optional, data set organization, DCB properties, new or existing data set, role of the data set during compilation.

3. Which three DD statements used during the compile step are specifically related to the three PARM options DECK, LIB, and LOAD? Describe the relationship in each case between the option and the JCL statement. Which PARM options require a DD statement to be coded during the execution of the program? In each case what DDname should be specified on the DD statement for each option?

4. Several COBOL copy libraries are to be concatenated. List at least three factors that are used to determine the order in which the DD statements should be coded. Prioritize the factors from most important to least important in determining the order of the data sets in the concatenation.

5. With the *COBOL Programmer's Guide* make a list of all available COBOL PARM options. Make a comparable list of all available PL/I PARM options. Why do specific options exist with one compiler and not the other? Which are the significant omissions with each compiler?

6. The statements COPY ALPHA and COPY BETA IN SECOND are used to identify COPY members in different libraries. The accompanying JCL is shown following Example 1. How can the two members be correctly referenced without using the COPY member name in DDname clause?

7. List several specific programming situations where the use of COPY statements would be appropriate.

8. In the COBUCG procedure expansion shown in Example 3 estimate the number of COBOL source statements that the compiler is capable of processing based on the SPACE parameter coded on the SYSLIN statement.

9. The PARM option COUNT requires a great deal of overhead. What situations would justify its usage? Should it ever be used with a production program?

Chapter 18

The Linkage Editor

Overview

The Linkage Editor and the Loader (which is discussed in the next chapter) are two essential processing programs on MVS systems. They are usually called service programs rather than utility programs. One of these two programs must be used along with a language translator in the process of turning an application program written in a high level language or assembler into a format in which it can actually be executed. Both the Linkage Editor and Loader are themselves language independent since neither of them processes source code as input.

Typically a program is either coded in a high level language such as COBOL and PL/I or written in assembler. A large programming system may have modules written in several different languages. In all of these situations language translators turn the source code into object modules. As discussed in Chapter 17, an object module is the primary output from a language translator.

What happens to an object module after it is created? Initially if a cataloged procedure is used the object module is stored on disk as a temporary data set. This data set could be made permanent, but this is rarely done since the object module is almost always processed further in a subsequent job step. Additional processing is required because an object module is not in a format suitable for execution. There are two specific reasons why an object module needs more processing: it usually contains unresolved external references, and some value within it may need to be relocated.

External References

All subroutine calls (external references) within an object module need to be resolved before the module can be successfully executed. Language translators do not resolve external references. These references in the object code may be explicit or implicit. Explicit references include all of the subroutine calls inserted into the source code by the programmer of the module. Implicit references consist of subroutine calls to sections of previously translated code that are stored in a permanent system library of either load or object modules. Implicit references are inserted into an object module during translation by the compiler. Almost all modern compilers insert these subroutine calls. There are many common programming situations which arise during translation that cause the compilers to insert a CALL statement rather than code the actual machine instructions. Every compiler has a library of (load module) subroutines for this purpose. This library is usually named SYS1.xxxLIB where xxx denotes the high level language used. For example, SYS1.COBLIB is the COBOL library. There are several hundred members supplied by IBM in SYS1.COBLIB. In fact, it may be impossible to write a COBOL program that does not call one or more of these subroutines (see Exercise 14). Each subroutine name starts with the letters ILBO. In addition, an installation may add other members to SYS1.COBLIB. These would need to be explicitly referenced in the source code.

All external references, both explicit and implicit, must be resolved before the successful execution of the module can take place. When an unresolved external reference is encountered during execution it usually causes a S0C1 abend to occur. Information concerning external references is stored in the External Symbol Dictionary (ESD). There are three types of ESD entries: the names of control sections, entry points, and the names of subroutines coded on CALL statements. A control section is a module that cannot be decomposed further into sub–modules. Control section is an assembler language term.

Relocation Dictionary

Some addresses may require adjustment or recalculation before an object module can be turned into an executable format. Every object module contains a listing of such addresses. This listing is called the Relocation Dictionary (RLD).

The Role of the Linkage Editor and Loader

Both resolving of external references and address adjusting must take place prior to attempting to execute the code in the object module. The Linkage Editor and Loader are designed to handle these two functions. One of these programs must be selected to process an object module. Both programs can also accept load modules as input.

Both the Linkage Editor and Loader create load modules as their primary output. Load modules are sections of code that are capable of being brought into memory in their present state and then executed. Unlike object modules, load modules do not require further processing. Hence the fundamental role of the Linkage Editor and Loader can be defined as follows: to take object modules, existing load modules, and additional directions called control statements as input, tie them together, and produce load modules as output.

The difference between object and load modules should be emphasized. An object module is composed of 80 byte logical records which contain non-executable machine code. It is produced by a language translator and may be either a sequential data set or a member of a card-image library. A load module contains executable machine language. It is produced by the Linkage Editor or Loader, and if it is to be stored on disk it must be a member of a partitioned data set. A load module must be created either directly in main memory or as a member of a pds. The records within a load module have an undefined record format. When stored on a 3330 or 3350 disk they ordinarily have a physical record length equal to one track on the disk volume where they are stored. Since object modules contain 80 byte logical records they can be concatenated with card images. Load modules cannot be concatenated to either object modules or control statements, which also consist of 80 byte records. The physical characteristics of a load module place some restrictions on where they can be specified in a Linkage Editor job step. Some of the exercises at the end of this chapter describe how more detailed information on the similarities and distinctions between object and load modules can be determined.

Since both the Linkage Editor and Loader produce load modules, either can be used to prepare a program for execution. However, in some situations the load module that is created is to be executed immediately and in other situations it is to be stored in a load module library for later execution in a following jobstep or in a future job.

The process of turning source code into a load module is depicted graphically in Figure 18–1.

Besides turning object modules into load modules, both the Linkage Editor and Loader are capable of performing a wide range of functions using both object and load modules as input. Some of the more important of these Linkage Editor functions will be discussed in detail in this chapter. The comparable material for the Loader is presented in Chapter 19. Some types of processing with the Linkage Editor and Loader are not discussed in this book. See the *Linkage Editor and Loader* manual for more details.

The Linkage Editor will first be examined in considerable detail. The Loader will then be compared and contrasted with the Linkage Editor. This chapter and the next will make evident not only how these programs work, but also which of the two is more appropriate for a particular application.

General Functions of the Linkage Editor

The functions that the Linkage Editor can perform are divided into two general categories, linking and editing. A person with limited MVS experience or anyone whose usage of the Linkage Editor is restricted to the cataloged procedures will probably

FIGURE 18–1

Turning Source Code into a Load Module

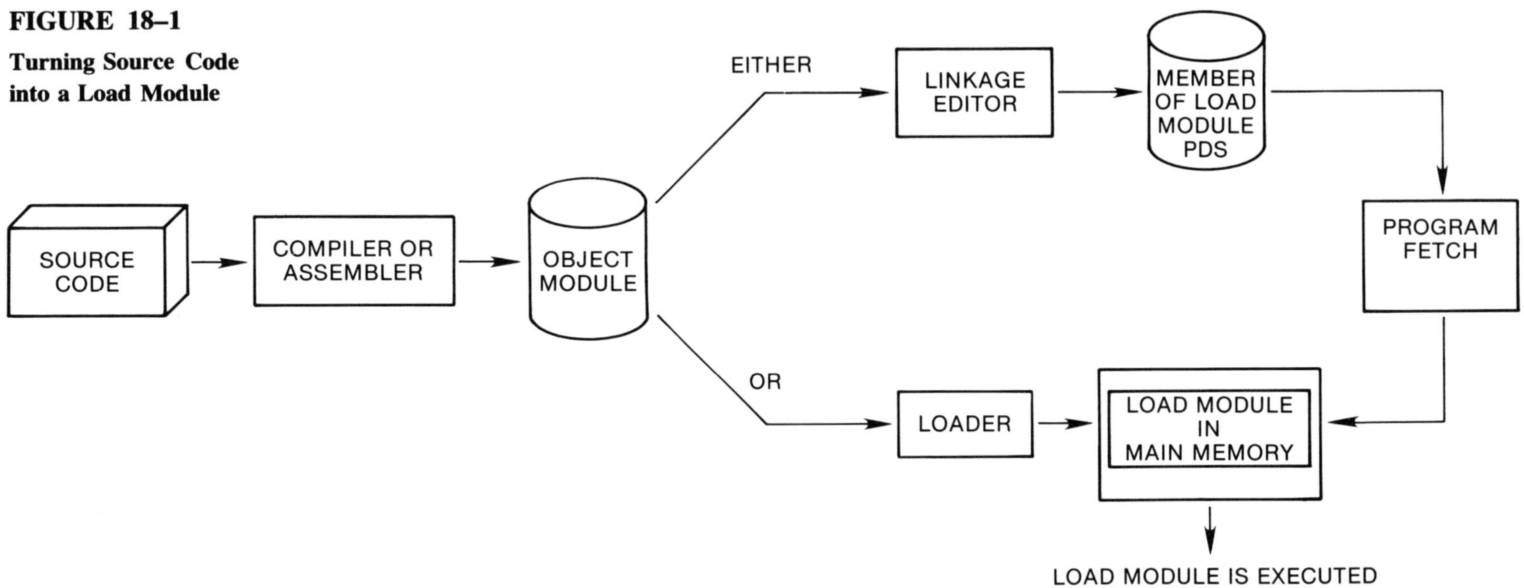

deal almost entirely with the linking functions. However, the Linkage Editor is capable of performing a wide range of powerful editing functions. Some of these functions will be discussed later in this chapter. The primary emphasis in this chapter concerns the linking aspect of the Linkage Editor.

No matter whether linking or editing is being performed, certain data sets are required with every invocation of the Linkage Editor. There are four required data sets that must always be present and four other types of data sets that may also be coded. These latter four categories involve either concatenation or multiple user selected DDnames. The eight data set types will be discussed individually. Note that two of the eight are actually categories that can contain multiple data set occurrences under distinct programmer chosen DDnames. These two require the use of control statements.

Required Data Sets

The four data sets that must always be coded when the Linkage Editor is used have DDnames of SYSPRINT, SYSUT1, SYSLMOD, and SYSLIN. SYSPRINT and SYSUT1 have the same basic roles as with the language translators.

SYSPRINT is the message data set. It is almost always written to the printer. The actual format and content of the message data set are determined by several of the PARM options which can be specified on the EXEC statement. The three PARM options LIST, XREF, and MAP determine the information written to the SYSPRINT data set. The greatest amount of information is provided when LIST and XREF are both coded. All diagnostic, warning, and error messages are written regardless of the options selected.

SYSUT1 is a work data set. It should be a sequentially organized disk data set. Only UNIT and SPACE parameters need be specified on its DD statement. The DCB values for SYSUT1 are supplied by the Linkage Editor.

SYSLMOD identifies the primary output data set. It must reference a pds which contains only load modules. The Linkage Editor will place every load module created during the jobstep into this library. The member names in the library can be specified in either of two ways: one member name may be coded on the SYSLMOD DD statement following the pds name, or multiple member names may be included on control statements. When multiple load modules are produced in a single jobstep, control statements must be used to give names to all members (except possibly the last). This is necessary because MVS JCL syntax permits only one member name on a DD statement.

When the library referenced on the SYSLMOD statement is first created, DCB values of RECFM=U and BLKSIZE=one track should be specified. If the library is created in a Linkage Editor jobstep rather than with IEFBR14, the DCB values need not be specified as they will be automatically supplied by the Linkage Editor. If the SYSLMOD library exists prior to the jobstep currently referencing it the value coded for the first DISP subparameter will determine if a member is to be added to the pds or replace an existing member in the library with the same name. This is discussed further in Chapter 12.

SYSLIN identifies the primary input to the Linkage Editor. Unlike the first three data sets described above, there are many variations in the manner in which this data set supplies the input. SYSLIN may identify a sequential disk or tape data set, a member of a pds, an in-stream data set, or a concatenation of several of these. Each data set may in turn contain object modules, control statements, or both. For example, with four DD statements concatenated SYSLIN could identify a sequential data set containing an object module, two members of a pds (each of which also contains object modules), and an in-stream data set containing control statements. No matter what the format of the data set is, it can contain only object modules and/or control statements. Note that load modules cannot be specified directly as input to the Linkage Editor; they must be referenced indirectly through the control statements. This occurs because control statements and object modules have similar DCB values which are not present with load modules. When a load module is specified directly one of the following messages may occur:

```
IEW0294  DDNAME PRINTED HAD SYNCHRONOUS ERROR
IEW0594  INPUT DATA SET BLKSIZE IS INVALID
```

Optional Data Sets

Of the four optional types of data sets used with the Linkage Editor, two must have the same DDnames whenever they are coded. The remaining two can be used only with control statements.

SYSLIB identifies an automatic call library. The role of this library is to supply object and load modules that are used to resolve external references in the primary input. For example, if the statement CALL 'ALPHA' appeared in the primary input (of a COBOL program) but there was no subroutine or entry point in the primary input named ALPHA, then after all the primary input was processed ALPHA would be considered an unresolved external reference. It is the role of SYSLIB to identify the libraries that are to be searched to resolve external references. Any library coded on the SYSLIB statement must be either an object module library or a load module library. If several libraries are concatenated together they must all be the same type; object and load module libraries cannot be mixed together. Both types can be specified in the same link edit step, but one or the other type must be referenced through the control statements discussed below. The modules supplied by SYSLIB are referred to as secondary input. A careful distinction should be made between automatic call libraries and automatic copy libraries. Call libraries contain object or load modules and copy libraries contain source code.

SYSIN identifies any additional primary input that is to be concatenated to the SYSLIN data set. The DDname SYSIN has no required role with the Linkage Editor. Rather, SYSIN is commonly used when the Linkage Editor is invoked in a cataloged procedure. The SYSIN input almost always consists entirely of control statements. The SYSIN data set is convenient because of the JCL restriction that prohibits in-stream data sets in cataloged procedures. The concatenation to the SYSLIN data set occurs because of a DDNAME=SYSIN parameter specified on the SYSLIN DD statement inside the cataloged procedure. This is illustrated in Example 1.

Example 1: One of the most common programming situations involving the Linkage Editor is a cataloged procedure containing two steps, a compile (or assemble) followed by a link edit. An xxxyCL procedure is ordinarily available with each language translator. C stands for compile and L for link edit. The characters xxx and y have the standard meanings with procedure names as described in Chapter 8. For example, starting with an assembler language source program a load module is created by coding

```
//A      EXEC   ASMFCL
//ASM.SYSIN      DD   *
  assembler source program
/*
//LKED.SYSLMOD DD   DSN=LOADMODU.PDS(PROG1),DISP=OLD
```

This will result in the following JCL listing where the statements beginning with XX are supplied by the cataloged procedure:

```
//A       EXEC   ASMFCL
XXASM     EXEC   PGM=IFOX00,PARM=OBJ,REGION=128K
XXSYSPRINT        DD   SYSOUT=A,DCB=BLKSIZE=1089
XXSYSLIB          DD   DSN=SYS1.MACLIB,DISP=SHR
XXSYSUT1          DD   UNIT=VIO,SPACE=(1700,(600,10))
XXSYSUT2          DD   UNIT=VIO,SPACE=(1700,(600,10))
XXSYSUT3          DD   UNIT=VIO,SPACE=(1700,(600,10))
XXSYSPUNCH        DD   DUMMY
XXSYSGO           DD   DSN=&&OBJSET,UNIT=SYSDA,
XX              DISP=(MOD,PASS),SPACE=(80,(200,50))
//ASM.SYSIN       DD   *
XXLKED EXEC PGM=IEWL,PARM=(XREF,LIST,LET),REGION=128K,
XX              COND=(8,LT,ASM)
XXSYSLIN          DD   DSN=&&OBJSET,DISP=(OLD,DELETE)
XX                DD   DDNAME=SYSIN
//LKED.SYSLMOD DD   DSN=LOADMODU.PDS(PROG1),DISP=OLD
X/SYSLMOD         DD   DSN=NULLFILE,DISP=SHR
XXSYSUT1          DD   DSN=&&SYSUT1,UNIT=SYSDA,
XX              SPACE=(1024,(50,20))
XXSYSPRINT        DD   SYSOUT=A
```

There is no LKED.SYSLIB DD statement since there is no assembler automatic call library. The assembler does not insert implicit subroutine calls into the source code. Notice that the output from the assembler (the object module stored in &&OBJSET) is the primary input to the Linkage Editor and that additional input can be supplied by coding an LKED.SYSIN DD statement. On MVS systems a warning message is issued if the DDNAME=SYSIN forward reference is not used when the procedure is invoked. The message is

```
IEF686I DDNAME REFERRED TO ON DDNAME KEYWORD IN PRIOR STEP
        WAS NOT RESOLVED
```

This message is strictly informatory and can usually be ignored. Try to determine why the BLKSIZE value was coded on the assembler message data set.

Before discussing the two remaining types of data sets that can be coded with the Linkage Editor, consider the following examples which illustrate almost all of the Linkage Editor notions discussed thus far.

Example 2: The other common procedure that involves the Linkage Editor has the format xxxyCLG. It contains the same first two steps as the xxxyCL procedure. However, there is also a third step that executes the load module constructed in the second step. During the link edit step the SYSLMOD statement identifies a new temporary load module library. Most commonly the only DD statements needed with the procedure are a SYSIN statement for the first step and DD statements for every data set the program uses during the third step. Hence to compile, link edit, and execute a COBOL program that reads master file records and prints them the following coding is sufficient:

```
//A           EXEC COBUCLG
//COB.SYSIN   DD   *
     COBOL source code here
/*
//GO.MASTER   DD   DSN=MASTER.FILE,DISP=SHR
//GO.REPORT   DD   SYSOUT=A
```

The SYSLMOD DD statement in step 2 and the EXEC statement in the final step are often coded in the procedure as

```
XXLKED.SYSLMOD  DD  DSN=&&LOADSET(GO),DISP=(,PASS),
XX                 UNIT=SYSDA,SPACE=(CYL,(1,1,1))
XXGO               EXEC PGM=*.LKED.SYSLMOD
```

Notice that the program is identified by a referback.

The next example illustrates a common programming situation that can readily be handled without using a cataloged procedure.

Example 3: Suppose there is a main COBOL program, COBOL1, which calls two external subroutines, COBSUB (written in COBOL) and PLISUB (written in PL/I). The COBOL program is in an object module library called OBJMAIN, and both subroutines are in the load module library LOADSUB. The coding needed to combine the main object module and the two load modules together into a single load module called MAINPRO is the following:

```
//LINKEDIT  EXEC PGM=IEWL,PARM='LIST,XREF,LET'
//SYSPRINT   DD  SYSOUT=A
//SYSUT1     DD  UNIT=SYSDA,SPACE=(CYL,1)
//SYSLIN     DD  DSN=OBJMAIN(COBOL1),DISP=SHR
//SYSLMOD    DD  DSN=LOADMAIN(MAINPRO),DISP=(NEW,CATLG),
//           UNIT=SYSDA,SPACE=(CYL,(1,,2)),VOL=SER=DISK01
//SYSLIB     DD  DSN=LOADSUB,DISP=SHR
//           DD  DSN=SYS1.COBLIB,DISP=SHR
```

The name of the Linkage Editor program is usually IEWL or HEWL. Both are traditionally pronounced "you'll". Like the language translators, the Linkage Editor program is kept in the system load module library, which is named SYS1.LINKLIB. The primary input is member COBOL1 in the library OBJMAIN. All subroutine calls in COBOL1 are resolved by searching the directories of the two automatic call libraries specified with SYSLIB. It is unnecessary to include the PL/I automatic call library since the PL/I subroutine has already been link edited, and all its external references from that library have been resolved. The PL/I library is called SYS1.PLIBASE, not SYS1.PLILIB. Here the pds LOADSUB contains the two programs that are explicitly called by COBOL1. SYS1.COBLIB is used to resolve any subroutine calls inserted in the COBOL code that have not been resolved to this point. There will always be such calls in the main COBOL program to get storage, perform initialization, handle data conversions, etc. Whether there are any of these unresolved subroutine calls in the two external subroutines will depend on the values that were coded when they were turned into load modules. One output load module is generated by the above code. Its name and the library in which it is a member are both specified on the SYSLMOD statement. Note that the library itself is being created in this step. SYSLIN and SYSLMOD each identify one member of a library, but SYSLIB references two entire libraries. Finally, note that neither external subroutine is explicitly mentioned anywhere in this code. A member name should never be coded on a SYSLIB DD statement.

Example 4: Suppose that the same load module constructed in Example 3 is to be created entirely from source code. Beginning with three source programs, two in COBOL and one in PL/I, create the load module MAINPRO that was constructed above. Assume that the LOADSUB library exists prior to running this job. The COBUCL and PLIXCL cataloged procedures contain SYSPRINT, SYSUT1, SYSLIN, and SYSLIB statements in their Linkage Editor (LKED) step, and hence these four DD statements do not need to be coded. In both procedures the SYSLIN data set will identify the object module created in the compile step. The SYSLMOD statement is coded to specify where the load module is to be stored, and it overrides the //LKED.SYSLMOD DD DSN=NULLFILE statement in the cataloged procedure.

```
//A          EXEC     COBUCL
//COB.SYSIN      DD   *
    source code for COBSUB goes here
/*
//LKED.SYSLMOD DD   DSN=LOADSUB(COBSUB),DISP=OLD
//B          EXEC     PLIXCL
//PLI.SYSIN      DD   *
    source code for PLISUB goes here
/*
//LKED.SYSLMOD DD   DSN=LOADSUB(PLISUB),DISP=OLD
//LINKEDIT EXEC     COBUCL
//COB.SYSIN      DD   *
    source code for COBOL1 goes here
/*
```

```
//LKED.SYSLMOD DD  DSN=LOADMAIN(MAINPRO),
//               DISP=(NEW,CATLG),UNIT=SYSDA,
//               SPACE=(CYL,(1,,2)),VOL=SER=DISK01
//LKED.SYSLIB  DD  DSN=LOADSUB,DISP=SHR
//             DD  DSN=SYS1.COBLIB,DISP=SHR
```

Executing a Load Module

No matter which of the previous two coding segments is used, load module MAINPRO in pds library LOADMAIN is now ready to be executed. This can be done in three different ways. The first of these is as follows:

```
//FIRST   EXEC  PGM=MAINPRO
//STEPLIB  DD   DSN=LOADMAIN,DISP=SHR
//  any additional DD statements used during execu-
    tion should be specified here. Their DDnames need
    not be prefaced by GO.
```

Notice that a STEPLIB DD statement is present to inform the system where the program that is to be executed is stored. Without this information MAINPRO could not be located and this jobstep would abend with a system 806-4 completion code and the accompanying message LOAD MODULE NOT FOUND. This message will result if STEPLIB is not specified, if the wrong STEPLIB data set is coded, or if the name of the PGM is misspelled. Note that the program (PGM) identified to be run on an EXEC statement is a load module. The terms *program* and *load module* can be used interchangeably.

Coding the following JCL will also permit MAINPRO to be executed.

```
//       JOB Statement
//JOBLIB DD DSN=LOADMAIN,DISP=SHR
.
.
.
//SECOND EXEC PGM=MAINPRO
//  any additional DD statements used during execution
    should be specified here.
```

A thorough discussion of the role of the JOBLIB and STEPLIB DD statements is given in Chapter 21. In the present situation either a JOBLIB or STEPLIB DD statement must be coded. Otherwise, only the system load module library is searched for the member identified by PGM.

The third way in which the load module MAINPRO may be executed is by coding the following:

```
//THIRD    EXEC   PGM=*.LINKEDIT.LKED.SYSLMOD   or
//THIRD    EXEC   PGM=*.LINKEDIT.SYSLMOD
//   any additional DD statements used during execution
     should be specified here
```

The referback format assumes the existence of a previous jobstep called LINKEDIT and a procedure step called LKED which contains a DD statement with the DDname SYSLMOD. If such names are not present in the job stream a syntax error will result during the JCL syntax scan. If they are present the data set identified on that DD statement will be executed by the system. Problems will result if only the library name is coded on the referenced statement. A member name must also be coded. When a referback (*) is coded with the PGM parameter no JOBLIB or STEPLIB DD statement is necessary to locate the PGM to be executed. One or both may be coded for other purposes. The second EXEC statement is used when LINKEDIT is not a procedure.

Control Statements

For many typical programming situations, such as a compile and link-edit or a compile, link-edit, and go, coding the six data sets described above will usually suffice. However, for most sophisticated Linkage Editor processing control statements are required. These control statements may either be coded in the SYSLIN data set or in a data set concatenated to it. A procedure statement with DDname SYSIN is commonly used for this purpose and specified with the DDNAME parameter.

The Linkage Editor control statements discussed in this chapter can be grouped into three categories. Some are used in linking modules together, some are concerned primarily with editing, and some are used to create overlay structures. This is the order in which they will be discussed. Linking is the most important function and creating overlays is the least important.

All control statements have the same format. An operator is coded starting in column 2 (or anywhere to the right of column 2). The operator is followed by one or more spaces. After the spaces operands are coded, separated by commas. The operand field can extend through column 71. If necessary operands can be continued on the next line by placing any non-blank character in column 72, breaking off the coding after an operand and its following comma, and continuing with the next operand on the following statement in column 16. In practice continuation is rarely needed. Embedded blanks in the operand field cause the rest of the statement to be treated as comments.

Five important control statements used to request additional features during Linkage Editor processing are discussed below.

NAME is used to give a name to the load module being created in the present job step. The name is entered into the directory of the pds specified on the SYSLMOD statement. NAME must be coded when more than one load module is created in a single job step. The value coded with NAME is often called the *true name* of the member.

ALIAS can be used to specify up to fifteen additional names for any load module created by the Linkage Editor. These names are also placed in the directory of the SYSLMOD pds and may be used to subsequently reference the module. All ALIAS names reference the same single copy of the load module as does the true name.

Example 5: The NAME and ALIAS control statements are used to give three names to the load module created by the Linkage Editor.

```
ALIAS   SECOND,THIRD
NAME    PROG123
```

Following this any of the EXEC statements shown here may be used to execute the load module. Each EXEC statement should be followed by a STEPLIB DD statement or a JOBLIB DD statement must be coded.

```
//A  EXEC  PGM=SECOND    or
//A  EXEC  PGM=PROG123   or
//A  EXEC  PGM=THIRD
```

ENTRY is used to specify where execution of a load module is to begin if there are several places within the output load module that could be the first statement executed. All of the programming languages permit execution to begin at an internal point within the load module. It is also a good idea to specify every ENTRY name on an ALIAS statement. This guarantees that all references to the entry point can be successfully resolved. Otherwise information about entry points is not stored in the load module library directory. When this happens subroutine calls to existing entry points may remain unresolved.

INCLUDE is used to identify additional primary input to the Linkage Editor. This identification is made indirectly and consists of listing the DDnames of DD statements. The DD statements identify either sequential data sets (containing object modules and/or more control statements) or partitioned data sets (containing object modules and/or control statements or load modules). It is only through the INCLUDE control statement that load modules can be specified as primary input to the Linkage Editor for additional processing. The syntax of the INCLUDE statement can use any of the following three formats:

```
INCLUDE    DDname1(member name)
INCLUDE    DDname2(member name1,member name2,etc)
INCLUDE    DDname3
```

The third format cannot be used with load modules. Any combination of these three formats can also be coded on the same statement. Hence, the following INCLUDE statement is valid:

```
INCLUDE DD1(ALPHA,BETA),OBJMOD,DD2(A),DD1(GAMMA)
```

Notice that a data set is identified through a DDname on an INCLUDE statement in the same way that a data set used by a COBOL program is identified on a SELECT-ASSIGN Statement.

LIBRARY is used to specify additional data sets that may be required to resolve external references. It is possible to be more precise about how an external reference is to be resolved with the LIBRARY control statement than can be done with a SYSLIB statement. Like the INCLUDE statement, the LIBRARY statement contains operands that reference additional DD statements. The syntax of the LIBRARY statement includes two of the same formats as the INCLUDE statement.

```
LIBRARY DDname1(member name)
LIBRARY DDname2(member name1,member name2,etc)
```

Again, two or more DDnames can be coded on the same library statement. Either object or load modules can be referenced with the LIBRARY control statement. The LIBRARY statement supplies secondary input.

With the exception of the NAME statement the control statements can usually be specified in any order. However, a NAME statement delimits a group of control statements. All statements following the NAME statement refer to the next load module being created in the jobstep. It is the NAME statement that permits the creation of multiple load modules in one invocation of the Linkage Editor. For example, if three NAME control statements are present, either three or four load modules are created, depending on whether the third NAME statement is the last statement in the control data set. If it is not a NAME statement, the fourth load module should be given its name on the SYSLMOD statement.

Example 6: To illustrate the use of control statements Example 3 will be recoded in a different way. Recall that a main COBOL program currently stored as an object module in the library OBJMAIN, COBOL1, calls two external subroutines, COBSUB and PLISUB, both of which are in the load module library LOADSUB. The primary input data set will be specified through a control statement. This will require that an additional DD statement be coded. Note that the member of the pds is coded on a control statement but the pds itself is identified in the JCL. Only the SYSLIN statement needs to be changed from the code in Example 3.

```
//SYSLIN     DD  *
    INCLUDE  DD1(COBOL1)
/*
//DD1        DD  DSN=OBJMAIN,DISP=SHR
```

The code in this example is valid whether COBOL1 is an object module or a load module. However, in Example 3 COBOL1 must be an object module since a load module cannot be coded on the SYSLIN statement.

If COBOL1 had been a sequential data set rather than a pds member the above code would be replaced by the following:

```
//SYSLIN     DD   *
    INCLUDE   DD1
/*
//DD1           DD   DSN=COBOL1,DISP=SHR
```

Here COBOL1 must be an object module since the control statement syntax specifies a sequential data set. This code assumes that COBOL1 is the name of the data set but not necessarily the name of the object module it contains.

Example 7: Again using Example 3 for comparison, another type of change will be made. The member name will be supplied on a control statement rather than through JCL. This causes the SYSLMOD and SYSLIN statements to be changed.

```
//SYSLMOD       DD   DSN=LOADMAIN,DISP=....
//SYSLIN        DD   DSN=OBJMAIN(COBOL1),DISP=SHR
//              DD   *
    NAME   MAINPRO
/*
```

When using the NAME control statement a replacing option can be coded. If NAME MAINPRO(R) had been specified above then the existing member called MAINPRO in the pds LOADMAIN would be automatically replaced by this new member. If the replacing option is coded and there is no existing member with the same name in the pds library the new member will still be successfully added. Most information provided for a data set by an application program can also be specified through JCL. Hence the DISP parameter value OLD also specifies automatic replacement with a pds member. This is discussed in Chapter 12.

When the Linkage Editor places a load module in a library one of four messages is printed. The message is determined by two factors, whether the replacing option is coded and whether an existing module with the same name is already present in the load module library.

(R) Coded	*Existing Member*	*Message*
NO	NO	MAINPRO NOW ADDED TO DATA SET
NO	YES	EXISTING MEMBER IN LIBRARY WILL TRY TO ADD THIS MEMBER AS TEMPNAME
YES	NO	MAINPRO DOES NOT EXIST BUT HAS BEEN ADDED TO DATA SET
YES	YES	MAINPRO NOW REPLACED IN DATA SET

What happens if a member is given a name on both the SYSLMOD statement and with a NAME control statement? In this case the value coded with NAME has precedence. This is consistent with DCB subparameter values where the value coded in the program is used rather than the comparable value in the JCL. If a member name is not coded in either place the Linkage Editor will supply the name TEMPNAME. It is not good programming practice to allow this to happen. The member names in a pds directory are unique. Whenever the message data set identifies a load module as TEMPNAME, examine the output from that step carefully for additional problems.

Example 8: It is possible to identify both the main program and the two external subroutines with control statements. If this approach is used the code in Example 3 becomes

```
//SYSLIN      DD   *
     INCLUDE   DD1(COBOL1)
     INCLUDE   DD2(COBSUB,PLISUB)
/*
//DD1         DD   DSN=OBJMAIN,DISP=SHR
//DD2         DD   DSN=LOADSUB,DISP=SHR
//SYSLIB      DD   DSN=SYS1.COBLIB,DISP=SHR
```

Example 9: Switching the order of the two INCLUDE statements in Example 8 could lead to disastrous results. Suppose this is done. When the resulting load module is executed it probably will begin executing in the first subroutine. Since it is assumed that the subroutines are to execute only when called by the main program, an abend will probably result. To specify where execution should begin within a load module an ENTRY statement can be coded. Here we will assume that the name of the entry point (module name) and the member name are exactly the same. When possible this is a good safe practice to use. The control statements in Example 8 are replaced by the following:

```
//SYSIN DD *
     ENTRY COBOL1
     INCLUDE   DD2(PLISUB)
     INCLUDE   DD2(COBSUB),DD1(COBOL1)
/*
```

Under most conditions execution begins in the first module referenced in the primary input. However, this can always be overridden by coding an ENTRY control statement. If a load module is link edited a second time the entry point information is not retained. Hence ENTRY should be specified in all such subsequent link edits. The ENTRY statement may be coded anywhere before the NAME statement.

Example 10: Still another way to handle this section of code involves the LIBRARY control statement. Here specific external references can be resolved from the pds identified on the LIBRARY control statement. While the INCLUDE statement identifies either primary input, the main program, or subroutines, the LIBRARY statement identifies external references (secondary input) only. Hence the main program should not be referenced on a LIBRARY statement.

```
//SYSLIN     DD  *
    INCLUDE  DD1(COBOL1)
    LIBRARY  DD2(PLISUB,COBSUB)
/*
//DD1        DD  DSN=OBJMAIN,DISP=SHR
//DD2        DD  DSN=LOADSUB,DISP=SHR
//SYSLIB     DD  DSN=SYS1.COBLIB,DISP=SHR
```

The above coding implies that all external references in COBOL1 will be resolved using the libraries coded with SYSLIB except for the two references to PLISUB and COBSUB. These members are to be located in the data set coded on the DD2 DD statement. The LIBRARY statement can be used to expedite locating specific modules. It is unnecessary to search the SYSLIB pds directories for members coded on LIBRARY statements. The LIBRARY statement can also enable the correct member to be found if several members with the same name exist in different libraries concatenated on the SYSLIB statement. If the LIBRARY statement is not used the first member found within the concatenation is used even if it is not the desired member.

If the LIBRARY statement specifies just a member name enclosed in parentheses this means that the listed member is not to be linked to the SYSLIN input. It will remain an unresolved external reference. In the previous example, suppose that for some reason program logic in COBOL1 is such that for the foreseeable future no subroutine calls will be made to PLISUB. Hence to ignore it during the link edit code

```
LIBRARY   DD2(COBSUB),(PLISUB)
```

In this case the external reference to PLISUB will not be resolved. If at some future time PLISUB is again needed MAINPRO and PLISUB can be link edited together.

A third variation of the LIBRARY statement causes an external reference to remain unresolved for the lifetime of the module. Its syntax is

```
LIBRARY    *(member name)
```

At this point all of the data sets that interact with the Linkage Editor have been discussed. They can be pictured as shown in Figure 18–2.

Example 11: In this example two load modules are to be created in a single job step. The first is the same load module created in Example 3; the second is the same load module minus the PLISUB subroutine. This code illustrates the use of the NAME control statement to delimit the statements needed to construct one load module. The first five control statements build the load module MAINPRO. In order, it consists of modules PLISUB, COBOL1, COBSUB and all required ILBO subroutines. The remaining control statements create load module MAINSEC. COBSUB is located through the automatic call library.

```
//A        EXEC  PGM=IEWL,PARM='LIST,XREF,LET'
//SYSPRINT DD   SYSOUT=A
//SYSUT1   DD   UNIT=SYSDA,SPACE=(CYL,1)
//SYSLMOD  DD   DSN=LOADMAIN,DISP=OLD
//MAIN     DD   DSN=OBJMAIN,DISP=SHR
//SUB      DD   DSN=LOADSUB,DISP=SHR
//SYSLIB   DD   DSN=SYS1.COBLIB,DISP=SHR
//         DD   DSN=LOADSUB,DISP=SHR
//SYSLIN   DD   *
    INCLUDE  SUB(PLISUB)
    ENTRY  COBOL1
    INCLUDE  MAIN(COBOL1)
    LIBRARY  SUB(COBSUB)
    NAME  MAINPRO(R)
    ALIAS  BACKUP
    INCLUDE  MAIN(COBOL1)
    LIBRARY  (PLISUB)
    NAME  MAINSEC
/*
```

FIGURE 18–2

Data Sets That Interact with the Linkage Editor

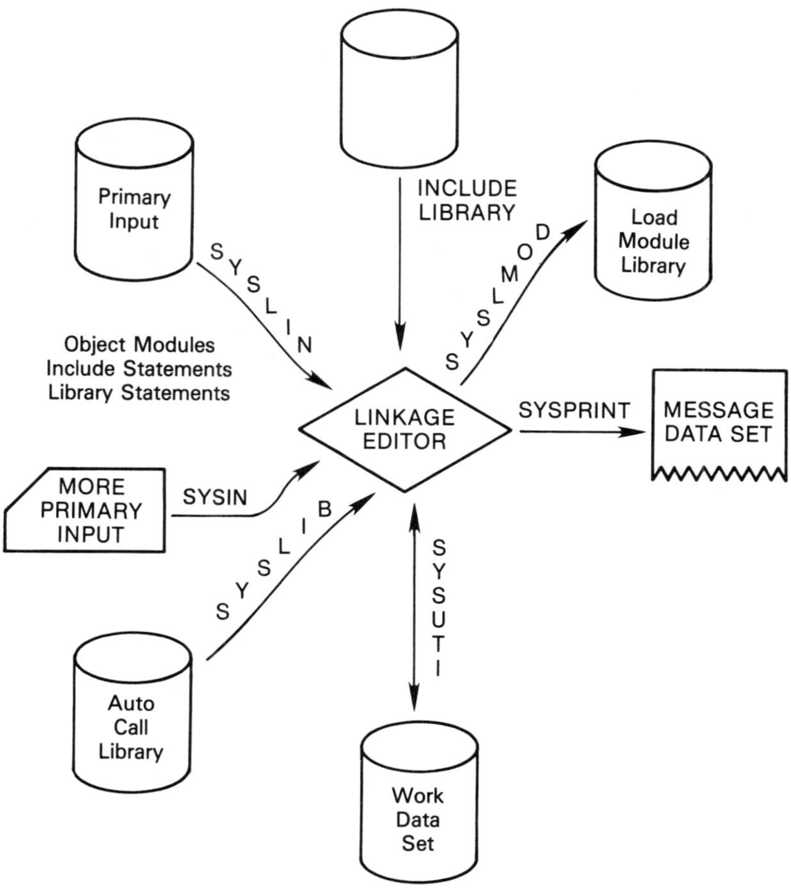

PARM Options with the Linkage Editor

A large number of PARM values may be coded when using the Linkage Editor. The most commonly coded values are discussed below. Any or all of the keywords described below can be coded on the EXEC statement. The values coded apply to all load modules created during the jobstep. Standard JCL rules for coding PARM values apply. The format is:

```
//stepname EXEC PGM=IEWL,PARM='value1,value2,...,valueN'
```

If the Linkage Editor is being used as one step in a cataloged procedure it is necessary to qualify the PARM parameter. For example, to compile and link-edit a COBOL program code

```
//stepname EXEC  COBUCL,PARM.COB='value1,...,valueN',
//      other COB operands,PARM.LKED='value1,...,valueM',
//      other LKED operands
```

The three PARM values LIST, MAP, and XREF determine the contents of the SYSPRINT data set. If none of them are coded the bare minimum of diagnostic and error messages is written. Coding both LIST and XREF creates the maximum amount of SYSPRINT output.

LIST

All of the control statements are printed on the SYSPRINT data set. If LIST is not coded it is necessary to examine the SYSLIN source statements to determine the control statements used. To minimize debugging problems, it is a good idea to code LIST whenever control statements are used. LIST is routinely a default value with procedures that use the Linkage Editor.

MAP

A map or table of contents of all modules that make up the new load module is printed. For each module its length in bytes, relative starting address, and all entry points within it are listed.

XREF

For each external reference (subroutine call) in the load module being created an entry is printed telling if, how, and where that reference was resolved. The module map described with MAP is also printed. Since XREF implies MAP there is no need to specify both options. XREF is frequently coded in a procedure that uses the Linkage Editor.

LET

Every load module created by the Linkage Editor is marked as either executable or not executable. This is done by setting a bit in the pds directory entry for that member to the appropriate value. If the Linkage Editor detects major errors when creating a load module it will conclude that the load module cannot be subsequently executed with any hope that the execution will succeed. On the other hand, some relatively minor errors can also cause a module to be marked not executable. The most common such occurrence involves creating a load module when one or more external references cannot be resolved. For example, this occurs if a main program that calls several subroutines is compiled and link-edited before the subroutines are available. Clearly the subroutine references cannot be resolved but the programmer knows that when the subroutines are subsequently supplied the module will be executable. The two PARM values, LET and NCAL, deal with this situation.

LET causes a load module to be marked as executable even if the Linkage Editor detects minor errors while creating the module. These minor errors are denoted by a condition code of 4 or 8. It is the programmer's responsibility to subsequently correct these problems before the module is executed. LET is often coded as a default PARM value in the cataloged procedure steps that use the Linkage Editor.

In the situation described above, if the main program is executed and its subroutines are not present the main program will abend when it attempts to call the subroutine (usually with an OC1 abend). There are other situations where relatively minor errors will also cause the Linkage Editor to mark a module as not executable. This includes two forms of the LIBRARY control statement and the NCAL option discussed below. In all cases LET overrides these conditions.

If LET is not coded and the Linkage Editor marks a module not executable the load module cannot be executed. Attempting to do so will cause a S706 abend, which is accompanied by the message LOAD MODULE MARKED NOT EXECUTABLE.

NCAL or CAL

NCAL specifies that the automatic call library will not be used to resolve references during this jobstep. The module will be marked executable even if unresolved external references exist. It is unnecessary to code a SYSLIB statement or any LIBRARY control statements. This option can be used to postpone resolving references until a subsequent jobstep or the load module is ready to be executed. For example, suppose several COBOL programs are to be stored as separate load modules and all call the same group of SYS1.COBLIB subroutines. Considerable disk storage may be saved by not linking the subroutines until execution time. CAL is the default value. It specifies that the automatic call library will be used to resolve all external references left unresolved after the primary input is processed, except for those references handled by LIBRARY control statements.

The remaining PARM values deal with a wide variety of topics. Although many PARM values are described some have been omitted. For the complete list see the *Linkage Editor and Loader* manual.

OVLY

This specifies that an overlay structure is to be created by the Linkage Editor. The final section in this chapter describes overlay structures.

XCAL

This is applicable only with an overlay structure. Hence OVLY must also be coded. The load module will be marked executable even if invalid exclusive references have been made between the module segments. OVLY and XCAL are discussed again at the end of this chapter.

RENT

The module is marked re–entrant. This means that more than one task can be executing the module (program) at the same time. Such a load module should never modify itself. Most system software is re–entrant. The Linkage Editor cannot determine if a module is actually re–entrant. It assumes the value supplied by the programmer is correct.

REUS

The module is marked reusable. This means that it can be executed by only one task at a time.

REFR

The module is marked refreshable. The module can be replaced by a new copy during execution.

AC=x

This sets an authorization code that determines what system resources the module can use. The default is AC=0 and implies minimal resources. AC can assume values from 0 to 255.

ALIGN

Each control section is aligned on a 2K boundary.

Editing Features

The editing features of the Linkage Editor can be used to modify existing load modules or object modules. Any external symbol within a module can be changed. Usually an external symbol is either an external name (the name of a control section or an entry point) or an external reference (a subroutine call). Other types of external symbols are possible when using PL/I or assembler. Only the three types of external symbols mentioned above are covered here.

Three types of editing are permitted with the Linkage Editor:

— The name of any external symbol may be changed. The CHANGE control statement is used for this purpose.

— One control section can replace another. The new control section can either have the same name as the old one or a different name. If the names are the same no additional control statements are coded. With different names a REPLACE statement must be used.

— Entire control sections may be deleted. Likewise, entry points may be deleted. The REPLACE control statement is used in both cases.

All of these module modifications will be illustrated using the two modules shown in Figure 18–3.

Here the External Symbol Dictionary (ESD) for module AMODULE will contain the entries ALPHA, A1, B1, B2, and BETA. The ESD entries associated with BMODULE are BETA, B1, C1, and B2. Both AMODULE and BMODULE are members of the load module library LOADLIB.

To clarify the distinction between a module name and the name of the pds member that contains the module, note that CALL 'BETA' is issued to reference the subroutine, not CALL 'BMODULE'. A Linkage Editor control statement for the subroutine should be written as INCLUDE DD1(BMODULE) rather than INCLUDE DD1(BETA).

FIGURE 18–3
ESD Entries for Modules ALPHA and BETA

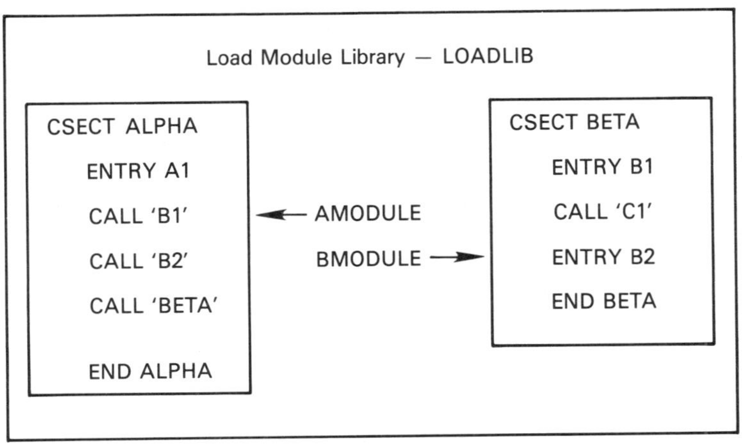

CHANGING AN ESD ENTRY

When a CHANGE statement is coded all symbols being modified must occur on the module referenced immediately following the CHANGE statement. This module can physically follow the CHANGE statement (for an object module) or be identified on an INCLUDE statement (for a load module or an object module). The scope of the CHANGE statement extends only through the first module encountered after the statement itself. If the symbol to be altered does not occur in the first module or if the CHANGE is followed by a control statement other than INCLUDE, the CHANGE statement has no effect on the symbol. No messages are printed in any case. Rather, the module map must be examined to see if the change was successful.

Example 12: The CHANGE control statement will be used to alter the names of three external symbols in module AMODULE. The name of the CSECT itself will be changed to NEWALPHA, entry point A1 will become NEWA1, and external reference B1 will be renamed NEWB1. The relevant JCL and control statements are

```
//A EXEC   PGM=IEWL,PARM='LIST,XREF,LET'
//SYSPRINT DD SYSOUT=A
//SYSUT1    DD UNIT=3380,SPACE=(CYL,(1,1))
//SYSLMOD   DD DSN=LOADLIB,DISP=OLD
//SYSLIN    DD *
  ENTRY    NEWALPHA
  CHANGE   ALPHA(NEWALPHA),B1(NEWB1),A1(NEWA1)
  INCLUDE  SYSLMOD(AMODULE)
  NAME     NEWAMODU(R)
/*
```

The NAME statement changes the name of the member in the pds directory. No matter what type of external symbol is to be changed the syntax of the CHANGE statement calls for listing the old symbol followed by the new symbol in parentheses. Note that all symbols to be changed occur on the next module referenced. If subsequent INCLUDE statements are present the CHANGE will have no effect on them. The entry point for the module is specified using its new value since the old no longer exists following the step. Since only editing is taking place no SYSLIB statement is necessary. Notice that the three PARM options LIST, XREF, and LET have been coded on the EXEC statement. Why is it a good idea to have coded these three values with this example? Try to justify the reasons for each of the three for this specific example.

The same results as in Example 12 can be achieved by making two minor changes. The INCLUDE control statement becomes

```
  INCLUDE DD1(AMODULE)
```

and one additional DD statement

```
//DD1     DD DSN=LOADLIB,DISP=SHR
```

is added. This approach uses more coding but is clearer. Example 12 uses the DDname SYSLMOD for two distinct purposes: to identify the output pds and the library referenced on an INCLUDE statement.

If an attempt is made to link edit NEWAMODU and BMODULE together following Example 12 CALL 'NEWB1' will generate an unresolved external reference. It will be necessary to change entry point B1 in BMODULE with a separate CHANGE statement. However, if modules AMODULE and BMODULE are initially linked together only one CHANGE statement is necessary. Here the CHANGE would be in effect throughout the entire module, which includes both control sections. Editing functions are in effect throughout all the control sections comprising the load module. However, symbols in other modules must have their values changed with additional CHANGE control statements in order to correctly reference the new symbols.

MODIFYING AN ENTIRE CONTROL SECTION

There are two ways in which an entire CSECT can be changed (where the CSECT is assumed to be just one control section within a multi CSECT load module). If the load module contains just one CSECT the following still holds but there are easier ways to make the modifications.

Control section replacement is handled in different ways depending on whether the control sections involved have the same name or not. Initially assume that an existing control section is to be replaced by a new control section with exactly the same name. The key to using this technique involves understanding the order in which the Linkage Editor constructs an output load module. Input modules are processed one at a time in the order in which they appear in the control statements. If two input modules have the same name the first one encountered is made a part of the output module. The second (and any subsequent) module with the same name is ignored. In addition, no message is printed concerning the duplication. Hence to replace an existing module by one with the same name specify both as input and be certain that the replacement module occurs first.

Example 13: Suppose modules AMODULE and BMODULE have been link-edited together to form FINALMOD. It is now necessary to replace BMODULE by a new module with the same name. After the new BMODULE has been recompiled it is passed to the Linkage Editor as an object module in the data set BMODULE. To get the new module to replace the old, code the following statements:

```
                                                 Input Module Supplied
//SYSLMOD   DD   DSN=LOADLIB,DISP=OLD
//SYSLIN    DD   DSN=BMODULE,DISP=SHR           BMODULE (NEW) Added
//          DD   *
  ENTRY    AMODENTR
  INCLUDE  SYSLMOD(FINALMOD)                    AMODULE (OLD) Added
  NAME     FINALMOD(R)                          BMODULE (OLD) Replaced
/*
```

Notice that there is no mention of replacement anywhere in the control statements. If the control section BMODULE had been placed in data set XYZ then the name BMODULE would not occur anywhere in this job step. An ENTRY statement is necessary since the order of the two modules within FINALMOD has been reversed.

Example 14: Suppose that BMODULE is now to be replaced by a module with a different name. Here the REPLACE control statement is used to identify the two modules. To modify Example 13 suppose that the replacement for BMODULE is a sequential data set that was created by the compiler and is named &&OBJECT. It contains the control section NEWBMOD. Now the SYSLIN data set is coded as follows:

```
                                                     Input Module Supplied
//SYSLMOD DD   DSN=LOADLIB,DISP=OLD
//SYSLIN  DD   DSN=&&OBJECT,DISP=SHR                 NEWBMOD (NEW)
//           DD *
  ENTRY      ALPHA
  REPLACE    BMODULE(NEWBMOD)
  INCLUDE    SYSLMOD(FINALMOD)                       AMODULE (OLD)
  NAME       FINALMOD(R)                             BMODULE (OLD)
/*
```

Just as with the CHANGE control statement, REPLACE is coded immediately before the INCLUDE statement that references BMODULE. Here all references within the original FINALMOD are automatically changed to reference the new module. All references to BMODULE from outside FINALMOD must be corrected with additional CHANGE control statements.

DELETING A CONTROL SECTION OR ENTRY POINT

Two of the three types of ESD entries, CSECTs and entry points, may be deleted. A CALL statement can be modified but not deleted.

Example 15: An entire control section can be deleted by using the REPLACE control statement. Here the module to be deleted is listed as the module to be replaced but no new replacement value is specified. The REPLACE control statement can also be used to delete an entry point. Here REPLACE is used to delete BMODULE from FINALMOD. The control statements shown here also delete entry point A1 along with the BMODULE control section. Both A1 and BMODULE are located using the information on the following INCLUDE statement.

```
//SYSLMOD   DD DSN=LOADLIB,DISP=OLD
//SYSLIN    DD *
  ENTRY     ALPHA
  REPLACE   BMODULE,A1
  INCLUDE   SYSLMOD(FINALMOD)
  NAME      FINALMOD(R)
/*
```

Overlay Programming

The Linkage Editor can be used to decompose a large program into parts in order to reduce its total storage requirements. This technique is useful when a limited amount of memory is available or when a program is extremely large. However, with the development of virtual storage systems overlay programming techniques have become far less important than they used to be. In the future overlay programming may in fact become a theoretical notion that is rarely employed.

To illustrate an overlay structure consider a program that consists of three control sections called A, B, and C. Both A and B are 100K bytes in length and C is 80K bytes. If the entire program is loaded into memory it occupies 280K bytes. At some installations job classes are different for programs that require over 256K of memory. Suppose, however, that B and C are independent of each other. That is, when one of the two is executing the other need not be present in memory. In this situation the Linkage Editor can be used to develop an overlay structure that will enable the program to run in well under 280K bytes. This process is pictured in Figure 18–4.

Since B and C do not interact in any manner only one of the two needs to be in memory at any one time. Figure 18–4 is called a *tree*. This tree implies that there can be subroutine calls from A to B and A to C but no subroutine calls between B and C. Hence if 200K bytes of memory are available for running the program and the proper subroutine (B or C) is loaded into memory when required, the program should execute correctly. In essence this is the basic idea in overlay programming: decompose a program into control sections and then determine which control sections are independent of one another. These independent control sections can then be loaded into memory only when required. Additionally, since they are independent the same location can be used to hold any of them. This is possible since only one will be in memory at a specific time. In the example above it is important to realize that B and C can never be in memory at the same time. This in turn prohibits subroutine calls from B to C or from C to B. The XCAL PARM option can be used to override this.

When using overlay programs control sections are grouped into segments. A segment is the smallest group of control sections that must be dealt with as a group during program execution. If three control sections comprise a segment all must be loaded into memory when one of them is invoked. In the example above A, B, and C are segments that each contain one control section. In every overlay structure there

FIGURE 18–4
An Overlay Structure

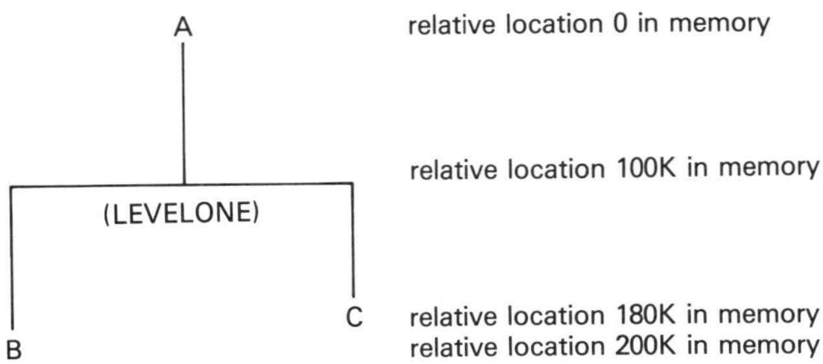

FIGURE 18–5

A More Complicated Tree Diagram

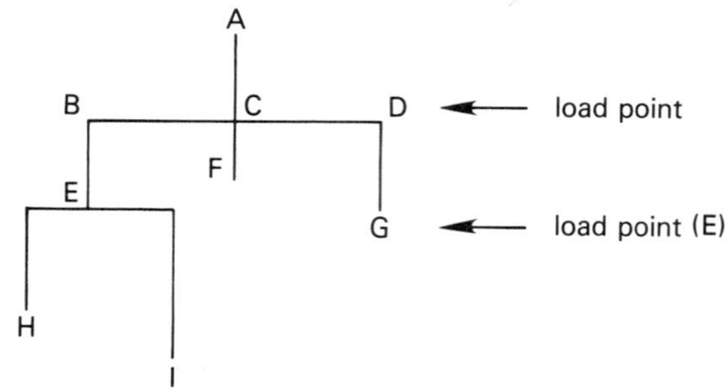

is one segment that must be in memory throughout execution. In the example above this is A. It is called the *root segment*. When a particular segment must be loaded into memory all segments between it and the root segment must also be in memory. Segments below it in the tree diagram need not be in memory, however. The collection of all segments between the root segment and a given segment is said to form a *path*. A and B form a path, as do A and C. Consider the more complicated tree diagram shown in Figure 18–5. Here A B E H forms a path. Hence when H is required during execution A, B, and E must also be in memory. A D G is also a path, as is A D. When D is in memory A must also be present, since it is above D in this diagram. Since G is below D in the tree diagram it need not be present until it is called.

In the first diagram it may have appeared that A, B, and C could be executed in 200K bytes of memory. This is not exactly true. There is some additional overhead necessary to keep track of the segments currently in memory (and also which segments can overlay other segments).

Example 16: It is a very simple process to use the Linkage Editor to create the overlay structure for A, B, and C as pictured in Figure 18–4. First compile each of the three COBOL programs and store them in an object module pds as individual members. Call this pds OVLYPDS. Now use the following control statements with the Linkage Editor:

```
//OVERLAY  EXEC    PGM=IEWL,PARM='OVLY,LIST,LET,XREF'
//SYSPRINT  DD     SYSOUT=A
//SYSUT1    DD     UNIT=SYSDA,SPACE=(CYL,5)
//SYSLIB    DD     DSN=SYS1.COBLIB,DISP=SHR
//OVLYDD    DD     DSN=OVLYPDS,DISP=SHR
//SYSLMOD   DD     DSN=&&LOADMOD(RUN),DISP=(,PASS),
//                UNIT=SYSDA,SPACE=(CYL,(2,1,1))
//SYSLIN    DD     *
  ENTRY    ALPHA
  INCLUDE  OVLYDD(A)
  OVERLAY  LEVELONE
  INCLUDE  OVLYDD(B)
  OVERLAY  LEVELONE
  INCLUDE  OVLYDD(C)
/*
```

Here ALPHA is an entry point in the root control section A. The format of the INCLUDE statement is the same as for a non-overlay structure. For example, member A will be located in the pds identified on the statement with DDname OVLYDD. The OVERLAY control statement is responsible for building the desired overlay structure. The format of the OVERLAY control statement is

```
  OVERLAY   symbolic name
```

Here symbolic name identifies a relative location in memory where the next module referenced is to be loaded. In the code above the root segment is loaded at relative address 0. It is not preceded by an OVERLAY statement. The statement OVERLAY LEVELONE means assign the symbolic name LEVELONE to the location in memory where control section B will be loaded. In this example it will be approximately relative address 100K. Module B is located and made part of the output load module. The next OVERLAY statement contains the same symbolic name. This means that when C is brought into memory it will be loaded at exactly the same address. This is all the coding that is required. All other details are handled automatically by the Linkage Editor during the creation of the module. The overlay structure is then used when the module is executed. Note that the PARM value OVLY must be coded. Otherwise the Linkage Editor will not acknowledge that the OVERLAY control statement is valid. The address denoted by LEVELONE is called a *load point*. If this module is to be reprocessed by the Linkage Editor the overlay structure must be reconstructed, since it is not retained.

The INSERT control statement is available to simplify the control statements needed for an overlay structure. The INSERT statement can be used to move a control section to its proper location in the overlay structure.

Example 17: Suppose that A, B, and C have been compiled and the three object modules are stored in the sequential data set &&OBJECT. In this case the SYSLIN data set may be coded as follows:

```
//SYSLIN  DD    DSN=&&OBJECT,DISP=(OLD,PASS)
//        DD    *
  ENTRY   ALPHA
  INSERT  A
  OVERLAY ONE
  INSERT  C
  OVERLAY ONE
  INSERT  B
/*
```

Notice that any valid symbolic names may be used for load points. Note also that the order of inserting B and C is not important. The INSERT statement takes the object modules from their original locations and repositions them to where they are required. This code could also be written without a concatenation, as follows:

```
//OVLYDD    DD   DSN=&&OBJECT,DISP=(OLD,PASS)
//SYSLIN    DD   *
  ENTRY     ALPHA
  INSERT    A
  OVERLAY   LOADPT
  INSERT    B
  OVERLAY   LOADPT
  INSERT    C
  INCLUDE   OVLYDD
/*
```

Here the format of the INCLUDE statement implies that a sequential data set is defined on the statement with the DDname OVLYDD.

Exercises

1. What restrictions apply when specifying a load module as part of the primary input to the Linkage Editor which do not hold when an object module is part of the primary input? What are the different ways in which a load module can be specified as part of the secondary input? Are all of these also allowed with an object module?

2. Write a program in COBOL or PL/I which calls a short assembler subroutine. For both the main program and the subroutine dump out the object modules that are produced. Use the PRINT command with the IDCAMS utility to do this. Determine what a given statement in the original source code has become in the object module. Locate the external symbol dictionary entries in the object modules.

3. Take the two object modules created in the previous exercise and link edit them together to form one load module. Use IDCAMS to examine the structure of this module. Determine the differences between this load module and the two object modules used to create it.

4. Try to execute an object module that is stored in an object module library. What happens? Why do you suppose this occurs? Try to execute an object module stored as a sequential data set. Do the same results occur?

5. Why must load modules be stored in libraries? Why can't a sequential data set be a load module? The sequential data set could be created with the same dcb properties as the pds except for data set organization.

6. Write the code to produce a load module out of the following existing modules:

Module 1	Source code in COBOL	member ALPHA in ALIB
Module 2	Object code in PL/I	member BETA in BLIB
Module 3	Load module in Assembler	member GAMMA in CLIB

   Execute the resulting load module after giving it the name DELTA. The main program is BETA.

7. Suppose a load module called ALPHA in a pds called ALIB is to be executed. Determine four distinct ways in which this execution can be requested. It was created by the Linkage Editor in the previous step.

8. In Example 3 under what conditions is it unnecessary to code a SYSLIB DD statement?

9. Execute the load module XYZ in library ALPHA using a backward reference. The load module was placed in the library when the cataloged procedure PLIXCL was invoked on an EXEC statement that read

```
//FIRST  EXEC PLIXCL,TIME=(,30),COND=EVEN
```

10. An attempt is made to reference a load module with an INCLUDE control statement. Load module ALPHA is in member ALIB, which is a load module library. However, the Linkage Editor gives the error message IEW0294 DDNAME PRINTED HAD SYNCHRONOUS ERROR. What is causing the trouble? The relevant code is

```
//SYSLIN DD *
    INCLUDE DD1  (ALPHA)
/*
//DD1    DD   DSN=ALIB,DISP=SHR
```

11. Under what conditions is it reasonable to code a member name on the SYSLMOD statement and also include a NAME control statement in the same jobstep as part of the primary SYSLIN input? Determine at least two distinct situations where this might be meaningful.

12. Suppose there is a very large program called ALPHA that calls twenty-six subroutines. These have member names A, B, C,...,Z in the load module library LETTERS. Compile the main program and resolve all external references except those that involve the vowels, A, E, I, O, and U. The main program and the subroutines are in the same library and all the code is in COBOL.

13. Given the collection of libraries and members shown in Figure 18–6, in which each member name is also the module name, determine which sections of code shown below will successfully produce output modules with all external references resolved. Assume that the statements:

```
//A   EXEC PGM=IEWL,PARM='LET,LIST,XREF'
//SYSPRINT DD SYSOUT=A
//SYSUT1 DD UNIT=VIO,SPACE=(CYL,5)
```

FIGURE 18–6
Exercise 13

OBJLIB
A (COBOL) B (PL/I) C (BAL) M (FORTRAN)

LOADLIB
M (COBOL) N (COBOL and PL/I) P (BAL) Q (COBOL, PL/I, and BAL) A (COBOL)

are always coded as shown. Also assume that each object module calls all of the load modules written in the same language. Furthermore the modules are called in reversed collating sequence order based on their names. Draw a picture of the output module structure showing the relative order of the modules in the output structure.

(a)
```
//SYSLIB   DD   DSN=SYS1.COBLIB
//         DD   DSN=OBJLIB
//         DD   DSN=LOADLIB
//SYSLIN   DD
       INCLUDE SYSLMOD(B)
       NAME NEWA
/*
//SYSLMOD DD   DSN=LOADLIB
```

(b)
```
//SYSLIB   DD   DSN=SYS1.PLIBASE
//         DD   DSN=SYS1.ASMLIB
//         DD   DSN=SYS1.COBLIB
//SYSLIN   DD   *
       LIBRARY SYSLMOD(M)
       INCLUDE SYSLMOD(A)
       LIBRARY SYSLMOD(B)
       ENTRY B
/*
//SYSLMOD DD   DSN=LOADLIB
```

14. Complete JCL Job Listing, Example 3 in Chapter 19 shows the cross reference listing and module map generated by link editing a COBOL main program and a subroutine together. Determine the members of SYS1.COBLIB that were linked into the output module. Determine the function performed by each subroutine. This information can be found in the *COBOL Programmer's Guide*. Try to write a COBOL program that makes at most two subroutine calls to SYS1.COBLIB.

15. Describe several specific conditions that will cause a load module created by the Linkage Editor to not be added to the SYSLMOD library. Consider data set and member names and the physical characteristics of the library.

Chapter 19

The Loader

Overview

The Loader program is the alternative to using the Linkage Editor when preparing object and load modules for execution. Like the Linkage Editor, the Loader is used after language translation is completed and before actual program execution begins. The output from both programs is a module that is ready to be executed. The Loader is not capable of performing many of the major processing functions that the Linkage Editor can perform. In particular, the Loader uses fewer DD statements. It does not use any control statements and a smaller number of PARM options can be coded with it than with the Linkage Editor.

Since both the Linkage Editor and the Loader produce a load module structure that is ready to be executed, which program should be used in a specific situation? The most important difference between the Loader and the Linkage Editor is that a load module created by the Linkage Editor is stored on disk as a member of a pds library, while the Loader builds a comparable load module structure in main memory. Because of this the load module built by the Linkage Editor is permanent and can be executed more than one time in later steps and later jobs. In contrast, the load module structure created by the Loader must be executed immediately in the same step in which it is constructed. In addition, the output from the Loader is a program that can be executed only once.

When new programs are being written, debugged, and tested they must be frequently recompiled. There is no reason to create a permanent load module if the program must be changed before it is run again. Hence the Loader is commonly used during program development. Conversely, with a production program that is run on a regular schedule the Linkage Editor is used to create a permanent load module. There is no reason to recompile such a program every time it must be run. Rather, the load module is merely executed with a new set of data.

There are several significant reasons for using the Loader rather than the Linkage Editor. The single most important advantage in using the Loader is that it can process an object or load module through execution in one step. It reduces editing and loading time by approximately 50% compared to using the Linkage Editor and then later moving the load module into memory. Because the Loader contains fewer options, the necessary coding is easier to understand and write. Since the Loader ordinarily uses only three data sets it requires less disk storage than the Linkage Editor, which uses five data sets.

When using the Loader two programs are actually executed during the job step. First, the Loader itself creates a load module structure out of the input it is given. After the Loader is finished control is passed to the module it created in memory. This module is then executed. Recall that every load module created by the Linkage Editor is initially placed in a pds. When the load module is to be executed in a subsequent step or job it must be brought into memory by program "fetch."

Data Sets Used with the Loader

Three data sets may be used with the Loader. They have DDnames of SYSLIN, SYSLIB, and SYSLOUT. Only the SYSLIN data set is required. Although SYSLIB and SYSLOUT are optional, both are usually coded. The SYSLIN and SYSLIB data sets perform the same basic functions with the Loader as they do with the Linkage Editor. Although the Loader itself is a member of the system load module library (SYS1.LINKLIB), a STEPLIB DD statement is frequently coded when using the Loader. However, the library it identifies is not needed until the module constructed by the Loader is executing.

The SYSLIN data set identifies the primary input to the Loader. This input can include object modules, load modules, or a combination of the two. All primary input data sets are concatenated together and each must be specified either as a sequential data set or a pds member. An entire pds library should not be included in the concatenation. Since control statements are not available both object and load modules are permitted as primary input. This is one of the few instances where object and load modules may both be included in the same concatenation. Recall that with the Linkage Editor all load modules in the primary input must be identified with control statements.

The DDname SYSLIB identifies the automatic call libraries. The SYSLIB data sets supply the secondary input used to resolve external references that remain after all of the primary input has been processed. SYSLIB should identify either object module libraries or load module libraries. The two types of libraries should not be concatenated together on the SYSLIB statement. The Loader does not contain any feature that is equivalent to the Linkage Editor LIBRARY control statement. However, external references can be resolved from one additional location, the system

Link Pack Area (LPA) in main memory. The LPA was discussed in Chapter 1. Modules in the LPA can be executed in their present locations. They do not need to be copied to the Loader's region in memory. If the RES option is coded on the PARM parameter references will be resolved first from the LPA then from the libraries coded with SYSLIB. If the same member name occurs within several libraries the first one within the concatenation is processed.

To resolve an external reference with SYSLIB two conditions must be met. The reference must be a member name or alias in the pds directory and must also be an external name in the External Symbol Dictionary of the pds member with that name. If the second condition is not met the member is processed but the external reference remains unresolved. External references resolved by the Linkage Editor do not need to meet such stringent conditions.

Example 1: An object module called MAINPGM is stored in the temporary data set &&ALPHA. MAINPGM calls three external subroutines named FIRST, SECOND, and THIRD. FIRST is a member of the load module library SYS1.XYZ and SECOND is a member of the load module library SYS1.ABC. There is also a module called SECOND in SYS1.XYZ. THIRD is a load module in the system LPA. To resolve the three references successfully the SYSLIB statement is coded as shown below. Note that the wrong SECOND subroutine will be retrieved if the order of the last two DD statements in the concatenation is reversed. SYS1.COBLIB (the COBOL automatic call library) is always needed in order to resolve the references inserted in the COBOL object module by the COBOL compiler. Notice that the names of the main program and subroutines do not appear anywhere in the JCL for the step. PARM=RES is coded to locate the THIRD subroutine.

```
//A      EXEC PGM=LOADER,PARM=RES
//SYSLIB DD   DSN=SYS1.COBLIB,DISP=SHR
//            DD   DSN=SYS1.ABC,DISP=SHR
//            DD   DSN=SYS1.XYZ,DISP=SHR
//SYSLIN DD   DSN=&&ALPHA,DISP=(OLD,DELETE)
//     additional DD statements needed by the Loader
//     and for program execution
```

The same result can be obtained by specifically identifying the main program and subroutines FIRST and SECOND as the primary input. Here it is assumed that &&ALPHA has a BLKSIZE value at least as large as either of the two load module libraries. Ordinarily a load module has a larger blocksize than an object module. With this approach the SYSLIN and SYSLIB statements are coded as shown below.

```
//A      EXEC PGM=LOADER,PARM=RES
//SYSLIB DD   DSN=SYS1.COBLIB,DISP=SHR
//SYSLIN DD   DSN=&&ALPHA,DISP=(OLD,DELETE)
//            DD   DSN=SYS1.XYZ(FIRST),DISP=SHR
//            DD   DSN=SYS1.ABC(SECOND),DISP=SHR
//     additional DD statements needed by the Loader
//     and for program execution
```

It is possible that the load module created by this code will not be identical to the load module created by the previous code. In each case the subroutines may be placed in the output module in a different order. A third approach is to list either or both of the subroutines before the main program in the SYSLIN data set. If this is done an entry point must be specified.

The DDname SYSLOUT identifies the message data set used by the Loader. Diagnostic, warning, and error messages are written to the SYSLOUT data set. Additional optional information can also be printed. The contents of the SYSLOUT data set are determined by the PARM options coded on the EXEC statement. If the PARM option NOPRINT is coded the message data set is not opened. If the PARM option MAP is coded a module map is printed. SYSLOUT is an unusual DDname for a message data set since SYSPRINT almost universally identifies this data set. With major IBM software products, only the Loader and Sort/Merge programs do not use SYSPRINT to identify the message data set. In addition, many application programs use the DDname SYSPRINT to identify a printed output data set. This is especially common with PL/I programs. Recall that when the Loader is used two programs are executed in the same job step. The DD statements for both programs are coded together. Hence it is possible to have both the Loader and the application program writing messages to the same data set. SYSLOUT was probably selected as a DDname because it is highly unlikely that an application program would arbitrarily use the name.

Linkage Editor Data Sets and Options Not Used by the Loader

There are two additional data sets that must be coded with the Linkage Editor. However, neither SYSUT1 or SYSLMOD are used with the Loader. Because the output load module is constructed in main memory rather than on disk, no SYSUT1 data set is needed. Likewise, there is no need for a SYSLMOD DD statement since no output load module is written to a pds on disk. Since control statements are not permitted modules or DD statements cannot be identified with INCLUDE and references cannot be resolved with LIBRARY control statements. Since no NAME statements are possible only one load module can be created by the Loader in a jobstep. It is not permitted and also makes no sense to assign an ALIAS to the output since it is not a pds member and cannot be referenced in a later step. If control statements are coded with the Loader they are ignored except for printing a diagnostic message which states that they are not supported. Since the Loader does not support many of the Linkage Editor options it has only three major advantages over the Linkage Editor: it is cheaper and faster and easier to use.

Loader PARM Values

Some types of information supplied by the Linkage Editor control statements can also be specified when using the Loader. However, PARM values rather than control statements must be used. An entry point for the load module is specified by coding EP=entry point name. Coding NAME=name gives the module a name that will identify it to the system. The default name is **GO, and it is acceptable for most applications. If several modules with the same name are included as part of the SYSLIN data set the first is used and the others are ignored. This is the only Loader feature comparable to the editing control statements available with the Linkage Editor.

The PARM options LET, CALL, NCAL, and MAP function in the same way as when coded with the Linkage Editor. However, if LET is coded and unresolved references exist they cannot be subsequently resolved by the Loader or Linkage Editor in a later step. However, they can be dynamically resolved during execution by using a STEPLIB DD statement. A dynamic subroutine call must be resolved during execution, while a static call can be resolved from the automatic call library prior to execution. The distinction between standard (static) subroutine calls and dynamic subroutine calls is further discussed in Chapter 21. If NCAL is coded NORES is implied, and no automatic search of the LPA will be made. Similarly, if RES is coded CALL is implied.

Table 19–1 shows the PARM options available with the Loader along with a brief description of their roles. The common default values are underlined. However, an installation may select its own default values. The PARM description applies to the underlined values except for MAP and LET.

The data sets that interact with the Loader and the application program it creates in memory are represented graphically in Figure 19–1.

TABLE 19–1
PARM Options Available with the Loader

Option	*Description*
PRINT or NOPRINT	If NOPRINT is coded the SYSLOUT data set is not opened. Otherwise informatory and diagnostic messages print on the SYSLOUT data set.
MAP or NOMAP	The SYSLOUT data set contains a module map.
RES or NORES	The system LPA is searched to resolve external references. Heavily used load modules are stored in the LPA.
CALL or NCAL	The automatic call library(s) is searched to resolve external references. If NCAL is coded the SYSLIB data set is not opened.
LET or NOLET	The LET option functions basically the same as when coded with the Linkage Editor. An output module is marked as executable even if the Loader detected minor errors while constructing it.
EP=	EP identifies the entry point of the load module created. Hence the main module need not be coded first in the primary input.
NAME=	This determines the name used to identify the loaded program to the system.
SIZE=	SIZE determines the number of bytes of virtual storage available to the Loader and the application program it creates.

FIGURE 19–1
Data Sets That Interact with the Loader

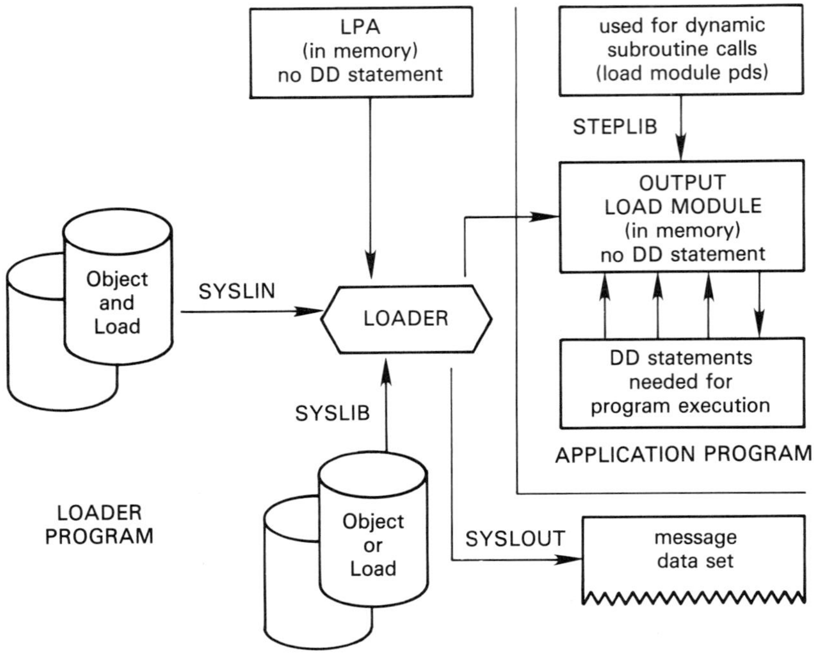

Using the Loader

Four examples are presented to illustrate the use of the Loader. The first example does not use a cataloged procedure, but the remaining three do. Frequently a language translator is used in the first step of a procedure and the Loader is used in the second step. Such procedures are commonly named xxxyCG where xxx identifies the compiler or assembler and y the specific version of the language translator. CG stands for Compile and Go. With an xxxyCG procedure all of the DD statements ordinarily used by the Loader (SYSLIN, SYSLIB, SYSLOUT, and STEPLIB) are included in the procedure. Hence none of them need be coded unless a statement must be overridden. In Example 4 the Loader is used in a final jobstep following the procedure. It could have been included in a procedure here. Example 1 in Chapter 8 shows the Loader DD statements that are usually included in the COBUCG procedure.

Example 2: An object module contained in the data set &&ALPHA is to be executed. The Loader is used to construct the load module. The original source code was written in COBOL. The program processes two data sets during execution: an instream data set with DDname CARDS is read and a data set with DDname SYSPRINT is printed. If the SYSLIN data set contained a load module the job stream in this example would still be valid.

```
//B        EXEC PGM=LOADER,PARM='MAP,RES,CALL,LET'
//STEPLIB   DD  DSN=SYS1.COBLIB,DISP=SHR
//          DD  DSN=DYNAMIC.SUBLIB,DISP=SHR
//SYSLOUT   DD  SYSOUT=A
//SYSLIB    DD  DSN=SYS1.COBLIB,DISP=SHR
//SYSLIN    DD  DSN=&&ALPHA,DISP=(OLD,DELETE)
//SYSPRINT DD  SYSOUT=A
//CARDS     DD  *
  instream data set
/*
```

With this group of PARM options external references will first be resolved from the LPA and then from SYS1.COBLIB. The STEPLIB DD statement permits dynamic external subroutine calls that occur during execution to be resolved from SYS1.COBLIB and DYNAMIC.SUBLIB. A STEPLIB DD statement is necessary when dynamic subroutine calls are explicitly or implicitly coded in the COBOL program. The main program makes such a call to both of the libraries in the concatenation. The COBOL automatic call library should be coded with STEPLIB when COBOL diagnostic options such as STATE and FLOW are specified during compilation. There is no required order among the DD statements for the jobstep. However, STEPLIB is traditionally coded first in any jobstep. Here it is followed by the three data sets used by the Loader. The data sets used by the application program are coded last. Since this is not a procedure there is no reason to qualify the final two DDnames with GO. DDname qualification outside of a procedure is ignored. If the input to the Loader had actually been a load module then it would have been a member of a pds. Hence DSN=&&PDS(ALPHA) could be coded on the SYSLIN DD statement. In this case the name of the load module program contained in member ALPHA need not also be ALPHA.

Example 3: An assembler program is to be assembled and executed using the cataloged procedure ASMFCG. Additionally, a PARM value is coded with the GO step in order to pass data from the EXEC statement to the executing program. Care must be taken to separate the Loader PARM options from the PARM values that are being passed to the executing program. Remember that the GO step results in two programs being executed. When both programs require a PARM parameter, code PARM.GO='value1, . . .,valueN/value1, . . .,valueM'. If no Loader options are coded follow the beginning apostrophe with a slash (/) and the PARM values for the executing program.

```
//C     EXEC  ASMFCG,PARM.ASM=OBJ,
//      PARM.GO='MAP,LET,CALL/12345ABC'
//ASM.SYSIN  DD  *
  Assembler source statements go here
/*
//GO.xxx data sets required during program execution
//GO.yyy
```

This example assumes that all of the data sets needed by the Loader are included in the cataloged procedure.

Example 4: Compile and link edit a PL/I subroutine. Following step D1 load module ONE is contained in the pds &&SUB. It will be subsequently called by a main COBOL program in the final step. Step D2 compiles the COBOL program. The Loader message data set is to be suppressed during the final step. The second and third steps could be performed by the COBUCG procedure. However, the approach here is used for clarity.

```
//D1        EXEC  PLIXCL
//PLI.SYSIN     DD  *
    The PL/I subroutine source code goes here
/*
//LKED.SYSLMOD DD  DSN=&&SUB(ONE),DISP=(NEW,PASS),UNIT=SYSDA,
//                  SPACE=(CYL,(1,,1))
//D2     EXEC  COBUC,PARM.COB=STATE
//COB.SYSLIN    DD  DSN=&&MAIN,DISP=(NEW,PASS),UNIT=SYSDA,
//               SPACE=(CYL,1)
//COB.SYSIN     DD  *
    COBOL main program goes here
/*
//D3       EXEC PGM=LOADER
//STEPLIB DD  DSN=SYS1.COBLIB,DISP=SHR
//SYSLOUT DD  DUMMY
//SYSLIN  DD  DSN=&&MAIN,DISP=(OLD,PASS)
//SYSLIB  DD  DSN=&&SUB,DISP=(OLD,PASS)
//        DD  DSN=SYS1.COBLIB,DISP=SHR
//        DD  DSN=SYS1.PLIBASE,DISP=SHR
//DDname  DD  All data sets required during execution
// ...        by either the COBOL or PL/I programs
// ...        should be coded here.
```

Example 5: A COBOL program reads records from a master file and produces an edited report. The program requires two complex calculations which are performed by an assembler program that consists of two modules or control sections (CSECTS). The assembler source code is contained in the cataloged sequential disk data set ASM.SOURCE. The load module generated from the assembler program is placed into a pds library called &&TEMP. The cataloged procedure COBUCG is used to create and execute the complete system. Note that the automatic call library statement used with the Loader is overridden.

```
//E1             EXEC ASMFCL
//ASM.SYSIN      DD  DSN=ASM.SOURCE,DISP=SHR
//LKED.SYSLMOD DD  DSN=&&TEMP(ALPHA),DISP=(,PASS),
//              SPACE=(CYL,(1,,1)),UNIT=SYSDA
//E2             EXEC COBUCG,PARM.COB='STATE,FLOW',PARM.GO=MAP
//COB.SYSIN     DD *
       COBOL main program goes here
/*
```

```
//GO.SYSLIB     DD   DSN=SYS1.COBLIB,DISP=SHR
//              DD   DSN=&&TEMP,DISP=(OLD,PASS)
//GO.REPORT     DD   SYSOUT=A
//GO.MASTER     DD   DSN=PAYROLL.MASTER,DISP=SHR
//GO.SYSDBOUT    DD   SYSOUT=A
```

Module Maps

The module map produced by the Loader is printed in a different format than the module map produced by the Linkage Editor. Additionally, the Loader does not print a(XREF) cross reference listing. With both module maps every entry resolved from an automatic call library is followed by an asterisk. With the Loader all entries retrieved from the LPA are followed by two asterisks. Primary input is not followed by an asterisk with either program.

Complete JCL Job Listing: Example 3 A main program written in COBOL calls an assembler subroutine. In step A the assembler subroutine is compiled and link edited. In step B the COBOL program is compiled, processed by the Loader, and executed. The module map produced by the Loader is printed. The abbreviations SD and LR stand for control section and label reference respectively. In step C the original COBOL program is again compiled and then link edited with the XREF option specified. In step D the load module is executed. The JCL should be carefully examined, especially the overriding statements in the procedures. The message data sets produced by the Loader and Linkage Editor should be contrasted. The output produced by the application programs in steps B and D is not shown but is identical in both steps.

Exercises

1. ABC is an object module created from assembler source code. It calls two subroutines, PQR and XYZ. PQR is an object module originally written in COBOL and XYZ is a load module initially written in PL/I. The subroutines are members of the libraries PDS.COB and PDS.PLI respectively. Two data sets with DDnames SYSPRINT and MASTER are used during execution. The following code attempts to use the Loader to combine the three modules and then execute the resulting program. Find and correct all of the syntax and logic errors in this code.

```
//DISASTER EXEC PGM=LOADER,PARM='MAP,RES,NCAL,LET',EP=ABC
//STEPLIB    DD   DSN=PDS.COB,DISP=SHR
//           DD   DSN=SYS1.PLIBASE,DISP=SHR
//SYSPRINT   DD   SYSOUT=A
//SYSLIB     DD   DSN=SYS1.ASMLIB,DISP=SHR
//           DD   DSN=SYS1.PLILIB,DISP=SHR
//           DD   DSN=PDS.PLI,DISP=SHR
//           DD   DSN=PDS.COB,DISP=SHR
//SYSLIN     DD   DSN=ABC,DISP=SHR
//MASTER     DD   DSN=OLD.MASTER,DISP=OLD
```

FIGURE 19–2

JCL Job Output, Example 3

```
                                  J E S 2   J O B   L O G

-------- JOB 1878   IEF097I LARRY    - USER ACS1125  ASSIGNED
15.13.52 JOB 1878   IEF677I WARNING MESSAGE(S) FOR JOB LARRY    ISSUED
15.13.52 JOB 1878   $HASP373 LARRY     STARTED - INIT  2 - CLASS B - SYS 8000
15.13.52 JOB 1878   IEF403I LARRY - STARTED - TIME=15.13.52
15.14.19 JOB 1878   IEF404I LARRY - ENDED - TIME=15.14.19
15.14.19 JOB 1878   $HASP395 LARRY     ENDED

 1   //LARRY   JOB  (XXXXXXXXXXXXXX),LARRY,MSGCLASS=D,CLASS=B,PRTY=8            JOB 1878
     ***ROUTE PRINT I6670                                                            002
 2   //A   EXEC  ASMFCL                                                             0030
     ***********************************************************************       0040
     *** AN ASSEMBLER SUBROUTINE IS COMPILED AND LINK-EDITED INTO THE               0050
     *** LOAD MODULE LIBRARY CODED ON SYSLMOD. BOTH THE CSECT AND THE               0060
     *** MEMBER ARE CALLED REALIO. THE SUBROUTINE DOES I/O FOR THE MAIN             0070
     *** COBOL PROGRAM. IT IS CALLED FROM SEVERAL DIFFERENT PLACES.                 0080
     ***********************************************************************       0090
 3   XXASMFCL   PROC MAC='SYS1.MACLIB',MAC1='SYS1.ASISTMAC',OUT=$               00000100
 4   XXASM      EXEC PGM=IEV90,PARM=OBJECT,REGION=1024K                         00000200
 5   XXSYSLIB   DD DSN=&MAC,DISP=SHR                                            00000300
 6   XX         DD DSN=&MAC1,DISP=SHR                                           00000400
 7   XXSYSUT1   DD UNIT=VIO,SPACE=(1700,(600,10))                               00000500
 8   XXSYSUT2   DD UNIT=VIO,SPACE=(1700,(600,10))                               00000600
 9   XXSYSUT3   DD UNIT=VIO,SPACE=(1700,(600,10))                               00000700
10   XXSYSPRINT DD SYSOUT=&OUT,DCB=BLKSIZE=1089                                 00000800
11   XXSYSPUNCH DD DUMMY                                                        00000900
12   XXSYSLIN   DD DSN=&&OBJSET,UNIT=VIO,SPACE=(80,(200,50)),                   00001000
     XX            DISP=(MOD,PASS)                                              00001100
13   //ASM.SYSIN DD *                                                               0100
14   XXLKED     EXEC PGM=IEWL,PARM=(XREF,LET,LIST,NCAL),REGION=192K,            00001200
     XX            COND=(8,LT,ASM)                                              00001300
15   XXSYSLIN   DD DSN=&&OBJSET,DISP=(OLD,DELETE)                               00001400
16   XX         DD DDNAME=SYSIN                                                 00001500
17   //LKED.SYSLMOD DD DSN=ACSSTU.LARRYJCL.LIB,DISP=(NEW,PASS),UNIT=SYSDA,          0590
     //            SPACE=(CYL,(1,,1)),VOL=SER=WORK01                                0600
     X/SYSLMOD  DD DSN=NULLFILE                                                 00001600
18   XXSYSUT1   DD UNIT=VIO,SPACE=(CYL,5)                                       00001800
19   XXSYSPRINT DD SYSOUT=&OUT                                                  00002000
20   //LKED.SYSIN   DD *                                                            0610
21   //B     EXEC  COBUCG,PARM.COB='STATE',                                           0640
     //            REGION.COB=600K,PARM.GO='MAP,PRINT,LET'                          0650
     ***********************************************************************       0660
     *** THE COBOL PGOGRAM ALPHA IS COMPILED AND THEN THE LOADER IS                 0670
     *** USED TO PREPARE IT FOR EXECUTION. SUBROUTINE CALLS TO REALIO               0680
     *** ARE RESOLVED BY THE LOADER.                                                0690
     ***********************************************************************       0700
22   XXCOBUCG   PROC REG=128K                                                   00000200
23   XXCOB      EXEC PGM=IKFCBL00,REGION=128K,PARM='CLIST'                      00000400
24   XXSYSPRINT DD SYSOUT=$                                                     00000600
25   XXSYSUT1   DD UNIT=VIO,SPACE=(460,(700,100))                               00000800
26   XXSYSUT2   DD UNIT=VIO,SPACE=(460,(700,100))                               00001000
27   XXSYSUT3   DD UNIT=VIO,SPACE=(460,(700,100))                               00001200
28   XXSYSUT4   DD UNIT=VIO,SPACE=(460,(700,100))                               00001400
29   XXSYSPUNCH DD DUMMY,DCB=(RECFM=F,BLKSIZE=80)                               00001600
30   XXSYSLIN   DD DSNAME=&LOADSET,DISP=(MOD,PASS),                             00001800
     XX            UNIT=VIO,SPACE=(80,(500,100))                                00002000
31   XXSYSLIB   DD DSN=SYS1.COBFDLIB,DISP=SHR                                   00002200
32   XXSYSUDUMP DD SYSOUT=$                                                     00002400
33   //SYSIN        DD  *                                                           0710
34   XXGO       EXEC PGM=ISULOADR,COND=(5,LT,COB),REGION=&REG                   00002600
35   //GO.STEPLIB DD                                                                0870
     X/STEPLIB  DD DSN=SYS1.COBLIB,DISP=SHR                                     00002800
36   //            DD DSN=ACSSTU.LARRYJCL.LIB,DISP=(OLD,PASS)                       0880
37   XXSYSLIN   DD DSNAME=*.COB.SYSLIN,DISP=(OLD,DELETE)                        00003000
38   XXSYSLOUT  DD SYSOUT=$                                                     00003200
39   //GO.SYSLIB  DD                                                                0890
     X/SYSLIB   DD DSN=SYS1.COBLIB,DISP=SHR                                     00003400
40   //            DD DSN=ACSSTU.LARRYJCL.LIB,DISP=(OLD,PASS),                      0900
     //            VOL=SER=WORK01,UNIT=SYSDA                                        0910
41   XXSRTCDS   DD DUMMY,DCB=BLKSIZE=80                                         00003600
42   //FNOTB        DD DUMMY                                                        0920
43   //SYSPRINT     DD SYSOUT=*                                                     0930
44   //SYSDBOUT     DD SYSOUT=$                                                     0940
45   //SYSOUT       DD SYSOUT=$                                                     0950
46   //C     EXEC  COBUCL,PARM.COB=STATE,PARM.LKED='LET,LIST,XREF'                  0960
     ***********************************************************************       0970
     *** THE SAME LOAD MODULE STRUCTURE CREATED BY THE LOADER IN THE                0980
     *** PREVIOUS STEP IS NOW BUILT BY THE LINKAGE EDITOR. AGAIN REALIO             0990
     *** AND THE ILBO SUBROUTINES ARE FOUND IN THE AUTOMATIC CALL LIBRARY           1000
     ***********************************************************************       1010
47   XXCOB EXEC PGM=IKFCBL00,REGION=128K,PARM='CLIST,XREF'                      00000200
48   XXSYSPRINT DD SYSOUT=$                                                     00000400
49   XXSYSPUNCH DD DUMMY,DCB=(RECFM=F,BLKSIZE=80)                               00000600
50   XXSYSUT1   DD UNIT=VIO,SPACE=(460,(700,100))                               00000800
51   XXSYSUT2   DD UNIT=VIO,SPACE=(460,(700,100))                               00001000
52   XXSYSUT3   DD UNIT=VIO,SPACE=(460,(700,100))                               00001200
53   XXSYSUT4   DD UNIT=VIO,SPACE=(460,(700,100))                               00001400
54   XXSYSLIN   DD DSNAME=&LOADSET,DISP=(MOD,PASS),UNIT=VIO,                    00001600
     XX            SPACE=(80,(500,100))                                         00001800
55   XXSYSLIB   DD DSN=SYS1.COBFDLIB,DISP=SHR                                   00002000
56   //SYSIN        DD  *                                                           1020
```

```
57      XXLKED EXEC PGM=IEWL,REGION=192K,PARM='XREF,LIST,LET',COND=(5,LT,COB)   00002200
58      XXSYSLIN   DD DSN=&LOADSET,DISP=(OLD,DELETE)                            00002400
59      XX         DD DDNAME=SYSIN                                              00002600
60      //LKED.SYSLMOD DD DSN=&&X(TEST),DISP=(,PASS),UNIT=SYSDA,                    1180
        //       SPACE=(1,(1,,1))                                                   1190
        X/SYSLMOD  DD DSN=NULLFILE,DISP=OLD                                     00002800
61      //LKED.SYSLIB DD                                                            1200
        X/SYSLIB   DD DSN=SYS1.COBLIB,DISP=SHR                                  00003000
62      //               DD DSN=ACSSTU.LARRYJCL.LIB,DISP=SHR                        1210
63      XXSYSUT1   DD UNIT=VIO,SPACE=(1024,(50,20,1))                           00003200
64      XXSYSPRINT DD SYSOUT=$                                                  00003400
65      //D    EXEC PGM=*.C.LKED.SYSLMOD                                            1220
        ****************************************************************            1230
        *** THE LOAD MODULE CREATED IN THE PREVIOUS STEP IS NOW EXECUTED.           1240
        *** IT IS IDENTIFIED BY THE REFERBACK ON THE EXEC STATEMENT.                1250
        *** THE SAME DD STATEMENTS ARE NEED FOR EXECUTION AS IN STEP B.             1260
        *** A CONDITION CODE OF 99 MENAS SUCCESSFUL EXECUTION.                      1261
        ****************************************************************            1270
66      //SYSPRINT  DD SYSOUT=$                                                     1280
67      //SYSDBOUT  DD SYSOUT=$                                                     1290
68      //SYSOUT    DD SYSOUT=$                                                     1300
69      //FNOTB     DD DUMMY                                                        1310
        //                                                                          1320

 STMT NO. MESSAGE
-
    5      IEF653I SUBSTITUTION JCL - DSN=SYS1.MACLIB,DISP=SHR
    6      IEF653I SUBSTITUTION JCL - DSN=SYS1.ASISTMAC,DISP=SHR
   10      IEF653I SUBSTITUTION JCL - SYSOUT=$,DCB=BLKSIZE=1089
   19      IEF653I SUBSTITUTION JCL - SYSOUT=$
   34      IEF653I SUBSTITUTION JCL - PGM=ISULOADR,COND=(5,LT,COB),REGION=128K
   65      IEF686I DDNAME REFERRED TO ON DDNAME KEYWORD IN PRIOR STEP WAS NOT RESOLVED
IEF236I ALLOC. FOR LARRY ASM A
IEF237I 143  ALLOCATED TO SYSLIB
IEF237I 262  ALLOCATED TO
IEF237I VIO  ALLOCATED TO SYSUT1
IEF237I VIO  ALLOCATED TO SYSUT2
IEF237I VIO  ALLOCATED TO SYSUT3
IEF237I JES2 ALLOCATED TO SYSPRINT
IEF237I DMY  ALLOCATED TO SYSPUNCH
IEF237I VIO  ALLOCATED TO SYSLIN
IEF237I JES2 ALLOCATED TO SYSIN
IEF142I LARRY ASM A - STEP WAS EXECUTED - COND CODE 0000
IEF285I   SYS1.MACLIB                                  KEPT
IEF285I   VOL SER NOS= SYS003.
IEF285I   SYS1.ASISTMAC                                KEPT
IEF285I   VOL SER NOS= ISU010.
IEF285I   SYS86329.T151352.RA000.LARRY.R0000001        DELETED
IEF285I   SYS86329.T151352.RA000.LARRY.R0000002        DELETED
IEF285I   SYS86329.T151352.RA000.LARRY.R0000003        DELETED
IEF285I   JES2.JOB01878.S0000106                       SYSOUT
IEF285I   SYS86329.T151352.RA000.LARRY.OBJSET          PASSED
IEF285I   JES2.JOB01878.SI000101                       SYSIN
IEF373I STEP /ASM     / START 86329.1513
IEF374I STEP /ASM     / STOP  86329.1513 CPU    0MIN 00.63SEC SRB    0MIN 00.02SEC VIRT  1024K SYS   492K
IEF236I ALLOC. FOR LARRY LKED A
IEF237I VIO  ALLOCATED TO SYSLIN
IEF237I JES2 ALLOCATED TO
IEF237I 14C  ALLOCATED TO SYSLMOD
IEF237I VIO  ALLOCATED TO SYSUT1
IEF237I JES2 ALLOCATED TO SYSPRINT
IEF142I LARRY LKED A - STEP WAS EXECUTED - COND CODE 0000
IEF285I   SYS86329.T151352.RA000.LARRY.OBJSET          DELETED
IEF285I   JES2.JOB01878.SI000102                       SYSIN
IEF285I   ACSSTU.LARRYJCL.LIB                          PASSED
IEF285I   VOL SER NOS= WORK01.
IEF285I   SYS86329.T151352.RA000.LARRY.R0000004        DELETED
IEF285I   JES2.JOB01878.S0000107                       SYSOUT
IEF373I STEP /LKED    / START 86329.1513
IEF374I STEP /LKED    / STOP  86329.1514 CPU    0MIN 00.09SEC SRB    0MIN 00.00SEC VIRT   192K SYS   444K
IEF236I ALLOC. FOR LARRY COB B
IEF237I JES2 ALLOCATED TO SYSPRINT
IEF237I VIO  ALLOCATED TO SYSUT1
IEF237I VIO  ALLOCATED TO SYSUT2
IEF237I VIO  ALLOCATED TO SYSUT3
IEF237I VIO  ALLOCATED TO SYSUT4
IEF237I DMY  ALLOCATED TO SYSPUNCH
IEF237I VIO  ALLOCATED TO SYSLIN
IEF237I 148  ALLOCATED TO SYSLIB
IEF237I JES2 ALLOCATED TO SYSUDUMP
IEF237I JES2 ALLOCATED TO SYSIN
IEF142I LARRY COB B - STEP WAS EXECUTED - COND CODE 0000
IEF285I   JES2.JOB01878.S0000108                       SYSOUT
IEF285I   SYS86329.T151352.RA000.LARRY.R0000005        DELETED
IEF285I   SYS86329.T151352.RA000.LARRY.R0000006        DELETED
IEF285I   SYS86329.T151352.RA000.LARRY.R0000007        DELETED
IEF285I   SYS86329.T151352.RA000.LARRY.R0000008        DELETED
IEF285I   SYS86329.T151352.RA000.LARRY.LOADSET         PASSED
IEF285I   SYS1.COBFDLIB                                KEPT
```

(continued)

```
IEF285I   VOL SER NOS= ISU004.
IEF285I   JES2.JOB01878.S0000109                     SYSOUT
IEF285I   JES2.JOB01878.SI000103                     SYSIN
IEF373I STEP /COB     / START 86329.1514
IEF374I STEP /COB     / STOP  86329.1514 CPU    0MIN 00.30SEC SRB    0MIN 00.00SEC VIRT   136K SYS   636K
IEF236I ALLOC. FOR LARRY GO B
IEF237I 140  ALLOCATED TO STEPLIB
IEF237I 14C  ALLOCATED TO
IEF237I VIO  ALLOCATED TO SYSLIN
IEF237I JES2 ALLOCATED TO SYSLOUT
IEF237I 140  ALLOCATED TO SYSLIB
IEF237I 14C  ALLOCATED TO
IEF237I DMY  ALLOCATED TO SRTCDS
IEF237I DMY  ALLOCATED TO FNOTB
IEF237I JES2 ALLOCATED TO SYSPRINT
IEF237I JES2 ALLOCATED TO SYSDBOUT
IEF237I JES2 ALLOCATED TO SYSOUT
IEF142I LARRY GO B - STEP WAS EXECUTED - COND CODE 0099
IEF285I   SYS1.COBLIB                                KEPT
IEF285I   VOL SER NOS= SYS000.
IEF285I   ACSSTU.LARRYJCL.LIB                        PASSED
IEF285I   VOL SER NOS= WORK01.
IEF285I   SYS86329.T151352.RA000.LARRY.LOADSET       DELETED
IEF285I   JES2.JOB01878.S0000110                     SYSOUT
IEF285I   SYS1.COBLIB                                KEPT
IEF285I   VOL SER NOS= SYS000.
IEF285I   ACSSTU.LARRYJCL.LIB                        PASSED
IEF285I   VOL SER NOS= WORK01.
IEF285I   JES2.JOB01878.S0000111                     SYSOUT
IEF285I   JES2.JOB01878.S0000112                     SYSOUT
IEF285I   JES2.JOB01878.S0000113                     SYSOUT
IEF373I STEP /GO      / START 86329.1514
IEF374I STEP /GO      / STOP  86329.1514 CPU    0MIN 00.15SEC SRB    0MIN 00.02SEC VIRT   128K SYS   444K
IEF236I ALLOC. FOR LARRY COB C
IEF237I JES2 ALLOCATED TO SYSPRINT
IEF237I DMY  ALLOCATED TO SYSPUNCH
IEF237I VIO  ALLOCATED TO SYSUT1
IEF237I VIO  ALLOCATED TO SYSUT2
IEF237I VIO  ALLOCATED TO SYSUT3
IEF237I VIO  ALLOCATED TO SYSUT4
IEF237I VIO  ALLOCATED TO SYSLIN
IEF237I 148  ALLOCATED TO SYSLIB
IEF237I JES2 ALLOCATED TO SYSIN
IEF142I LARRY COB C - STEP WAS EXECUTED - COND CODE 0000
IEF285I   JES2.JOB01878.S0000114                     SYSOUT
IEF285I   SYS86329.T151352.RA000.LARRY.R0000009      DELETED
IEF285I   SYS86329.T151352.RA000.LARRY.R0000010      DELETED
IEF285I   SYS86329.T151352.RA000.LARRY.R0000011      DELETED
IEF285I   SYS86329.T151352.RA000.LARRY.R0000012      DELETED
IEF285I   SYS86329.T151352.RA000.LARRY.LOADSET       PASSED
IEF285I   SYS1.COBFDLIB                              KEPT
IEF285I   VOL SER NOS= ISU004.
IEF285I   JES2.JOB01878.SI000104                     SYSIN
IEF373I STEP /COB     / START 86329.1514
IEF374I STEP /COB     / STOP  86329.1514 CPU    0MIN 00.30SEC SRB    0MIN 00.00SEC VIRT   136K SYS   644K
IEF236I ALLOC. FOR LARRY LKED C
IEF237I VIO  ALLOCATED TO SYSLIN
IEF237I DMY  ALLOCATED TO
IEF237I 26C  ALLOCATED TO SYSLMOD
IEF237I 140  ALLOCATED TO SYSLIB
IEF237I 14C  ALLOCATED TO
IEF237I VIO  ALLOCATED TO SYSUT1
IEF237I JES2 ALLOCATED TO SYSPRINT
IEF142I LARRY LKED C - STEP WAS EXECUTED - COND CODE 0000
IEF285I   SYS86329.T151352.RA000.LARRY.LOADSET       DELETED
IEF285I   SYS86329.T151352.RA000.LARRY.X             PASSED
IEF285I   VOL SER NOS= WORK03.
IEF285I   SYS1.COBLIB                                KEPT
IEF285I   VOL SER NOS= SYS000.
IEF285I   ACSSTU.LARRYJCL.LIB                        DELETED
IEF285I   VOL SER NOS= WORK01.
IEF285I   SYS86329.T151352.RA000.LARRY.R0000013      DELETED
IEF285I   JES2.JOB01878.S0000115                     SYSOUT
IEF373I STEP /LKED    / START 86329.1514
IEF374I STEP /LKED    / STOP  86329.1514 CPU    0MIN 00.13SEC SRB    0MIN 00.02SEC VIRT   192K SYS   444K
IEF236I ALLOC. FOR LARRY D
IEF237I 26C  ALLOCATED TO PGM=*.DD
IEF237I JES2 ALLOCATED TO SYSPRINT
IEF237I JES2 ALLOCATED TO SYSDBOUT
IEF237I JES2 ALLOCATED TO SYSOUT
IEF237I DMY  ALLOCATED TO FNOTB
IEF142I LARRY D - STEP WAS EXECUTED - COND CODE 0099
IEF285I   SYS86329.T151352.RA000.LARRY.X             KEPT
IEF285I   VOL SER NOS= WORK03.
IEF285I   JES2.JOB01878.S0000116                     SYSOUT
IEF285I   JES2.JOB01878.S0000117                     SYSOUT
IEF285I   JES2.JOB01878.S0000118                     SYSOUT
IEF373I STEP /D       / START 86329.1514
IEF374I STEP /D       / STOP  86329.1514 CPU    0MIN 00.05SEC SRB    0MIN 00.00SEC VIRT    16K SYS   288K
IEF285I   ACSSTU.LARRYJCL.LIB                        KEPT
IEF285I   VOL SER NOS= WORK01.
IEF237I 26C  ALLOCATED TO SYS00001
IEF285I   SYS86329.T151418.RA000.LARRY.R0000001      KEPT
IEF285I   VOL SER NOS= WORK03.
IEF285I   SYS86329.T151352.RA000.LARRY.X             DELETED
IEF285I   VOL SER NOS= WORK03.
IEF375I  JOB /LARRY   / START 86329.1513
IEF376I  JOB /LARRY   / STOP  86329.1514 CPU    0MIN 01.65SEC SRB    0MIN 00.06SEC
RCS176I  1125 01515000
```

```
                                                    VS LOADER
OPTIONS USED - PRINT,MAP,LET,CALL,RES,NOTERM,SIZE=98304,NAME=**GO

    NAME   TYPE  ADDR          NAME   TYPE  ADDR          NAME   TYPE  ADDR          NAME   TYPE  ADDR          NAME   TYPE  ADDR

 ALPHA       SD  11C010      ILBOSRV *   SD  11C5A8      ILBOSRVO*   LR  11C5B2      ILBOSR3 *   LR  11C5B2      ILBOSR5 *   LR  11C5B2
 ILBOSR   *  LR  11C5B2      ILBOSRV1*   LR  11C5B6      ILBOSTP1*   LR  11C5B6      ILBOST  *   LR  11C5BA      ILBOSTPO*   LR  11C5BA
 ILBODBG  *  SD  11CA50      ILBODBGO*   LR  11CA82      ILBODBG1*   LR  11CA86      ILBODBG2*   LR  11CA8A      ILBODBG3*   LR  11CA8E
 ILBODBG4*   LR  11CA92      ILBODBG5*   LR  11CA96      ILBODBG6*   LR  11CA9A      ILBODBG7*   LR  11CA9E      ILBODSP *   SD  11D8B0
 ILBODSPO*   LR  11D8B2      ILBODSSO*   LR  11D8B2      REALIO  *   SD  11E2B8      ILBOCOMO*   SD  11E550      ILBOCOM *   LR  11E550
 ILBOCMM  *  SD  11E6C0      ILBOCMMO*   LR  11E6C2      ILBOCMM1*   LR  11E6C6      ILBOBEG *   SD  11EA60      ILBOBEGO*   LR  11EA62
 ILBOMSG  *  SD  11EBE8      ILBOMSGO*   LR  11EBEA

 TOTAL LENGTH     2CD8
 ENTRY ADDRESS  11C010


  H96-LEVEL LINKAGE EDITOR OPTIONS SPECIFIED LET,LIST,XREF
           DEFAULT OPTION(S) USED -  SIZE=(262144,65536)


                                                  CROSS REFERENCE TABLE

 CONTROL SECTION                              ENTRY

   NAME      ORIGIN  LENGTH                     NAME     LOCATION     NAME     LOCATION     NAME     LOCATION     NAME     LOCATION
 ALPHA          00     594
 ILBOCOMO*     598     16D
                                              ILBOCOM       598
 ILBODBG *     708     E60
                                              ILBODBGO      73A      ILBODBG1      73E      ILBODBG2      742      ILBODBG3      746
                                              ILBODBG4      74A      ILBODBG5      74E      ILBODBG6      752      ILBODBG7      756
 ILBODSP *    1568     A08
                                              ILBODSPO     156A      ILBODSSO     156A
 ILBOSRV *    1F70     4A4
                                              ILBOSRVO     1F7A      ILBOSR5      1F7A      ILBOSR3      1F7A      ILBOSR       1F7A
                                              ILBOSRV1     1F7E      ILBOSTP1     1F7E      ILBOST       1F82      ILBOSTPO     1F82
 REALIO  *    2418     294
 ILBOBEG *    26B0     188
                                              ILBOBEGO     26B2
 ILBOCMM *    2838     399
                                              ILBOCMMO     283A      ILBOCMM1     283E
 ILBOMSG *    2BD8     100
                                              ILBOMSGO     2BDA


 LOCATION   REFERS TO SYMBOL   IN CONTROL SECTION                LOCATION   REFERS TO SYMBOL   IN CONTROL SECTION
     2C8             ILBOSRVO        ILBOSRV                          2CC            ILBODBGO          ILBODBG
     2D0             ILBOSR5         ILBOSRV                          2D4            ILBODBG4          ILBODBG
     2D8             ILBODSPO        ILBODSP                          2DC            REALIO            REALIO
     2E0             ILBOSRV1        ILBOSRV                          258            ILBOCOMO          ILBOCOMO
     7B4             ILBOCMMO        ILBOCMM                         1420            ILBOFLWO         $UNRESOLVED(W)
    1424             ILBOFLW2       $UNRESOLVED(W)                   1428            ILBOTEF3         $UNRESOLVED(W)
    142C             ILBOSTNO       $UNRESOLVED(W)                   1434            ILBOTCOO         $UNRESOLVED(W)
    196C             ILBOCMMO        ILBOCMM                         22FC            ILBOCOM           ILBOCOMO
    2300             ILBOCMMO        ILBOCMM                         2304            ILBOBEGO          ILBOBEG
    2308             ILBOMSGO        ILBOMSG                         230C            ILBOSND2         $UNRESOLVED(W)
    231C             ILBOSTTO       $UNRESOLVED(W)                   27F0            ILBOPRMO         $UNRESOLVED(W)

 ENTRY ADDRESS        00

 TOTAL LENGTH      2CD8
****TEST      DOES NOT EXIST BUT HAS BEEN ADDED TO DATA SET     AMODE 24
RMODE IS 24
AUTHORIZATION CODE IS         0.
```

2. List the DDnames that may be coded while using the Loader. For each DDname list the following information for the accompanying data set: required or optional, permissible data set organizations, DCB properties, new or existing data set, and the role of the data set with the Loader.

3. Describe the conditions that should be evaluated when deciding whether the Loader or the Linkage Editor is more appropriate for a specific application. List specific programming situations where one of the two is preferred.

4. Determine the differences between the SYSLIN, SYSLIB, and SYSLOUT data sets used with the Loader and the three corresponding data sets used with the Linkage Editor.

5. Suppose a PL/I program has been compiled and stored as member MAIN1 in the object module library PLI.OBJ. Use the Loader to resolve all external references and then execute the resulting module. The program copies records from a disk data set to tape and prints diagnostic messages. There are no explicit subroutine calls in the source code. Replace the Loader with the Linkage Editor and write the code to achieve the same results.

6. Suppose that in Example 1 the two subroutines FIRST and SECOND are members of object module libraries rather than load module libraries. Use the Loader to resolve all external references, and then execute the resulting module.

7. Implement the following experiment to determine whether the Loader makes more than one pass through the SYSLIB automatic call libraries when resolving external references. Write a short main module which calls subroutine SUB1, a member of load module library A. In turn SUB1 calls SUB2, which is in a second load module library called B, and SUB2 calls SUB3, which is also in library A. Examine the output structure produced to determine the manner in which the Loader resolves external references.

8. When resolving references from an automatic call library, why must a different set of conditions be used with the Linkage Editor than with the Loader? Why does the Linkage Editor allow more flexible conditions? It does not require that the name of the pds member agree with an ESD entry. Identify several coding restrictions that exist with the Loader because ALIAS control statements are not available.

9. ALPHA is a load module in the pds COBOL.LOAD. The Linkage Editor has marked it as executable. Can the Loader be used to execute ALPHA? If so write the necessary code. What would occur if the module had been marked as not executable by the Linkage Editor?

10. Suppose that the assembler source program in Example 5 is used to create an object module rather than a load module. Thus the first step uses ASMFC rather than ASMFL. Can the desired results still be achieved just by coding the COBUCG procedure? Are there any restrictions on the names of the two CSECTS in the assembler program?

11. ALPHA and BETA are object and load modules respectively that were created from COBOL source code. ALPHA is the main program. It calls the subroutine BETA. Use the Loader to bring ALPHA into memory and then execute it successfully. The call to BETA is a dynamic subroutine call. Thus there is no CALL 'BETA' statement in ALPHA.

12. Suppose that ALPHA and BETA are the same as in the previous exercise. The Linkage Editor is used to place them both in the same load module called MAIN. Both were brought in with INCLUDE statements and BETA was referenced first. Use the Loader to execute MAIN.

13. How can overlay programming be performed without using the Linkage Editor? Consider the use of section numbers in a COBOL program.

14. For each PARM option described in Table 19–1, identify the comparable Linkage Editor feature.

Chapter 20

Flow of Control

Overview

The COND parameter controls the flow of execution in a job with two or more steps. COND may be coded on the JOB or EXEC statements. On the EXEC statement it determines whether the step should be executed or bypassed. On the JOB statement COND determines whether all remaining steps in the job should be bypassed. Since the effect of coding COND on the JOB statement is so drastic it is more commonly coded on EXEC statements.

Clearly there are situations where the outcome of one step will dictate which of the subsequent steps should be skipped. A familiar example of this is a three-step job to compile, link-edit, and then execute a COBOL program. If significant errors are detected during the compile there is no reason to execute the last two steps. If the compile is successful but the link-edit fails the program will ordinarily not be executed. The three EXEC statements can be coded as follows:

```
//COB  EXEC   PGM=IKFCBL00,(no COND test on compile
 .            since it is the first step)
 .
 .
//LKED EXEC   PGM=IEWL,COND=(test results of compile)
 .
 .
 .
//GO   EXEC   PGM=*.LKED.SYSLMOD,COND=(test compile and
              link edit results)
```

A job step need not fail or abend in order to influence which subsequent steps are to be executed. IF-THEN-ELSE logic can determine which steps are executed in an MVS job stream.

FIGURE 20–1

Dynamically Modifying the Flow of Control with the COND parameters

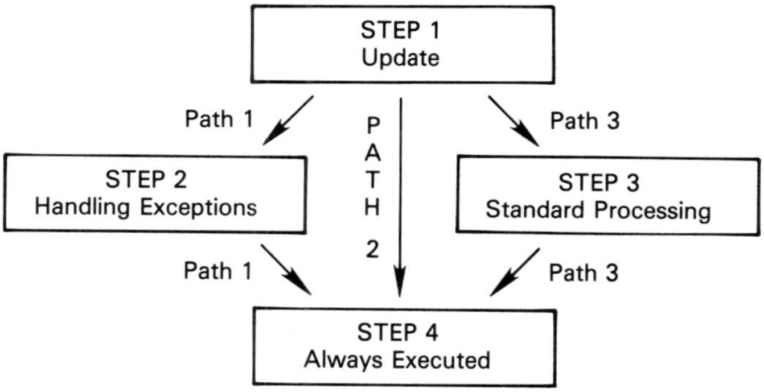

Example 1: Suppose a master file update is the first step of a four-step job. The second step is to be executed only when certain exceptional conditions are detected during the first step. The third step is to be executed on those occasions when the exceptional conditions do not occur in the first step. Hence the first step must perform some function that will allow exactly one of the next two steps to execute. A further condition is that if the first step abends the next two steps are to be skipped. The fourth step is to be executed no matter what occurs in the first three steps, including abends. The COND parameter allows such decisions to be made as a job is running. There are three possible groups of steps which may be executed, as pictured in Figure 20–1.

Here each of the lines denotes one of the three possible logic paths that may result during execution.

Return Codes

Every program that executes without abending returns a condition code to the system. The terms *condition code* and *return code* are used interchangeably. Condition code values are standardized for most IBM system software: compilers, utilities, Linkage Editor, and Loader. The values that are commonly assigned and their approximate meaning are as follows:

Return Code Value	*Meaning*
0	Successful execution
4	Warning—minor errors detected, execution may succeed
8	Severe errors—successful execution unlikely
12	Severe errors—successful execution impossible
16	Disaster—executing program unable to continue

Although these are the five standard condition code values, any number from 0 to 4095 can be used as a condition code. When values outside this range are used unpredictable results may occur. For the IBM system software the condition code values are automatically generated.

To effectively control the flow of execution in a job stream two questions must be answered. How does a user written application program issue a condition code in each of the three major programming languages? How does a job step test the condition codes issued in earlier steps? The first of these questions does not involve JCL.

COBOL, PL/I, and Assembler all allow the application programmer to determine the return code. In COBOL coding

```
MOVE value TO RETURN-CODE.
```

places value in the special register RETURN-CODE. Here value may range from 0 to 4095. Hence, to have a COBOL program issue a return code of 1234 code the statement

```
MOVE 1234 TO RETURN-CODE.
```

The default value for RETURN-CODE is 0. RETURN-CODE is a two byte field.

In PL/I coding

```
CALL PLIRETC(value);
```

causes the program to return value as its condition code. As with COBOL a default value of 0 is provided. To have a PL/I program return the condition code 335 code

```
CALL PLIRETC(335);
```

To set a condition code in an assembler program place the value of the condition code in register 15. This can be done in many ways, including

```
LA   15,value
```

and

```
L   15,=F'value'
```

This should be executed immediately before returning control to the system or the calling program. For example,

```
LA   15,100
```

sets the condition code to 100. If register 15 is not explicitly assigned a value its contents will still be used to set the return code. This can result in a strange value with no real meaning being printed in the messages and allocations section of a listing.

In order to determine the return code sent to the system examine message IEF142I. Its format is

```
IEF142Ijobname stepname - STEP WAS EXECUTED - COND CODE xxxx
```

This should be contrasted with the message that is printed when a program abends.

```
IEF142Ijobname stepname - COMPLETION CODE -
       SYSTEM=code1   USER=code2
```

This message will never be printed by a program that terminates normally. Ordinarily code1 and code2 give some indication of the reason for the abend.

Now that it is clear how to set a return code in an application program, the process of evaluating it in subsequent steps will be discussed. This procedure is handled entirely through JCL.

COND Parameter Syntax

The condition code issued by a job step can be tested by the COND parameter on the JOB statement and subsequent EXEC statements. The results of these tests will determine whether the step will be skipped or executed. The syntax of the COND parameter is

```
COND=((test1),(test2),...,(test8))
```

The tests are not true positional subparameters since they can be coded in any order without affecting the results or generating a syntax error. Hence, by default they are keyword subparameters that are not of the standard format keyword=value. If only one test is coded the outer parentheses are unnecessary. If more than eight tests are coded a JCL syntax error occurs. Each test has one of two formats. The most common format is

```
test=(numeric value,operator,previous stepname)
```

Here the three sub-subparameters are positional.

Numeric values can range from 0 to 4095. The six operators that can be coded are

GT greater than

GE greater than or equal

EQ equal

LT less than

LE less than or equal

NE not equal

The previous stepname identifies a stepname that occurred earlier in the job stream. The return code from the step is used in the test. A previous stepname must be qualified whenever it identifies a procedure. For most tests the result is either true or false. Under some conditions the test is not performed. When the result of a test is true the step will be skipped; when the result is false it may be executed. This reverse logic causes considerable difficulty in understanding the COND parameter. Many people consider COND the single most confusing JCL parameter. Up to eight tests can be coded on a single COND parameter. If any of the tests coded with COND is true the step is skipped. All of the tests performed must be false for the step to execute. If COND is not coded no tests are made and steps are executed normally. If the third operand in a test is omitted that test is made against all of the return codes from previous job steps that have executed. The first and second positional sub-subparameters do not have default values and must be coded. When COND is coded on the JOB statement the results are interpreted differently.

The examples below illustrate the COND parameter. The next nine examples assume that a two-step job with jobstep names AA and BB is to be run. The first five examples assume that step AA does not abend and supplies a return code that is tested in step BB.

Example 2: If AA returns a condition code between 0 and 100 inclusive then BB is to be executed.

```
//BB    EXEC   PGM=BPGM,COND=(100,LT,AA)
```

The COND parameter asks the question: "Is 100 less than the code returned by step AA?" Since 100 is less than all numbers from 101 through 4095, any of these values cause step BB to be skipped. Since the statement "100 is less than X" is false for every value of X between 0 and 100, all of these values will permit step BB to be executed. The same results can also be achieved by coding either of two additional COND parameters:

```
COND=(101,LE,AA)        or        COND=(100,LT)
```

The second of these is equivalent only because BB is the second step in the job.

Example 3: Execute BB whenever AA returns a code other than 13 or 50.

```
//BB   EXEC   PGM=BPGM,COND=((13,EQ,AA),(50,EQ,AA))
```

To verify that this COND parameter gives the desired results select a test point for every interval or end point that is involved in a COND test.

Interval or End Point	*Test 1 13=AA*	*Test 2 50=AA*	*Combined Test Results*	*Skip or Execute*
0-12	F	F	F	Execute
13	T	F	T	Skip
14–49	F	F	F	Execute
50	F	T	T	Skip
51-4095	F	F	F	Execute

This is a very simple way to verify that the correct COND value is coded. Divide the range of numbers from 0 to 4095 into intervals and end points using all the numeric values coded in the COND tests to do the division. If this technique shows that the results are incorrect a good rule of thumb is to simply reverse the inequalities in those intervals or points that are wrong.

Example 4: Execute BB only when AA returns a code between 5 and 10 inclusive.

```
//BB   EXEC   PGM=BPGM,COND=((5,GT,AA),(10,LT,AA))
```

Use the interval test described in the last example to verify that the COND values are correct. Use 0–4, 5, 6–9, 10, 11–4095 for numeric values. Under all conditions it is a good idea to verify the extreme values carefully since that is where most errors occur.

Another technique that can be used to determine the appropriate COND parameter is to write tests for when the step is not to be run. Those that evaluate to TRUE are equivalent to executing the step with the FALSE value. When AA is less than or equal to 11 or AA is greater than or equal to 4 the step should be skipped. Hence coding

```
COND=((11,LE,AA),(4,GE,AA))
```

will also work. Clearly this is equivalent to the test described above. Some people prefer this approach when writing COND parameters.

Example 5: Execute BB no matter what value AA returns. This requires writing a COND parameter that always evaluates to false.

```
//BB   EXEC   PGM=BPGM,COND=(4095,LT,AA)
```

The COND parameter could also be coded as COND=(0,GT). The same result occurs if no COND parameter is coded.

Example 6: Skip BB no matter what value AA returns. Here a COND test must be written that always evaluates to true.

```
//BB   EXEC   PGM=BPGM,COND=(4095,GE)
```

COND=(0,LE,AA) gives the same result.

Abend Processing

The previous discussion and examples assume that step AA does not abend. The rules change if an abend occurs while a job is running. What happens when a jobstep abends? The COND parameters on all steps following the abend are examined. Unless the COND parameter contains one of the special tests EVEN or ONLY that step will be skipped. This abend evaluation is done on a step-by-step basis. This is the second format that a COND test can assume. EVEN and ONLY are mutually exclusive. If both are coded a syntax error results. If one of them is coded a maximum of seven standard tests can be made. As with the standard tests, EVEN and ONLY can be coded in any order.

Unless COND with EVEN or ONLY is coded the system has no way of knowing if an abend in an earlier step will affect the present step. The programmer supposedly can determine if steps following an abend can be meaningfully processed.

Coding COND=(. . .,EVEN, . . .) means that the present step should be run even if a previous step abended. If other tests are coded with EVEN and one or more of them is true the step will still be skipped. EVEN is a meaningless test unless a prior step has abended.

Example 7: Step BB is to be executed even if step AA abends.

```
//BB   EXEC   PGM=BPGM,COND=EVEN
```

Example 8: BB is to be executed even if step AA abends. However, if AA returns a code greater than 16 step BB will be skipped.

```
//BB   EXEC   PGM=BPGM,COND=(EVEN,(16,LT,AA))        or
                       COND=((17,LE,AA),EVEN)
```

Coding COND=(. . .,ONLY, . . .) means that the present step should be executed ONLY if a previous jobstep has abended. As with EVEN, if other tests are coded and one or more of them is true the step will be skipped. Unlike EVEN, the ONLY test is not ignored if an abend has not occurred.

Example 9: Run step BB only when step AA abends.

```
//BB   EXEC   PGM=BPGM,COND=ONLY
```

Example 10: Run step BB whenever step AA abends or returns a code of 13 or 50. This is tricky! Examine the following code carefully.

```
COND=(EVEN,(13,GT,AA),(13,LT,AA),(50,GT,AA),(50,LT,AA))
```

Except for handling the abend processing, this is the opposite of the situation described in Example 3. This illustrates how a simple situation can lead to some very involved coding. Is this an example of a condition that is impossible to test?

Summary of COND on EXEC Statements

Six important points should be kept in mind when determining if a step will be executed.

1) A step that abends does not issue a condition code. Tests involving a step that abended are ignored. Hence such tests will never cause a step to be skipped.

2) A step that is skipped because of the COND parameter on its EXEC statement does not issue a condition code. Subsequent tests involving such a step will be ignored.

3) If no COND parameter is coded no tests will be made. If no prior steps abended the present step will be executed. If an abend has occurred it will be skipped.

4) Coding COND on the EXEC statement for a procedure applies it to every step within the procedure. To restrict the COND value to just one step code COND.procstepname=(tests).

5) To apply a specific test to one step within a previous procedure code the COND parameter as COND=(numeric value,operator,stepname.procstepname).

6) By coding COND=EVEN on every step in an N-step job each of the N steps can be executed and abend!

There are several things that will cause execution of a jobstep to be skipped even though COND=(. . .,EVEN, . . .) is coded. These include

- if any other tests coded on the COND parameter are true
- if requests for resources such as TIME and REGION cannot be satisfied
- if requested space on a disk volume is not available
- if a requested data set cannot be found
- if COND tests on the JOB statement are true
- if JCL syntax errors are found during the initial scan by the Job Scheduler no steps will be executed.

Coding COND on the JOB Statement

COND can also be coded on the JOB statement. Here again one to eight tests may be made. All tests must consist of pairs rather than triples. EVEN and ONLY are not permitted on the JOB statement. Thus COND is coded as

```
COND=((numeric value,operator),(numeric value,operator),...)
```

After a step is executed tests are made against the condition code returned. If any test on the JOB statement COND parameter is true all of the remaining steps in the job are skipped. If all tests are false then the COND parameters coded on the next EXEC statement determine whether that step will be executed. Unlike some JCL values that can be associated with both the JOB statement and individual EXEC statements (JOBLIB/STEPLIB, JOBCAT/STEPCAT, and most keyword parameters), neither COND parameter causes the other to be ignored. Rather, both are in effect. COND on the EXEC statement can cause a single job step to be skipped. COND on the JOB statement can cause all remaining steps to be skipped.

Example 11: If any step within a multi-step job yields a condition code other than 0, skip all of the remaining steps in the job.

```
//JOBNAME   JOB ---,COND=(0,NE)
```

Detailed COND Parameter Examples

A more involved five-step job stream is used to illustrate most of the points discussed above. The job consists of a cataloged procedure COBUCLG and the two programs used in the examples above. Two of the three EXECs in the procedure have COND parameters coded. There is never any reason to code COND on the first step in a job.

```
//CLG    PROC
//COB    EXEC  PGM=IKFCBL00                COBOL compiler
---
//LKED   EXEC  PGM=IEWL,COND=(5,LT,COB)    Linkage Editor
---
//GO     EXEC  PGM=*.LKED.SYSLMOD,COND=((5,LT,COB),
//             (8,LT,LKED))                Program Execution
```

When this procedure is invoked the COBOL program must compile successfully or with warnings or both following steps will be skipped. Likewise, if serious problems occur during the link-edit the GO step will not be executed.

Example 12: Run the above job with the following flow of control logic now in effect. If the second procedure step returns a code of 8 skip the GO step and all subsequent steps. If the GO step returns a code between 6 and 9 inclusive execute Step AA, otherwise execute Step BB.

```
//CLG EXEC COBUCLG,COND.GO=((8,EQ,LKED),(5,LT,COB))
//AA  EXEC PGM=APGM,COND=((8,EQ,CLG.LKED),
//         (6,GT,CLG.GO),(9,LT,CLG.GO))
//BB  EXEC PGM=BPGM,COND=((8,EQ,CLG.LKED),
//         (6,EQ,CLG.GO),(7,EQ,CLG.GO),
//         (8,EQ,CLG.GO),(9,EQ,CLG.GO))
```

Example 13: For the same job stream as in Example 12 modify the code. The linkage editor should be run only if the compiler returns an 8. The GO step should be run if the compiler returns an 8 and the Linkage Editor a zero. If the GO step is not executed or abends run step AA. If the GO step runs with a code of 8 or if any prior step abends run BB. If any step returns a code of 4000 every remaining step in the job should be skipped.

```
//          JOB     ---,COND=(4000,EQ)
//CLG       EXEC    COBUCLG,COND.LKED=(8,NE,COB),
//                  COND.GO=((8,NE,COB),(0,NE,LKED))
//AA        EXEC    PGM=APGM,COND=((EVEN,(8,EQ,CLG.COB),
//                  (0,EQ,CLG.LKED))
//BB        EXEC    PGM=BPGM,COND=((8,NE,CLG.GO),EVEN)
```

Note in particular the two tests that are made with Step AA to determine whether the GO step in the procedure was executed. This code will allow Step AA to execute if any earlier step abended.

Interaction Between the COND Parameter and Other JCL Parameters

The COND parameter interacts with three other topics in JCL not yet discussed. Two of these are the RESTART and RD parameters which are covered in Chapter 22. Restarting a job may require some additional planning. In addition, some COND values may have to be changed before a job can be rerun.

The COND parameter also results in additional complications when used with Generation Data Sets. Generation Data Sets use a relative number for identification. If some steps that create such data sets are skipped those relative numbers are skipped and problems can result.

Exercises

1. Write the appropriate COND parameters for all four steps to implement Example 1. Assume the program executed in Step 1 was written in COBOL. Describe the logic employed within the program that is used to help implement these results.

2. Study the following job stream:

```
//A     EXEC   PGM=A

//B     EXEC   COBUCL,COND.COB=(EVEN,(25,LT,A)),
//           COND.LKED=((30,LT,A),(22,LE,COB))

//C     EXEC   FORTGCG,COND.FORT=((35,GE,A),ONLY,
//          (32,LT,B.COB)),COND.GO=((300,EQ),EVEN,
//          (300,NE,FORT))
```

Fill in the following table with either RUN or SKIP depending on whether the step is executed or not. The A values are the condition codes generated when the first step is executed. The values on the far right are the condition codes returned if that step is executed. For example, if the COBOL compiler is executed a return code of 8 results.

Job Step	*Return Code From Step A*				*Return Code If Executed*
A	4	28	300	OC1 Abend	
B - COB					8
B - LKED					16
C - FORT					8
C - GO					40

3. Draw a flow chart to depict those factors that will affect whether a given step in a job stream will actually be executed. Assume this is the Nth step in an N-step job. How do the coded COND values and the results of other steps determine whether step N will actually be executed?

4. Why can't the COND parameter be omitted in Example 6 as it was in Example 5?

5. In Example 8, two equivalent COND parameters are shown. How many other variations of the COND parameter give exactly the same results?

6. In Example 12, how will the values coded change if the range from 6 to 9 is replaced by a range of 6 to 16?

7. Use the internal testing technique described with Example 3 to verify that the COND values in Example 12 are correct.

8. In Example 13, what modifications can be made in order to accomplish the same results without coding the COND parameter on the JOB statement?

9. In Example 13, Step AA is not to be executed if one specific step out of the three prior job steps abended. Does the existing code actually perform this test? How can an attempt be made to determine whether one prior job step out of many actually abended?

10. When running the job described in Example 13, what is the maximum number of steps that can abend? Can two or more abends occur in the same job step?

11. Two possible COND parameters are coded with each of Examples 5 and 6. With each example one of the parameter values may not always give the correct results. Which of the two values will always work in each example? How can the other value fail to work under some conditions? Hint: Consider return codes provided by an assembler program.

12. Describe programming situations where it is reasonable to code the COND parameter on the JOB statement. Under what conditions is it reasonable to code COND=ONLY on an EXEC statement?

Chapter 21

System Searches

Overview

This chapter gathers together a considerable amount of material that is touched upon in various places in this book. When a job is submitted for execution one of the major responsibilities of the Job Scheduler is to locate all of the data sets and library members that the job requires. The data sets and library members coded in the job stream fall into three categories. These include data sets to be processed, programs to be executed, and procedures to be invoked. Data sets are identified on DD statements. Programs and procedures are coded on EXEC statements. In this chapter the search the Job Scheduler uses to find these three classes of objects is discussed in detail. The material in the chapter is very important; an MVS user unfamiliar with system searches makes many serious coding errors and usually writes too much unnecessary JCL. Data sets are discussed first, then programs, and finally procedures.

The Creation and Subsequent Location of Data Sets

Every DD statement in a job stream identifies a data set. In order for the job to create or use a data set its location must be determined. Five parameters are important in this process: DSN, DISP, UNIT, VOL, and LABEL. All data sets can be placed in one of four categories.

1. Dummy data sets.

2. Unit record data sets—these include both in-stream and SYSOUT data sets.

3. Disk data sets.

4. Tape data sets.

Dummy data sets are identified on a DD statement by coding either the positional parameter DUMMY or DSN=NULLFILE. Since no I/O is performed with a dummy data set it is unnecessary for the system to locate the data set. If DSN, DISP, UNIT, VOLUME, or LABEL parameters are also coded on the DD statement they are ignored.

Unit record data sets are identified either by one of the two positional parameters (* and DATA) or by SYSOUT. Both * and DATA imply that an in-stream data set follows the DD statement. The value coded with SYSOUT determines the printer or punch that is used to create the output data set. Since all in-stream and SYSOUT I/O is actually done to or from a spool data set it is the responsibility of the Job Scheduler and the Job Entry Subsystem to keep track of these data sets. By examining the allocation messages it is apparent that system names have been generated for them.

Both disk and tape data sets are created and located in the same manner. There are two steps in this process. First, for an existing data set the system must determine the volume where it resides; for a new data set the system must select the volume where it is to reside. Second, the specific location on the volume must then be determined. There are four DD parameters that control the location and creation of disk data sets: DSN, DISP, UNIT, and VOLUME. With tape data sets LABEL is also used. For a disk data set the volume table of contents (VTOC) is used to determine the exact location on the volume. This is done after the volume itself is identified. For a tape data set the file sequence number and label format subparameters of the LABEL parameter determine where on the tape volume the data set is located. Unlike a disk, a tape volume does not have a table of contents describing the data sets it contains. Hence the two additional subparameters must be supplied to enable the system to locate a tape data set. Only the VTOC is needed with a disk data set. Recall that file sequence numbers can be interpreted differently depending on the values coded for the label format of a tape data set.

There are three ways to identify the specific volume that contains a data set. (1) The VOLUME parameter may be coded on the DD statement. When VOLUME is coded UNIT is also usually coded. The UNIT parameter is unnecessary when the VOL=REF form of the VOLUME parameter is coded. In this case UNIT information is taken from the DD statement or data set identified by the referback. (2) If the data set is cataloged the VOLUME and UNIT information can be provided by the catalog. For tape data sets the file sequence number is also stored in the catalog. (3) If the data set has been passed then the system has stored VOLUME and UNIT information in the pass table. For tape data sets the file sequence number and format are also stored in the pass table. For simplicity it is convenient to think of both a catalog and the pass table as directories which contain three or more fields for each data set identified. They are pictured graphically in Figure 21–1.

FIGURE 21–1

Catalog and Pass Table

Catalog (System Wide Data Sets)

DSNAME	UNIT	VOLUME	File Sequence Number (tape only)	possibly other information
ALPHA	3380	DISK99	. . .	. . .
A.B.C.	TAPE	ABCDEF	2	. . .

Pass Table (or Pass Mechanism — Job Restricted Data Sets)

DSNAME	UNIT	VOLUME	File Sequence Number (tape only)	Data Set Format (tape only)	other fields
ALPHA	3380	DISK99	. . .	. . .	. . .
A.B.C.	TAPE	ABCDEF	2	SL	. . .

For a cataloged or passed data set the information needed to locate the data set is already available in the system. It need not be coded on a DD statement. How does the system determine whether to look in a catalog or the pass table for the location of the data set? If VOLUME is coded on the data set's DD statement the system will not look in a catalog or pass table. If VOLUME is not coded it will search these objects for information about the data set. When a data set is initially created UNIT and VOLUME information must be supplied by the DD statement. Often both parameters are explicitly coded. Alternatively, a UNIT parameter can be coded which makes a non-specific volume request. In this case the system selects one volume in a given UNIT class. Following creation the data set can then be cataloged or passed or both.

When referencing a data set that has been either cataloged or passed it is unnecessary to code UNIT and VOLUME parameters. A fundamental axiom associated with JCL is that "the more JCL written, the greater the chance of syntax errors." Why code redundant information that can take extra runs to debug? There is also the possibility that an unnecessary VOLUME or UNIT value will be an incorrect value. Balanced against these possible programmer errors is the fact that referencing a data set through a catalog or pass table is slightly slower than going directly to the volume.

Example 1: Suppose that two data sets called X and Y are to be created. X may be either cataloged or passed. Y is to be a kept data set. The following JCL is used to create X and Y:

```
//A     EXEC   PGM=IEFBR14
//DD1   DD    DSN=X,DISP=(NEW,PASS),UNIT=SYSDA,VOL=SER=WORK01,
//      SPACE=(TRK,1)
//DD2   DD    DSN=Y,DISP=(NEW,KEEP),UNIT=SYSDA,VOL=SER=WORK02,
//      SPACE=(TRK,1)
```

Now suppose these data sets are referenced in a variety of ways. in the next step.

```
//DD1   DD   DSN=X,DISP=OLD,VOL=SER=WORK02,UNIT=SYSDA
//DD2   DD   DSN=X,DISP=OLD,VOL=SER=WORK01,UNIT=SYSDA
//DD3   DD   DSN=X,DISP=OLD
//DD4   DD   DSN=Y,DISP=OLD
//DD5   DD   DSN=Y,DISP=OLD,VOL=SER=WORK02,UNIT=SYSDA
```

For both DD1 and DD4 the system will report

```
IEF212 dsname DATA SET NOT FOUND
```

and cancel the job. In this case the message will print only for DD1 since it is coded first in the step. When a single data set cannot be located no additional processing is performed. The VOLUME parameter value is incorrect on DD1. Since Y is neither passed nor cataloged UNIT and VOL information must be coded on DD4. For DD2 the system will go directly to the VTOC of volume WORK01 without examining the pass table. For DD3 the system will go first to the pass table. There it will determine that X is on volume WORK01. It will then go to the VTOC on WORK01. Hence both DD2 and DD3 successfully determine the location of X. DD3 contains half as much code. For DD5 both VOLUME and UNIT parameters must be coded since the data set is neither cataloged nor passed. If X is always to be located through the pass table or a catalog there is no reason to request a specific volume when X is created.

Clearly both a catalog and the pass table contain some identical information. However, there are significant distinctions between them. A data set has an entry in the pass table only for the duration of the job that passed the data set. There can be multiple entries in the pass table for the same data set name. If a data set is passed several times in a single jobstep there will be one entry for each time it is passed. In subsequent steps a data set can be referenced from the pass table only as many times as it has been previously passed. Within a single jobstep a temporary data set can be referenced only once through the pass table. Catalogs store information about permanent data sets. The data set names in a catalog must be unique. However, since an MVS system can contain multiple catalogs the same data set name can occur in more than one catalog. There is no limit to the number of times a data set can be referenced through its catalog entry. With a VSAM catalog structure the catalog may contain additional information about the data set. Some of this information is not stored in the pass table. Conversely, there are some fields in the pass table that are not included in a catalog.

When an existing data set name is coded on a DD statement without accompanying UNIT and VOLUME parameters the pass table is searched first. If there is no entry in the pass table the catalog structure is searched. There are four ways in which a catalog can be associated with a data set.

1) The application program may actually identify the catalog by name within the source code. This is extremely rare, but is possible with the IDCAMS utility.

2) JOBCAT and STEPCAT DD statements may be coded. These two statements perform one specific function. They identify a catalog (data set) that is used to

locate or catalog other data sets in the job or jobstep respectively. When both are coded only STEPCAT is used. Hence JOBCAT is in effect for all steps for which no STEPCAT statement is coded. The data sets identified on JOBCAT and STEPCAT DD statements are themselves VSAM cataloged data sets. Hence only DSN and DISP should be coded on these two statements. Both JOBCAT and STEPCAT may identify a concatenation of catalogs.

3) The first level of qualification of a data set name can match the name of a VSAM user catalog or be an alias for the name of a user catalog. If either of these possibilities occurs the user catalog is searched for the data sets entry.

4) The final level of catalog searched is the System Master Catalog. On an MVS system there is one master catalog, and it must be a VSAM data set. Many installations allow only user catalogs and system data sets as entries in the master catalog. There are several important reasons why this is done.

Catalogs are an important topic in their own right. The order of catalog search is the only topic discussed in detail in this book. However, two points should be mentioned. Most installations have numerous user catalogs and one VSAM master catalog. There are non-VSAM catalogs also (called CVOLs), but they are becoming increasingly rare.

Example 2: To illustrate how catalog search takes place consider the following three-step job. Assume there are three user catalogs in the system, CATA, CATB, and CATC. To the right of the JCL is a list of the catalogs searched in an attempt to locate the data set. If the data set is located in a particular catalog the remaining entries are not searched.

JCL Coded	*Catalogs Searched*
`//JOBCAT   DD   DSN=CATA,DISP=SHR`	Master
`//A      EXEC   PGM=FIRST`	
`//DD1       DD   DSN=CATB.ABCDEF,DISP=SHR`	CATA,CATB,Master
`//DD2       DD   DSN=A.B.C,DISP=SHR`	CATA,Master
`//DD3       DD   DSN=CATA.XYZ,DISP=SHR`	CATA,Master
`//B      EXEC   PGM=SECOND`	
`//STEPCAT DD   DSN=CATB,DISP=SHR`	Master
`//          DD   DSN=CATC,DISP=SHR`	Master
`//DD4       DD   DSN=CATA.XYZ,`	CATB,CATC,CATA,
`//               DISP=(OLD,PASS)`	Master
`//DD5       DD   DSN=A.B.C,DISP=SHR,`	no catalog search
`//               UNIT=3350,VOL=SER=DISK99`	
`//C      EXEC   PGM=IDCAMS`	
`//SYSIN     DD   *`	
`    DEFINE  CLUSTER...  CATALOG(CATB)`	CATB,CATA,Master
`/*`	

Note that for DD1, DD2, DD3, and DD4 the pass table will be searched prior to examining any catalog. The above example can be modified to illustrate this. The last two DD statements in step A can be recoded as

```
//DD2      DD   DSN=A.B.C,DISP=(OLD,PASS)
//DD3      DD   DSN=CATA.XYZ,DISP=(OLD,PASS)
```

When this is coded CATA.XYZ on DD4 is located through its entry in the pass table. No catalog is searched. Since DISP=(OLD,PASS) is coded on DD4 a new entry is placed in the pass table for CATA.XYZ. It is not used in the third step and is removed from the pass table when the job ends. Data set A.B.C also has an entry in the pass table. However, it is not used on DD5 since UNIT and VOL are coded.

When DISP=(xxx,CATLG) is coded the order of catalog search specified above is used to determine in which catalog to place an entry for the data set. A catalog cannot be used if it currently contains a data set with the same name. Automatic data set replacement is not permitted with a catalog. Recall that member replacement can be done with a pds. If a data set cannot be cataloged the message

```
IEF287 dsname NOT CATALOGED X
```

is printed. The most common reason for this message is that there is an existing cataloged data set with the same name.

An entry is placed in the pass table every time DISP=(xxx,PASS) is coded. Recall that there is one pass table for each job executing and duplicate data set names may occur in it. A reference is resolved by the first entry whose name satisfies the reference. This need not be the desired data set. When a data set is retrieved via the pass table one entry for the data set is removed from the table. Every entry for a data set is removed from the pass table when the job in which it is coded finishes execution. A cataloged data set may also be passed. Note that this may be advantageous because of the order of search.

In summary, if UNIT and VOL parameters are coded then only that specific volume is searched for the data set. If UNIT and VOL are not coded searching begins with the pass table. If necessary it continues through the catalog hierarchy. To further illustrate this process consider the following example.

Example 3: Data sets X, Y, and Z are on volume WORK01. The three DD statements below contain the code needed to

1) UNCATLG the cataloged data set X,

2) CATLG the kept data set Y, and

3) DELETE the cataloged data set Z.

```
//C     EXEC    ---
//DD1    DD   DSN=X,DISP=(OLD,UNCATLG)
//DD2    DD   DSN=Y,DISP=(OLD,CATLG),UNIT=3350,VOL=SER=WORK01
//DD3    DD   DSN=Z,DISP=(OLD,DELETE)
```

On DD1 UNIT and VOL must not be coded. Otherwise the catalog structure will not be accessed, and an uncatalog operation cannot be performed. If Y was previously passed UNIT and VOL are not needed on DD2. With DD2 access through the catalog is impossible. Two messages are generated for DD3. Z is first uncataloged and then deleted.

Suppose Z is to be deleted (scratched) but not uncataloged. To do this code the following:

```
//DD3   DD   DSN=Z,DISP=(OLD,DELETE),UNIT=3350,VOL=SER=WORK01
```

The VTOC entry for Z is removed but the catalog entry remains. Suppose an attempt is made to create a data set called Z on WORK01. If DISP=(NEW,CATLG) is coded the new data set becomes associated with the existing catalog entry. If an attempt is made to create a cataloged data set called Z on any other volume subsequent problems can develop.

The Creation and Subsequent Location of ProGraMs (PGMs)

The library used to hold a load module is determined when the Linkage Editor creates it. When attempting to locate the PGM values coded on EXEC statements the Job Scheduler may examine any of four different locations in the system. These are the JOBLIB and STEPLIB DD statements, if present, the System Link Pack Area (LPA), and the system load module libraries. The JOBLIB and STEPLIB DD statements parallel the role in which the JOBCAT and STEPCAT DD statements are used to locate cataloged data sets. Recall that JOBCAT and STEPCAT reference catalogs which identify a collection of data sets. JOBLIB and STEPLIB identify load module libraries. Recall that load module and PGM are equivalent terms. Hence these two DD statements identify a load module library whose directory is searched for the member name coded on the EXEC statement. When both JOBLIB and STEPLIB are coded only the STEPLIB is used for that jobstep. Both JOBLIB and STEPLIB permit concatenation of load module libraries.

Suppose neither JOBLIB nor STEPLIB is coded. In this case the search for the PGM is restricted to the LPA and the system load module library. At most installations this library is named SYS1.LINKLIB. It contains important programs used on the system, including compilers, assemblers, the Linkage Editor, the Loader, IDCAMS, utilities, Sort/Merge program, etc. Placing them in SYS1.LINKLIB makes locating them as straightforward as possible. Additionally, whenever the system first searches either JOBLIB or STEPLIB and fails to find the member, then the LPA and finally SYS1.LINKLIB is searched.

Example 4: To illustrate searching for programs consider the following three-step job. As in Example 2, the actual order in which the search takes place is listed on the right.

JCL Coded	Order of Search
`//JOBLIB   DD   DSN=LIBA,DISP=SHR`	
`//A        EXEC PGM=STEPA`	LIBA and
`...`	SYS1.LINKLIB
`//B        EXEC PGM=STEPB`	
`//STEPLIB  DD   DSN=LIBB,DISP=SHR`	LIBB(but not LIBA) and
`...`	SYS1.LINKLIB
`//C        EXEC PGM=IEWL`	SYS1.LINKLIB only
`//STEPLIB  DD   DSN=SYS1.LINKLIB,DISP=SHR`	
`//SYSLMOD  DD   DSN=LOADLIB(MEMBER),DISP=OLD`	
`...`	
`//D        EXEC PGM=*.C.SYSLMOD`	Library coded on
`...`	SYSLMOD statement
	in previous step

A JOBLIB statement is usually coded only when there are several PGMs in the job stream contained in the same private library(s). Notice that coding SYS1.LINKLIB on the STEPLIB statement in step C shortens the search time. The referback in step D references a specific load module created in a previous step.

The Job Scheduler looks in one other place for PGMs—the System Link Pack Area. This area is in main memory and is discussed in Chapter 1. It contains heavily used system routines. The system looks here after STEPLIB and JOBLIB and before SYS1.LINKLIB, so the search order listed in the previous example should be modified to reflect this. The other three places searched are all disk libraries. The specific programs placed in the LPA are selected by the systems programming staff.

One program may dynamically invoke a second program while executing. Here dynamic means that the second program has not been link edited into the executing load module structure. The PGM name is not present anywhere in the job stream JCL. One common place where this occurs is when a COBOL program abends and debugging options such as STATE and FLOW have been coded. The routines these options call are not usually link edited into the main program. A COBOL CALL statement of the form CALL variable-name is a second example. Dynamically invoked programs are located using the same order of search as those programs explicitly coded on EXEC statements. Because of this the STEPLIB statement coded with an executing COBOL module often identifies SYS1.COBLIB, the COBOL automatic call library.

The Creation and Location of Procedures

The third object in the job stream that must be located is a procedure or PROC. There are two types of procedures, cataloged and in-stream. In-stream procedures are restricted to the job in which they are coded. They are included along with the other JCL statements. See Chapter 8 for more specific details. The general format of an in-stream procedure is

```
procname  PROC
          . . .
          body of the procedure
          . . .
          PEND
```

Cataloged procedures are global and are available to any jobs executing in the system. The name of a cataloged procedure is its member name in a pds library. Cataloged procedure libraries must be identified as such to the system. There is a system procedure library. On almost all MVS systems it is called SYS1.PROCLIB. Multiple system procedure libraries can be created. A specific procedure library is selected on the /*JOBPARM or //*MAIN statement. Recall that /*JOBPARM is a JES2 statement. The value coded here:

```
/*JOBPARM    PROC=xx
```

gives the DDname of the statement in the JES2 procedure which identifies a library.

The hierarchy of search for a procedure is as follows:

1) In-stream procedures are examined first.

2) With JES2 the library identified on the /*JOBPARM statement is searched next if coded. With JES3 the library on the //*MAIN statement is searched if coded.

3) If no JOBPARM or MAIN library is coded then the default procedure library SYS1.PROCLIB is searched.

Procedures are created in two ways. In-stream procedures can be included as part of any job stream. They exist only within a single job. Cataloged procedures are members of card image libraries. Typically utilities such as IEBUPDTE and IEBGENER are used to place members in the libraries. JES2 or JES3 determines whether libraries other than SYS1.PROCLIB are to be used as system procedure libraries.

System Search Summary

Since volumes are listed in the allocation messages questions about the location of data sets can be answered. However, there are no allocation messages showing where PROCs and PGMs are found. For all three classes of object, failure to find a coded value results in the job being cancelled or abending. The three messages associated with this are as follows:

Object	*Message*
data set (DSN)	IEF212 dsname DATA SET NOT FOUND
program (PGM)	IEA703 MODULE ACCESSED module name accompanied by an S806-4 abend specified module not found
procedure (PROC)	IEF612 PROCEDURE NOT FOUND

FIGURE 21–2
Search for Procedures

Search for PROCEDURES

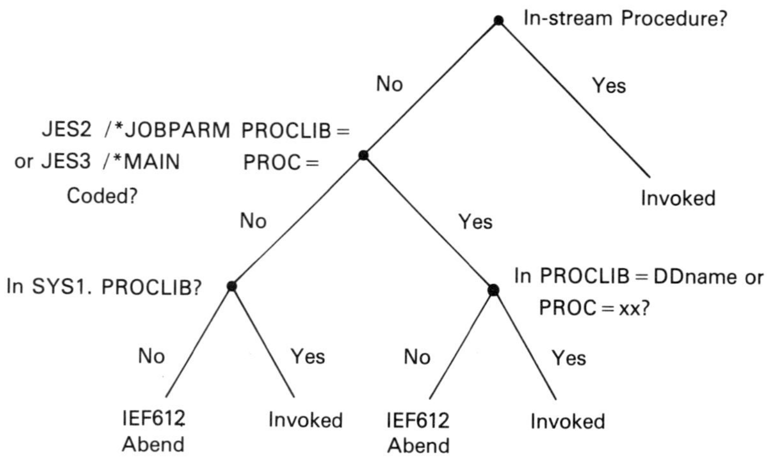

The IEF messages are written by the Job Scheduler. With both data sets and procedures the job is cancelled. The IEA message is written by the Supervisor. Since an abend occurs the COND parameter can be used to execute subsequent steps.

Figures 21–2, 21–3, and 21–4 serve as flow charts for the order of search for procedures, programs, and data sets.

The IEFBR14 Utility

IEFBR14 is the simplest possible utility program to use. It is not a true' utility, such as the IEB and IEH utilities discussed later in this book. It uses no control statements or PARM values, and it requires no DD statements. IEFBR14 is often called the null utility. It executes only two significant instructions. First, it returns a condition code of zero for the jobstep. Second, it ends. The name of the utility decomposes into IEF and BR14. IEF is the identifier for the Job Scheduler. BR14 refers to the assembler language instruction BR 14, which ends a program or subroutine and returns control to the program that had called it. When IEFBR14 finishes executing control is returned to MVS and the next step or job begins execution.

IEFBR14 performs no actual processing and it does not require any DD statements or control information of any type. Rather, the basic function performed by the utility is to serve as a placeholder to which DD statements may be attached. Recall that except for several special DDnames (JOBLIB, JOBCAT, and SYSCHK, etc.) every other DD statement is processed with the EXEC statement that immediately precedes it. Since IEFBR14 does not open any data sets, no records can be added, deleted, or modified to any of the data sets coded on the DD statements coded with it. All of the functions performed with IEFBR14 can also be performed without it. It is strictly a convenience feature like procedures.

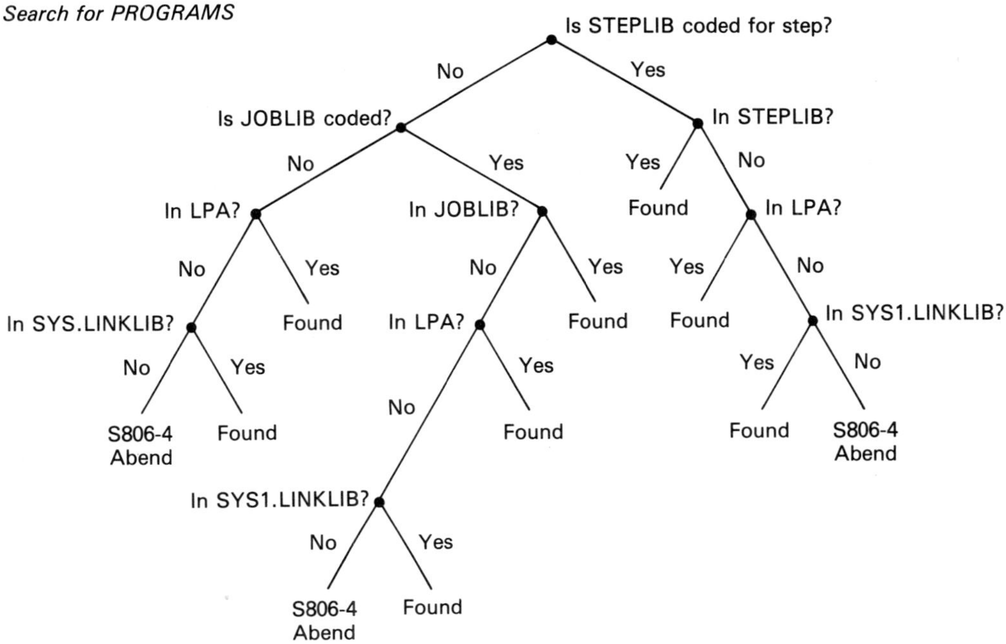

FIGURE 21–3
Search for Programs

Concatenation is permitted on JOBLIB and STEPLIB statement.

Same order of search is used for PGM = program and dynamically invoked programs.

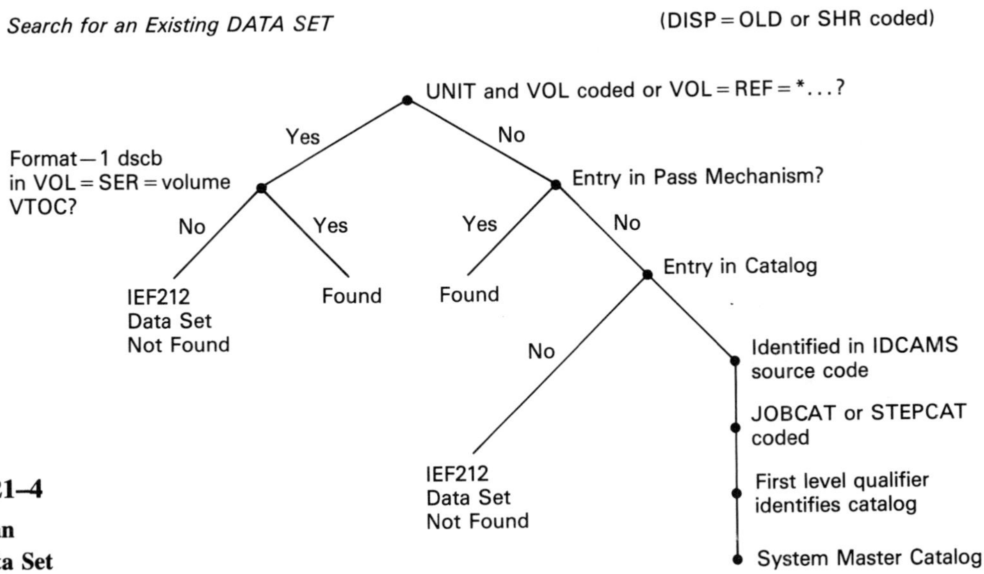

FIGURE 21–4
Search for an Existing Data Set

The major functions performed by IEFBR14 are listed here. A disk data set can be created. That is, a VTOC entry is written, and optional space may be allocated on the volume. In any subsequent processing, the DISP parameter must imply an existing data set. The status of an existing data set may be changed in a number of ways. In each case, no other processing is performed. An existing uncataloged data set may be cataloged, name permitting. A cataloged data set may have its catalog entry removed (uncataloged). An uncataloged data set may be scratched or deleted. A cataloged data set may be deleted even though its catalog entry remains. It may also be uncataloged and deleted using just one DD statement. A temporary data set may be made permanent if its DSN value will permit this. For any existing data set, it may be passed, and an entry placed in the pass mechanism. A passed data set may have one of its entries in the pass mechanism removed. These functions are illustrated in the following three examples.

Example 5: Three disk data sets and one standard label tape data set are created in this step. The disk data sets will consist of two sequential and one partitioned data set. The sequential data sets, X and Y, will be passed and cataloged respectively, while the partitioned data set will be permanent but uncataloged. The tape data set will also be passed. A non-specific volume request is made on the statement with DDname DD2. No member names are coded with the pds on DD3.

```
//A   EXEC PGM=IEFBR14
//DD1  DD  DSN=X,DISP=(NEW,PASS),UNIT=SYSDA,SPACE=(CYL,1),
//         VOL=SER=DISK01
//DD2  DD  DSN=Y,DISP=(NEW,CATLG),UNIT=SYSDA,
//         SPACE=(TRK,(1,1))
//DD3  DD  DSN=Z,DISP=(NEW,KEEP),UNIT=SYSDA,
//         SPACE=(CYL,(1,,36)),VOL=SER=DISK02
//DD4  DD  DSN=W,DISP=(NEW,PASS),UNIT=TAPE,VOL=SER=TAPE01,
//         LABEL=(1,SL)
```

Example 6: Four changes are made in the status of the four data sets created in the previous example. Data set X is cataloged. Data set Y is uncataloged and deleted. An entry is placed in the pass table for data set Z. The entry in the pass table for data set W is removed.

```
//B   EXEC PGM=IEFBR14
//DD1  DD  DSN=X,DISP=(OLD,CATLG)
//DD2  DD  DSN=Y,DISP=(OLD,DELETE)
//DD3  DD  DSN=Z,DISP=(OLD,PASS),UNIT=SYSDA,VOL=SER=DISK02
//DD4  DD  DSN=W,DISP=(OLD,KEEP or DELETE)
```

Example 7: Several additional examples of processing with IEFBR14 are shown here. In addition, this example illustrates that both new and existing data sets can be processed in the same IEFBR14 jobstep.

```
//C    EXEC PGM=IEFBR14
//DD1  DD   DSN=X,DISP=(OLD,UNCATLG)
//DD2  DD   DSN=Z,DISP=(OLD,KEEP)
//DD3  DD   DSN=X,DISP=(OLD,DELETE),UNIT=SYSDA,VOL=SER=DISK01
//DD4  DD   DSN=X,DISP=(,PASS),UNIT=SYSDA,SPACE=(TRK,0)
```

The first DD statement uncatalogs data set X, but does not delete the data set. The second DD statement turns a temporary data set into a permanent data set. The data set is located using the pass table. The third DD statement deletes the VTOC entry for data set X. Because of the first DD statement, it is necessary to code UNIT and VOL with the third statement. A new data set called X is created and passed on the last DD statement. A VTOC entry is created for X, but no space is allocated.

Any of the previous three examples can be modified by recoding the EXEC statement in the manner shown here.

```
//STEPX   EXEC PGM=IEFBRXX
```

None of the examples contain a STEPLIB or JOBLIB DD statement. Hence, only SYS1.LINKLIB is searched for a load module named IEFBRXX. Since the library contains no member with this name, the supervisor abends the step with an S806-4 abend–LOAD MODULE NOT FOUND. However, following the abend, the disposition processing of the data set is still performed. The third DISP subparameter determines the action taken following an abend. Since no third subparameters were coded the second subparameter is used as a default value. Hence, the same result occurs as specified above unless the data set was passed. For passed data sets other factors control the processing.

The IBM manuals imply that a major function of IEFBR14 is that it can be used to syntax check the JCL (DD statements) in a job stream for syntax errors without actually executing any of the steps. IEFBR14 is probably slightly superior for detecting JCL errors than coding TYPRUN=SCAN on the JOB statement. However, this method contains subsequent overhead and TYPRUN=SCAN does not. Specifically, a clean-up job or jobstep may have to be run to undo the data set statuses created by the original IEFBR14 job.

Exercises

1. The following job stream contains two jobsteps (two EXEC programs and numerous DD statements). For those statements whose numbers are listed below explain the order of search (and how it terminates if possible) for the particular data set or member referenced on that JCL statement. For some of these (e.g., 1) it is impossible to determine from the coding when if ever the search is successfully terminated. For others (e.g., 2) it should be apparent where the system will locate the required object. Consider catalogs, VTOCs, libraries, tables, etc. in your searches. Irrelevant DD parameters are not shown.

```
//JOBLIB   DD DSNZLIB, DISP=SHR
//A      EXEC  PGM=X            (1)
//STEPLIB DD DSN=XLIB,DISP=SHR
//         DD DSN=YLIB,DISP=SHR
//DD1      DD DSN=X,DISP=(NEW,CATLG),VOL=SER=WORK01,...
//DD2      DD DSN=X,DISP=(NEW,KEEP),VOL=SER=WORK02,...
//DD3      DD DSN=X,DISP=(NEW,PASS),VOL=SER=WORK03,...
//B      EXEC PGM=Y           (2)
//DD4      DD DSN=X,DISP=SHR        (3)
//DD5      DD DSN=X,VOL=SER=WORK02,DISP=SHR,... (4)
//DD6      DD DSN=X,VOL=SER=WORK01,DISP=SHR,... (5)
//DD7      DD DSN=X,DISP=OLD
```

2. Determine where the system looks for each of the objects coded below. Begin with the first item that must be located.

```
//ABCDEFG   JOB  . . .a typical jobcard here
/*JOBPARM   PROCLIB=PROCDD12
//JOBLIB    DD DSN=AAA,DISP=SHR,UNIT=3350,VOL=SER=WORK04
//JOBCAT    DD DSN=BBB,DISP=SHR
//*
//IDCAMS    PROC PROG=
//A         EXEC PGM=A
//STEPLIB   DD DSN=XX,DISP=SHR,VOL=SER=WORK02,UNIT=3350
//DD1       DD DSN=ALPHA,DISP=(OLD,PASS)
//DD2       DD DSN=ALPHA,DISP=(NEW,KEEP),VOL=SER=WORK10,
//             UNIT=DISK,...
//DD4       DD DSN=ALPHA,DISP=OLD,VOL=SER=WORK02,UNIT=DISK
//          DD DDNAME=MU
//DD5       DD DSN=EPSILON.ALPHA,DISP=SHR
//*
//B         EXEC PGM=&PROG
//DD1       DD DSN=ALPHA,DISP=OLD
//STEPCAT   DD DSN=YY,DISP=SHR
//DD2       DD DSN=BETA,DISP=(NEW,CATLG),UNIT=3350,...
//DD3       DD DSN=*.A.DD2,DISP=SHR,VOL=SER=WORK14,
//             UNIT=DISK
//DD4       DD DSN=ZETA(ALPHA),DISP=(OLD,KEEP)
//DD5       DD DSN=ALPHA,VOL=REF=*.A.STEPLIB,DISP=SHR
//          PEND
//*
//A         EXEC  IDCAMS,PROG=B
//MU        DD DATA,DLM=
  ...
//B.DD2     DD DSN=PI,DISP=OLD
//B.MU      DD DSN=MU,DISP=SHR
//SYSIN     DD *
  ...
/*
```

```
//*
//B          EXEC   AARDVARK
//*
//C          EXEC   COBUCLG
//SYSIN      DD *
//GO.SYSOUT DD SYSOUT=$
//SYSIN       DD DSN=NULLFILE,DISP=SHR
//*
//IDCAMS      EXEC PGM=IDCAMS
//SYSIN       DD DUMMY
//
```

3. Can a data set be processed in the same jobstep with both new and existing DISP values specified on two distinct DD statements? Either IEFBR14 or any other program can be used.

4. Can a member of a pds be processed by IEFBR14. If yes, give an example. If no, why not?

5. Describe the physical appearance of the tape data set created in Example 5. Show all tape marks and IBGs.

Chapter 22

Dumps, Checkpoints, and Restarts

Overview

Printing and reading abend dumps remains a significant topic on MVS systems. This chapter discusses the three types of abend dumps available, the information each type contains, and how each of the three can be printed. Interpreting the information contained in the dumps is not discussed in this book. The three types of abend dumps are identified by coding specific reserved DDnames. Abend dumps are not related to Checkpoints or Restarts.

Checkpoints are used to store important information at periodic intervals in a program that executes for a long period of time. In case the program does not complete successfully it may be possible to restart it from one of the checkpoints rather than rerunning the entire job from the beginning. Checkpoints are necessary only with programs that perform a significant amount of processing. Checkpoints are identified in the JCL either by specific DDnames or the CHKPT DD parameter.

Restarts allow a program that abended to be restarted at a later time. When restarted, the program may begin executing at the first step within the job or at a specific later jobstep. If checkpoints were taken when the program was initially run a wider range of restarting options is available. A specific checkpoint within a given step can be selected as the location where the program is to be restarted.

Abend Dumps

When an executing program abends three basic options are available to help the programmer determine the reason for the abend. The *System Messages* and *System Codes* manuals contain a general explanation of abend causes. In some situations this information clarifies the reason for the abend. Additionally, all of the major programming languages contain facilities that can be used to help determine the specific cause of the abend. For example, COBOL contains the STATE and FLOW options. The STATE option identifies the statement that was executing when the abend occurred. The FLOW option prints out the order in which major parts of the COBOL program had executed prior to the abend. Usually tools such as these are sufficient to determine the cause of an abend.

The third approach used to determine the reason for an abend is to print an abend dump and then examine it. Ordinarily dump reading requires more effort and considerably more skill on the part of the programmer than using the facilities built into the application programming language. Over the last decade there has been a gradual decline in the use of dump reading to determine the causes of abends. This trend will probably continue and even accelerate. However, dump reading will never completely disappear. There are several important reasons for this. First, some abends will defy every other attempt at determining their cause. Some SOC4 abends fall into this category. This abend often follows a major alteration of the load module code itself and the destruction of the built-in debugging facilities from the programming language. Dump reading is used as the last resort when no other alternative remains. Second, by examining a dump a programmer can learn a great deal about the format of an executing application program. From studying a printed copy of the load module generated by the program, considerable information can be gained that will help when writing and debugging future programs and understanding MVS systems. With a COBOL program the PMAP compile option should be coded when examining a dump. Finally, some installations prohibit the use of options such as STATE and FLOW with production programs. If such programs abend the dump must be examined to determine the reason.

The abend dump for a large program can fill a great deal of paper. Unless there are plans to use the dump for one of the reasons described above there is no sense in printing it. It is assumed that the typical MVS programmer does not want an abend dump to print by default. Hence, unless a dump is specifically requested it will not be printed. To request that an abend dump be printed one of three special DDnames must be coded in the jobstep where the abend occurred. The three DDnames are SYSUDUMP, SYSABEND, and SYSMDUMP. SYSUDUMP contains the least information, and SYSMDUMP contains the most. To further reflect the fact that most programmers are not interested in printing an abend dump, the common cataloged procedures frequently do not contain any of the three special DDnames. Two or more of the DDnames may be coded in the same step. When this is done the last DDname coded is the one used.

If none of the three DDnames are coded an IEF142 message is printed which contains the abend code and the job step in which the abend occurred. If special debugging aids have been requested the program that abended will print additional information.

The three types of abend dumps supply different types and amounts of information. In addition, the actual format for all three dumps is determined by the installation when the system is generated. Specific options can be defined for each of the three types of dumps. This information is placed in SYS1.PARMLIB, an important system library. The options determine the parts of the application program and the remainder of the system that are to be printed.

SYSUDUMP produces the minimum amount of output. The load module itself is printed along with three items familiar to an assembler language programmer, the program's save area, the register contents, and the program status word. In addition, various control blocks and the SWA for the program are also printed. All information included in the dump is formatted prior to being printed. For abends that do not take place during an I/O operation a SYSUDUMP is usually sufficient to determine the reason for the abend.

The SYSABEND dump contains all of the information provided by a SYSUDUMP dump. In addition, SYSABEND also contains the LSQA and additional control blocks related to the I/O the program is performing. This is also a formatted dump.

The SYSMDUMP is the most comprehensive of the three dumps. In addition to almost all of the information provided by a SYSABEND dump the SYSMDUMP dump contains the MVS nucleus, SQA, LSQA, and several other areas. A SYSMDUMP is not formatted. Hence it should be written to tape or disk. A program is then used that formats the SYSMDUMP information prior to printing.

The JCL required to print a SYSUDUMP or SYSABEND abend dump is the same except for the DDname. A disk or tape data set is specified with a SYSMDUMP. Two conditions must be met to produce an abend dump: one of the three following DDnames must be coded and an abend must occur during the jobstep.

```
//SYSUDUMP   DD   SYSOUT=A
//SYSABEND   DD   SYSOUT=A
//SYSMDUMP   DD   DSN=&&DUMP,DISP=(,PASS),...
```

To print the SYSMDUMP abend dump, the AMDPRDMP service aid program can be used in a later step.

Example 1: A two-step job is to be run. If an abend occurs during the first step a SYSUDUMP dump is to be produced. If an abend occurs during the second step a SYSABEND dump is to be printed. Because COND=EVEN is coded both dumps could be printed.

```
//A      EXEC PGM=EDITPGM
//SYSUDUMP   DD   SYSOUT=A
 ...other DD statements used with step A
//B      EXEC PGM=UPDATE,COND=EVEN
//SYSABEND   DD   SYSOUT=A
 ...other DD statements used with step B
//
```

The SYSUDUMP and SYSABEND statements are listed first only to call attention to them. There is never any required ordering for the DD statements coded with an EXEC PGM statement.

Checkpoints

Overview

Checkpoints are only important for programs that execute for a long period of time. If a program executes for a great deal of time and abends just before completion the entire job may have to be rerun. This is exceedingly wasteful of computer resources. There are many important application programs whose execution time is measured in hours. Checkpoints are used to avoid having to completely rerun a lengthy job from the beginning. A checkpoint is a 'snapshot' of the major information in the program after it has performed a specific amount of work.

In theory an application program could take its own checkpoints. It could save essential information on disk or tape. This information could then be used if it became necessary to restart the program from that point. However, since checkpoints are such an important notion the facilities are available within all three major programming languages to request them. If a CHKPT macro instruction is executed a checkpoint is taken. CHKPT can be coded directly in an assembler program. In a COBOL program this is accomplished by coding the RERUN clause. A data set must be supplied to hold the records written as the checkpoints are taken.

Each checkpoint that is taken is written to the disk or tape data set identified by the DDname specified with the application program. The default DDname is SYSCHK. Each checkpoint is numbered consecutively from 1. The checkpoint records are preceded by the identifier C0000001, C0000002, ..., etc. The first step in working with checkpoints is requesting that they be taken and storing them for later use.

If the job completes execution successfully the checkpoints that were taken will not be needed. However, if for any reason the job abended it can be restarted from the last checkpoint taken. In order to successfully do this two things must be done: a restart request must be made that specifies restarting at a checkpoint, and the data set that holds the checkpoint records must be available when the job is restarted.

JCL for Checkpoints

The reserved DDname SYSCHK is used to identify a checkpoint data set. The data set coded with SYSCHK or a programmer selected DDname should have been used to hold the checkpoint records that were written while the job was initially executing. The same data set is then used again when the job is restarted. The checkpoint data set is ignored if the RESTART parameter is not coded on the JOB statement. The SYSCHK statement must be placed between the JOB statement and the first EXEC statement. If a JOBLIB statement is present SYSCHK is coded after it. When the job is restarted the SYSCHK statement must be placed immediately in front of the first EXEC statement.

The DD parameter CHKPT can be used to take checkpoints with multi-volume data sets. When CHKPT=EOV is coded a checkpoint is taken each time the end of a volume is reached. The checkpoints can be requested when both writing and reading data sets. If several data sets are concatenated together as input CHKPT=EOV must be specified on every DD statement in the concatenation.

When CHKPT=EOV is used in a job a DD statement with DDname SYSCKEOV must also be coded. The SYSCKEOV statement is used to hold the end of volume checkpoint records. This DD statement must be coded in the same job step where CHKPT=EOV is coded.

Example 2: A large multi-volume disk data set is to be read. Checkpoints should be taken after every volume is processed. This can be accomplished by coding

```
//A     EXEC PGM=XYZ
//SYSCKEOV DD DSN=CHKPTDS,DISP=(MOD,CATLG),UNIT=SYSDA
//MASTER   DD DSN=FINANCIL.RECORDS,DISP=SHR,
//            UNIT=3380,VOL=SER=(DISK01,DISK02,DISK03,
//            DISK04),CHKPT=EOV
...
```

It is important that MOD be coded as the first DISP subparameter. Otherwise the checkpoint records will overwrite one another.

Restarts

Overview

Restarting a job is controlled by the RD and RESTART parameters. The RD parameter may be coded on the JOB and EXEC statements, but the RESTART can be coded only on the JOB statement. The two parameters are closely related. In addition, the RESTART and RD parameters are strongly related to checkpoint data sets.

RD

RD stands for the restart definition parameter. The RD parameter may be coded on both the JOB and EXEC statements. When coded on the JOB statement it overrides the RD value coded on an EXEC. The RD parameter performs two functions. First, it determines how the automatic step restart facilities are to be used with the CHKPT macro. Second, it determines whether automatic restart is permitted or suppressed.

Automatic restarts require a job journal. There are four values that may be coded with RD. These are R, RNC, NC, and NR. Coding RD=R or RD=RNC on either the JOB or EXEC statement forces journaling by JES2. The four RD values are explained below.

RD=R If the job step abends automatic step restart is permitted. However, if a checkpoint has been executed the job will restart at the last checkpoint. R provides the most flexibility of the four RD values.

RD=RNC Automatic step restart is permitted. However, automatic and deferred checkpoint restarts are not allowed.

RD=NC Automatic step restarts are not permitted. Additionally, automatic and deferred checkpoint restarts are not allowed. NC provides the least flexibility of the four RD values.

RD=NR NR gives the same results as NC. However, checkpoints can be established. It will then be possible later to rerun the job from the checkpoint. Hence a deferred checkpoint restart may be used in a second job.

RESTART

The RESTART parameter is used to resubmit a job for execution. Execution may start at the beginning of a job step or at a checkpoint within the step. There are several instances where restarting a job must be handled very carefully. Restarts can cause problems when Generation Data Sets are created during the job. The same data sets should not be created twice, which can occur from executing the same step two times with Generation Data Sets. Likewise, complications can arise when restarts are used with jobs where either the COND parameter or backward references are coded. These types of problems are related to the fact that information is referenced in steps that are not being executed when the job is restarted. This is the opposite of the problem involving Generation Data Sets. Three RESTART formats are available to restart a job at the beginning of a step.

Format	*Meaning*
RESTART=*	Restart from within the first jobstep.
RESTART=stepname	This format and the next identify a specific jobstep to use for restarting.
RESTART=stepname.procstepname	

RESTART=* is one instance where an asterisk is not used to reference a value coded earlier in the job stream. All three of the RESTART formats cause the job to restart at the beginning of the step identified. However, all three formats can also be modified to restart at a checkpoint within a jobstep. In this case the RESTART parameter has two positional subparameters. It is coded as RESTART=(first parameter as above, checkpoint-id) where checkpoint-id specifies where within the step the restart is to begin. When restarting within a job step it is necessary to include a SYSCHK DD statement. The checkpoint-id must be identified as C000000i.

Example 3: A two-step job is to be restarted at the fourth checkpoint taken in the second step. The checkpoints are contained in the sequential data set DSN = CHECK.POINTS.

```
//JOB123   JOB (accounting information),LARRY,
//         RESTART=(BETA,C0000004),other parameters
//JOBLIB   DD   DSN=LOADLIB,DISP=SHR
//SYSCHK   DD   DSN=CHECK.POINTS,DISP=OLD
//ALPHA   EXEC PGM=X
   ...
//BETA    EXEC PGM=Y
   ...
```

Exercises

1. Write a short COBOL program that will abend when executing. Run the program three times to produce each type of abend dump. Examine the resulting output. Code all three of the dump DDnames in the same step. Which of the dumps are printed?

2. This exercise considers why many installations prohibit using STATE and FLOW options. Recompile the COBOL program used in the previous exercise. Specify the STATE option during the compile. Rerun the program again to get a SYSUDUMP printed listing. Examine the second dump to see how it differs from the first dump. Recompile the COBOL program a third time with the FLOW option specified during the compile. Examine the SYSUDUMP created by running this program to see how it differs from the first two.

3. A one-step job takes checkpoints. Write the relevant code to create the checkpoints on an SL tape data set. Suppose the job abends. Write the relevant code to permit a checkpoint restart.

Chapter 23

The Sort/Merge Utility

Overview

Sorting is one of the most common programming functions. Sorting consists of ordering a collection of records based on the values in one or more fields. Often a data set sorted in one order must be resorted in a different manner for a second application. The basic premise of sorting is always the same: impose a specific order on the logical records in the data set.

In this chapter one major approach to sorting is examined. IBM supplies a Sort/Merge program that easily handles most common sorting applications. The program itself is usually classified as a utility program. It can also be classified as a service program like the Linkage Editor or Loader. The Sort/Merge program differs from the IEB/IEH utilities in several significant ways. It gives the programmer more options to choose from and is easier to use. It is described in its own manual, *DFSORT Application Programming Guide*. The system sort is used more frequently than most other utilities.

Several software vendors supply comparable sort programs for large IBM computer systems. The most popular of these is SYNCSORT, which is marketed by Syncsort, Inc. From a programmer's point of view the IBM Sort/Merge program and SYNCSORT are almost identical. In 1984 IBM changed the name of their system sort program from Sort/Merge to DFSORT and upgraded the program itself to make it more competitive. The material in this chapter includes information on both DFSORT and the Sort/Merge program. The Sort/Merge program can be thought of as a subset of DFSORT.

Fundamental Sorting Techniques

There are three general approaches to sorting: (a) writing a sort from scratch, (b) invoking the Sort/Merge program from within a COBOL, PL/I, or Assembler program, and (c) using the Sort/Merge program in a separate jobstep. In a non-academic setting approach (a) is rarely used. To write a sort program is time consuming. The sort itself will probably be less efficient than the sort provided by either approach (b) or (c). Approach (a) should only be undertaken if the data set to be sorted has some special property that the user-written sort can take advantage of. Whenever a user sort has been written two questions must always be asked. Does the sort always work correctly? How does its performance compare to the existing Sort/Merge program that is available? Writing a sort can teach a person a great deal about programming techniques. However, this practice is usually restricted to courses in data structures and programming languages. A user sort is rarely employed in a production data processing environment.

The Sort/Merge program can be called from an application program written in COBOL, PL/I, or Assembler. Thus approach (b) guarantees a sort that obviously works and is also moderately efficient. Most features of the Sort/Merge program are available in this setting. Some options may not be permitted because of the language restrictions. For example, referencing individual bits is quite difficult in a COBOL–invoked sort. These minor disadvantages are often outweighed by the additional flexibility the language provides. Pre- and post-processing of records can be handled readily in either COBOL or PL/I. This type of processing used to be very difficult if only the Sort/Merge program was used. Now with DFSORT it is rarely necessary to call the Sort program from within an application program written specifically for that purpose. More details on invoking the Sort in a COBOL application program are discussed in the last section of this chapter.

There are several drawbacks to approach (b). Unless some unusual processing is required along with the sort operation it is wasteful to write an application program merely to call the Sort/Merge program. It also requires learning some extra features of the language, especially for COBOL. Few introductory programming language courses cover the SORT verb in COBOL or CALL PLISORTx in PL/I in sufficient depth to handle common sort situations. Remember that when SORT SD-name is coded in COBOL or CALL PLISORTx is coded in PL/I a call to the Sort/Merge utility occurs. If no processing other than sorting is to be done it is unreasonable to write an application program to do it.

Approach (c) involves executing the Sort/Merge utility directly. Clearly, every possible option is available when this approach is used. It is necessary to code only JCL and control statements. An efficient sort is guaranteed, the user has some control of the sorting technique selected, and it is unnecessary to compile an application program.

Some problems can occur with approach (c). Under some circumstances pre- and post-editing of records can be more difficult than with approach (b). Some processing of this type must be handled by external subroutines that are user written and stored in a load module library. The Sort/Merge utility does require a knowledge of JCL. However, no more is actually required than in (b). For a person trying to learn JCL the Sort/Merge utility is an excellent program to use for practice.

Fundamental Sort/Merge Utility Information

Through JCL and control statements at least four items must be supplied to the Sort/Merge utility each time it is invoked. These include a minimum of three DD statements.

— Where are the records that are to be sorted? The input data set used by the Sort/Merge program is identified by a DD statement with DDname SORTIN.

— Where should the sorted records be written? DDname SORTOUT identifies the output data set. A printed listing of the sorted records can be gotten by coding the SYSOUT parameter on the SORTOUT statement.

— How are the records to be sorted? The SYSIN data set identifies the control information related to the key fields. Like SORTIN and SORTOUT, a SYSIN DD statement is required.

— What resources are available to the Sort/Merge program? The amount of main storage and disk work space that are provided have a strong bearing on the efficiency of the sort. In general, the more storage available the more efficient the sort. Disk work space is identified on DD statements with DDnames of SORTWK01, SORTWK02, SORTWK03, etc. Although the SORTWKxx DD statements are optional, they are usually required when sorting a large data set.

The fields within the record that are used in ordering the data set are called key fields. These fields are prioritized. The one of most importance is called the major key field. The second most important is the first minor key, the third most important the second minor key, etc. The records are then sorted into ascending or descending order based on the value in each record's major key field. If two records have the same major key value the first minor key value is used to determine ordering. If both the major and first minor values are the same the second minor key value is used, etc.

Example 1: Suppose a collection of records is to be sorted using the values in three fields. There is one record for each employee in a large company. The first field is state of residence. This is a two byte character field used as the major key. Ascending order is used. Hence Alabama employees are listed first and Wyoming employees last. The first minor key is a three byte numeric character (zoned decimal) field which contains the employee's age. The second minor key is a five byte packed decimal field which holds the person's salary. Descending order is used with both of the minor keys.

The actual details of specifying how the records are to be sorted can now be explained. It is necessary to identify the key fields and establish the priority among them. Four values must be specified with each key field. They are coded as positional subparameters. They answer the following questions: Where does a key field begin? How many bytes are in the field? What is the format of the data in the field? Is the key field value to be used to sort the records in ascending or descending order? For all of the keys this information is coded on one control statement. Describing the details of the sort requires no knowledge of JCL. It is necessary only to know the characteristics of the data set and how it is to be ordered.

The SORT Control Statement

In order to illustrate the syntax of a control statement consider the following example.

Example 2: It is required to sort a data set of 60 byte records. As stated above, four specific values are required for each key field in the sort. This information is summarized in Table 23–1.

The control statement used to encode this information is

```
SORT FIELDS=(6,2,CH,A,15,3,CH,D,45,5,PD,D)
             \________/ \________/ \________/
               major      minor      minor
                key       key 1      key 2
```

This is the most common format of the SORT control statement. The four values associated with the major key are listed first. If there is a first minor key its four fields follow next. Next come the four fields for the second minor key, etc. Up to 255 keys can be coded. Key fields may overlap one another. One key may be embedded in a second key. All key fields must be contained in the first 4092 bytes of a record. No keys are permitted in the variable length portion of records that are not present in some records. The total length of all keys must be less than or equal to 4092 bytes. SORT control statements may be continued by coding a non-blank character in column 72. The continued statement must begin in column 16.

The complete job stream needed to perform the sort operation can now be defined. The IBM Sort/Merge program is usually called ICEMAN. It is a member of SYS1.LINKLIB. To sort the 60 byte input data set using the above control statement, the following should be coded:

```
//B        EXEC PGM=ICEMAN
//SYSOUT    DD  SYSOUT=A
//SORTIN    DD  DSN=EMPLOYEE.MASTER,DISP=SHR
//SORTOUT   DD  DSN=NEW.EMPLOYEE.SORTED,DISP=(NEW,CATLG),
//              SPACE=(CYL,(10,2)),UNIT=SYSDA,
//              DCB=(EMPLOYEE.MASTER)
//SYSIN     DD  *
    SORT FIELDS=(6,2,CH,A,15,3,CH,D,45,5,PD,D)
/*
//SORTWK01 DD   UNIT=SYSDA,SPACE=(CYL,5)
//SORTWK02 DD   UNIT=SYSDA,SPACE=(CYL,5)
//SORTWK03 DD   UNIT=SYSDA,SPACE=(CYL,5)
```

TABLE 23–1
Key Field Information in the SORT Control Statement

Key Field	*Starting Byte Location*	*Length in Bytes*	*Data Format*	*Desired Ordering*
Major key	6	2	character	ascending
Minor key 1	15	3	numeric character	descending
Minor key 2	45	5	packed decimal	descending

Three SORTWK DD statements have been coded to provide work space on disk. Space for work data sets should always be requested in cylinders. Small requests are rounded up to cylinders. The DCB values for the sorted output data set are taken from the labels of the cataloged input data set. Notice that the message data set is called SYSOUT rather than SYSPRINT. Along with the Loader, the Sort/Merge program is the other major IBM software product that does not use SYSPRINT as the DDname for the message data set. With DFSORT the message data set can also be identified with the DDname SORTMSG.

Example 3: Produce a printed listing of every employee in the company ordered by salary from lowest to highest. Only the SORTOUT and SYSIN DD statements need to be changed from the last example. They become

```
//SORTOUT   DD  SYSOUT=A
//SYSIN     DD  *
  SORT FIELDS=(45,5,PD,A)
/*
```

The four fields in the SORT control statement are examined in more detail below. Each field is positional. No default values are associated with any of the four.

The first subparameter is starting location. This value denotes a location, not a displacement. A record begins with byte one. Ordinarily fields begin on a byte boundary. Bit values can be specified by coding X.Y where Y is a value from zero to seven. Bit values are considered displacements. A key field that begins in the 5th bit of the 99th byte of a record will have a location of 99.4. When sorting variable length records and VSAM data sets four bytes must be added to the actual starting location value. This compensates for a Record Description Field which precedes the record. In the case of a VSAM data set the Sort/Merge utility constructs this field preliminary to sorting.

The second subparameter is key field length. The length of a key field can be expressed in bytes as an unsigned integer N or as a combination of bytes and bits N.M. The same comments on N and M hold here as with starting location as regards the range of possible values and displacement.

The third subparameter is the data format. A complete list of the data formats available with the Sort/Merge program is shown in Table 23–2. Note that AQ is not really a data type; it specifies that data are to be ordered with a user-chosen collating sequence.

TABLE 23–2
Data Formats Available with the Sort/Merge Program

Value	*Data Format*	*Permissible Field Length (in bytes)*
CH	(EBCDIC character, unsigned)	1 – 4092
ZD	(zoned decimal, signed)	1 – 32
PD	(packed decimal, signed)	1 – 32
FI	(fixed decimal, signed)	1 – 256
BI	(binary, unsigned)	1 bit – 4092
AC	(character ASCII, unsigned)	1 – 256
CSL	(numeric, leading separate sign)	2 – 256
CST	(numeric, trailing separate sign)	2 – 256
CLO	(numeric, leading overpunch sign)	1 – 256
CTO	(numeric, trailing overpunch sign)	1 – 256
ASL	(numeric, ASCII, leading separate sign)	2 – 256
AST	(numeric, ASCII, trailing separate sign)	2 – 256
AQ	(character EBCDIC, user collating sequence)	1 – 256

Any combination of data formats can be included in a single sort statement. The sum of the lengths of the fields must be less than or equal to 4092 bytes.

The fourth subparameter determines the order. Three possible values can be coded. A identifies an ascending key, D is descending, and E means that the key will first be modified and then sorted into ascending order.

In addition to the field parameter several additional operands can be coded on a SORT control statement. All SORT statement operands are keyword and can be coded in any order.

FORMAT-Data Format

This operand can be coded only when every key field in the FIELD parameter has the same data type. The data format subparameters can then be factored out of the FIELD operand. Suppose in Example 2 that the second minor key contains character data as do the other two keys. Then the SORT control statement can be written

```
SORT FIELDS=(6,2,A,15,3,D,45,5,D),FORMAT=CH
```

FILSZ=En or FILSZ=n

Here n is an estimate of the number of records to be sorted. Coding this value allows the Sort/Merge program to more efficiently sort the data set. IBM recommends that this operand always be coded. If E is omitted then n should be the exact number of records to be sorted.

SKIPREC=n

This operand causes the first n input records to be omitted from the sort operation. If it is known that the first n records are already sorted it may be more efficient to sort the remaining records and then merge the two sorted data sets together. SKIPREC can also be used to ignore one or more control records at the beginning of a data set.

EQUALS

This keyword operand specifies that records with identical keys in the input data set will be in the same relative order in the output data set. Otherwise two such records could have their order switched during the sort. When EQUALS is coded the sort is said to be stable. The sort program includes a temporary four byte field with each input record. It contains a sequence number which can be used to distinguish between records with equal keys. In addition to the extra four bytes of overhead an additional pass through the data must be made. The sum of all the keylengths used in the sort may be as large as 4088. The length and location of the key fields are not changed on the SORT control statement.

Example 4: The same records are to be sorted as in Example 2. The same three keys are to be used. However, all keys are now assumed to contain character data and all keys are to be sorted into ascending order. Records with identical key values are not to have their order switched during the sort. There are approximately 8000 records in the input data set and the first two records are to be skipped. To accomplish this the control statement becomes

```
 SORT FIELDS=(6,2,A,15,3,A,45,5,A),EQUALS,                  X
                SKIPREC=2,FORMAT=CH,FILSZ=E8000
```

Notice that, although CH can be factored from the FIELDS statement, the A subparameter value cannot. E8000 is coded because it is an approximate value.

Referencing Individual Bits as Part of a Sort Key

In all the previous examples the first two FIELDS operands identified byte values. Both the starting location and the length of a key field can also be specified as bit values. With both operands the format for doing this is X.Y. Here X is a byte value and Y is a bit value ranging from 0 to 7. When coded with the starting location Y represents a displacement. Hence 3.1 identifies the second bit in the third byte. Note that this is contradictory to the way byte values are interpreted. When coded with the length, a non zero Y value denotes the number of bits in the rightmost byte in the key field. However, X and X.0 have the same meaning. Thus to sort records using the 12 bits which begin with the rightmost hexadecimal character in byte 15 as the key field, code the following SORT control statement:

```
SORT FIELDS=(15.4,1.4,BI,A)
```

When bit values are specified for either the starting location or length operand the format operand should be binary (BI). If the key field contains character data then two FIELD statements can be specified to accomplish the same sort. This is illustrated in the next example.

Example 5: The 11 hexadecimal characters (5½ bytes) that begin at byte 20 are to be used as the key field to sort the records in a data set into ascending order. Assume that bytes 20 through 25 contain character (alphabetic) data. Hence the first four bits (the leftmost) in each byte in the key field represents a hexadecimal C, D, or E. To sort these records into ascending order either of the following statements may be coded:

```
SORT FIELDS=(20,5.4,BI,A)                    or
SORT FIELDS=(20,5,CH,A,25,0.4,BI,A)
```

To determine which of the above statements is the most efficient sort a very large data set with both approaches and examine computer utilization statistics.

Alternate Collating Sequences

By default the Sort/Merge program bases all non-numeric sorting operations on the EBCDIC collating sequence. The EBCDIC representation consists of the 256 hexadecimal values 00, 01, 02, . . ., FE, FF. In terms of the standard printable characters the EBCDIC collating sequence consists of the blank (hex 40), special characters, alphabetics (A-Z as C1, . . .,C9,D1, . . .,D9,E2, . . . E9), and numerics (0-9 as F0,. . .,F9). With the Sort/Merge program it is easy to temporarily reorder this sequence in any way desired. The ALTSEQ control statement is coded to select a different collating sequence. This statement specifies how each EBCDIC hexadecimal value is to be interpreted during the sort. It does not change the value of the input data. The format for the assignment of a new collating sequence is as follows:

```
ALTSEQ   CODE=(xxyy,xxyy,xxyy,...)
```

Here xx is the regular hexadecimal representation in EBCDIC and yy is the EBCDIC representation into which xx is to be translated for the duration of the sort operation. For example, to modify the position of the blank character (hex 40) so that it collates after the alphabetic characters but before the numeric characters code:

```
ALTSEQ   CODE=(40EA)
```

Since Z is represented in hexadecimal as E9 and the first numeric is F0, blank now comes directly after the letters in the altered collating sequence. The ALTSEQ statement must be coded after a SORT FIELDS (or MERGE FIELDS) control statement. The type of change made by an ALTSEQ statement can also be performed in a COBOL program using the COLLATING SEQUENCE IS alphabet-name clause in the SORT verb or OBJECT-COMPUTER portion of the program.

Example 6: Create a new collating sequence to sort the records in a data set. All consonants should precede all vowels. Hence during the sort the alphabet becomes BCDFG . . . XYZAEIOU. Further, assume that the first twelve bytes in each record are to be used as the key. The records are to be sorted into ascending order. All of this can be accomplished by coding

```
SORT FIELDS=(1,12,AQ,A)
ALTSEQ CODE=(C1EA,C5EB,C9EC,D6ED,E4EE)
```

The new values, EA through EE, are all non-printable characters. Note that the accompanying SORT statement must specify a format of AQ. Otherwise the ALTSEQ statement will be ignored but no warning messages will be issued by the DFSORT program. Instead the key field will be collated as standard character data.

Only one ALTSEQ statement may be coded during a sort operation. It is used with all key fields coded on the SORT statement where AQ is the format. Modifying the collating sequence is often a convenient tool for simplifying many programming situations. An installation may define a default alternate collating sequence which is in effect when AQ is coded without an ALTSEQ control statement. If ALTSEQ is coded it overrides the default alternate sequence.

Modifying Sort Input and Output

To this point, unless SKIPREC was coded the sorting operations have involved ordering all the records in the input data set. Additionally, the format of an output record has remained the same as its input format (the sort orders all the records but does not change their content). However, it is possible to selectively reject some input records other than the first ones in the data set. They will not appear in the sorted output data set. Also, the content of the records can be changed during the sort operation.

Until recently such processing was commonly done by invoking the SORT in a COBOL or PL/I program. In COBOL, INPUT and OUTPUT PROCEDURES are used for this purpose. In PL/I, PLISORTx is used where x = B, C, or D. The latest version of DFSORT can perform much of this processing itself. It is rarely necessary to write an application program for such processing. There are five control statements involved in modifying sort input. They are MODS, INCLUDE, OMIT, INREC, and OUTREC. MODS is the most flexible but the most difficult to use. INCLUDE and OMIT perform the same function. Likewise, INREC and OUTREC both perform a second function.

MODS is used to transfer control to user-written modules. This is ordinarily done at either the E15 or E35 exit. These are the names for the sort exits used for input and output processing. E15 and E35 are written in the message data set to identify where input and output processing is taking place. The actual sorting occurs following E15 and before E35 processing. The format of the control statement is

```
MODS exit=(member name,bytes of storage used,DDname,exit-code)
     code
```

Although any number of exit operands can be coded, two is ordinarily the maximum. Usually either E15 or E35 or both are specified in the MODS statement. The member name identifies a load module. The library that contains the module is coded on the DD statement identified by DDname. Hence module identification is similar to using an INCLUDE statement with the Linkage Editor. The exit-code must be specified as either C or N. C means that the module is written in COBOL, while N specifies that it is not a COBOL program.

Example 7: Suppose two modules have been written in COBOL to perform processing at the E15 and E35 exits. They are called INPUTX and OUTPUTY respectively. Both are members of the load module library SORT.STUFF. To use these routines in a sort code the following:

```
//SYSIN   DD   *
       SORT statement
       MODS E15=(INPUTX,8500,DD1,C),E35=(OUTPUTY,9750,DD1,C)
/*
//DD1      DD   DSN=SORT.STUFF,DISP=SHR
```

The size of the load modules can be determined by examining the Linkage Editor message data set printed when the module is created.

The complete details needed to create the modules identified on the MOD control statements are covered in the DFSORT manual.

The INCLUDE and OMIT control statements are mutually exclusive; only one of them may be coded during a sort operation. Both statements are used to determine which records will be output from the sort. Both have the following format:

```
INCLUDE or OMIT COND=(test1,AND or OR,test2,AND or OR,test3...)
```

The symbols & and | can be used in place of AND and OR respectively. Each test has the specific format shown in Figure 23–1.

FIGURE 23–1
INCLUDE or OMIT Test Subparameters

```
(location1,length1,format1,OPERATOR,location2,length2,format2) or
 └──────── Field 1 ────────┘         └──────── Field 2 ────────┘

(location1,length1,format1,OPERATOR,constant value)
 └──────── Field 1 ────────┘         └─ Field 2 ─┘
```

The possible OPERATOR values are EQ, NE, GT, LT, GE, and LE. These have the same meanings as when used with the JCL COND parameter. Field 1 must be located in the input records. Field 2 must be located within the input records or be a constant value. In the first format two data fields in the record are compared. With a constant value the triple is replaced by a single operand. The standard Boolean logic is used to evaluate the results.

Example 8: The records in a data set are to be passed to the sort program only if they satisfy one of two conditions: the value coded in the first three bytes of the record must either match the value coded in bytes 10 through 12 or be a value larger than 100. This is coded as follows:

```
INCLUDE   COND=(1,3,ZD,EQ,10,3,ZD,OR,1,3,ZD,GT,100)
```

Example 9: Any record that contains a vowel in byte 5 is not to appear in the output from the sort. These records can be rejected by coding

```
OMIT   COND=(5,1,CH,EQ,'A',OR,5,1,CH,EQ,'E',OR,                    X
             5,1,CH,EQ,'I',OR,5,1,CH,EQ,'O',OR,                    X
             5,1,CH,EQ,'U')
```

or

```
OMIT   COND=(5,1,EQ,'A',OR,5,1,EQ,'E',OR,5,1,EQ,'I',OR,            X
            5,1,EQ,'O',OR,5,1,EQ,'U'),FORMAT=CH
```

The third technique used to modify the record's input to a sort involves physically changing the record's contents. The INREC and OUTREC statements are used to do this. In format and purpose they are similar to the RECORD FIELD statements that are used with IEBGENER. The permissible operations are to change the location of fields within the records, delete fields, and pad fields with blanks or binary zeroes. The format of both statements consists of two to four subparameters for each field placed in the output records. This is coded as follows:

```
INREC or OUTREC   FIELDS=(x1,a1,b1,y1,x2,a2,b2,y2),...
```

The a and b fields are required. The a value identifies the first byte of a field in the input records. The b value identifies the length of the field which begins with byte a. The input field described by the a and b values is moved to the output record. It is aligned following any other fields that have previously been moved. Additionally, an x field may be coded as H, F, or D. This specifies that the field is to be aligned on a halfword, fullword, or doubleword boundary. Any unused space in the record is initialized to binary zeroes. The y means that a constant field should be inserted into the output record in front of the field. Here y must be coded as nX or nZ where n is the number of bytes of either blanks (X) or binary zeroes (B).

Example 10: 50 byte records are input to the sort program. Preliminary to sorting, the contents of the first half and last half of each record are to be switched.

Additionally, ten bytes of spaces are to be used to separate the two parts of the record. This is done by coding

```
INREC   FIELDS=(26,25,1,25,10X)
```

When either INCLUDE or OMIT is to be used it is coded before INREC.

Example 11: The records in the data set used in Example 2 are to be both selected for sorting and modified preliminary to the sort. The complete set of control statements to do this is the following:

```
//SYSIN    DD *
   INCLUDE COND=(6,2,CH,NE,'AL',AND,6,2,CH,NE,'HA')
   INREC FIELDS=(6,2,15,3,45,5)
   SORT FIELDS=(1,2,CH,A,3,3,CH,D,6,5,PD,D)
/*
//SORTOUT DD DSN=NEW.EMPLOYEE.SORTED,DISP=(,CATLG)
//           SPACE=(CYL,(10,2)),UNIT=SYSDA,
//           DCB=(LRECL=10,BLKSIZE=1000,RECFM=FB)
```

All data fields in the records are to be deleted except for the three key fields themselves. In addition, all records for people living in Alaska or Hawaii are to be ignored preliminary to the sort. Finally, the DCB parameter must be coded with SORTOUT or default values will be assigned using the dcb from the input records.

Merging

The Sort/Merge program allows up to 32 sorted data sets to be used as input in a merge operation. A single output data set is created. The syntax of the MERGE control statement is identical to the SORT statement. Hence it is coded as

```
MERGE FIELDS=(a,b,c,d,...,a,b,c,d),other options    or
MERGE FIELDS=(a,b,d,...,a,b,d),FORMAT=c,other options
```

The a,b,c, and d fields are identical to those coded on the SORT statement. As with the SORT, the format subparameters can be factored out of the FIELDS statement. Several options available with the SORT statement cannot be used with MERGE. These include EQUALS, SKIPREC, and DYNALLOC. For a merge the FILSZ operand refers to the total number of records in all the input data sets. The SORTIN DDname is replaced by a group of DDnames of the form SORTINxx where xx denotes a value from 01 to 32. Work data sets are not needed for a MERGE operation.

Example 12: It is necessary to merge three sorted input data sets, all of whose records have the same format as in Example 2. The input data sets have names ALPHA, BETA, and GAMMA.

```
//A   EXEC   DFSORT
//SORTIN01   DD   DSN=ALPHA,DISP=SHR
//SORTIN02   DD   DSN=BETA,DISP=SHR
//SORTIN03   DD   DSN=GAMMA,DISP=SHR
//SORTOUT    DD   DSN=OUTPUT.DATASET,DISP=(NEW,CATLG),UNIT=3380,
//                SPACE=(CYL,(10,5))
//SYSIN      DD   *
       MERGE FIELDS=(6,2,CH,A,15,3,CH,D,45,5,PD,D)
/*
```

Variable Length Records

DFSORT can be used to process data sets that contain variable length records. Such data sets may be non-VSAM or VSAM KSDS or ESDS. One significant change occurs when sorting or merging variable length records. The four bytes of overhead which precede each logical record must be considered during the sort operation. For non-VSAM records these four bytes hold the Record Descriptor Word field (RDW). With VSAM data sets a temporary four byte RDW is constructed for each logical record. The information placed in this RDW is taken from the RDF control field associated with the record.

Sorting With a COBOL Application Program

To perform a sort operation with a COBOL program an SD must be defined and the SORT verb coded. To perform processing equivalent to that done with the Sort/Merge utility in Example 2 the following should be coded:

```
SELECT SORT-SD
     ASSIGN TO UT-S-SORTWK.
SELECT INPUT-MASTER
     ASSIGN TO UT-S-SORTIN.
SELECT OUTPUT-SORTED-MASTER
     ASSIGN TO UT-S-SORTOUT.
...
SD  SORT-SD.
...
    05 FILLER        PIC X(5).
    05 STATE-KEY     PIC X(2).
    05 FILLER        PIC X(7).
    05 AGE-KEY       PIC 9(3).
    05 FILLER        PIC X(27).
    05 SALARY-KEY    PIC S9(9) COMP-3.
    05 FILLER        PIC X(11).
PROCEDURE DIVISION.
```

```
MOVE 'SORTMSG' TO SORT-MESSAGE.
SORT SORT-SD
    ASCENDING KEY IS STATE-KEY
    DESCENDING KEY IS AGE-KEY
    DESCENDING KEY IS SALARY-KEY
    USING INPUT-MASTER
    GIVING OUTPUT-SORTED-MASTER
```

The accompanying JCL contains the following DD statements which are necessary for this sort operation:

```
//SORTMSG   DD   SYSOUT=A
//SORTIN    DD   DSN=EMPLOYEE.MASTER,DISP=SHR
//SORTOUT   DD   DSN=NEW.EMPLOYEE.SORTED,DISP=(NEW,...
//SORTWK01 DD   UNIT=SYSDA,SPACE=(CYL,5)
//SORTWK02 DD   UNIT=SYSDA,SPACE=(CYL,5)
//SORTWK03 DD   UNIT=SYSDA,SPACE=(CYL,5)
```

Exercises

For each of the first twelve exercises, assume that there is a cataloged data set with DSN = SORTINPT which contains four fields defined as follows:

Starting Location	*Length*	*Data Type*	*Field Description*
1	9	Numeric Character	Social Security number
10	14	Alphabetic Character	Last Name
24	2	Signed Packed Decimal	Number of Fields following
26	55	Zoned Decimal	(0 to 11 five byte fields)

The four fields are identified as fields one to four in the exercises. There are approximately 10,000 records in the data set.

1. Sort these records using Number of Fields as the major key, Last Name as the first minor key, and Social Security number as the second minor key. Use ascending order except with the major key. A stable sort should be performed.

2. Use DFSORT to print all of the records in SORTINPT such that records with even Social Security numbers are listed first. There is no additional ordering among the records. How can the even/odd order be reversed so that the records with odd Social Security numbers are listed first? Suppose that standard numeric ascending order is required within the even/odd categories. How must the control statements be altered?

3. Modify the previous exercise by grouping records into three categories and printing them. The particular category is determined by the remainder when the last digit of the Social Security number is divided by three. The possible remainders are 0, 1, and 2. List all records associated with a remainder of 2 first, and all those with a remainder of 0 last.

4. Sort the records in the SORTINPT data set into ascending order. Use the absolute value of the number in Number of Fields as the key. Assume Number of Fields contains negative values and zeroes in some records.

5. Sort the records in the SORTINPT data set into ascending order using Last Name as the key field. All characters in the collating sequence should retain their position except for letters of the alphabet (their collating order should be reversed). Hence interchange A with Z, B with Y, etc.

6. During the next sort operation make two changes in the collating sequence. All Social Security numbers that begin with a 3 should collate first. The rest retain their usual order: 0, 1, 2, 4, . . . 9. Bytes 2 through 9 collate in their regular order. Additionally, for the packed decimal field 0, 5, and 8 should collate first, followed by the remaining digits in their usual order. Sort the records using Social Security number as the major key and Number of Fields as the minor key.

7. Which types of non-sequential non-VSAM data sets can be sorted with the Sort/Merge utility? Which types of VSAM data sets can be sorted with the Sort/Merge utility?

8. Some of the data in the alphabetic character field are in lower case, the rest are in upper case. However, both should be interpreted as the same value for the sort (i.e., 'a' and 'A' should both mean the same thing). Successfully sort the records in the data set even though this problem exists.

9. If the value in field three is 0 the record is to be omitted from the sort. If it is a negative number it is to be omitted unless it has a single significant digit (i.e., −1 to −9). When all of these records are rejected sort the data set in ascending order using the third field as the key.

10. Run a three-step sort system to order the records into ascending order based on the value in the third key field. In step 1 sort the non-negative records into ascending order and place them into a temporary data set. Do the same thing with the absolute value of the negative numbers. In the third step merge the two temporary data sets together.

11. Suppose a sort is to be performed using the same key fields and ordering as in Exercise 1. However, assume that the records in SORTINPT are variable length. Assume that the value in Number of Fields specifies the actual number of five byte fields that follow. Write the complete job step to perform this sort.

12. Suppose a sort is to be performed using the same key fields and ordering as in Exercise 1. The only difference is that SORTINPT is a VSAM KSDS. Write the complete jobstep to perform this Sort.

13. Comment on similarities and differences between the Linkage Editor INCLUDE and LIBRARY control statements and the Sort/Merge MODS control statement. Consider both syntax and purpose.

14. Verify that the COBOL code at the end of the chapter used to perform a Sort operation and the Sort/Merge program in Example 2 are equivalent. Do any minor differences exist between them?

PART III

Utilities

Chapter 24

The IBM Utilities

Overview

IBM supplies a collection of approximately fifteen programs that perform a wide range of common programming functions. Collectively these programs are known as the IEB/IEH utilities. Over half of these utilities are exceedingly useful and are heavily used by application and system programmers. This set of utilities is thoroughly studied in this and the next seven chapters. The remaining utilities are used infrequently and will be mentioned only briefly.

There are several reasons for studying this collection of utility programs.

1) They serve as an example of the types of utilities that are available with all computer systems. A DEC, Apple, or IBM PC computer will have its own set of utilities although their scope may not be the same as the IEB/IEH utilities. There is no reason to write an application program to perform the function of a utility. Hence it is important to know what utilities are available on a computer system and what functions they can perform.

2) This particular group of utilities is the most heavily used in the world because of its association with IBM 360, 370, and 30xx computers. Anyone using these computers should take the time to become familiar with these utilities. More on how these utilities can be used to a programmers' advantage is discussed with the individual utilities.

3) A primary goal of this book is to help develop proficiency with JCL. The only way this can be achieved is by writing a great deal of JCL. The easiest way to

do this is by writing multi-step jobs using utilities. Such job streams are of manageable size compared to the job streams that consist of application programs. To do the exercises included in Part III of this book requires a strong background in MVS JCL. This is why Part I is a prerequisite for this section of the book.

4) Studying and using the IEB/IEH utilities strengthens one's knowledge of MVS system concepts. These concepts include data set organizations, record formats, and disk and tape data sets. This is why Part II is a prerequisite for this section of the book.

The fifteen IEB/IEH utilities can be divided into two categories: data set utilities and system utilities. In general the utilities in each group perform different types of functions. However, the two categories have some overlapping functions. The system utility IEHMOVE can be used to copy a data set from one volume to another. This is a task ordinarily associated with a data set utility. The data set utility IEBPTPCH can be used to perform the system utility function of printing the directory of a partitioned data set (pds).

All of the utilities were developed several years prior to IBM's introduction of VSAM. None of them are meant to be used with VSAM data sets. If a utility function is required for a VSAM data set the IDCAMS utility should be used.

The following guidelines are recommended for selecting the appropriate type of utility. Use the non-VSAM utilities only with non-VSAM data sets. Use the IDCAMS utility with VSAM data sets. Avoid using non-VSAM utilities with VSAM data sets. The IEB/IEH utilities usually will not work with VSAM data sets. Some IDCAMS functions will work with non-VSAM data sets. The number of such functions will continue to grow during the next few years. The *Access Methods Service Manual* identifies the functions that IDCAMS can perform with VSAM and non-VSAM data sets.

The guidelines for selecting a utility are summarized in Table 24–1.

The Data Set Utilities

The basic function of the data set utilities is to manipulate the records in data sets. They can be used to copy entire data sets, copy portions of a data set, edit the records in a data set, update selected records in a data set, process individual pds members

TABLE 24–1
Selecting the Correct Type of Utility

Utility Type	*VSAM Data Sets*	*Non-VSAM Data Sets*
IDCAMS	always correct	can occasionally be used (for details consult manual; usage will become more widespread)
IEB and IEH utilities	should not be used	always correct

or an entire pds, create test data, compare data sets, and perform many other functions. The IBM manual *OS/VS2 MVS Utilities* classifies nine utilities as data set utilities. Seven of these will be discussed in this and the next five chapters: IEBCOMPR, IEBCOPY, IEBDG, IEBGENER, IEBISAM, IEBPTPCH, and IEBUPDTE. The others, IEBEDIT and IEBTCRIN, are almost never used by an application programmer.

Brief descriptions of the primary functions performed by the seven data set utilities discussed in this book are listed below.

Utility	*Primary Function*
IEBCOMPR	Determine if two sequential or two partitioned data sets are identical
IEBCOPY	Maintain partitioned data set libraries
IEBDG	Generate test data
IEBGENER	Copy and edit sequential data sets
IEBISAM	Copy or print ISAM data sets
IEBPTPCH	Print or punch the records in a sequential data set
IEBUPDTE	Modify partitioned and sequential data sets

The System Utilities

The system utilities also perform a wide range of functions. These functions include manipulating and displaying three fundamental components of the system: catalogs, partitioned data set directories, and disk volume tables of contents (VTOCs). Other functions performed by the system utilities include initialization of disk and tape volumes, moving or copying groups of data sets that all begin with the same data set name qualifiers, and dumping disk fields to the printer. There are six system utilities discussed in the *MVS Utilities* manual. Five of these are discussed in Chapters 30 and 31 in this book: IEHDASDR, IEHINITT, IEHLIST, IEHMOVE, and IEHPROGM. The sixth, IEHATLAS, is almost never used by an application programmer.

Brief descriptions of the primary functions performed by the five system utilities discussed in this book are listed below.

Utility	*Primary Function*
IEHDASDR	Initialize, analyze, and dump disk volumes
IEHINITT	Initialize Standard Label tape volumes
IEHLIST	Print the contents of VTOCs, pds directories, and catalogs
IEHMOVE	Move and copy sequential and partitioned data sets
IEHPROGM	Modify the contents of VTOCs, pds directories, and catalogs

General Utility Information

The degree to which each of the twelve utilities is examined in this book varies considerably. Some such as IEBGENER and IEHLIST are discussed in almost as much detail as in the *MVS Utilities* manual. Hopefully the presentation in this book is clearer than that in the manual. Some of the less frequently used utilities, such as IEBCOMPR and IEHDASDR, are briefly studied. The author's likes and dislikes influence the amount of coverage given to each utility. In particular IEHMOVE is somewhat deemphasized in this book in favor of IEBCOPY and IEBGENER, because these two utilities require a wider range of JCL.

All data set and system utilities are stored in the system load module library, which is called SYS1.LINKLIB. The member name under which the utility is stored in the library directory lists the category into which it falls. All data set utilities begin with the letters IEB, while all system utilities start with IEH.

Every utility follows the general format shown below.

```
//stepname    EXEC  PGM=utility-name
//SYSPRINT     DD   SYSOUT=A
//DDname1      DD     ---
//DDname2      DD     these additional DD statements
//DDname3      DD     are used to identify data sets
   .                  or volumes that will be used
   .                  during the utility job step
   .
//DDnameN      DD     ---
//SYSIN        DD   * (or DATA, DUMMY,
                        DSN=sequential data set or
                        DSN=pds(member))

control statements which are directions to the util-
ity (and possibly user data) are included with SYSIN

/*
```

The two DD statements SYSPRINT and SYSIN are required with almost every utility. The utility-name is coded as either IEBxxxxx or IEHxxxxx depending on the category to which the utility belongs. With some of the utilities a PARM value may be coded on the EXEC statement.

The SYSPRINT DD statement identifies a message data set that should be coded with every utility. Ordinarily the message data set is sent to a printer where a report with 121 bytes per line is produced. This report lists the control statements along with diagnostic and error messages. The message data set may be sent to other output devices or dummied out. If blocking is used the blocksize should be a multiple of 121. The usefulness of the message data set varies considerably among the utilities. For example, IEBUPDTE and IEBCOPY supply clear, user-friendly messages. IEBGENER messages are often quite difficult to understand. IEHLIST control statements do not print in the message data set.

Although the SYSIN DD statement is required with almost every utility, it may be dummied out with some of them. All control statement data sets must be sequentially organized.

The order of the DD statements associated with any of the utilities is completely arbitrary. Traditionally SYSPRINT is placed after the EXEC statement and SYSIN is listed last. If a utility is made part of a cataloged procedure the SYSIN statement is usually supplied when the procedure is invoked.

Other than the SYSPRINT, and SYSIN statements, it is difficult to make generalities regarding utility DD statements. Every utility has its own quirks. The people who designed and developed the utilities did not enforce any true consistency among the utilities. Had this been done it would be much easier to use the utilities. After studying the material in Chapters 24 through 31 it may be helpful to make a list of the most prominent inconsistencies found within the group of utilities.

Some utilities require specific additional DD statements, while others require none. Consider a DD statement with the DDname SYSUT1. Approximately two-thirds of the utilities require this DD statement. With one utility SYSUT1 denotes a work data set. With most it identifies the input data set. With the remaining utilities SYSUT1 has no specific meaning. The DDnames SYSUT1, SYSUT2, SYSUT3, and SYSUT4 all have specific roles with some utilities and should not be chosen as arbitrary utility DDnames. The majority of the IEB utilities permit concatenation of the input data sets.

The parameters found on a DD statement associated with a utility are no different from those used elsewhere in JCL. The standard syntax and logic of JCL are followed throughout. There is, however, one major difference between the parameters coded with a system utility and those used with a data set utility. A system utility DD statement references an entire volume, while a data set utility DD statement references an individual data set or data sets. Different parameters are coded in each situation.

With most of the IEH utilities temporary data sets cannot be used unless the complete data set name as generated by the system is coded.

SYSIN Control Statements

The DDname SYSIN identifies a sequentially organized data set containing 80 byte records called control statements. Control statements specify the functions being performed by the utility in a given step and are necessary because of the wide variety of functions some utilities perform. Some control statements contain special processing options while others reference additional DD statements in the JCL; still others invoke rarely used exotic options.

The utility control statements are not JCL statements. Their format is similar to IBM assembly language. A control statement may contain four fields, but only the operator is always required. The label and comments are (with a single exception) optional. Control statements have the following format:

```
label     operator     keyword-operands     comments
```

The label serves no purpose except for documentation, and is rarely included. However, it is required with one utility, IEHINITT. When present the label should begin in column 1 and consist of one to eight alphanumeric characters. The operator identifies the type of control statement used. Two very important utilities (IEBGENER and IEBPTPCH) allow their most important operator to be coded only once during a job step. The number of operands present depends on the function being performed. All operands are keyword (their format is: operand1 = value1, operand2 = value2,etc.) and are separated by commas. Commas are used to separate the keyword parameters and spaces are used to separate the statement fields. When an operand is assigned an expression that contains multiple values, the values must be enclosed in parentheses. For example, operand1 = (value1,value2,value3).

The expression keyword = device = list occurs with some IEH utility control statements. The keyword should be VOL, FROM, or TO. Device is a device type coded on the UNIT parameter, such as SYSDA, TAPE, 3350, or 3380. VOL = SER = volser is a JCL parameter, not a control statement operand.

Continuing a Control Statement

To continue a control statement over more than one line place any non-blank character in column 72 on the statement being continued and start the continuation in column 16 of the next statement. The statement being continued can be interrupted either in column 71 or after any keyword operand and its following comma. The error messages that result when continuation is done incorrectly are often misleading and difficult to understand. For this reason it is a good defensive programming practice to try to avoid continuation altogether. Some of the utilities (IEBGENER, IEBPTPCH) do not have as many continuation restrictions. They do not require the continuation character in column 72, and the continued statement may begin anywhere between column 4 and column 16. With most of the IEH utilities, including IEHLIST and IEHPROGM, both of which often require continuation the complete set of continuation rules must be followed. In general the IEB utilities use the same basic continuation rules as JCL, while IEH utilities follow assembler language continuation rules.

Exercises

1. Describe the basic differences between data set and system utilities in terms of the functions each group performs. Describe the basic differences between the two classes of utilities and their use of JCL and control statement syntax. How does continuation differ between the two classes of utilities?

2. List the important data set utilities and the functions they perform. List the important system utilities and the functions they perform.

3. Suppose a person did not know whether a given program was classified as a data set or system utility. How can the appropriate classification be determined by examining the JCL

statements coded in the job step? Classification can be determined either by the EXEC statement or by the DD statements.

4. Identify the role and the dcb properties (LRECL, RECFM, DSORG, and BLKSIZE) associated with the DDnames SYSPRINT, SYSIN, and SYSUT1 when they are used with an IEB/IEH utility.

5. The IEBGENER utility is one of the best known IEB/IEH utilities. It contains the GENERATE operator. GENERATE must be coded exactly once, on the first control statement. Under these circumstances, why is a GENERATE operator necessary?

6. Each of the following control statements contains one or more major syntax errors. Find and correct the errors. Assume each operator begins in column 2.

```
a. GENERATE   MAXFLDS=1 MAXLITS=10 MAXGPS=1
b. LISTVTOC   DSNAME=&&TEMP,VOL=3380=DISK01,FORMAT
c. PRINT      MAXFLDS=10,,TOTCONV=XE
d. SCRATCH    DSNAME=A.B.C,VOL=SER=DISK01,PURGE
e. LABEL      GENERATE    MAXFLDS=2,MAXNAME=2, COMMENTS
f. SCRATCH    DSNAME=A.B.C,PURGE,                      X
                       VOL=SYSDA=WORK01
g. COPY       ALPHA,3380,SYSDA
h. RECORD     FIELD=(80,1,),IDENT=(5,'XXXXX',3)
```

Chapter 25

IEBGENER

Overview

The major uses of IEBGENER are:

— Copy any 'sequential like' data set, including pds members and relative data sets

— Edit the records in any 'sequential like' data set

— Create a pds and load it with one or more members in a single job step; add one or more members to an existing pds in a single job step

— Change the logical record length, blocksize, and record format of the records in a data set

— Create variable length records out of fixed length input records

— Use in-stream records to create output records of any permissible size or record format

The utility IEBGENER (or GENER) is perhaps the best known of the IBM utilities and one of the easiest to use. Its primary function is to copy a data set from one I/O device to another. For example, GENER can be used to create a backup tape copy of a sequential disk data set. It can also be used to list the records in a disk data set to the printer. These two examples typify the situations in which IEBGENER is usually invoked. A number of coding examples that illustrate the complete copy process are covered below. After this process becomes clear some of the advanced functions of IEBGENER will be considered.

Copying a Sequential Data Set

IEBGENER can be used to copy any data set with sequential organization, including a partitioned data set member or a relative data set, to an output device. The code to do this is

```
//stepname  EXEC  PGM=IEBGENER
//SYSPRINT  DD    SYSOUT=A
//SYSUT1    DD    input  data set parameters
//SYSUT2    DD    output data set parameters
//SYSIN     DD    DUMMY
```

The IEBGENER message data set does not usually provide a lot of information. If the copy operation is successful the simple statement

```
PROCESSING ENDED AT EOD
```

is printed. No other SYSPRINT output is produced. When errors occur the resulting messages are frequently difficult to decipher. Because there are no control statements in this example SYSIN has been dummied out. Control statements are unnecessary when the entire input data set is copied and no records are to be edited. Both SYSUT1 and SYSUT2 must always be coded. They identify the input and output data sets respectively. SYSUT1 can identify a collection of concatenated data sets. DCB information must be coded for SYSUT2 or the DCB values associated with SYSUT1 will be assigned to it by default. When this occurs the message

```
IEB352I WARNING: OUTPUT RECFM/LRECL/BLKSIZE COPIED FROM INPUT
PROCESSING ENDED AT EOD
```

is printed in the SYSPRINT data set. The examples below show a complete copy operation.

Example 1: A cataloged disk data set called ALPHA.ONE is to be backed-up to a nine track 6250 BPI standard tape volume. ALPHA.ONE contains card images.

```
//A          EXEC  PGM=IEBGENER
//SYSPRINT   DD    SYSOUT=A
//SYSUT1     DD    DSN=ALPHA.ONE,DISP=SHR
//SYSUT2     DD    DSN=ALPHA.BACKUP,DISP=(NEW,KEEP),
//           UNIT=TAPE,VOL=SER=ABC123,LABEL=(1,SL),
//           DCB=(LRECL=80,RECFM=FB,BLKSIZE=4000,DEN=4)
//SYSIN      DD    DUMMY
```

This job step results in a copy of the records in ALPHA.ONE being written to the first data set on tape volume ABC123. If the DCB information is not specified with SYSUT2, IEBGENER will copy the LRECL, BLKSIZE, and RECFM values from the SYSUT1 data set labels.

Example 2: Copy the records in ALPHA.ONE to the disk volume DISK22 and give the new data set the name BETA.TWO. The coding to do this is exactly the same as in Example 1 except for the SYSUT2 statement, which is changed to

```
//SYSUT2    DD  DSN=BETA.TWO,DISP=(NEW,CATLG),UNIT=3350,
//          VOL=SER=DISK22,SPACE=(CYL,1),DCB=(SYS1.PROCLIB)
```

Here the DCB information for BETA.TWO is copied from the data set label of the cataloged data set SYS1.PROCLIB.

Example 3: The records in ALPHA.ONE are to be listed to the printer. Again only the SYSUT2 statement needs to be changed from the coding given in Example 1. It should be

```
//SYSUT2      DD   SYSOUT=A,DCB=BLKSIZE=800
```

Example 4: The two data sets ALPHA.ONE and ALPHA.TWO (a permanent uncataloged disk data set on volume DISK99) are to be listed to the card punch. The SYSUT1 and SYSUT2 statements necessary to do this are

```
//SYSUT1      DD   DSN=ALPHA.ONE,DISP=SHR
//            DD   DSN=ALPHA.TWO,DISP=SHR,UNIT=3350,
//            VOL=SER=DISK99
//SYSUT2      DD   SYSOUT=B,DCB=BLKSIZE=80,OUTLIM=2000
```

Note that the two data sets that are being used to produce the punched cards have been concatenated together as the SYSUT1 data set. Both data sets are assumed to contain card images. It is always a good idea to code the OUTLIM DD parameter when using the card punch. Whenever data sets are concatenated the one with the largest blocksize must be listed first. Additionally, all of them should have the same logical record size and record format.

The four preceding examples illustrate how to use IEBGENER to copy an entire data set from one I/O device to another. In any of the examples records could have been chosen that contained other than 80 bytes. The final two examples of complete sequential copying illustrate some additional capabilities of IEBGENER.

Example 5: A member called PLIXCG of the partitioned data set SYS1.PROCLIB is to be copied to an existing cataloged pds called SYS1.BACKUP. The SYSUT1 and SYSUT2 DD statements are coded as follows:

```
//SYSUT1       DD   DSN=SYS1.PROCLIB(PLIXCG),DISP=SHR
//SYSUT2       DD   DSN=SYS1.BACKUP(PLIXCG2),DISP=OLD
```

Here member PLIXCG is copied from the input pds, given the member name PLIXCG2, and added to the output pds. An existing member named PLIXCG2 will be replaced by the new member. If the parameters on SYSUT2 are changed to SYSOUT=A the records in member PLIXCG will be printed instead.

Example 6: IEBGENER is to be made into a cataloged procedure. A cataloged procedure is created that can be used to list the contents of any sequentially organized data set to the printer. When the cataloged procedure is invoked a SYSUT1 statement that identifies the input data set must be supplied.

```
//F           EXEC   PGM=IEBGENER
//SYSPRINT    DD     SYSOUT=A
//SYSUT2      DD     DSN=SYS1.PROCLIB(GENER),DISP=OLD
//SYSUT1      DD     DATA
//GENER       EXEC   PGM=IEBGENER     *
//SYSPRINT    DD     SYSOUT=A         *
//SYSUT2      DD     SYSOUT=A         *
//SYSIN       DD     DUMMY            *
/*
//SYSIN       DD     DUMMY
```

Note that the four statements followed by asterisks are an in-stream data set that will be placed in the system procedure library SYS1.PROCLIB and given the member name GENER. To use this cataloged procedure to list the records in the data set ALPHA.ONE code the following two statements:

```
//A           EXEC   GENER
//SYSUT1      DD     DSN=ALPHA.ONE,DISP=SHR
```

The complete JCL stream that results is:

```
//A           EXEC   GENER
XXGENER       EXEC   PGM=IEBGENER     *
XXSYSPRINT    DD     SYSOUT=A         *
XXSYSUT2      DD     SYSOUT=A         *
XXSYSIN       DD     DUMMY            *
//SYSUT1      DD     DSN=ALPHA.ONE,DISP=SHR
```

For more information on procedures see Chapter 8.

Using IEBGENER Control Statements

Control statements must be used when editing data, processing only some of the records in the SYSUT1 data set, or adding multiple members to a pds in one job step. Several rarely used functions that also involve control statements will be mentioned only in the exercises. These include standard user data set labels and user-written exit routines.

The first control statement in an IEBGENER job step always has the following format:

```
GENERATE    MAXFLDS=w,MAXLITS=x,MAXNAME=y,MAXGPS=z
```

All of the keywords are optional.

The operator GENERATE identifies this statement as the first control statement associated with IEBGENER. Exactly one GENERATE statement should be coded and it must precede all other control statements. The four keyword operands can be specified in any order and only those required for the specific application need be coded. The values assigned to the four keyword parameters are selected as follows:

MAXFLDS the number of FIELD operands coded on subsequent RECORD control statements

MAXLITS the number of literal characters appearing within FIELD operands on subsequent RECORD control statements

MAXNAME the number of pds member names and aliases that occur on subsequent MEMBER control statements

MAXGPS the number of IDENT operands appearing on subsequent RECORD control statements

For all four of these keywords a value greater than that actually required will also work. However, coding a value too small will generate an error message. For this reason the values for w, x, y, and z are often determined after the subsequent MEMBER and RECORD statements have been coded. The error message

```
IEB342I INVALID SPACE ALLOCATION
```

seems misleading and suggests a lack of disk storage. However, internal tables are set up with the size that is specified on the GENERATE statement. The error message occurs on the control statement that causes one of these four totals to be exceeded. When this size is exceeded in a particular control statement IEBGENER is out of space internally. GENERATE is not needed unless one or both of the MEMBER and RECORD statements are coded.

The MEMBER Control Statement

This statement is used to create partitioned data set members. Its format is

```
MEMBER  NAME=(pds member name,alias1,alias2,...)
```

Here pds member name is the entry that is stored in the directory for this member. Aliases (which are optional) are also stored in the directory for this member when coded on this statement. Parentheses are not necessary if alias values are not coded. The MEMBER statement is unnecessary when adding just one member to a pds in a given job step. In this case the member can be identified on the SYSUT2 DD statement.

The RECORD Control Statement

This statement is used to edit data sets. Its format is

```
RECORD FIELD=(a1,b1,c1,d1),FIELD=(a2,b2,c2,d2),. . .
       IDENT=(x,'y',z),FIELD=(an,bn,cn,dn), . . .
```

The RECORD statement can optionally contain one IDENT operand and any number (including 0) of FIELD operands. The IDENT operand and the FIELD operands can be coded in any order. However, the values within both types of operands are positional subparameters and must be coded in the order defined below. If a value is omitted a comma must be coded to denote its position. As with JCL, if one or more final trailing subparameters are omitted it is unnecessary to code commas for them. The values of the four FIELD subparameters are as follows:

ai The number of characters being moved or inserted into the output records is specified first.

bi This subparameter has two possible meanings. If an integer is coded it denotes the starting location in the input records where the ai characters begin. If a literal within quotes is coded it means that those characters will be inserted into the output records.

ci This means that data conversion is to be performed. Either PZ or ZP can be coded. They specify converting data from packed decimal to zoned decimal and from zoned decimal to packed decimal respectively. The default is that no conversions are performed.

di This number identifies the starting location in the output records where the ai characters are to be moved.

The examples below clarify these definitions.

```
FIELD=(10,1,,30)      (MAXFLDS must also be coded)
```

Ten bytes of data from the SYSUT1 data set records will be moved. These ten bytes begin with byte 1 and include bytes 2 through 10. They will be made part of the output data set records occupying bytes 30 through 39. Note that no data conversion is necessary and the third subparameter is omitted.

```
FIELD=(5,'*****',,76)     (MAXFLDS and MAXLITS
                          must also be coded)
```

Here five asterisks will be inserted into the output records. They will occupy bytes 76 to 80.

IEBGENER can be used to create packed decimal output from character input. Suppose that FIELD=(4,'1234',ZP) is coded on a control statement. Then three bytes will be inserted into the output records. They will occupy the first three bytes of each output record and will contain the packed decimal value 01 23 4F. Since the fourth subparameter was omitted the default value of 1 is used. Likewise, 1 is the default for the second positional subparameter. Hence FIELD=(100) gives the same results as FIELD=(100,1,,1). The default value for the first subparameter is 80.

The IDENT operand is used to determine when the end of a collection of logical records has been reached. It tests every SYSUT1 record looking for a matching pattern. The record that contains this pattern will be the last record in the data set to be processed by this RECORD statement. Additional SYSUT1 records will be processed differently or not at all. The values x, y, and z have the following meanings:

x the number of characters in the search pattern. x must be less than 9.

y the specific characters that comprise the search pattern. The y value must be enclosed in apostrophes.

z the leftmost byte location in the SYSUT1 records of the x bytes that make up the field to be examined.

For example, if IDENT=(5,'COBOL',20) is coded then each record in the input data set will be checked to see if 'COBOL' occurs in bytes 20 to 24. If and when such a record is found it becomes the last record created with the FIELD specifications given on that control statement. When adding multiple members to a pds in one job step the IDENT statement can be used to determine the last record placed in a pds member. The next three examples illustrate all the GENERATE, MEMBER, and RECORD control statements.

Example 7: The input data set consists of card images. In one job step the 80 byte records are used to create three members in a pds. All input records beginning with the first and continuing until a record with '$$$' in bytes 78 to 80 will become member ALPHA. The records following the '$$$' record, up to and including a record with '****' in bytes 5 to 8, will become member BETA. The remaining input records will become member GAMMA.

```
//G           EXEC  PGM=IEBGENER
//SYSPRINT    DD    SYSOUT=A
//SYSUT1      DD    *
. . .         input card images
. . .
. . .   $$$
    ****
. . .
. . .
/*
```

```
//SYSUT2     DD DSN=NEWPDS,
//           DISP=(NEW,CATLG),UNIT=3350,
//           VOL=SER=DISK25,SPACE=(CYL,(1,,36)),
//           DCB=(LRECL=80,BLKSIZE=6160,RECFM=FB)
//SYSIN      DD    *
    GENERATE  MAXNAME=4,MAXGPS=3
    MEMBER   NAME=ALPHA
    RECORD   IDENT=(3,'$$$',78)
    MEMBER   NAME=(BETA,B2)
    RECORD   IDENT=(4,'****',5)
    MEMBER   NAME=GAMMA
/*
```

Note that, in addition to everything specified above, B2 has been made an alias for BETA, requiring MAXNAME=4. The MAXGPS value is one larger than actually required. Since there are no FIELD operands on the RECORD control statements, a complete copy is performed with each member. If the pattern '$$$' does not occur in the final three bytes of any of the input records only one pds member, ALPHA, will be created and the rest of the control statements will be ignored.

Example 8: The disk data set ALPHA.THREE contains 100 byte records. These records will be used to create the data set ALPHA.EDIT.

```
//H          EXEC   PGM=IEBGENER
//SYSPRINT   DD     SYSOUT=A
//SYSUT1     DD     DSN=ALPHA.THREE,DISP=SHR
//SYSUT2     DD     DSN=ALPHA.EDIT,DISP=(NEW,CATLG),
//           UNIT=SYSDA,SPACE=(TRK,5),DCB=(LRECL=110,
//           BLKSIZE=1100,RECFM=FB)
//SYSIN      DD     *
    GENERATE  MAXFLDS=6,MAXLITS=15
    RECORD   FIELD=(40,1,,41),FIELD=(9,41,ZP,81),
             FIELD=(5,'*****',,86),FIELD=(40,60,,1),
             FIELD=(10,50,,91),
             FIELD=(10,'ABCDEFGHIJ',,101)
/*
```

Here the 110 byte SYSUT2 record is constructed using four fields from the input record (one of which is first converted) and two literal fields. Note that bytes 60 to 99 in the input record become bytes 1 to 40 in the output record. Input bytes 1 to 40 move to locations 41 to 80. The nine byte zoned decimal number occupies five bytes when packed. Finally, bytes 50 to 59 move to locations 91 to 100. The two literals supply values for the remaining 15 bytes.

This example shows how IEBGENER can be used to change the logical record length of a data set. Note that some data from the original records does not appear in the output records. Other fields have been moved to different locations within the output record. New fields can be introduced by defining them in FIELD statements.

Suppose that the GENERATE statement had contained MAXFLDS=4. In this case IEBGENER would stop processing when it encountered the fifth FIELD operand.

To change this code so the output records would be made into a member in a pds, change the SPACE parameter on the SYSUT2 statement to SPACE=(TRK,(5,,1)), insert an additional control statement after the GENERATE statement, and modify the GENERATE statement. The first two control statements should be coded as follows:

```
GENERATE   MAXFLDS=6,MAXLITS=15,MAXNAME=1
MEMBER   NAME=ALPHAMEM
```

Example 9: It is possible to use all the control statements together in one job step. Here an in-stream data set will be used to create a multiple member pds. Before each member is created its records will be edited, and each member will have its records edited differently. Additionally, both types of data conversion will be included.

Suppose that three members are to be placed into an output library. All records from the beginning of the SYSUT1 data set through the record that contains 'ABCDE' in bytes 10 through 14 are to become member MEM1. The following records up to the one with 'MNOPQ' in bytes 10 through 14 are to be MEM2. The remaining records are to be MEM3.

```
//I          EXEC  PGM=IEBGENER
//SYSPRINT   DD    SYSOUT=A
//SYSUT1     DD    *
   input card images
/*
//SYSUT2     DD    DSN=EDIT.PDS,DISP=(NEW,CATLG),
//           UNIT=3350,VOL=SER=ABC234,DCB=(LRECL=80,
//           RECFM=FB,BLKSIZE=1600),SPACE=(CYL,(1,,36))
//SYSIN      DD    *
   GENERATE   MAXFLDS=10,MAXNAME=4,MAXLITS=50,MAXGPS=2
   MEMBER     NAME=(MEM1,NEBULAR)
   RECORD     IDENT=(5,'ABCDE',10),
              FIELD=(30,1,,51),
              FIELD=(30,51,,1),
              FIELD=(20,'********************',,31),
              FIELD=(5,'HELLO',,39)
   MEMBER     NAME=MEM2
   RECORD     FIELD=(5,10,PZ,6),
              FIELD=(9,1,,51),
              FIELD=(9,1,ZP,1),
              IDENT=(5,'MNOPQ',51),
              FIELD=(9,15,ZP,15),
              FIELD(25,'$$$$$$$$$$$$$$$$$$$$$$$$$',,20),
   MEMBER     NAME=(MEM3)
   RECORD     FIELD=(70,1,,11)
/*
```

To determine exactly what results from this job step run the above code. Be careful to include the character strings 'ABCDE' and 'MNOPQ' in the appropriate locations in the SYSUT1 data set. Try to place packed and zoned numbers in the input fields that specify them. Recall that some printable characters have EBCDIC representations that are valid packed decimal numbers. After running the job use IEBPTPCH or IDCAMS to display the three output members in hexadecimal. Try to account for every byte value found in the three members. Some of the results may surprise you.

Creating Variable Length Records from Fixed Length Input

Along with IEBDG, IEBGENER can be used to create a data set with variable length records out of input that is fixed length. Without using one of these two utilities it is ordinarily necessary to write an application program to perform this function. Two examples will illustrate this technique.

The IDENT and FIELD keyword parameters are used to create the variable length records. All consecutive records that have the same length can be grouped together by IDENT parameters. The FIELD parameters can be used to specify the logical record length with variable length records.

Example 10: Suppose that a card image data set is used to create variable length records. The first three records are to be 50 bytes in length. The fourth record is to be 10 bytes. These are followed by two records each 40 bytes in length. All of the remaining records are to be 75 bytes in length.

```
//J         EXEC PGM=IEBGENER
//SYSPRINT DD SYSOUT=A
//SYSUT1    DD *
  record 1
  record 2
  record 3                               column 51-->$$
  record 4@@<--column 11
  record 5
  record 6                     column 41-->##
  record 7
  other records
  . . .
//SYSUT2  DD  DSN=VARIABLE.RECFM.DATASET,DISP=(NEW,PASS),
//        UNIT=SYSDA,SPACE=(TRK,1),
//        DCB=(LRECL=79,BLKSIZE=500,RECFM=VB)
//SYSIN  DD  *
      GENERATE   MAXFLDS=4,MAXGPS=3
      RECORD     FIELD=(50,1,,1),IDENT=(2,'$$',51)
      RECORD     FIELD=(10,1,,1),IDENT=(2,'@@',11)
      RECORD     FIELD=(40,1,,1),IDENT=(2,'##',41)
      RECORD     FIELD=(75)
/*
```

Notice that no IDENT parameter is necessary with the last group of variable length records. The delimiters may be characters within the variable length data itself if the records will permit this. With some data sets this may be inconvenient or impossible. Likewise, the delimiter may be any field from one to eight characters in length. The individual logical record lengths are determined by the FIELD operands.

The same approach can be used to create a data set with an undefined or spanned record format. In fact, the contents of the SYSIN data set remain exactly the same for each record format. Only the SYSUT2 statement needs to be modified. For example, to create a data set with an undefined record format code the DCB parameter as

```
DCB=(RECFM=U,BLKSIZE=75)
```

A data set with spanned unblocked records can be created with IEBGENER. Notice that this cannot ordinarily be done in COBOL.

Example 11: Variable length records larger than 80 bytes can also be created. Suppose the records created in the last example are all to be preceded by 70 bytes of additional data. Every odd record contains the character A in these 70 bytes, and every even record a B. These records are added to the SYSUT1 data set. They are interspersed with the original SYSUT1 records. Each group of two records will form one output record. Thus the SYSUT1 data set appears as follows:

```
//SYSUT1   DD   *
AAAAAAAAAAAAAAAAAAAAAAAAAAAAAAAAAAAAAAAAAAAAAAAAAAAAAAAAAAAA
original record 1
BBBBBBBBBBBBBBBBBBBBBBBBBBBBBBBBBBBBBBBBBBBBBBBBBBBBBBBBBBBB
original record 2
AAAAAAAAAAAAAAAAAAAAAAAAAAAAAAAAAAAAAAAAAAAAAAAAAAAAAAAAAAAA
original record 3                     column 51-->$$
 . . .
```

The SYSIN and SYSUT2 statements are also coded differently. The SYSUT2 blocksize must be a multiple of 160. The remaining JCL is as follows:

```
//STEP1    EXEC PGM=IEBGENER
//SYSPRINT DD   SYSOUT=A
//SYSIN     DD   DUMMY
//SYSUT2    DD   DSN=&&TEMP,DISP=(NEW,PASS),UNIT=SYSDA,
//        SPACE=(TRK,1),DCB=(LRECL=80,BLKSIZE=800,RECFM=FB)
```

It is necessary to use IEBGENER two more times to get the desired results. The first of these steps is used to change the logical record length to 160. This illustrates that logical record length is irrelevant to an I/O device. The final step creates variable length records out of the 160 byte logical records.

```
//STEP2     EXEC PGM=IEBGENER
//SYSPRINT DD   SYSOUT=A
//SYSUT1    DD   DSN=&&TEMP,DISP=(OLD,DELETE)
```

```
//SYSUT2    DD  DSN=&&TEMP2,DISP=(NEW,PASS),UNIT=SYSDA,
//      SPACE=(TRK,1),DCB=(LRECL=160,BLKSIZE=800,RECFM=FB)
//SYSIN     DD  DUMMY
//STEP3     EXEC PGM=IEBGENER
//SYSPRINT DD   SYSOUT=A
//SYSUT1    DD  DSN=&&TEMP2,DISP=(OLD,PASS)
//SYSUT2    DD  DSN=VARIABLE.RECFM.DATASET,DISP=(NEW,PASS),
//              UNIT=SYSDA,SPACE=(TRK,1),
//              DCB=(LRECL=149,BLKSIZE=1000,RECFM=VB)
//SYSIN     DD  *
  GENERATE MAXFLDS=8,MAXGPS=3
  RECORD   FIELD=(70),FIELD=(50,81,,71),IDENT=(2,'$$',131)
  RECORD   FIELD=(70),FIELD=(10,81,,71),IDENT=(2,'@@',91)
  RECORD   FIELD=(70),FIELD=(40,81,,71),IDENT=(2,'##',121)
  RECORD   FIELD=(70),FIELD=(75,81,,71)
/*
```

All of the above data sets with various record formats and record lengths can also be created by IEBDG.

Exercises

1. Suppose that SYS1.GENER is a cataloged sequential data set which occupies five tracks on a 3350 disk. Use IEBGENER to create a backup copy of this data set on tape. Place it on the 9-track 1600 BPI SL tape volume ABC123 as file number 2. Is it necessary to know the dcb values for SYS1.GENER to create the backup data set?

2. Perform the reverse of Exercise 1. The data set SYS1.GENER is file number 2 on the 9–track 1600 BPI SL tape volume TAPE22. Copy this data set to the 3350 disk volume DISK33. Is it necessary to know the dcb values for SYS1.GENER to create the disk data set?

3. There are ten records in the cataloged disk data set ALPHA. Use IEBGENER to print the first, third, fifth, seventh, and ninth records. This should be done in one job step if possible. The only known information about the records is that they contain a three digit sequence number in bytes 2 through 4. The values coded there are 001, 001, 002, 003, 005, 008, 013, 021, 034, and 055 respectively, the first ten Fibonacci numbers.

4. Use the same ten records described in Exercise 3 to create a partitioned data set and load five members into it. The five members should be created using the following records from ALPHA:

Member Name	*ALPHA Records*
A1	1
B2	2,3
C3	4,5,6
D4	6,7,8,9
E5	10

These members should be created in one job step if possible. Note that the exercise is much easier to do if the sixth record is placed in only one of the members.

5. Use IEBGENER to create a sequential disk data set composed of ten variable length records. These records should be as follows:

Record Number	*Length in Bytes*	*Character in Each Byte*
1,2	60	A
3,4,5	51	B
6	78	C
7,8,9,10	55	D

Code a minimal number of data and control statements in constructing this data set. Specify LRECL=82 in the DCB information on the SYSUT2 DD statement. No literals should be coded in the FIELD operands. Can the coding be simplified if literals are allowed in the FIELD operands?

6. Use IEBGENER to create a disk data set that contains variable length records as in Exercise 5. The only difference between the two data sets is that the logical record length here should be 100 bytes greater than in that exercise. Hence the first two records should now consist of 160 bytes of the character A. Again try to minimize the amount of coding in both the SYSIN and SYSUT1 data set. Create this data set in two different ways: with and without literals in the control statements. Which is easier?

7. Use IEBGENER to create a sequential disk data set that consists of 50 records of 13 bytes each. Each record should contain the following four fields:

Byte Location	*Data Value*
1–3	+1234 stored as a packed decimal
4–5	**
6–11	+12345 as a zoned decimal number
12–13	$$

8. Take the records created in the data set in Exercise 7 and use them to construct a partitioned data set that contains four members. This should be done in one job step. The first member should have the data values permuted so that '**' occupies the first two bytes of each record and the packed decimal number is the rightmost field. The second member should have records beginning with the zoned decimal number and ending with '**'. The third and fourth members should be similarly permuted. It should not be necessary to respecify any literals in the FIELD operands in the control statements.

9. There is a partitioned data set called SYS1.PDS. It contains two members A and B. Use IEBGENER to add a member to SYS1.PDS that will also be called A and will replace

the existing A. Is it necessary to use control statements to do this? Suppose it is necessary to replace both A and B with new members with the same names. Can IEBGENER be used to do this in one job step? See Chapter 12 for additional information on adding and replacing members in a pds.

10. Suppose A, B, and C are cataloged sequential data sets. All of them contain 80 byte records. With A 10 records comprise a block. With B 20 records comprise a block. With C 100 records comprise a block. Print out the contents of these three data sets in one job step using IEBGENER. What restrictions are necessary to accomplish this?

11. Read the material on User Labels in the IBM manual *OS/VS2 MVS Utilities* and then use IEBGENER to create a tape data set with four user labels. In a second job step use IEBGENER to dump the contents of the data set labels, both standard and user, to the printer. Repeat this with a disk data set.

12. Read the material on user-written exit routines in the IBM manual *OS/VS2 MVS Utilities*. Write an exit routine.

Chapter 26

IEBPTPCH

Overview

The major uses of IEBPTPCH are:

— Print or punch the records in a 'sequential like' data set, including pds members and relative data sets

— Print or punch the records in every member of a pds in one simple jobstep

— Print or punch the records in a direct data set

— Print or punch an edited version of a sequential data set, a single pds member, every member in a pds, a relative data set, or a direct data set

— Print or punch a pds directory

— Create a new data set by selecting every Nth record from an existing data set

IEBPTPCH (or PRINT-PUNCH) has many similarities with IEBGENER. It requires the same four DD statements and each has the same role. SYSPRINT is the message data set, SYSIN holds the control statements, SYSUT1 is the input data set, and SYSUT2 is the output data set. The MEMBER and RECORD control statements have the same basic meaning and syntax with both utilities, as do the keyword parameters MAXFLDS, MAXNAME, MAXGPS, and FIELD.

The primary function of both utilities is to copy a data set identified on the SYSUT1 statement to the I/O device specified on the SYSUT2 statement. With IEBPTPCH the SYSUT2 statement usually identifies the printer. Because there are so many similarities between the two utilities the decision of which to use for a particular application is determined by the differences between the two.

What are the major differences between GENER and PRINT-PUNCH? IEBPTPCH requires a control statement data set that can't be dummied out (as is possible with IEBGENER). With IEBPTPCH the SYSUT1 statement can identify a complete partitioned data set as well as a sequential data set. Because IEBGENER is restricted to sequentially organized input an individual pds member may be specified on its SYSUT1 statement, but not the entire pds. Most importantly, IEBPTPCH is intended primarily for listing a data set to the printer or card punch. The SYSUT2 statement may identify other output devices, but these are the two most frequently coded. This printed output can be made to look much nicer with PRINT-PUNCH than is possible with GENER.

Since the control statement data set is required with IEBPTPCH it is actually easier to use IEBGENER to list a data set to the printer. With IEBPTPCH the minimum code to print a sequential data set is

```
//A           EXEC  PGM=IEBPTPCH
//SYSPRINT    DD    SYSOUT=A
//SYSUT1      DD    DSN=INPUT.SEQ.DATA.SET,DISP=SHR
//SYSUT2      DD    SYSOUT=A
//SYSIN       DD    *
    PRINT
/*
```

This code lists the records in the cataloged data set INPUT.SEQ.DATA.SET to the printer. Either the PRINT or PUNCH control statement is required. Recall that with IEBGENER the SYSIN statement is dummied out for this task. Hence IEBPTPCH requires some extra code. Additionally, the output from IEBPTPCH is displayed in unedited format consisting of eight bytes of data, two spaces, the next eight bytes of data, two more spaces, etc. If the first several lines in this paragraph are printed using this format they will appear as shown in Figure 26–1.

To create this output the SYSUT1 data set identified a group of 40-byte records. The asterisks are printed by IEBPTPCH to identify the end of a logical record. Two asterisks denote the end of a physical record. This format may be acceptable for printing a hexadecimal dump but it is inconvenient for most other applications. In order for the contents of the records to be printed in contiguous bytes without the

FIGURE 26–1
The Output From IEBPTPCH is Displayed in Unedited Format

```
This cod   e lists    the reco   rds in t   he catal   *
oged dat   a set IN   PUT.SEQ.   DATA.SET   to the     *
printer.   Either t   he PRINT   or PUNCH   control    *
```

intervening blanks, several additions must be made to the above code. The single control statement should be replaced by

```
PRINT  MAXFLDS=1
RECORD FIELD=(40,1,,1)
```

As with IEBGENER, MAXFLDS means that one FIELD operand is present in the remaining control statements. The RECORD control statement specifies that 40 bytes of input data beginning in byte 1 will be listed to the printer beginning in column 1. When these control statements are coded the printed output records look exactly like the input records. Thus the output looks precisely the same as when IEBGENER is used with a SYSIN DD DUMMY statement. The RECORD statement assumes that the input data set is composed of 40 byte records. One subtle distinction still exists between the records created by the two utilities: one byte of carriage control information precedes each record created by IEBPTPCH whether the SYSUT2 statement identifies the printer or any other output device. The carriage control byte is used to control the print operation. It does not actually appear in the printed listing. This one byte field is not supplied with IEBGENER.

PRINT and PUNCH Control Statements

With IEBPTPCH the first control statement must contain the operator PRINT or PUNCH. Traditionally PRINT is associated with a printed listing of the SYSUT1 data set and PUNCH produces a punched card copy. Exactly one of these two operators must be specified every time IEBPTPCH is used. Where the output is actually placed depends on the parameter values coded on the SYSUT2 DD statement. For example, a data set can be printed on tape or punched on disk.

The real power of IEBPTPCH comes from the fact that there are a great many keyword operands that can be specified in the control statements to make the output data set look nice. There are eleven operands that may be specified on either the PRINT or PUNCH statement:

TYPORG — Either PS or PO may be specified depending on whether the input data is physical sequential or has partitioned organization. PS is the default.

TOTCONV — Either XE or PZ may be specified. XE means convert the output data set to hexadecimal, with each byte of data represented by 2 characters. PZ means convert packed decimal to zoned decimal. Note that zoned to packed conversion is not available. The default is that no data conversion is performed.

CNTRL — When specified with PRINT the values 1, 2, and 3 can be coded to represent single, double, and triple spacing of output, respectively.

When specified with PUNCH, the value 1 indicates the first stacker and the value 2 indicates the second stacker. The default is 1 with both PRINT and PUNCH.

STRTAFT — This specifies the number of records to be skipped in the SYSUT1 data set before the printing or punching actually begins.

STOPAFT — This specifies the number of records to be printed or punched before the print or punch operation is terminated.

SKIP — This denotes processing every Nth record when SKIP=N is coded. The default values for STRTAFT, STOPAFT, and SKIP result in the processing of every record in the data set.

PERFORM — A or M may be coded depending on whether ASA or machine carriage control characters are to be employed.

MAXFLDS — As with IEBGENER, this should be set to a number greater than or equal to the occurrences of the FIELD operand on subsequent RECORD statements.

MAXGPS — As with IEBGENER, this should specify a number greater than or equal to the occurrences of the IDENT operand on subsequent RECORD statements.

MAXLITS — This should be set to a value greater than or equal to the number of literal characters contained in all following IDENT operands. Note that MAXLITS with IEBGENER has a different meaning. Unlike IEBGENER, IEBPTPCH does not allow literals in a FIELD operand.

MAXNAME — This should be set to a value greater than or equal to the number of MEMBER control statements that follow. With IEBPTPCH this value will be equal to the number of NAME=member-name operands, since only one member-name can be specified on a MEMBER control statement. With IEBPTPCH MEMBER references an existing pds member; with IEBGENER it references a member that is to be created in the present jobstep.

In addition to the 11 keyword operands that may be specified with either PRINT or PUNCH there are two additional operands that may be specified only when PRINT is coded and two others that can be used only with PUNCH.

INITPG — This can be used with PRINT to specify the page number of the first page of output. The default value is 1.

MAXLINE — This is coded with PRINT and determines the maximum number of lines on a printed page. The default value is 55.

CDSEQ This can be coded with PUNCH to specify the beginning sequence number for punched output. Sequence numbers are coded in bytes 73 to 80.

CDINCR This also can be coded with PUNCH and is used in conjunction with CDSEQ. It specifies the value by which sequence numbers will be incremented.

Other Control Statements

Either PRINT or PUNCH may be followed by a TITLE statement which is used to supply a title for the SYSUT2 output. Up to two TITLE operators are allowed, with the second specifying a subtitle. The format of the TITLE statement is as follows:

```
TITLE ITEM=('message-1',byte-1),ITEM=('message-2',byte-2),
ITEM=('message-3',byte-3), . . .
```

Here 'message-i' denotes up to 40 bytes of character data. This data is to be printed or punched beginning at the location specified in byte-i. If a TITLE statement is coded it must follow the PRINT/PUNCH statement and precede any MEMBER or RECORD statements. The TITLE and subTITLE print on every output page.

In addition to PRINT, PUNCH, and TITLE, two other control statements are frequently used with IEBPTPCH. These are the MEMBER and RECORD statements. Both are used in practically the same way as with IEBGENER. The differences between the two utilities are examined below.

The MEMBER statement is coded

```
MEMBER  NAME=member-name  or  MEMBER  NAME=alias
```

Note that only one name may be specified with a MEMBER statement. IEBGENER allows multiple names to be specified on a single MEMBER statement; IEBPTPCH does not. The reason for this difference is that IEBGENER is only actually processing one member and all names except the first are aliases for that one member which is being created. Unlike IEBGENER, IEBPTPCH is retrieving an existing member, not creating a new member. Hence it is meaningless to code both a member name and its alias.

The RECORD statement is also very similar with both utilities. Its format with both is as follows:

```
RECORD  FIELD=(a1,b1,c1,d1),FIELD=(a2,b2,c2,d2),...
     IDENT=(x,'y',z),FIELD=(an,bn,cn,dn),...
```

As with IEBGENER, ai bytes of data are copied from the SYSUT1 data set and inserted beginning at byte location di in the SYSUT2 data set. The bi value gives the beginning byte location in the SYSUT1 records from which the ai bytes are taken. Unlike IEBGENER, literals are not allowed as bi values when using IEBPTPCH. The ci value denotes conversion. Two types are possible: character to hexadecimal and packed decimal to zoned decimal. Unlike IEBGENER, zoned to packed conversion cannot be performed. This is the second place where data conversion can be specified with IEBPTPCH.

Use with Sequential Data Sets

Example 1: The cataloged disk data set ALPHA.ONE contains 75 byte records. These records are to be listed to the printer, single-spaced, and printed in 75 contiguous bytes.

```
//A            EXEC   PGM=IEBPTPCH
//SYSPRINT     DD     SYSOUT=A
//SYSUT1       DD     DSN=ALPHA.ONE,DISP=SHR
//SYSUT2       DD     SYSOUT=A
//SYSIN        DD     *
        PRINT    TYPORG=PS,MAXFLDS=1
        RECORD   FIELD=(75,1,,1)
/*
```

Since PS is the default for data set organization the TYPORG is included only for documentation. The FIELD operand can be coded as FIELD=(75) since 1 is the default value for the second and fourth positional parameters specified above. The default for conversion is that none is performed.

Example 2: Print out the same records as in Example 1. This time printing should be in hexadecimal. The only change in the above code is to the control statements, which should now be written as

```
PRINT    MAXFLDS=1                or      PRINT TOTCONV=XE
RECORD   FIELD=(75,1,XE,1)
```

When data is printed in hexadecimal it always appears in the dump format of eight characters, two spaces, etc. When RECORD statements are coded along with TOTCONV=XE they take precedence over the TOTCONV operand.

Example 3: Again the records in ALPHA.ONE are to be listed to the printer. In addition, several keyword parameters are coded to modify the appearance of the printed output. The control statements are as follows:

```
PRINT    STRTAFT=5,SKIP=3,STOPAFT=500,
         CNTRL=2,INITPG=1,MAXLINE=20,MAXFLDS=1
TITLE    ITEM=('A LISTING OF DATASET ALPHA.ONE',25)
TITLE    ITEM=('SUBTITLE HERE',10),ITEM=('AND HERE',50),
           ITEM=('AND MORE HERE',70)
RECORD   FIELD=(75)
```

Here the records in the SYSUT1 data set are listed to the printer. After skipping the first five records every third record is printed until a total of 500 records have printed.

The records are double-spaced on pages that are numbered and contain a title and subtitle. A maximum of 20 lines are printed on each page.

Example 4: Once more the input is data set ALPHA.ONE. Punch out a deck of cards using the contents of bytes 2 to 73 from the SYSUT1 data set. These characters should be punched in columns 1 to 72 and the card deck should be sequenced in increments of ten beginning with 100. The control statements needed to do this are

```
PUNCH    MAXFLDS=1,CDSEQ=100,CDINCR=10
RECORD   FIELD=(72,2,,1)
```

Additionally, the SYSUT2 DD statement should now specify SYSOUT=B, the card punch.

Example 5: Print out the records in STOW, which is a member of the card image pds SYS1.MACLIB. The pertinent JCL and control statements may be coded as follows:

```
//SYSUT1      DD   DSN=SYS1.MACLIB,DISP=SHR
//SYSIN       DD   *
      PRINT    TYPORG=PO,MAXFLDS=1,MAXNAME=1
      MEMBER   NAME=STOW
      RECORD   FIELD=(80)
/*
```

Here the TYPORG keyword must be coded or the jobstep will fail.

Exactly the same results can be obtained by changing the SYSUT1 and SYSIN statements as follows:

```
//SYSUT1      DD   DSN=SYS1.MACLIB(STOW),DISP=SHR
//SYSIN       DD   *
      PRINT    MAXFLDS=1
      RECORD   FIELD=(80)
/*
```

When exactly one member of a pds is to be processed it may be identified either by the MEMBER control statement or through the DSN parameter in the SYSUT1 statement. With the first approach the SYSUT1 input is the entire pds. With the second approach the input is a sequential data set (a member of a pds).

Use with Partitioned Data Sets

Example 6: In one jobstep print the contents of three members of SYS1.MACLIB: STOW, BLDL, and FIND. Because of JCL syntax restrictions only one member name may be specified as part of the DSN parameter. Thus control statements are used to get the required listing

```
//SYSUT1     DD DSN=SYS1.MACLIB,DISP=SHR
//SYSIN      DD *
      PRINT    TYPORG=PO,MAXFLDS=3,MAXNAME=3
      MEMBER   NAME=STOW
      RECORD   FIELD=(80)
      MEMBER   NAME=BLDL
      RECORD   FIELD=(80)
      MEMBER   NAME=FIND
      RECORD   FIELD=(80)
/*
```

It is important not to specify a member on the SYSUT1 statement when MEMBER statements are coded. Notice that a RECORD control statement must follow every MEMBER statement if that MEMBER is to be edited. It is not possible to factor out the RECORD statement and have it apply to every preceding MEMBER statement. Additionally, the MEMBER statement should precede the RECORD statement(s) associated with it. The SYSUT1 statement must identify the entire pds. With this example every member is individually labeled by IEBPTPCH. In the next example no labeling is done.

Example 7: The same records can be printed without coding the MEMBER statements. The three members can be coded on three concatenated SYSUT1 DD statements. Like IEBGENER, IEBPTPCH allows input data sets that share the same data set organization and have similar DCB attributes to be concatenated. This should be the case for members of the same pds. With this approach the SYSUT1 and SYSIN statements are coded as follows:

```
//SYSUT1   DD DSN=SYS1.MACLIB(STOW),DISP=SHR
//         DD DSN=SYS1.MACLIB(BLDL),DISP=SHR
//         DD DSN=SYS1.MACLIB(FIND),DISP=SHR
//SYSIN    DD *
     PRINT  MAXFLDS=1
     RECORD FIELD=(80)
/*
```

This listing does not print the members' names above the members. Page breaks are also not performed between the members with this code.

Example 8: Print out the records in every member in SYS1.MACLIB. Here the SYSUT1 statement must identify the pds. No member name can be included on the SYSUT1 statement and no MEMBER statements need to be included in the control statements. Code the following:

```
//SYSUT1     DD   DSN=SYS1.MACLIB,DISP=SHR
//SYSIN      DD   *
      PRINT   TYPORG=PO,MAXFLDS=1
      RECORD  FIELD=(80)
/*
```

Since SYS1.MACLIB is usually a very large library, a rather lengthy listing could result if this job is actually run. If a TITLE control statement is coded it will be printed preceding the records in each member, along with the name of the member. If TYPORG = PO is not coded on the PRINT statement the jobstep will not run.

Example 9: IEBPTPCH can also be used to print out the directory of a pds. Along with IEHLIST and IDCAMS, it is one of the three utilities most commonly used to perform this important function. The code to print the directory of SYS1.MACLIB is very similar to that used in Example 8 to print the members.

```
//SYSUT1      DD  DSN=SYS1.MACLIB,DISP=SHR,
//              DCB=(RECFM=U,BLKSIZE=256)
//SYSIN       DD  *
      PRINT   TYPORG=PS,TOTCONV=XE
/*
```

Notice that the DCB information coded on SYSUT1 reflects the properties of the directory rather than of the member area of the pds. It is necessary to override the values in the data set labels which are for the members only. TYPORG = PS is coded because the directory is to be processed like a sequential data set which is separated from the member area by an End of File marker. The directory is usually printed in hexadecimal because much of the important information it contains will not print in character format. For a thorough discussion of the information contained in a pds directory see Chapter 12. Unlike IEHLIST, IEBPTPCH can be used with any type of pds without warning messages being printed for members that are not load modules.

Additional Examples

Example 10: Often when testing a new program the real data available is so voluminous as to require the construction of smaller test data sets. Suppose a group of multiple level control break COBOL programs are to be tested and the only real data available is a tape data set containing 100,000 sorted records. With IEBPTPCH it is possible to copy the tape data set to a disk data set and in the process copy only every one-hundredth record. This will give a more manageable file of 1,000 records to use in testing the COBOL programs. Note that a better cross section of records in the data set will probably result than if the first or last 1,000 records had been chosen. Here SYSUT2 identifies a disk data set and SKIP = 100 must be coded on the PRINT control statement. Selecting every Nth record is such a convenient feature that it is surprising that it cannot be done with any other utility (not even IDCAMS). Assuming that the input data is on standard label tape, the actual code is

```
//J          EXEC PGM=IEBPTPCH
//SYSPRINT    DD SYSOUT=A
//SYSUT1      DD DSN=TEST.TAPE.DATA,DISP=(OLD,KEEP),
//              UNIT=TAPE,VOL=SER=TAPE12
```

```
//SYSUT2      DD DSN=TEST.DISK.DATA,DISP=(NEW,CATLG),
//            UNIT=3380,VOL=SER=DISK99,SPACE=(CYL,5),
//            DCB=(LRECL=81,BLKSIZE=4050,RECFM=FB)
//SYSIN    DD *
     PRINT MAXFLDS=1,SKIP=100
     RECORD FIELD=(80)
/*
```

Since IEBPTPCH places one byte of carriage control in front of each output record, care must be taken not to treat this as the first byte of actual data. Since the output is going to disk, this byte is actually the first byte of each record. In addition, some of the records written to the SYSUT2 data set will be headings. These must be detected and discarded by the application programs or by a preliminary edit routine.

Example 11: Three members from the card image pds SYS1.ALPHA are copied to the printer. The first printed page should be numbered 7 since the first six pages of this report were printed in a prior job. The members are ALPHA, BETA, and GAMMA. Title every page of the output. Never print more than 15 lines from a given member. Print the records in BETA as single 80 byte fields, but print bytes 41 through 80 to the left of bytes 1 through 40 for members ALPHA and GAMMA. The necessary code to do this is the following:

```
//K           EXEC   PGM=IEBPTPCH
//SYSPRINT    DD     SYSOUT=A
//SYSUT1      DD     DSN=SYS1.ALPHA,DISP=SHR
//SYSUT2      DD     SYSOUT=A
//SYSIN       DD     *
    PRINT     TYPORG=PO,MAXFLDS=5,MAXNAME=3,
              INITPG=7,STOPAFT=15
    TITLE     ITEM=('A 1-40 BYTE TITLE GOES HERE',10),
              ITEM=('IT PRECEDES ALL 3 MEMBERS',40),
              ITEM=('MEMBER NAMES PRINT AUTOMATICALLY',70)
    MEMBER    NAME=ALPHA
    RECORD    FIELD=(40,41,,1),
              FIELD=(40,1,,41)
    MEMBER    NAME=BETA
    RECORD    FIELD=(80)
    MEMBER    NAME=GAMMA
    RECORD    FIELD=(40,41,,1),
              FIELD=(40,1,,41)
/*
```

Exercises

1. ALPHA is a cataloged sequential data set that contains 100 records each 85 bytes in length. This data set will also be referenced in the next four exercises. It is necessary to print out the records in ALPHA in two formats, first in hexadecimal and then in character format. Each listing should contain a title which uniquely identifies it. Use IEBPTPCH to generate the two listings. Can IEBPTPCH generate both listings in one jobstep? Suppose

the same title precedes each of the listings. Can they be generated in one jobstep? How could the same two listings be created using only IEBGENER? Can a title be included with IEBGENER?

2. Print out all records in ALPHA, beginning with the seventh and continuing through the fifty-fourth. Print exactly eight records per page of printed output. Include both a title and subtitle with each page of output. Print the data in contiguous bytes.

3. Print out all the records numbered 5,10,15,20,...,70,75 from ALPHA. Title the output and double space the records.

4. Produce a report listing the contents of record numbers 1,3,5,7,...,45,47,49,54,59,...,89,94,99 from ALPHA. This is the first twenty-five odd numbers and then every fifth number. The printed output should imply that the records were printed on adjacent pages even if this is not the case. Two jobsteps may be necessary to accomplish this.

5. Take the records in ALPHA and use them to create a second sequential data set. This new data set should be placed on disk and contain exactly one-half of the records in ALPHA. Those 50 records will be every other record in ALPHA starting with the second record, i.e., the even numbered records. Be certain to avoid inadvertently including either heading or carriage control information with the records being created. Several steps may be necessary, and several other utilities may be needed.

6. SYS1.X is a cataloged pds library that contains four members A,B,C, and D. All members contain card image data. This pds and its members will also be referenced in the next five questions. It is necessary to print out the records in member D in two formats, first in hexadecimal and then in character format. Each listing should contain a title that uniquely identifies it. Use IEBPTPCH to generate the two listings. Can IEBPTPCH generate both listings in one jobstep? Suppose the same title precedes each of the listings. Can they be generated in one jobstep? Compare your results to those from Exercise 1. How could the same two listings be created using only IEBGENER?

7. Use IEBPTPCH to print the contents of member C in the pds SYS1.X. Use an absolute minimum number of control statements to accomplish this.

8. Print out every member in SYS1.X. Start each member on a new page in the listing. Records in member A should be single spaced, those in B double spaced, those in C triple spaced, and those in D should print one per page.

9. Print all the members in SYS1.X except for member C.

10. Print the directory of SYS1.X. It should be printed in both character and hexadecimal. Which listing is the most useful?

11. Use IEBPTPCH to modify the records in member D by including sequence numbers in columns 73 through 80. This will result in a new copy of member D being written to the pds.

12. ALPHA.GDGX is a Generation Data Group. Use IEBPTPCH to print the records in every generation data set in ALPHA.GDGX. The data sets themselves should be printed in reverse chronological order.

13. ALPHA.RELATIVE is a relative data set that contains 80 byte records. List these records to the printer. The first ten bytes of each record consist of two 5 byte packed decimal numbers. When printed these values should be in unpacked format. The two fields should be reversed from the order in which they occur in each record. Could IEBPTPCH print these records if ALPHA.RELATIVE had been a true direct data set where each record was preceded by a disk KEY field?

14. ALPHA.VARI is a sequential disk data set that contains variable length records. Print the records in this data set. Some of the records exceed 200 bytes in length. The records should be printed in edited format. Use IEBGENER to do this also. Compare the differences in the output.

15. Use IEBGENER to create a sequential data set consisting of exactly five card image records. This data set may be on either tape or disk, but should be created with standard user labels. Can IEBPTPCH display the labels of a disk data set? Can IEBPTPCH display the labels of an SL or SUL tape data set?

16. Can IEBPTPCH be used to create a sequential data set of variable length records out of in-stream data? Is it possible to mimic the way this is done with IEBGENER?

17. Zoned to packed data conversion is supported by IEBGENER but not by IEBPTPCH. Why is this the case?

18. Identify every data set organization that may be coded on the SYSUT1 DD statement with IEBGENER and then IEBPTPCH. Comment on the differences between the two utilities. What data set organizations may be coded on the SYSUT2 statement with both utilities?

Chapter 27

IEBUPDTE

Overview

The major uses of IEBUPDTE are:

— Add or replace a complete member in a partitioned data set

— Add, delete, and modify the individual records in a pds member

— Add, delete, and modify the individual records in a sequential data set

— Number or renumber the records in a pds member or a sequential data set

There are two primary functions performed by IEBUPDTE: it can be used to add or replace members in pds libraries, and can also modify individual records in existing members in a pds library. The modifications can affect the entire member or just selected records within it. IEBUPDTE only accepts as input data sets with logical record lengths of less than or equal to 80 bytes.

This utility (usually known as UPDATE) shares a number of similarities with IEBGENER and IEBPTPCH. UPDATE has the same four required DDnames: SYS-

PRINT, SYSIN, SYSUT1, and SYSUT2. The four DD statements have the same roles with UPDATE as with GENER and PRINT-PUNCH.

UPDATE, however, places more restrictions on the types of data sets that may be coded with the SYSUT1 and SYSUT2 statements. Only partitioned or sequential (usually tape or disk) data sets are permitted as the input and output data sets. Partitioned data sets are used much more frequently with IEBUPDTE than sequential data sets. For this reason only the final two examples in this chapter cover the use of sequential data sets. In all of the other examples SYSUT1 and SYSUT2 will both identify partitioned data sets.

As with PRINT-PUNCH, the SYSIN control statement must be coded and cannot be dummied out. Unlike most other IBM utilities, SYSIN may contain data statements as well as control statements. A control statement must contain ./ in columns 1 and 2. Thus the format of every IEBUPDTE control statement is

```
./label   operator    keyword-operands    comments
```

If a label is coded it must begin in column 3. Never code ./ as the first two characters of a data statement when using IEBUPDTE.

Because data statements may be coded within the SYSIN data set, there are two primary sources of input with this utility. The other, of course, is the partitioned data set coded on the SYSUT1 statement. IEBUPDTE permits up to sixteen partitioned data sets to be concatenated together on the SYSUT1 statement. The standard rules for concatenation of libraries should be followed when using IEBUPDTE. The appropriate locations for input data are determined by the particular function used.

Unlike GENER and PRINT-PUNCH, situations exist where either the SYSUT1 or SYSUT2 statement can be omitted. One situation involves a PARM value that may optionally be coded on the EXEC statement. Either of two values may be assigned to the PARM: MOD or NEW. They should not be confused with the DISP subparameters with the same names. MOD is the default value. NEW specifies that all input to the utility will come from the SYSIN data set. Hence the SYSUT1 data set will not be used and it need not be coded. When MOD is coded input can come from either the SYSIN or SYSUT1 data set. If MOD is specified a SYSUT1 statement must be included even if it will not be used. If it is omitted IEBUPDTE will end with the message

```
IEB814I DDNAME SYSUT1 CANNOT BE OPENED.
```

The SYSUT2 statement need not be coded if the directory of the pds coded on the SYSUT1 DD statement remains unchanged during the step. This in turn can occur only when UPDATE is used to modify a member of the pds without having it moved to a new location within the pds. When UPDATE=INPLACE is coded on a CHANGE control statement this condition will be satisfied. This is explained in more detail below. For additional details on the structure and working of a pds see Chapter 12.

For most applications the following code will be used with IEBUPDTE:

```
//A        EXEC PGM=IEBUPDTE,PARM=NEW or PARM=MOD
//SYSPRINT DD  SYSOUT=A
//SYSUT1   DD  DSN=old-master-pds,DISP=SHR  (OM-old master)
//SYSUT2   DD  DSN=new-master-pds,DISP=OLD  (NM-new master)
//SYSIN    DD  *
./  function control statement
./  detail control statement

    in-stream data

./  function control statement

    in-stream data

./  end control statement
/*
```

The SYSUT1 DD statement need not be present when PARM=NEW is coded. The SYSUT2 DD statement should not be coded when there is exactly one function control statement and it contains the UPDATE=INPLACE operand. The SYSPRINT data set uses the abbreviations OM and NM in messages referring to the old master and new master partitioned data sets. These are the libraries coded on the SYSUT1 and SYSUT2 DD statements respectively. The message data set is very informative and user friendly with IEBUPDTE. It probably equals IEBCOPY in providing the best information. Some messages are printed entirely to the right of column 80. Hence, when examining IEBUPDTE output at a terminal such messages may be overlooked.

Function Control Statements

Every time UPDATE is used one of four control statements must be coded. These are known as function statements. More than one function statement can be coded in the same job step. The basic processing handled by each function statement is listed below.

ADD Add a member to the pds coded on the SYSUT2 statement. The records that will comprise the new member are contained in the SYSIN data set.

REPRO Add a member to the pds coded on the SYSUT2 statement. A member of the pds coded on the SYSUT1 data set is reproduced as the new member.

REPL Replace an existing member in the SYSUT2 pds data set. The replacement member's records are contained in the SYSIN data set. The entire old member is replaced.

CHANGE Modify a member in the SYSUT1 pds data set. The member is rewritten back to the same pds. Unlike REPL, CHANGE modifies individual records in a pds member.

To determine the role of each DD statement with the four function control statements consult Table 27–1.

No matter which of the four functions is coded several keyword operands may be specified. The six operands defined here are only some of the possible keywords. The ones that have been omitted are used very infrequently.

NAME = member name — NAME identifies the particular member that is being added to the pds (ADD and REPRO) or changed within the pds (REPL and CHANGE). The NAME parameter and the MEMBER parameter (defined below) are often confused.

LIST = ALL — This parameter specifies that every record within the member will be listed in the SYSPRINT data set. Messages explaining actions taken on individual records will also be printed. If LIST = ALL is not coded a less complete listing of the records in the member is given. It usually contains only those records that have been modified in this function step.

TABLE 27–1
Function Control Statements and DD Statements

Function Control Statement	*Role of SYSUT1 DD Statement*	*Role of SYSUT2 DD Statement*	*Role of SYSIN DD Statement*
ADD	not used; code PARM = NEW if only ADD functions performed	pds that will contain new member	in-stream data that holds the new member-to-be
REPRO	input pds (existing member)	pds that will contain new member	not used except for control statement
REPL	pds that contains member to be replaced	pds that will contain new member (same as SYSUT1)	in-stream data that holds the new member-to-be
CHANGE	input pds (existing member)	same as SYSUT1	in-stream data modifications for old member

SSI=xxxxxxxx — This keyword parameter stores four bytes of system status information. Code any eight hexadecimal digits. The contents of this field will be placed in the directory of the pds in the user data area following the membername and location. This four byte field can be used for any purpose selected by the programmer. As an example, SSI=02081588 could represent version two of this particular member which was placed into the pds on Aug 15, 1988. To subsequently examine the contents of a directory entry a utility such as IEBPTPCH, IEHLIST, or IDCAMS can be used.

LEVEL=xx — LEVEL can be used to specify two hexadecimal digits that represent the version number of this particular member. It is a subfield of SSI and is ignored if both are coded.

MEMBER=member-name — This keyword parameter is coded only when a sequential data set is made a member of a pds. The value coded is written in the directory as the name of the member. MEMBER can only be used with a CHANGE function control statement.

NEW=PO or PS — Coding PO means that a sequential data set is to be made a member of a pds. PS means that a sequential data set is to be created from a pds member. NEW=PO and MEMBER=member-name must be coded together. When both SYSUT1 and SYSUT2 are partitioned data sets this operand need not be coded.

It is strongly recommended that LIST=ALL always be coded when using IEBUPDTE. It is convenient to also code either SSI or LEVEL.

Detail Control Statements

Certain applications require that additional control statements be coded with the function statement. These extra statements are called detail statements. There are two detail statements: NUMBER and DELETE. NUMBER is used to number records in a data set or member that does not contain sequence numbers, or to renumber records that are currently sequenced. DELETE is used to physically delete records from a member or data set during a CHANGE operation.

There are several important keyword parameters that may be specified with detail statements. Again this is not an all-inclusive list, and just contains the most commonly used parameters.

NEW1=xxxxxxxx — This specifies an eight-digit sequence number which will be the sequence number on the first record in the member. This applies to a new member being added or an old member being renumbered.

INCR=xxxxxxxx This is used in conjunction with NEW1. It specifies the value by which sequence numbers will be incremented. NEW1 and INCR are similiar to CDSEQ and CDINCR with IEBPTPCH.

SEQ1=xxxxxxxx This value identifies the first record in a group that is to be renumbered or deleted.

SEQ2=xxxxxxxx This keyword is used along with SEQ1 and identifies the last of a group of records that is to be renumbered or deleted.

With all four of the above keyword parameters fewer than eight digits may be coded. Such a number is right justified and padded with leading zeroes. Hence INCR=25 and INCR=00000025 are equivalent.

INSERT=YES This specifies that the following group of logical records, all of which do not have sequence numbers, are to be inserted into the member.

COLUMN=xx This specifies that when a new logical record is designated to replace an existing logical record all bytes from column xx to the rightmost end of the statement are replaced. The default value is COLUMN=1. This causes the complete logical record to be replaced.

Other Control Statements

In addition to the four function statements and two detail statements there are two additional control statements that may be coded with UPDATE.

./ ENDUP This should be the last record coded in the control statement data set. It serves as the delimiter for this data set.

./ ALIAS NAME=alias name This statement allows the assignment of an alias to the pds member named in the function statement. Unlike IEBGENER, only one alias may be assigned on a control statement. Additional ALIAS statements after the first must follow any data statements when used with ADD, REPL, or CHANGE. When a member is replaced or changed existing aliases are not automatically updated to reference the new member unless they are listed again on an ALIAS statement.

Two typical sequences of control statements showing the syntax of both function and detail statements are examined below.

```
./      ADD      NAME=ALPHA,LIST=ALL,SSI=01081588
./      NUMBER   NEW1=100,INCR=50
```

The records used to create member ALPHA immediately follow these statements. They will be given sequence numbers of 00000100, 00000150, 00000200, etc. when written as member ALPHA. The value 01081588 will be stored in the directory and the complete member will be printed in the SYSPRINT data set.

```
./      CHANGE   NAME=BETA,LIST=ALL,SSI=02081587
./      DELETE   SEQ1=200,SEQ2=500
```

The records in BETA to be modified or added are coded immediately following the control statements. They must have sequence numbers greater than 200. In addition, all records from the record with sequence number 00000200 up to the record with sequence number 00000500 inclusive are deleted.

Detailed Usage of Function Statements

The remainder of this chapter examines the four function control statements. Examples are used to illustrate each of the four functions. In conjunction with each function, the corresponding row entry in Table 27–1 should be examined.

The ADD Function

The ADD function is used to insert a new member whose records are contained in the SYSIN data set into the pds specified on the SYSUT2 statement. It is assumed that there is no member in the pds with the same name as the member being added. However, if there is an old member with the same name it will be automatically replaced by the new member provided that DISP=OLD is coded on the SYSUT2 statement.

If an IEBUPDTE jobstep contains only ADD functions there is no reason to code a SYSUT1 DD statement. Since all input will come from the SYSIN data set the SYSUT1 data set will never be opened. When doing this be certain to specify PARM=NEW on the EXEC statement. Conversely, when PARM=NEW is coded only the ADD control statement can be used.

Example 1: The ADD function is used to resolve a common programming situation. Several JCL statements are to be made into a cataloged procedure. This will involve making the group of JCL statements a member of the system procedure library, SYS1.PROCLIB. The code to do this is as follows:

```
//A           EXEC PGM=IEBUPDTE,PARM=NEW
//SYSPRINT    DD   SYSOUT=A
//SYSUT2      DD   DSN=SYS1.PROCLIB,DISP=OLD
//SYSIN       DD   DATA
./   ADD   NAME=GENER,LIST=ALL,LEVEL=00
./   NUMBER   NEW1=100,INCR=50
//GENER        EXEC   PGM=IEBGENER              *
//SYSPRINT     DD     SYSOUT=A                  *
//SYSUT2       DD     SYSOUT=A                  *
//SYSIN        DD     DUMMY                     *
./   ALIAS   NAME=IEBGENER
./   ENDUP
/*
```

Here the group consisting of the four data records denoted by * is made a member of SYS1.PROCLIB and given the name GENER. Additionally, a listing of the records in the member will print in the message data set. The value 00 is stored in the user data area of the pds directory for member GENER. All of this is a direct consequence of the first control statement. The second control statement specifies that every record in the member will be numbered. The GENER EXEC statement will be 00000100, the SYSPRINT statement 00000150, etc. It is not required that a member be numbered when it is added to a pds, but it is a good practice. Unless it is numbered individual records within it cannot be subsequently modified by IEBUPDTE.

The same basic results can be obtained using IEBGENER rather than IEBUPDTE. In fact, Example 6 in Chapter 25 does just that. However, UPDATE is the preferred way to perform this function for two major reasons. First, UPDATE numbers records so that they can be subsequently referenced by those numbers. GENER cannot automatically number records. Second, the GENER message data set does not display a copy of the member after the addition. When LIST=ALL is coded IEBUPDTE does. To see the results produced by IEBGENER a second jobstep must be run. A minor advantage of UPDATE is its ability to write user information in the directory of the pds.

Note that SYSIN DD DATA was coded on the control data set since there were JCL statements in the input stream. Note also that an alias entry was placed in the directory of SYS1.PROCLIB so that coding either

```
//A    EXEC  GENER        or
//A    EXEC  IEBGENER
```

will result in the four records being inserted into the JCL stream. Any job that uses this cataloged procedure must supply the SYSUT1 DD statement. If either GENER, IEBGENER, or both existed as members in the pds prior to this jobstep, they will be replaced by this new code.

The REPRO Function

The REPRO function is very similar to the ADD function. A new member whose records currently comprise a member of the pds coded on the SYSUT1 statement will be placed in the pds specified on the SYSUT2 statement.

Example 2: To copy three members from the SYS1.MACLIB pds to a second pds called NEW.PDS code the following:

```
//B          EXEC   PGM=IEBUPDTE,PARM=MOD
//SYSPRINT   DD     SYSOUT=A
//SYSUT1     DD     DSN=SYS1.MACLIB,DISP=SHR
//SYSUT2     DD     DSN=NEW.PDS,DISP=OLD
//SYSIN      DD     *
./   REPRO NAME=STOW,LIST=ALL,LEVEL=01
./   REPRO NAME=BLDL,LIST=ALL,LEVEL=01
./   REPRO NAME=FIND,LIST=ALL,LEVEL=01
./   ENDUP
/*
```

Following this step NEW.PDS contains the three members STOW, BLDL, and FIND. Since PARM=MOD is the default it need not be coded.

The REPL Function

The REPL control statement uses an in-stream data set as input just as the ADD function does. The distinction between the two control statements is that REPL uses the input member to replace an existing member with the same name in the SYSUT2 pds. Since ADD can automatically replace existing members this is the least essential of the four function statements.

Example 3: Replace the member GENER that was put into SYS1.PROCLIB by the code specified with the ADD function in Example 1 with a revised version of GENER.

```
//C          EXEC   PGM=IEBUPDTE,PARM=MOD
//SYSPRINT   DD     SYSOUT=A
//SYSUT1     DD     DSN=SYS1.PROCLIB,DISP=SHR
//SYSUT2     DD     DSN=SYS1.PROCLIB,DISP=OLD
//SYSIN      DD     DATA
./   REPL   NAME=GENER,LIST=ALL,LEVEL=01
./   NUMBER   NEW1=50,INCR=100
//GENER      PROC   PDS=,MEMBER=                          *
//GENER      EXEC   PGM=IEBGENER                          *
//SYSPRINT   DD     SYSOUT=A                              *
//SYSUT1     DD     DISP=SHR,DSN=&PDS&MEMBER              *
./   ENDUP
/*
```

After jobstep C is run the four lines of JCL denoted by * become the new member GENER. The old member cannot be accessed by coding GENER. In the above situation the old member can still be accessed by specifying its alias IEBGENER, since it is unaffected by the code in this example. If ./ ALIAS NAME=IEBGENER had been coded before the ENDUP statement the alias would also have been modified.

The CHANGE Function

The last of the four function statements is CHANGE. It is the most complicated of the four. CHANGE is used to modify individual records within an existing pds member. The pds containing the member to be modified is specified on the SYSUT1 statement. The modified member replaces the original member in the pds specified on the SYSUT2 statement. The same pds should be coded on both DD statements.

What kind of modifications can be made to a pds member using CHANGE?

— New records can be inserted into the member.

— Existing records in the member can be deleted.

— Existing records in the member can be replaced entirely by new records with the same sequence numbers as the old records.

— Parts of existing records in the member can be replaced when the COLUMN parameter is coded.

— Records in the member can be renumbered. All of the records or just some of them may have their sequence numbers changed.

— Blocks of records that are unnumbered can be inserted into the member at any point. After being inserted they can be numbered. This numbering operation may force records that follow the inserted records to also be renumbered.

Example 4: Member ALPHA in the pds OLD.PDS contains six records. The records have sequence numbers 100, 150, 200, 250, 300, and 350. It is necessary to change ALPHA by modifying record 100, inserting records with sequence numbers 125 and 225, and deleting existing records with sequence numbers 200, 250, and 350. The jobstep to accomplish all this is reproduced below. The important features in the code are explained on the following page.

```
//D          EXEC PGM=IEBUPDTE
//SYSPRINT    DD   SYSOUT=A
//SYSUT1      DD   DSN=OLD.PDS,DISP=OLD
//SYSUT2      DD   DSN=OLD.PDS,DISP=OLD
//SYSIN       DD   *
./   CHANGE   NAME=ALPHA,LIST=ALL,LEVEL=03
new record    to replace existing record               00000100
new record    to be added                              00000125
./   DELETE   SEQ1=200,SEQ2=250
new record    to be added                              00000225
./   DELETE   SEQ1=350,SEQ2=350
./   REPRO    next function control statement
       . . .
./   ENDUP
/*
```

Although adds, deletes, and changes are all specified, they are listed in order by the sequence numbers on the records in the SYSIN data set. If records are specified out of order IEBUPDTE ends the CHANGE function statement with the message

```
IEB806I STATEMENT SEQUENCE ERROR.
```

If there are additional function statements IEBUPDTE will continue to process them. Whether a record is an add or replacement depends entirely on whether a record exists in the old member with a matching sequence number. In this example it is assumed that existing member ALPHA contains a record with sequence number 00000100 but does not contain records with sequence numbers 00000125 and 00000225.

When using the CHANGE function to add or replace records specify the complete eight digit sequence number in columns 73 to 80. Failure to do so will usually cause sequence errors to occur. However, it is not necessary to specify leading zeros with the parameters on a NUMBER or DELETE detail statement. If only one record is to be deleted specify the same value for both SEQ1 and SEQ2.

Both a SYSUT1 and a SYSUT2 statement must be coded even though they both identify the same data set. When CHANGE is specified other function statements may also be placed in the SYSIN data set as long as the UPDATE=INPLACE parameter is not coded with CHANGE.

Example 5: When the only changes to an existing member are record replacements a special form of the CHANGE function can be used. This is the UPDATE=INPLACE keyword parameter. The jobstep will fail if there is an attempt to add or delete records. The message printed is

```
IEB807I INVALID OPERATION
```

To replace records 100 and 200 in ALPHA the following code could be used:

```
//SYSUT1      DD  DSN=OLD.PDS,DISP=OLD
//SYSIN       DD  *
./  CHANGE    NAME=ALPHA,LIST=ALL,LEVEL=04,UPDATE=INPLACE
./  NUMBER    NEW1=100,INCR=5
replacement for record 100                        00000100
replacement for record 200                        00000200
./  ENDUP
```

With this code the two records in ALPHA are rewritten within the space currently occupied by member ALPHA. In addition, after the replacements are made all records in ALPHA are renumbered starting at 100 and incrementing by five. A new copy of member ALPHA in a different location within the pds is not made. Hence there is no reason to code a SYSUT2 statement. The TTR entry for ALPHA is unchanged. A new copy of the member is always created unless UPDATE=INPLACE is specified. When CHANGE with UPDATE=INPLACE is specified no other function statements are permitted in the SYSIN data set. In this example the records in member ALPHA are not renumbered until after the replacements are made.

Example 6: A third example illustrating CHANGE concerns inserting a block of four records into member ALPHA. None of the records are numbered. They are to be inserted following the record with sequence number 150 and are given sequence numbers 160, 170, 180, and 190. The code to do this is the following:

```
//SYSIN   DD   *
./   CHANGE   NAME=ALPHA,LIST=ALL,LEVEL=05
./   NUMBER   SEQ1=ALL,NEW1=160,INCR=10,INSERT=YES
the 4 records to be inserted follow here
./   ENDUP
```

Using Sequential Data Sets With IEBUPDTE

Sequential data sets may be specified on the SYSUT1 and SYSUT2 statements. When a sequential data set is coded it denotes that it is being made into a member of a pds or vice versa. Examples of each situation are given below.

Example 7: Member ALPHA is to be added to the pds OLD.PDS. The records that will comprise ALPHA are currently stored as a sequential data set. Two of the records in ALPHA are to be new logical records replacing those in the sequential data set. This example assumes that the records in the sequential data set are numbered.

```
//G             EXEC   PGM=IEBUPDTE,PARM=MOD
//SYSPRINT      DD     SYSOUT=A
//SYSUT1        DD     DSN=SEQ.DATA.SET,DISP=SHR
//SYSUT2        DD     DSN=OLD.PDS,DISP=OLD
//SYSIN         DD     *
./   CHANGE     NEW=PO,MEMBER=ALPHA,LIST=ALL,LEVEL=00
./   NUMBER     NEW1=25,INCR=25
replacement record for existing record 50       00000050
replacement record for existing record 250      00000250
./   ALIAS      NAME=AAAAASEQ
./   ENDUP
/*
```

Here a copy of the records in the sequential data set SEQ.DATA.SET will be added to the pds OLD.PDS with member name ALPHA and alias AAAAASEQ. The records are also renumbered starting at 25 and incremented by 25. Note that MEMBER and not NAME is specified on the CHANGE statement. Also note that the keyword parameter NEW is used to denote that the organization of a data set is being changed (in this case from sequential to partitioned).

Example 8: Member BETA in pds OLD.PDS will be used to create a sequential data set. Portions of selected records in BETA will be replaced by data coded in the SYSIN data set. Here it is also assumed that the records in BETA are numbered.

```
//H            EXEC   PGM=IEBUPDTE
//SYSPRINT     DD     SYSOUT=A
//SYSUT1       DD     DSN=OLD.PDS,DISP=SHR
//SYSUT2       DD     DSN=ANEW.SEQ.DATASET,
//             DCB=(LRECL=80,RECFM=F,BLKSIZE=80),
//             SPACE=(TRK,3),VOL=SER=DISK99,
//             UNIT=3350,DISP=(NEW,CATLG)
//SYSIN       DD  *
./  CHANGE    NEW=PS,NAME=BETA,LIST=ALL,COLUMN=30
replacement record for existing record 7        00000007
./  DELETE    SEQ1=13,SEQ2=19
replacement record for existing record 32       00000032
./  ENDUP
/*
```

Note that in this example NAME must be specified on the CHANGE statement, contrary to the previous example. Here the COLUMN keyword parameter means that columns 30 through 80 on the records with sequence numbers 00000007 and 00000032 will be replaced by the data coded above. Columns 1 through 29 on these two records will remain unchanged. LEVEL is not coded since the output is not a pds member.

IEBUPDTE is probably the most complicated data set utility. Five factors in the JCL are used to control the processing. These are the SYSIN, SYSUT1, and SYSUT2 DD statements, the PARM value, and the DISP value coded with an output pds. These factors interact to determine whether members can successfully be added or replace existing members.

Exercises

1. Use IEBUPDTE to copy the three members PLIXCG, COBUCG, and ASMFCG from SYS1.PROCLIB to a new pds that is being created in this jobstep. Call the new pds SYS1.XCG.

2. Use IEBUPDTE to copy two members from SYS1.PROC.BACKUP to SYS1.XCG. The members are to replace two existing members with the same names, PLIXCG and COBUCG.

3. Suppose that IEBUPDTE is not available. How can the functions required in Exercises 1 and 2 be performed? What utilities besides IEBUPDTE can be used to: a) create a pds and copy several specific members from an existing pds into it in one jobstep, or b) copy several members from one existing pds to another where the copied members are to replace existing members with the same name. Again several members should be replaced in one step if possible.

4. Suppose it is necessary to add several members to an existing pds. The members are to be called ALPHA and BETA. It is unknown if there are existing members with the same names in the destination pds. How can IEBUPDTE alone be used to add them to the destination pds regardless of whether members with those names are present? How can IEBGENER be used to perform the same function in one jobstep?

5. It is necessary to add two members to the system cataloged procedure library SYS1.PROCLIB. The contents of the two members are shown below. They are to be given the names A123 and B456 respectively.

```
first member
  //A123      PROC                                      00000010
  //A         EXEC PGM=IEFBR14                          00000020
  //DD1       DD   DISP=(OLD,DELETE),DSN=NULLFILE       00000030

second member
  //B456      PROC DATASET=                             00000010
  //A         EXEC PGM=IEBUPDTE,PARM=MOD                00000020
  //SYSPRINT  DD   SYSOUT=A                             00000030
  //SYSUT1    DD   DSN=&DATASET,DISP=OLD                00000040
  //SYSUT2    DD   DSN=&DATASET,DISP=OLD                00000050
```

Both of these members should be written exactly as shown above. However, it is unnecessary to actually include the sequence numbers on the SYSIN data statements. Include the date in the directory entry for each member and record them as version one of each member. Be certain that all the above records also print out in the message data set. Is there any way to add these two members to SYS1.PROCLIB with IEBUPDTE and not have their records print in the message data set?

Now use IEBGENER to add the same two members to SYS1.PROCLIB. Can the exact same results be achieved? Why or why not? List at least four advantages IEBUPDTE has over IEBGENER when adding multiple members to a card image pds. Are there any situations when IEBGENER must be used to add members to a pds due to coding limitations associated with IEBUPDTE? Discuss the possible roles of each of the two procedures.

6. Suppose that IEBCOPY is unavailable at a time when it is necessary to compress a pds. Originally pds ALPHA contained five members A, B, C, D, and E. B and D have since been deleted. Compress the member area in ALPHA to regain the wasted space associated with the deleted members. Use IEBUPDTE for the compression. Multiple jobsteps may be necessary. It is not an acceptable solution to create a copy of ALPHA on a different disk volume with members A, C, and E; it must be the original ALPHA that is eventually compressed.

7. COBUCLG is a member of SYS1.PROCLIB. Turn this member into a sequential data set. Although the member contains records with sequence numbers 60 and 80 these records should not be present in the new data set. There is a record with sequence number 70 in the member. All of the records following it should be resequenced in increments of 20.

8. Two existing cataloged sequential data sets, SEQ1 and SEQ2 are to be used to supply the records to create the two members MEM1 and MEM2 in the existing pds ALPHA. Use IEBUPDTE to do this in one job step if possible. Is there any other utility that can perform the same function in exactly one job step?

9. The card image pds SYS1.ABC contains a member ALPHA whose ten records are listed below.

```
AAA . . .                    AA010
BBB . . .                    BB020
CCC . . .                    CC030
. . .
III . . .                    II090
JJJ . . .                    JJ100
```

Modify this member by adding records with sequence numbers 65, 35, 5, and 15. Each of these records should contain 70 bytes of the letter K. Existing records 30 and 40 are to have their contents changed to 77 bytes of the letter X. The records with sequence numbers 10, 20, 60, 70, and 80 are to be deleted. All changes are to be done in one jobstep with a minimum of control statements.

10. Starting with the same ten records in member ALPHA as defined in exercise 9, change the contents of bytes 37 to 50 on records with sequence numbers 30, 50, and 70 to 14 bytes of the character Z. Also delete records 10, 20, and 40. Add three records that consist of 77 bytes of the letter Q. These records should follow the last record in the data set and have sequence numbers of 125, 150, and 175.

11. Again begin with the ten records in member ALPHA as defined in exercise 9. It is necessary to insert five records between records 40 and 50. These five records are currently stored in a disk data set called DISK.DATA. Insert these records numbering them as 42, 44, 46, 48, and 50. The existing record 50 is to be deleted.

12. Once again the records in member ALPHA in SYS1.ABC as defined in Exercise 9 are to be modified. This time the update is to be performed in place. Change the contents of every record with a sequence number that is a multiple of 20 into 77 bytes of the character U.

13. Create a data set that contains 1000 records with the following format. There is a four digit sequence number in bytes 1 through 4. The first record is numbered 0 and subsequent records are incremented by ten. The remaining 76 bytes of each record contain blanks. Use IEBUPDTE in a meaningful manner in the construction of these records.

14. Use IEBUPDTE to create a sequential data set (not a pds member) out of in-stream data. With several minor modifications this is similar to adding a member to a pds.

Chapter 28

IEBCOPY

Overview

The major uses of IEBCOPY are:

— Create a backup copy of a partitioned data set (pds)

— Unload a pds to tape

— Reload an unloaded pds

— Restrict any type of copy operation to specific members rather than the entire pds

— Merge several partitioned data sets together to produce a new pds or enlarge an existing pds

— Compress a pds

What specific functions can be performed by IEBCOPY? There are seven general categories that will be discussed here and illustrated in the examples. The following list can serve as a detailed table of contents for the examples in this chapter.

1. A backup copy of a pds can be created. This backup can also be used as a pds. The same function can be performed with IEBUPDTE, but it is then necessary to

specify every member name in the control statements. Backing up a pds should be contrasted with using IEBCOPY to unload a pds or using IEBPTPCH to list the records in every member in a pds to the printer.

2. A pds can be unloaded to either disk or tape. Ordinarily, a tape volume is used to hold the unloaded data set. Such an operation is performed for backup or transportability.

3. An unloaded copy of a pds can be reloaded back to disk and reconstructed as a pds. This operation is necessary in order to process the data set as a pds again. In its unloaded format, a pds is a sequential data set.

4. In contrast to case 1 (a full copy) there is also the selective copy operation used when only designated members need to be copied from an input pds to an output pds. These selected members may be added to the output pds, and given the same names they had in the input pds, added and given new names in the output pds, or automatically replace an existing member in the output pds with the same name. With a little more work most of these functions can also be performed by IEBUPDTE.

5. Several input partitioned data sets can be merged to form an output pds. This output pds may be created in the IEBCOPY jobstep or may exist prior to the merge. The members themselves are merged. The logical records within the members are not examined. There is little similarity with the merge process performed by DFSORT.

6. A compress operation can be performed on a pds to regain the wasted space that results from replacing and deleting members.

7. Combinations of the above functions can take place in the same job step. Each function can involve different partitioned data sets. Like IEBUPDTE, IEBCOPY can perform distinct functions in the same job step; while IEBGENER and IEBPTCH can perform only one function.

IEBCOPY is the last of the four major data set utilities to be discussed in depth. It has very few similarities with the three utilities already covered.

SYSPRINT still identifies the message data set and SYSIN the control statement data set. With IEBCOPY the SYSIN data set may be dummied out. The SYSPRINT messages are easy to understand and contain a good deal of extra informatory details about the pds processed. There is a loosening on the restrictions of DDnames when using IEBCOPY. SYSUT1 and SYSUT2 need not be coded as DDnames unless the control statement data set is dummied out. When this is done SYSUT1 and SYSUT2 identify the input and output data sets in exactly the same manner as with the other data set utilities.

When control statements are present any DDnames can be used to denote the input and output data sets. The keywords coded in the control statements specify whether a data set will be used for input or output. There can be any number of input and output data sets specified with just one IEBCOPY jobstep. However, concatenation of data sets is not allowed.

The single most significant fact about IEBCOPY's input and output data sets is that they are all partitioned data sets or unloaded copies of partitioned data sets. IEBCOPY's sole function is to manipulate partitioned data sets at the member level. By contrast, IEBUPDTE can manipulate a pds at both the member level and the record level and IEBGENER can only manipulate the records in a member. The most significant function involving partitioned data sets that IEBCOPY cannot perform is to create a multi-member pds out of in-stream data. IEBGENER and IEBUPDTE can both do this.

A sequential copy of a pds can be created with IEBCOPY. This copy, often used as a backup, may be written onto tape or disk. It obviously cannot be used as a pds when sequentially organized. However, it can later be transformed back to true pds format on disk.

This process of transforming a pds into a sequential data set is called unloading the pds. Invariably the unloaded data set is stored on tape. Except for loading and unloading of pds's, there are no situations where a sequential data set should be specified as an input or output data set with this utility.

Work Data Sets

Two work data sets are often required when using IEBCOPY. They are identified by DDnames of SYSUT3 and SYSUT4. SYSUT3 is used whenever there is insufficient virtual storage to process the members in the input pds. SYSUT4 is necessary if there is not enough virtual storage to process the directory of the output pds. With two exceptions (covered in the examples below) it is a good idea to code both of these data sets every time IEBCOPY is executed. Allocating several tracks for each of these data sets will guarantee sufficient space for all but the largest partitioned data sets. Only UNIT and SPACE parameters need to be coded for the SYSUT3 and SYSUT4 work data sets. If insufficient storage is requested for either data set a standard Sx37 abend will result.

IEBCOPY requires a large amount of virtual storage for some functions. The messages IEB133 and IEB135 imply that the utility should be run in a larger region. This frequently occurs during a compress operation.

Control Statements

For any IEBCOPY function the first control statement contains the COPY operator. Data sets used as input and output are identified on a control statement by the keyword parameters INDD and OUTDD. If INDD=DD1,OUTDD=DD2 is coded on a COPY statement then the DD statements with DDnames DD1 and DD2 will identify the input and output data sets respectively. Since every COPY statement contains the same operators, IEBCOPY cannot determine the function to be performed until the input and output data sets are examined. A sequential input data set identifies a load operation and a sequential output data set an unload operation. If both data sets are partitioned, a copy operation is performed. When the same data set is coded for both input and output, a compress is performed. Two sequential data sets are an invalid combination.

A full copy of every input pds member does not have to be performed each time IEBCOPY is used. A selective copy requires an additional control statement with the SELECT or EXCLUDE operator. The two operators are mutually exclusive within the same COPY operation, and will appear as follows:

```
COPY   INDD=dd1,OUTDD=dd2           FIRST COPY OPERATION
SELECT  MEMBER=(a,b,c,...)
SELECT  MEMBER=(m,n,o,...)
COPY   INDD=dd3,OUTDD=dd4           SECOND COPY OPERATION
EXCLUDE  MEMBER=(z,y,x,...)
```

Every operator and keyword operand used by IEBCOPY can be abbreviated to the first letter in its complete name. Hence the first two control statements above can also be coded as follows:

```
C   I=dd1,O=dd2
S   M=(a,b,c,...)
```

Notice that more than one copy operation may be specified in a jobstep. Each COPY operator marks the beginning of a new copy operation. For each COPY operation an output data set and one or more input data sets must be specified. A COPY operation can include any number of SELECT operators or one EXCLUDE operator. The complete JCL code needed with the above set of control statements is

```
//A         EXEC    PGM=IEBCOPY,REGION=500K
//SYSPRINT DD SYSOUT=A
//SYSUT3    DD UNIT=SYSDA,SPACE=(CYL,(1,1))
//SYSUT4    DD UNIT=SYSDA,SPACE=(CYL,(1,1))
//dd1       DD input  pds for first  copy operation
//dd2       DD output pds for first  copy operation
//dd3       DD input  pds for second copy operation
//dd4       DD output pds for second copy operation
//SYSIN     DD *
  COPY   INDD=dd1,OUTDD=dd2           FIRST COPY OPERATION
  SELECT  MEMBER=(a,b,c,...)
  SELECT  MEMBER=(m,n,o,...)
  COPY   OUTDD=dd4,INDD=dd3           SECOND COPY OPERATION
  EXCLUDE  MEMBER=(z,y,x,...)
/*
```

Several additional options are available when SELECT is coded. It is possible to select a member from an old pds and have it copied to a new pds giving it a different name. A member copied from an old pds can be designated to replace an existing member with the same name in the output pds. Finally, a member can be copied from one pds to another and be renamed to a value that will replace an existing member. The only other information specified with EXCLUDE is a listing of the members to be omitted from the copy operation.

Creating a Backup Copy of a Partitioned Data Set

Example 1: Create a full backup copy of the cataloged pds OLD.PDS. This backup copy should itself be a pds rather than an unloaded copy of OLD.PDS.

```
//A            EXEC   PGM=IEBCOPY
//SYSPRINT     DD     SYSOUT=A
//SYSUT3       DD     UNIT=SYSDA,SPACE=(TRK,(2,1))
//SYSUT4       DD     UNIT=SYSDA,SPACE=(TRK,(2,1))
//SYSUT1       DD     DSN=OLD.PDS,DISP=SHR
//SYSUT2       DD     DSN=NEW.PDS,DISP=(NEW,CATLG),
//             UNIT=3350,VOL=SER=DISK98,DCB=(OLD.PDS),
//             SPACE=(CYL,(5,,36))
//SYSIN        DD     DUMMY
```

Here the backup copy will have exactly the same DCB attributes as the original pds. It will have one track devoted entirely to directory blocks. For more information on the structure of a pds see Chapter 12.

Exactly the same results can be achieved by using control statements. With control statements, SYSUT1 and SYSUT2 are not required DDnames and will be replaced by DD statements with DDnames ALPHA and BETA respectively. The changes in the above code are shown below. There are no changes in the first three DD statements.

```
//ALPHA       DD     DSN=OLD.PDS,DISP=SHR
//BETA        DD     DSN=NEW.PDS,DISP=(NEW,CATLG),
//            UNIT=3350,VOL=SER=DISK98,DCB=(OLD.PDS),
//            SPACE=(CYL,(5,,36))
//SYSIN       DD     *
    COPY   INDD=ALPHA,OUTDD=BETA
/*
```

Unloading and Reloading Partitioned Data Sets

Example 2: Create an unloaded backup copy of OLD.PDS. To do this and place the resulting unloaded copy on disk only two very small changes in the original

Example 1 code are necessary. On the SYSUT2 DD statement change the SPACE parameter to reflect a sequential rather than a partitioned data set organization. For example, code SPACE=(CYL,5). The second change is to omit the DCB parameter, and let IEBCOPY supply all of the DCB values during an unload operation.

To place the unloaded data set on tape SYSUT2 should be rewritten as follows:

```
//SYSUT2    DD   DSN=NEW.UNLOADED.PDS,DISP=(NEW,KEEP),
//               UNIT=TAPE,VOL=SER=TAPE02,LABEL=(2,SL)
```

The unloaded pds becomes the second data set on the standard label tape volume TAPE02.

As with unloading to disk, no DCB parameter should be present. Let the utility provide the LRECL, RECFM, and BLKSIZE. Since an unloaded pds contains both directory and member area records in the same sequential data set, the record format cannot be fixed. Some type of variable format must be used. One other change should be made to the code in Example 1 to make it appropriate here. It is unnecessary to code SYSUT4 with an unload operation since there is no output pds directory present.

Notice that there is no change in the control statement data set for a backup or an unload operation. The message data set specifies the particular operation performed. Recall that IEBCOPY determines the desired operation by examining the control statements (if any) and the data set organization of the input and output data sets.

Example 3: A pds that had been previously unloaded to tape is now to be loaded back to pds format on disk. The unloaded data set is currently on tape. Use the following code for this:

```
//C           EXEC   PGM=IEBCOPY
//SYSPRINT    DD     SYSOUT=A
//SYSUT4      DD     UNIT=SYSDA,SPACE=(TRK,(2,1))
//TAPE        DD     DSN=NEW.UNLOADED.PDS,DISP=(OLD,KEEP),
//            UNIT=TAPE,VOL=SER=TAPE02,LABEL=(2,SL)
//DISK        DD     DSN=NEW.LOADED.DISK.PDS,UNIT=3350,
//            DISP=(NEW,CATLG),SPACE=(CYL,(5,,36)),
//            VOL=SER=DISK95
//SYSIN       DD     *
    COPY   INDD=TAPE,OUTDD=DISK
/*
```

Notice that no SYSUT3 statement is necessary since the input is not a pds. Note also that it is unnecessary to code a DCB parameter on either the tape or disk data set. It is unnecessary with the tape data set because SL processing is specified. IEBCOPY will provide the necessary values for the output disk data set. They will be the same values the pds had prior to the unload operation. Unloading from disk rather than tape is very similar to this example.

Selective Copy Operations

Complete JCL Job Listing: Example 4: Five members are to be copied from SYS1.PROCLIB to a private procedure pds called ACSSTU.PROCLIB. This pds has already been created in the previous job step by IEBUPDTE and two members, COBOLCOM and LINKAGEE, have been added to it. The five new members are COBUC, PLIXCG, SORTD, LKED, and ASMFC. The following code is used:

```
//D            EXEC   PGM=IEBCOPY
//SYSPRINT     DD     SYSOUT=A
//SYSUT3       DD     UNIT=SYSDA,SPACE=(CYL,1)
//SYSUT4       DD     UNIT=SYSDA,SPACE=(CYL,1)
//PROCLIB      DD     DSN=SYS1.PROCLIB,DISP=SHR
//MYLIB        DD     DSN=ACSSTU.PROCLIB,DISP=OLD
//SYSIN        DD     *
    COPY   OUTDD=MYLIB,INDD=PROCLIB
    SELECT MEMBER=(COBUC,PLIXCG,SORTD,LKED,ASMFC)
/*
```

In addition to copying the same five members some additional functions are to be performed. COBUC is to be given the name COBOLCOM in ACSSTU.PROCLIB and LKED the name LINKAGEE. There already is a COBOLCOM and LINKAGEE in ACSSTU.PROCLIB that must be replaced. There is no member PLIXCG in ACSSTU.PROCLIB. All of the above JCL remains the same but the SELECT control statement can now be coded in either of the two following ways:

```
SELECT   MEMBER=((COBUC,COBOLCOM),(PLIXCG,,R),SORTD,   X
         ASMFC,(LKED,LINKAGEE,R))
```
or
```
SELECT   MEMBER=((COBUC,COBOLCOM),(PLIXCG,,R),SORTD)
SELECT   MEMBER=(ASMFC,(LKED,LINKAGEE,R))
```

When this job is run the messages displayed in Figure 28–1 are written to the SYSPRINT data sets with IEBUPDTE and IEBCOPY. The JCL and allocation messages are also printed.

The possible formats that can be used with the MEMBER operand are shown in Table 28–1.

Merging Partitioned Data Sets

Four existing partitioned data sets contain the members shown in Figure 28–2. It is assumed that all four pds's have the same dcb values. These will be refered to in Example 5.

FIGURE 28–1

Complete JCL Job Listing: Example 4

```
                    J E S 2   J O B   L O G

-------- JOB 2181  IEF097I LARRY    - USER ACS1125  ASSIGNED
16.03.43 JOB 2181  $HASP373 LARRY    STARTED - INIT  1 - CLASS B - SYS 8000
16.03.43 JOB 2181  IEF403I LARRY - STARTED - TIME=16.03.43
16.03.50 JOB 2181  IEF404I LARRY - ENDED - TIME=16.03.50
16.03.50 JOB 2181  $HASP395 LARRY    ENDED
```

```
 1      //LARRY JOB (XXXXXXXXXXXXXX),LARRY,PRTY=8,MSGCLASS=D,CLASS=B          JOB 2181
        ***ROUTE PRINT 16670                                                       002
 2      //A       EXEC PGM=IEBUPDTE,PARM=NEW                                      0030
        ******************************************************************        0040
        *** IEBUPDTE IS USED TO ADD TWO MEMBERS TO THE CARD IMAGE LIBRARY         0050
        *** WHICH IS CREATED IN THIS STEP                                         0060
        ******************************************************************        0070
 3      //SYSPRINT DD  SYSOUT=$                                                   0080
 4      //SYSUT2   DD  DSN=ACSSTU.PROCLIB,DISP=(NEW,PASS),                        0090
        //             UNIT=SYSDA,SPACE=(CYL,(1,,5)),                             0100
        //             DCB=(LRECL=80,RECFM=FB,BLKSIZE=400)                        0110
 5      //SYSIN    DD *                                                           0120
 6      //B EXEC PGM=IEBCOPY                                                      0350
        ******************************************************************        0040
        *** IEBCOPY IS USED TO ADD AND MODIFY SEVERAL MEMBERS IN THE              0050
        *** LIBRARY CREATED IN THE PREVIOUS STEP.                                 0060
        ******************************************************************        0070
 7      //SYSPRINT DD SYSOUT=$                                                    0360
 8      //SYSUT3   DD UNIT=SYSDA,SPACE=(CYL,1)                                    0370
 9      //SYSUT4   DD UNIT=SYSDA,SPACE=(CYL,1)                                    0380
10      //PROCLIB  DD DSN=SYS1.PROCLIB,DISP=SHR                                   0390
11      //MYLIB    DD DSN=ACSSTU.PROCLIB,DISP=OLD                                 0400
12      //SYSIN    DD *                                                           0410
        //                                                                        0460
```

```
IEF236I ALLOC. FOR LARRY A
IEF237I JES2 ALLOCATED TO SYSPRINT
IEF237I 14D  ALLOCATED TO SYSUT2
IEF237I JES2 ALLOCATED TO SYSIN
IEF142I LARRY A - STEP WAS EXECUTED - COND CODE 0000
IEF285I   JES2.JOB02181.S0000104                     SYSOUT
IEF285I   ACSSTU.PROCLIB                             PASSED
IEF285I   VOL SER NOS= WORK02.
IEF285I   JES2.JOB02181.SI000101                     SYSIN
IEF373I STEP /A       / START 86329.1603
IEF374I STEP /A       / STOP  86329.1603 CPU    0MIN 00.08SEC SRB    0MIN 00.00SEC VIRT    32K SYS   396K
IEF236I ALLOC. FOR LARRY B
IEF237I JES2 ALLOCATED TO SYSPRINT
IEF237I 26D  ALLOCATED TO SYSUT3
IEF237I 14C  ALLOCATED TO SYSUT4
IEF237I 140  ALLOCATED TO PROCLIB
IEF237I 14D  ALLOCATED TO MYLIB
IEF237I JES2 ALLOCATED TO SYSIN
IEF142I LARRY B - STEP WAS EXECUTED - COND CODE 0000
IEF285I   JES2.JOB02181.S0000105                     SYSOUT
IEF285I   SYS86329.T160343.RA000.LARRY.R0000001      DELETED
IEF285I   VOL SER NOS= WORK04.
IEF285I   SYS86329.T160343.RA000.LARRY.R0000002      DELETED
IEF285I   VOL SER NOS= WORK01.
IEF285I   SYS1.PROCLIB                               KEPT
IEF285I   VOL SER NOS= SYS000.
IEF285I   ACSSTU.PROCLIB                             DELETED
IEF285I   VOL SER NOS= WORK02.
IEF285I   JES2.JOB02181.SI000102                     SYSIN
IEF373I STEP /B       / START 86329.1603
IEF374I STEP /B       / STOP  86329.1603 CPU    0MIN 00.11SEC SRB    0MIN 00.01SEC VIRT   128K SYS   396K
IEF375I  JOB /LARRY   / START 86329.1603
IEF376I  JOB /LARRY   / STOP  86329.1603 CPU    0MIN 00.19SEC SRB    0MIN 00.01SEC
RCS176I  1125 015150000
```

```
      SYSIN                          NEW MASTER                               IEBUPDTE LOG PAGE 0001

      ./ ADD NAME=COBOLCOM,LIST=ALL                                     0130
      ./ NUMBER NEW1=10,INCR=10                                         0140
                                     AAAAAAAAAAAAAAAAAAAAAAAAAAAAAAAAAAAAAAAAAAAAAAAAAAAAAAAAAAAA         00000010
                                     AAAAAAAAAAAAAAAAAAAAAAAAAAAAAAAAAAAAAAAAAAAAAAAAAAAAAAAAAAAA         00000020
                                     AAAAAAAAAAAAAAAAAAAAAAAAAAAAAAAAAAAAAAAAAAAAAAAAAAAAAAAAAAAA         00000030
                                     AAAAAAAAAAAAAAAAAAAAAAAAAAAAAAAAAAAAAAAAAAAAAAAAAAAAAAAAAAAA         00000040
                                     AAAAAAAAAAAAAAAAAAAAAAAAAAAAAAAAAAAAAAAAAAAAAAAAAAAAAAAAAAAA         00000050
                                     AAAAAAAAAAAAAAAAAAAAAAAAAAAAAAAAAAAAAAAAAAAAAAAAAAAAAAAAAAAA         00000060
                                     AAAAAAAAAAAAAAAAAAAAAAAAAAAAAAAAAAAAAAAAAAAAAAAAAAAAAAAAAAAA         00000070
                                     AAAAAAAAAAAAAAAAAAAAAAAAAAAAAAAAAAAAAAAAAAAAAAAAAAAAAAAAAAAA         00000080
                                     AAAAAAAAAAAAAAAAAAAAAAAAAAAAAAAAAAAAAAAAAAAAAAAAAAAAAAAAAAAA         00000090
                                     AAAAAAAAAAAAAAAAAAAAAAAAAAAAAAAAAAAAAAAAAAAAAAAAAAAAAAAAAAAA         00000100
                                     AAAAAAAAAAAAAAAAAAAAAAAAAAAAAAAAAAAAAAAAAAAAAAAAAAAAAAAAAAAA         00000110
IEB817I MEMBER NAME (COBOLCOM) NOT FOUND IN NM DIRECTORY.  STOWED WITH TTR.


      SYSIN                          NEW MASTER                               IEBUPDTE LOG PAGE 0002

      ./ ADD NAME=LINKAGEE,LIST=ALL                                     0260
      ./ NUMBER NEW1=10,INCR=10                                         0270
                                     BBBBBBBBBBBBBBBBBBBBBBBBBBBBBBBBBBBBBBBBBBBBBBBBBBBB                 00000010
                                     BBBBBBBBBBBBBBBBBBBBBBBBBBBBBBBBBBBBBBBBBBBBBBBBBBBB                 00000020
                                     BBBBBBBBBBBBBBBBBBBBBBBBBBBBBBBBBBBBBBBBBBBBBBBBBBBB                 00000030
                                     BBBBBBBBBBBBBBBBBBBBBBBBBBBBBBBBBBBBBBBBBBBBBBBBBBBB                 00000040
                                     BBBBBBBBBBBBBBBBBBBBBBBBBBBBBBBBBBBBBBBBBBBBBBBBBBBB                 00000050
                                     BBBBBBBBBBBBBBBBBBBBBBBBBBBBBBBBBBBBBBBBBBBBBBBBBBBB                 00000060
                                     BBBBBBBBBBBBBBBBBBBBBBBBBBBBBBBBBBBBBBBBBBBBBBBBBBBB                 00000070
IEB817I MEMBER NAME (LINKAGEE) NOT FOUND IN NM DIRECTORY.  STOWED WITH TTR.
IEB818I HIGHEST CONDITION CODE WAS 00000000
IEB819I END OF JOB IEBUPDTE.


                                     IEBCOPY MESSAGES AND CONTROL STATEMENTS

                     COPY    OUTDD=MYLIB,INDD=PROCLIB                                    0420
                     SELECT  MEMBER=((COBUC,COBOLCOM),(PLIXCG,,R),SORTD,            X    0430
                                ASMFC,(LKED,LINKAGEE,R))                                 0440
IEB167I  FOLLOWING MEMBER(S)  COPIED  FROM INPUT DATA SET REFERENCED BY PROCLIB  -
IEB154I  ASMFC    HAS BEEN SUCCESSFULLY  COPIED
IEB155I  LINKAGEE HAS BEEN SUCCESSFULLY  COPIED  AND IS A NEW NAME
IEB154I  PLIXCG   HAS BEEN SUCCESSFULLY  COPIED
IEB154I  SORTD    HAS BEEN SUCCESSFULLY  COPIED
IEB144I  THERE ARE 0000014 UNUSED TRACKS IN OUTPUT DATA SET REFERENCED BY MYLIB
IEB149I  THERE ARE 0000004  UNUSED DIRECTORY BLOCKS IN OUTPUT DIRECTORY
IEB147I  END OF JOB -00 WAS HIGHEST SEVERITY CODE
```

TABLE 28–1
Formats Used With the MEMBER Operand

Syntax	*Processing Performed*
MEMBER=(a)	Copy member a. It is to be named a in the output pds. Parentheses are unnecessary.
MEMBER=((a,b))	Copy member a. It is to be named b in the output pds.
MEMBER=((a,,R))	Copy member a. It is to replace an existing member a in the output pds.
MEMBER=((a,b,R))	Copy member a. It is to be named b and replace an existing member b in the output pds.
MEMBER=(a,,R)	Syntax error.
MEMBER=(a,R)	Copy members a and R. They will retain those names. The parentheses are necessary.

Example 5: Merge the members in the first three pds's into the fourth pds. Here PDSA is a partitioned data set containing members A, E, I, and W. PDSB contains members A, E, I, and O. PDSC contains members A, I, Q, and W. It is desired to merge the members from these three data sets into the existing pds PDSZ which currently contains three members A, I, and Q. This is coded as follows:

```
//E          EXEC  PGM=IEBCOPY
//SYSPRINT   DD    SYSOUT=A
//SYSUT3     DD    UNIT=SYSDA,SPACE=(TRK,(1,1))
//SYSUT4     DD    UNIT=SYSDA,SPACE=(TRK,(1,1))
//PDSA       DD    DSN=PDSA,DISP=SHR
//PDSB       DD    DSN=PDSB,DISP=SHR
//PDSC       DD    DSN=PDSC,DISP=SHR
//PDSZ       DD    DSN=PDSZ,DISP=OLD
//SYSIN      DD    *
     COPY   OUTDD=PDSZ,
            INDD=PDSA,
            INDD=PDSB,PDSC
/*
```

Since no SELECT or EXCLUDE statements are present a full copy will take place. The three partitioned data sets that are supplying input members will be searched in the order in which they are specified in the control data set. PDSA is searched and members E and W are copied to PDSZ. Members A and I are not added to PDSZ since members with those names are already present. Next, PDSB is searched and

FIGURE 28–2
Four Partitioned Data Sets

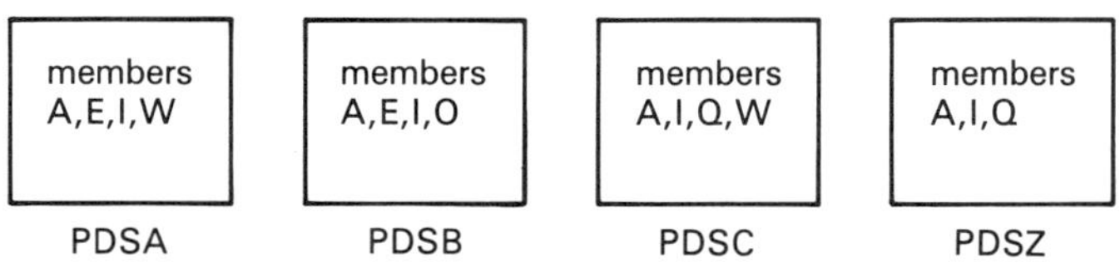

only member O is copied to PDSZ. Finally, the directory of PDSC is searched and since all member names found there are already present in PDSZ none are added. Notice that it is unnecessary to use column 72 to denote continuation with IEB-COPY.

Suppose one additional control statement is coded to specify the members that are to be added to PDSZ. The control statements now read as follows:

```
COPY   OUTDD=PDSZ,
       INDD=PDSA,PDSB,PDSC
SELECT   MEMBER=(A,E,I,O,W)
```

Since members A and I are already present they will never be selected. PDSA is searched and supplies members E and W. PDSB supplies member O. Since all members specified on the SELECT statement have been found at this point, PDSC is ignored.

A final modification would result in specifying the replace option with every member specified on the SELECT statement.

```
SELECT MEMBER=((A,,R),(E,,R),(I,,R),(Q,,R),(W,,R))
```

Here members A and I are copied from PDSA and replace the existing members in PDSZ with those names. Member Q from PDSC replaces existing member Q. There are no members named E and W that could be replaced.

PDS Compression

The single most common use of IEBCOPY is to compress a partitioned data set. Most MVS installations contain a large number of pds's that must be compressed on a periodic basis. Every pds that has had members replaced or deleted needs to be periodically compressed. A compression operation is the only way to reclaim the dead space in the member area of the pds. Without undergoing periodic compressions a pds may appear to be full when over 90% of its member area is dead space. Although a compression is the most complex operation IEBCOPY performs it requires the smallest number of JCL and control statements.

Example 6: The following code can be used to compress a pds:

```
//F           EXEC   PGM=IEBCOPY,REGION=500K
//SYSPRINT    DD     SYSOUT=A
//SYSUT3      DD     UNIT=SYSDA,SPACE=(TRK,(2,1))
//SYSUT4      DD     UNIT=SYSDA,SPACE=(TRK,(2,1))
//INOUT       DD     DSN=PDS.TO.COMPRESS,DISP=OLD
//SYSIN       DD     *
    COPY   INDD=INOUT,OUTDD=INOUT
/*
```

SELECT and EXCLUDE should not be coded when doing a compress. Remember to code a REGION parameter when compressing a large pds. At the completion of the compress operation the SYSPRINT data set will list the members that were moved and those that remained in place during the compression. The number of unused tracks and unused directory blocks in the pds will also be printed. It is unnecessary to code two DD statements to reference the single pds. As a final note, do not compress a pds when members in it are being used. For example, do not use the IEBCOPY program in SYS1.LINKLIB to compress SYS1.LINKLIB. Create a second copy of the program in some other library.

Additional IEBCOPY Features

Example 7: There are several additional features that can be used with IEBCOPY. They are utilized in the following section of code:

```
//G          EXEC   PGM=IEBCOPY
//SYSPRINT   DD     SYSOUT=A
//SYSUT3     DD     DSN=INPUT.PDS.MEMBERS,DISP=(NEW,PASS),
//           UNIT=SYSDA,VOL=SER=DISK95,SPACE=(80,(200,50))
//SYSUT4     DD     DSN=OUTPUT.PDS.DIRECTRY,DISP=(NEW,PASS)
//           UNIT=SYSDA,VOL=SER=DISK96,SPACE=(256,(20,5))
//INPUT1     DD     DSN=SYS1.PROCLIB,DISP=SHR
//INPUT2     DD     DSN=SYS1.PROCLIB2,DISP=SHR
//INPUT3     DD     DSN=MORE.PROCLIB,DISP=SHR
//OUTPUT     DD     DSN=ALL.PROCS.PDS,DISP=OLD
//SYSIN      DD     *
    COPY   INDD=INPUT1,OUTDD=OUTPUT,LIST=NO
    COPY   INDD=((INPUT2,R)),OUTDD=OUTPUT
    EXCLUDE  MEMBER=ABCDE,
             INDD=INPUT3,
    SELECT   MEMBER=((A,,R),(B,,R))
/*
```

Good approximations are attempted for both of the work data sets. Check the *MVS Utilities* manual for more information on this subject. Both work data sets have been passed and are available in subsequent steps. Examining these two data sets will contribute additional information as to how IEBCOPY works.

Multiple copy operations are specified in the control data set. In the first COPY operation every member in SYS1.PROCLIB is added to ALL.PROCS.PDS if a member with the same name does not exist in that pds. A listing of the members involved in the first copy operation is suppressed by coding LIST=NO. The second copy operation consists of two sub-steps. In the first of these all members from SYS1.PROCLIB2 are copied to ALL.PROCS.PDS and those whose names occur in the output pds will replace the existing member with the same name. Note that this replacement is at the data set level rather than at the member level. Member ABCDE will not be copied, however. The EXCLUDE statement marks the end of the first sub-step. The second sub-step specifies a new input pds from which additional selected members are to be included.

What potential dangers exist when using IEBCOPY?

1. Be certain to use IEBCOPY only with partitioned data sets for the input and output data sets unless doing a load or unload operation. No other data set organizations can be used.

2. Allow the utility sufficient space. This space consists of two types: the SYSUT3 and SYSUT4 work data sets and the actual region given to the program. The region size is especially important with a compress operation.

3. Do not use the same member name twice in a SELECT or EXCLUDE statement.

4. Do not code SELECT and EXCLUDE together in the same copy operation.

Exercises

1. SYS1.MACLIB is a card image library. Create a backup copy of SYS1.MACLIB and place it on disk volume WORK03. Call the backup copy SYS1.MACBACK. Do not use control statements in your code. Now create a second backup copy called SYS1.MACBACK2 on the same volume. Use control statements to do this. Suppose that for some reason IEBCOPY is not available and it is necessary to create a backup copy of SYS1.MACLIB. What other utilities could be used? Discuss the disadvantages and advantages associated with using other utilities to backup a very large partitioned data set.

2. As in Exercise 1, a backup copy of SYS1.MACLIB is to be placed on volume WORK03 and named SYS1.MACBACK. However, seven members that are part of SYS1.MACLIB are not to be included in the backup copy. The seven members are WRITEUP, DISKCOP, TAPECOP, BACKUP1, BACKUP2, BACKUP3, and BACKUP4. Write the necessary code to backup the pds. Do not use continuation in the control statements. Now accomplish the same results using exactly two control statements. Is it possible with IEBCOPY to create a backup copy of SYS1.MACLIB and omit seven members without coding any control statements?

3. A large pds called SYS1.MACBACK exists on volume WORK03. Several members have been deleted from it using IEHPROGM or IDCAMS. Write the code to compress the pds to reclaim the wasted space that the deleted members occupied. Under what conditions will the remaining active members occupy the same locations in the pds before and after the compress?

4. Copy every member in SYS1.MACLIB whose name begins with a vowel into a new pds that is being created in this step. Assume that IEHLIST has been used to produce a complete listing of all members in SYS1.PROCLIB. Suppose it is desired to write a more general segment of code that will accomplish the same results as were obtained by manually examining the IEHLIST output and using it to code the specific IEBCOPY control statements. Write a job stream that will create a pds whose members are the existing members in SYS1.MACLIB that begin with a vowel. The job stream should be general enough so that no manual intervention is necessary at any time to achieve correct results. Hint: Interface IEBCOPY, IEHLIST, and one or more application programs. Generalize

the job stream by specifying the vowels as a PARM value in your JCL and in no other place. Finally, modify your PARM value so that all members whose names do not begin with vowels are placed in the new pds.

5. Suppose ALPHA, BETA, and GAMMA are three partitioned datasets that all have the same dcb characteristics. They contain card images and are blocked with a blocking factor of ten. Each pds contains the members listed below.

Pds	*Members*	*New Names for the Members*
ALPHA	*A*, B	A, B1
BETA	A, *C*	A1, C
GAMMA	A, *B*, C	A2, B, C1

Use IEBCOPY to create a pds called DELTA which will contain just the three italicized members. Do this in one jobstep if possible. Using IEBGENER create a pds called DELTA which will contain the three members italicized above and no others. Do this in one jobstep if possible.

6. Merge the three existing partitioned data sets ALPHA, BETA, and GAMMA from Exercise 5 to create a new pds called DELTA which will contain all seven of the existing members. The names of the members in DELTA should be as shown above. Do this in one jobstep if possible. What will occur if the members in the three pds's contain different dcb characteristics?

7. Unload SYS1.PROCLIB to a 9–track 6250 BPI tape. Call it PROCLIB.UNLOAD. Unload all of SYS1.PROCLIB to tape except for members COBUC, COBUCL, and COBUCLG. This second unloaded data set should be the second data set on the same tape volume. Call it PROCLIB.SECOND. Suppose five members of SYS1.PROCLIB are each unloaded to tape. Can these members be loaded back to disk as part of a pds? Can this be done using IEBCOPY?

8. An unloaded pds called PROCLIB.UNLOAD exists on volume TAPE23. Recreate the initial pds on disk volume DISK34. Can the tape data set be loaded back to disk with several members excluded in the process?

9. Create a card image library and place five members in it called A, B, C, D, and E. Each member should consist of exactly three unblocked records. Print out the directory of the pds. Now use IEHPROGM or IDCAMS to delete members B and D. Use IEBCOPY to compress the pds. Prior to examining the IEBCOPY message data set, determine where within the pds members C and E will now be located. Use the IEBCOPY listing to verify your conjecture. Note that the exact location the members will occupy depends on the number of directory blocks in the pds.

10. Merge disk data set ALPHA and unloaded tape data set BETA (both are partitioned data sets). If the same member name occurs in both include only the member in ALPHA. Will it be necessary to first load BETA to disk? Can the results be accomplished in one jobstep?

11. Take an existing pds and unload it to tape. Code your own DCB parameters on the DD statement for the tape. Will IEBCOPY perform the unload successfully with your values? If the unload is performed successfully what dcb values are written on the tape data set labels—yours or a different set of values? What dcb values does IEBCOPY select for an unload operation? To determine the dcb values on a tape label use IEBGENER to copy them to the printer. Repeat this exercise, but unload the pds to disk rather than tape. First use a 3350 disk and then a 3380 disk.

12. A large pds is to be unloaded to tape. Is it reasonable to first compress it in order to save space on the tape? Create a jobstream to examine the format of an unloaded pds that originally contained deleted and modified members. Are the deleted members actually unloaded with the rest of the pds members? Is it possible to compress an unloaded pds? Does an unload operation followed by a load equal a compress operation?

13. ALPHA and BETA are two existing partitioned data sets. Copy all members from ALPHA to BETA. If an existing member in BETA has the same name as a member in ALPHA the ALPHA member is to replace it. All other members from ALPHA are to retain their original names when added to BETA.

14. As in Exercise 13, ALPHA and BETA are existing partitioned data sets. Copy into BETA only those members in ALPHA with names that do not match member names in BETA. These members should retain their original names.

15. Create a partitioned data set and add three members to it. All three members should contain fixed length unblocked records, but all three should have different logical record lengths. Choose 10, 80, and 500 bytes for the three logical record length values. Use IEBCOPY to create a backup copy of this pds. Does IEBCOPY successfully backup the pds? Describe conditions under which IEBCOPY will successfully backup such a pds and conditions under which it will fail. Hint: Reread Chapter 10 on construction of the Data Control Block and Chapter 12 on partitioned data sets.

16. Concatenate SYS1.PROCLIB and SYS1.MACLIB together as an input data set. Select several members from each (COBUCG, PLIXCLG, STOW, BLDL, and FIND) in the process of creating a new pds. Determine if IEBCOPY supports any processing of concatenated input data sets.

17. Rerun Example 4 and dump out the directory of ACSSTU.PROCLIB after the IEBUPDTE job step and again after the IEBCOPY step. In each case account for all the information contained in the directory especially the TTR values.

Chapter 29

IEBDG, IEBISAM, and IEBCOMPR

Overview

The major uses of IEBDG are:

— generate test data usually in the form of a sequential data set

— easily create variable, undefined, and spanned records (IEBGENER can also do this but requires more work)

— modify an existing sequential or ISAM data set by creating a second data set whose records contain the modifications

— create an ISAM data set out of sequential input

— create BDAM data sets with key fields

The major uses of IEBISAM are:

— create a backup ISAM data set

— unload an ISAM data set

— reload an unloaded ISAM data set

— print the records in an ISAM data set

The major uses of IEBCOMPR are:

— determine if the records in two sequential data sets are identical

— determine if the members in two partitioned data sets and the records they contain are identical

In this chapter the three remaining IEB utilities are examined. This includes IEBDG, IEBISAM, and IEBCOMPR. Both IEBISAM and IEBCOMPR are simple with few coding options available. IEBDG differs from these utilities in that it contains many control statement coding options. With the exception of IEBUPDTE it is probably the most difficult IEB utility to completely master. Since IEBDG does not enjoy the widespread popularity of the four utilities previously examined some of its features are not discussed in this book. Many programmers infrequently or never use this utility. As with any program that is rarely used, its features and options become forgotten. Because of this it often seems easier to write an application program rather than learn or relearn how to perform the same function with IEBDG. Hopefully the material presented in this chapter will make it easier and faster to perform the common IEBDG functions than to accomplish the same results by writing a COBOL or PL/I program.

IEBDG

In this book only the most important IEBDG features are discussed. The first two uses listed above are the most common reasons for using IEBDG. Both of the first two functions can also be performed with IEBGENER. In some cases, IEBGENER may be a better choice. Several situations where both utilities can be used are covered in the exercises at the end of the chapter. Even in the cases where IEBGENER requires more control statement code or more planning on the programmer's part it is still usually selected over IEBDG. This is due to the unfamiliarity of working with IEBDG.

The last two uses for IEBDG listed above cannot be performed with IEBGENER. In fact, no other utility can create an ISAM data set out of sequential input. This is the only major function that IEBISAM cannot perform with an ISAM data set. Likewise, no other utility can create a BDAM data set where a disk KEY field is written in front of each record. Other utilities can be used to create a relative BDAM data set. When creating either an ISAM or BDAM data set with keys, a programmer has two reasonable choices: either write an application program or use IEBDG. Using an exit routine written in assembler a BDAM data set with keys can also be created with IEBGENER. However, this involves as much work as writing an application program.

When using IEBDG the only required DDnames are SYSPRINT and SYSIN. Unlike all of the four utilities previously discussed, SYSPRINT need not be coded.

However, if it is not coded no message data set is written. SYSPRINT should always be coded until all syntax errors are removed from the control statements. The IEBDG error and informatory messages are easily understandable. When an error occurs most messages clearly isolate its exact byte location in the control statement. Like IEB-UPDTE, this utility permits both control statements and data within the SYSIN data set. Unlike IEBUPDTE, in practice in-stream data sets are rarely coded with the SYSIN control statements and in general can be avoided.

Input and Output Data Sets

Other than SYSIN and SYSPRINT, all other data sets used by IEBDG may have arbitrary DDnames. A control statement is used to identify and classify a particular DDname and the data set it references as either input or output. At least one output data set must be identified in a job step. However, any number of output data sets may be created in a single job step. The data used to create a record in an output data set can come from any of three possible sources. These are the following:

I An input data set may be identified by its DDname on a control statement. It may reside on disk or tape or be an in-stream data set.

II An in-stream data set may be included as a part of the SYSIN control statement data set.

III Data may also be created as the result of a request on a control statement. This is a common source of input data with IEBDG.

Data from any or all three of the sources is used to create output records. This is illustrated in Figure 29–1.

FIGURE 29–1

Creating Output Records From Three Input Sources

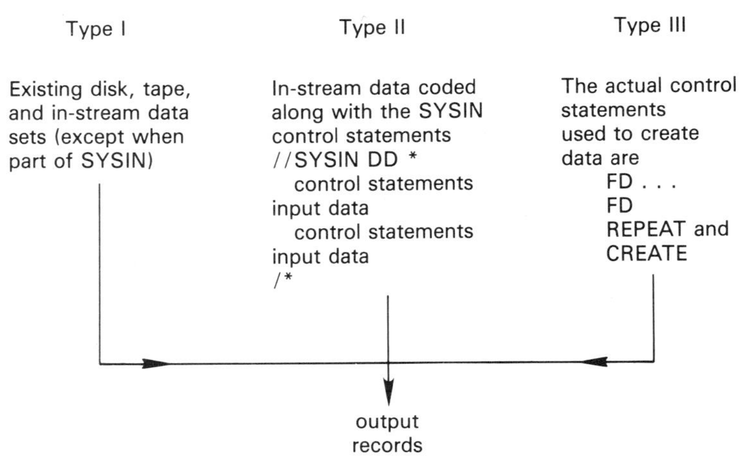

Any number of input triples (or parts of them) can be used repeatedly to create additional output data sets. A new output data set can be created on disk, tape, a printer, or on cards.

Control Statements

Five types of control statements can be coded.

DSD This operator serves two purposes. First, it is used to identify the input and output data sets through their DDname value. Additionally, each DSD denotes the beginning of a set of control statements. Each set creates exactly one output data set. When all of the output is generated from control statements and in-stream (SYSIN) data (types III and II in Figure 29–1) no input data sets are identified on a DSD statement.

FD This operator identifies a data field. The values commonly coded on an FD control statement are the name of the field, its location, the type of data it contains, and an initial value. Unlike the DSD operator, no FD operators need be coded. However, when this is the case all input must come from an existing data set or in-stream (SYSIN) records (types I and II in Figure 29–1). In this situation it is often just as easy to use IEBGENER to create an output data set. When an FD is defined with one set of control statements it can then be used with all subsequent sets of control statements in the job step.

CREATE The CREATE operator uses the previously defined sources of input to build output records. The specific types of input that are used are identified with this statement. Ordinarily one or more FD fields are grouped together on this statement to form output records.

REPEAT This operator is used to group together CREATE statements in order to easily establish patterns in the output records. REPEAT is not a required operator. It is the least frequently coded control statement.

END This marks the end of a group of control statements. END must be coded. Any number of control statement groups can be coded in a single IEBDG job step. DSD is always the first control statement in the group and END is the last.

The control statements shown below are used to create two output data sets.

//SYSIN DD * identifies the control statement data set

DSD references the first output data set. There is no input data set

FD references a first data field

FD	references a second data field
CREATE	uses just the two previous FDs to create output records
END	denotes the end of the first set of control statements. The output data set is created.
DSD	references a second output data set and two input data sets, one on disk and one on tape
FD	references a third data field
REPEAT	specifies that the next two CREATE statements are to be grouped together and repeated a specified number of times
CREATE	uses the disk input data set and all three FDs defined above to create output records
CREATE	uses only the first and third FDs to create output records with a different format
CREATE	uses the tape data set as input and the third FD to create output records. This CREATE statement is not within the scope of the REPEAT statement.
END	denotes the end of the second set of control statements. The second output data set is created.

The DSD Statement

The DSD statement contains the DDnames that identify the output data set and (optionally) one or more input data sets. Like IEBCOPY, IEBDG may use arbitrary DDnames for input and output data sets. The complete syntax is

```
DSD    OUTPUT=(DDname1),INPUT=(DDname2,DDname3,...,DDnameN)
```

As with all IEBDG parameters, OUTPUT and INPUT are keyword and may be coded in any order. Most frequently only one input data set is referenced. DDname1 should not be the same as any of the input DDnames. SYSIN and SYSPRINT should not be used as either input or output DDnames.

Example 1: Suppose it is desired to take records from an input data set called ALPHA and modify them by changing the values in bytes 61 through 70. The modified records are used to create an output data set called BETA. The following can be coded:

```
//A        EXEC PGM=IEBDG
//SYSPRINT DD   SYSOUT=A
//DDOUT     DD   DSN=BETA,DISP=(NEW,CATLG),...
//DDIN      DD   DSN=ALPHA,DISP=SHR
//SYSIN     DD   *
  DSD       OUTPUT=(DDOUT),INPUT=(DDIN)
  FD        this statement identifies the values that are to be
            placed in bytes 61 through 70 of the ALPHA
            records
```

The FD Statement

The FD statement is used to create output data strictly from control statements. Entire records may be created using just FD statements. Additionally, FD statements can be used to modify fields in existing data sets. Five keyword operands are frequently coded with FD statements. These operands are used to give the field a name (NAME=field name), specify its length in bytes (LENGTH=number-of-bytes), identify where it is to be placed in an output record (STARTLOC=byte location), and the actual value to be placed in the field. This initialization value can be assigned in two different ways. Either the FORMAT or PICTURE keyword may be coded. They cannot both be specified on the same FD statement. The syntax of the FORMAT statement is FORMAT=pattern where pattern denotes one of eight possible values or actions. These values are defined in Table 29–1 and illustrated in Figure 29–2.

TABLE 29–1
Pattern Value Definitions

Abbreviation	*Description*
SL	Shift Left
SR	Shift Right
TL	Truncate Left
TR	Truncate Right
FX	Fixed
RP	Ripple
RO	Roll
WV	Wave

FIGURE 29–2
Illustration of the Eight Pattern Actions

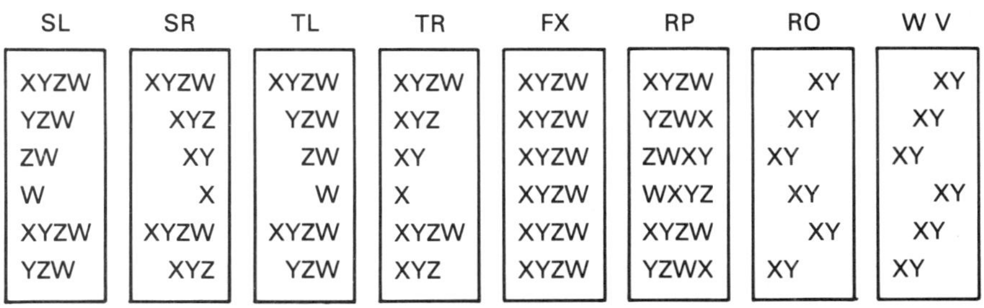

To illustrate the eight actions assume that a field contains the four bytes XYZW. The contents of the field after processing with each of the eight action types is shown in Figure 29–2. FX is the default. For RO and WV assume that only XY is used to clarify the processing.

The PICTURE keyword is coded in one of three ways.

```
PICTURE=length,'character string'   or
PICTURE=length,P'decimal number'    or
PICTURE=length,B'decimal number'
```

The latter two formats are used to code a decimal number using packed or binary representation. To create a 1 byte field and initialize it to 255 (i.e., hexadecimal FF) code:

```
FD  NAME=DELBYTE,LENGTH=1,STARTLOC=1,PICTURE=1,B'255'     (*)
```

Note the unusual syntax of the PICTURE keyword operand. It contains two positional subparameters. However, they are not enclosed together in an outer set of quotes or parentheses. To create a 3 byte field that begins in column two and contains the value +1 any of the following can be coded:

```
FD NAME=KEYFLD,LENGTH=3,STARTLOC=2,FORMAT=ZD
FD NAME=KEYFLD,LENGTH=3,STARTLOC=2,FORMAT=ZD,CHARACTER=1
FD NAME=KEYFLD,LENGTH=3,STARTLOC=2,FORMAT=AL,CHARACTER=1
FD NAME=KEYFLD,LENGTH=3,STARTLOC=2,FORMAT=AN,CHARACTER=1
```

When FORMAT=ZD is coded the default value is +1. With the other three patterns CHARACTER must be coded since 1 is not the default with any of them. This example can be extended by including an additional parameter that will cause the value in the field to be incremented by a fixed amount each time an output record is created. For example, to generate the numbers 1,3,5,7,9,... in field KEYFLD in the output records include the keyword parameter INDEX=2 on the FD statement. Likewise, to generate multiples of five in the field code the following:

```
FD NAME=KEYFLD,LENGTH=3,STARTLOC=2,FORMAT=ZD,               (*)
   CHARACTER=0,INDEX=5
```

To create a 77 byte field that begins in byte 5 and initialize it to binary zeroes code the following:

```
FD  NAME=FILLER,LENGTH=77,STARTLOC=5                        (*)
```

Since neither PICTURE nor FORMAT is coded the field is initialized to a default value of all binary zeroes. If FORMAT=AL is coded, the value ABC... XYZABC...XYZABC...XY is placed in the field.

The CREATE Statement

At this point it is clear how input records can be identified on the DSD statement and how the FD is used to build a particular output field. The CREATE statement is used to construct the actual output records. The syntax of this statement is

```
CREATE    QUANTITY=x,NAME=(FDname1,FDname2,...,FDnameN)
```

Here x determines the number of output records to be created. NAME identifies the FDs that are used to construct these output records. For example, to create 100 records each 81 bytes in length using the three FDs described above and identified by (*) code

```
CREATE    QUANTITY=100,NAME=(DELBYTE,KEYFLD,FILLER)
```

The records generated will contain the following data:

	In Hexadecimal	*In Character*
Byte	010 20 30 40506 81	123456...81
Record 1	FFF0F0F00000...00	.000...
Record 2	FFF0F0F50000...00	.005...
Record 3	FFF0F1F00000...00	.010...

Notice that the INDEX operand that was coded on the KEYFLD statement causes the value in that field to be incremented by five.

Example 2: At this point all of the coding discussed above can be summarized as a complete example. Using only control statements create a sequential data set and load it with 100 81 byte records which have the format and values described in the three fields denoted by (*) above.

```
//B         EXEC PGM=IEBDG
//SYSPRINT DD   SYSOUT=A
//DDOUT     DD   DSN=KEYED.DATA.SET,DISP=(NEW,CATLG),
//               UNIT=3350,VOL=SER=DISK99,SPACE=(TRK,1),
//               DCB=(LRECL=81,BLKSIZE=6156,RECFM=FB)
//SYSIN     DD   *
  DSD       OUTPUT=(DDOUT)
  FD        NAME=DELBYTE,LENGTH=1,STARTLOC=1,PICTURE=1,  X
            B'255'
  FD        NAME=KEYFLD,LENGTH=3,STARTLOC=2,FORMAT=ZD,   X
            CHARACTER=0,INDEX=5
  FD        NAME=FILLER,LENGTH=77,STARTLOC=5
  CREATE    QUANTITY=100,NAME=(DELBYTE,KEYFLD,FILLER)
  END
/*
```

Example 3: Several major changes are to be made to the records created in Example 2. The output records are now used to create an ISAM data set. Each record is to be marked as active. Hence a value other than HIGH-VALUES (X'FF') is to be placed in the first byte of each record. Finally, the last 77 bytes of each record are to contain the character X rather than LOW-VALUES. This can be accomplished by coding

```
//C         EXEC PGM=IEBDG
//SYSPRINT DD   SYSOUT=A
//DDOUT     DD   DSN=ISAM.DATA.SET,DISP=(NEW,CATLG),
//          UNIT=3350,VOL=SER=DISK99,SPACE=(CYL,1),
//          DCB=(LRECL=81,BLKSIZE=81,RECFM=F,KEYLEN=3,
//          RKP=1,DSORG=IS,OPTCD=L)
//SYSIN     DD   *
  DSD       OUTPUT=(DDOUT)
  FD        NAME=DELBYTE,LENGTH=1,STARTLOC=1
  FD        NAME=KEYFLD,LENGTH=3,STARTLOC=2,FORMAT=ZD,                X
            CHARACTER=0,INDEX=5
  FD        NAME=FILLER,LENGTH=77,STARTLOC=5,CHARACTER=X
  CREATE    QUANTITY=100,NAME=(DELBYTE,KEYFLD,FILLER)
  END
/*
```

Since the delete byte field (DELBYTE) is not assigned a value it contains hexadecimal zeroes. The ISAM record keys are multiples of five.

Example 4: The same ISAM data set as in the last example will be created. However, here it will be assumed that Example 2 has already been run and data set KEYED.DATA.SET exists. Note that this is a sequential data set. This leads to a slight simplification in the control statements. Here, the first byte is supplied from an FD literal and the remaining 80 bytes are taken from the input data set. This is accomplished with the FROMREC operand.

```
//D         EXEC PGM=IEBDG
//SYSPRINT DD   SYSOUT=A
//DDIN      DD   DSN=KEYED.DATA.SET,DISP=SHR
//DDOUT     DD   DSN=ISAM.DATA.SET,DISP=(NEW,CATLG),
//               UNIT=3350,VOL=SER=DISK99,SPACE=(CYL,1),
//               DCB=(LRECL=81,BLKSIZE=81,RECFM=F,KEYLEN=3,
//               RKP=1,DSORG=IS,OPTCD=L)
//SYSIN     DD   *
  DSD       OUTPUT=(DDOUT),INPUT=(DDIN)
  FD        NAME=DELBYTE,LENGTH=1,STARTLOC=1
  FD        NAME=RESTREC,LENGTH=80,STARTLOC=2,FROMREC=DDIN
  CREATE    QUANTITY=100,NAME=(DELBYTE,RESTREC)
  END
/*
```

Example 5: A data set is to be created and loaded with 400 records. These records are of three distinct types. The first two records are of type A, the third of type B, and the fourth of type C. Each additional group of four records follows this same pattern. Each record type contains all records of the same length. However, the three record types all have different logical record lengths. With all three types of records the first ten bytes are an alphabetic field. With type A the remaining 40 bytes are an alphanumeric field. With type B bytes 11 through 70 can be any arbitrary collating sequence characters. The remaining 15 bytes of a type B record are to contain three five byte packed decimal fields. Hence type A records are 50 bytes in length, type B are 85 bytes, and type C only 10 bytes. The ease with which this data set can be created should be contrasted with the difficulties that would have to be overcome with IEBGENER or any other utility. A major reason why IEBDG can do this so efficiently is the REPEAT statement. A second reason is that the CREATE statement establishes logical record length when creating variable length records. The complete code is as follows:

```
//E          EXEC PGM=IEBDG
//SYSPRINT DD   SYSOUT=A
//DD1         DD   DSN=OUTPUT.DATA.SET,DISP=(NEW,CATLG),
//                 UNIT=3350,VOL=SER=DISK98,SPACE=(CYL,2),
//                 DCB=(LRECL=89,RECFM=VB,BLKSIZE=6160)
//SYSIN       DD   *
  DSN       OUTPUT=(DD1)
  FD        NAME=ALPHA,FORMAT=AL,LENGTH=10
  FD        NAME=ALNUM,FORMAT=AN,LENGTH=40
  FD        NAME=COLLATE,FORMAT=CO,LENGTH=60
  FD        NAME=PACKED,FORMAT=PD,LENGTH=05
  REPEAT    QUANTITY=100,CREATE=3
  CREATE    QUANTITY=2,NAME=(ALPHA,ALNUM)
  CREATE    QUANTITY=1,NAME=(ALPHA,COLLATE,                   X
            PACKED,PACKED,PACKED)
  CREATE    QUANTITY=1,NAME=(ALPHA)
  END
/*
```

IEBISAM

Overview

IEBISAM is the simplest of the utilities discussed to this point. It requires only three DD statements. They have required DDnames of SYSPRINT, SYSUT1, and SYSUT2. These statements have the same meaning as with the other IEB utilities. They identify the message, input, and output data sets respectively. The SYSUT1 data set must identify either an ISAM data set or an unloaded sequential copy of an ISAM data set. SYSUT2 must identify either an ISAM data set, an unloaded copy of an ISAM data set, or a printed listing of an ISAM data set.

TABLE 29–2

The Roles of SYSUT1 and SYSUT2 with IEBISAM

PARM Value	*Description of the SYSUT1 Data Set*	*Description of the SYSUT2 Data Set*
COPY	existing ISAM data set	new ISAM data set
UNLOAD	existing ISAM data set	unloaded sequential data set
LOAD	unloaded sequential data set	reloaded ISAM data set
PRINTL	existing ISAM data set	printed sequential data set

IEBISAM does not have a control statement data set. Instead the particular function to be performed is identified with the PARM parameter on the EXEC statement. Four functions may be performed with IEBISAM. They are identified by PARM values of COPY, LOAD, UNLOAD, and PRINTL respectively. COPY is used to create a backup copy of an existing ISAM data set. The backup copy is a second ISAM data set. UNLOAD is also used to create a backup copy of an existing ISAM data set. However, the unloaded data set has sequential organization and is usually written on tape. LOAD is used to reload an unloaded ISAM data set back to disk. Following a LOAD operation it is again an ISAM data set. PRINTL is used to print the records in an ISAM data set. By default the records print in hexadecimal. To print them as character 'PRINTL,N' must be coded. Only one function can be performed by IEBISAM in a single step.

The roles of SYSUT1 and SYSUT2 with each of the four PARM values are summarized in Table 29–2.

COPY Operation

IEBISAM is one of two IEB utilities that can create a new ISAM data set. The major restriction is that the new data set must be a backup copy of an existing indexed sequential data set. Creating an ISAM data set out of sequential input cannot be done with IEBISAM. Rather, IEBDG must be used. During the COPY operation logically deleted records are not copied. In addition, records in the overflow area are moved to the prime area in the new data set. Different DCB values can be associated with the new ISAM data set.

Example 6: The existing cataloged ISAM data set ISAM.DATASET is to be used to create a new ISAM data set. The new data set will contain a reorganized version of the old data set.

```
//A         EXEC PGM=IEBISAM,PARM=COPY
//SYSPRINT DD  SYSOUT=A
//SYSUT1    DD  DSN=ISAM.DATASET,DISP=SHR,DCB=DSORG=IS
//SYSUT2    DD  DSN=NEW.ISAM.DATASET,DISP=(NEW,CATLG),
//              UNIT=3350,VOL=SER=DISK02,SPACE=(CYL,10),
//              DCB=(DSORG=IS,BLKSIZE=250,OPTCD=LY,
//              CYLOFL=5)
```

UNLOAD Operation

An UNLOAD operation is performed for purposes of backup and transportability. An unloaded data set is almost always stored on tape. In addition to the records that comprise the data set, necessary control information is also unloaded. This information is required in order to later recreate the original data set. An unloaded ISAM data set should have a logical record length of 80 bytes.

Example 7: The same ISAM data set used in the last example is to be unloaded to tape volume TAPE99. It is to be the second standard label data set on the volume. This can be done by coding

```
//B         EXEC PGM=IEBISAM,PARM=UNLOAD
//SYSPRINT  DD   SYSOUT=A
//SYSUT1    DD   DSN=ISAM.DATASET,DISP=SHR,DCB=DSORG=IS
//SYSUT2    DD   DSN=UNLOADED.DATASET,DISP=(NEW,KEEP),
//               UNIT=TAPE,VOL=SER=TAPE99,LABEL=(2,SL),
//               DCB=(LRECL=80,BLKSIZE=2000,RECFM=FB)
```

LOAD Operation

An unloaded data set can be restored to its original indexed organization by performing a LOAD operation. Different DCB values can be associated with the loaded data set than were stored with it originally. Obviously it would be unlikely that values such as LRECL, KEYLEN, and RECFM=F or V would change during a LOAD operation.

Example 8: The unloaded data set created in the last example is to be loaded back to disk as an ISAM data set.

```
//C         EXEC PGM=IEBISAM,PARM=LOAD
//SYSPRINT  DD   SYSOUT=A
//SYSUT1    DD   DSN=UNLOADED.DATASET,DISP=OLD,
//               UNIT=TAPE,VOL=SER=TAPE99,LABEL=(2,SL)
//SYSUT2    DD   DSN=RELOADED.ISAM.DATASET,DISP=(,PASS),
//               UNIT=3350,VOL=SER=DISK02,SPACE=(CYL,10),
//               DCB=(DSORG=IS,BLKSIZE=500,CYLOFL=2)
```

PRINTL Operation

A print operation is used to produce a listing of the records in an ISAM data set. Neither IEBGENER nor IEBPTPCH can produce such a listing. Two formats are available, hexadecimal and character. For character the complete PARM value must be enclosed in apostrophes.

Example 9: Print the record in the ISAM data set named ISAM.DATASET in character format.

```
//D          EXEC PGM=IEBISAM,PARM='PRINTL,N'
//SYSPRINT    DD  SYSOUT=A
//SYSUT1      DD  DSN=ISAM.DATASET,DISP=SHR
//SYSUT2      DD  SYSOUT=A
```

To print the records in hexadecimal the PARM value must be coded as PARM= PRINTL.

IEBCOMPR

Overview

IEBCOMPR is the final IEB utility discussed in this book. It is the simplest and also the least frequently used IEB utility. It performs two functions. For two sequential data sets it determines whether they contain identical records. For two partitioned data sets it determines whether all the member names in one are also contained in the other, and for each pair of members whether they contain identical records. IEBCOMPR uses four DD statements with DDnames SYSPRINT, SYSUT1, SYSUT2, and SYSIN. SYSUT1 and SYSUT2 denote the two input statements being compared. Both must identify sequential data sets or partitioned data sets. The SYSIN control data set is required but may be dummied out. The only output produced by IEBCOMPR is written to the SYSPRINT message data set.

Control Statements and Messages

Only one control statement is available. It contains the COMPARE operator and the TYPORG keyword parameter. Either TYPORG=PS or TYPORG=PO must be coded. TYPORG=PS is the default and in this case the SYSIN data set can be dummied out. If comparable records being compared are unequal both records are printed in the message data set in hexadecimal. They are labeled as coming from either the SYSUT1 or SYSUT2 data set. Their logical and physical record numbers are also printed.

Examples Using IEBCOMPR

Example 10: IEBCOMPR is used to determine whether the contents of two cataloged data sets are identical. This can be done as follows:

```
//A          EXEC PGM=IEBCOMPR
//SYSPRINT DD   SYSOUT=A
//SYSUT1     DD   DSN=SEQNTL1,DISP=SHR
//SYSUT2     DD   DSN=SEQNTL2,DISP=SHR
//SYSIN      DD   DUMMY
```

The control statement is not necessary when comparing two sequential data sets.

Example 11: Determine whether PDS1 and PDS2 contain identical members which in turn contain identical records. PDS1 is a cataloged data set while PDS2 is kept.

```
//B          EXEC PGM=IEBCOMPR
//SYSPRINT DD   SYSOUT=A
//SYSUT1     DD   DSN=PDS1,DISP=SHR
//SYSUT2     DD   DSN=PDS2,DISP=SHR,UNIT=DASD,VOL=SER=DISK95
//SYSIN      DD   *
   COMPARE   TYPORG=PO
/*
```

If PDS1 contains members A, E, I, O, and U and PDS2 contains members A, I, and U then only the pairs of members named A, I, and U will be compared by the utility.

Conclusion

IEBCOMPR is used for several purposes. It can be used to determine if a copy operation was performed successfully. Hence it could be run following an IEBGENER or IEBCOPY jobstep. In actuality it is highly unlikely that either utility will not copy correctly and also not inform the programmer of problems. IEBCOMPR can also be used to determine whether two data sets are identical so that one of them can be deleted. A third use occurs in an academic environment: Student programming assignments can be structured in such a way that two copies of the output are produced. One copy is printed and the second written to disk. The one written to disk can then be compared with a master data set on disk which contains the correct results. Incorrect records will be automatically flagged.

Exercises

1. Create a sequential data set which consists of 100 byte records. The first ten bytes should consist of two five byte integer fields. The rest of the record should contain only alphabetic characters. Write 50 records in the data set. No two records should be identical. Use IEBDG.

2. Create a sequential data set containing the same variable length records as in the data set in Example 10 in Chapter 25. Use IEBDG.

3. Create an ISAM data set whose records contain the same three fields as in Exercise 1. Place an additional byte in front of each record for a delete byte. Hence the records are now 101 bytes each.

4. Take the records in the last exercise and modify them somewhat to create an ISAM data set with variable length records. Every third record starting with the first will contain all four fields (101 bytes). Every third record starting with the second will contain only the first 11 bytes. The remaining records will contain only the first six bytes.

5. Create a BDAM data set that contains disk KEY fields.

6. Use IEBDG to create a pds and add three members to it. All three members should have different LRECL,BLKSIZE, and RECFM values. Try to do this in one step.

7. Use IEBDG to create a data set with the following DCB values: RECFM=VS, LRECL=100, and BLKSIZE=40. Create the same data set with a COBOL program.

8. IEBISAM performs four basic functions with an ISAM data set. Which utilities can be used to perform one or more of these functions with a partitioned data set? Which utilities can be used to perform one or more of these functions with a direct data set?

9. Use IEBDG to create and load an ISAM data set. The records should have the following properties:

```
LRECL=101    BLKSIZE=202    RECFM=FB    OPTCD=ILMY
KEYLEN=5     RKP=10
```

   Load 1000 records into the data set. Use IEHDASDR or ADRDSSU to dump out the entire data set. The data set can also be created by an application program.

10. Can IEBDG be used to update the ISAM data set created in the last exercise.

11. Determine some additional situations in which IEBCOMPR can be meaningfully used.

12. Use IEBGENER to copy a disk data set to tape. In a second step determine if the disk and tape data sets contain the same records.

13. Use IEBGENER or IEBUPDTE to create a pds and place four members in it. Use IEB-COPY to create on the same volume a second pds that contains only two of the four members. Use IEBCOMPR to compare the two pds's.

Chapter 30

IBM System Utilities

Overview

This chapter and the next continue the study of IBM utilities. Five additional utilities remain to be discussed. There is a great difference between the functions associated with these five utilities and the functions discussed in the previous chapters. The utilities in the previous chapters were data set utilities. Their names began with the letters IEB. In this chapter and the next every utility name begins with the letters IEH. These are categorized as system utilities. The five utilities studied here are IEHLIST, IEHPROGM, IEHMOVE, IEHINITT, and IEHDASDR.

The system utilities process a different type of information than the data set utilities. System utilities can be used to work with three major components of any MVS computer system: catalogs, the Volume Tables of Contents (VTOCs) found on every disk volume, and pds directories. The system utilities are used to examine, change, and display information in these three system components. System utilities can also be used to initialize tape and disk volumes. One system utility, IEHMOVE, duplicates many of the features available with IEBGENER, IEBCOPY, and IEBUPDTE. IEHMOVE also contains a few additional options not found with any of the IEB utilities.

IEH Utility DD Statements

SYSPRINT and SYSIN retain the same roles that they have with the data set utilities. However, the remaining DD statements are quite different from their data set utility counterparts. Most system utility DD statements reference a volume rather than a data set. A DSN parameter should not be coded on DD statements that reference an entire volume. Rather, the following three parameters are ordinarily specified: UNIT=unit, VOL=SER=volser, and DISP=OLD. These are usually the only three parameters coded. Individual data sets are identified through control statements rather than through DD statements. Just as there is ordinarily no reason to code two DD statements with the same DSN value on both, it is unnecessary to specify two DD statements that reference exactly the same volume. Only one DD statement need be coded for each volume no matter how many times the volume is referenced in the control statements. System utility control statements do not identify the DDname which in turn identifies a specific volume. Rather, a volume identified on a control statement must be coded on one DD statement in the job step. Some system utilities require a permanently mounted volume. If no such volume is specifically identified as a consequence of the utility control statements then one extra DD statement must be included to reference such a volume. Temporary data set names that begin with && or & should be avoided with the IEH utilities.

IEH Utility Control Statements

Some of the system utilities require a control statement operand of the form VOL=device-type=volser. Note that this is not part of a JCL statement. To identify the 3350 disk volume ALPHA1 on a control statement code VOL=3350=ALPHA1, not VOL=SER=ALPHA1. However, the accompanying DD statement must contain VOL=SER=ALPHA1 as a parameter. When referencing a multi-volume data set the format VOL=device-type=(volser1,volser2, . . .) is used. The accompanying JCL must also reference volser 1 and volser2.

A second IEH control statement keyword parameter that causes confusion because of its similarity with a JCL parameter is DSNAME. The abbreviation DSN is not allowed on a control statement although it is syntactically correct on a JCL statement. Since data sets should not be identified through IEH Utility JCL, the value specified with DSNAME identifies the data set to be referenced. Since data sets are not identified on JCL statements with system utilities, the character string 'DSN' is not coded anywhere within an IEH utility jobstep. Some system utilities also require an operand of the form FROM=device=volser or TO=device=volser. Because these are not similar to JCL code fewer problems occur with them than with the two other control statement operands.

When coding the system utility control statements the complete set of utility continuation rules must be followed. There are three important rules. End the operand field after a keyword parameter and its following comma. For a statement being continued place a continuation character in column 72. Resume the continuation in column 16 of the next statement. In the examples that follow paper width does not allow placing an X in column 72. Rather, the X is the rightmost character in a statement. All continued statements do begin in column 16 in the examples. Recall that a far less restrictive set of rules for continuation is used with most IEB utilities.

IEHLIST - Printing System Information

Overview

This utility is used to print out the following three types of system information:

— List the information in an OS catalog.

— List the information in the directory of a pds.

— List the information in the VTOC of a disk volume.

Any combination of these three listings can be printed in the same jobstep, and each type may be requested any number of times. The three listings are identified by the operators LISTCTLG, LISTPDS, and LISTVTOC respectively.

Listing OS Catalog Entries

IEHLIST can be used to list all the entries in an OS catalog that are part of a fully qualified data set name. An OS catalog is also called a CVOL. The printed listing includes two or three additional information fields along with every data set name. These contain unit and volume information for the data set and (for tape data sets only) file sequence number.

Example 1: Print all entries found in the OS catalog that is contained on volume DISK01.

```
//A           EXEC   PGM=IEHLIST
//SYSPRINT    DD     SYSOUT=A
//CATLGVOL    DD     UNIT=3350,VOL=SER=DISK01,DISP=OLD
//SYSIN       DD     *
   LISTCTLG   VOL=3350=DISK01
/*
```

Note that the control statement contains the keyword operand with the format VOL=device=volser, not VOL=SER=volser. Confusing these two is a very common programming error with system utilities. This is the only operand that should be coded with LISTCTLG. Notice also that there is no significance to the DDname CATLGVOL. In fact, any name could have been used. LISTCTLG is used only with OS catalogs. It cannot be used with a VSAM master catalog or VSAM user catalog. To list the entries in a VSAM catalog use the LISTCAT command with the IDCAMS utility.

Listing PDS Directories

IEHLIST can also be used to list the entries in the directory of a pds. Such a listing may be printed in either a hexadecimal dump format or in a more readable character format. Additionally, whenever two or more pds's are contained on the same disk volume all of their directories can be printed with a single control statement.

Three utilities are commonly used to print out the contents of a pds directory: IDCAMS, IEHLIST, and IEBPTPCH. No matter which of the three utilities is employed the directory information printed includes the member names, their locations within the pds, and any additional user data stored in the directory with an individual member. Both IEBPTPCH and IDCAMS print out the contents of the entire directory, including three additional pieces of information not supplied by IEHLIST:

1) The number of bytes used to hold meaningful data in each directory block. Ordinarily part of every 256 byte directory block is unused and may contain garbage.

2) The last member name in the directory, which always consists of eight bytes of binary ones. The address of this entry is given as three bytes of binary zeroes (LOW-VALUES), an invalid address.

3) The contents of all directory blocks are printed, not just those that contain meaningful data. For a detailed analysis of the information in a pds directory see Chapter 12.

The directory listings supplied by IDCAMS and IEBPTPCH are unformatted. Primarily for this reason, most application programmers prefer the IEHLIST report.

Example 2: Produce a printed listing of the directories of the pds SYS1.MACLIB and also the pds ANOTHER.PDS. They are stored on volumes DISK01 and WORK01 respectively.

```
//B          EXEC  PGM=IEHLIST
//SYSPRINT   DD    SYSOUT=A
//DD1        DD    UNIT=3350,DISP=OLD,VOL=SER=WORK01
//DD2        DD    UNIT=3350,DISP=OLD,VOL=SER=DISK01
//SYSIN      DD    *
   LISTPDS   DSNAME=SYS1.MACLIB,VOL=3350=DISK01,DUMP
   LISTPDS   DSNAME=ANOTHER.PDS,VOL=3350=WORK01,FORMAT
/*
```

The DSNAME and VOL operands are required. A third operand is used to select the format of the printed output. The first directory will be printed in DUMP format, which is an unedited hexadecimal listing. The second directory will be printed as a comprehensive edited listing. The edited listing is much easier to read than the listings supplied by IEBPTPCH and IDCAMS.

The formatted listing produced by IEHLIST is meant to be used with a load module pds. If used with a pds whose members were not created by the linkage editor the message

```
IEH112 - MEMBER OF SPECIFIED PDS NOT CREATED BY LINKAGE
         EDITOR - DUMP OPTION OUTPUT GENERATED
```

is printed along with each such member. The test IEHLIST uses to determine whether the message is to be printed is whether the directory entry for the member is less than 34 bytes in length. The value 34 implies creation by the linkage editor, although this need not actually be the case. In practice IEHLIST can be used with any type of pds and the IEH112 message can be safely ignored.

A pds directory printed by IEHLIST has two significant advantages over comparable listings produced by IEBPTPCH or IDCAMS. Only IEHLIST produces a formatted report. In addition, IEHLIST specifies all properties that apply to a load module, such as whether it is reentrant, reusable, executable, etc.

Example 3: Produce the same listing as in Example 2 under the conditions that both pds's are on the same volume and an unedited hexadecimal listing is required for both. Code the following:

```
//C           EXEC  PGM=IEHLIST
//SYSPRINT    DD    SYSOUT=A
//DISK01      DD    UNIT=3350,DISP=OLD,VOL=SER=DISK01
//SYSIN       DD    *
   LISTPDS        DSNAME=(ANOTHER.PDS,SYS1.MACLIB),             X
                  VOL=3350=DISK01
/*
```

There are three changes from the code in Example 2. The names of the data sets have been factored onto a single control statement. This is valid since both data sets are on the same volume. Up to ten data sets located on the same volume can be coded on one control statement. Second, since neither DUMP nor FORMAT is coded the default (DUMP) is in effect. DISK01 rather than DD1 is used as the DDname on the statement referencing volume DISK01. By using this naming convention JCL and control statement errors are minimized. It is a simple matter to check for a one–to–one correspondence between VOL parameters in the control statements and DDnames in the JCL. The IEHLIST control statements are never displayed in the SYSPRINT listing. This makes debugging them more difficult when errors occur.

Listing VTOC Entries

IEHLIST can be used to print a partial or complete listing of the entries in a given disk Volume Table of Contents. IEHLIST is the only utility discussed in this text that performs this important function. For an explanation of the types of information contained in a VTOC listing see Chapter 15.

There are three formats available with a VTOC listing. Two of the three are the same as with LISTPDS. DUMP provides an unedited hexadecimal listing and FORMAT provides a comprehensive edited listing. If neither is requested the default is a third format, an abbreviated edited listing.

If the DSNAME operand is not coded a complete listing of every data set on the volume is supplied. When DSNAME is coded the listing is restricted to just those data sets. As with LISTPDS, up to ten data set names can be coded on the same control statement as long as all the data sets are on the same volume. Hence VOL is the only required operand. If DSNAME is coded it must identify one to ten data sets that reside on the VOL=device-type=volser volume. Either FORMAT, DUMP, or the default (which is neither) may be requested.

Example 4: List the VTOC information for the data sets SYS1.MACLIB and ANOTHER.PDS, both of which are on volume DISK01. The information should be printed in edited format. Next, list the VTOC information for the sequential data set SEQUENTL.DATASET, also on volume DISK01. Finally, print out the complete VTOC for volume DISK03 in abbreviated edited format. In this example the data sets listed on the first two LISTVTOC statements can be factored onto a single statement if all are to be printed with the same format.

```
//D          EXEC  PGM=IEHLIST
//SYSPRINT DD      SYSOUT=A
//DISK01     DD    UNIT=3350,VOL=SER=DISK01,DISP=OLD
//DISK03     DD    UNIT=3350,VOL=SER=DISK03,DISP=OLD
//SYSIN      DD    *
   LISTVTOC      DSNAME=(SYS1.MACLIB,ANOTHER.PDS),                  X
                 VOL=3350=DISK01,FORMAT
   LISTVTOC      DSNAME=SEQUENTL.DATASET,VOL=3350=DISK01
   LISTVTOC      VOL=3350=DISK03
/*
```

Any combination of LISTCTLG, LISTPDS, and LISTVTOC can be coded in the same jobstep. This is illustrated in the final IEHLIST example.

Example 5: List the directory of SYS1.MACLIB, the VTOC entry for SYS1.MACLIB, the catalog on volume DISK03, and the VTOC entry for every data set on volume DISK03.

This can be done as follows:

```
//E          EXEC  PGM=IEHLIST
//SYSPRINT DD      SYSOUT=A
//DISK01     DD    UNIT=3350,VOL=SER=DISK01,DISP=OLD
//DISK03     DD    UNIT=3350,VOL=SER=DISK03,DISP=OLD
//SYSIN      DD    *
   LISTPDS       DSNAME=(SYS1.MACLIB),VOL=3350=DISK01,             X
                 FORMAT
   LISTVTOC      DSNAME=SYS1.MACLIB,VOL=3350=DISK01,FORMAT
   LISTCTLG      VOL=3350=DISK03
   LISTVTOC      VOL=3350=DISK03
/*
```

IEHPROGM - Modifying System Information

Overview

IEHLIST is used to display information stored in catalogs, pds directories, and VTOCs. IEHPROGM is a very powerful system utility that is used to modify the information stored in these three system components. Because of the functions IEHPROGM performs it should be used carefully. It is very easy to inadvertently damage or destroy a data set when using IEHPROGM.

In this book five IEHPROGM functions are covered. Some additional relatively obscure functions can also be performed by IEHPROGM. For information on the other functions that IEHPROGM can perform consult the *MVS Utilities* manual. The five functions discussed in this text are listed below.

Function	*Object of the Function*
Scratch	a data set from a VTOC or a member from a pds directory
Rename	a data set or a member of a pds
Catalog	a non-VSAM kept data set
Uncatalog	a non-VSAM cataloged data set
Build	a generation index or base table to allow Generation Data Group processing

Scratching a Data Set

A scratch operation is meaningful only with disk data sets. To scratch a data set means to remove the format-1 data set control block (dscb) entry from the VTOC of the disk volume on which the data set resides. The space previously occupied by the data set is then available for reallocation. Sequential, ISAM, direct, and partitioned data sets can all be scratched. If the data set contains an unexpired expiration date an additional operand (PURGE) must be coded. IEHPROGM can also be used to scratch password protected non-VSAM data sets.

A data set may also be scratched by coding DISP=(OLD,DELETE) on the DD statement that identifies the data set. Such a JCL statement may be coded as part of an IEFBR14 jobstep or added to any jobstep. Clearly it requires less coding to delete a data set using JCL disposition processing than it does to code a separate IEHPROGM step. However, there is a major disadvantage with the JCL approach. If the data set specified for deletion cannot be located by the system (for any reason including programmer coding error) the message

```
IEF212 dsname DATA SET NOT FOUND
```

is printed, and the job is immediately terminated. When IEHPROGM is used and a data set cannot be found a non-zero condition code results. However, the job continues to execute. In this situation the COND parameters on the EXEC statements of the following steps can be used to determine which steps should execute in the remainder of the job. Any following functions in the IEHPROGM jobstep will also be executed.

When a JCL statement is used to scratch a non-cataloged data set UNIT and VOLUME parameters must be coded on the DD statement. If the data set is cataloged coding DISP=(OLD,DELETE) on the DD statement causes the data set to first be uncataloged and then deleted. Two allocation messages are printed in this situation.

```
IEF285    dsname    UNCATALOGED
IEF285    dsname    DELETED
```

After a data set is scratched the space it formerly occupied is added to the available freespace on the volume. Other data sets being created on this volume may use this space. This process involves modifying the format-5 DSCB.

Surprisingly, it is possible to access the records in a data set even after it has been scratched as long as the space the data set previously occupied has not been reallocated and written to. Access can be accomplished by coding a JCL statement with the following parameters:

`DISP=(NEW,x),` where x=KEEP, CATLG, or PASS

`VOL=SER=volume` where volume is the volume that contained the scratched data set

`SPACE=(ABSTR,address)` where address is the location on the volume where the data set was stored prior to being scratched. See Chapters 7 and 15 for more details on using ABSTR with the SPACE parameter.

To use this technique it is necessary to know the address on the disk volume where the data set formerly resided. IEHLIST can be used to determine the address of a disk data set. This approach allows access to the contents of any data set that has been deleted. To prevent someone from examining the contents of a deleted data set one safeguard is to overwrite the data set before deleting it. With VSAM data sets IDCAMS can be used to overwrite a data set with binary zeroes prior to scratching it. This is an expensive process but it is worthwhile with important data sets.

Scratching a PDS Member

When a member of a pds is scratched the entry for that member is removed from the pds directory. However, the space the member occupied is not available for reallocation. The space remains unusable until the pds is compressed.

A pds member cannot be scratched through JCL alone. It is a common misconception that the following code will delete member BETA from the cataloged pds ALPHA:

```
//A        EXEC     PGM=IEFBR14
//DD1      DD       DSN=ALPHA(BETA),DISP=(OLD,DELETE)
```

Rather, this code deletes the entire pds. This occurs because the second DISP subparameter value applies to the entire data set, not just the member. See Chapter 7 for more information on the DISP parameter. The values coded with the second and third DISP subparameters are always unrelated to the processing performed with the member name coded on the DD statement.

The only difference between the IEHPROGM control statement used to scratch a data set and the code used to scratch a member is that the latter contains one additional operand, the member name. The following example illustrates scratching both a complete data set and a pds member.

Example 6: Scratch data set ALPHA1 on volume DISK01, and scratch members BETA and GAMMA in the pds ZETA. ZETA resides on disk volume DISK99. ZETA has an expiration date which has not yet occurred.

```
//F          EXEC  PGM=IEHPROGM
//SYSPRINT   DD    SYSOUT=A
//DISK01     DD    UNIT=3350,VOL=SER=DISK01,DISP=OLD
//DISK99     DD    UNIT=3350,VOL=SER=DISK99,DISP=OLD
//SYSIN      DD    *
   SCRATCH       DSNAME=ALPHA1,VOL=3350=DISK01
   SCRATCH       DSNAME=ZETA,VOL=3350=DISK99,PURGE,             X
                 MEMBER=BETA
   SCRATCH       MEMBER=GAMMA,VOL=3350=DISK99,PURGE,            X
                 DSNAME=ZETA
/*
```

When performing a scratch operation both the DSNAME and VOL parameters must be coded. PURGE is required only for a data set with an unexpired expiration date. The MEMBER operand is coded only with a pds member. Multiple member names cannot be coded with a single MEMBER operand.

There is one other way to scratch a pds member or a complete data set. Both operations can be done with the IDCAMS utility by using the DELETE command. No other utility program can delete a pds member. No other utility program can explicitly delete a data set using only control statements.

Renaming a Data Set

IEHPROGM can be used to change the name of a data set. This operation consists of modifying the data set control block (dscb) entry in the VTOC to reflect the new name chosen. The old dscb entry is physically deleted and a new dscb is created. The records in the data set itself remain unchanged. They occupy the same location on the disk volume.

A catalog is not accessed during a renaming operation. If a cataloged data set is renamed the name in the catalog no longer agrees with the entry in the dscb on the volume. When the data set is subsequently accessed problems can occur whether the old name or new name is used. Of course, if the access does not involve the catalog and the new name is used the data set will be found. If the catalog is used either the data set will not be found or an S213 abend will result. To successfully rename a cataloged data set three operations must be performed. The old name is first uncataloged. The name of the data set is then changed. Finally, the new name is cataloged. These three steps are illustrated in Example 10.

Unlike the scratch operation, it is impossible to directly rename a data set by coding only JCL statements. If IEHPROGM is not used several IEB/IEH utilities are necessary to rename a data set on a disk volume.

Renaming a PDS Member

A pds member can also be renamed. The directory is modified by adding an entry which contains the new name of the member and deleting the entry for the old member name. No other directory information is changed. No changes are made to the member area of the pds. The member name being renamed may be a true name or an alias. Because no other directory information is changed except for the member name, the new name retains the same status as the old name. When a true name entry is changed all of its aliases remain unchanged. All of the existing alias entries still point to the same location in the pds.

Example 7: Rename the data set ALPHA.BETA to A.B.C. In the same step rename member FIRST to LAST in pds ZETA. ALPHA.BETA is on volume DISK05 and ZETA is on volume DISK99. ZETA has an unexpired expiration date.

```
//G          EXEC  PGM=IEHPROGM
//SYSPRINT DD      SYSOUT=A
//DISK05   DD      UNIT=3350,VOL=SER=DISK05,DISP=OLD
//DISK99   DD      UNIT=3350,VOL=SER=DISK99,DISP=OLD
//SYSIN    DD      *
   RENAME        DSNAME=ALPHA.BETA,NEWNAME=A.B.C,                  X
                 VOL=3350=DISK05
   RENAME        DSNAME=ZETA,MEMBER=FIRST,                         X
                 VOL=3350=DISK99,NEWNAME=LAST
/*
```

As with a scratch operation, the DSNAME and VOL operands must be coded with a rename operation. NEWNAME is required to supply the new name for the data set or pds member. MEMBER identifies the member whose name is to be changed.

The IDCAMS utility can be used to rename a data set or a pds member. The ALTER command is used for both functions.

Cataloging and Uncataloging Data Sets

IEHPROGM can be used to catalog an existing data set. The system will select the appropriate catalog in which to make the entry for the data set. See Chapter 21 for information on how the system selects the appropriate catalog. Any existing kept data set may be cataloged as long as there is no data set with the same name currently in the catalog.

IEHPROGM may also be used to uncatalog a cataloged non-VSAM data set. When a data set is uncataloged its dscb entry remains unchanged. When uncataloging a data set the VOL operand should not be coded on the control statement. Likewise, since for this operation all accessing is through the catalog, no DD statement need be supplied to identify the volume that contains the data set.

Non-VSAM data sets can also be cataloged and uncataloged entirely through JCL statements. When cataloging an existing data set it is necessary to supply UNIT and VOLUME parameter values. However, UNIT and VOLUME should not be coded when uncataloging a data set. The advantages and disadvantages of using JCL versus IEHPROGM to catalog and uncatalog data sets are the same as those for scratching data sets. JCL requires less coding but errors are less significant with IEHPROGM. It should again be noted that IDCAMS can also catalog and uncatalog data sets.

Example 8: Catalog data set A.B.C on volume DISK05 and uncatalog the data set XX.YY.ZZ on volume DISK06. Both are non-VSAM data sets.

```
//H           EXEC   PGM=IEHPROGM
//SYSPRINT    DD     SYSOUT=A
//DISK05      DD     UNIT=3350,DISP=OLD,VOL=SER=DISK05
//SYSIN       DD     *
  CATLG       DSNAME=A.B.C,VOL=3350=DISK05
  UNCATLG     DSNAME=XX.YY.ZZ
/*
```

Note that one operand is used for an uncatalog operation and two operands are used for a catalog operation.

Example 9: Use JCL to perform the same functions specified in Example 8.

```
//I      EXEC PGM=IEFBR14
//DD0    DD   DSN=A.B.C,DISP=(OLD,CATLG),UNIT=3350,
//                 VOL=SER=DISK05
//DD1    DD   DSNAME=XX.YY.ZZ,DISP=(OLD,UNCATLG)
```

If UNIT and VOLUME parameters are coded on the DD1 statement the data set will not be uncataloged. The message IEF287 will be printed.

Example 10: This example uses all the control statements discussed to this point in one jobstep. The pds ALPHA is to have its name changed to MU. ALPHA is cataloged. Member ZETA within ALPHA is to have its name changed to RHO, and member PI is to be deleted. The first and last control statements are necessary to keep the catalog information in agreement with the VTOC of the volume.

```
//J           EXEC   PGM=IEHPROGM
//SYSPRINT    DD     SYSOUT=A
//DISK05      DD     VOL=SER=DISK05,DISP=OLD,UNIT=3350
//SYSIN       DD     *
   UNCATLG        DSNAME=ALPHA
   RENAME         DSNAME=ALPHA,NEWNAME=MU,VOL=3350=DISK05
   RENAME         DSNAME=MU,MEMBER=ZETA,VOL=3350=DISK05,         X
                  NEWNAME=RHO
   SCRATCH        DSNAME=MU,MEMBER=PI,VOL=3350=DISK05
   CATLG          DSNAME=MU,VOL=3350=DISK05
/*
```

Generation Data Groups

At present IEHPROGM is still being used on some systems to create Generation Data Group base tables. This function is now more commonly performed with IDCAMS. With both utilities the GDG name and the number of entries in the base table are specified.

Example 11: With IEHPROGM create a Generation Data Group called ALPHA that can hold up to four entries.

```
//K           EXEC PGM=IEHPROGM
//SYSPRINT    DD      SYSOUT=A
//DISK01      DD      UNIT=3350,VOL=SER=DISK01,DISP=OLD
//SYSIN       DD      *
   BLDG       INDEX=ALPHA,ENTRIES=4
/*
```

Exercises

IEHLIST

1. Print an edited listing of the directories of SYS1.PROCLIB and SYS1.LINKLIB. Notice that in the SYS1.PROCLIB listing the message IEH112 MEMBER OF SPECIFIED PDS NOT CREATED BY LINKAGE EDITOR is printed preceding every member in the pds. What specific criteria determine whether this message is produced? How can it be removed from the SYS1.PROCLIB listing? Is it possible that this message will print with some but not all of the members in a particular pds?

2. After reviewing Chapter 18 print out a formatted listing of a pds directory whose members were created by the Linkage Editor. Examine these entries and determine the specific information contained in each one. It will probably be necessary to consult the IBM *Linkage Editor and Loader* manual. How will IEHLIST print a pds directory entry of a member that was created by the Loader?

3. Use IEBGENER or IEBUPDTE to create a pds and place several members and their aliases in this pds in one step. Include as much user data as possible with each directory entry. Now use IEHLIST to examine this directory information. How many different directory listings can be produced by IEHLIST for this pds? Which one of these contains the most useful information?

4. Write a job to print out the contents of every member in SYS1.PROCLIB that begins with the four letters PLIX. Make the jobstream independent and flexible. That is, the job should work correctly without the necessity to first examine a printed listing of the pds directory. It should also be possible to run the job with any other four letters by making one (or at most two) coding changes in the job. Using a PARM value is the easiest way to accomplish this. Finally, generalize the job to find all pds members whose first N characters are a specific character string. Here N ranges from one to eight. Using symbolic parameters will allow even the pds itself to become a variable. Can this function be performed using any utility other than IEHLIST?

5. Print an edited listing of the names of all data sets on disk volume WORK99. Other than an edited listing of this information, what other types are possible? How can they be requested?

6. Modify the previous exercise to print out the names of just those data sets on volume WORK99 that begin with a first level qualifier of ACCOUNT2. The job that produces this listing should run successfully without the necessity of a person examining a printed listing of the data sets on the volume and then modifying the job. In fact, the character string ACCOUNT2 should be coded exactly once in the job. It should be a PARM value for a specific application program. Modify this job to print out the records in every data set on the volume whose name begins with the identifier ACCOUNT2. Hint: What utilities can print the contents of multiple data sets (perhaps with unlike DCB characteristics) in a single job step? If this modification proves too difficult, assume that all data sets on the volume are cataloged.

7. Create a data set where SPACE=(TRK,(1,2)) is coded. Write sufficient records to use the primary and most of the secondary space allocations. Use IEHLIST to examine the VTOC entry for this data set. Determine where on the volume the space was actually allocated. For more information on VTOC entries see Chapter 16.

8. To determine the number of physical records in a disk data set examine the PTR field in the VTOC entry for the data set. Use IEBGENER to create a disk data set. Manually determine the number of physical records it contains and then use IEHLIST to confirm your answer. How can the number of physical records in a tape data set be determined? What utility should be used for this function?

9. Print out the contents of the CVOL catalog CAT12345 on volume SYS123. If there is only one catalog in the system is it necessary to specify the volume?

10. Use IEHLIST to produce a listing of all cataloged data sets in the system that contain the letters ABCD as their complete second qualifier. With a VSAM catalog, can the same thing be done using IDCAMS? If so how? If not why not?

11. Create a non-VSAM sequential data set and catalog it in a CVOL. Now create the same non-VSAM data set and catalog it in a VSAM catalog. Display the entries stored in each catalog. What information is the same in both catalogs? How do the two catalog entries differ?

12. Use the IEHLIST functions with the system residence volume and with data sets on that volume. Determine whether a less restrictive amount of control statement and JCL coding is necessary when referencing this volume.

13. Print out the VTOC entry for every data set in the system whose name starts with the qualifier ABCDEF. Specify two approaches depending on whether the system has a VSAM catalog structure or not. Discuss whether all the data sets are cataloged (this simplifies things) or not. Modify the job to restrict it to data sets on a specific group of volumes.

IEHPROGM

14. Use IEHLIST, IEHPROGM, and one or more user–written programs to delete all cataloged data sets on volume WORK98 that contain a 1 in their first level qualifiers. Modify the job to delete all data sets on volumes WORK97 and WORK98 that contain a 1 in their first level qualifiers.

15. COBUC, PLIXC, and SORTD are three members of the system procedure library SYS1.PROCLIB. Rename COBUC giving it the name PLIXC. Member PLIXC should still be in the library, but now it can only be referenced by its alias PLIALIAS.

16. Suppose that member COBUC was to be renamed SORTD. If SORTD contained two aliases SORT123 and SORT456 which would be elevated to true name status? What criteria are used to decide this?

17. A COBOL copy library contains two members ALPHA and BETA. A single COBOL program will use each of the members for the same purpose but on different occasions. If COBOL had macro capabilities like PL/I or Assembler something like COPY &MEMBER could be specified. Here &MEMBER represents a symbolic parameter that can be assigned the value ALPHA or BETA. Unfortunately, this is not possible with COBOL. How can a job be constructed to copy the required member under the restriction that the COBOL program itself is not to be modified no matter which member is needed?

18. XYZ is a cataloged disk data set on volume WORK98. To uncatalog and delete it the following job step is run:

```
//A      EXEC  PGM=IEFBR14
//DD1    DD    DSN=XYZ,DISP=(OLD,DELETE),UNIT=3350,
//             VOL=SER=WORK98
```

What actually happens? What IEF messages are printed? At this point how can IEHPROGM be used to achieve the originally desired results? Can IEFBR14 be used to do the same thing? If so how? How should the original IEFBR14 have been coded?

19. A pds contains three members A, B, and C. It is desired to rename them in the following circular manner: A is to be renamed B, B becomes C, and C turns into A. Write the appropriate IEHPROGM control statements to accomplish this in one jobstep.

20. Member A contains two aliases B and C. It is desired to rename A to ANEW. Will the two aliases continue to reference the old or the new copy of A (i.e., ANEW)? Suppose that, rather than renaming A, A is replaced by a new member also named A. Ordinarily the two aliases will still reference the old copy of A. How can this same problem be handled with other utilities such as IEBUPDTE or IEBGENER?

21. Two members A and B of the pds ALPHA are to be modified as follows: A is to become the alias of B and B is to be renamed A, forcing A to be renamed B. Can this be done? If so how?

22. Use IEFBR14 to delete member COBUC from SYS1.PROCLIB. Assume you have the authorization to do this. Comment on any unusual problems that develop when running the job.

23. Assume that XYZ is a cataloged multi-volume disk data set. It resides on ALPHA1 (which includes the primary allocation), ALPHA2, and ALPHA3. Uncatalog and delete the parts of the data set on volumes ALPHA2 and ALPHA3. Is it possible to uncatalog and delete only the primary allocation?

24. An ISAM data set is created using three distinct DD statements for the data, index, and overflow areas. The syntax of JCL prohibits cataloging the data set during its creation. Use IEHPROGM to turn it into a cataloged data set called ISAM.DATA which resides on volume DISK01.

25. Use IEHPROGM to create a GDG base entry sufficient to hold a maximum of ten Generation Data Sets. What options can be coded along with this? Under what conditions should IEHPROGM rather than IDCAMS be used to create a GDG base entry?

26. Examine the functions that IEHPROGM performs with a data set. Which of these functions can also be done by IEFBR14? For a function that can be done by both what test should be used to determine the appropriate utility for a specific application? Are there any functions that can be performed by IEFBR14 but not by IEHPROGM?

Chapter 31

IEHMOVE, IEHINITT, and IEHDASDR

Overview

The remaining three IEH utilities are discussed in this chapter. Unlike IEHLIST and IEHPROGM, there are no similarities between IEHMOVE, IEHINITT, and IEHDASDR. IEHMOVE is the only one of the three that is heavily used by application programmers. IEHINITT performs only one function. IEHDASDR performs many functions but only one is of interest to application programmers.

The major functions performed by IEHMOVE are the following:

— Move a data set from one volume to another. When the move is successfully completed the original data set is scratched.

— Copy a data set from one volume to another. The original data set still exists after the copy operation.

— Move a partitioned data set from one volume to another. During the move operation specific members may be included, excluded, or renamed. The original pds is scratched.

— Copy a partitioned data set from one volume to another. During the copy operation specific members may be included, excluded, or renamed. The original pds still exists after the copy operation.

— Move a collection of cataloged disk data sets. The group of data sets is determined using one or more common qualifiers in the data set name. The original data sets are scratched.

— Copy a collection of cataloged disk data sets. The original data sets still exist after the copy operation.

— Move every data set on a disk volume to another disk volume.

— Copy every data set on a disk volume to another disk volume.

One function is performed by IEHINITT:

— Write the volume label to initialize a standard label tape volume.

Only one IEHDASDR function is discussed in this book:

— Print the complete contents of a disk data set including all of the accompanying overhead.

IEHMOVE

Overview

IEHMOVE is one of the most powerful and flexible IEB/IEH utilities. Some of the functions it performs overlap several of the data set utilities, especially IEBGENER and IEBCOPY. It is the only IEB/IEH utility that permits the generic processing of a collection of data sets. It is also the only IEB/IEH utility that supports the dynamic creation of data sets. Here dynamic means that it is not necessary to code an accompanying DD statement that identifies the new data set by name. Both generic processing and dynamic data set allocation can also be performed by the VSAM utility program IDCAMS. Like IEBCOPY, IEHMOVE can perform multiple diverse data set utility functions in a single step.

IEHMOVE performs eight basic functions. In this chapter each function is illustrated with an example. Four of the IEHMOVE functions are classified as move operations and four are copy operations. The distinction between a move and a copy operation is very important. Suppose a data set A resides on volume WORK01. The following describes the difference between move and copy operations:

Operation	*Result of Operation*
Move A to WORK02	Data set A is copied to volume WORK02. The original data set A is then automatically scratched from WORK01 following the successful completion of the operation.
Copy A to WORK02	Data set A is copied to volume WORK02. However, the original data set A remains on WORK01.

Except for IEBCOMPR all of the IEB utilities perform copy operations. However, their input data sets can be deleted by coding DISP=(OLD,DELETE) on the accompanying DD statement.

A single data set is one of the four categories of objects that can be moved or copied. However, IEHMOVE cannot move or copy ISAM or VSAM data sets. Thus, IEHMOVE can be used to process sequential, direct access, and partitioned data sets. The remaining three categories of objects that can be moved and copied are: all or some of the individual members in a partitioned data set, a collection of cataloged disk data sets with similar names, and an entire volume of data sets. Hence the basic information contained on an IEHMOVE control statement is the following:

Major Operation	*Object Type*		*Specific Object*	*To and From*	*Supplemental*
MOVE or COPY	DSNAME PDS DSGROUP VOLUME	or or or	dsname or part of name or volume	identify the source and destination volumes used	additional qualifying information like member names

The MOVE PDS and COPY PDS operations may be further qualified by a second control statement. These statements perform the same basic functions as the SELECT and EXCLUDE operators with IEBCOPY. These additional control statements and their functions are as follows:

Operation	*Result of Operation*
INCLUDE	used to include specific pds members by name
EXCLUDE	used to exclude specific pds members by name
REPLACE	used to replace an existing member by one with the same name
SELECT	used to include specific pds members and if desired rename them

When using IEHMOVE three DD statements must always be coded. As usual SYSPRINT identifies the message data set and SYSIN identifies the control statement data set. Unlike with IEBCOPY and IEBGENER, the SYSIN data set cannot be dummied out. When using IEHMOVE, SYSUT1 identifies a work data set which is required. Recall that the DDname SYSUT1 has been used with several previous programs to identify a work data set. However, with IEHMOVE the parameters coded with SYSUT1 should not describe a new temporary data set. Rather, the standard three parameters that are coded to reference a volume with an IEH utility should be used. These are UNIT, VOL, and DISP=OLD. SPACE and DSN are not coded.

For all of the examples considered in this chapter assume that the following data sets reside on the volumes listed in Table 31–1.

TABLE 31–1
Data Sets Used With IEHMOVE Examples and Exercises

Volume	*Data Set*	*Status*	*DSORG*	*Other Information*
WORK01	A.B	cataloged	PS	
(disk)	A.C	cataloged	PS	
	A.X	cataloged	PO	members ALPHA, BETA, GAMMA
	A.Y	kept	PO	members DELTA, ALPHA
	B.A	cataloged	DA	direct data set
	B.B	kept	DA	relative data set
WORK02	A.C	kept	PS	
(disk)				
TAPE01	A1	kept	PS	
(SL tape)	A2	kept	PS	
	A3	kept	PS	

Copying and Moving Sequential, Direct, and Partitioned Data Sets

Example 1: Three data sets on WORK01 are to be copied to different volumes. A.B should be copied to WORK02 and A.C to WORK03. Since both existing data sets are cataloged the two new data sets will be kept. In addition, kept data set B.B is to be copied to WORK03. IEHMOVE will allocate space on WORK02 and WORK03 for the new data sets. This allocation is based on the present size of the data set on WORK01. Notice that although new disk data sets are being created, no DSN, DISP=NEW, or SPACE parameters appear on any DD statement. This can be done as follows:

```
//A          EXEC PGM=IEHMOVE
//SYSPRINT    DD  SYSOUT=A
//SYSUT1      DD  UNIT=3380,VOL=SER=WORK04,DISP=OLD
//WORK01      DD  UNIT=3380,VOL=SER=WORK01,DISP=OLD
//WORK02      DD  UNIT=3380,VOL=SER=WORK02,DISP=OLD
//WORK03      DD  UNIT=3380,VOL=SER=WORK03,DISP=OLD
//SYSIN       DD  *
       COPY   DSNAME=A.B,TO=3380=WORK02
       COPY   DSNAME=A.C,TO=3380=WORK03
       COPY   DSNAME=B.B,TO=3380=WORK03,FROM=3380=WORK01
/*
```

Since both A.B and B.A are cataloged it is unnecessary to code a FROM keyword parameter with their control statements. On the other hand, volume information must be provided to locate the B.B data set which is not cataloged.

Example 2: The same three data sets used in the last example are now to be moved rather than copied. The catalog entries should be updated following the move.

Every JCL statement remains exactly the same. Only the control statements need to be changed from the previous example. They now become

```
MOVE    DSNAME=A.B,TO=3380=WORK02
MOVE    DSNAME=A.C,TO=3380=WORK03
MOVE    DSNAME=B.B,TO=3380=WORK03,FROM=3380=WORK01
```

Copying and Moving Groups of Cataloged Data Sets

Example 3: All cataloged data sets that have a first level qualifier of A are to be copied to disk volume WORK03. IEHMOVE will allocate space for all of the new data sets. Data sets A.B, A.C, and A.X will be copied. Data sets A.C and A.Y are ignored since they are not cataloged. All data sets are referenced through the system catalogs. The complete job step to accomplish this is as follows:

```
//C          EXEC PGM=IEHMOVE
//SYSPRINT    DD  SYSOUT=A
//SYSUT1      DD  UNIT=3380,VOL=SER=WORK05,DISP=OLD
//WORK01      DD  UNIT=3380,VOL=SER=WORK01,DISP=OLD
//WORK02      DD  UNIT=3380,VOL=SER=WORK02,DISP=OLD
//WORK03      DD  UNIT=3380,VOL=SER=WORK03,DISP=OLD
//SYSIN       DD  *
    COPY     DSGROUP=A,TO=3380=WORK03
/*
```

Example 4: All cataloged data sets with a first level qualifier of A are to be moved to disk volume WORK03. The catalog entry for each data set should be changed if necessary. For each data set IEHMOVE will allocate the necessary disk space. The only change from the last example is the control statement. It now becomes

```
MOVE    DSGROUP=A,TO=3380=WORK03
```

Copying and Moving Partitioned Data Sets and Their Members

Example 5: The partitioned data set A.X is to be copied to volume WORK02. Only members ALPHA and BETA are to be copied. BETA is to be renamed NEWBETA in the new pds. Here the space for the new pds will be preallocated in the prior jobstep. Additionally, a copy of the entire pds is to be unloaded to tape volume TAPE01. Note that IEBCOPY can also perform the same operations in a single jobstep. The complete jobstream for all of this is shown below. Since a control statement is continued an X is placed in column 72 and the continuation resumes in column 16.

```
//EE0         EXEC PGM=IEFBR14
//DD1          DD   DSN=A.X,DISP=(NEW,KEEP),
//             UNIT=3380,VOL=SER=WORK02,SPACE=(CYL,(5,1,10))
//E           EXEC PGM=IEHMOVE
//SYSPRINT     DD   SYSOUT=A
//SYSUT1       DD   UNIT=3380,VOL=SER=WORK05,DISP=OLD
//WORK01       DD   UNIT=3380,VOL=SER=WORK01,DISP=OLD
//WORK02       DD   UNIT=3380,VOL=SER=WORK02,DISP=OLD
//TAPE01       DD   DSN=BACKUP.PDS,DISP=(NEW,KEEP),
//             UNIT=TAPE,VOL=SER=TAPE01,LABEL=(2,SL)
//SYSIN        DD   *
    COPY          PDS=A.X,FROM=3380=WORK01,TO=3380=WORK02
    SELECT        MEMBER=(ALPHA,(BETA,NEWBETA))
    COPY          PDS=A.X,FROM=3380=WORK01,TO=TAPE=TAPE01,      X
                  TODD=TAPE01,UNLOAD
/*
```

The DD statement for the tape data set is an exception to the format of a standard IEH utility DD statement. In addition, the COPY control statement specifies an unload operation. When moving or copying a pds IEHMOVE duplicates many of the functions that IEBCOPY performs. The last example illustrated a selective copy of a pds to disk and unloading a pds to tape. The next example illustrates two additional functions that IEBCOPY can perform.

Example 6: The unloaded pds on tape volume TAPE01 is to be reloaded to disk. In addition, all members of the pds A.X on volume WORK01 except for ALPHA are to be moved to volume WORK02. Since this is a move operation the source pds will be automatically deleted. By excluding ALPHA it can no longer be referenced on either volume. The second MOVE operation identifies the file sequence number on the FROM operand.

```
//F           EXEC PGM=IEHMOVE
//SYSPRINT     DD   SYSOUT=A
//SYSUT1       DD   UNIT=3380,VOL=SER=WORK05,DISP=OLD
//WORK01       DD   UNIT=3380,VOL=SER=WORK01,DISP=OLD
//WORK02       DD   UNIT=3380,VOL=SER=WORK02,DISP=OLD
//TAPE01       DD   DSN=BACKUP.PDS,DISP=OLD,
//             UNIT=TAPE,VOL=SER=TAPE01
//SYSIN        DD   *
    MOVE          PDS=A.X,FROM=3380=WORK01,TO=3380=WORK02
    EXCLUDE       MEMBER=ALPHA
    MOVE          DSNAME=TAPE01,TO=3380=WORK01,                 X
                  FROM=TAPE=(TAPE01,2),FROMDD=TAPE01
/*
```

Copying and Moving Entire Disk Volumes

The last of the four major functions performed by IEHMOVE is to copy or move all of the data sets from one disk volume to another. Only disk volumes may be referenced during these operations. Clearly an application programmer would not perform these last two functions as frequently as the six functions previously discussed. Moving and copying all the data sets on a volume are illustrated in the final two examples.

Example 7: Every data set that resides on volume WORK01 is to be copied to volume WORK02. Every data set on volume WORK03 is to be copied to volume WORK04.

```
//G          EXEC PGM=IEHMOVE
//SYSPRINT    DD   SYSOUT=A
//SYSUT1      DD   UNIT=3380,VOL=SER=WORK05,DISP=OLD
//WORK01      DD   UNIT=3380,VOL=SER=WORK01,DISP=OLD
//WORK02      DD   UNIT=3380,VOL=SER=WORK02,DISP=OLD
//WORK03      DD   UNIT=3380,VOL=SER=WORK03,DISP=OLD
//WORK04      DD   UNIT=3380,VOL=SER=WORK04,DISP=OLD
//SYSIN       DD   *
    COPY     VOLUME=3380=WORK01,TO=3380=WORK02
    COPY     VOLUME=3380=WORK03,TO=3380=WORK04
/*
```

Example 8: Every data set that resides on volume WORK01 is to be moved to volume WORK02. Two changes must be made to the code in Example 7. First, the DD statements for WORK03 and WORK04 are not needed. Also, the single control statement now becomes

```
  MOVE   VOLUME=3380=WORK01,TO=3380=WORK02
```

IEHINITT

Overview

The IEHINITT utility performs one function: it writes volume labels on reels of magnetic tape. It performs no other function. It can be used with IBM standard labels or ANSI labels. IEHINITT is not used with NL tape volumes. It is this utility that identifies a tape as containing standard labels. Any number of tapes can be labeled in a single jobstep. A potential danger with using IEHINITT is that it can overwrite the volume label on any existing volumes, destroying the contents of the volume. For this reason its use is sometimes restricted.

Following an IEHINITT jobstep the total information written on the tape volume will consist of the following:

Field	*Contents of Field Starting with Byte 1*	*Physical Description*
Volume label	VOL1volser	First 80 byte block
First data set header	HDR1	Second 80 byte block
Tape mark		Denotes end of tape

Here volser is the name of the volume provided by IEHINITT. When data is eventually placed on the volume the first data set header receives its remaining 76 bytes of data and the second header record for the data set overwrites the tape mark. More information on standard label tapes is contained in Chapter 16.

Control Statements

IEHINITT contains only one control statement. Its format is

```
DDname   INITT   SER=xxxxxx
```

Here the INITT operator is preceded by the label field which must begin in column one. Here again the label is written as DDname since the label must match a DDname in the jobstep. The label field is required. The SER operand is required and contains the volume's serial number. Most commonly this is a numeric value. However, alphabetics and special characters are allowed. Two other operands may be coded with INITT. OWNER=yyyyyyyyyy can be used to identify the owner of the volume. NUMBTAPE=n can be used to initialize n tape volumes with one control statement. In this case the SER value must be numeric. It is used for the first volume and repeatedly incremented by one for the remaining volume serial numbers.

DD Statements

IEHINITT requires SYSPRINT for the message data set and SYSIN for the control statements. Each INITT control statement has a label field that must identify a DD statement. Such a DD statement should contain two parameters DCB=DEN=density and UNIT. No other parameters can be meaningfully coded.

Initializing One Volume With an INITT Statement

Example 9: Two tape volumes are to be initialized with standard labels. They will have volume serial numbers of 123456 and ABCDEF and densities of 6250 and 1600 BPI respectively. An optional owner value is included with ABCDEF.

```
//A          EXEC PGM=IEHINITT
//SYSPRINT DD   SYSOUT=A
//TAPE1      DD   DCB=DEN=4,UNIT=(TAPE,1,DEFER)
//TAPE2      DD   DCB=DEN=3,UNIT=(TAPE,1,DEFER)
//SYSIN      DD   *
TAPE1      INITT  SER=123456
TAPE2      INITT  SER=ABCDEF,OWNER=LBRUMBAUGH
/*
```

Initializing Multiple Tape Volumes

Example 10: Here four tape volumes are to be initialized with serial numbers of 999001, 999002, 999003, and 999004. All are to have 6250 BPI density. This is done with the NUMBTAPE keyword parameter.

```
//B          EXEC PGM=IEHINITT
//SYSPRINT DD   SYSOUT=A
//XYZ        DD   DCB=DEN=4,UNIT=(TAPE,1,DEFER)
//SYSIN      DD   *
XYZ        INITT SER=999001,NUMBTAPE=4
/*
```

IEHDASDR

Overview

The IEHDASDR utility is a very powerful system utility. However, it will be only briefly discussed in this book. There are two reasons for this. First, most of the functions it performs are not used by application programmers. These include analyzing and assigning values to fields associated with disk volumes. Second, most of the functions performed by IEHDASDR can also be performed by the ADRDSSU utility. ADRDSSU shares many syntax properties with IDCAMS.

IEHDASDR and ADRDSSU are both capable of performing one very important function that is of interest to application programmers. Both utilities can be used to obtain a printed listing of the complete contents of a disk data set. This listing includes all of the information on a track, including COUNT and KEY field values, the R0 record, etc. Hence both utilities allow a complete examination of a data set rather than just the logical records. Frequently questions arise as to how a particular data set organization is stored on disk or what type of processing actually takes place during a given operation. Such questions are difficult or impossible to answer merely by examining the logical records in the data set. In such situations IEHDASDR or ADRDSSU can be used. Both utilities are suggested when solving some of the exercises in Chapters 13 and 14.

Examining a Disk Data Set

Example 11: A partitioned data set's directory is to be printed. The listing should include COUNT and KEY fields and the R0 records. No other IEB/IEH utility can provide this information. The location and extent of the data set on disk must be given as two CCHH values.

```
//A          EXEC PGM=IEHDASDR
//SYSPRINT DD   SYSOUT=A
//DD1        DD   UNIT=3350,VOL=SER=WORK01,DISP=OLD
//SYSIN      DD   *
  DUMP            FROMDD=DD1,TODD=SYSPRINT,BEGIN=00020000,              X
                  TODD=00020005
/*
```

Exercises

1. What are the major functions that IEBCOPY performs that cannot be done with IEH-MOVE? Can IEHMOVE compress a pds? Of the eight major functions performed by IEHMOVE, which cannot be done with IEBCOPY? Compare the functions performed by the SELECT and EXCLUDE operators with IEBCOPY to the INCLUDE, EXCLUDE, REPLACE, and SELECT operators with IEHMOVE.

2. Which of the eight major functions performed by IEHMOVE can also be performed by IEBGENER? Distinguish between MOVE and COPY operations performed with IEBGE-NER. Which other utilities can process more than one data set with a single control statement as IEHMOVE can with DSGROUP? Which other utilities can process every data set on a disk volume?

3. Under what conditions would the MOVE VOLUME and COPY VOLUME operations most likely be performed?

4. Use IEHMOVE to copy a true direct data set with disk KEY fields. Use IEHDASDR or ADRDSSU to print the new copy of the data set. Examine the COUNT and KEY fields. What other utilities can be used to copy a true direct data set?

5. Why must a SYSIN data set necessarily be coded with IEHMOVE when some comparable operations with IEBCOPY do not require control statements?

6. Write the necessary DD statements and control statements to perform the following functions. Use the data set names and volumes in Table 31–1 to obtain any necessary additional information. Whenever possible use IEHMOVE.

    a. Unload the pds A.X to tape volume TAPE01. Make it the first standard label data set on the volume.

b. Move the pds A.X to disk volume WORK02.
c. Copy member DELTA in pds A.Y to disk volume WORK02.
d. Copy every disk data set with a first level qualifier of B to disk volume WORK02.
e. Move all cataloged data sets whose first two qualifiers are A.B to disk volume WORK02.
f. Merge the members in A.X and A.Y to form a new pds called A.Z.
g. Copy the three standard label data sets on tape volume TAPE01 to disk volume WORK01.
h. Move every data set from disk volumes WORK01 and WORK02 to WORK03.

7. Initialize a reel of standard label 6250 BPI tape with a serial number of 111222.

8. In a single step initialize five reels of standard label 6250 BPI tape with serial numbers of 000111, 000112, 000113, 000991, and 000992. All of the volumes have an owner named AAAARDVARK.

9. Approximately ten tape volumes are to be labeled at 1600 BPI. All have serial numbers that consist entirely of alphabetic characters. Four tape drives are available for this. Use a minimum number of DD statements to perform the labeling by specifying multiple units on one statement.

10. For each of the functions listed below, select the appropriate utility or service program (IEBxxx, IEHxxx, IEFBR14, Sort/Merge, ADRDSSU, IDCAMS, Loader, Linkage Editor, or none of these) to perform the specific function required in one jobstep. Supply all possible answers in each case. Some questions do not have a unique answer. Most utilities occur as answers more than once.

a. Create a true direct (the COBOL term) data set from card image input.
b. Copy 752 (of the 756) members of SYS1.MACLIB into a new pds.
c. Create an ISAM data set using sequential input.
d. Create variable length QSAM records from sequential input.
e. Create a relative (the COBOL term) data set from sequential input.
f. Create a multiple members pds, out of sequential input.
g. Copy SYS1.LINKLIB to tape.
h. List the records in a relative data set. Edit and title the listing.
i. Create packed decimal data out of character input.
j. Unload an ISAM data set to tape.
k. Delete member COBUCG from SYS1.PROCLIB.
l. Determine if a backup of SYS1.LINKLIB worked successfully. There are approximately 1000 members in SYS1.LINKLIB.
m. Print the contents of the directory of SYS1.COBLIB.
n. Add a new member to SYS1.LINKLIB from ''sequential input''!
o. Compress SYS1.PROCLIB.
p. Print every record in every member in the pds named SYS1.DATALIB.
q. Unload SYS1.ACSCTLG1 (a VSAM user catalog) to tape.
r. Merge the records in three pds members together to form a fourth member. Maintain alphabetical order on a key field within each member.
s. Merge the members in three existing pds's together to form a new pds.
t. Move a load module from disk to main memory.

u. Alter the catalog to reflect the actual contents of a VSAM data set.
v. Unload member COBUCG of SYS1.PROCLIB to tape.
w. Print the COUNT fields found on a 3350 disk.
x. Uncatalog a disk data set, but do not delete it. No other processing is to be done.
y. Create a new data set by selecting every fifth record from an existing sequential data set.
z. Create an object module data set out of card image COBOL source code.

Chapter 32

Using the IDCAMS Utility with Non-VSAM Data Sets

Overview

In addition to the IEB/IEH utilities, there is one other essential utility on MVS systems. It is called IDCAMS, which is pronounced either I-′D-cams or ′id-cams. It is more powerful and flexible than most of the IEB/IEH utilities combined. IDCAMS was introduced in the early 1970s in conjunction with the VSAM data set organizations. It was initially developed for use primarily with VSAM data sets. Some of the functions performed by IEB/IEH utilities on non-VSAM data sets could also be performed by IDCAMS. In the ensuing years more IEB/IEH functions have been added to IDCAMS. In the future the role of the IEB/IEH utilities will continue to diminish in importance while IDCAMS will assume more of their functions. For example practically every IEHPROGM function can now also be performed by IDCAMS. The relationship between IEB/IEH utilities, IDCAMS, and data set organizations is summarized in Table 24–1. Two IBM manuals are needed to completely describe the IDCAMS utility: *Data Facility Extended Function: Access Method Services Reference* (SC26-3967) and *Data Facility Extended Function: Access Method Services Administration and Services* (SC26-3966).

IDCAMS uses only two required data sets. The DDnames SYSPRINT and SYSIN identify the message and control statement data sets respectively. Unlike with the IEB/IEH utilities, SYSPRINT consists of variable length records. The specific default values are RECFM = VBA, LRECL = 125, and BLKSIZE = 629. Smaller logical record values should not be specified. Neither F nor FB should be coded with RECFM as both are ignored and VB is substituted. SYSIN is required and must identify one or more control statements in order for meaningful processing to be performed. The *Access Method Services Reference* manual describes several PARM options that may be coded on the IDCAMS EXEC statement. This same information can also be coded on an IDCAMS control statement.

With some types of control statements, printed output may be directed to a data set other than SYSPRINT. There are several situations, described below in the discussions of PRINT and LISTCAT commands when it is convenient to do this.

Control statements are used to perform specific functions with IDCAMS. Many control statements can be used only with VSAM data sets. Some parameters are meaningful only with a particular data set organization. There are five important control statements that overlap the functions performed by the IEB/IEH utilities. The basic role of each of the five types of control statements is shown in Table 32–1 along with the IEB/IEH utilities whose functions they overlap. There are two general types of IDCAMS control statements. The five discussed here are called function control statements. The other type is called a modal control statement.

Multiple function control statements can be coded in a single IDCAMS jobstep. The commands are executed independently of one another unless they are being used to perform several different functions with the same data set. Each function returns a condition code. The code values and their meanings are basically the same as with the standard IBM software codes: 0 means success, 4 is a warning, 8 is a severe error, 12 is a nonrecoverable error, and 16 is a disaster. The highest condition code returned by any function during the jobstep is printed in the job listing as the condition code for the step. The *Access Method Services Reference* manual describes how the flow of control within an IDCAMS jobstep itself can be dynamically modified by using modal commands to interrogate the condition codes returned by the previous individual function statements. This is similar to using the COND parameter with jobsteps.

TABLE 32–1

Relationship Between IEB/IEH Utilities and IDCAMS Functions

Type of IDCAMS Control Statement	*Overlapping IEB/IEH Utilities*	*Basic Functions Performed*
REPRO	IEBGENER IEBISAM	Copy sequential, ISAM, and direct data sets
PRINT	IEBPTPCH IEBGENER IEBISAM	Print the records in non-VSAM data sets
LISTCAT	IEHLIST	Print catalog information for non-VSAM data sets
ALTER	IEHPROGM IEFBR14	Modify catalog and data set status values; change the names of data sets and pds members
DELETE	IEHPROGM IEFBR14	Uncatalog and delete data sets; delete pds members

Example 1: In a single jobstep the REPRO command is used to create a back-up copy of an existing data set. Following this PRINT displays the records in the new data set and DELETE scratches the original data set. The JCL needed to do this is shown below. The actual parameters for the three control statements are not included. The condition codes are shown to the right of each function statement. Here, it can be assumed that the DELETE did not work correctly and the REPRO generated a warning.

```
//A         EXEC PGM=IDCAMS
//SYSPRINT DD   SYSOUT=A
//OLDDATA  DD   parameters for the existing data set
//NEWDATA  DD   parameters for a new (back-up) data set
//SYSIN    DD   *
   REPRO    create a back-up copy       condition code=4
   PRINT    the new data set            condition code=0
   DELETE   the existing data set       condition code=8
/*
```

The condition code for the complete jobstep is 8.

Dynamically Allocating Data Sets

With the IEB utilities, a DD statement must be coded for every data set the utility processes. Parameters coded on the DD statement supply information that is used to locate the data set. This information can identify a disk VTOC, a catalog, the pass mechanism, or several other possibilities. The DD statement also identifies where information about the data set should be placed during disposition processing after the step ends. With the IEH utilities, control statements are used to identify data sets by specifying unit and volume information. IDCAMS allows an alternative method of identifying a data set without having to code a DD statement to identify it. It consists of coding only the data set name on a control statement. No additional information is required. When the function statement is processed, the data set is dynamically allocated.

All dynamically allocated data sets are located through their catalog entry. This can always be done with VSAM data sets since they must be cataloged. However, with non-VSAM data sets a previous jobstep or job must be used to catalog a data set before it can be dynamically allocated. There are several advantages to using dynamic allocation. First, no accompanying DD statement is necessary. This minimizes the possibility of JCL syntax errors. Second, a job cannot be cancelled because a data set is not found or a duplicate data set name is coded. Finally, the data set is not allocated to the job until it is actually needed, if it is actually needed. With JCL, the data set is allocated preliminary to the execution of the step.

There are also several significant disadvantages that exist when using dynamic allocation. First, as previously mentioned the data set must be cataloged. Second, since no DISP parameter is coded a default value of OLD is supplied. This prohibits other jobs from using the data set concurrently. This is a bad practice with important system data sets that are needed only for input. Likewise, if a data set is currently in use it cannot be dynamically allocated. Many data sets used by on-line systems such as CICS are always in use when the system is up. Additional DD parameters cannot be coded with a dynamically allocated data set. For example, with a printed data set it may be desirable to code the FREE, COPIES, or OUTLIM parameters, etc. However, this cannot be done on the function statement that dynamically allocates a data set. Likewise, JCL must be used to concatenate data sets. In-stream and SYSOUT data sets cannot be dynamically allocated. Following the step the only DISP value possible with a dynamically allocated data set is KEEP. Despite these drawbacks dynamic allocation is an important concept with the REPRO and PRINT commands. Unless a specific restriction in the above list or something comparable applies, dynamic allocation should be used.

IDCAMS Syntax

IDCAMS control statements use a free format syntax where information may be coded between columns 2 and 72 inclusive. Control statements begin with an operator which identifies the function or command to be performed. One or more positional or keyword parameters and subparameters are then coded. The parameters must be separated from one another by commas, spaces, and comments. Spaces are used most commonly. Likewise, the operator or command must be separated from the first parameter by spaces, a comma, or a comment. Hence, the following REPRO statements perform the same function and are all syntactically correct.

```
REPRO   INFILE(DD1),OUTFILE(DD2),COUNT(100)
REPRO   INFILE(DD1)  OUTFILE(DD2)  COUNT(100)
REPRO   COUNT(100),   INFILE(DD1)  /*COMMENT*/   OUTFILE(DD2)
```

Almost all parameters are keyword. Positional parameters must be coded before all keyword parameters. Keyword parameters use the syntax keyword(value) and keyword(value1 . . . value2 . . . valueN) with multiple subparameters. The subparameters ordinarily are positional. Hence, with the above REPRO statements INFILE, OUTFILE, and COUNT are keywords with values DD1, DD2, and 100 respectively.

Comments may be included on an IDCAMS statement using the same syntax as with PL/I: /* comment field */. It is essential to remember to code the */ or the following parameters and control statements will be treated as comments until the */ characters are encountered on a subsequent statement. Complete lines of comments may be inserted within the control statements. Furthermore, blank statements can be inserted among the control statements to enhance readability.

Control statements may be continued. This is done most commonly by specifying a hyphen as the rightmost non-blank character on every statement that is to be continued. The hyphen should be replaced by a plus sign if the statement is to be continued and a specific value on the statement is also to be continued. The end of a function statement is identified either by a line that does not end in a continuation character or a line that ends with a semicolon. Three additional syntactically correct versions of the REPRO control statement that was coded above are shown below to illustrate continuation and termination of statements. In all of the examples the REPRO statement is immediately followed by a PRINT statement to illustrate how the end of one function statement is separated from the beginning of the next one.

```
REPRO            -    REPRO-              REPRO INFILE(DD1)-
  INFILE(DD1)    -      INFILE(DD1)-            OUTFILE(DD2)-
  OUTFILE(DD2)   -      OUTFILE(D+              COUNT(100);
  COUNT(100)            D2)-              PRINT INFILE(DD2)
PRINT            -      COUNT(100)
  INFILE(DD2)         PRINT-
                        INFILE(DD2)
```

Most programmers prefer to code only one parameter per line. For readability, keywords on continued statements should begin in the same column and the hyphens and plus signs should also be coded in the same column. For all of these reasons the code on the left is preferred. Note that the semicolon can be used as an alternative to coding nothing to delimit the complete statement. This is another similarity between PL/I and IDCAMS.

When coding a continued statement care must be taken if either a comment or a blank line is included in the continuation. In both cases, the line itself must still contain a hyphen as the rightmost non-blank character. If this is not done, the continuation is ended. Hence a correct way to code a comment and blank statement within a continued REPRO statement is as follows:

```
          REPRO                       -
          INFILE(DD1)                 -
    /* REPRO CREATES A BACK-UP */     -
          OUTFILE(DD2)                -
                                      -
          COUNT(100)
```

The REPRO Command

The REPRO command is the IDCAMS equivalent of IEBGENER. REPRO does not contain features equivalent to the GENERATE, RECORD, and MEMBER control statement options available with IEBGENER. However, the basic copy operation itself is similar.

Example 2: An input disk data set is used to create a back-up, output data set. Example 1 in Chapter 25 used IEBGENER to create a back-up copy on tape of a disk data set. The same function can be performed with REPRO as follows:

```
//A          EXEC PGM=IDCAMS
//SYSPRINT DD   SYSOUT=A
//INDD       DD   input data set parameters
//OUTDD      DD   output data set parameters
//SYSIN      DD   *
     REPRO INFILE(INDD)   OUTFILE(OUTDD)
/*
```

Here, INFILE and OUTFILE identify DDnames that are equivalent to the SYSUT1 and SYSUT2 data sets respectively with IEBGENER.

The following parameters are used with REPRO when processing non-VSAM data sets. Three of the first four discussed have the same roles with the PRINT command.

To identify the input data set, either INFILE or INDATASET is required. Keyword abbreviations are shown on the right.

```
INFILE(DDname)              IFILE(DDname)        or
INDATASET(dsname)           IDS(dsname)
```

To identify the output data set, either OUTFILE or OUTDATSET (or their abbreviations) must be coded.

```
OUTFILE(DDname)             OFILE(DDname)        or
OUTDATASET(dsname)          ODS(dsname)
```

Only the input and output data sets are required with REPRO. All of the remaining parameters are optional. There are five parameters that may be used with non-VSAM data sets. Some combinations are mutually exclusive.

Parameter	*Function*
SKIP(n)	Skip the first n records in the input data set before beginning the copy operation.
COUNT(n)	Copy a maximum of n records into the output data set and then terminate the copy operation.
ENVIRONMENT(DUMMY)	When copying an ISAM data set, logically deleted records are included in the copy operation when DUMMY is coded.
FROMKEY(key value) TOKEY(key value)	FROMKEY and TOKEY are used only with ISAM data sets. They determine the first and last records to be copied from the input data set. A partial key value identifies a generic key. Only the leftmost bytes in the record key must match the value coded.

SKIP and FROMKEY are mutually exclusive, as are COUNT and TOKEY. ENVIRONMENT must be coded as a qualifier to the input parameter. SKIP and COUNT can be used with sequential, indexed, and direct data sets while ENVIRONMENT,

FROMKEY, and TOKEY are restricted to ISAM data sets. To illustrate the REPRO parameters, Example 2 is completed in a variety of ways.

Example 3: The cataloged disk data set ALPHA.ONE is to be backed-up to a standard label tape. DCB values for the new data set will be taken from the labels of ALPHA.ONE.

```
//C          EXEC PGM=IDCAMS
//SYSPRINT    DD   SYSOUT=A
//DD1         DD   DSN=ALPHA.ONE,DISP=SHR
//DD2         DD   DSN=ALPHA.BACKUP,DISP=(NEW,PASS),
//                 UNIT=TAPE,VOL=SER=TAPE99,LABEL=(1,SL),
//                 DCB=(ALPHA.ONE)
//SYSIN       DD   *
    REPRO     INFILE(DD1)    -
              OUTFILE(DD2)
/*
```

By using dynamic allocation, the DD1 DD statement can be omitted and the control statement recoded as shown below:

```
   REPRO   INDATASET(ALPHA.ONE)   OUTFILE(DD2)
```

Here, ALPHA.ONE has a disposition of OLD. Since the output data set is being created in this step, it cannot be dynamically allocated. However, if the tape data set had been created and cataloged in a previous jobstep with IEFR14, both DD1 and DD2 may be omitted and the REPRO statement is coded as

```
   REPRO   IDS(ALPHA.ONE)   ODS(ALPHA.BACKUP)
```

Example 4: The records in ALPHA.ONE and ALPHA.TWO are used to create a new disk data set called BETA. The first five records in ALPHA.ONE are not to be copied and a maximum of 1000 records are to be copied to the new data set. ALPHA.TWO is a permanent uncataloged data set. It is located using the catalog information stored with ALPHA.ONE.

```
//D          EXEC PGM=IDCAMS
//SYSPRINT DD   SYSOUT=A
//ALPHA     DD   DSN=ALPHA.ONE,DISP=SHR
//          DD   DSN=ALPHA.TWO,DISP=SHR,VOL=REF=(ALPHA.ONE)
//DDB       DD   DSN=BETA,DISP=(,PASS),UNIT=SYSDA,
//               SPACE=(CYL,(10,1)),DCB=(ALPHA.ONE)
//SYSIN     DD   *
    REPRO   IFILE(ALPHA)     -
            OFILE(DDB)       -
            SKIP(5)          -
            COUNT(1000)
/*
```

Even if ALPHA.TWO had been a cataloged data set, dynamic allocation should not be used with the input data set because of the concatenation operation.

Example 5: Suppose that ALPHA.ONE is a cataloged ISAM data set. The key field is last name. Only those records where the last name begins with a letter in the second half of the alphabet (N-Z) are to be copied to an existing ISAM data set. Dummy records are to be included in the copy operation. Since only one letter is specified with FROMKEY the copy operation begins with the first record that starts with the letter N. If no key field begins with N, the first record that begins with a letter that follows N identifies the beginning of the copy operation. Notice that the statement with DDname ALPHA is never used.

```
//E         EXEC PGM=IDCAMS
//SYSPRINT DD   SYSOUT=A
//ALPHA     DD   DSN=ALPHA.ONE,DISP=SHR
//BETA      DD   DSN=ISAM.DATASET,DISP=(MOD,KEEP),
//               UNIT=SYSDA,VOL=SER=WORK01,
//               DCB=(DSORG=IS,OPTCD=L,CYLOFL=5,BLKSIZE=100,
//               RECFM=F)
//SYSIN     DD   *
    REPRO   IDS(ALPHA.ONE ENVIRONMENT(DUMMY)) -
            OFILE(BETA)     -
            FROMKEY(N)
/*
```

The PRINT Command

The PRINT command can be thought of as a special case of the REPRO command in much the same way that many functions of IEBPTPCH can be thought of as a subset of IEBGENER. Although neither is a true subset, both PRINT and IEBPTPCH are ordinarily used to copy an input data set to a printer. When processing non-VSAM data sets, every parameter described with REPRO is valid with and maintains the same meaning with PRINT except for OUTDATASET. Hence, the possible values that can be coded with PRINT may be summarized as follows:

Input Data Set	*Output Data Set*	*Processing Options*	*Output Format*
INFILE(DDname) INDATASET(dsname)	default(SYSPRINT) OUTFILE(DDname)	SKIP(n records) or FROMKEY(keyvalue1) COUNT(n records) or TOKEY(keyvalue2) ENVIRONMENT(DUMMY)	HEX CHAR DUMP
One of these is required.	If OUTFILE is not coded, the default is used.	Any combination of these three groups may be coded data set organization permitting.	DUMP

Input data sets are identified in exactly the same manner as with REPRO. Ordinarily the output from a PRINT command is sent to the SYSPRINT message data set. This is sufficient in most cases and no keyword parameter is required. However, OUTFILE may be coded and has the same meaning as with REPRO. OUTFILE is most frequently used in order to code some of the many DD parameters that are available with a SYSOUT data set. The five additional processing options parameters have exactly the same meanings as with REPRO.

The actual format of the output produced by PRINT is controlled by specifying either CHARACTER (CHAR), HEX, or DUMP. CHAR prints all standard printable characters and represents nonprintable characters with a decimal point. HEX represents every EBCDIC value by its two character hexadecimal representation. DUMP is the default and produces a combination of CHAR and HEX. When DUMP is coded, the leftmost 2/3 of the listing contains the HEX representation while the remainder contains the CHAR representation.

Example 6: The records in the cataloged data sets ALPHA.ONE and ALPHA.TWO are to be printed. ALPHA.ONE, a sequential data set, is to be printed in DUMP format and ALPHA.TWO, an ISAM data set, in character format. The control statements needed to do this are:

```
PRINT IDS(ALPHA.ONE)
PRINT IDS(ALPHA.TWO) CHAR
```

Here the ease of coding a dynamic allocation should be balanced against any processing difficulties that it might cause for other programmers.

Suppose that only the first 500 records in ALPHA.ONE are to be printed in hexadecimal format and the first 500 records in ALPHA.TWO are to be skipped before printing begins. Furthermore, processing should end when a record with a key field value of SMITH is reached.

```
PRINT IDS(ALPHA.ONE) HEX COUNT(500)
PRINT IDS(ALPHA.TWO) DUMP SKIP(500) TOKEY(SMITH)
```

Example 7: Three members of SYS1.PROCLIB are to be printed in character format. The necessary control statement and DD statements are coded as follows:

```
//PRNTPROC   DD   DSN=SYS1.PROCLIB(COBUC),DISP=SHR
//           DD   DSN=SYS1.PROCLIB(COBUCL),DISP=SHR
//           DD   DSN=SYS1.PROCLIB(COBUCLG),DISP=SHR
//SYSIN      DD   *
     PRINT   INFILE(PRNTPROC)   CHAR
/*
```

The same results can be achieved by coding three separate PRINT statements. This would result in a more readable listing but still not comparable to IEBPTPCH.

The most common reason for coding OUTFILE is to request additional DD parameters with the printed copy of the data set. For example, suppose 25 copies of the data set ALPHA.ONE are to be printed. Furthermore, a maximum of 1000 lines should be printed from ALPHA.TWO.

```
//DD1      DD   SYSOUT=A,COPIES=25
//DD2      DD   SYSOUT=D,OUTLIM=1000
//SYSIN    DD   *
    PRINT IDS(ALPHA.ONE)  OFILE(DD1)  CHAR
    PRINT IDS(ALPHA.TWO)  OFILE(DD2)  HEX
/*
```

Example 8: Along with IEHLIST and IEBPTPCH, IDCAMS can print the directory of a pds. The actual code is very similar to that used with IEBPTPCH. With both utilities, the directory is processed as a sequential data set which ends when the EOF mark for the directory is encountered. Both utilities produce an unformatted listing that contains all the information in the directory. To print the directory of SYS1.PROCLIB, the following should be coded:

```
//H          EXEC PGM=IDCAMS
//SYSPRINT DD   SYSOUT=A
//PDSDIREC DD   DSN=SYS1.PROCLIB,DISP=SHR,
//              DCB=(RECFM=U,BLKSIZE=256)
//SYSIN      DD   *
     PRINT IFILE(PDSDIREC) DUMP
/*
```

The LISTCAT Command

LISTCAT is used only with cataloged data sets. Its role is to display some or all of the information in a system catalog for a given data set. LISTCAT requires no additional DD statements to locate the data set. All of the data sets are identified on control statements. However, there is no actual dynamic allocation because the records in the data set are not processed. Rather, only the catalog entry itself is retrieved. Like IEHLIST, LISTCAT can only be used to display information. Values cannot be modified. Only user catalogs and the system VSAM master catalog can be accessed by LISTCAT.

The parameters used with LISTCAT are the following for non-VSAM data sets:

Identify Data Sets	*Amount of Information*	*Destination of Printed Listing*
ENTRIES(dsname1 . . . dsnameN)	NAME	default(SYSPRINT)
LEVEL(dsname1 . . . dsnameN)	ALL	OUTFILE(DDname)

ALL supplies the complete amount of information found in the catalog for the data set. NAME supplies the minimum amount of information. NAME is the default. Several additional Amount values are not discussed here.

In rare instances a printed listing produced by LISTCAT is not sent to the message data set. This is usually done only when multiple copies of the listing are required.

LISTCAT, ALTER and DELETE all permit multiple data sets to be coded on a single DD statement. Either the ENTRIES or LEVEL parameter must be used to identify the data set(s) whose catalog entries are to be displayed. With ENTRIES, a complete data set name may be coded and a generic listing may be gotten by replacing one level of qualification with an asterisk. To list the catalog entries for the data sets ALPHA, BETA, and GAMMA, code:

```
LISTCAT   ENTRIES(ALPHA BETA GAMMA)   ALL
```

or

```
LISTCAT   ENT(ALPHA,BETA,GAMMA)   ALL
```

To list the catalog entries for every cataloged data set whose name consists of two levels of qualification, the first of which is ALPHA, code:

```
LISTCAT   ENTRIES(ALPHA.*)   ALL
```

The LEVEL parameter produces a generic listing of all data sets whose initial qualifiers match those coded. Any number of trailing qualifiers are valid. Like ENTRIES, one of the coded qualifiers may be replaced by an asterisk. Hence, LEVEL produces a generic listing in two different directions. Both ENTRIES and LEVEL illustrate the advantages associated with using consistent qualifier values when naming data sets. They can then be easily processed as a group by commands like LISTCAT. (The ALTER and DELETE commands discussed below also support generic processing.)

Example 9: The following LISTCAT commands are used to illustrate the different types of generic processing available with ENTRIES and LEVEL. The fundamental difference between the two parameters concerns the number of levels of qualification to which the generic processing applies. With ENTRIES an * applies to only one level of qualification. With LEVEL if * is the rightmost qualifier coded, it may identify any number of trailing qualifiers. Suppose that the following are all cataloged data set names.

X
X.Y
X.Z
X.W
X.Y.A
X.Y.B
X.Y.A.B

LISTCAT Command Keyword Parameter	*Data Sets Identified*
ENTRIES(X.*.A)	X.Y.A
ENTRIES(X.*)	X.Y, X.Z, X.W
LEVEL(X.Y)	X.Y.A, X.Y.B, X.Y.A.B
ENTRIES(X.Y.*)	X.Y.A, X.Y.B
LEVEL(X)	all data sets except X
ENTRIES(*.Y)	X.Y

The ALTER Command

ALTER is used to modify information concerning an existing data set. Most of the ALTER parameters cannot be used with non-VSAM data sets. Basically, ALTER is used to change information stored in a system catalog. With non-VSAM data sets, only the name itself is commonly altered. Recall that the RENAME control statement with IEHPROGM can be used for the same purpose.

ALTER performs one other important function that can also be done with IEHPROGM. A pds member can be renamed. Again, the actual syntax depends on whether the pds is cataloged.

Example 10: The cataloged data set ALPHA is to be renamed NEW.ALPHA. ALPHA is a pds. Member BETA in ALPHA is to be renamed NEWBETA. The control statements needed to accomplish this in the same jobstep are:

```
ALTER   ALPHA   NEWNAME(NEW.ALPHA)
ALTER   NEW.ALPHA(BETA)   NEWNAME(NEW.ALPHA(NEWBETA))
```

The ALTER command permits generic processing. To change the names of all cataloged data sets with a first level qualifier of ALPHA to a first level qualifier of BETA code the following

```
ALTER   ALPHA./   NEWNAME(BETA./)
```

Here all data sets are assumed to have two qualifiers in their names. The * may be coded anywhere in the data set name. It does not have to be the last qualifier.

The DELETE Command

The DELETE command can be used to perform a number of important functions. The two SCRATCH functions performed by IEHPROGM can also be done with IDCAMS. This consists of deleting any non-VSAM data set or any pds member. Furthermore, with cataloged data sets the data set is uncataloged and then deleted.

With non-VSAM data sets scratch is a more appropriate term than delete. Data sets with one or more identical qualifiers can be generically deleted by the DELETE command provided that they are cataloged. By coding one additional parameter a data set whose expiration date has not been reached can also be deleted. Multiple data sets can also be deleted with one statement without using generic processing.

For the remainder of this section assume that ALPHA.X, ALPHA.Y, ALPHA.Z.A, ALPHA.W.A, and ALPHA.Q.A are existing cataloged data sets. ALPHA.Q.A is a pds that contains members named BETA and GAMMA. ALPHA.X and ALPHA.Y contain expiration dates that have not occurred.

Example 11: The five data sets described above can be deleted in a variety of ways. An individual statement can be coded for every data set as follows:

```
DELETE ALPHA.X   PURGE
DELETE ALPHA.Y   PURGE
DELETE ALPHA.Z.A
DELETE ALPHA.W.A
DELETE ALPHA.Q.A
```

It is necessary to code PURGE with every data set that has an expiration date that has not occurred. Multiple data sets can also be deleted on a single control statement. The above five statements can be recoded as:

```
DELETE (ALPHA.X ALPHA.Y) PURGE
DELETE (ALPHA.Z.A ALPHA.W.A ALPHA.Q.A)
```

Here, the parentheses are necessary since more than one data set is coded. All of the data sets can be deleted on a single statement. Here, PURGE is unnecessary with three of the data sets but must be coded:

```
DELETE (ALPHA.X ALPHA.Y ALPHA.Z.A ALPHA.W.A ALPHA.Q.A) PURGE
```

Example 12: Generic processing can be used to more easily delete the five data sets. To delete all data sets with a first level qualifier of ALPHA and a third level qualifier of A, the following may be coded:

```
DELETE  ALPHA.*.A
```

Generic processing can also be used to delete all data sets with a first level qualifier of ALPHA and any second level qualifier by coding

```
DELETE PURGE
```

Example 13: DELETE can be used to delete a member from a pds. Here, member BETA in ALPHA.Q.A is deleted by coding

```
DELETE ALPHA.Q.A(BETA)
```

Exercises

1. Which of the IDCAMS commands support generic processing where only part of the data set name is coded? Discuss the range of processing allowed and the limitations associated with each of the commands. Why do the remaining IDCAMS commands not support generic processing?

2. Which IDCAMS commands optionally permit dynamic allocation of the input and output data sets? What are the major advantages provided by dynamic allocation? What are the significant disadvantages?

3. SYS1.PROCLIB is a cataloged data set. Print out all the information in the catalog for the pds SYS1.PROCLIB. Now use IDCAMS to print out the directory of SYS1.PROCLIB in dump format. Print out COBUCLG, a member of SYS1.PROCLIB. Print it just in character format. Suppose that SYS1.PROCLIB had not been cataloged. In what ways would the above three functions be performed: printing catalog information, directory contents, and specific members. For the member only, 20 copies are to be printed.

4. Use IDCAMS to create a cataloged disk data set and load it with 30 records from an instream data set. Now create a tape data set using the records in the disk data set for input. Both copy operations should be done in the same step. Can any of the data sets be dynamically allocated?

5. Use IDCAMS to print a listing of all cataloged data sets in the system that have two levels of qualification in their names, the first of which is SYS1. Print out the names of all cataloged data sets whose second level qualifier is COBLIB.

6. Change the name of SYS1.COBLIB to SYS1.AUTOMATC.CALLLIB. Change the names of all cataloged data sets whose first level of qualification is SYS1 to a name that begins with SYSTEMS and whose second qualifier remains the same. STOW and BLDL are two members of the pds SYS1.MACLIB. Change their member names to STORE and BUILDIT respectively. Can this be done with IDCAMS if SYS1.MACLIB is not cataloged? Is there any difference in changing the true name of a member versus an alias name?

7. Delete members STOW, BLDL, and FIND from the pds SYS1.MACLIB. Delete the data sets ALPHA, ALPHA.BETA, ALPHA.BETA.GAMMA, and ALPHA.BETA.GAMMA.DELTA. Use a minimum of control statements and keyword parameters. Delete every cataloged data set whose first level of qualification is ALPHA. Suppose X is the name of an uncataloged disk data set. How can X be deleted (scratched)?

8. X.Y.Z is a disk data set that consists of 300 records. Except for the first and last 50 all of them are to be copied to a new sequential data set created in the same jobstep. Suppose that X.Y.Z is an ISAM data set. What changes will this create during the copy operation? No logically deleted records should be copied. Can IDCAMS be used to create an ISAM data set?

9. In Example 4 dynamically allocate the data set ALPHA.ONE.

INDEX

A

Abend dumps, 72, 378, 379–81
Abend processing, 5, 357–58
Access methods, 182–84
  blocking, 184–88
  buffering, 184–88
ACCODE parameter, 85, 133
Accounting Information parameter, 35
  in JOB Statement, 49
ACCOUNT parameter, 65
AC-x, 326
ADD function, 438, 442–43
Addresses, conversion of virtual to real, 12–13
ADDRSPC parameter, 50, 65
  in JOB statement, 50
AFF format, 108–9
ALIAS NAME control statement, 441–42
ALIAS statement, 318, 340
ALIGN, 326
ALTER command, 519
ALTSEQ control statement, 392, 393
ALX subparameter, 120
Amdahl, 6
Ampersand, use of, for coding, 89, 162, 164
AMP parameter, 85, 132
Anticipatory buffering, 186
ANY, 72
APOST, 304
Apostrophes, use of, for coding, 43, 49, 50, 89
Application programs, use of, to handle I/O operations, 6
ASP (Asymmetric Multiprocessing System), 17
Assembler, 3, 4
  DDnames in, 300
Asterisk, use of, in coding, 300
/*, 89, 90

B

Backup copy, creating, of partitioned data set, 455
Basic Operating System (BOS), 6
BATCH, 304–5
BDAM, 247
  data sets, 181
BLDL macro, 215, 219, 223–24
BLDL table, 14–15
BLKSIZE subparameters, 125
Blocking, 184–85, 253, 268–69
BLP with tape data sets, 278, 280
BSAM, 219, 247
Buffering, 184–88
BUFNO subparameter, 129
BUFTEK subparameter, 129
Burroughs computers, 7
BURST parameter, 59, 86, 92

C

CAL, 325, 341
CANCEL, 72
CARDS parameter, 57, 72
Cartridge tape drives, 288–89
Cataloged data sets, copying and moving groups of, 500
Cataloged procedures, 31, 152, 370–71
CATLG, 115
CCHHR value, 261
CDINCR, 428
CDSEQ, 428
C field, 217, 218
Change bit, 13
CHANGE function, 439
Chapping, 16
CHARS parameter, 86, 92
Checkpoints, 5, 378, 381
  JCL for, 381–82
CHKEOV parameter, 132
CHKPT parameter, 86, 381, 382
CICS, 21
CICS task, 21
CKPTPGS parameter, 59
CLASS parameter, 50–51, 73, 97
  in JOB statement, 50–51
CLIST, 301
CNTL parameter, 86, 133–34
CNTRL, 426–27
COBOL, 3
  application programs, 3–4
  paging in, 14
  sorting with, 397–98
  SORT verb in, 386
COBOL compiler, 292
COBOL PARM options, 300–1
  APOST, 304
  BATCH, 304–5
  CLIST, 301
  COUNT, 302–3
  DECK, 303
  FLOW, 302
  LIB, 304
  LISTER, 304
  LOAD, 303
  PMAP, 302
  SEQ, 303
  SIZE, 301
  STATE, 302
  SXREF, 303
  XREF, 303
COBUCG, 345
COLUMN control statement, 441
Comment field, 32
  JCL syntax rules for, 32
Comment statement, 26–27, 32
  coding of, 39–40
Common Area, 14–15
Common Service Area (CSA), 14
Concatenation, 168–69
COND parameter, 36, 41–42, 352–53
  coding of, on EXEC statement, 352, 358–59
  coding of, on JOB statement, 352, 359–60
  examples, 360–61
  interaction between, and other JCL parameters, 361
  syntax, 355–57
Condition code, 353
CONTIG subparameter, 120
Control statement, 317–23
  continuing, 408
COPIES parameter, 57, 59, 86, 93
COPY, 54
COPYG parameter, 59
COPY library, 293
COPY operation, 476

COUNT, 302–3
COUNT DATA format, 259, 260–61
COUNT KEY DATA format, 259, 261
CREATE control statement, 469, 470, 473–75
CSECT, 218
CVOLs, 367
CYLOFL subparameter, 129

D

Data control block, 192–93
  construction of, 193–96
  programming techniques related to, 197
DATA parameter, 87, 88–91
Data set(s). *See also* Direct data sets; Disk data sets; ISAM data sets; Non-VSAM data sets; Partitioned data sets; Relative data sets; Tape data sets
  cataloging and uncataloging, 491–92
  concatenating, 168–69
  creation and subsequent location of, 363–69
  renaming, 489–90
  scratching, 487–88
  use of, with loader, 338–40
Data set organization, 179
  direct data sets, 181
  ISAM data sets, 180–81
  partitioned data sets (PDS), 181–82
  relationship between record formats and, 209–10
  sequential data sets, 180
Data set utilities, 404–5
DCB parameter, 36, 85, 123–24, 286
  BLKSIZE (block size) subparameter, 125
  BUFNO subparameter, 129
  BUFTEK subparameter, 129
  CYLOFL subparameter, 129
  DEN subparameter, 129
  DSORG (data set organization) subparameter, 127–29
  EROPT subparameter, 129
  KEYLEN subparameter, 129
  LIMCT subparameter, 130
  LRECL (logical record length) subparameter, 124–25
  NTM subparameter, 130
  OTCD subparameter, 130
  RECFM (record format) subparameter, 125–27
  RKP subparameter, 130
  special formats for, 131–32
DD (Data Definition) statement, 21–22, 25–26, 29
  adding and overriding, 155–57
  aligning of operators, 39
  backward and forward references, 83–84
  coding of, 39, 41, 77
  DATA parameter, 87, 88–91
  Delimiter statement, 88
  DLM parameter, 89–91
  DUMMY parameter, 87
  DYNAM parameter, 87
  functions of, 77–80
  keyword parameters, 84–87
  name field on, 31
  operand field, 32
  overriding, 167–68
  positional parameters, 87–91
  reserved names for, 80–81
  syntax, 82–83
  SYSOUT parameter, 87, 91
  unnecessary and duplicate, 80
DDname, 31
DDNAME parameter, 134–35
DD parameters
  for disk and tape data sets, 85–86, 99–144
  positional, 87–91
  for printed and in-stream data sets, 86
DEADLINE, 73
Deadline scheduling, 19
DECK, 303
DEFAULT parameter, 97
DELETE, 116–17, 519–20
Delimiter Statement, 88
Demand paging, 13
DEN subparameter, 129
Dependent job control, 19
DEST parameter, 60, 86
Detail control statements, 440–41
DFSORT, 385, 386, 397
Direct data sets, 181, 246–47
  creation of, 248–50
  JCL for, 251–52
  programming considerations, 247–48
  updating, 250–51
Disk data sets, 259–60
  DD statement parameters for, 85–86, 132–44
  disk format, 260–62
  disk timing considerations, 270–71
  examining, 505
  and JCL, 263–64
  numeric calculations, 264–68
  reasons for blocking, 268–69
  3380 disk drive, 269–70
  volume table of contents (VTOC), 264
Disk Operating System (DOS), 5, 6
Dispatching priority, 11, 18
DISP parameter, 85, 112–13, 285, 363
  first subparameter values, 114
  second and third subparameters, 115–17
DLM parameter, 86, 89–91
Documentation, role of Comment statement in, 26–27
Dollar sign, use of, in coding, 51
DOS/VS, 8
DPRTY parameter, 65–66
DSD control statement, 469, 470–71
DSID parameter, 86, 135
DSNAME parameter, 85, 99–100
  permanent data set names, 101–2
  properties of, 102–3
  referencing parts of a data set, 103–4
  temporary data set names, 100–1
DSN parameter, 285, 363
DSORG subparameter, 127–29, 252
DUMMY parameter, 87
DUMP, 72
Duplicate slot numbers, 256–57
DYNALLOC, 396
Dynamic Address Translation (DAT), 12–13
Dynamically allocating data sets, 510–11
DYNAMNBR parameter, 66
DYNAM parameter, 87

E

EBCDIC collating sequences, 392
END control statement, 469, 470
ENDUP control statement, 441
ENTRY statement, 318
EQUALS, 391, 396
EROPT subparameter, 129
Error handling, 5
EXAMINE, 14
EXCP, 187
EXEC (Execute) statement, 21, 22, 25, 29, 63–64
  ACCOUNT parameter, 65
  ADDRSPC parameter, 65
  coding of, 39, 41
  DPRTY parameter, 65–66
  DYNAMNBR parameter, 66
  format of, 63
  keyword parameters, 65–68
  modifying parameters, 160–61
  name field on, 30
  operand field, 31–32
  PARM parameter, 66–67
  PERFORM parameter, 67
  PGM parameter, 64
  PROC parameter, 64
  REGION parameter, 68
  summary of COND on, 358–59
  TIME parameter, 68
  use of stepnames, 63
External Symbol Dictionary (ESP), 308, 327

F

FCB parameter, 60, 86
FD control statement, 469, 470, 471–72
FIELD parameter, 419–21, 424
FIELDS statement, 396
FIND macro, 215, 219, 224–25
Fixed BLDL Table, 15
Fixed length records, 203
FLASH parameter, 86, 94
F-level assembler, 292, 300
FLOW, 302
Flow of control, 352–53
  abend processing, 357–58
  coding COND on the JOB statement, 359–60
  COND parameter syntax, 355–57
  interaction between COND parameter and other JCL parameters, 361
  return codes, 353–55
  summary of COND on EXEC statements, 358–59
FLOW option, 379
FORMAT statement, 71–72
Frame, 12
FREE parameter, 86, 156
Function control statements, 438–40

G

GENER, 410. *See also* IEBGENER
GENERATE statement, 414
Generation data groups, 492
Generation data sets, 361
Generic processing, 102
GROUP parameter, 51
  in JOB statement, 51

H

Hashing algorithm, 249, 250
HASP (Houston Automatic Spooling Program), 17
Header fields, 200
HOLD, 54
HOLD parameter, 73, 86, 95

I

IBM
  manuals, 4
  operating systems, 5–6
IBM 360, 6
IBM system utilities, 481, 403–4
  continuing a control statement, 408
  data set utilities, 404–5
  general utility information, 406–7
  IEH utility control statements, 482
  IEH utility DD statements, 481–82
  SYSIN control statements, 407–8
  system utilities, 405
ICEMAN, 388
IDCAMS utility, 90, 116, 367
  syntax, 511–12
  utility, use of, with non-VSAM data sets, 508–20
IDENT parameter, 419–21
IEBCOMPR utility, 406, 478
  control statements and messages, 478
  examples using, 478–79
IEBCOPY utility, 406, 451–53, 462–63
  control statements, 453–55
  creating backup copy of partitioned data set, 455
  merging partitioned data sets, 457–61
  multiple copy operations, 462
  PDS compression, 461–62
  selective copy operations, 457
  unloading and reloading partitioned data sets, 455–57
  work data sets, 453
IEBDG utility, 467–69
  control statements, 469–70
  CREATE statement, 473–75
  DSD statement, 470–71
  FD statement, 471–72
  input and output data sets, 468–69
IEBGENER utility, 395, 406, 408, 410–11, 453
  copying sequential data set, 411–413
  creating variable length records from fixed length input, 419–21
  MEMBER control statement, 414–15
  RECORD control statement, 415–19
  using control statements, 413–14
IEBISAM utility, 475–76
  COPY operation, 476
  LOAD operation, 477
  PRINTL operation, 477–78
  UNLOAD operation, 477
IEBPTPCH utility, 408, 424–26
  PRINT control statements, 426–28
  PUNCH control statements, 426–28
  use of, with partitioned data sets, 430–32
  use of, with sequential data sets, 429–30
IEBUPDTE utility, 217, 406, 436–38
  ADD function, 442–43
  ALIAS NAME control statement, 441–42
  CHANGE function, 445–47
  detail control statements, 440–41
  ENDUP control statement, 441
  function control statements, 438–40
  REPL function, 444
  REPRO function, 443–44
  using sequential data sets with, 447–48
IEBWPOTE utility, 453
IEFBR14 utility, 372–75
IEF message code, 33
IEHATLAS utility, 405
IEHDASDR utility, 405, 406, 504
  examining disk data set, 505
IEHINITT utility, 405, 408, 502–3
  control statements, 503
  DD statements, 503
  initializing multiple tape volumes, 504
  initializing volume with INITT statement, 503–4
IEHLIST utility, 405, 406, 483
  listing OS catalog entries, 483
  listing PDS directories, 484–85
  listing VTOC entries, 485–86
IEHMOVE utility, 405, 406, 497–99
  copying and moving data sets, 499–501
  copying and moving entire disk volumes, 502
IEHPROGM utility, 116, 405, 487
  cataloging and uncataloging data sets, 491–92
  generation data groups, 492
  renaming data set, 489–90
  renaming PDS member, 490
  scratching data set, 487–88
  scratching PDS member, 488–89
IEH utility control statements, 482
IEH utility DD statements, 481–82
INCLUDE statement, 318–19
INCR, 441
INITPG control statement, 427
INITT statement, 503
  initializing one volume with, 503–4
INREC, 393, 395
INSERT control statement, 441
INSPECT, 14
In-stream data sets, 88
  DD statement parameters for, 86–87
In-stream procedures, 31, 152–54, 370–71
INTRDR, 91
I/O concepts, and JCL, 188–90
I/O (input/output) management, 5
IORATE, 73
ISAM (Indexed Sequential Access Method), 228
ISAM data sets, 180–81, 228–29
  adding records randomly, 235–37
  components of, 229–31
  problems with, 243
  random processing, 234–35
  random rewriting, 237
  sequential data set creation, 231–33
  sequential processing on existing, 233–34

ISAM data sets—*cont.*
  size of, as larger than one cylinder, 238–43

J

JCL (Job control language), 3
  advantages of knowing, 24–25
  for checkpoints, 381–82
  and the COBOL compiler, 297–99
  disks and, 263–64
  and I/O concepts, 188–90
  nonuser friendliness of, 22
  problems with learning, 23–24
  relative order of, 27
  role of, in MVS system, 21–27
  syntax in, 23; *see also* JCL syntax
  use of, for direct data sets, 251–52
  use of, for relative data sets, 256
JCL coding standards, 39–43
JCLHOLD, 54
JCL statement, 21
  continuing, 37–39
  types of, 25–26
JCL syntax, 17, 22, 23
  apostrophes in, 43
  coding of parameters in, 43–44
  coding of variable length character strings, 43
  coding standards in, 39–43
  comment field, 32
  continuing a JCL statement, 37–39
  field summary, 32–34
  name field, 29–31
  operand field, 31–32
  operand parameters, 34–35
  operation field, 31
  parentheses in, 43
  periods in, 44
  subparameters, 35–37
JES2
  development of, 17
  differences between JES3 and, 19
JES2 control statements
  JOBPARM, 57–58
  Message statement, 58–59
  OUTPUT statement, 59–60
  overview of, 56–57
  PRIORITY statement, 60
  ROUTE statement, 60–61
  SETUP statement, 61
  XEQ statement, 61
JES2 job scheduling, 11
JES3
  development of, 17
  differences between JES2, 19
JES3 control statements, 70–71
  FORMAT statement, 71–72
  MAIN statement, 72–74
  NET statement, 74–75
JGLOBAL, 72
JLOCAL, 72
JOBCAT, 366–67, 369
Job Entry System (JES), 17–18
  differences in, 19
JOBLIB, 369–70, 381
Job management, 5
JOBPARM, 57–58
JOBPARM statement, 72
Job Scheduler, 8–9, 10, 17
  interpretation of JCL statements by, 23
  responsibilities of, 363
  role of, in checking JCL syntax, 33–34
JOB statement, 21, 22, 25, 29
  accounting information, 35, 49
  ADDRSPC parameter, 50
  CLASS parameter, 50–51
  coding COND on, 359–60
  coding of, 39, 40–41
  GROUP parameter, 51
  MSGCLASS parameter, 51
  MSGLEVEL parameter, 51–52
  name field on, 30
  NOTIFY parameter, 52
  operand field, 32
  PASSWORD parameter, 52–53
  PERFORM parameter, 53
  Programmer Name field, 49–50
  PRTY parameter, 53
  REGION parameter, 53
  TIME parameter, 54
  TYPRUN parameter, 54
  USER parameter, 55
Job stream, 21, 22
JOURNAL parameter, 73

K

KEYLEN subparameter, 129
Keyword parameter, 31, 34–35, 36
  coding of, for JOBPARM, 57–58
  coding of, for OUTPUT statement, 59–60
  for DD statements, 85–87
  for EXEC statements, 65–68
  for JOB Statement, 48

L

LABEL parameter, 85, 121, 287–88, 363
  file sequence number, 121
  label type, 121–22
  protecting data sets, 122–23
LABEL subparameters, 115
Language translators, 292–342
  JCL and the COBOL compiler, 297–99
  optional data sets, 296–97
  PL/I and assembler data sets and DDnames, 300
  required data sets, 293–96
LET, 325, 341
Level of qualification, 101, 102
LEVEL, 440
LIB, 304
LIBRARY statement, 319–23, 340
LIMCT subparameter, 130, 252
LINECT parameter, 57
LINES parameter, 57, 72
Linkage editor, 169, 307. *See also* Loader
  changing ESD entry, 328–30
  control statements, 317–23
  editing features of, 327
  executing a load module, 316–17
  external references, 308
  general functions of, 309, 311
  optional data sets, 312–16
  overlay programming, 331–34
  PARM options with, 324–26
  relocation dictionary, 308
  required data sets, 311–12
  role of, 308–9
LIST, 324
LISTCAT command, 517–19
LISTER, 304
LIST function, 439
LOAD, 303
Loader, 169, 337–38. *See also* Linkage editor
  data sets used with, 338–40
  linkage editor data sets and options not used by, 340
  module maps, 345
  PARM values, 240–41
  role of, 308–9
  using, 242–45
Load module, executing, 316–17
LOAD operation, 477
Local System Queue Area (LSQA), 15
Logical record, 184
LRECL subparameter, 124–25

M

Main memory, principle areas in, 14–15
MAIN statement, 72–74
MAP, 324, 341
MAXFLDS, 414, 424, 425, 427
MAXGPS, 414, 424, 427
MAXLINE, 427
MAXLITS, 414, 427
MAXNAME, 414, 424, 427

MEMBER control statement, 414–15, 424
MEMBER parameter, 440
Message statement, 58–59
Microcode, 8
MOD, 114
MODIFY parameter, 86, 95
MODS, 393, 394
Module maps, 345
MSGCLASS parameter, 51
  in JOB statement, 51
MSGLEVEL parameter, 51–52
  in JOB statement, 51–52
MSVGP parameter, 86, 156–57
Multiple Virtual Storage (MVS) operating system, 3, 5
  evolution of present, 6–8
  job control language in, 4
  and job scheduling, 11
  major concepts of, 8–9
  prioritizing system utilization, 9–11
  record formats, 199
  role of JCL in, 21–27
  utilities in, 4
Multiprocessing, 7
Multiprogramming, 7
MVS operating system. *See* Multiple Virtual Storage
MVS/XA, 7
  storage capacity of, 12
MXIG subparameter, 120

N

Name field, 216
  JCL syntax rules for, 29–31
NAME function, 439
NAME statement, 317–18, 340
National Advanced Systems (NAS), 6
NCAL, 325, 340
Net, 74
NET statement, 74–75
NEW, 440–41
NL tape data sets, 278
NOLOG parameter, 57
Non-VSAM data sets, using IDCAMS with, 508–20
NON-VSAM record formats. *See* Record formats
NOTIFY parameter, 52
  in JOB statement, 52
NTM subparameter, 130
Null statement, 26, 32, 89
  coding of, 41

O

Object module, 292
OMIT, 393, 394
Operand field, JCL syntax rules for, 31–32
Operand parameters, 31. *See also* Keyword parameters; Positional parameters; Symbolic parameters
  types of, 34–35
Operating systems, for the IBM, 5–6
Operation field, JCL syntax rules for, 31
OPTCD subparameters, 251, 252
Optional data sets, use of, with linkage editor, 312–16
OS catalog, listing entries, 483
OS/MFT (multiprogramming with a Fixed Number of Tasks), 6–7
OS/MVT (Multiprogramming with a Variable Number of Tasks), 7
OS/VS1, 7
OS/VS2, 7
OTCD subparameter, 130
OUTLIM parameter, 87, 95
OUTPUT DD parameter, 95–96
OUTPUT parameter, 87
OUTPUT statement, 29, 31, 59–60, 96–97
  coding of, 39
OUTREC, 393, 395
Overlay programming, 331–34
Overriding within a concatenation, 32
OVLY, 326

P

Page, 12
Pageable BLDL Table, 14–15
Pageable Link Pack Area (PLPA), 14
Page fault, 12, 13
Page stealing, 12
Paging, 11, 12–14
Parameters. *See* Keyword parameters; Positional parameters; Symbolic parameters
Parentheses, use of, for coding, 32, 43
PARM options, with the linkage editor, 324–26
PARM parameter, 66–67
Partitioned data sets (PDS), 181–82, 212–13
  advantages of using, to group data sets, 220–21
  automatic replacement, 222
  backup copy of, 455
  BLDL macro, 223–24
  compression, 461–62
  copying and moving groups of, 500–1
  creating, 213–15
  directory, 215–19
  disadvantages of using, 221–22
  FIND macro, 224–25
  listing directories, 484–85
  member
    renaming, 490
    scratching, 488–89
  macros for manipulation of, 222–26
  member area, 219–20
  merging with IEBCOPY, 457–61
  unloading and reloading, 455–57
  use of IEBPTPCH with, 430–32
  STOW macro, 225–26
PASS, 115
PASSWORD parameter, 52–53
  in JOB statement, 52–53
Path, 332
PCB parameter, 94
PEND statement, 29, 31, 32, 152–54
PERFORM, 427
PERFORM parameter, 53, 67
  in JOB statement, 53
PGM parameter, 64
Physical record, 184
PL/I, 3, 4, 90
  DD names, 300
  PLISORTx, 386
PL/I optimizing compiler, 292
Plug Compatible Machines (PCM), 6
Plus sign, use of, for coding, 32
PMAP, 302
Positional parameters, 31, 34, 35, 36
  in JOB Statement, 48
Primary Control Program (PCP), 6
PRINT control statements, 426–28, 515–17
Printed data sets, 425
  DD statement parameters for, 86–87
  keyword parameters for, 92–96
PRINTL operation, 477–78
Priority aging, 19
PRIORITY statement, 60
Priority value, assigning to jobs, 9–10
Private Area, 15
PROC, 73
Procedures, 31, 150–51
  adding and overriding DD Statements, 155–57
  cataloged, 31, 152, 370–71
  concatenating data sets within, 168–69
  developing, 160
  dynamic modification of, 154–55
  modifying EXEC parameters, 160–61
  multi-step, 157–58
  overriding individual parameters, 158–59
  overriding subparameters, 159–60
  in-stream, 31, 152–54, 370–71
  symbolic parameter positional and keyword syntax, 165–67
  symbolic parameters, 161–64

Procedures—*cont.*
symbolic parameters and overriding DD statements, 167–68
symbolic parameter syntax, 164–65
types of, 152
PROCLIB parameter, 57
PROCNAME, 31
PROC parameter, 64, 73
PROC statement, 29, 31, 152–54
coding of, 40
Program address space, 12
Programmer Name field, 49–50
in JOB Statement, 49–50
ProGraMs (PGMs), creation and subsequent location of, 369–70
PROTECT parameter, 86, 157
PRTY parameter, 53
in JOB statement, 53
PUNCH control statements, 425, 426–28

Q

QISAM access method, 233–34
QNAME parameter, 86, 137
QSAM, 219
Queue, 9
Queue processing, 18

R

RACF (Resource Access Control Facility) program, 51, 52, 53
Random processing, 234–35
Random record additions, 235–37
Random rewriting, 237
RD (restart definition) parameter, 65, 361, 382–83
Real memory, 11–12
Real storage, 11
Real storage address, 12
RECFM (record format) parameter, 125–27
RECORD control statement, 415–19
Record formats, 199–200, 247
advantages and disadvantages of V, U, and S, 200–1
fixed length records, 203
relationship between data set organization and, 209–10
spanned records, 207–210
specifying, 201–3
undefined records, 207
variable length records, 203–7
Recovery management, 5
Reference bit, 13
Referbacks, 103
REFR, 326
REGIONAL I data set, 252–53
REGION parameter, 53, 68
in JOB statement, 53
Relative data sets, 252–53
creating, 254–55
duplicate slot numbers, 256–57
JCL for, 256
programming considerations, 253–54
updating, 255–56
Relocation Dictionary (RLD), 308
RENT, 326
REPEAT control statement, 469, 470
REPL function, 438, 444
REPRO command, 512–15
REPRO function, 438, 443–44
Required data sets, use of, with linkage editor, 311–12
Resource Manager, 16
RESTART parameter, 58, 361, 381, 383–84
Restarts, 5, 378, 382
RD parameter, 361, 382–83
RESTART parameter, 361, 383–84
Return codes, 353–55
REUS, 326
REWRITE, 255–56
RKP subparameter, 130
ROOM parameter, 58
ROUND subparameter, 120
Root segment, 332
ROUTE statement, 60–61

S

SCAN, 54
Scheduler Work Area (SWA), 15
Segment, 12
SEQ, 303
SEQ control statements, 441
Sequential data sets, 180
copying of, with IEBGENER, 411–13
creation of, 231–33
use of, with IEBUPDTE, 447–48
use of IEBPTPCH with, 429–30
Sequential processing, 233–34
SETUP, 73–74
SETUP statement, 61
SHR, 114
Single Virtual Storage (SVS), 7
SIZE, 301
SKIP, 427
SKIPREC, 391, 396
Slot, 12
SL tape data sets, 277–78
SORTIN, 387
Sort/Merge utility, 385
alternate collating sequences, 392–93
EQUALS, 391
format data format, 390
fundamental information, 387–88
fundamental sorting techniques, 386
merging, 396–97
modifying sort input and output, 393–96
referencing individual bits as part of sort key, 391–92
SKIPREC = n, 391
SORT control statement, 388–90
sorting with COBOL application program, 397–98
variable length records, 397
SORTOUT, 387
SORTWK DD statements, 387, 389
SPACE parameter, 85, 117–18, 286, 296
ABSTR format of, 120–21
ALX subparameter, 120
CONTIG subparameter, 120
cylinders, tracks, and blocks, 118–20
MXIG subparameter, 120
RLSE subparameter, 120
ROUND subparameter, 120
Spanned records, 207–9
SRM control, 16
SSI, 440
STATE, 302
STATE option, 379
STDWTR, 91
STEPCAT statement, 366–67, 369
coding of, 41
STEPLIB statement, 343, 369–70
coding of, 41
STOPAFT, 427
STOW macro, 215, 219, 225–26
STRING, 14
STRTAFT, 427
Subparameters, 35–37
overriding, 159–60
SUBSYS parameter, 86, 138
Swapping, 12
SXREF, 303
Symbolic parameters, 31, 32, 34, 35, 161–64
and overriding DD statements, 167–68
syntax, 164–67
SYNCSORT, 385
SYSABEND, 72, 379, 380
SYSCKEOV, 382
SYSCHK, 381–82
SYSIN, 293, 387, 424, 437, 452
SYSIN control statements, 407–8, 469
SYSLIB, 293–94, 312, 338–39
SYSLIN, 294–95, 300, 311, 312, 338
SYSLMOD, 311, 340
SYSLOUT, 338, 340
SYSMDUMP, 379, 380
SYSOUT data set, 18
SYSOUT parameter, 85, 87, 91

SYSPRINT, 296, 311, 340, 424, 436–37, 452
SYSPRINT DD statement, 406
SYSPUNCH, 296
SYSTEM, 72
System Area, 14
System Link Pack Area (LPA), 369
System Queue Area (SQA), 14
System Resource Manager (SRM), 9, 16
  and allocation of resources, 18
  components of, 16
  use of DPRTY value by, 65
System searches, 363, 371–72
  creation and location of, 370–71
  creation and subsequent location of data sets, 363–69
  creation and subsequent location of ProGraMs, 369–70
  IEFBR14 utility, 372–75
System utilities, 405
SYSUDUMP, 72, 297, 379, 380
SYSUT1, 296, 311, 340, 424, 437, 442, 444, 445, 446, 447, 448
SYSUT2, 296, 424, 437, 442, 443, 444, 445, 446, 447, 448
SYSUT3, 296, 453
SYSUT4, 296, 453

T

Tape data sets, 273–74
  blocking, 280–81
  BLP with, 278, 280
  cartridge tape drives, 288–89
  DD statement parameters for, 85–86, 132–44
  JCL for, 285–88
  NL, 278
  processing guidelines, 284–85
  processing multi-volume, 288
  representing data on tape, 274–76
  SL, 277–78, 279
  SUL and LTM, 283–84
  tape I/O operations, 282–83
  types of, 276–77
Tape I/O operations, 282–83
Tape Operating System (TOS), 6
Task management, 5
TCAM (TeleCommunications Access Method), 137
TERM parameter, 86, 138
3380 disk drive, 269–70
TIME parameter, 54, 58, 68
  in JOB statement, 54
TITLE statement, 428
TOTCONV, 426
TRANSLATE, 14
Tree, 331
TSO (Time Sharing Option), 52
TSO/SPF, 25
TTR field, 216, 218
TYPORG, 426
TYPRUN parameter, 54
  in JOB statement, 54

U

UCS parameter, 60, 87, 96
UNCATLG, 116
Undefined records, 207
UNIT parameter, 85, 104, 286, 363, 364, 365
  AFF format, 108–9
  conditions for coding, 106–7
  Group names and device types, 104–5
  second and third positional subparameters, 107–8
  system device addresses, 105–6
  VIO data sets, 109
UNLOAD operation, 477
UPDATE, 73, 436–37, 438
User data field, 217
USER parameter, 55
  in JOB statement, 55

V

Variable length records, 203–7
VIO data sets, 109
Virtual address, 12
Virtual Machine (VM) operating system, 5
Virtual memory, 11, 12
Virtual storage (VS) operating system, 7, 11–12
  types of memory in, 11–12
VOL parameter, 85, 104, 109–10, 286, 363–66
  conditions for coding, 112
  VOL=REF subparameter, 110–11
  VOL=SER subparameter, 110–11
  VOL subparameters, 111–12
Volume table of contents (VTOC), 99, 264
  listing entries, 485–86
VSAM catalog structure, 366, 367
VTAM (Virtual TeleCommunications Access Method), 137

W

WARNING, 72
Workload manager, 16

X

XCAL, 326
XEQ statement, 61
XREF, 303, 324